JUN − 3 2013

17 (10)

W9-CMZ-964

ANCIENT ISRAEL

THE FORMER PROPHETS: JOSHUA, JUDGES, SAMUEL, AND KINGS

ALSO BY ROBERT ALTER

ANCIENT ISRAEL

THE FORMER PROPHETS: JOSHUA, JUDGES, SAMUEL, AND KINGS

A Translation with Commentary

ROBERT ALTER

W · W · Norton & Company

NEW YORK LONDON

For information about permission to reproduce selections from this book,
write to Permissions, W. W. Norton & Company, Inc.,
500 Fifth Avenue, New York, NY 10110

For information about special discounts for bulk purchases, please contact
W. W. Norton Special Sales at specialsales@wwnorton.com or 800-233-4830

Manufacturing by RR Donnelley, Harrisonburg
Book design by Margaret M. Wagner
Production manager: Julia Druskin

Library of Congress Cataloging-in-Publication Data

Bible. O.T. Former Prophets. English. Alter. 2013.
Ancient Israel : the Former Prophets : Joshua, Judges, Samuel and Kings : a translation
with commentary / Robert Alter. — 1st ed.
p. cm.
Includes bibliographical references.
ISBN 978-0-393-08269-2 (hardcover)
1. Bible. O.T. Former Prophets—Commentaries. I. Alter, Robert. II. Title.
BS1286.5.A3A48 2013
222'.077—dc23
2013000932

W. W. Norton & Company, Inc.
500 Fifth Avenue, New York, N.Y. 10110
www.wwnorton.com

W. W. Norton & Company Ltd.
Castle House, 75/76 Wells Street, London W1T 3QT

1 2 3 4 5 6 7 8 9 0

for

HADAS

CONTENTS

KINGS

ACKNOWLEDGMENTS

RESEARCH AND SECRETARIAL assistance for the initial phase of this project was provided by funds from the Class of 1937 Chair at the University of California, Berkeley. The bulk of this project was funded by an emeritus research grant from the Mellon Foundation, and I am especially grateful for the generosity of the Mellon support. I am again in debt to Janet Livingstone for her dedicated work as typist. My friend and colleague Ron Hendel reviewed the manuscript and gave me the benefit of his superb command of the scholarship on the Bible and the ancient Near East. Daniel Fisher vetted the translation against the Hebrew, hunting down inadvertent omissions and other lapses. Any slips, of course, in regard to the translation or the notes, that were not caught are my own responsibility.

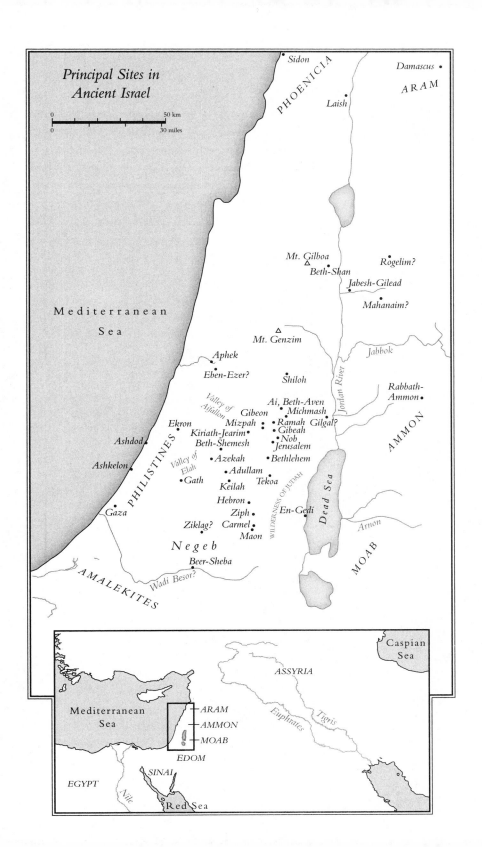

Principal Sites in
Ancient Israel

0   50 km

0   30 miles

Sidon •

Damascus •

PHOENICIA

ARAM

Laish •

Mt. Gilboa △

Rogelim? •

Beth-Shan •

Jabesh-Gilead •

Mediterranean
Sea

Mahanaim? •

Mt. Genzim △

Jabbok

Aphek •

Eben-Ezer? •

Shiloh •

Rabbath-
Ammon •

Valley of
Aijalon

Ai, Beth-Aven •
Michmash •

Gibeon •

Mizpah •

Ramah • Gilgal?

Jordan River

AMMON

Ekron •

Kiriath-Jearim •

• Gibeah

• Nob

Ashdod •

Beth-Shemesh •

• Jerusalem

Ashkelon •

PHILISTINES

• Azekah

• Bethlehem

Valley of
Elah

• Adullam

Dead Sea

• Gath

Keilah •

Tekoa •

WILDERNESS OF JUDAH

Hebron •

Gaza •

Ziph •

En-Gedi •

Ziklag? •

Carmel •

Maon •

Arnon

N e g e b

MOAB

Beer-Sheba •

AMALEKITES

Wadi Besor?

Caspian
Sea

ASSYRIA

Mediterranean
Sea

ARAM

Euphrates

Tigris

AMMON

MOAB

EDOM

EGYPT

SINAI

Nile

Red Sea

INTRODUCTION

To many readers, the rubric *The Former Prophets* may be puzzling. Some will not recognize it as the designation of a part of the Bible with which they are familiar. Some will wonder which prophets are involved, for the figures we usually think of as prophets like Jeremiah and Ezekiel are nowhere in evidence, and Isaiah has only a late walk-on appearance toward the end of 2 Kings. Then, the question poses itself: Former to what? Or even, what did they do after they stopped being prophets?

This conventional English title is a literal translation of the Hebrew *nevi'im ri'shonim*. In the canonical Hebrew division of the Bible into three parts, *nevi'im*, the Prophets, was the middle section. This large unit comprised two halves, the Former Prophets, which were narrative books, and the Latter Prophets, which were hortatory and predominantly poetic. The founders of Jewish tradition seem to have thought of the first of these two units as prophetic literature because they imagined it as having been composed by various of the so-called "writing prophets." This is not a view in any way embraced by modern scholarship. More plausible grounds for calling this sequence of narratives the Former Prophets is that from Samuel onward figures identified as prophets keep popping up, for the most part to frame the narrative with prophecies of doom. (This is not true for Joshua and Judges. The sole exception is Deborah in Judges 4, who is called a "prophet-woman," *ishah nevi'ah*, but she is not shown exercising that vocation.)

Biblical scholars, since the work in Germany by Martin Noth in the middle of the twentieth century, have adopted a more precise though less pronounceable designation for the large narrative from Joshua and Judges to Samuel and Kings: the Deuteronomistic History. In the late seventh century BCE, a major revolution in the religion of ancient Israel was effected when, in the course of renovation work on the temple in the reign of King Josiah, a long scroll was purportedly discovered (see 2 Kings 22–23), referred to as "this book of teaching," *sefer hatorah hazeh.* Most scholars since the early nineteenth century have concluded that it was a version of Deuteronomy, and surmise that it was actually composed around this time by reformers in Josiah's court. It put forth a new insistence on the exclusivity of the cult in the Jerusalem temple, vehemently polemicized against the use of any image or icon in worship, and proposed a system of historical causation in which the survival of a given king and of the covenanted people was strictly dependent on their loyalty—above all, cultic loyalty—to their God. All this was cast in language that highlighted certain formulaic phrases—"to love the LORD your God with all your heart and with all your might," "to keep His statutes, His commands and His dictates"—and in a distinctive rhetoric that, unlike other biblical prose, favored long periodic sentences and the oratorical insistence of anaphora—that is, emphatic repetition.

At the same time that Deuteronomy proper (which would acquire some additional layers when it was edited in the Babylonian exile only a few decades after its initial promulgation in 621 BCE) was exhorting the people to follow what it deemed to be the right path, writers in this same circle sought to make sense of the history of the nation in the revelatory light of the new reforming book. A religious intellectual—it may actually have been a whole group, but for the sake of convenience, scholarship refers to him schematically as the Deuteronomist—who was swept up in Josiah's reforms set out to assemble a more or less continuous version of the national history from the conquest of the land to his own time, covering roughly six centuries. This first Deuteronomistic historian does not envisage the destruction of the southern kingdom (the northern kingdom of Israel had disappeared a century earlier, in 721 BCE, at the hands of the Assyrians) or of the cutting off of the Davidic dynasty, so it is plausible to date him to the late seventh century BCE. Then, in the view of most scholars, a second and more or less final edition of the Deuteronomistic History was executed in the Babylonian exile after 586 BCE, probably just a few decades later (it contains as yet no vision of a return to Zion), incorporating an account of the devastation of the kingdom of Judah and the humiliation, mutilation, and exile of its last king.

An elusive question about this entire chain of books is what exactly was the role played by the Deuteronomist in their composition. Some scholars are inclined to speak of him as the "author" of the history, a writer who utilized older textual and perhaps also oral materials but edited them and reworked them freely according to his own ideological bent. I find this view implausible. The Deuteronomist clearly drew on a wide variety of pre-existing texts, some of them probably preserved in royal archives, from annals to folktales and legends to the most artfully articulated historical narratives. He punctuated these disparate materials, especially in the Book of Kings, with formulaic assertions—often reminiscent of the language of Deuteronomy—of his own interpretation as to why particular historical events happened as they did. But there is abundant evidence that the old stories resisted the pressure of his insistent interpretation, showing their own view of things, and that for the most part he did not feel at liberty to tamper with the literary documents he had inherited.

Let me cite one central instance. Nearly a third of the Former Prophets is devoted to the story of Saul and David (1 Samuel 8–2 Kings 2). As a literary composition, this story manifestly antedates the Deuteronomist, perhaps even by as much as three centuries. It also happens to be one of the greatest pieces of narrative in all of Western literature. Biblical scholars have a lamentable habit of referring to it as "royal propaganda," and also of breaking it down into purportedly disparate sources in a fashion that does violence to its powerful continuities of style, image, motif, and character. Though David is clearly represented as a divinely elected king in this narrative, he is also seen quite strikingly in all his human weakness, in his relentlessness, and in his moral ambiguity—hardly a figure of royal propaganda. And in regard to the issue of historical causation, events here are the consequence of human actions; in the preponderance of these stories there is nothing miraculous and there is no divine intervention. When the aged king is dying, he calls Solomon to his bedside and instructs him to use his "wisdom" to get rid of two men against whom David has a score to pay off, and who also might well threaten Solomon's throne. This final gesture, worthy of a mafia chieftain, was evidently too much for the Deuteronomist, so he inserted before David's hit list a whole swatch of dialogue, in which David, deploying an uninterrupted pastiche of Deuteronomistic phrases, piously enjoins Solomon to walk in God's ways and keep His commands. What the editor did not feel free to do was to change the inherited text or delete the parts of it he found objectionable.

This combination of tendentious editorial framing with an assemblage of disparate narrative texts from different periods and probably different regions of the country has been a source of debate and perplexity among scholars. General readers, on the other hand, may be grateful for the extravagant heterogeneity of these books. Each has its own distinctive character. The first half of Joshua is an account of conquest and destruction, enlivened by the tale of Rahab and the two spies and the fall of Jericho; the second half is a mapping out of the tribal territories in which the supposedly conquered land now appears far from fully conquered. The Book of Judges comprises a series of episodes of martial derring-do in the sundry struggles of the tribes with the surrounding peoples, and it includes the unforgettable cycle of stories about the Herculean folk-hero Samson. After the anarchic period recorded in Judges, Samuel recounts the founding of the monarchy in the long, continuous story—which is the artistic pinnacle of these books—of David from brilliant youth to the sad infirmity of old age. It is in Samuel, as the German scholar Gerhard von Rad argued seven decades ago, that the writing becomes properly historical, liberated from the heavy dependence on legend and sheer authorial invention. The Book of Kings, in more miscellaneous fashion, and with more conspicuous interventions of the Deuteronomist, continues the historical narrative, tapping the royal annals of both kingdoms but also liberally introducing folktales and legends, especially visible in the cycle of stories about Elijah and Elisha.

What results from this amalgam is a richly overflowing miscellany. It incorporates folk memories or fantasies about ideal and magically powerful figures; historical accounts of deadly court intrigues; representations of the intricate and dangerous complexities of life in the political realm; and reports of the great powers surrounding the small kingdoms of Israel and Judah and of their military campaigns in the land of Canaan. Over it all hovers the somber awareness of the Deuteronomist that these two nation-states, located at the crossroads of aggressive empires to the east and to the south, lived under constant threat and in the end might not endure. What did endure, embodied in the stories themselves, was the people's memories, their vision of God and history and national purpose. All these, preserved in their Hebrew texts, they would one day bring back from exile as the potent instrument of an unprecedented national revival.

JOSHUA

TO THE READER

THE BOOK OF JOSHUA, sandwiched in between the grand oratory of Deuteronomy and the vivid accounts of guerilla warfare and civil war in Judges, is a text that many modern readers may find off-putting. Its early chapters do include two memorable episodes—the expedition of the two spies to Jericho and the miraculous destruction of the walls of Jericho that enables its conquest. The prevailing sense, however, of the first half of the book is ruthlessness, and the general effect of the second half is tedium. Nowhere in the Bible is there a more palpable discrepancy between the values and expectations of the ancient Near Eastern era in which the book was written and those of twenty-first-century readers.

Joshua is really two books, symmetrically divided into twelve chapters each. The first of these we may call the Book of Conquests. It appears to be predominantly the work of the school of Deuteronomy, though it is not altogether uniform, and there is evidence that other sources have been drawn on, some of them probably older than Deuteronomy. The second half of Joshua can be given the rubric the Book of Apportionments. Its provenance is largely Priestly, though it ends with an emphatic Deuteronomistic flourish. There is some narrative material in the last three chapters, but the bulk of it is devoted to mapping out the sundry tribal territories in elaborate detail.

This book as a whole is offered as a historical account of the conquest of the land and the division of its territories, but the connection with history of both its large components is tenuous. Archeologists in the earlier twentieth century were often bent on confirming the biblical record through their discoveries, but that project has not stood the test of time. What the last several decades of archeological investigation have established is that there was no sweeping conquest of Canaan by invaders from the east in the late thirteenth century BCE—which would have been the time of Joshua—and that many of the towns listed as objects of Israelite conquest were either uninhabited at this time or did not come under Israelite rule till considerably later. Jericho, the gateway town in the Jordan Valley and the one whose conquest has become etched in collective memory, was an important fortified city in the Middle Bronze Age (two or three centuries before the putative time of Joshua), but in the late thirteenth century it was an abandoned site or at most not much more than a large village without walls. Lachish, another important town said to have been taken by Joshua's forces, fell under Israelite domination only during the period of the monarchy.

The fact that this narrative does not correspond to what we can reconstruct of the actual history of Canaan offers one great consolation: the blood-curdling report of the massacre of the entire population of Canaanite towns—men, women, children, and in some cases livestock as well—never happened. Some reflection on why these imagined mass murders are included in the book may provide a sense of the aim of the pseudo-historiographical project of the Book of Joshua. The *ḥerem*, the practice of total destruction that scholars call "the ban" (a usage adopted in the present translation), was not unique to ancient Israel, and there is some evidence that it was occasionally carried out in warfare by other peoples of the region. The question is why the Hebrew writers, largely under the ideological influence of Deuteronomy, felt impelled to invent a narrative of the conquest of the land in which a genocidal onslaught on its indigenous population is repeatedly stressed.

Deuteronomy, which crystallized as a canonical book during and after the sweeping religious reforms of King Josiah—the purported discovery of the book took place in 621 BCE—articulates an agenda of uncompromising monotheism that insists on two principal points: the exclusive centralization of the cult in Jerusalem and the absolute separation of the Israelites from the Canaanite population. There is an underlying connection between these two emphases: the worship of YHWH in sundry local sanctuaries and on rural hillside altars was liable to be more susceptible to the influences of Canaanite paganism, or so the Deuteronomist seems to have feared, than a central cult in Jerusalem overseen by a priestly bureaucracy and under the shadow of the monarchy. One strong expression of the program to separate the population is the injunction to carry out the ban in the conquest of the land, an undertaking that at the fictional time of the writing of Deuteronomy (the thirteenth century BCE) had not yet begun. The Book of Joshua, then, which is offered as a report of the subsequent conquest, presents as a historical account the implementation of that wholesale slaughter of the indigenous population in town after town.

This gruesome story is intended as an explanation of a circumstance observed by audiences of the book in the seventh century and later—that by then a non-Israelite Canaanite population was only vestigially in evidence. Where, one might wonder, did all these peoples—seven in the traditional enumeration repeatedly invoked here—go? Joshua's answer is that they were wiped out in the conquest, as Deuteronomy had enjoined. But the narrative of the *h.erem* is a cover-up as well as an explanation. If the Canaanites seem to have disappeared, it was not because they were extirpated but because they had been assimilated by the Israelites, who had come to exercise political dominion over large portions of the land. There is good reason to assume that the Canaanites intermarried with the Israelites (a taboo for the Deuteronomist), had all kinds of social and economic intercourse with them, and shared with them many of their religious practices as well as many elements of their theology.

This story, then, of the annihilation of the indigenous population of Canaan belongs not to historical memory but rather to cultural memory, a concept that Ronald Handel has aptly applied to biblical literature in his book *Remembering Abraham*. That is to say, what is reported as the national past is grounded not in the factual historical experience of the nation but in the image of the nation that the guardians of the national literary legacy seek to fix for their audiences and for future generations. Thus, Israel is represented in this narrative as "a people that dwells apart" (Numbers 23:9), though in historical actuality its life was intricately entangled not only with the sundry peoples of Canaan but also with the cultures of Egypt to the south and of Mesopotamia to the east.

The story of the Gibeonites recounted in Chapter 9 is in this regard an instructive case in point. The audience of the story, we may safely infer, would have been aware of the Gibeonites as a group of different ethnic stock from the Israelites yet "dwelling in their midst"—that is, having close social and economic relations with them, perhaps of the subservient order indicated in the biblical account. But what were they doing there if the systematic plan of the conquest was to wipe out all traces of the indigenous inhabitants of the land? This difficulty is resolved by the account here of the subterfuge of the Gibeonites: disguising themselves as representatives of a people living in a distant country and hence not subject to the ban, they trick the Israelites into making a binding pact of peaceful coexistence with them, and hence for all future times they must be spared. The ostensible exception to the programmatic rule of total destruction is thus given a narrative explanation or etiology.

What should also be observed about the story of the conquest in Joshua is that it is a vision of overwhelming military triumph. It is a triumph that is repeatedly attributed to God's power, not to Israel's martial prowess (though a couple of the reported episodes do show cunning tactical moves on the part of the Israelites). That notion is perfectly in keeping with the Deuteronomistic view of historical causation, in which God causes Israel to prevail when it is loyal to the covenant and brings defeat on the people when Israel betrays its commitment to God. The message, however, of an irresistible sweep of the Israelite forces through the land of Canaan addresses a geopolitical situation of the Israelite nation that was quite the opposite. It was the historical fate of Israel to sit at the bloody crossroads between powerful empires to the east and the south with some dire threats from the north as well. This chronic predicament came to seem much graver in the span of years from the destruction by Assyria of the northern kingdom of Israel in 721 BCE to the conquest of the southern kingdom of Judea by Babylonia in 589 BCE—the very period in which the early nucleus of Deuteronomy was formulated and when the book as a whole achieved its first general recension. What must have been in the minds of a good many Judeans after 721 BCE was that national existence itself was a highly contingent affair, that the people which had come to think of itself as chosen by God for a grand destiny, as the Patriarchal narratives in Genesis repeatedly asserted, could easily suffer disastrous defeat, bitter exile, perhaps even extinction. Whatever the rousing promises and consolations of theology, it would have been difficult to dismiss the awareness of imperial powers that could bring to bear overwhelming force on the tiny Israelite nation. The story of the conquest, then, served as a counter-move in the work of cultural memory: Israel had entered its land in a stirring triumphal drive as a power before which no man could stand. The theological warrant for this vision, antithetical as it was to the historical facts, was that as long as Israel remained faithful to all that its God had enjoined upon it, the people would be invincible.

Against this general background of theological explanation of historical events, the story of Achan in Chapter 7 is meant to play an exemplary role. Achan violates the ban, which is represented as an obligation imposed by God. The direct consequence is military defeat, and Israel cannot continue on its triumphal progress until the transgressor is singled out and punished by death. That punishment grimly extends to his entire family, as if the guilt were a kind of contagion that infected everyone in immediate contact with him and thus had to be ruthlessly expunged. If the transgression of a single person can have such dire widespread effects, how much more so when large numbers of the people backslide. This is the prospect raised by Joshua in his two valedictory addresses (Chapters 23 and 24). The emphasis of both these speeches is heavily Deuteronomistic: Joshua fears that the Israelites will intermarry with the surrounding peoples and worship their gods; he expresses doubt as to whether Israel will be up to the challenge of faithfulness to this demanding God—"You will not be able to serve the LORD, for He is a holy God. He is a jealous God, He will not put up with your crimes and your offenses" (24:19). Though his audience responds with a solemn pledge of fealty, the somber prospect has been evoked that Israel will betray its God and therefore suffer cataclysmic defeat and exile. In this fashion, there is a tension between the first twelve chapters of Joshua and the conclusion of the book, a contradiction between the vision of a grand conquest and the threat of national disaster.

Some of that tension is also detectable in the discrepancy between the Book of Conquests and the Book of Apportionments. The function of the elaborate drawing of tribal borders in the second of these two texts is to convey a sense of a systematic and orderly division of the land. Because the determination of the tribal territories is made by lot (*goral*), which is a divinely inspired oracular device, the clear implication is that God dictates the boundaries within which the sundry tribes are to live. The aim is to provide theological authentication and solidity to the existing tribal territories. In fact, there were likely to have been ad hoc arrangements marked by a good deal of fluidity, with tribes encroaching on one another's territories, migrating in pursuit of better pastureland

and tillable soil, and, at least in the case of Dan, being completely displaced by political circumstances. The mapping of boundaries, however, also incorporates several indications that the conquest of the land was not as comprehensive as the first twelve chapters of Joshua might lead one to conclude. This chronicle concedes that there were instances in which the Israelites were unable "to dispossess"—which is to say, conquer and destroy—the local Canaanites, an uncomfortable circumstance that the writer seeks to mitigate by noting that these unsubdued populations were reduced to the status of forced laborers as they continued to live alongside the Israelites.

The Book of Joshua thus registers a double awareness of Israel's historical predicament. The people had been promised the land by God, and its success in establishing an autonomous state, which very quickly became two states, over a large portion of Canaan was testimony to the fulfillment of that promise. The fulfillment is inscribed in the first half of the book. The conquest, however, was not total, and its permanency was menaced by a series of foreign powers. The book translates this contradiction into theological terms: Israel in the flush of its military triumph is imagined as staunchly loyal to its God, with the single exception of Achan; Israel, having taken possession of the land and drawn its boundaries, is seen as teetering on the brink of future disloyalties that will entail disastrous consequences. Though the tension between the two halves of the book is arguably an artifact of the redactional process that joined two different sources, the effect is to produce a dialectical perspective on the history of the nation. The Book of Judges follows logically from this because there it is vividly clear that Israel's tenure in the land before the monarchic period is unstable, that much of the Israelite population is either subject to foreign domination or exposed to the attacks of marauders. Accounting for the incompleteness of the conquest, which is already adumbrated in the latter part of Joshua, will become the task of the book that follows.

CHAPTER 1

And it happened after the death of Moses servant of the Lord, that 1
the Lord said to Joshua son of Nun, Moses's attendant, saying: "Moses 2
My servant is dead. And now, arise, cross this Jordan, you, and all this
people, to the land I am about to give to them, to the Israelites. Every 3
place where the sole of your foot treads, to you I have given it, as I spoke
to Moses, from the wilderness and this Lebanon to the Great River, the 4

---

1. *And it happened after the death of Moses.* These opening words are an explicit
device to create a direct link with the end of Deuteronomy, which reports the
death of Moses (Deuteronomy 34:5ff.), and the beginning of this book, in
which Joshua takes up Moses's task.

servant of the Lord. This identifying phrase, reiterated in this initial passage,
is a formal epithet for Moses, also used in Deuteronomy. Joshua is called his
"attendant," as he is in Numbers 11:28; the implication is that the attendant of
the Lord's servant will now assume the role of his master.

2. *this Jordan . . . this people.* The repeated use of the deictic *zeh*, "this" (and
again in verse 4, "this Lebanon") is positional. God is addressing Joshua across
the Jordan from Canaan. First, He points to "this Jordan," across which Joshua
will have to take the people, then to "this people," whom Joshua must lead, and
then to "this Lebanon," marking the northern limits of the land.

4. *from the wilderness and this Lebanon to the Great River, the River Euphrates.*
These are utopian—or perhaps one should say fantastic—borders never occupied by Israel and never within its military capacity to occupy.

River Euphrates, the whole land of the Hittites, and to the Great Sea,
5 where the sun sets, will be your territory. No man will stand up against
you all the days of your life. As I was with Moses, I shall be with you.
6 I shall not let go of you and I shall not forsake you. Be strong and stalwart, for you will make this people inherit the land that I vowed to their
7 fathers to give to them. But you must be very strong and stalwart to keep
and do according to all the teaching that Moses My servant charged
you. You shall not swerve from it to the right or the left, so that you may
8 prosper wherever you go. This book of teaching shall not depart from
your mouth, and you shall murmur it day and night, so that you may
keep to do according to all that is written in it; then you will make your
9 ways succeed and then you will prosper. Have I not charged you, 'Be
strong and stalwart'? Do not be terror-stricken and do not cower, for the
LORD your God is with you wherever you go."

10,11 And Joshua charged the people's overseers, saying: "Pass through the
midst of the camp and charge the people, saying, 'Prepare yourselves
provisions, for in three days you are to cross this Jordan to come to take

---

the whole land of the Hittites. This can scarcely be the region in Asia Minor
that was once the center of a Hittite empire. There were Hittite immigrants
scattered through Canaan from an early period. Shmuel Ahituv proposes that
the phrase reflects a usage in neo-Assyrian texts where it indicates everything
west of the Euphrates, including the Land of Israel.
to the Great Sea. The "Great Sea" is, as elsewhere, the Mediterranean.

6. *Be strong and stalwart.* This reiterated exhortation clearly reflects the military
setting of this initial charge by God to Joshua, who is commander-in-chief of
the army about to invade the land.

8. *This book of teaching shall not depart from your mouth.* The book in question
is almost certainly Deuteronomy, and the phrasing of the entire verse is strongly
Deuteronomistic.

10. *the people's overseers.* This is the same term used in the Exodus story
(5:10ff.). It derives from a verb meaning to document or record, and so it is not
necessarily a specialized military term.

11. *three days.* This is a conventional time-span in biblical narrative for an
interval of relatively short duration.

hold of the land that the LORD your God is about to give you to take hold of it.'" And to the Reubenites and to the Gadites, and to the half-tribe 12 of Manasseh, Joshua said: "Recall the word that Moses servant of the 13 LORD charged you, saying, 'The LORD your God is about to grant you rest and will give you this land. Your wives, your little ones, and your herds 14 shall dwell in this land that Moses has given you across the Jordan, but you shall cross over arrayed for combat before your brothers, all the mighty warriors, and you shall help them, until the LORD grants rest to 15 your brothers like you and they too take hold of the land that the LORD their God is about to give to them, and you shall return to the land of your holding and take hold of it, which Moses servant of the LORD has given to you across the Jordan where the sun rises.'" And they answered 16 Joshua, saying, "All that you charged us we will do, and wherever you send us we will go. As in all that we heeded Moses, so we will heed you. 17

---

13. *Recall the word that Moses . . . charged you.* The episode of the two and a half tribes that chose to settle on land east of the Jordan is initially reported in Numbers 32.

   grant you rest. The verb here has the obvious technical sense of granting respite from previously hostile neighboring peoples.

14. *arrayed for combat.* The Hebrew ḥamushim appears to derive from the word for "five," and it has been plausibly explained as referring to a battle formation, with troops on all four sides and a unit of fighting men inside the rectangle. In modern Hebrew, it means "armed."

17. *As in all that we heeded Moses, so we will heed you.* The Israelites in fact were repeatedly rebellious against Moses, but it is best to view this declaration of unswerving loyalty as an idealized representation of the people, not as an intended irony.

18 Only may the LORD your God be with you as He was with Moses. Every man who flouts your command and does not heed your word in all that you charge him shall be put to death. Only be strong and stalwart."

---

18. *Every man who flouts your command . . . shall be put to death.* What appears to be reflected in these stern words is the strictness of military justice: Israel is about to enter into battle, and whosoever does not obey the commander's orders will be summarily executed.

Only be strong and stalwart. The opening section of Joshua comprises four speeches: God to Joshua, Joshua to the people's overseers, Joshua to the trans-Jordanian tribes, and the response of the trans-Jordanian tribes to Joshua. These interlocked speeches are meant to convey a sense of perfect solidarity on the eve of the conquest of the land. Thus, the concluding words of the tribal spokesman exactly echo God's twice asserted exhortation to Joshua, with the addition of the emphatic *raq,* "only."

CHAPTER 2

And Joshua son of Nun sent out in secret two men as spies from Shittim, 1
saying, "Go, see the land, and Jericho." And they went and they came
to the house of a whore-woman whose name was Rahab, and they slept
there. And it was said to the king of Jericho, saying, "Look, men of the 2
Israelites have come here tonight to search out the land." And the king of 3
Jericho sent to Rahab, saying, "Bring out the men who have come to you,
who came to your house, for they have come to search out the whole land."

---

1. *two men as spies*. The two spies evoke the two spies in the story in Numbers
13–14. Joshua and Caleb son of Jephunneh, who did not come back with a fearful report like their ten companions. This story, then, on the eve of the conquest,
is framed as a pointed reversal of the failed spy mission in Numbers: there the
Israelites quail before the gigantic inhabitants of the land; here a Canaanite
woman reports that the inhabitants of the land quail before the Israelites.

    Shittim. This place-name means "The Acacias."

    the house of a whore-woman . . . and they slept there. Sometimes biblical usage
adds "woman" in this fashion to the designation of profession. "Whore," in turn,
seems to be used neutrally, not as a term of opprobrium. Though she may merely
be providing the two men lodging, the narrative coyly plays with the sexual
meaning of the verb *shakhav*, which also means simply to lie down, to sleep, or
spend the night. Similarly, the verb "come to," used in verse 3 and verse 4, also
has a sexual meaning when the object of the preposition is a woman. In fact,
Rahab in answering the king's inquiry may be saying that the two men were
merely her customers, and hence she had no idea that they might be spies.

3. *the whole land*. The king adds "whole" to the report that has been brought to
him: these spies have come on an extensive reconnaissance mission. Jericho is
a city-state, the prevalent political form in Canaan in this era, and would have
governed surrounding territory.

4   And the woman had taken the two men and hidden them, and she said,
    "The men indeed came to me and I did not know from where they were.
5   And as the gate was about to close at dark, the men went out. I know
    not where the men went. Pursue them quickly, for you can overtake
6   them." And she had taken them up to the roof and had hidden them
7   in the stalks of flax laid out for her on the roof. And the men pursued
    them along the Jordan by the fords, and they closed the gate when the
8   pursuers had gone out after them. They had not yet bedded down when
9   she went up to them on the roof. And she said to the men, "I know that
    the LORD has given you the land, and that your terror has fallen upon

---

4. *the woman had taken the two men and hidden them*. The sense of the verb is
evidently pluperfect: she had hidden the spies before the arrival of the king's
emissaries.

   as the gate was about to close at dark. The gates of the walled city were locked
at nightfall.

5. *Pursue them quickly, for you can overtake them*. In this shrewd maneuver,
Rahab simultaneously makes herself sound like a loyal subject of Jericho and
encourages the king's men to leave her house immediately, heading in what she
correctly calculates will be the wrong direction.

6. *stalks of flax laid out for her on the roof*. The flax would have been laid out on
the roof to dry in the sun. Hiding in the flax stalks may be a reminiscence of
baby Moses hidden (the same Hebrew verb) in the ark among the bulrushes.

7. *along the Jordan by the fords*. This, as Rahab has rightly surmised, would be
the most plausible route of pursuit because the men from Jericho are aware
that the Israelites are encamped east of the Jordan and assume that the spies
will try to reach a ford over which they can cross to return to their people.

9. *your terror has fallen upon us and . . . all the dwellers of the land quail before
you*. Rahab is directly quoting the Song of the Sea (Exodus 15:15–16), merely
reversing the order of terms in the poem: "all the dwellers of Canaan quailed. /
Terror and fear did fall upon them." Her words are a verbatim confirmation of
the assertion in the Song that the great news of the event at the Sea of Reeds
reached the Canaanites and dismayed them.

us and that all the dwellers of the land quail before you. For we have 10
heard how the LORD dried up the waters of the Sea of Reeds before you
when you came out of Egypt, and what you did to the two Amorite kings
across the Jordan, to Sihon and to Og, whom you put to the ban. And 11
we heard, and our heart failed, and no spirit arose in any man before
you, for the LORD your God, He is God in the heavens above and on
the earth below: And now, pray, vow to me by the LORD, for I have done 12
kindness with you, that you, too, shall do kindness with my father's
house and give me a faithful sign, and let my father and mother live, 13
and my brothers and my sisters, and all that is theirs, and save our lives
from death." And the men said to her, "Our own lives in your stead to 14
die! So long as you do not tell of this mission of ours. And so, when the
LORD gives us this land, we shall do faithful kindness with you." And 15
she lowered them with a rope through the window, for her house was in
the outer wall, and in the wall she dwelled. And she had said to them, 16

---

10. *what you did to the two Amorite kings*. This triumph, reported in Numbers
21, at the other end of the story of Wilderness wanderings from the victory at
the Sea of Reeds, is a recent event, perhaps having occurred in the last few
months before the present narrative moment.

11. *for the LORD your God, He is God in the heavens above and on the earth
below*. Rahab is cast as a good monotheist, persuaded of the LORD's supreme
sovereignty, as the Israelites are expected to be, by His dramatic intervention
in history.

14. *Our . . . lives in your stead to die!* This drastic offer expresses their recognition of the awesome solemnity of the vow they are taking.

15. *for her house was in the outer wall*. Many fortified cities in the region had
a double wall, and most interpreters understand the seemingly redundant *qir
haḥomah* ("wall of the wall") as an indication of the outer wall. In this way, being
lowered by a rope from her window enables them to get out of the city even
though the gate is locked.

16. *And she had said to them*. The context requires construing the verb here,
and at the beginning of the next verse, as pluperfects. Otherwise, one is left
with the absurd situation of this dialogue taking place at a distance, both parties
shouting, after she has lowered them with the rope.

"Go to the high country, lest the pursuers encounter you, and hide there
three days until the pursuers come back. Then you may go on your way."
17 And the men had said to her, "We will be clear of this vow that you made
18 us vow. Except, when we come into the land, this scarlet cord you must
tie in the window through which you lowered us, and your father and
your mother and all your father's house you must gather to you within
19 the house. And so, whosoever comes out of the doors of your house to
the street, his blood shall be on his head, and we will be clear. But whoever will be with you in the house, his blood is on our head if any hand
20 should touch him. And should you tell of this mission of ours, we will

---

Go to the high country. This is the mountainous area to the west of the Jordan
Valley and in the opposite direction from the one taken by the pursuers. The
terrain would also have afforded hiding places.

three days. As in Chapter 1, the time span is formulaic, but it is also a plausible interval to wait until the pursuers have given up the chase.

17. *We will be clear of this vow.* Having stated that they are prepared to die in
her stead should they violate the terms of the vow, they now stress that they will
have no obligation to carry it out unless she strictly adheres to her own terms
that they stipulate.

18. *this scarlet cord you must tie in the window.* This is a purely practical stipulation: the attackers need a sign to know which house they are to spare. The
scarlet cord recalls the scarlet cord attached to the hand of the newborn twin
Zerah in Genesis 38:28 and probably also the blood smeared on the lintel to
ward off the Destroyer in Exodus 12:13.

20. *And should you tell of this mission of ours, we will be clear of your vow.* The
concluding statement regarding a release from the vow concerns the vital interest of the two spies rather than the practical provision for the safety of Rahab
and her family.

be clear of your vow that you made us vow." And she said, "According   21
to your words, so shall it be." And she sent them off and they went, and
she tied the scarlet cord in the window. And they went and came to the   22
high country and stayed there three days, until the pursuers went back.
And the pursuers searched all along the way and did not find them.
And the two men went back and came down from the high country   23
and crossed over to Joshua son of Nun and recounted to him all that
had befallen them. And they said to Joshua, "Yes, the LORD has given   24
all the land into our hands, and what's more, all the dwellers of the land
quail before us."

---

21. *she tied the scarlet cord in the window.* Though it is possible to understand
this as an act she performs later, it may be that, mindful of the grave warning
of the two men, she hastens to affix the agreed-on sign as soon as they leave,
though she knows the attack will not come for at least several days.

22. *all along the way.* This would be the road parallel to the Jordan.

23. *crossed over.* Now they take a ford across the Jordan back to the Israelite
camp.

24. *all the dwellers of the land quail before us.* They are directly quoting one of
those inhabitants, Rahab, who in turn is quoting the Song of the Sea. Thus the
line from the poem becomes a kind of refrain that punctuates the middle and
the end of this episode.

CHAPTER 3

^I And Joshua rose early in the morning, and they journeyed on from Shittim and came to the Jordan, he and all the Israelites, and they spent
² the night there before they crossed over. And it happened at the end of three days that the overseers passed through the midst of the camp.
³ And they charged the people, saying, "When you see the Ark of the Covenant of the LORD your God, with the levitical priests carrying it,
⁴ then you shall journey from your place and go after it. But keep a distance between you and it, about two thousand cubits in measure. Do not come close to it. So that you may know the way in which you should
⁵ go, for you have not passed over this way in time past." And Joshua

---

1. *crossed over*. The verb *'avar*, which means either to cross over or, as in verse 2 and verse 4, to pass through or over, is repeated eight times in this chapter, thus marking the episode as a portentous liminal moment when the people of Israel cross over from their long Wilderness wanderings into the land they have been promised.

2. *at the end of three days*. The recurrence of this formulaic interval suggests a certain symmetry with the experience of the spies, who hide out in the high country for three days.

3. *the Ark of the Covenant*. The Ark contains the stone tablets of the Law. It is imagined as both a sacred and a magical object, and as such is also a numinous vessel carried into battle, as one sees in the early chapters of Samuel.

4. *But keep a distance*. The Ark, saturated with divine aura, is also a dangerous object. In 2 Samuel 6, when Uzza puts his hand on the Ark to prevent it from slipping from the cart in which it is carried, he is struck dead.
   about two thousand cubits. This would be a little over half a mile.

said, "Sanctify yourselves, for tomorrow the LORD will do wonders in
your midst." And Joshua said to the priests, saying, "Carry the Ark of 6
the Covenant, and cross over before the people." And they carried the
Ark of the Covenant and went before the people. And the LORD said 7
to Joshua, "This day I shall begin to make you great in the eyes of all
Israel, so they may know that as I was with Moses, I shall be with you.
And you, charge the priests, bearers of the Ark of the Covenant, saying, 8
'When you come to the edge of the waters of the Jordan, you shall stand
still in the Jordan.'" And Joshua said to the Israelites, "Draw near and 9
hear the words of the LORD your God." And Joshua said, "By this you 10
shall know that a living God is in your midst, and He will utterly dispossess before you the Canaanite and the Hittite and the Hivite and the
Perizzite and the Girgashite and the Amorite and the Jebusite. Look, 11
the Ark of the Covenant of the Master of all the earth is about to cross

---

7. *as I was with Moses, I shall be with you.* The "wonder" that God is about to
perform will in fact replicate a miracle done for Moses.

9–10. *And Joshua said . . . And Joshua said.* As a rule, when the formula for the
introduction of dialogue is repeated without an intervening response from the
second party, the repetition indicates some difficulty in response—puzzlement,
amazement, embarrassment, and so forth. Here the repetition has a purely
dramatic function. Joshua invites the people to draw close; they do so, scarcely
having an opening to say anything to him; then, when his audience is gathered
around him, Joshua goes on to give detailed instructions.

10. *the Canaanite and the Hittite.* In all, seven peoples are mentioned, fill-
ing out the formulaic number. The list itself is heterogeneous: Canaanite
and Amorite are general designations for the inhabitants of this territory; the
Hittites are immigrants from Asia Minor who were probably not a distinctive
Canaanite people in any political sense; little is known about the Perizzites and
the Girgashites, though the latter may have come from Asia Minor. In any case,
the enumeration of seven peoples does reflect a historical memory of Canaan
divided up among small city-states.

11. *Master of all the earth.* This is not an epithet that occurs in the Torah, and
since designations of the deity are important indicators of sources, its use may
point to a literary source distinct from those of the Pentateuch.

₁₂ over the Jordan before you. And now, take for yourselves twelve men
₁₃ from the tribes of Israel, one man from each tribe. And so when the
footsoles of the priests, bearers of the Ark of the LORD, Master of all the
earth, rest in the waters of the Jordan, the waters of the Jordan coming
₁₄ down from above will be cut off and stand up as a single mound." And
it happened, when the people journeyed forth from its tents to cross the
Jordan, with the priests, bearers of the Ark of the Covenant before the
₁₅ people, and when the bearers of the Ark reached the Jordan and the feet
of the priests, bearers of the Ark, were immersed in the water's edge—
the Jordan being full to all its banks throughout the harvest days—

---

12. *take for yourselves twelve men from the tribes of Israel.* These men play no
role in what immediately follows, though in the next chapter they are assigned
the task of placing twelve stones in the riverbed. Though this verse could be
construed as a prolepsis, it is more likely that it was erroneously transposed in
copying from the next section of the story, where it is duplicated in 4:2.

13. *the waters of the Jordan coming down.* This formulation harbors an etymological pun. The Jordan, *Yarden,* is called that because it "comes down" (verbal
stem y-r-d) from mountain heights in the north to the Dead Sea, the lowest
point on the face of the earth.

14–16. *And it happened. . . .* The syntax of these three verses, constituting
one long run-on sentence, is quite untypical of biblical prose, and its use here
builds a sense of climactic fulfillment as the miracle is enacted.

15. *the Jordan being full to all its banks throughout the harvest days.* This rather
awkward parenthetical clause, still further complicating the syntax, appears to
be an effort to explain a difficulty. As we learned in Chapter 2, there are numerous fords across the Jordan, and the two spies obviously used one of those to
cross back and forth. But the story needs an impassable Jordan to enable the
miracle of immobilizing its waters, and so we are reminded that in this moment
at the beginning of the spring (in the month of Nissan), the river would have
been overflowing after the winter rains. The reference to harvest days is a little
puzzling because early April is too soon for a harvest. Perhaps the phrase means
to say that this high level of the Jordan continues until the end of the first harvest in late May-early June.

the water coming down from above stood still, rose up in a single mound, 16
very far off from the town of Adam which is by Zanethan, and the water
going down to the Arabah Sea, the Salt Sea, was completely cut off, and
the people crossed over opposite Jericho. And the priests, bearers of the 17
Ark of the LORD's Covenant, stood firm on dry ground in the middle of
the Jordan, with all Israel crossing over on dry ground until the whole
nation finished crossing the Jordan.

---

16. *rose up in a single mound*. These words are the clearest indication that this
incident is a repetition of the drying up of the Sea of Reeds because the rare
term *ned*, "mound," is used, as it is in the Song of the Sea, Exodus 15:8. History
for the biblical writers moves forward but also repeats itself in significant patterns. This notion prepared the way for later typological conceptions of history.

very far off from the town of Adam which is by Zanethan. This odd and seemingly gratuitous specification of a place at some distance from the reported
event is a strategy of "documenting" the miracle by locating it along geographical coordinates.

the Arabah Sea. The Arabah is the geological rift through which the Jordan
runs.

17. *dry ground*. The Hebrew here, *ḥaravah*, is a different word from *yabashah*,
"dry land," the term used in Exodus 14–15 and also in Genesis.

CHAPTER 4

1 And it happened, when the whole nation had finished crossing over
2 the Jordan, that the Lord said to Joshua, saying, "Take for yourselves
3 from the people twelve men, one man from each tribe, and charge them,
saying, 'Carry from here, from the Jordan, from the place where the feet
of the priests stand firm, twelve stones and bring them across with you
and set them down at the encampment where tonight you will spend
4 the night.'" And Joshua called to twelve men whom he had readied
5 from the Israelites, one man from each tribe. And Joshua said to them,
"Cross over before the Ark of the Lord your God into the middle of the
Jordan and each of you lift up one stone on his shoulder according to
6 the number of the tribes of Israel, so this may be a sign in your midst:
Should your children ask you tomorrow, saying 'What are these stones
7 to you?' you shall say, 'That the waters of the Jordan were cut off before
the Ark of the Lord's Covenant, when it was crossing over the Jordan,
the waters of the Jordan were cut off, and these stones became a memo-
8 rial for the Israelites forever.'" And thus did the Israelites do, as Joshua
had charged them, and they carried twelve stones from the Jordan as
the Lord had spoken to Joshua, according to the number of the tribes
of Israel, and they brought them across with them to the encampment
9 and set them down there. And Joshua set up twelve stones in the middle

---

6. *Should your children ask you tomorrow.* This is a liturgical or, as some put
it, catechistic formula, which has fairly close parallels in Exodus 12:26–27;
Exodus 13:14–15; and Deuteronomy 6:20. "Tomorrow" is, of course, a homey
idiom for "in future times." The commemorative stones become a didactic
occasion for recounting the ancient miracle to future generations.

9. *And Joshua set up twelve stones in the middle of the Jordan.* This second set of
twelve stones looks redundant. There may have been a competing account of the

of the Jordan in the place where the feet of the priests, bearers of the
Ark of the Covenant, had stood, and they have been there to this day.
And the priests, bearers of the Ark of the Covenant, were standing in   10
the Jordan until all the mission that the LORD had charged Joshua to
speak to the people was finished, as all that Moses had charged Joshua.
And the people hurried and crossed over. And it happened, when all   11
the people had finished crossing over, that the Ark of the LORD, and
the priests with it, crossed over before the people. And the Reubenites   12
and the Gadites and the half-tribe of Manasseh crossed over in battle
array before the Israelites as Moses had spoken to them, about forty   13
thousand, vanguard of the army, crossed over before the LORD for battle
to the plains of Jericho. On that day the LORD made Joshua great in the   14
eyes of all Israel, and they feared him as they had feared Moses all the

---

event in which the conveyers of the traditional material felt that the more appropriate memorial was on the very spot where the feet of the priests had stood,
and the redactor decided to include both versions. This would, however, be an
underwater memorial scarcely visible except when the Jordan was nearly dry.
But see the next comment on the question of the stones' visibility.

and they have been there to this day. This is an explicitly etiological tag absent
in the report about the other set of twelve stones. It leads one to wonder whether
there in fact might have been a pattern of stones in the riverbed detectable from
the surface around which this story was woven.

10. *as all that Moses had charged Joshua.* This clause is puzzling because Moses
clearly had no role in instructing Joshua about the procedure for crossing the
Jordan. The clause does not appear in the Septuagint, and one suspects a
scribe inadvertently added it here because it was a set formula, and akin to the
concluding clause of verse 12, where the reference to Moses is appropriate.

14. *feared him.* The context makes clear that the force of the verb is not an
experience of fright but reverence or, perhaps more specifically, acceptance of
his authority. After the enactment of a miracle that closely corresponds to the
great miracle performed for Moses at the Sea of Reeds, Joshua's position as
legitimate leader is fully confirmed.

15,16 days of his life. And the LORD said to Joshua, saying, "Charge the priests, bearers of the Ark of the Covenant, that they come up from the Jordan."
17 And Joshua charged the priests, saying, "Come up from the Jordan."
18 And it happened when the priests, bearers of the Ark of the LORD's Covenant, came up from within the Jordan, that the priests' footsoles pulled up onto dry ground and the waters of the Jordan went back to
19 their place and flowed as in time past over all its banks. And the people had come up from the Jordan on the tenth of the first month, and they
20 camped at Gilgal at the eastern edge of Jericho. And these twelve stones
21 that they had taken from the Jordan, Joshua set up at Gilgal. And he said to the Israelites, saying, "When your children ask their fathers tomorrow,

---

16. *Ark of the Covenant*. Here a different term *'edut* ("witnessing") is used, but it appears to be a synonym for *brit*, "covenant."

19. *on the tenth of the first month*. This is the month of Nissan, approximately corresponding to April. The tenth of Nissan is four days before the Passover festival.
    the eastern edge of Jericho. This would mean the edge of Jericho's territory.

20. *And these twelve stones . . . Joshua set up at Gilgal*. The name Gilgal means "circle" (although it is given a secondary etymology in the next episode), and so we may assume that the stones were set up in a circle. Gilgal was an important cultic site in the first two centuries of the monarchy and figures significantly in the stories of Samuel, Elijah, and Elisha. As with other sacred places in ancient Israel, it may well have been a locus of pagan worship before it was taken over by the Israelites. There is some likelihood, then, that the stones arrayed in a circle were originally *matseivot*, cultic steles, and that the story is framed to make them integral to the monotheistic narrative.

saying, 'What are these stones?' you shall inform your children, saying, 22
'On dry land Israel crossed over this Jordan. For the LORD your God 23
dried up the waters of the Jordan before them until they crossed over,
as the LORD your God had done to the Sea of Reeds, which He dried
up before us until we crossed over, so that all the peoples of the earth 24
might know the hand of the LORD, for it is strong, so that you might fear
the LORD your God at all times.'"

---

22. *dry land.* Here *yabashah* is used, the term that occurs in Exodus 14–15.

23. *which He dried up before us.* The switch from third person ("dried up the
waters of the Jordan before them") to first person plural reflects the operation
of the commemorative ritual: it was the Israelites of Joshua's generation who
experienced the miracle at the Jordan, but all Israel of every generation—beginning with everyone over twenty who was with Moses, the generation that has
purportedly died out—participates in the defining moment of the parting of the
Sea of Reeds, replicated at the Jordan.

24. *so that all the peoples of the earth might know the hand of the LORD.* This
theme is similar to the one reiterated in the narrative of the Ten Plagues in
Exodus. Its validity will then be confirmed in the first verse of Chapter 5, which
in all likelihood is the actual conclusion of this narrative unit.

so that you might fear the LORD your God at all times. The repetition of "so
that," *lema'an*, inscribes a causal chain: the other nations recognize the power
of the God of Israel through this great miracle, and Israel fears, or reveres, its
God both through the direct experience of the miracle and through its confirmation in the eyes of the surrounding peoples.

CHAPTER 5

And it happened, when the Amorite kings who were across the Jordan
to the west, and all the Canaanite kings who were by the sea, heard that
the LORD had dried up the waters of the Jordan before the Israelites
until they crossed over, their heart failed and there was no longer any
spirit within them before the Israelites.

2 At that time the LORD said to Joshua, "Make you flint knives and again
3 circumcise the Israelites a second time." And Joshua made flint knives
4 and he circumcised the Israelites at the Hill of Foreskins. And this is the
reason that Joshua circumcised them: all the people who had come out
of Egypt, all the males, the men of war, had died out on the way in the
5 Wilderness when they came out of Egypt. For all the people who came
out were circumcised, but all the people who were born in the Wilderness on the way when they came out of Egypt were not circumcised.

---

2. *flint knives*. The story takes place in the late Bronze Age and was composed
sometime in the Iron Age, but flint knives are introduced precisely because
they are archaic, and hence the appropriate implements for this ritual act.
In the enigmatic story of the Bridegroom of Blood, Exodus 4:24–26, Moses's
wife takes a flint knife to circumcise their son, and the phrase "on the way"
that is used in this story appears three times there in relation to the lack of
circumcision.

4. *Joshua circumcised them*. The object of the verb in this clause, "them," is
merely implied.
   the males, the men of war. This is an indication of age, twenty years old
being the beginning point for military service. This generation, now died out,
is about to be replaced by a new generation of adult males who will carry out
the campaign of invasion.

For forty years did the Israelites go in the Wilderness until the whole 6
generation was finished, the men of war coming out of Egypt, who had
not heeded the LORD's voice, as the LORD had vowed to them not to
show them the land that the LORD had vowed to their fathers to give
to us, a land flowing with milk and honey. And their sons He put up in 7
their stead, them did Joshua circumcise, for they were uncircumcised,
as they had not been circumcised on the way. And it happened when 8
the whole nation had finished being circumcised, they remained in their
place until they revived. And the LORD said to Joshua, "I have rolled 9
away from you the shame of Egypt," and the name of the place has
been called Gilgal to this day. And the Israelites encamped at Gilgal and 10
performed the Passover rite on the fourteenth day of the month, in the

---

6. *the whole generation.* The Masoretic text reads "the whole nation," which is
surely too sweeping, but several Hebrew manuscripts as well as the Targum
show "generation" instead of "nation."

who had not heeded the LORD's voice. The specific reference is to the pusillanimous report of the ten spies, an episode already invoked in the story of the
two spies who go to Jericho. The ten spies in fact use the formula of a land
flowing with milk and honey.

7. *they had not been circumcised.* Literally, "they had not circumcised them."

8. *they remained in their place until they revived.* It must be said that, in realistic
terms, circumcision of all the fighting men just three days before battle is joined
would be a rather imprudent measure. But the writer is focusing on the state
of ritual purity necessary for the celebration of Passover and for the conduct
of warfare, and so he is prepared to have us assume that all the men are fully
recovered and ready for action after three days.

9. *I have rolled away from you the shame of Egypt.* The verb here, *galoti*, is an
etymological pun on Gilgal, a word that can mean either circle or, as in this
instance, wheel. The "shame of Egypt" may have a double sense, referring to
slavery—now, as free men entered into the covenant of Abraham, the Israelites
are ready to conquer their own land—and to their uncircumcised condition,
which was not the case while they were in Egypt but was entailed by their
flight from Egypt and their wanderings, during which it was not feasible to
circumcise the male infants.

10. *performed the Passover rite.* Of all the stipulated festival sacrifices, it was the
Passover that confirmed a person's full participation in the community of Israel.

11 evening, on the plains of Jericho. And they ate from the yield of the land
    from the day after the Passover sacrifice, flatbread and parched grain
12 on that very day. And the manna ceased on the day after, when they ate
    from the yield of the land, and the Israelites no longer had manna, and
    they ate from the produce of the land of Canaan in that year.

13 And it happened when Joshua was at Jericho that he raised his eyes and
    saw, and look, a man was standing before him, his sword unsheathed in
    his hand. And Joshua went toward him and said to him, "Are you ours
14 or our foes'?" And he said, "No. For I am the commander of the LORD's

---

For a male, being circumcised was a necessary condition for taking part in the
rite, as is made clear in Exodus 12:44. The celebration of the first Passover
took place on the eve of the departure from Egypt, and so this second Passover
marks the liminal moment of leaving the Wilderness for the land as the first
Passover marks the leaving of Egypt for the Wilderness.

11. *they ate from the yield of the land.* Evidently, the Israelite troops have been
foraging in the territory adjacent to Jericho. The substitution of the produce
of the land for the manna is another marker of the end of the Wilderness
experience.

13. *at Jericho.* The Hebrew particle b^e, which usually means "in," here must
refer to the vicinity of Jericho, which Joshua may be reconnoitering.
    and look, a man was standing before him. This is a crystal-clear instance of
the use of the presentative *hineh*, "look," as a shifter to the character's visual
perspective. The as yet unidentified figure is thus called "a man" because that
is how he appears to Joshua.
    Are you ours or our foes'? The translation seeks to emulate the compactness
of the Hebrew, *halanu 'atah 'im-letsareinu.* This brisk wording is beautifully
appropriate to the military context, as a sentry might urgently challenge an
unknown figure, wasting no words.

14. *I am the commander of the LORD's army.* This is a bit of fleshed-out mythology not attested to elsewhere. God, who is not infrequently a warrior God, is
often referred to as the LORD of Armies, but elsewhere there are no indications that He has an officer staff. This piece of imagining is perfectly apt in a
dedication scene for Joshua because the LORD's emissary can address him as
(superior) commander to commander.

army. Now have I come." And Joshua fell on his face to the ground and did obeisance, and he said to him, "What does my master say to his servant?" And the commander of the LORD's army said to Joshua, "Take 15 off your sandal from your foot, for the place on which you stand is holy." And so Joshua did.

Now have I come. This pronouncement, just two words in the Hebrew, is meant to sound portentous: now is the beginning of my great mission of conquest in which you will serve as my human deputy.

15. *Take off your sandal from your foot, for the place on which you stand is holy.* This is a direct quotation of God's words to Moses at the Burning Bush, Exodus 3:5, with the marginal difference that both "sandal" and "foot" are plurals in the Exodus story (here the singular usage implies the plural and might be thought of as a kind of synecdoche). The alignment of the present episode with the one of Moses at Mount Horeb points to differences as well as similarities. Both stories are dedication episodes as a leader is about to embark on his mission. But Moses is addressed by God Himself, as is appropriate for the greatest of prophets and the lawgiver, and at the site is a miraculously burning bush, proleptic of the moment when this very mountain will be enveloped in lightning during the great epiphany. Joshua is the legitimate heir of Moses but a lesser figure and no prophet, so he is addressed by the commander of the LORD's army, not by God Himself, and there is no pyrotechnic display on this holy ground.

CHAPTER 6

And Jericho was shut tight before the Israelites—no one came out and
no one went in. And the LORD said to Joshua, "See, I have given into
your hand Jericho and its king and the mighty warriors. And you shall go
round the town, all the men of war, encircling the town once. Thus you
shall do six days. And seven priests shall bear seven ram's horns before
the Ark, and on the seventh day you shall go round the town seven times
and the priests shall blow the ram's horns. And so, when the horn of the
ram sounds a long blast, when you hear the sound of the ram's horn, all
the people shall let out a great shout, and the wall of the town shall fall
where it stands, and the people shall go up, every man straight before
him." And Joshua son of Nun called to the priests and said to them,
"Bear the Ark of the Covenant, and seven priests shall bear seven ram's

---

2. *and the mighty warriors.* The Masoretic text lacks "and," which has been
added in the translation.

3. *town.* At most, Jericho would have had a scant few thousand inhabitants. So
"city" is an exaggeration.

4. *seven priests . . . seven ram's horns . . . on the seventh day . . . seven times.* The
rite devised to bring down the walls of the town involves a quadrupling of the
sacred number seven. But the destruction of the town is also an anti-creation
story: six days they go round the wall, and on the climactic seventh day, it col-
lapses and the town is reduced to rubble.
   ram's horns. These were primitive trumpets that produced a shrill and piercing sound. They were used to assemble troops in battle and at coronations.

5. *the people.* Given the military context, *'am* may have its secondary sense of
"troops."

horns before the Ark of the Covenant." And he said to the people, "Cross 7
over and go round the town, and the vanguard will cross over before the
Ark of the Lord." And it happened as Joshua spoke to the people that 8
the seven priests bearing the seven ram's horns before the Lord crossed
over and blew on the ram's horns, with the Ark of the Lord's Covenant
going after them. And the vanguard was going before the priests who 9
were blowing the ram's horns, and the rearguard was going behind the
Ark as they went and blew the ram's horns. And Joshua had charged the 10
people, saying, "You shall not shout and you shall not let your voice be
heard, and no word shall come out of your mouths until the moment I
say to you, 'Shout,' and then you shall shout." And the Ark of the Lord 11
went round the town encircling it once, and they came to the camp
and spent the night in the camp. And Joshua rose early in the morning, 12
and the priests bore the Ark of the Lord. And the seven priests bearing 13
seven ram's horns before the Ark of the Lord went along blowing the
ram's horns, with the vanguard going before them and the rearguard
going behind the Ark of the Lord, along they went blowing the ram's
horns. And they went round the town once on the second day, and they 14
returned to camp—so did they do six days. And it happened on the sev- 15
enth day that they rose early as dawn broke and went round the town
in this fashion seven times. Only on that day did they go round the city
seven times. And it happened when the priests blew the ram's horns for 16
the seventh time that Joshua said to the people "Shout! For the Lord
has given the town to you. And the town and all that is within it shall be 17
under the ban to the Lord, except that Rahab the whore shall live and

---

9. *blowing*. The consonantal text seems to read "they blew," but the Masoretic
marginal correction properly has this as *toq'ey*, "blowing."

10. *until the moment*. The literal sense of the Hebrew is "until the day," but the
word for "day," *yom*, is often a fluid indicator of time.

17. *the ban*. This total prescription of destruction, *ḥerem*, of the conquered city,
which means annihilating its population and its animals and, at least in this
instance, dedicating all objects of value to the Lord's treasury, is the grimmest
aspect of this triumphalist story. The enactment of the *ḥerem* is in keeping with
the reiterated injunction in Deuteronomy to exterminate the native population
of Canaan. That project is what Moshe Weinfeld has called a "utopian" plan

whoever is with her in the house, for she hid the messengers whom we
18 sent. Only you, you must keep from the ban, lest you covet and take of
the ban and put the camp of Israel under the ban and stir up trouble for
19 it. And all the silver and gold and vessels of bronze and iron shall be holy
20 to the LORD, they shall enter into the LORD's treasury." And the people
shouted and blew the ram's horns, and it happened when the people had
heard the sound of the ram's horn, the people let out a great shout, and
the wall fell where it stood, and the people went up into the town, every

---

because it is highly unlikely that it was ever acted upon. For the Deuteronomist, it
is a brutal way of expressing the absolute separation from the pagan population—
a separation that never really occurred—called for in his program of uncompromising monotheism, and the hallmark of the Deuteronomist is often detectable
in Joshua. The ḥerem was not an Israelite invention, as there is archeological
evidence that it was sometimes practiced by various Canaanite peoples.

except that Rahab the whore shall live and whoever is with her in the house.
There is, of course, a contradiction here with the story of the collapse of the
wall. If the wall around the town collapsed, how could Rahab, whose house was
in the wall, have been saved, and what good would the scarlet thread, which
implied protection against conscious human destroyers, have done? The medieval Hebrew commentator David Kimchi tried to save the consistency of the
text by proposing that only one part of the wall fell, through which breach the
Israelites entered the town, though all the encircling with ram's horns certainly
leads one to imagine that the entire wall came down. One suspects that the story
of the two spies and the story of the ram's horns reflect two different traditions
about the conquest of Jericho. Indeed, if the plan was to bring down the walls
miraculously, there would scarcely have been any need to reconnoiter the town
and the surrounding terrain, and the tale of the spies appears to assume a scenario in which the Israelite warriors will break into the city using conventional
means of warfare.

18. *lest you covet.* The received text reads, "lest you put under the ban," *pen
taḥarimu,* which doesn't make much sense. The translation follows the Septuagint, which appears to have used a Hebrew text that showed *pen taḥmedu* (a
reversal of consonants and a *dalet* for the similar-looking *reish*), "lest you covet."

20. *the people let out a great shout, and the wall fell where it stood.* Attempts have
been made to recover a historical kernel for this fabulous event by proposing
that it records the memory of an earthquake that leveled Jericho. (In fact, Jericho was built on a seismic fault and has been subject to earthquakes over the
ages.) But nothing in the telling of the tale remotely suggests an earthquake.

man straight before him, and they took the town. And they put under 21
the ban everything that was in the town, from man to woman, from lad
to elder, and to ox and sheep and donkey, by the edge of the sword. And 22
to the two men who had spied out the land Joshua had said, "Go into the
house of the whore-woman, and bring the woman out from there and all
that is hers, as you vowed to her." And the young spies came and brought 23
out Rahab and her father and her mother and her brothers and all that
was hers, and all her clan they brought out, and they put them outside
the camp of Israel. And the town they burned in fire and everything 24
in it. Only the silver and the gold and the vessels of bronze and iron
they placed in the treasury of the LORD's house. And Rahab the whore 25

The ground is not said to move, and the destruction occurs through the deployment of sevens and the ram's horns' blasts and the shouting. One can also
dismiss the idea of shock waves of sound splitting the walls as a scientific non-
starter. The whole point of the story is its miraculous character. Almost everywhere in biblical narrative, Israel triumphs not through any martial powers,
which get scant representation, but because God battles for Israel (compare
the Song of the Sea, the Song of Deborah, and Moses' upraised arms in the
defeat of the Amalekites). This story, then, is framed to vividly illustrate how
the Israelite conquest of the first principal Canaanite town in the Jordan Valley
is entirely due to the spectacular intervention of the LORD, Who gives Joshua
the detailed instructions for the procedures of circumambulating the town with
the Ark and the ram's horns. It should also be noted that the extensive archeological exploration of Jericho indicates that its conquest by Joshua could not
have taken place. There was a very old town on this site, but it was destroyed
by the Middle Bronze Age, and at the putative time of Joshua's conquest in
the Late Bronze Age, toward the end of the thirteenth century BCE, there had
been no walled town on this site at least for a couple of centuries. The writer
no doubt had in mind Jericho's antiquity—it is one of the oldest cities in the
world—and its role as eastern gateway to Canaan, but historically it could not
have been an object of Joshua's conquest.

23. *the young spies*. Only here are they identified as *ne'arim*, "lads" or young men,
thought it is possible that the term has its secondary sense of "elite soldiers."

24. *the LORD's house*. This phrase is an anachronism—in general, it refers to
the temple—because at the time of the conquest there would have been only
a portable sanctuary, not referred to as a "house."

and her father's house and all that was hers Joshua kept alive, and she has dwelled in the midst of Israel to this day, for she hid the messengers 26 that Joshua had sent to spy out Jericho. And Joshua imposed a vow at that time, saying, "Cursed be the man before the LORD who will arise and rebuild this town, Jericho.

> With his firstborn shall he found it,
> and with his youngest set up its portals."

27 And the LORD was with Joshua, and his fame was throughout the land.

---

25. *she has dwelled in the midst of Israel to this day.* This clause must mean that Rahab's descendants have dwelled in the midst of Israel to this day. It is thus an etiological note, explaining how a particular Canaanite clan came to be naturalized Israelites.

26. *Cursed be the man . . . who will . . . rebuild this town.* The reason for the implacability toward Jericho is not entirely clear since there is no indication that its inhabitants perpetrated war crimes, as did the Amalekites in Exodus. Perhaps this should be understood in the context of the miraculous destruction of the walls: that event is a token for the laying low of the inhabitants of the land before the invading Israelites (something that never happened historically), and so as a sign and symbol of the whole conquest, the town razed through divine intervention should never be rebuilt.
With his firstborn shall he found it / and with his youngest set up its portals. The solemnity of the vow is reinforced by casting this dire prediction in a line of poetry. Rashi nicely catches the narrative progression from the first verset to the second: "At the beginning of the foundation when he rebuilds it, his firstborn son will die, whom he will bury and go on until the youngest dies at the completion of the work, which is setting up the portals." In 1 Kings 16–34, it is recorded that at the time of Ahab, "Hiel of Beth-El rebuilt Jericho. With Abiram, his firstborn, he founded it, and with Segub his youngest he set up its portals, according to the word of the LORD that He spoke through Joshua son of Nun." Joshua's curse may have been formulated to explain a calamitous event that occurred three and a half centuries later.

CHAPTER 7

Ａnd the Israelites violated the ban, and Achan son of Carmi, son of 1
Zabdi, son of Zerah from the tribe of Judah took from the ban, and the
LORD's wrath flared against the Israelites.

And Joshua sent men from Jericho to Ai, which is by Beth-Aven to the 2
east of Bethel, and he said to them, saying, "Go up and spy out the
land," and the men went up and spied out Ai. And they came back to 3
Joshua and said to him, "Let not the whole people go up. Let about two
thousand men or three thousand men go up and strike Ai. Do not weary
the whole people there, for they are few." And about three thousand 4

---

1. *the Israelites violated the ban . . . Achan . . . took from the ban.* This conjunction of subjects intimates why, in the harsh retribution of this episode, Achan
must be extirpated: his violation of the ban imparts guilt, as though by contagion, to the whole people, as the defeat at Ai will immediately demonstrate.

3. *about two thousand men or three thousand men.* Boling's contention that
'elef here is not a number but means a "contingent," perhaps no more than
twenty or thirty men, may be supported by the fact that thirty-six deaths in
the defeat are regarded as a catastrophic loss. This is not, however, conclusive
evidence because the Israelites are supposed to carry out the conquest virtually
unscathed, as at Jericho. Boling's claim that the particle *kᵉ* before the number
means "precisely" and not, as it usually does, "about," is dubious because the
alternative of "two or three," whether thousand or contingents, suggests approximation, not exactitude.

men from the people went up there, and they fled before the men of Ai.
5 And the men of Ai struck down about thirty-six of them and pursued
them from before the gate as far as Shebarim and struck them down
6 on the slope. And the people's heart failed and turned to water. And
Joshua tore his robes and flung himself on his face to the ground before
the Ark of the LORD till evening—he and the elders of Israel—and they
7 put dust on their heads. And Joshua said, "Alas, O Master LORD, why
did You insist on bringing this people across the Jordan to give us into
the hand of the Amorite and to destroy us? Would that we had been
8 content to dwell across the Jordan. I beseech you, my Master, what
9 should I say after Israel has turned tail before its enemies? And the
Canaanites and all the dwellers in the land will hear and draw round us
and cut off our name from the earth. And what will You do for Your great
10 name?" And the LORD said to Joshua, "Rise up. Why have you fallen on
11 your face?" Israel has offended and also has broken My covenant that I
charged them and also has taken from the ban and also stolen and also

---

5. *pursued them from before the gate.* The evident strategy is a sudden sortie
from the gate of the town, taking the besiegers, who are too few in number, by
surprise.

7. *why did You insist on bringing this people across the Jordon to give us into the
hand of the Amorite and to destroy us?* Joshua's complaint is distinctly reminiscent of the complaints of the Israelites in the Wilderness to Moses, asking him
why he brought them into the Wilderness to perish instead of leaving them in
peace in Egypt. The echo may suggest that Joshua is not quite as fit a leader
as Moses.

9. *the Canaanites.* There is a loose interchange of reference between "Amorites"
and "Canaanites."
   And what will You do for Your great name? God's reputation as all-powerful
deity is contingent on the success of His chosen people. Moses uses the same
argument when God in His anger threatens to wipe out Israel.

11. *also . . . also . . . also . . . also.* These repetitions of *gam*—which equally has
the sense of "even" or "actually"—vividly express God's wrathful indignation.

denied it and also put it in their bags. And the Israelites have not been 12
able to stand up against their enemies. They have turned tail before
their enemies, for they themselves have come under the ban. I will not
continue to be with you if you do not destroy the banned things from
your midst. Rise, sanctify the people, and say 'Sanctify yourselves for 13
the morrow, for thus the LORD God of Israel has said, There are banned
things in your midst, O Israel! You will not be able to stand up against
your enemies until you remove the banned things from your midst. And 14
you shall draw near in the morning according to your tribes. And it
shall be, that the tribe on which the LORD lets the lot fall shall draw
near according to its clans, and the clan on which the LORD lets the lot
fall shall draw near according to its households, and the household on
which the LORD lets the lot fall shall draw near according to its men.
And it shall be, that he on whom the lot falls for taking the banned 15
things shall be burned in fire, he and all that is his, because he broke
the LORD's covenant and because he has done a scurrilous thing in
Israel.'" And Joshua rose early in the morning and brought Israel near 16
according to its tribes, and the lot fell on the tribe of Judah. And he 17
brought near the clans of Judah, and the lot fell on the clan of Zerah,
and he brought near the clan of Zerah, and the lot fell on Zabdi. And 18
he brought near his household according to the men, and the lot fell on

---

12. *they themselves have come under the ban*. Through the contamination of
having taken objects devoted to destruction, they have become subject to
destruction. The word "themselves" has been added in the translation for the
sake of clarity.

14. *draw near*. This is a technical term for approaching the Ark of the Covenant.
    lets the lot fall. The verb repeatedly used in this section also means "to catch"
or "to trap." What is involved in this process is an oracular device—most likely
the Urim and Thummim—that yields a binary yes / no answer, thus serving to
select one from many.

17. *the clans of Judah*. The received text has "the clan of Judah," but a tribe is
not a clan. Several Hebrew manuscripts show the more plausible plural form.

19 Achan son of Carmi son of Zerah of the tribe of Judah. And Joshua said to Achan, "My son, show honor, pray, to the LORD God of Israel, and make confession to Him, and tell me, pray, what you have done. Do not
20 conceal it from me." And Achan answered Joshua and said, "Indeed, it is I who offended against the LORD God of Israel, and thus and so I
21 have done. I saw in the booty a fine fur mantle and two hundred shekels of silver and an ingot of gold fifty shekels in weight, and I coveted them and took them, and there they are, buried in the ground within my tent,
22 and the silver is underneath them." And Joshua sent messengers and they ran to the tent, and there it was buried in his tent, with the silver
23 underneath it. And they took these from within the tent and brought them to Joshua and to all the Israelites, and he presented them before

---

19. *My son, show honor, pray, to the* LORD *God of Israel, and make confession to Him.* Joshua's language in addressing Achan is cunningly gentle, suggesting he intends to draw in his interlocutor and then lead him to divulge his crime. He begins by calling Achan "my son," elsewhere an affectionate form of address in the Bible; he uses the polite particle of entreaty, *na'*, "pray," and at first does not mention guilt but rather honoring God. The idiom for "make confession," *ten todah*, more frequently means "to give thanks," so it sounds almost as though Joshua were about to say something quite positive to the man who will be made to confess his guilt and then undergo horrendous punishment.

20. *Indeed, it is I who offended.* Achan's immediate and full confession is probably best explained by his awareness that the oracle has singled him out, the lot falling on him alone of all the multitude of Israel, and so he feels he has no choice but to admit his guilt. Joshua's ostensibly fatherly approach to him may also make him sense that he is a member of this community now gravely endangered by his act, and hence he must make restitution, whatever the price.

thus and so I have done. Though this is an idiom that can be used in place of a detailed account, here it is proleptic: the precise content of "thus and so" is laid out in the next verse.

21. *a fine fur mantle.* The Masoretic text reads "a fine Shinar mantle," neatly rendered in the King James Version as "a goodly Babylonish garment" because Shinar is another name for Babylon. There is no evidence that Shinar specialized in exporting fine apparel, and this translation reads instead of *shin'ar*, deleting the middle consonant, *sei'ar*, "hair" or "fur."

the LORD. And Joshua took Achan son of Zerah and the silver and the   24
mantle and the ingot of gold and his sons and his daughters and his ox
and his donkey and his flock and his tent and all that was his, and all
Israel was with him, and he brought them up to the Valley of Achor.
And Joshua said, "Even as you have stirred up trouble for us, the LORD   25
shall stir up trouble for you on this day." And all Israel pelted them
with stones and burned them in fire and pelted them with stones. And   26
they piled up over him a great heap of stones to this day, and the LORD
turned back from His blazing wrath. Therefore is the name of that place
called the Valley of Achor to this day.

---

24. *And Joshua took Achan . . . and the silver and the mantle . . . and his sons and
his daughters . . .* The lining up in a single syntactic string of human beings,
material treasure, and animal possessions is disturbing. The evident assumption about the family members is that they have been contaminated by Achan's
violation of the ban, and hence they must perish with him. One notes that
Achan has considerable possessions (the donkey and ox may well be collective
nouns), which makes his crime all the more heinous. The collective punishment is nevertheless troubling.

   the Valley of Achor. This means the Valley of Trouble, making the end of
this story an etiological tale about the origin of the place-name. It may have
been originally called the Valley of Trouble for entirely different reasons—for
example, because its terrain was treacherous or bleak and barren.

25. *burned them in fire and pelted them with stones.* The burning may refer only
to the material objects because it was not customary to burn bodies after stoning. The repeated clause about pelting with stones seems redundant.

26. *Therefore is the name of that place called.* This is an explicit etiological
formula.

CHAPTER 8

A nd God said to Joshua, "Do not be afraid and do not cower. Take with you all the combat troops and rise, go up to Ai. See, I have given in your hand the king of Ai and his people and his town and his land. And you shall do to Ai as you did to Jericho and to its king. Only its booty and its cattle you may plunder. Set up for yourself an ambush against the town behind it." And Joshua arose, and all the combat troops with him, to go up to Ai. And Joshua chose thirty thousand men, sturdy warriors, and sent them out at night. And Joshua charged them, saying, "See, you are to lie in ambush against the town behind the town. Do not keep very far

---

2. *Only its booty and its cattle you may plunder.* Ai, like Jericho, is to be put to the ban, its structures burned and all its inhabitants massacred, but an exception is made for booty, which the conquering Israelites are allowed to take.

3. *the combat troops.* Throughout this episode, *'am*, elsewhere "people," clearly has this military sense.
    thirty thousand men. The very large number here for men in an ambush is cited by proponents of the idea that *'elef* must refer to a small contingent and does not mean a thousand. But highly exaggerated numbers are often used in ancient narrative, and the sense of "contingent" in the count of the deaths of the town's inhabitants in verse 30 is problematic.

4. *behind the town.* This would be west of the town. The main gates of the town are evidently on the eastern side, and the main Israelite camp is northeast of the city.

4.–8. Although God had said he would deliver Ai to Joshua, it is Joshua's shrewdness as a strategist that brings about the fall of the town. The elaboration of the details of military strategy is untypical of biblical narrative. Scholars have pointed out a similarity not only in strategy but also in wording between this story and the account of the siege of Gibeah in the civil war reported in Judges 20, and it is generally thought that this story draws on the one in Judges. Joshua

away from the town, and all of you must be on the ready. And I and the ₅
troops that are with me, we shall draw near the town, and so, when they
come out toward us as before, we shall flee from them, and they will ₆
come out after us till we draw them away from the town, for they will
think, 'They are fleeing from us as before,' and we shall flee from them.
And you will rise from the ambush and take hold of the town, and the ₇
LORD your God will give it into your hand. And so, when you seize the ₈
town, you will set fire to the town, according to the word of the LORD
you will do. See, I have charged you." And Joshua sent them off, and ₉
they went to the ambush, and they stayed between Bethel and Ai to the
west of Ai. And Joshua spent that night among the troops. And Joshua ₁₀
rose early in the morning and marshaled the troops, he and the elders
of Israel, before the troops, to Ai. And all the combat troops who were ₁₁
with him went up and approached and came opposite the town, and they
camped to the north, with the ravine between them and Ai. And he took ₁₂
about five thousand men and set them as an ambush between Bethel and
Ai to the west of the town. And they put the troops, the whole camp, to ₁₃
the north of the town, and its covert contingent, to the west of the town.

---

shrewdly capitalizes on the previous defeat of the Israelites at Ai by seeming to
repeat the same tactical error, positioning his troops in front of the town gate
and then retreating. This time, however, he hides an attack unit behind the
town that will move forward against it once the armed men of the town have
been drawn out in pursuit of the main body of Israelites.

10. *before the troops*. This phrase looks odd and may reflect a scribal error.

12. *And he took about five thousand men*. This verse seems to replicate verses 3–4
using a different (somewhat more plausible) number—5,000 instead of 30,000.
It also puts the sending out of the ambush troops after the general encampment,
not before it. Two different versions may have been awkwardly spliced together.

13. *And they put the troops, the whole camp*. Like the translation, the wording
of the Hebrew is a bit clumsy and the syntax ambiguous.
  its covert contingent. The Hebrew *'aqev* usually means "heel." There is no
evidence that it means "rearguard," as some claim, and an ambush is not a rearguard. It is equally questionable that it could mean "far edge," again an inap-
propriate term for ambush. The translation follows the Targum of Jonathan,
Rashi, and Kimchi, in relating *'aqev* to *'oqbah*, a term that suggests deviousness
and that might apply to an ambush.

14 And Joshua spent that night in the valley. And it happened, when the king of Ai saw it, that the men of the town hurried early morning and came out toward Israel to do battle, he and all his troops, at the set place opposite the Arabah. He did not know there was an ambush against him 15 behind the town. And Joshua and all Israel were routed before them 16 and fled on the road to the wilderness. And all the troops who were in the town were mustered to pursue Joshua, and were drawn away from 17 the town. And not a man remained in the town, in Ai, who did not go 18 out after Israel, and they left the town open and pursued Israel. And the LORD said to Joshua, "Reach out with the javelin that is in your hand toward Ai, for into your hand I shall give it," and Joshua reached out with 19 the javelin that was in his hand toward the town. And the ambushers rose quickly from their place and ran as his hand reached out, and they entered the town and took it, and they hurried and set the town on fire. 20 And the men of Ai turned behind them and saw and, look, smoke was rising from the town toward the heavens, and they had no place in any direction to flee, while the troops who had fled to the wilderness became 21 the pursuers. And Joshua and all Israel saw that the ambushers had taken the town and that the smoke from the town was rising, and they struck

---

Joshua spent that night. The Masoretic text reads *wayelekh,* "walked," but a few manuscripts show *wayalen,* "spent the night," which seems more plausible.

14. *the Arabah.* This is the north-south rift of the Jordan Valley and is equivalent to the wilderness several times mentioned in this episode.

15. *were routed.* The obvious implication in context is: pretended to be routed. The verb used *wayinag'u* (literally, "were smitten / plagued") comes instead of the expected *wayinagfu,* and may be influenced by the parallel passage in Judges 20, where the same verbal stem is employed in a different sense.

18. *Reach out with the javelin that is in your hand.* The exact nature of the weapon, *kidon,* is in dispute. (Modern Hebrew has adopted it as the term for bayonet.) Some scholars think it is a kind of scimitar. In any case, the outstretched *kidon* is both a signal for the men in the ambush to move against the town and a magical act pointedly reminiscent of Moses's upraised staff in the battle against Amalek reported in Exodus 17.

21. *the ambushers.* The Hebrew term *ha'orev* can refer either to the ambush or, as a collective noun, to the combatants carrying out the ambush.

down the men of Ai. And these had come out of the town toward them 22
so that they were in the midst of Israel, who were on both sides, and they
struck them down till they left among them no remnant or survivor. And 23
the king of Ai they caught alive and brought him forth to Joshua. And 24
it happened, when Israel had finished killing all the inhabitants of Ai in
the field, in the wilderness where they had pursued them, all of them by
the edge of the sword to the last of them, all Israel turned back to Ai and
struck it with the edge of the sword. And all who fell on that day, men 25
and women, came to twelve thousand, all the people of Ai. And Joshua 26
did not pull back his hand that he had reached out with the javelin until
he had put all the inhabitants of Ai under the ban. Only the cattle and 27
the booty of that town did the Israelites plunder, according to the word of
the LORD that He charged to Joshua. And Joshua burned Ai and turned 28
it into an everlasting heap, a devastation to this day. And the king of Ai 29
he impaled on a pole till eventide, and when the sun was setting, Joshua
give orders, and they took his corpse down from the pole and flung it
by the entrance of the town gate and put over it a pile of stones to this

---

22. *And these had come out of the town toward them*. These are the ambushers,
who, having put the town to the torch, now attack its troops outside, who are
caught in a pincer movement between the main Israelite force and the ambushers (whether 5,000 or 30,000). The reference to no place to flee in verse 20
may be out of chronological order because it makes good sense here, when the
men of Ai are attacked from both sides.

24. *turned back to Ai and struck it with the edge of the sword*. The gruesome
reality of this report is as follows: the ambushing force, after setting fire to the
town and then coming out to join in the attack on the troops of Ai, now comes
back with the main Israelite camp to the town to slaughter the women and
elders and children left there.

29. *impaled on a pole*. This is the form of execution that many modern scholars think likely. But the traditional rendering of "hanged on a tree" remains a
distinct possibility.
    *they took his corpse down from the pole and flung it by the entrance of the
town gate*. The use of the verb "flung" is a clear indication that this is not an
honorable burial, though the biblical prohibition against leaving a body hanging
overnight is preserved. The place of burial may point toward the area in front
of the gates of the town where the Israelites were killed in their earlier attack.

30 day. Then did Joshua build an altar to the LORD God of Israel on Mount
31 Ebal, as Moses the servant of the LORD had charged the Israelites, as
it is written in the book of the teaching of Moses, "an altar of whole
stones, over which no iron has been brandished," and they offered up
on it burnt offerings to the LORD, and they sacrificed well-being sacri-
32 fices. And he wrote there on the stones the repetition of the teaching
33 of Moses, which he had written in the presence of the Israelites. And
all Israel and its elders and its overseers and its judges were standing
on both sides of the Ark opposite the levitical priests, bearers of the Ark
of the Covenant of the LORD, sojourner and native alike, over against
Mount Gerizim, and its other half over against Mount Ebal, as Moses,
34 servant of the LORD, had formerly charged to bless Israel. And afterward
he read out all the words of the teaching, the blessing and the curse,
35 according to all that is written in the book of the teaching. There was no
word of all that Moses had charged that Joshua did not read out before
the whole assembly of Israel and the women and the little ones and the
sojourners who went in their midst.

---

30. *Then did Joshua build an altar*. This textual unit invokes the two mountains
of blessing and curse mentioned in Deuteronomy 11:26–32, and is a direct
implementation of the command in Deuteronomy 27:2–3, "on the day that
you cross the Jordan into the land that the LORD your God is about to give you,
you shall set up great stones and coat them with plaster. And you shall write
on them the words of this teaching . . ." But the placement of the episode
has puzzled both ancient and modern commentators. Temporally, it does not
happen right after the crossing of the Jordan as it should, and geographically,
the Israelites at Ai are not opposite Mount Ebal and Mount Gerizim.

31. *an altar of whole stones, over which no iron has been brandished*. This is an
approximate quotation of Exodus 20:25.

32. *the repetition of the teaching of Moses*. The Hebrew *mishneh torat mosheh*
refers to Deuteronomy (that Greek name itself being a rendering of the Hebrew
mishneh torah). The Deuteronomist behind this story is clearly promoting the
interests of his own privileged text.

CHAPTER 9

And it happened when all the kings heard who were beyond the 1
Jordan, in the high country and in the lowland and along the whole
shore of the Great Sea opposite Lebanon, the Hittite and the Amorite,
the Canaanite, the Perizzite, the Hivite and the Jebusite, that they gath- 2
ered together to do battle with Joshua and with Israel in united resolve.
And the inhabitants of Gibeon had heard what Joshua did to Jericho 3
and to Ai. And they on their part acted with cunning and provisioned 4
themselves and took worn-out sacks for their donkeys and worn-out and
cracked and trussed-up wineskins, and worn-out and patched sandals 5

---

1. *beyond the Jordan*. Since all the peoples enumerated here are Canaanites
living on the western side of the Jordan, this phrase would have to mean beyond
the Jordan from the viewpoint of the Israelites coming from the eastern side,
though elsewhere it almost always refers to trans-Jordanian territory.

2. *in united resolve*. The literal sense of the Hebrew is "with one mouth." It is
historically quite unlikely that the divided city-kingdoms of Canaan could have
constituted themselves as a single united force.

4. *they on their part acted with cunning*. In context, the "on their part" (or "too")
must refer to the immediately preceding story of the conquest of Ai. There the
Israelites used the cunning of the ambush strategy to destroy the town; here,
by contrast, cunning is used by the Gibeonites to save themselves.
   provisioned themselves. The Masoretic text reads *wayitstayru*, which might
mean "they painted themselves"—that is (perhaps), "they disguised themselves." An emendation yields *wayitsdaydu* (the letters *reish* and *dalet* look quite
similar), which seems more plausible, especially given the prominence of the
cognate noun *tsayid*, "provisions," in this episode.
   trussed-up. The wineskins are held together with cords or strips of leather
because they are falling apart.

on their feet and worn-out cloaks upon them, and all the bread of their
6 provision was dry and moldy. And they went to Joshua at the Gilgal camp
and said to him and to the men of Israel, "We have come from a far-
7 away land, and now seal a pact with us." And the men of Israel said to
the Hivites, "Perhaps you dwell in our midst, so how can we seal a pact
8 with you?" And they said to Joshua, "We are your servants." And Joshua
9 said to them, "From where are you and from where do you come?" And
they said to them, "From a very far-away land, your servants have come
through the fame of the LORD your God, for we have heard the report of
10 Him and all that He did in Egypt, and all that He did to the two Amorite
kings who were across the Jordan, to Sihon king of Heshbon and to Og
11 king of Bashan which is in Ashtaroth. And our elders and all the inhabitants of our land said to us, saying, 'Take in your hand provisions for the
way and go to them and say to them, We are your servants, and now
12 seal a pact with us.' This bread of ours we took still warm as provisions
from our homes on the day we went out toward you, and now, look, it is
13 dry and has turned moldy. And these wineskins that we filled were new,
and now they are cracked, and these cloaks of ours and our sandals have

---

6. *We have come from a far-away land*. With the evidence of the just consummated destruction of Jericho and Ai, the Gibeonites seem aware that the Israelites are embarked on a campaign to annihilate the indigenous population
of Canaan, and so they adopt the subterfuge of pretending to be from a land
far from Canaan. This entire story is in fact an elaborate etiological tale that
betrays the shaky historical basis of this canonical account of the conquest.
Deuteronomy, with its call for a radical separation from the pagan peoples of
the land, enunciated a program of genocide. Such a program was never actually
carried out, and the situation of Israel among the Canaanites was by and large
the opposite: the two populations frequently mingled, and the Israelites were
often open to cultural and religious influences from the Canaanite peoples.
The author of this episode was trying to resolve a contradiction: a particular
group of Canaanites—the Gibeonites—were not only living cheek by jowl with
the Israelites but were performing subservient duties at an Israelite sanctuary
at Gibeon. The story comes to explain how the Gibeonites were not wiped out,
as the program of total destruction dictated, and how they came to play a role
in an Israelite cultic place.

9. *a very far-away land*. Pushed by Joshua, they add "very" to their previous
words.

worn out from the very long way." And the men took from their provi- 14
sions, and they did not inquire of the LORD. And Joshua made peace 15
with them, and sealed a pact with them to preserve their lives, and the
chieftains of the community made a vow to them. And it happened at 16
the end of three days after they had sealed the pact with them, that they
heard that they were neighbors and were dwelling in their midst. And 17
the Israelites journeyed forth and came to their towns on the third day,
and their towns were Gibeon and Chephirah and Beeroth and Kiriath-
Jearim. But the Israelites did not strike them down, for the chieftains 18
of the community had made a vow to them in the name of the LORD
God of Israel, and all the community complained against the chieftains.
And all the chieftains said to the whole community, "We have made a 19
vow to them in the name of the LORD God of Israel, and now we cannot
touch them. This let us do to them, letting them live, that there be no 20
fury against us for the vow we made to them." And the chieftains said 21
of them, "Let them live, and they will be hewers of wood and drawers

---

14. *And the men took from their provisions.* It may seem puzzling that Israelites
should want to eat the dry and moldy bread of the Gibeonites, but Kimchi
is probably right in surmising that breaking bread—even virtually inedible
bread—with the strangers was a way of ritually confirming a treaty of peace
with them.

they did not inquire of the LORD. This is the technical idiom for inquiring
of an oracle. Without such guidance, Joshua and the Israelites are taken in by
the deception.

17. *on the third day.* Though this is the formulaic number for relatively short
journeys, it is also an implication that the Gibeonite towns are well within the
borders of Canaan.

19. *We have made a vow to them . . . and now we cannot touch them.* Vows made
in the name of the deity—compare the story of Jephthah's daughter in Judges
11—are irrevocable and cannot be renegotiated.

20. *fury.* The Hebrew *qetsef* means divine rage, characteristically manifested
in a plague.

21. *hewers of wood and drawers of water.* These are menial workers at the lowest
point in the social hierarchy, as is clear in Deuteronomy 29:9–10: "You are stationed here today all of you before the LORD your God, your heads, your tribes,

of water for the whole community, as the chieftains have said of them."
22 And Joshua called to them and spoke to them, saying, "Why did you
deceive us, saying, 'We are very far-away from you,' when you dwell in
23 our midst? And now, you are cursed, and no slave or hewer of wood or
drawer of water for the house of my God will cease to be among you."
24 And they answered Joshua and said, "For it was indeed told to your servants that the LORD your God had charged Moses to give all the land to
you and to destroy the inhabitants of the land before you. And we were
25 very afraid for our lives because of you, and so we did this thing. And
now, here we are in your hand. What is good and what is right in your
26 eyes to do to us, do." And he did thus to them and saved them from the
27 hand of the Israelites, and they did not kill them. And on that day Joshua
made them hewers of wood and drawers of water for the community and
for the LORD's altar to this day, at the place He was to choose.

---

your elders and your overseers, every man of Israel. Your little ones, your wives,
and your sojourner who is in the midst of your camps, from the hewer of your
wood to the drawer of your water."

23. *for the house of my God.* In verse 21, it was "for the whole community." In
historical fact, the Gibeonites could conceivably have performed these functions in both the sacred and the profane realm.
   will cease to be among you. Literally, "will not be cut off from you."

24. *For it was indeed told to your servants.* In this fiction, the Gibeonites somehow have been given a full report of the promise of the land and the program
of genocide articulated in Deuteronomy.

26. *saved them from the hand of the Israelites.* This formulation may suggest that,
despite the solemn vow, there was some popular sentiment among the Israelites, outraged by this deception, to destroy the Gibeonites. The quick maneuver
of the chieftains implemented by Joshua to make them menial servants would
be devised to fend off such an assault.

27. *to this day.* This is the formal marker of the etiological tale: if you wonder
why the Gibeonites are hewers of wood and drawers of water for the Israelites,
this story explains it.
   at the place He was to choose. This phrase in Deuteronomistic texts invariably
refers to Jerusalem, but it is a misplaced editorial tic here because the sanctuary in question is located at Gibeon.

CHAPTER 10

And it happened when Adoni-Zedek king of Jerusalem heard that 1
Joshua had taken Ai and put it under the ban, as he had done to Jericho
and its king, so had he done to Ai and its king, and that the inhabitants of
Gibeon had made peace with Israel and were in their midst, that he was 2
very afraid, for Gibeon was a big town, like one of the royal towns, and it
was bigger than Ai, and all its men were warriors. And Adoni-Zedek king 3
of Jerusalem sent to Hoham king of Hebron and to Piram king of Jarmuth, Japhia king of Lachish, and Debir king of Eglon, saying, "Come 4
up to me and help me, and let us strike Gibeon, for it has made peace
with Joshua and with the Israelites." And the five Amorite kings, the 5
king of Jerusalem, the king of Hebron, the king of Jarmuth, the king of
Lachish, the king of Eglon, gathered together, they and all their camps,
and they encamped against Gibeon and did battle against it. And the 6
men of Gibeon sent messengers to Joshua at the Gilgal camp, saying,
"Do not let go of your servants. Come up quickly to us and rescue us
and help us, for all the Amorite kings who live in the high country have

---

1. *Adoni-Zedek.* The name means "master of justice" or "master of victory," and
as several medieval Hebrew commentators note, it is probably a hereditary title
rather than a proper name. Malchizedek king of Salem (probably a variant of
"Jerusalem"), mentioned in Genesis 15:18, has a similar titular name, which
means "king of justice" or "king of victory."

2. *like one of the royal towns.* Even though there is no monarchy in Gibeon, its
size and importance make it the equivalent of a royal town.

6. *Do not let go of your servants.* That is, hang on to us; do not leave us in the lurch.
    help us. The simple verb "to help" also has technical sense, exhibited in many
psalms and in narrative contexts such as this, which is to render military support.

7 gathered against us." And Joshua came up from Gilgal, he and all the
8 combat troops with him, and all the valiant warriors. And the LORD said
to Joshua, "Do not fear them, for I have given them into your hand.
9 No man of them will stand up before you." And Joshua came against
10 them suddenly—all night long he had come up from Gilgal. And the
LORD panicked them before Israel, and they struck them a great blow at
Gilgal, and they pursued them on the road of the ascent to Beth-Horon,
and they struck them down as far as Azekah and as far as Makkedah.
11 And it happened when they fled before Israel, that they were on the
descent from Beth-Horon when the LORD flung down on them great
stones from the heavens as far as Azekah, and those who died from the
12 hailstones were many more than the Israelites killed by the sword. Then
did Joshua speak to the LORD on the day the LORD gave the Amorites
over to the Israelites, and he said in the sight of Israel:

---

7. *the combat troops . . . all the valiant warriors.* These terms probably indicate
that Joshua led elite troops, the ancient Near Eastern equivalent of comman-
dos, on this mission.

9. *Joshua came against them suddenly.* By marching all night long the considerable distance from Gilgal to Gibeon, he is able to carry out a surprise attack,
perhaps just at daybreak.

10. *and the LORD panicked them.* This is a vivid illustration of the system of
dual causation sometimes adopted by the biblical writers. The soldiers of the
alliance of five kings are of course in the first instance panicked by Joshua's
surprise attack, a shrewd tactical maneuver, but now the panic is explained as
God's direct intervention.

11. *the descent from Beth-Horon.* This is the same steep road that is called
"ascent" in the previous verse, now imagined from Beth-Horon looking down
rather than the other way around.
   great stones from the heavens. This wording gives the initial impression of an
entirely supernatural event, but then it is explained naturalistically as a reference to hailstones. Even so, the hailstones would have had to be improbably
big in order to be lethal.

"O sun in Gibeon halt,
            and the moon in Ajalon Valley."
And the sun halted   13
            and the moon stood still
                        till the nation wreaked vengeance on its foes.

Is it not written in the Book of Yashar?—"And the sun stood still in the   14
middle of the heavens and did not hasten to set for a whole day. And there
was nothing like that day before it or after it, in the LORD's heeding the
voice of a man, for the LORD did battle for Israel." And Joshua went back,   15
and all Israel with him, to the Gilgal camp. And those five kings fled and   16
hid in a cave at Makkedah. And it was told to Joshua, saying, "The five   17
kings have been found hiding in the cave at Makkedah. And Joshua said,   18
"Roll great stones over the mouth of the cave, and set men over it to guard
them. As for you, do not stand still. Pursue your enemies and cut them   19
down from behind. Do not let them enter their towns, for the LORD your

---

12. *O sun in Gibeon halt.* The reason for the prayer is explained in the next
verse: the sun is to halt its movement across the sky and the moon not to appear
in its place in order to give Joshua a long extension of daylight in which to hunt
down and destroy his enemies.

14. *the Book of Yashar.* This lost text is also mentioned in 2 Samuel 1:18 as the
literary source in which David's elegy for Saul and Jonathon appears. It is safe
to assume that it is a very old book, largely poetic or even epic, in which martial
themes are prominent. The name *yashar* would appear to mean "the upright,"
though Shmuel Ahituv, mindful of the practice of calling books by their opening
words, interestingly proposes that it could mean "he sang" (revocalizing *yashar*
as *yashir*).
    And the sun stood still. This translation construes the remainder of this verse
as a continuation of the quotation from the Book of Yashar. It does not scan as
poetry, but the language is elevated, with epic flourishes.
    did not hasten to set. Psalm 19 imagines the sun racing across the sky like a
warrior running on his path, and that mythological imagery is probably behind
the verb "hasten" here.

19. *cut them down from behind.* The verb *zanev*, derived from *zanav*, "tail,"
means etymologically "to cut off the tail." It is used in Deuteronomy 25:18.

20 God has given them into your hand." And it happened when Joshua and the
Israelites had finished striking them a very great blow, to the last of them,
21 that a remnant of them survived and entered the fortified towns. And
the troops came back safely to the camp to Joshua, no man so much as
22 snarled at the Israelites. And Joshua said, "Open the mouth of the cave,
23 and bring these five kings out to me from the cave." And so they did,
and they brought those five kings out to him from the cave—the king of
Jerusalem, the king of Hebron, the king of Jarmuth, the king of Lach-
24 ish, the king of Eglon. And it happened when they brought out those
kings to Joshua, that Joshua called out to all the men of Israel and said
to the captains of the men of war who had gone with him: "Put your feet
on the necks of these kings." And they drew near and put their feet on
25 their necks. And Joshua said to them, "Do not fear and do not cower. Be
strong and stalwart, for thus shall the LORD do to all your enemies with
26 whom you do battle." And afterward Joshua struck them down and put
them to death, and he impaled them on five poles, and they remained

---

20. *to the last of them*. More literally, "until they came to an end." But as the next
clause makes clear, this actually means that they were almost entirely wiped
out but some escaped.

21. *no man*. The Hebrew says "to no man," but the prefix *le* is probably a dittography triggered by *le yisra'el*, "at [or to] Israel."

24. *Put your feet on the necks of these kings*. As both Egyptian and Assyrian art
abundantly demonstrate, this was a symbolic gesture by the victors for subju-
gating the defeated enemies.

26. *he impaled them on five poles*. Since it would be somewhat odd to hang a
dead body by the neck, this particular verse offers credibility to the view that
the Hebrew verb in question when applied to an execution means to impale,
not to hang. Impaling the body for public display would be an act of shaming.

impaled on the poles till evening. And it happened as the sun was set- 27
ting that Joshua gave the command and they took them down from the
poles and flung them into the cave in which they had hidden, and they
put great stones over the mouth of the cave, to this very day. And Joshua 28
took Makkedah on that day and struck it and its king with the edge of
the sword and every living thing within it. He left no survivor, and he
did to the king of Makkedah as he had done to the king of Jericho. And 29
Joshua moved on, and all Israel with him, from Makkedah to Libnah,
and he did battle with Libnah. And the Lord gave it as well into the 30
hand of Israel with its king, and he struck it with the edge of the sword
and every living thing within it. He left no survivor, and he did to its king
as he had done to the king of Jericho. And Joshua moved on, and all 31
Israel with him, from Libnah to Lachish, and he camped against it and
did battle against it. And the Lord gave Lachish into the hand of Israel, 32
and he took it on the second day and struck it by the edge of the sword

---

27. *to this very day*. This is again the etiological tag—the story explains why one
finds great stones piled over the mouth of the cave at Makkedah.

28. *and Joshua took Makkedah on that day and struck it and its king*. Here begins
a catalog of Joshua's conquests, conveyed in more or less identical formulas,
and probably from a different literary source.

32. *And the Lord gave Lachish into the hand of Israel*. This notation is still
another indication of the tenuous relation to history of this account of the
conquest because extra-biblical evidence shows that in the thirteenth century
BCE (the time of Joshua) and well beyond it, Lachish was not in Israelite
hands. Altogether, this report of a lightning campaign in which a large swath
of the land was conquered does not accord with the archeological record for
the history of this period. One might also observe an internal contradiction
between the catalogue of conquests and the episode that precedes it. One of
the five kings put to death at the Makkedah cave is the king of Jerusalem, the
very man who organized the anti-Israelite alliance. One would expect that the
conquest of Jerusalem should then logically figure in this account, but it was
of course general knowledge that Jerusalem remained in Jebusite hands until
over two centuries later, when it was taken by David. One suspects that the
source from which the catalog of conquests was drawn knew nothing of an
Adoni-Zedek king of Jerusalem who played a central role in these battles, and
that the redactor did not reconcile the two accounts.

33 and every living thing within it, as all that he had done to Libnah. Then did Horam king of Gezer come up to help Lachish, and Joshua struck him down, and all his troops with him, till he left no survivor of him.
34 And Joshua moved on, and all Israel with him, from Lachish to Eglon,
35 and they camped against it and did battle against it. And they took it on that day and struck it with the edge of the sword and every living thing within it. On that day he passed it under the ban as all he had done to
36 Lachish. And Joshua went up, and all Israel with him, from Eglon to
37 Hebron, and they did battle against it. And they took it and struck it with the edge of the sword, and its king and all its towns and every living thing within it. He left no survivor, as all he had done to Eglon, and he put it
38 under the ban and every living thing within it. And Joshua, and all Israel
39 with him, turned back to Debir and did battle against it. And he took it, and its king and all its towns, and he struck them with the edge of the sword, and he put under the ban every living thing within it. He left no survivor. As he had done to Hebron, so he did to Debir and its king and
40 as he had done to Libnah and to its king. And Joshua struck the whole land, the high country and the Negeb and the lowland and the slopes and all their kings. And he left no survivor of it. And every breathing
41 thing he put under the ban as the Lord God of Israel had charged. And Joshua struck them from Kadesh-Barnea to Gaza, and the whole land of
42 Goshen to Gibeon. And all these kings and their land Joshua took in one
43 fell swoop, for the Lord God of Israel did battle for Israel. And Joshua, and all Israel with him, turned back to the Gilgal camp.

---

40. *the Negeb and the lowland.* In David's time, much of the Negeb was dominated by the Amalekites, and the lowland was Philistine territory.

41. *from Kadesh-Barnea.* This would be extravagantly far to the south, in the northern part of the Sinai peninsula.

42. *in one fell swoop.* Literally, "one time" or "at once." This hyperbolic flourish again raises the problem of historicity.

CHAPTER 11

And it happened when Jabin king of Hazor heard, that he sent to Jobab   1
king of Madon and to the king of Shimron and the king of Achshaph,
and to the kings who were in the north, in the high country and in the   2
Arabah, south of Chinneroth, and in the lowland and in Naphoth-Dor
on the west, the Canaanite from the east, and to the west, and the   3
Amorite and the Hittite and the Perizzite and the Jebusite in the high
country, and the Hivite below Hermon in Mizpah land. And they sallied   4
forth, they and all their camps with them, troops more numerous than
the sand that is on the shore of the sea in number, and very many horses

---

1. *when Jabin king of Hazor heard.* Though no grammatical object for the verb
appears, the obvious sense is that he heard of Joshua's initial conquests. The
pointed parallel with 10:1 makes this clear. Altogether, this whole chapter
appears to have been composed to create a symmetrical complement to the
account of the defeat of the southern alliance in the previous chapter. Here,
the alliance is one of northern kings. The reach of this new conquest, going all
the way to Sidon in Lebanon and, to the south on the Mediterranean coast, to
Misrephoth-Mayim, is scarcely historical, and it seems devised to convey the
idea of the completeness of the conquest of the land.

Hazor. This was an important city in northeastern Canaan in the Middle
Bronze Age, a memory perhaps reflected in making its king the leader of the
alliance, but by Joshua's time it had become a relatively small town.

2. *Chinneroth.* This is the same place as Kinneret, the Sea of Galilee.

3. *Hermon.* This is a mountain to the northeast, on the border between present-
day Israel and Syria.

5 and chariots. And all these kings joined forces and came and camped
6 together by the Waters of Merom to do battle with Israel. And the LORD
said to Joshua, "Do not fear them, for tomorrow at this time I shall cause
all of them to be slain before Israel. Their horses you will hamstring
7 and their chariots you will burn in fire." And Joshua, and all the combat
troops with him, came against them suddenly at the Waters of Merom,
8 and fell upon them. And the LORD gave them into the hand of Israel,
and they struck them down and pursued them to Greater Sidon and to
Misrephoth-Mayim and to Mizpeh Valley to the east, and they struck
9 them down until no survivor was left of them. And Joshua did to them as
the LORD had said to him, their horses he hamstrung and their chariots
10 he burned in fire. And Joshua came back at that time and took Hazor,
and its king he struck down with the sword. For Hazor in those days
11 was chief of these kingdoms. And he struck down every living person

---

5. *the Waters of Merom*. The location is in the high country of north-central
Canaan.

6. *their horses you will hamstring and their chariots you will burn in fire*. The
chariot, a formidable instrument of warfare, was not generally adopted by the
Israelites, who were essentially guerilla fighters from the high country, for
another two centuries. These Canaanite chariots in all likelihood were made
out of wood, hence the burning. As to hamstringing of the horses, Boling and
others think this was a cunning strategy to disable the horses at the onset of the
battle, though it is not entirely clear how easy it would have been for the Israelite warriors to get close enough to the chariots in order to maim the horses.
Alternately, they might have hamstrung the horses after the victory in order to
make sure they would not be used again to draw chariots, a possibility encouraged by the previous verse in which the enemy troops appear to be defeated
before the hamstringing.

7. *came against them suddenly at the Waters of Merom*. This is the same strategy
of surprise attack used against the southern alliance, with the enemy caught
unawares at its own encampment.

11. *living person . . . breathing person*. The two Hebrew terms, *nefesh* and *neshamah*, are phonetically and semantically related. *Nefesh* is the life-breath and,
by extension, the living person; *neshamah* explicitly means breath or anything
that breathes.

who was in it with the edge of the sword, putting it under the ban. No
breathing person was left, and he burned Hazor in fire. And all the towns 12
of these kings and all their kings Joshua took and struck them down with
the edge of the sword, he put them under ban as Moses servant of the
LORD had charged. Only all the towns standing on their mounds Israel 13
did not burn, except for Hazor alone that Joshua burned. And all the 14
booty of these towns and the cattle the Israelites plundered. Only the
human beings they struck down with the edge of the sword until they
had destroyed them—they left no breathing person. As the LORD had 15
charged Moses His servant, so Moses charged Joshua, who neglected
nothing of all that the LORD had charged Moses. And Joshua took all 16
this land, the high country and all the Negeb and all the land of Goshen
and the lowland and the Arabah and the high country of Israel and its
lowland, from Mount Halak going up to Seir as far as Baal-Gad in the 17
Lebanon valley beneath Mount Hermon. And their kings he captured
and struck them down and put them to death. Many days Joshua did 18
battle with these kings. There was no town that made peace with the 19
Israelites except the Hivites dwelling in Gibeon. Everything they took in

---

13. *the towns standing on their mounds*. The "mound," *tel*, is the heaped up
layers of earlier habitation on which old cities stand. (It has become a technical archeological term.) What the expression may mean in context is towns of
notable antiquity, though that is not entirely certain.

15. *As the LORD had charged Moses*. The genocidal imperative is spelled out
several times in Deuteronomy.

16. *the high country of Israel*. This rather odd phrase, matched in verse 21 with
"the high country of Judah," probably reflects an awareness of the division into
a southern and northern kingdom after the death of Solomon.

17. *Mount Halak*. Boling wittily and accurately observes that this could be
translated as Bald Mountain.

18. *Many days*. The Hebrew *yamim* is an elastic indicator of time, and so it
could mean here months or even years.

20 battle. For it was from the LORD to harden their heart for battle against
   Israel, so that they would be put under the ban with no mercy shown
   them in order that they be destroyed, as the LORD had charged Moses.
21 And Joshua came at that time and cut down the Anakites from the high
   country, from Hebron, from Debir, from Anab, and from the high country of Judah and from all the high country of Israel, with their towns,
22 Joshua put them under the ban. No Anakites were left in the land of the
23 Israelites. Only in Gaza, in Gath, and in Ashdod did they remain. And
   Joshua took the whole land according to all that the LORD had spoken to
   Moses. And Joshua gave it in estate to Israel according to their divisions
   by their tribes. And the land was at rest from war.

---

20. *For it was from the* LORD *to harden their heart for battle against Israel.* This
is one of two verbs used in the exodus story for the hardening or toughening of
the heart of Pharaoh. There, the divinely instigated obduracy was in order to
enable the display of God's overwhelming power. Here it is to provide grounds
for wiping out the indigenous population.

21. *the Anakites.* Though in the present context this looks like a gentilic designation, in other biblical texts the word refers to giants.

22. *Only in Gaza, in Gath, and in Ashdod did they remain.* These are three of the
five Philistine towns on the southern part of the Mediterranean coast. Goliath
the Philistine was, of course, a giant, though the Hebrew *'anaq* is not attached
to him in the story in 1 Samuel 17. It is conceivable that the association of
huge physical proportions with the Anakites derives from a perception that the
Philistines, of original Aegean stock, were bigger than the indigenous population of Canaan though archeological evidence suggests the Canaanites were
also big. The Philistines invaded the coastal areas around 1200 BCE, but later
writers (as in Genesis) imagined them as longtime residents of the coastal strip.

CHAPTER 12

Ａnd these are the kings of the land whom the Israelites struck down   1
and whose land they took hold of, across the Jordan where the sun
rises, from Wadi Arnon to Mount Hermon and all the Arabah to the
east: Sihon king of the Amorites who dwelled in Heshbon, who ruled   2
from Aroer on the banks of Wadi Arnon and within the wadi, and half
of Gilead as far as Wadi Jabbok, border of the Ammonites, and the   3
Arabah as far as Lake Chinneroth to the east and as far as the Arabah
Sea, the Salt Sea, to the east, by way of Beth-Jeshimoth, and to the
south below the slopes of Pisgah. And the region of Og king of Bashan,   4
from the remnant of the Rephaim, who dwelt in Ashtaroth and in Edrei,
and ruled over Mount Hermon and Salkah and all of the Bashan as far   5

---

1. *And these are the kings of the land whom the Israelites struck down . . . across the Jordan where the sun rises.* The second half of the Book of Joshua, which begins in the next chapter, essentially abandons narrative to offer, after this catalogue of conquests, a tabulation of the apportioning of the land according to tribal divisions. Only in the three concluding chapters do we return to narrative. The first six verses of this chapter report the victories of Moses over the sundry trans-Jordanian kings that are narrated in Numbers. The remainder of the chapter gives us a list of Joshua's victories west of the Jordan.

3. *Lake Chinneroth.* As before, this is a variant form of Lake Kinneret, or the Sea of Galilee.

4. *the remnant of the Rephaim.* Some scholars think this term originally referred to elite warriors. In biblical usage it can mean either "shades," which is scarcely a relevant sense here, or "giants." In Deuteronomy 3:11, Og is reported to have possessed gigantic proportions.

as the border of the Geshurite and the Maacathite and half of Gilead,
6 the border of Sihon king of the Amorites. Moses servant of the LORD
and the Israelites struck them down, and Moses servant of the LORD
gave it as an inheritance to the Reubenites and to the Gadites and to
7 the half-tribe of Manasseh. And these are the kings of the land whom
Joshua and the Israelites struck down on the other side of the Jordan to
the west, from Baal-Gad in the Lebanon valley as far as Mount Halak,
which goes up toward Seir. And Joshua gave it to the tribes of Israel as an
8 inheritance according to their divisions. In the high country and in the
lowland and in the Arabah and on the slopes and in the wilderness and
in the Negeb of the Hittite, the Amorite, the Canaanite, the Perizzite,
the Hivite, and the Jebusite:
9   the king of Jericho—one,
       the king of Ai which is alongside Bethel—one,
10   the king of Jerusalem—one,
       the king of Hebron—one,
11   the king of Jarmuth—one,
       the king of Lachish—one,
12   the king of Eglon—one,
       the king of Gezer—one,
13   the king of Debir—one,
       the king of Geder—one,

---

6. *Moses servant of the* LORD *gave it as an inheritance.* By the time this material
was edited, late in the seventh century BCE or in the sixth century, the Israelites no longer had possession of this trans-Jordanian region. The list thus serves
as a kind of ideal map of sovereignty in times past.

9. *the king of Jericho—one.* This system of tallying is unusual. The evident aim
is to arrive at a complete sum of all the conquests. Though, as we have seen,
the historical reality of much of this account is in doubt, the numbering of
thirty-one kings does accurately reflect a historical situation in which Canaan
was splintered into a large number of city-kingdoms controlling quite small territories. Even if these rulers actually bore the title of king, they probably were
closer to what today would be thought of as tribal war-lords. This list obviously
picks up names from the preceding narrative report, though it also includes
several kings not mentioned earlier.

the king of Hormah—one,   14
the king of Arad—one,
the king of Libnah—one,   15
the king of Adullam—one,
the king of Makkedah—one,   16
the king of Bethel—one,
the king of Tapuah—one,   17
the king of Hepher—one,
the king of Aphek—one,   18
the king of Sharon—one,
the king of Madon—one,   19
the king of Hazor—one,
the king of Shimron-Merom—one,   20
the king of Achshaph—one,
the king of Taanach—one,   21
the king of Megiddo—one,
the king of Kedesh—one,   22
the king of Jokneam in Carmel—one,
the king of Dor in Naphoth-Dor—one,   23
the king of Goiim in Gilgal—one,
the king of Tirzah—one,   24
all the kings were thirty-one.

CHAPTER 13

1 A nd Joshua was old, advanced in years. And the LORD said to him,
"You are old, advanced in years, and very much of the land remains to
2 take hold of. This is the land remaining: all the provinces of the Phi-
3 listines and all of the Geshurites, from the Shihor, which faces Egypt,
to the region of Ekron to the north, it is reckoned Canaanite. The five
Philistine overlords, the Gazite, and the Ashdodite, the Ascolonite, the
4 Gittite, and the Ekronite. And the Avvites on the south, all the Canaan-

---

1. *very much of the land remains to take hold of.* There is a tension between
the section that begins here and the previous account of Joshua's conquest. In
the preceding chapters, one gets the impression of a grand sweep of victories
in which the Israelite forces led by Joshua took town after town, virtually the
whole land. But the audience of this narrative was well aware that there were
substantial regions of the land that for long periods were not controlled by the
Israelites, and this awareness is registered here.

2. *all the provinces of the Philistines.* In fact, the Philistines did not establish
their pentapolis along the Mediterranean shore, having arrived perhaps from
the Aegean, until a generation or more after the putative time of Joshua.

3. *overlords.* The Hebrew *seren* is in all likelihood a loanword from the Philistine
language. Some scholars think it is cognate with the Greek *tyrranos.*
   the Avvites. These are an indigenous Canaanite people bordering on Philistine territory who remained unconquered by the Philistines.

ite land from Arah of the Sidonians to Aphek, which is on the Amorite
border, and the land of the Giblite, and all of Lebanon to the east, from 5
Baal-Gad below Mount Hermon to the approach to Hammath. All the 6
inhabitants of the high country from Lebanon to Misrephoth-Mayim, all
the Sidonians, I Myself will dispossess them before the Israelites, only
to make it fall in estate to Israel as I have charged you. And now, divide 7
this land in estate among the nine tribes and the half-tribe of Manasseh,
with whom the Reubenites and the Gadites took their estate that Moses 8
gave them across the Jordan to the east, as Moses servant of the LORD
gave them, from Aroer, which is on the banks of Wadi Arnon, and the 9
town that is in the wadi, and the plain from Medeba to Dibon, and all 10
the towns of Sihon king of the Amorites, who reigned in Heshbon, to
the border of the Ammonites, and Gilead and the territory of the Geshu- 11
rites and the Maacathites, and all of Mount Hermon and all Bashan to
Saleah, and all the kingdoms of Og in Bashan, who reigned in Ashtaroth 12
and in Edrei—he remained from the remnant of the Rephaim, and

---

4. *from Arah*. The received text reads "and from Arah." Arah is not a known
place-name, and some emend it to Acco, which was a Sidonian town. Strenu-
ous scholarly efforts have been made, and will not be recapitulated here, to
identify all the towns and regions. Some names in the list nevertheless defy
identification, and there are elements in the geographical indications that
seem scrambled.

7. *the nine tribes and the half-tribe of Manasseh*. These are the tribes that settled
west of the Jordan, the other two and a half tribes remaining on the east side
of the Jordan.

8. *with whom the Reubenites and the Gadites took their estate*. That is, these two
tribes plus the other half of the tribe of Manasseh. The more likely historical
scenario is not that Israelites settled east of the Jordan in the original conquest
but that they migrated there by stages later in search of land.

10. *border*. The Hebrew *gevul* sometimes means "border" and sometimes "territory" or "region," the meaning shifting in this chapter.

12. *he remained from the remnant of the Rephaim*. See the comment on 12:4.

13 Moses struck them down and dispossessed them. But the Israelites did
not dispossess the Geshurites and the Maacathites, and Geshur and
14 Maacath have dwelled in the midst of Israel to this day. Only to the tribe
of Levi he gave no estate. The fire-offerings of the LORD God of Israel,
15 they are its estate, as He had spoken to it. And Moses gave to the tribe
16 of the Reubenites according to its clans, and it became their territory
from Aroer, which is on the banks of Wadi Arnon, and the town that is
17 in the wadi and the whole plain to Medeba. Heshbon and all its towns
that are on the plain, Dibon and Bamoth-Baal and Beth-Baal-Meon,
18,19 and Jaza and Kedemoth and Mephaath, and Kiriathaim and Sibma and
20 Zereth-Shahar on the Mountain of the Valley, and Beth-Peor and the
21 slopes of Pisgah and Beth-Jeshimoth, and all the towns of the plain and
all the kingdom of Sihon king of the Amorites, who reigned in Heshbon,
whom Moses struck down—and the princes of Midian, Evi and Rekem
and Zur and Hur and Reba, princes of Sihon who dwelled in the land.
22 And Balaam son of Beor, the soothsayer, the Israelites killed by the
23 sword with the rest of their slain. And the border of the Reubenites was
the Jordan. This was the estate of the Reubenites by their clans, the
24 towns and their hamlets. And Moses had given it to the tribe of Gad
25 and to the Gadites by their clans, and it became their territory: Jazer and

---

13. *Maacath.* This is either a variant, archaic form of Maachah or a scribal error.
dwelled in the midst of Israel. As elsewhere, this phrase does not mean that
they were geographically integrated with Israel but that they had peaceful relations with the Israelites.

14. *the fire-offerings of the* LORD *God of Israel, they are its estate.* A substantial
part of these sacrifices was not burnt and thus was available to the Levites as
food. This verse, reiterated at the end of the chapter, probably reflects a Deuteronomistic background in which the cult has been centralized in Jerusalem.

22. *Balaam son of Beor.* The killing off of Balaam, who in Numbers 22–24
delivered, against his own intention, a grand prophecy of blessing about Israel,
may reflect a nationalist nervousness over the prominence of this Aramean
soothsayer. Lest one think he lived happily ever after once he had returned to
his native land, here he is included among the victims of the conquest.

all the towns of Gilead and half of the land of the Ammonites as far as
Aroer, which is just before Rabbah, and from Heshbon as far as Ramoth- 26
Mizpeh, and Betonim, and from Mahanaim to the border of Lidber, and 27
in the Valley, Beth-Haran and Beth-Nimrah and Succoth and Zaphon,
the rest of the kingdoms of Sihon king of Heshbon, from the Jordan and
its border to the edge of the Sea of Chinnereth across the Jordan to the
east. This is the estate of the Gadites according to their clans, the towns 28
and their hamlets. And Moses gave it to the half-tribe of Manasseh and 29
it went to the half-tribe of the Manassites according to their clans, and 30
their territory was from Mahanaim, all of Bashan, all the kingdom of Og
king of Bashan, and all of Havvoth-Jair, which is in Bashan, sixty towns,
and half of Gilead and Ashtaroth and Edrei, the royal towns of Og in 31
Bashan, to the sons of Machir son of Manasseh, to half of the sons of
Machir according to their clans. These were what Moses apportioned 32
in estate in the plains of Moab across the Jordan to the east of Jericho.
But to the tribe of Levi Moses gave no estate—the Lord God of Israel, 33
He is their estate, as He had spoken to them."

CHAPTER 14

1   And these are what the Israelites took in estate in the land of Canaan,
    which Eleazar the priest and Joshua son of Nun and the patriarchal
2   heads of the Israelite tribes gave them in estate, in the portion of their
    estate, as the LORD had charged through Moses for the nine and a half
3   tribes. For Moses had given an estate to the two and a half tribes across
4   the Jordan, but to the Levites he gave no estate in their midst. For the
    sons of Joseph were two tribes, Ephraim and Manasseh. And they gave
    no share in the land to the Levites except for towns to dwell in and
5   their pastures for their livestock and their possessions. As the LORD had
    charged Moses, so did the Israelites do, and they divided up the land.
6   And the Judahites came forward to Joshua in Gilgal, and Caleb son
    of Jephunneh the Kenizzite said to him, "You yourself know the word
    that the LORD spoke to Moses man of God about me and about you in

---

1. *in the land of Canaan*. As the next two verses make clear, this phrase indicates the land west of the Jordan.

4. *except for towns to dwell in*. These towns were a practical concession to the Levites from the other tribes and not inalienable territory.

6. *And the Judahites came forward*. Although what is in question is the inheritance of Caleb, head of one of the clans of Judah, it is also regarded as a tribal issue because he is part of the tribe.
    You yourself know. Caleb uses the emphatic form in which the personal pronoun is added before the conjugated verb, because Joshua was there with him, joining him in the positive minority report against the fearful assessment of the other ten spies.

Kadesh-Barnea. I was forty years old when Moses servant of the LORD 7
sent me from Kadesh-Barnea to spy out the land, and I brought him
back word just as I thought. But my brothers who came up with me 8
made the people's heart faint, yet I followed after the LORD my God.
And Moses vowed on that day, saying, 'The land on which your foot 9
trod shall surely be yours in estate, and your sons', for all time, for you
have followed after the LORD my God.' And now, look, the LORD has 10
kept me alive, as He had spoken, forty-five years since the LORD spoke
this word to Moses while Israel went in the wilderness. And now, look,
I am eighty-five years old. I am still today as strong as the day Moses 11
sent me. As my vigor then is my vigor now, for battle and for command.

---

7. *brought him back word*. This phrase is used in the spy narrative in Numbers
13:26.

just as I thought. That is, honestly. The literal sense is "as it was with my
heart."

8. *made the people's heart faint*. The literal sense of the Hebrew is "made the
people's heart melt," but in English that phrase unfortunately suggests gushing
sentiment. The same idiom is used in the recapitulation of the story of the spies
in Deuteronomy 1:25.

I followed after the LORD my God. The literal sense of the idiom is "I filled
after." The clear meaning is to carry out implicitly the will or command of
someone. The same expression is used in the original story of the spies in
Numbers 14:24.

10. *I am eighty-five years old*. The Talmudic sages, calculating that the incident
of the spies took place two years into the forty years of wilderness wandering,
conclude from this that the conquest of the land took seven years.

11. *As my vigor then is my vigor now, for battle and for command*. The region
around Hebron still requires conquering, as Caleb's words in verse 12 show.
The idiom rendered as "command" is literally "to go out and to come back," and
it means to lead troops in battle.

12 And now, give me this mountain, as the Lᴏʀᴅ spoke on that day, for you yourself heard on that day that there were giants there and great fortified towns. Perhaps the Lᴏʀᴅ will be with me and I shall dispossess them

13 as the Lᴏʀᴅ has spoken." And Joshua blessed him and gave Hebron to

14 Caleb son of Jephunneh in estate. Therefore has Hebron been in estate to Caleb son of Jephunneh the Kenizzite to this day because he followed

15 after the Lᴏʀᴅ God of Israel. And the name of Hebron formerly was Kiriath-Arba—he was the biggest person among the giants. And the land was at rest from war.

---

12. *you yourself heard on that day that there were giants there*. The narrative context makes clear that the Hebrew *'anaqim* is not in this instance a gentilic ("Anakites") but means "giants," the adversaries of daunting proportions before whom the ten fearful spies felt themselves to be like grasshoppers.

14. *Therefore*. As often elsewhere the Hebrew *'al-ken* introduces an etiological explanation.

15. *Kiriath-Arba*. The Hebrew name means "city of four"—perhaps, as many scholars have inferred, because it was divided into four neighborhoods. But here "Arba" is construed as a man's name—the largest of the indigenous giants.

CHAPTER 15

And the portion for the Judahites according to their clans was south- 1
ward to the border of Edom, the Wilderness of Zin on the far south.
And their southern boundary was from the edge of the Salt Sea, from 2
the tongue that turns southward. And it extended to the south, to the 3
ascent of Akrabbim, and passed on to Zin and went up from the south
to Kadesh-Barnea, and passed on to Hezron and went up to Addar and
swung round to Karka. And it passed on to Azmon and extended to the 4
Wadi of Egypt, and the far reaches of the border came to the sea. This
shall be for you the southern boundary. And the boundary to the east 5
is the Salt Sea south of the Jordan, and the boundary on the northern
side from the tongue of the Sea to the mouth of the Jordan. And the 6
boundary went up to Beth-Hoglah and passed on north of Beth-Arabah,
and the boundary went up to the Stone of Bohan son of Reuben. And 7

---

1. *the portion.* The Hebrew *goral* means "lot"—evidently, an aleatory device
used to portion out the various territories—and through metonymy, it also
means what is indicated by the lot, the portion or share.

southward to the border of Edom. What begins here and runs through the
chapter is an elaborate geographical tracing of Judah's tribal territory. The general reader can scarcely be expected to follow all these details, and any reader
would need a complicated map to do it. What is noteworthy is the inordinate
amount of space devoted to Judah's possessions, which appear to cover most
of central and southern Israel from the Jordan to the Mediterranean. As many
scholars have inferred, this account probably reflects a later period—seventh
century?—when a centralized monarchy coming from the tribe of Judah governed the entire southern kingdom, with Jerusalem as its capital. The towns
in this list are so numerous that many of them were probably not much bigger
than substantial villages. Some of the names are well-known, can be confidently
located, and are sites of important biblical events. Others remain elusive.

the boundary went up to Debir from the Valley of Achor and turned north to Gilgal, which is opposite the Ascent of Adummim, which is south of the wadi, and the boundary passed on to the waters of Ein-
8 Shemesh, and its far reaches were to Ein-Rogel. And the boundary went up to the Vale of Ben-Hinnom to the flank of the Jebusite on the south, which is Jerusalem, and it went up to the mountain-top which overlooks the Vale of Ben-Hinnom to the west, which is at the end
9 of the Valley of Rephaim to the north. And the border swung round from the mountain-top to the spring of the Waters of Nephtoah and extended to the towns of the high country of Ephron, and the bound-
10 ary swung round to Baalah, which is Kiriath-Jearim. And the boundary turned from Baalah westward to Mount Seir and passed on northward to the flank of Mount Jearim, which is Kesalon, and went down to
11 Beth-Shemesh and passed on to Timnah. And the boundary extended to the flank of Ekron to the north, and the boundary swung round to Shikkron and passed on to Mount Baalah and extended to Jabneel,
12 and the far reaches of the boundary were to the sea. And the western boundary—the Great Sea. And this boundary is the boundary of the
13 Judahites all around, according to their clans. And Caleb the son of Jephunneh was given a share in the midst of the Judahites at the behest of the LORD through Joshua—Kiriath-Arba, father of the giant, which is
14 Hebron. And Caleb dispossessed from there the three sons of the giant,
15 Sheshai and Ahiman and Talmai, offspring of the giant. And he went up from there to the inhabitants of Debir, and the name of Debir formerly
16 was Kiriath-Sepher. And Caleb said, "Whoever strikes Kiriath-Sepher
17 and takes it, to him I shall give Achsah my daughter as wife." And Othniel son of Kenaz, Caleb's brother, took it, and he gave him Achsah his

---

9. *Baalah, which is Kiriath-Jearim.* This, like at least one other item on the list, cites first an old pagan name and then its replacement (which means "Forest City").

13. *Caleb.* He was the other one of the twelve spies, besides Joshua, who brought back an encouraging report about the land, and Hebron with the surrounding territory was to be his reward.

17. *Othniel.* He is to become the first of the Judges.

daughter as wife. And it happened when she came, that she enticed 18
him to ask a field of her father, and she alighted from the donkey, and
Caleb said to her "What troubles you?" And she said, "Give me a pres- 19
ent, for you have given me desert-land, and you should give me springs
of water." And he gave her the upper springs and the lower springs. This 20
is the estate of the tribe of the Judahites according to their clans. And 21
the towns at the edge of the Judahites by the boundary of Edom to the
south were Kabzeel and Eder and Yagur. And Kinah and Dimonah and 22
Adadah. And Kedesh and Hazor and Ithnan. Ziph and Telem and Beal- 23,24
oth. And Hazor-Hadattah and Kerioth-Hezron, which is Hazor. Amam 25,26
and Shema and Moladah. And Hazar-Gaddah and Heshmon and 27
Beth-Pelet. And Hazar-Shual and Beersheba and Beziothiah. Baalah 28,29
and Iim and Ezem. And Eltolad and Kesil and Hormah. And Ziklag 30,31
and Madmenah and Sansanah. And Lebaoth and Shilhin and Ain and 32
Rimmon. All the towns with their pasturelands came to twenty-nine.
In the lowland: Eshtaol and Zorah and Ashnah. And Zanoah and Ein- 33,34
Gannim, Tapuah and Einan. Jarmuth and Adullam, Socoh and Azekah. 35
And Shaaraim and Aditaim and Gederah and Gederothaim—fourteen 36
towns with their pastureland. Zenan and Hadashah and Migdal-Gad. 37
And Dilan and Mizpeh and Joktheel. Lachish and Bozkath and Eglon. 38,39
And Cabbon and Lahmas and Kithlish. And Gederoth, Beth-Dagon, 40,41
and Naamah and Makkedah—sixteen towns with their pasturelands.
Libnah and Ether and Ashan. And Iphtah and Ashmah and Nezib. And 42,43,44
Keilah and Achzib and Mareshah—nine towns with their pasturelands.

---

18. *she enticed him to ask a field of her father.* The Septuagint reads "he enticed
her," which makes the sequence of events easier to follow, but perhaps one
should hew to the philological principle of adopting the more difficult reading. In that case, Achsah enticed her husband but then did the asking herself,
perhaps because Othniel's request was rebuffed.

19. *present.* More literally, "blessing."
    desert-land. In the Hebrew "Negeb-land," the Negeb serving as the model for
arid country. The term is associated by etymology with dryness.

45,46 Ekron with its hamlets and its pasturelands. From Ekron westward,
  47 all that is by Ashdod, with their pasturelands. Ashdod, its hamlets and
     its pasturelands, Gaza, its hamlets and its pasturelands, to the Wadi
  48 of Egypt, and the Great Sea is the boundary. And in the high country,
  49 Shamir and Jattir and Socoh. And Dannah and Kiriath-Sannah, which
50,51 is Debir. And Anab and Eshtamoa and Ani m. And Goshen and Holon
  52 and Giloh—eleven towns with their pasturelands. Arab and Dumah and
53,54 Eshan. And Janim and Beth-Tapuah and Aphekah. And Humtah and
     Kiriath-Arba, which is Hebron, and Zior—nine towns with their pas-
55,56 turelands. Maon, Carmel, Ziph, and Juttah. And Jezreel and Jokneam
  57 and Zanoah. Kain, Gibeah, and Timnah—ten towns with their pas-
58,59 turelands. Halhul, Beth-Zur and Gedor. And Maaroth and Beth-Anot
  60 and Eltekon—six towns with their pasturelands. Kiriath-Baal, which
  61 is Kiriath-Jearim, and Rabbah—two towns with their pasturelands. In
  62 the Wilderness, Beth-Arabah, Middin, and Secacah. And Nishban and
  63 Salt Town and Ein-Gedi—six towns with their pasturelands. But the
     Jebusites, the inhabitants of Jerusalem, the Judahites were not able to
     dispossess, and the Jebusites have dwelled alongside the Judahites to
     this day.

---

46. *Ekron . . . Ashdod*. These towns, like Gaza and Ashdod in the next verse,
are Philistine cities. They could scarcely have been allotted to Judah in the
thirteenth century, though by the time this list was compiled, the Philistines
had long been vanquished.

63. *But the Jebusites, the inhabitants of Jerusalem, the Judahites were not able
to dispossess*. The writer is obliged to make this notation because it was well-
known that Jerusalem remained in Jebusite hands until David conquered it,
more than two centuries after the time of Joshua.
  and the Jebusites have dwelled alongside the Judahites to this day. This second
clause is somewhat misleading after the first clause. It could not mean, as
it may appear, that the Jebusites were never conquered but rather that after
having been conquered by David, many of them remained as land-holding residents of the city. See the account of David's purchase of the threshing floor of
Araunah the Jebusite for use as a cultic site in 12 Samuel 24:18–25)—he buys
it and does not take it by right of conquest.

CHAPTER 16

A nd the portion for the sons of Joseph came out—from the Jordan at 1
Jericho to the Waters of Jericho to the east of the wilderness that goes
up from Jericho through the high country of Beth-El. And it went out to 2
Beth-El, Luz, and passed on to the boundary of the Ataroth Archite. And 3
it went down westward to the boundary of the Japhletite as far as the
boundary of lower Beth-Horon and as far as Gezer, and its far reaches
were to the Sea. And the sons of Joseph, Manasseh and Ephraim, took 4
their estates. And the boundary of the Ephraimites according to their 5
clans—the boundary of their estate on the east was Ataroth Addar as far
as Upper Beth-Horon. And the boundary went out to the Sea, to Mich- 6
methath on the north, and the boundary swung round to the east of
Taanath-Shiloh, and passed through it to the east of Janoah. And it went 7
down from Janoah to Ataroth and to Naarath and touched on Jericho
and came out at the Jordan. From Tapuah the boundary goes westward 8
to Wadi Kanah, and its far reaches are to the Sea. This is the estate of

---

1. *And the portion for the sons of Joseph came out.* As above, the Hebrew *goral*,
"portion," refers both to the aleatory device used to indicate the portion of territory and to the result of using the device—that is, the portion itself. In this
instance, the verb "came out" refers to the toss of the oracular stone rather than
to the boundary.

2. *Beth-El, Luz.* The received text brackets these two names together, but in
Genesis 28:19 we are informed that Luz was the older name that was replaced
by Beth-El.

9 the Ephraimite tribe according to its clans. And the towns set apart for the Ephraimites within the estate of the Manassite—all the towns and their
10 pasturelands. And they did not dispossess the Canaanites dwelling in Gezer, and the Canaanites have dwelled in the midst of Ephraim to this day, and they became forced laborers.

---

9. *the towns set apart for the Ephraimites within the estate of the Manassite.* This indication suggests that not all the tribal boundaries were hard and fast, and that there were sometimes enclaves of one tribe within the territory of another tribe.

10. *they became forced laborers.* In keeping with the historiographical agenda of the writers, whatever Canaanite population that is not destroyed or driven out becomes subjugated to the Israelites. It is questionable whether this corresponds to historical reality.

CHAPTER 17

And the portion for the tribe of Manasseh, for he was Joseph's first-   1
born, to Machir Manasseh's firstborn, father of Gilead, for he was a
man of war—Gilead and Bashan were his. And to the remaining sons   2
of Manasseh according to their clans, to the sons of Abiezer and to the
sons of Helek and to the sons of Asriel and to the sons of Shechem
and to the sons of Hepher and to the sons of Shemida—these are the
male offspring of Manasseh son of Joseph according to their clans.
And Zelophehad son of Hepher son of Gilead son of Machir son of   3
Manesseh did not have sons but daughters, and these are the names
of his daughters: Mahlah and Noa, Hoglah, Milkah, and Tirzah. And   4
they approached Eleazar the priest and Joshua son of Nun and the
chieftains, saying, "The LORD charged Moses to give us an estate in
the midst of our kinsmen." And he gave them at the LORD's behest
an estate in the midst of their father's kinsmen. And the shares of   5

---

1. *for he was Joseph's firstborn.* Hence the clan of Machir is alotted the choice
region of Gilead and Bashan. But the further notation about Machir as "a man
of war" suggests that it was the military prowess of the clan that enabled it to
take hold of this territory.

3. *And Zelophehad . . . did not have sons but daughters.* This report of the inheritance of the daughters of Zelophehad picks up the story that appears in Numbers 27:1–11, echoing some of its language.

4. *kinsmen.* The Hebrew *aḥim* here has to have its extended sense and cannot
mean "brothers" because these five women have no brothers.

5. *the shares . . . fell out.* The verb here reflects the use of a lottery or some kind
of aleatory device, but the term for "shares," *ḥavalim,* also means "ropes" and

Manasseh fell out as ten, besides the land of Gilead and Bashan that is
6 across the Jordan. For the daughters of Manasseh took an estate in the
   midst of his sons, and the land of Gilead went to the remaining sons of
7 Manasseh. And the boundary of Manasseh was from Asher to Mich-
   methath, which is by Shechem, and the boundary went southward to
8 the inhabitants of Ein-Tapuah. The land of Tapuah was Manasseh's,
9 but Tapuah to the boundary of Manasseh was the Ephraimites'. And
   the boundary went down to Wadi Kanah south of the wadi. These
   towns were Ephraim's in the midst of the towns of Manasseh, and the
   boundary of Manasseh was north of the wadi, and its far reaches were
10 to the Sea, south of Ephraim and north of Manasseh, and the Sea was
   its boundary, and they touched Asher from the north and Issachar from
11 the east. And within Issachar and Asher, Manasseh had Beth-She'an
   and its hamlets and Ibleam and its hamlets and the inhabitants of Dor
   and its hamlets and the inhabitants of Taanach and its hamlets and the
12 inhabitants of Megiddo and its hamlets—the three regions. And the
   Manassites were unable to take hold of these towns, and the Canaan-
13 ites went on dwelling in this land. And it happened when the Israelites
   grew strong, that they subjected the Canaanites to forced labor, but
14 they did not absolutely dispossess them. And the sons of Joseph spoke
   to Joshua, saying, "Why did you give me in estate one portion and one
   share when I am a numerous people, and until now the LORD has

---

has the sense of share or portion of land because ropes were used to measure
out the land.

10. *south of Ephraim*. This phrase is confusing because the text is describing
the boundaries of Ephraim.

12. *take hold of these towns*. The Hebrew verb means "dispossess." Either a logical object such as "inhabitants" has dropped out of the text, or the verb is used
here in the sense it has in a different conjugation (*yarash* instead of *horish*), "to
take hold of."

14. *why did you give me*. It is fairly common in biblical dialogue assigned to
collective speakers to use the first person singular.
   and until now. The Hebrew wording is obscure and the text may be corrupt.

blessed me?" And Joshua said to them, "If you are a numerous people,   15
go up to the forest and clear it for yourself there in the land of the Perizzite and the Rephaim, for the high country of Ephraim is too cramped
for you." And the sons of Joseph said, "The high country is not enough   16
for us, and there are iron chariots among all the Canaanites who dwell
in the valley land, those in Beth-She'an and its hamlets and those in the
Valley of Jezreel." And Joshua said to the house of Joseph, to Ephraim   17
and to Manasseh, saying, "You are a numerous people and you have
great power. You shall not have just one portion. But the high country   18
shall be yours, for it is forest and you shall clear it, and its far reaches
will be yours, for you shall dispossess the Canaanites, though they have
iron chariots and though they are strong."

---

15. *go up to the forest and clear it.* There is archeological evidence that a good
deal of deforestation took place in this period in the high country, with the trees
replaced by terraced agriculture.

   the land of the Perizzite and the Rephaim. This geographical designation is
obscure and may reflect a scribal error.

16. *there are iron chariots among all the Canaanites.* These armored vehicles,
readily deployed in the valleys but not in mountainous regions, give a military
advantage to the Canaanites over the Israelites, who, by and large, conducted
warfare in guerilla style. (The characterization of "iron," however, may be an
exaggeration because the archeological evidence indicates that Canaanite chariots were primarily built of wood.) Thus the members of the Joseph tribes fear
that they will not be able to overcome the Canaanites in the flatlands.

17. *You are a numerous people and you have great power.* Joshua seizes on the
very phrase the Josephites have used to claim more territory and employs it in
a double sense: as a numerous people, you deserve more than a single portion,
and as a numerous people, you have the power to conquer the Canaanites.

CHAPTER 18

1   A nd the whole community of Israelites assembled at Shiloh and they set up the Tent of Meeting there, and the land was conquered before 2 them. And there remained seven tribes among the Israelites that had 3 not taken the share of their estate. And Joshua said to the Israelites, "How long will you be idle about coming to take hold of the land that 4 the LORD God of your fathers has given to you? Set out for yourselves three men to a tribe, that I may send them and they may rise up and go about the land and write it out according to their estate, and come 5 to me. And they shall share it out in seven parts. Judah will stay by its territory in the south, and the house of Joseph will stay by its territory 6 in the north. As for you, you shall write out the land in seven parts and bring them back to me here, and I shall cast a lot for you here before

---

1. *And the whole community of Israelites assembled at Shiloh*. This marks a shift from the role of the encampment at Gilgal as the national assembly place. Shiloh, as its representation in the early chapters of 1 Samuel indicates, was a central sanctuary, until its destruction by the Philistines sometime in the eleventh century BCE. Placing the Tent of Meeting there would have confirmed its centrality. In subsequent narratives, the Tent of Meeting is not mentioned but rather the Ark of the Covenant, which would have been within the Tent of Meeting.

2. *And there remained seven tribes*. If one subtracts Judah, Reuben, Ephraim, Manasseh, and Levi, all of which have already been accounted for, seven tribes are left to be given their tribal territories.

6. *write out the land*. Still more literally, this would be "write the land." The obvious sense is to draw up a set of notations of the boundaries of the tribal territories.
   I shall cast a lot for you here before the LORD. The drawing up of tribal boundaries by the representatives of the seven tribes is then to be confirmed by divine

the LORD our God. But the Levites have no share in your midst, for the 7
LORD's priesthood is their estate." And Gad and Reuben and the half-
tribes of Manasseh had taken their estate across the Jordan to the east,
which Moses servant of the LORD had given them. And the men rose 8
up and went off, and Joshua charged those who went to write out the
land, saying, "Up, go about in the land and write it out and come back
to me, and here I shall cast the lot for you before the LORD in Shiloh.
And the men went off and passed through the land and wrote it out 9
by towns into seven parts in a scroll, and they came back to Joshua, to
the camp at Shiloh. And Joshua cast the lot for them in Shiloh before 10
the LORD, and Joshua shared out the land to the Israelites according
to their portions. And the lot of the tribe of the Benjaminites fell out, 11
and the territory by their lot came out between the Judahites and the
Josephites. And they had the boundary on the northern edge from the 12
Jordan, and the boundary went up to the flank of Jericho on the north
and went up to the high country westward, and its far reaches were the
Wilderness of Beth-Aven. And the boundary passed on from there to 13
the flank of Luz, which is Bethel, to the south, and the boundary went
down to Atroth Addar in the high country that is south of Lower Beth-
Horon. And the boundary swung round south toward the sea of the high 14
country which is opposite Beth-Horon to the south, and its far reaches
were at Kiriath-Baal, which is Kiriath-Jearim, town of the Judahites.
This was the western edge. And the southern edge was from the border 15
of Kiriath-Jearim, and the boundary went out westward, and went out to
the Spring of the Waters of Naphtoah. And the boundary went down to 16
the edge of the high country which is opposite the Vale of Ben-Hinnom,

---

lot. As Shmuel Ahituv has shown, the use of such a lottery for the division of
land was widespread in the ancient Near East.

10. *cast the lot.* The Hebrew text here uses a different verb from the one in
verse 6, but both mean to cast or fling, suggesting that the mechanism for the
lot involved dice-like objects.

11. *fell out.* Literally, "went up."

16. *Vale of Ben-Hinnom . . . the Valley of Rephaim.* The Hebrew uses two different words for "valley," *gei'* and *'emeq.* It is possible that the former designates a

which is in the Valley of Rephaim to the north, and it went down the
Vale of Hinnom to the flank of the Jebusites on the south and down to
17 Ein-Rogel. And it swung round from the north and went out to Ein-
Shemesh and went out to Geliloth, which is over against the Ascent of
18 Adummim, and it went down to the Stone of Bohan son of Reuben. And
it passed on northward to the flank opposite the Arabah and went down
19 to the Arabah. And the boundary passed on northward to the flank of
Beth-Hoglah to the edge of the Jordan, and the far reaches of the boundary northward were at the tongue of the Salt Sea at the southern end of
20 the Jordan. This was the southern boundary. And the Jordan marked its
boundary at the eastern edge. This was the estate of the Benjaminites by
21 its boundaries all around, according to their clans. And the towns that
were the Benjaminite tribe's were Jericho and Beth-Hoglah and Emek-
22,23 Keziz, and Beth-Arabah and Zemaraim and Bethel, and Avvim and Parah
24 and Ophrah, and Chephar-Ammonah and Ophni and Geba—twelve
25,26 towns and their pasturelands. Gibeon and Ramah and Beeroth, and
27 Mizpeh and Chephirah and Mozah, and Rekem and Irpeel and Taralah,
28 and Zela-Eleph, and the Jebusite, which is Jerusalem, Gibeath, Kiriath-
Jearim. Fourteen towns and their pasturelands—this was the estate of
the Benjaminites according to their clans.

---

smaller topographical entity. Both valleys are within the perimeters of modern-
day Jerusalem, though they would have been outside the city to the west in
ancient times.

28. *Jerusalem*. It is a little surprising that Jerusalem, conquered from the
Jebusites by David, who was a Judahite, is here assigned to the tribe of Benjamin. It has been suggested that this apportionment reflects a later period, when
the unity of Benjamin and Judah, the two southern tribes, was firmly established and the old rivalry between the two, registered in the Book of Samuel,
had long since vanished.

Kiriath-Jearim. The Masoretic text reads *qiryat 'arim*, "Kiriath towns" (or "city
of towns"). This translation adopts a proposal, in part based on the Septuagint,
that a haplography occurred, with the original text reading *qiryat ye'arim 'arim*,
"Kiriath-Jearim, [fourteen] towns."

CHAPTER 19

And the second lot fell out for Simeon, for the tribe of the Simeonites   1
according to their clans, and their estate was within the estate of the
Judahites. And they had in their estate Beersheba and Sheba and Mola-   2
dah, and Hazar-Shual and Belah and Ezem, and Eltolad and Bethul and   3, 4
Hormah, and Ziklag and Beth-Marcaboth and Hazar-Susah, and Beth-   5, 6
Lebaoth and Sharuhen—thirteen towns and their pasturelands. Ayin,   7
Rimmon, Ether and Ashan—four towns and their pasturelands, and   8
all the pasturelands that are around these towns as far as Baalath-Beer,
Ramath-Negeb—this is the estate of the tribe of the Simeonites according to their clans. The estate of the Simeonites was from the territory of   9
the Judahites, for the share of the Judahites was too large for them, and
the Simeonites took an estate within their estate. And the third lot fell   10
out for the Zebulunites according to their clans, and the boundary of
their estate was as far as Sarid. And their boundary went up westward   11
to Maralah and touched Dabbesheth and touched the wadi which is
opposite Jokneam. And it turned back from Sarid eastward where the   12
sun rises to the boundary of Cisloth-Tabor, and it went out to Dabereth
and went up to Japhia. And from there it passed on eastward, toward the   13
sunrise, to Gath-Hepher, Ittah, Kazin, and it went out and swung round
to Neah. And the boundary on the north turned round to Hannathon,   14

---

1. *their estate was within the estate of the Judahites.* Unlike the other tribes,
Simeon did not have a territory with clearcut boundaries but rather enclaves
within the territory of Judah. This situation is reflected in the curse Jacob pronounces on Simeon and Levi: "I will divide them in Jacob, / disperse them in
Israel" (Genesis 49:7). (Levi's dispersal was manifested in its having no tribal
territory, only Levitical towns.) The anomaly of the portion assigned to Simeon
is explained in verse 9.

15 and its far reaches were the Vale of Iphtah-El, and Kattath and Nahalal
and Shimron and Idalah and Bethlehem—twelve towns and their pas-
16 turelands. This is the estate of the Zebulunites according to their clans,
17 these towns and their pasturelands. The fourth lot fell out for Issachar,
18 for the Issacharites according to their clans. And their boundary was to
19 Jezreel and Chesulloth and Shunem, and Hapharaim and Shion and
20,21 Anaharath, and Rabbith and Kishon and Ebez, and Remeth and Ein-
22 Gannim and Ein-Haddah and Beth-Pazzez. And the boundary touched
Tabor and Shahazimah and Beth-Shemesh, and the far reaches of their
boundary were at the Jordan—sixteen towns and their pasturelands.
23 This is the estate of the Issacharites according to their clans, and the
24 towns and their enclosures. And the fifth lot fell out to the tribe of the
25 Asherites according to their clans. And their boundary was Helkath and
26 Hali and Beten and Akshaph, and Alammelech and Amad and Mishal.
27 And it touched Carmel on the west and Shihor-Libnath. And it turned
back to Beth-Dagon where the sun rises and touched Zebulun and the
Vale of Iphtah-El on the north, Beth-Emek and Neiel, and the boundary
28 came out to Cabul on the north, and Ebron and Rehob and Hammon
29 and Kanah, as far as Greater Sidon. And the boundary turned back to
Ramah and as far as the fortress city of Tyre, and its far reaches, and
the boundary turned back to Hosah, and its far reaches were the Sea,
30 Mehebel, to Achzib, and Ummah and Aphek and Rehob—twenty-two
31 towns and their pasturelands. This is the estate of the tribe of Asherites
32 according to their clans—these towns and their pasturelands. For the
Naphtalites the sixth lot came out, for the Naphtalites according to their
33 clans. And their boundary was from Heleph, from Elon-in-Zaananim
and Adami-Nekeb and Jabneel as far as Kum, and its far reaches were
34 at the Jordan. And the boundary turned back westward to Aznoth-Tabor
and went from there to Hukok and touched Zebulun from the south and

---

27. *the Vale of Iphtah-El*. The Masoretic text here reads "the sons of Iphtah-
El," a noun that doesn't make sense as the object of the verb "touched." This
translation reflects the reading of the Septuagint.

28. *as far as Greater Sidon*. The territory of Asher could not have included
Sidon, a Phoenician city, but perhaps the qualifier "greater" is meant to suggest
something like the far southern reach of the region controlled by Sidon.

touched Asher from the west and Judah at the Jordan where the sun
rises. And the fortress towns were Ziddim, Zer, Hammath, Rakkath, and   35
Chinnereth, and Adamah and Ramah and Hazor, and Kedesh and Edrei   36,37
and Ein-Hazor, and Iron and Migdal-El, Horam, Beth-Anath and Beth-   38
Shemesh—nineteen towns and their pasturelands. This is the estate   39
of the tribe of the Naphtalites according to their clans, the towns and
their pasturelands. For the tribe of the Danites according to their clans   40
the seventh lot came out. And the territory of their estate was Zorah   41
and Eshtaol and Ir-Shemesh, and Shaalbim and Ajalon and Ithlah, and   42,43
Elon and Timnathah and Ekron, and Eltekeh and Gibthon and Baalath,   44
and Jehud and Benei Brak and Gath-Rimmon, and the Jarkon Waters   45,46
and Rakkon by the boundary over against Joppa. And the territory of the   47
Danites fell from their hands. And the Danites went up and did battle
with Leshem and took it. And they struck it with the edge of the sword
and took hold of it and dwelled in it. And they called Leshem Dan, like
the name of Dan their forefather. This is the estate of the tribe of the   48
Danites according to their clans—these towns and their pasturelands.

And they finished taking possession of the land according to its bound-   49
aries, and the Israelites gave Joshua son of Nun an estate in their midst.

---

47. *And the territory of the Danites fell from their hands.* More literally: "went out
from them." Their original territory was in the southwestern region bordering
on Philistine country—a location reflected in the stories about Samson, who
was a Danite. At some relatively early point, perhaps as early as the twelfth
century BCE, the Danites were forced out of their original tribal territory and
migrated to the far north of the country, where they conquered a new area for
settlement. This northern location is reflected in the story of Micah's idol in
Judges 18. The reading of this verse in the Septuagint shows a report that might
be the original version or might be an explanatory gloss: "The Danites did not
dispossess the Amorites, who forced them into the high country. The Amorites
did not let them come down into the plain, and their territory was too confin-
ing for them."
    Leshem. Elsewhere, this town is called Layish.

49. *the Israelites gave Joshua son of Nun an estate in their midst.* One infers that
Joshua waited until all the tribes had been allocated their territories before he
took his own estate. As Shmuel Ahituv notes, his portion was a special assign-
ment of territory to the commander-in-chief.

50 At the behest of the Lord they gave him the town that he had asked for, Timnath-Serah in the high country of Ephraim, and he rebuilt the
51 town and dwelled in it. These are the estates that Eleazar the priest and Joshua son of Nun and the heads of the Israelite tribes conferred by lot in Shiloh before the Lord at the entrance to the Tent of Meeting. And they finished sharing out the land.

---

50. *rebuilt*. The Hebrew verb ordinarily means "to build," but in contexts where the object is in ruins, as may be the case here because of conquest, it can mean "rebuild."

CHAPTER 20

And the Lord spoke to Joshua, saying: "Speak to the Israelites, saying, 1,2 'Set aside for yourselves the towns of asylum about which I spoke to you through Moses where a murderer, one who strikes down a person 3 in errance, without intending, may flee, and they will be an asylum for you from the blood avenger. And he may flee to one of these towns and 4 stand at the gateway to the town and speak his words in the hearing of the elders of that town, and they will take him to them into that town and give him a place and he will dwell with them. And should the blood 5 avenger pursue him, they will not hand the murderer over to him, for he struck down his fellow man without intending, and he had not been

---

1. *the towns of asylum about which I spoke to you through Moses.* The laws for the town of asylum are laid out in Numbers 35 and restated, in somewhat different terms, in Deuteronomy 19. Although the literary formulation of the laws here was probably done two or three centuries after the founding of the monarchy, the laws themselves reflect the tribal period when there was no centralized judicial authority, and vendetta justice prevailed in cases of murder or manslaughter.

3. *a murderer.* The Hebrew *rotseah*, which generally means "murderer," also encompasses "manslayer," as in the present context. Perhaps it is used to stress the gravity of destroying a life, even unintentionally.

in errance, without intending. This duplication of language brings together the term used in Numbers with the one used in Deuteronomy.

blood avenger. The literal sense of this designation is "blood redeemer." That idiom reflects an archaic notion that when the blood of one's kin is shed, it has been lost to—or perhaps drained away from—the family, and it must be "redeemed" by shedding the blood of the killer.

6 his enemy in times past. And he shall dwell in that town until he stands
before the community in judgment, until the death of the high priest
who will be in those days. Then the murderer shall return and come to
7 his town and to his home and to the town from which he had fled." And
they dedicated Kedesh in the Galilee in the high country of Naphtali
and Shechem in the high country of Ephraim and Kiriath-Arba, which
8 is Hebron, in the high country of Judah, and across the Jordan from
Jericho, to the east, Bezer in the wilderness on the plain, from the tribe
of Reuben and Ramoth in Gilead from the tribe of Gad and Golan in
9 Bashan from the tribe of Manasseh. These were the towns marked out
for all the Israelites and for the sojourners sojourning in their midst to
flee there, anyone striking down a person in errance, that he not die by
the hand of the blood avenger, until he stand before the community.

---

6. *until he stands before the community in judgment, until the death of the high priest.* These look suspiciously like contradictory terms. The fugitive has already received what amounts to a verdict of innocent when the elders accept his plea in the gateway of the town (the place of judgment). If a general amnesty obtains after the death of the high priest, why does the fugitive have to stand trial a second time? It is possible that the writer responsible for this passage was uneasy with the idea of a blanket exculpation at the time of the death of the high priest and wanted to emphasize that the fugitive's innocence had to be determined by judicial proceedings.

and to the town from which he had fled. This phrase seems redundant after "to his town." Perhaps one should drop the "and" and read it as an explanatory apposition, "to his town . . . . to the town from which he has fled."

9. *to flee there, anyone striking down a person in errance, that he not die by the hand of the blood avenger.* This phraseology repeats the language of the beginning of this section in an envelope structure.

until he stand before the community. He stands before the community to be judged, as verse 6 makes explicit. Here at the end, no mention is made of the death of the high priest, perhaps because the writer wanted to emphasize judicial proceedings, not amnesty.

CHAPTER 21

And the heads of the patriarchal houses of the Levites approached 1
Eleazar the priest and Joshua son of Nun and the heads of the patriarchal houses of the Israelite tribes, and they spoke to them in Shiloh in 2
the land of Canaan, saying, "The LORD charged through Moses to give
us towns in which to dwell and their fields for our cattle." And the Isra- 3
elites gave these towns and fields to the Levites from their estate at the
behest of the LORD. And the lot came out for the Kohathite clans, and 4
by lot the sons of Aaron the priest from the Levites had thirteen towns
from the tribe of Judah and from the tribe of Simeon and from the tribe
of Benjamin. And the remaining Kohathites had by lot ten towns from 5
the tribe of Ephraim and from the tribe of Dan and from the half-tribe
of Manasseh. And the sons of Gershon according to their clans had by 6
lot thirteen towns from the tribe of Issachar and from the tribe of Asher
and from the tribe of Naphtali and from the half-tribe of Manasseh in
Bashan. The sons of Merari according to their clans had twelve towns 7
from the tribe of Reuben and from the tribe of Gad and from the tribe

---

2. *The* LORD *charged . . . to give us towns.* It is difficult to assess to what extent
the list of levitical towns reflects historical reality. It is improbable that the
Levites actually had forty-eight of their own settlements, or that the other tribes
would have ceded that much real estate to them. Ahituv plausibly suggests that
what they were given was quarters within the towns, which continued to be
part of the domain of the host tribe.

4. *the sons of Aaron the priest.* Through verse 19, we have the apportionment
of towns to the priests (*kohanim*). What follows is the apportionment to the
Levites, who make up the rest of the tribe of Levi.

8 of Zebulun. And the Israelites gave to the Levites by lot these towns and
9 their fields as the LORD had charged through Moses. And they gave from
the tribe of the Judahites and from the tribe of the Simeonites these towns
10 which will here be called by name. And it came to the sons of Aaron
for the Kohathite clans from the sons of Levi, for theirs was the first
11 lot, and they gave them Kiriath-Arba father of Anak, which is Hebron,
12 in the high country of Judah, and its fields around it. And the town's
open land and its pastureland they gave to Caleb son of Jephunneh in
13 his holding. And to the sons of Aaron the priest they gave the town of
asylum for the murderer, Hebron and its fields, and Libnah and its fields,
14,15 and Jattir and its fields and Eshtamoa and its fields, and Holon and its
16 fields and Debir and its fields, and Ain and its fields and Juttah and its
fields, and Beth-Shemesh and its fields—nine towns from these tribes.
17 And from the tribe of Benjamin, Gibeon and its fields and Geba and its
18,19 fields, Anathoth and its fields and Almon and its fields—four towns. All
the towns of the sons of Aaron, the priest, were thirteen towns and their
20 fields. And for the clans of the Kohathites, the remaining Levites of the
21 Kohathites, the towns of their lot were from the tribe of Ephraim. And
they gave the towns of asylum for the murderer, Shechem and its fields
22 in the high country of Ephraim and Gezer and its fields, and Kibzaim
23 and its fields and Beth-Horon and its fields—four towns. And from the
24 tribe of Dan, Elteta and its fields, Gibthon and its fields, Ajalon and its
25 fields, Gath-Rimmon and its fields—four towns. And from the half-tribe
of Manasseh, Taanach and its fields and Gath-Rimmon and its fields—
26 two towns. All the towns and their fields were ten for the remaining
27 Kohathites. And to the Gershonites from the clans of the Levites, from
the half-tribe of Manasseh the asylum town for the murderer, Golan in

---

8. *these towns and their fields*. In an agricultural economy, the houses within
the town would have been places of residence but not sites from which income
could be generated. Hence the need to have a share in the fields outside the
town where crops could be grown or flocks pastured. For these areas outside
the town, three terms are used: *migrash*, "field," as here; *ḥatseir*, "pastureland,"
evidently an enclosed field; and (verse 12) *sadeh*, "open land," probably extending beyond the *migrashim*.

21. *towns of asylum*. As this list makes clear, all the towns of asylum are levitical
towns, but many others assigned to the Levites are not towns of asylum.

Bashan and its fields and Beeshterah and its fields—two towns. And 28
from the tribe of Issachar, Keshion and its fields, Dobrath and its fields,
Jarmuth and its fields, Ein-Gannim and its fields—four towns. And from 29,30
the tribe of Asher, Mishal and its fields, Abdon and its fields. Helkath 31
and its fields and Rehob and its fields—four towns. And from the tribe 32
of Naphtali, the town of asylum for the murderer, Kedesh in the Galilee
and its fields and Hammath-Dor and its fields and Kartan and its fields—
three towns. All the towns of the Gershonites according to their clans 33
were thirteen towns and their fields. And for the clans of the remaining 34
Merarites, from the tribe of Zebulun, Jokneam and its fields, Kartah and
its fields, Dimnah and its fields, Nahalal and its fields—four towns. And 35,36
from the tribe of Gad, the town of asylum for the murderer, Ramoth in
Gilead and its fields, and Mahanaim and its fields, Heshbon and its fields 37
and Jazer and its fields—all the towns were four. All the towns for the 38
remaining Merarites according to their clans that were their lot came
to twelve towns. All the towns of the Levites within the holdings of the 39
Israelites were forty-eight towns and their fields. These towns, each town 40
and its fields all around, thus these towns were. And the LORD gave to 41
Israel the whole land that He had vowed to give to their fathers, and they
took hold of it and dwelled in it. And the LORD granted them rest round 42
about, as all that He had vowed to their fathers, and no man of all their
enemies could stand against them—the LORD delivered all their enemies
in their hand. Nothing failed of all the good things that the LORD had 43
spoken to the House of Israel—everything came about.

---

36. *And from the tribe of Gad.* In between the end of the preceding verse and
these words, some Hebrew manuscripts insert the following: "and from the
tribe of Reuben Bezer and its fields and Johzah and its fields, Kedemoth and
its fields, and Mephath and its fields—four towns."

40. *These towns, each town and its fields all around, thus these towns were.* The
syntax of the Hebrew is rather crabbed, but this seems to be the sense of the
verse.

43. *Nothing failed.* The literal sense of the Hebrew is "nothing fell."
   the good things. The Hebrew uses a singular noun and it could also be understood to mean "the good word."

CHAPTER 22

Then did Joshua call to the Reubenites and the Gadites and to the half-
2 tribe of Manesseh, and he said to them, "You have kept all that Moses,
servant of the LORD, charged you, and you have heeded my voice in all
3 that I have charged you. You have not forsaken your brothers for many
days until this day, and you have kept the watch of the LORD your God.
4 And now the LÔRD your God has granted rest to your brothers, as He
had spoken to them, so now turn and go off to your tents, to the land
of your holding that Moses, servant of the LORD, gave to you across
5 the Jordan. Only watch carefully to do the command and the teaching
that Moses, servant of the LORD, charged you, to love the LORD your
God and to walk in all His ways, to keep His commands and to cling to
6 Him and to serve Him with all your heart and with all your being." And
Joshua blessed them and sent them off, and they went to their tents.

---

1. *Then did Joshua call.* Boling aptly describes the Hebrew phrasing *'az yiqra'
yehoshu'a* as "an expansive opening to a climactic unit." The small stylistic flourish in the translation seeks to mirror this effect.
   the Reubenites and the Gadites and the half-tribe of Manasseh. The book
began with the necessity for the trans-Jordanian tribes to join their brothers in
the conquest of the land west of the Jordan. Now that the conquest is complete, we come back to these tribes, in an envelope structure, as they are sent
back to their own territory.

3. *for many days.* These are the days, or period, of the conquest.

4. *granted rest.* As elsewhere, this idiom indicates subduing all enemies.

5. *to do the command and the teaching . . . to keep His commands and to cling to
Him and to serve Him with all your heart and with all your being.* This string of
phrases is a hallmark of Deuteronomistic prose.

And to the half-tribe of Manasseh Moses had given land in Bashan, 7
and to the other half Joshua gave land with their brothers west of the
Jordan. And what's more, when Joshua sent them off to their tents and
blessed them, he said to them, saying, "With many possessions return 8
to your tents and with very abundant livestock, with silver and with gold
and with bronze and with iron and with a great many cloaks. Share the
booty of your enemies with your brothers." And the Reubenites and 9
the Gadites and the half-tribe of Manasseh turned back and went from
Shiloh, which is in the land of Canaan, to go to the land of Gilead, to
the land of their holding in which they had taken hold at the behest of
the LORD through Moses. And they came to the Jordan districts that 10
are in the land of Canaan, and the Reubenites and the Gadites and the
half-tribe of Manasseh built there a great altar to be seen by all. And 11
the Israelites heard, saying, "Look, the Reubenites and the Gadites and
the half-tribe of Manasseh have built an altar over against the land of
Canaan in the Jordan districts across from the Israelites." And the Isra- 12
elites heard, and all the community of the Israelites assembled at Shiloh
to go up against them as an army. And the Israelites sent Phineas son 13
of Eleazar the priest to the Reubenites and to the Gadites and to the
half-tribe of Manasseh, and ten chieftains were with him, one chieftain 14
for a patriarchal house for each of the tribes of Israel, each the head
of a patriarchal house for the clan-groups of Israel. And they came to 15
the Reubenites and to the Gadites and to the half-tribe of Manasseh
and spoke with them, saying: "Thus said the whole community of the 16
LORD: 'What is this violation that you have committed against the God
of Israel, to turn back today from the LORD by building for yourselves an

---

9. *Share the booty of your enemies.* The source of the great abundance of possessions just listed is here spelled out.

10. *the Jordan districts.* These lie evidently alongside the Jordan, though one
cannot determine a precise location.
    to be seen by all. The words "by all" have been added in the translation because
of the requirements of English usage. The literal sense is "a great altar for sight."

16. *Thus said.* This is the so-called messenger-formula, regularly used to introduce the text of a message, whether oral or written.
    to turn back today from the LORD by building for yourselves an altar. The idiom
"to turn back" is repeated five times in this single episode, always in the sense

17 altar to rebel today against the LORD? Is the crime of Peor, from which
we have not been cleansed to this day, too little for us, as the scourge
18 came upon the community of the LORD? As for you, you turn back today
from the LORD, and it will happen that should you rebel today against
the LORD, tomorrow His fury will be against the whole community of
19 Israel. And if indeed the land of your holding is unclean, cross over
to the land of the LORD's holding where the LORD's sanctuary dwells
and take a holding within it, but do not rebel against the LORD, and
against us do not rebel, in your building yourselves an altar other than
20 the altar of the LORD our God. Did not Achan son of Zerah violate the
ban, and the fury was against the whole community of Israel while he,
21 a single man, did not perish through his crime?'" And the Reubenites
and the Gadites and the half-tribe of Manasseh answered and spoke to

---

of "to fall away from," "to abandon." The objection to building an altar east of
the Jordan is a little odd because regional altars were permissible in this period,
and the trans-Jordanian territory, allotted by God through Moses to the two and
a half tribes, could not plausibly be defined as "unclean" land. There was, however, an officially authorized altar in front of the sanctuary at Shiloh, and this
new altar was thought to set up illegitimate competition to the cis-Jordanian
one. Many scholars have detected a Priestly agenda in this story.

17. *the crime of Peor, from which we have not been cleansed to this day*. This episode, which involves an orgiastic sexual rite in which Israelite men are lured by
Midianite women, is recounted in Numbers 25. The punishment for the transgression is a plague that sweeps through the ranks of Israel. The Israelites' claim
here that they still have not been cleansed of the crime of Peor may reflect
some present-day epidemic, which is construed theologically as continuing
punishment for that initial crime. Perhaps, then, the Israelites understand the
erection of an altar east of the Jordan, where the hinterland is pagan, as the top
of a slippery slope leading to corruption by pagan practices.

19. *an altar other than the altar of the LORD our God*. Though the first part of this
verse introduces the notion of trans-Jordan as an "unclean" land, the emphasis
here is on the idea that there should be no alternative to the nationally recognized shrine at Shiloh.

20. *Achan*. Achan's transgression in violating the ban (Chapter 7) is comparable
to the putative transgression of the tribes east of the Jordan only in regard to
its consequences—it is not the transgressor but the whole people that suffers
because of the violation.

the heads of the clan-groups of Israel: "God of gods is the LORD. God of   22
gods is the LORD! He knows, and Israel shall know. If in rebellion and
in violation against the LORD, to build us an altar to turn back from the   23
LORD, do not rescue us this day. And if to offer up on it burnt offering
and meal offering, and if to prepare on it well-being offerings—let the
LORD seek it out. Or if not from concern for one thing we have done   24
this, saying, 'Tomorrow your sons will say to our sons, saying, What do
you have to do with the LORD God of Israel, when the LORD has fixed a   25
boundary, the Jordan, between you and us, O Reubenites and Gadites?
You have no share in the LORD.' And your children will prevent our
children from fearing the LORD. And so we thought, 'Let us act, pray, to   26
build an altar not for burnt offerings and not for sacrifices, but let it be   27
a witness between you and us and for our generations after us to do the
service of the LORD before Him with our burnt offerings and our sacrifices and our well-being offerings, that your children say not tomorrow
to our children, You have no share in the LORD.' And we thought, when   28
it happens that our generations tomorrow say to us, we shall say, 'See
the image of the LORD's altar that your forefathers made, not for burnt
offerings and not for sacrifices but as a witness between you and us. Far   29

---

22. *God of gods is the* LORD. This solemn, repeated pronouncement marks the
beginning of a sacred vow in which the two and a half tribes declare the innocence of their intentions before God and Israel.

He knows, and Israel shall know. The difference in tense is significant: God
knows that we did not intend to betray Him in building this grand altar, and
when we have finished making our declaration, Israel will know as well.

23. *do not rescue us this day.* If in fact the building of the altar was meant as an
act of rebellion against God, let your assembled army destroy us.

25. *your children will prevent our children from fearing the* LORD. The phrase
"fearing the LORD" does not indicate an inner state of piety but rather participation in the national cult: the cis-Jordanian tribes, seeing that the two and a
half tribes live beyond the Jordan in territory that the Israelite majority may not
regard as an intrinsic part of the land, will exclude them from nation and cult.

28. *See the image of the* LORD's *altar.* The altar we have built is a symbolic altar,
the image or simulacrum (*tavnit*) of the LORD's altar that we, like you, recognize
as the authorized site of public worship.

be it from us to rebel against the LORD and to turn back today from the LORD to build an altar for burnt offerings and for meal offerings and for sacrifice other than the altar of the LORD our God which is before

30 His sanctuary.'" And Phineas the priest, and the chieftains of the community and the heads of the clan-groups of Israel with him, heard what the Reubenites and the Gadites and the Manassites had spoken, and it

31 was good in their eyes. And Phineas son of Eleazar the priest said to the Reubenites and to the Gadites and to the Manassites, "Today we know that the LORD is in our midst, for you have not committed this violation against the LORD, and so you have saved the Israelites from the LORD's

32 hand." And Phineas son of Eleazar the priest, and the chieftains with him, turned back from the Reubenites and from the Gadites, from the land of Gilead to the land of Canaan, to the Israelites, and they brought

33 back word to them. And the thing was good in the eyes of the Israelites, and the Israelites blessed God, and they did not think to go up as an army to lay ruin to the land in which the Reubenites and the Gadites

34 were dwelling. And the Reubenites and the Gadites called the altar Witness, "for it is a witness among us that the LORD is God."

---

31. *and so you have saved the Israelites from the LORD's hand.* That is, you have saved us from attacking you without warrant, an act that would then have brought down retribution on us.

33. *the Israelites blessed God, and they did not think to go up as an army to lay ruin to the land.* This concluding narrative episode of the Book of Joshua is a story of civil war averted and national reconciliation, whereas the Book of Judges concludes with the story of a bloody civil war.

34. *called the altar Witness.* The received text says only "called the altar," but some Hebrew manuscripts as well as the Targum Yonatan show the more coherent text with the additional word as it is translated here. Rashi arrives at the same conclusion by inferring an ellipsis: "This is one of the abbreviated biblical texts, and it is necessary to add to it one word: 'and the Reubenites and the Gadites and the Manassites called the altar Witness.'"

CHAPTER 23

And it happened many years after the Lord had granted rest to Israel from all their enemies round about that Joshua grew old, advanced in years. And Joshua called to all Israel, to its elders and to its chieftains and to its judges and to its overseers. And he said to them, "I have grown old, advanced in years. As for you, you have seen all that the Lord your God has done to all these nations before you, for the Lord your God, it is He who did battle for you. See, I have made all these remaining nations fall to you in estate according to your tribes, and all the nations that I cut off, from the Jordan to the Great Sea where the sun goes down. And the Lord your God, it is He Who will drive them back before you and dispossess them before you, and you will take hold of their land

---

1. *after the Lord had granted rest to Israel from all their enemies.* This ringing declaration is subverted by the threat of exile that hovers over the end of the chapter. This is a tension that runs through both Joshua and Judges: God has enabled Israel to conquer all its enemies, yet the land is not completely conquered, and enemies threaten both within it and from surrounding nations. Even in this passage, the conquest of the Canaanite peoples alternates between being a completed process, as here, or a future activity, as in verse 5.

2. *I have grown old, advanced in years.* As several commentators have noted, Joshua's valedictory address stands in a line with those of Moses, Samuel, and David.

4. *all the nations that I cut off.* The Hebrew of this verse seems a little scrambled, with this clause appearing after "from the Jordan." In addition, "the Great Sea" lacks "to" in the Hebrew, and the preposition has been supplied in the translation.

6 as the LORD your God has spoken to you. And you must be very strong
to keep and to do all that is written in the book of Moses's teaching, not
7 to swerve from it to the right or to the left, not to come among these
nations that remain alongside you, nor to invoke the name of their gods
8 nor swear by them nor worship them and bow to them. But to the LORD
9 your God you shall cling as you have done till this day. And the LORD
has dispossessed before you great and mighty nations, and you—no man
10 has stood before you till this day. One man of you pursues a thousand,
for the LORD your God, it is He Who does battle for you as He spoke to
11 you. And you must be very careful for your own sake to love the LORD
12 your God. For should you indeed turn back and cling to the rest of these
remaining nations alongside you and intermarry with them and come
13 among them, and they among you, you must surely know that the LORD
your God will no longer dispossess these nations before you, and they
will become a trap and a snare for you and a whip against your side and
thorns in your eyes, until you perish from this good country that the
14 LORD your God has given you. And, look, I am about to go today on the
way of all the earth, and you know with all your heart and with all your
being that not a single thing has failed of all the good things that the
LORD your God has spoken about you. Everything has befallen you, not

---

6. *you must be very strong to keep and to do all that is written in the book of
Moses's teaching.* Here, as in much of the speech, the phraseology is strongly
reminiscent of Deuteronomy. In the book as a whole, the presence of the Deuteronomist is palpable but intermittent. As editor, he appears to have wanted
to put his strong imprint on the conclusion.

13. *a whip against your side.* The Masoretic text reads *leshotet*, which would
mean, implausibly, "to roam." The assumption of this translation is that the
second *tet* is a dittography and hence the Hebrew originally read *leshot*, "as a
whip."

14. *I am about to go . . . on the way of all the earth.* David on his deathbed,
1:Kings 2:2, uses the same language.
   not a single thing. This could also be construed as "not a single word."

a single thing of it has failed. And it shall be, just as every good thing   15
that the LORD your God has spoken of you has befallen you, so shall
the LORD bring upon you every evil thing until He destroys you from
this good country that the LORD your God has given you. When you   16
overturn the pact of the LORD your God that He charged you and you
go and worship other gods and bow to them, the wrath of the LORD will
flare against you, and you will perish swiftly from the good land that He
has given you.

---

15. *until He destroys you from this good country.* The term for "country," *'adamah*,
often means "soil," and its use here might reflect a desire to introduce a connotation of the land's fruitfulness. The notion that Israel will be driven from its
land if it betrays its pact with God is pre-eminently Deuteronomistic. The years
after 621 BCE, with the Assyrian and then the Babylonian threat uppermost in
the minds of the Judeans as well as the memory of the uprooting of the northern kingdom of Israel a century earlier, were a time when, with good reason,
national existence in the Land of Israel had come to seem painfully precarious.

CHAPTER 24

And Joshua gathered all the tribes of Israel at Shechem, and he called
to the elders of Israel and to its chieftains and to its judges and to its overseers, and they stood forth before God. And Joshua said to all the people:
"Thus said the LORD God of Israel: 'Your forefathers dwelled across the
Euphrates long ago—Terah father of Abraham and father of Nahor, and
they served other gods. And I took your father Abraham from across the
Euphrates and led him to the land of Canaan, and I multiplied his seed
and gave him Isaac. And I gave to Isaac Jacob and Esau, and I gave to
Esau the high country of Seir to take hold of, but Jacob and his sons went
down to Egypt. And I sent Moses and Aaron, and I struck Egypt with

---

1. *And Joshua gathered all the tribes.* The book appropriately ends with a renewal
of the covenant between Israel and its God, followed by the obituary notices
for Joshua and Eleazar.

2. *Your forefathers dwelled across the Euphrates . . . and they served other gods.*
Joshua's recapitulation of national history begins all the way back with Abraham's
ancestral family in Mesopotamia. ("Euphrates" in the Hebrew, as elsewhere in
biblical usage, is "the River"). But he immediately reminds his audience that
before Abraham these people were idolators, for the danger of backsliding into
idolatry is uppermost in his mind throughout the speech.

4. *Jacob and Esau.* It is noteworthy that Esau, together with his territorial inheritance, is mentioned with Jacob. There may be a gesture of restitution here for
Jacob's stealing the paternal blessing.

5. *I struck Egypt with plagues that I wrought in its midst.* The Hebrew text
shows what looks like a small glitch: "I struck Egypt with plagues as [or "when,"
ka'asher] I wrought in its midst." The Septuagint has a smoother reading: "I
struck Egypt with plagues as I wrought signs in its midst."

plagues that I wrought in its midst, and afterward I brought you out. And I brought your forefathers out of Egypt, and you came to the sea, 6 and the Egyptians pursued your forefathers with chariots and horsemen in the Sea of Reeds. And they cried out to the LORD, and He put a veil 7 of darkness between you and the Egyptians and brought the sea against them, and it covered them, and your own eyes saw that which I wrought against Egypt, and you dwelled in the wilderness many years. And I 8 brought you to the land of the Amorites dwelling across the Jordan, and they did battle against you, and I gave them into your hand, and you took hold of their land, and I destroyed them before you. And Balak son of 9 Zippor king of Moab rose up and did battle against Israel, and he sent out and called Balaam son of Beor to curse you. And I was unwilling to 10 listen to Balaam, and in fact he blessed you, and I saved you from his hand. And you crossed the Jordan and came to Jericho, and the lords 11 of Jericho did battle against you—the Amorite and the Perizzite and the Canaanite and the Hittite and the Girgashite, the Hivite and the

---

7. *a veil of darkness.* The Hebrew *ma'afel*, cognate to the more common *'apheilah,* "darkness," is unique to this verse. The clear reference is to the pillar of cloud in Exodus.

8. *the land of the Amorites dwelling across the Jordan.* These are the trans-Jordanian kings vanquished by Israel under Moses, as reported in Numbers and in Deuteronomy.

9. *Balak . . . did battle against Israel.* Because no actual battle is reported in Numbers 22:34, some commentators have claimed that a variant tradition is reflected here, but this is an unnecessary inference. Balak clearly saw Israel as his enemy and sought to destroy it using the curses of a professional hexer as his weapon of choice.

11. *the Amorite and the Perizzite and the Canaanite and the Hittite and the Girgashite, the Hivite and the Jebusite.* It is odd that all the seven peoples of Canaan are introduced here as though they had fought at Jericho, whereas no mention of a Canaanite alliance appears in the Jericho story. Perhaps Jericho, as the gateway town of Canaan and the first conquered, triggered the invocation of all these peoples, in a kind of synecdoche.

12 Jebusite. And I gave them into your hand. And I sent the hornet before you, and it drove them from before you—the two Amorite kings—not by
13 your sword and not by your bow. And I gave you a land in which you had not toiled and towns that you had not built, and you dwelled in them; from vineyards and olive groves that you did not plant you are eating the
14 fruit.' And now, fear the LORD and serve Him in wholeness and truth, and put away the gods that your forefathers served across the Euphrates
15 and in Egypt, and serve the LORD. And if it be evil in your eyes to serve the LORD, choose today whom you would serve, whether the gods that your forefathers served across the Euphrates or whether the gods of the Amorites in whose land you dwell, but I and my household will serve
16 the LORD." And the people answered and said, "Far be it from us to for-
17 sake the LORD to serve other gods. For the LORD our God, it is He Who brings our forefathers and us up from the land of Egypt, from the house of slaves, and Who has wrought before our eyes these great signs and guarded us on all the way that we have gone and among all the peoples
18 through whose midst we have passed. And the LORD drove out before us all the peoples, the Amorites, inhabitants of the land. We, too, will serve

---

12. *the hornet.* This is the traditional understanding of *tsir'ah*, leading some scholars to claim that noxious insects were actually used as weapons. But, on etymological grounds, as I proposed in comments on Exodus 23:28 and Deuteronomy 7:20, the term could mean "the Smasher," a mythological rather than a zoological entity.

13. *you are eating the fruit.* "Fruit" is implied by ellipsis. Pointedly, the verb for enjoying the fruit of vineyard and olive grove switches from past to a present participle, emphasizing to the audience that they themselves are benefitting from the conquest.

14. *in wholeness and truth.* Many construe these two Hebrew nouns as a hendiadys, having the sense of "in absolute truth."

15. *whether the gods that your forefathers served . . . or . . . the gods of the Amorites.* There is surely a note of sarcasm here: if you really want to serve foreign gods, just take your pick between Mesopotamian and Canaanite deities.

18. *all the peoples, the Amorites.* "Amorites" is sometimes a particular people and sometimes a general rubric for the sundry peoples of Canaan.

the Lord, for He is our God." And Joshua said to the people, "You will 19
not be able to serve the Lord, for He is a holy God. He is a jealous God,
He will not put up with your crimes and your offenses. For should you 20
forsake the Lord and serve alien gods, He shall turn back and do harm
to you and put an end to you after having been good to you." And the 21
people said to Joshua, "No! For we will serve the Lord." And Joshua said 22
to the people, "You are witnesses for yourselves that you have chosen
the Lord to serve Him." And they said, "We are witnesses." "And now, 23
put away the alien gods that are in your midst, and bend your hearts to
the Lord God of Israel." And the people said to Joshua, "The Lord we 24
will serve and His voice we will heed." And Joshua sealed a pact for the 25
people on that day and set it for them as statute and law at Shechem.
And Joshua wrote these things in the book of God's teaching, and he 26
took a great stone and set it under the terebinth that is in God's sanctuary. And Joshua said to all the people, "Look, this stone shall be witness 27
for us because it has heard all the Lord's sayings that He spoke to us,
and it shall be witness to you lest you deny your God." And Joshua sent 28
the people each man to his estate.

---

19. *You will not be able to serve the Lord, for He is a holy God.* In the face of
the people's solemn declaration to remain faithful to the God of Israel, Joshua
expresses grave doubt: YHWH is a holy God, making severe demands of exclusive loyalty, and I don't believe you will be able to meet these demands. This
view sets the stage for the series of idolatrous backslidings in Judges.

25. *set it for them as statute and law.* The same phrase is used in Exodus 15:25.

26. *the book of God's teaching.* This is a new designation, on the model of "the
book of Moses's teaching" and so can refer either to Deuteronomy or to the Five
Books of Moses, unless what Joshua writes is an appendix to them.

27. *this stone shall be witness.* Commemorative stone markers confirming trea-
ties appear a number of times in the Hebrew Bible and were common in much
of the ancient Near East.

29 And it happened after these things that Joshua son of Nun servant of
30 the Lord died, a hundred ten years old. And they buried him in the
territory of his estate in Timnath-Serah, which is in the high country of
31 Ephraim north of Mount Gaash. And Israel served the Lord all the days
of Joshua and all the days of the elders who outlived Joshua and who
32 had known all the acts of the Lord that He wrought for Israel. And the
bones of Joseph, which the Israelites had brought up from Egypt, they
buried in Shechem in the plot of land that Jacob had bought from the
sons of Hamor for a hundred *kesitahs*, so that it became an estate for
33 the sons of Joseph. And Eleazar the son of Aaron died, and they buried
him on the hill of Phineas his son, which had been given to him in the
high country of Ephraim.

---

29. *servant of the Lord*. Here at the end Joshua is given the same epithet as
Moses.

    a hundred ten years old. The narrative pointedly alots Joshua ten years fewer
than Moses, using instead the Egyptian number for a very full life-span.

33. The received text of Joshua ends on a relatively harmonious note of renewal
of the covenant and the death in ripe old age of the military leader Joshua and
the priestly leader Eleazar. But the ancient Greek translator used a Hebrew
text that concludes more discordantly with the following verse, which confirms
Joshua's doubts and looks forward to Judges: "And the Israelites went each
man to his place and to the town, and the Israelites served Ashtoreth and the
Ashtaroth and the gods of the peoples round about them, and the Lord gave
them into the hand of Eglon king of Moab, and he ruled over them eighteen
years." Though a variant manuscript might have added this report in order to
create a bridge with the beginning of Judges, it seems more likely that a scribe
or an editor deleted it out of motives of national piety, so as not to conclude the
book with an image of Israel's shame.

JUDGES

TO THE READER

L IKE SO MANY BIBLICAL BOOKS, Judges reflects an editorial splicing together of disparate narrative materials. Some of these materials, at least in their oral origins, could conceivably go back to the last century of the second millennium BCE, incorporating memories, or rather legendary elaborations, of actual historical figures. In any case, the redaction and final literary formulation of these stories are much later—perhaps, as some scholars have inferred, toward the end of the eighth century BCE, some years after the destruction of the northern kingdom in 721 BCE and before the reforms of King Josiah a century later.

The word *shofet*, traditionally translated as "judge," has two different meanings—"judge" in the judicial sense and "leader" or "chieftain." The latter sense is obviously the relevant one for this book, though the sole female judge, Deborah, in fact also acts as a judicial authority, sitting under the palm tree named after her. The narrative contexts make perfectly clear that these judges are ad-hoc military leaders—in several instances, guerilla commanders—but it would have been a gratuitous confusion to readers to call this text the Book of Chieftains or even to designate these figures in the text proper as chieftains or leaders rather than judges.

The first two chapters are both a prologue to what follows and a bridge from the end of the Book of Joshua. They incorporate a report of Joshua's death and an account of the incompletion of the conquest of the land, for which at least two rather different explanations are offered. The unconsummated conquest sets the stage for the sequence of stories in which Israel is sorely oppressed by enemies on all sides—the Philistines based on the coastal plain, the Midianites and the Moabites to the east, and the Canaanites in the heartland of the country. From the latter part of Chapter 3 to the end of Chapter 12, there is a formulaic rhythm of events: Israel's disloyalty to its God, its oppression by enemies as punishment for the dereliction, the crying out to God by the Israelites, God's raising up a judge to rescue them. This process of "raising up" leaders is what led Max Weber to borrow a term from the Greek and call a political system of this sort charismatic leadership. That is, the authority of the leader derives neither from a hereditary line nor from election by peers but comes about suddenly when the spirit of the LORD descends upon him: through this investiture, he is filled with a sense of power and urgency that is recognized by those around him, who thus become his followers.

The pattern remains the same, but for some of the judges we have no more than a bare notice of their name and their rescuing Israel (see, for example, the very first judge, Othniel son of Kenaz, 3:9–10) whereas for others we are given a detailed report of an act of military prowess (Ehud) or a whole series of narrative episodes (Gideon, Jephthah). The story of the fratricidal Abimelech breaks the sequence of judge narratives but provides foreshadowing of the bloody civil war at the end of the book.

The last in the series of judges is Samson, who is in several ways quite unlike those who precede him. Only Samson is a figure announced by pre-natal prophecy, with the full panoply of an annunciation type-scene. Only in the case of Samson is the first advent of the spirit of the LORD indicated not by a verb of descent (*tsalaḥ*) or investment (*labash*) but of violent pounding (*pa'am*). Unlike the other judges, Samson acts entirely alone, and his motive for devastating the Philistines is personal vengeance, not an effort of national liberation. Most strikingly, only Samson among all the judges exercises supernatural power. It seems likely, as many scholars have concluded, that the sequence of episodes about Samson reflects folkloric traditions concerning a Herculean, quasi-mythological hero, though the narrative as it has been formulated shows evidence of subtle literary craft. In any case, the Samson stories, editorially placed as the last in the series of judge-narratives, exemplify the breakdown of the whole system of charismatic leadership. Samson, battling alone with unconventional weapons or with his bare hands, more drawn to the sexual arena than to national struggle, hostilely confronted by fellow Israelites, sowing destruction all around him to the very end, like the fire with which he is associated from before his conception, is a figure of anarchic impulse: the man is whom the spirit of the LORD pounds mows down enemies but offers no leadership at all for his people, which may be a final verdict on the whole system of governance by charismatic warriors represented in the preceding episodes of the book.

The Samson narrative suggests that the shape given to Judges by its editors may be more purposeful than is often assumed. What follows the Samson cycle is the bizarre story of Micah's idol (Chapters 17 and 18) and then the grisly tale of the concubine at Gibeah who is gang-raped to death by the local Benjaminites, leading to a costly civil war between Benjamin and the other tribes (Chapters 19–21). These two blocks of material are often described as an appendix to the Book of Judges, and though it is true that they differ strikingly in subject matter and to some extent in style from the stories about the judges, they also show significant connections as well both with the immediately preceding Samson narrative and with the book as a whole. Divisiveness in the Israelite community, adumbrated in Samson's confrontation with the men of Judah, is vividly manifested both in the story of Micah and that of the concubine. Micah's narrative begins with his stealing eleven hundred shekels (the exact amount that the Philistines offer to Delilah) from his mother. Part of this purloined fortune, returned to his mother, is used to create a molten image of dubious monotheistic provenance, which will then become an object of contention. The displaced Danites, arriving on the scene as a military contingent, have no compunction about confiscating a whole set of cultic objects and buying off the young Levite whom Micah has hired to minister in his private sanctuary. The Danites then go on to conquer a new northern town in which to settle their southern tribe, but this is hardly a story that ends with the land quiet for forty years: tensions, verging on a clash of arms, between Micah and the Danites; dishonestly and deception; venality and the ruthless pursuit of personal and tribal self-interest—such far-from-edifying behavior dominates the story from beginning to end.

The morality exhibited in the book's concluding narrative is even worse. Another Levite, considerably more egregious than the one engaged by Micah, ends up re-enacting the story of Sodom with a bitter reversal. In this tale devoid of divine intervention, there are no supernatural beings to blind the brutal sexual assailants; the Levite pushes his concubine out the door to be raped all night long; and when he finds her prostrate on the threshold in the morning, he brusquely orders her to get up so that they can continue their journey, not realizing at first that she has expired. His remedy for this atrocity is as bad as the violation itself: he butchers her body into twelve parts that he sends out to the sundry tribes to rouse their indignation against Benjamin, and the ensuing civil war, in which the other tribes suffer extensive casualties, comes close to wiping out the tribe of Benjamin. Unbridled lust, implacable hostility, and mutual mayhem provide ample warrant for the implicitly monarchist refrain of these chapters: "In those days there was no king in Israel. Every man did what was right in his own eyes."

Anarchy and lust link these stories directly with the Samson narrative. But the theme of violence, threatened in Micah's story, shockingly realized in the narrative that follows, ties in the concluding chapters of Judges with everything that precedes them in the book. Judges represents, one might say, the Wild West era of the biblical story. Men are a law unto themselves—"Every man did what was right in his own eyes." There are warriors who can toss a stone from a slingshot at a hair and not miss; a bold left-handed assassin who deftly pulls out a short sword strapped to his right thigh to stab the Moabite king in the soft underbelly; another warrior-chieftain who panics the enemy camp in the middle of the night with the shock and awe of piercing ram's-horn blasts and smashed pitchers.

All this is certainly exciting in a way that is analogous to the gun-slinger justice of the Wild West, but there is an implicit sense, which becomes explicit at the end of the book, that survival through violence, without a coherent and stable political framework, cannot be sustained and runs the danger of turning into sheer destruction. In the first chapter of the book, before any of the judges are introduced, we are presented with the image of the conquered Canaanite king, Adoni-Bezek, whose thumbs and big toes are chopped off by his Judahite captors. This barbaric act of dismemberment, presumably intended to disable the king from any capacity for combat, presages a whole series of episodes in which body parts are hacked, mutilated, crushed. King Eglon's death by Ehud's hidden short sword is particularly grisly: his killer thrusts the weapon into his belly all the way up to the top of the hilt, and his death spasm grotesquely triggers the malodorous release of the anal sphincter.

Women are also adept at this bloody work: there is a vividly concrete report of how Jael drives the tent peg through the temple of Sisera the Canaanite general and into the ground; another woman, this one anonymous, smashes the head of the nefarious Abimelech with a millstone she drops on him from her perch in a besieged tower. Samson's slaughter of a thousand Philistines with a donkey's jawbone is surely a messy business of smashing and mashing—no neat spear's thrust here—though descriptive details are not offered. The grand finale of Samson's story, in which thousands of Philistine men and women, together with the Israelite hero, are crushed by the toppling temple, is an even more extensive crushing and mangling of bodies.

Against this background, one can see a line of imagistic and thematic continuity from the maiming of Adoni-Bezek at the very beginning of the book to the dismembering of the concubine at the end. That act of chopping a body into pieces, of course, is intended as a means to unite the tribes against Benjamin and its murderous rapists, but there is a paradoxical tension between the project of unity—unity, however, for a violent purpose—and the butchering of the body, the violation of its integrity, which in the biblical world as in ours was supposed to be respected through burial. The famous lines that Yeats wrote at a moment of violent upheaval in European and Irish history precisely capture the thematic thrust of Judges:

> Things fall apart; the centre cannot hold;
> Mere anarchy is loosed upon the world,
> The blood-dimmed tide is loosed. . . .

After this dark impasse to which the Book of Judges comes, it will be the task of the next great narrative sequence, which is the Book of Samuel, concluding in the second chapter of 1 Kings, to imagine a political means to create a center and leash the anarchy. That goal is in part realized, but the undertaking itself is an arduous one; and because these stories turn increasingly from legend and lore to a tough engagement in history, even as a center begins to hold, the blood-dimmed tide is never stemmed.

CHAPTER 1

And it happened after the death of Joshua that the Israelites inquired 1
of the LORD, saying, "Who will go up for us first against the Canaanite to
do battle with him?" And the LORD said, "Judah shall go up. Look, I have 2
given the land into his hand." And Judah said to Simeon his brother, "Go 3
up with me in my portion, and let us do battle with the Canaanite, and I,
too, shall go with you in your portion." And Simeon went with him. And 4
Judah went up, and the LORD gave the Canaanite and the Perizzite into
their hand, and they struck them down in Bezek—ten thousand men.

---

1. *And it happened after the death of Joshua*. These words are a pointed repetition of the formula that begins the Book of Joshua, "And it happened after the death of Moses."

the Israelites inquired of the LORD. This idiom indicates inquiry of an oracle in all likelihood, the *urim* and *thummim*, which could be used to yield a yes-no answer or to select an individual from a group. Some commentators have suggested that after Joshua's death, there was no longer a central leader with access to God and hence the oracular device was necessary.

2. *Judah shall go up*. The prominence of Judah in the vanguard of the conquest patently reflects a later period when Judah was the seat of the Davidide monarchy and the chief remaining tribe. The report here moves from Judah's military success in the south to the failures of the other tribes in the north.

3. *Simeon his brother*. This indication of fraternity and military cooperation probably derives from a moment in later history when Simeon was closely allied with or assimilated in Judah.

4. *ten thousand men*. Like almost all numbers in biblical narrative, this is formulaic, meant to indicate a large group. The reference to "seventy kings" in verse 7

5 And they found Adoni-Bezek in Bezek and did battle with him, and
6 they struck down the Canaanite and the Perizzite. And Adoni-Bezek
   fled, and they pursued him and seized him, and they chopped off his
7 thumbs and his big toes. And Adoni-Bezek said: "Seventy kings, their
   thumbs and their big toes chopped off, used to gather scraps under my
   table. As I have done, so has God paid me back." And they brought him
8 to Jerusalem, and he died there. And the Judahites did battle against
   Jerusalem, and they took it and struck it down with the edge of the
9 sword, and the town they set on fire. And afterward the Judahites went
   down to do battle with the Canaanite dwelling in the high country and

---

is similarly formulaic, though it does register the fact that Canaan was divided
among many small city-kingdoms, which were often at war with one another.

5. *Adoni-Bezek*. This name, which means "master of Bezek," appears to be a
hereditary title rather than a proper noun.

6. *They chopped off his thumbs and his big toes*. The mutilation, which on
the evidence of Adoni-Bezek's own words in the next verse, was evidently
a common practice, is both a humiliation and a means of permanently preventing the captured leader from becoming a combatant again because he
would be unable to wield a bow or sword or run on the battlefield. It should
be observed, moreover, that this grisly detail is an apt thematic and imagistic
introduction to Judges, the most violent of all the books of the Bible. In the
stories that follow, swords will be thrust into bellies, tent pegs into heads;
people will be variously mashed and crushed; and toward the end of the book,
the dismembered parts of a murdered woman's body will be sent out to the
sundry tribes in order to ignite a civil war. The mutilation of the king, then,
introduces us to a realm of political instability in which both people and
groups are violently torn asunder.

7. *And they brought him to Jerusalem, and he died there*. This notation and the
one in the next verse about the total destruction of Jerusalem by Judah are a
puzzlement. It is contradicted here by verse 2 1, in which it is said that Judah
was unable to drive out the Jebusites but continued to co-exist with them. 2
Samuel 5 reports, with some historical plausibility, that it was David who conquered Jerusalem from the Jebusites (probably two centuries after the putative
time of the events in Judges). One suspects that the Judahite writer was swept
up by the momentum of his own historical moment: Jerusalem had long been
the capital city of the Davidic monarchy, and so it was difficult for the writer to
imagine that it had not been part of the initial conquest of his tribe.

the Negeb and the lowland. And Judah went against the Canaanite 10
dwelling in Hebron—and the name of Hebron was formerly Kiriath-
Arba—and they struck down Sheshai and Achiman and Talmai. And 11
they went from there against the inhabitants of Debir—and the name
of Debir was formerly Kiriath-Sepher. And Caleb said, "Whoever strikes 12
Kiriath-Sepher and takes it, to him I shall give Achsah my daughter as
wife." And Othniel son of Kenaz, Caleb's younger brother, took it, and 13
he gave him Achsah as wife. And it happened when she came, that 14
she enticed him to ask a field of her father, and she alighted from the
donkey, and Caleb said to her, "What troubles you?" And she said to 15
him, "Give me a present, for you have given me desert-land, and you
should have given me springs of water." And Caleb gave her the upper
springs and the lower springs. And the sons of the Kenite, the father- 16
in-law of Moses, came up from the Town of Palms with the Judahites
from the Wilderness of Judah which is in the Negeb of Arad, and they
went and dwelled with the people. And Judah went with Simeon his 17
brother and they struck down the Canaanite dwelling in Zephath and
put it under the ban, and they called the name of the town Hormah.

---

12. *Whoever strikes Kiriath-Sepher and takes it, to him I shall give Achsah my
daughter as wife.* The story here, including the two previous verses, repeats in
virtually identical language the story told in Joshua 15:13–19. The offer of the
hand of the daughter to the victorious hero is an obvious folkloric motif and
recurs in the episode of David and Goliath.

13. *Othniel.* He is to become the first judge.

15. *desert-land.* The term *negev* (rendered elsewhere in this translation as the
place-name "Negeb") means terrain that supports little or no vegetation, probably deriving from a verbal stem that means "dry" or "desolate." The region in
the southern part of the Land of Israel is that sort of terrain and hence is given
the geographical name Negeb. Another term, *midbar*, is represented in this version, as it is in most English translations, as "wilderness" because it includes
land in which animals can graze.

16. *the Town of Palms.* On the basis of other biblical occurrences, this is Jericho.

17. *Hormah.* The name puns on *ḥerem*, "ban."

18 And Judah took Gaza and its territory and Ashkelon and its territory and
19 Ekron and its territory. And the LORD was with Judah, and he took pos-
    session of the high country, but he was not able to dispossess the inhab-
20 itants of the valley, for they had iron chariots. And they gave Hebron to
    Caleb as Moses had spoken, and he dispossessed from there the three
21 sons of the giant. But the Jebusite dwelling in Jerusalem, the Benjami-
    nites did not dispossess, and the Jebusite has been dwelling with the
22 Benjaminites in Jerusalem to this day. And the sons of Joseph, too, went
23 up to Bethel, and the LORD was with them. And the House of Joseph
24 scouted out Bethel—and the name of the town was formerly Luz. And
    the lookout saw a man coming out of the town and said to him, "Show
    us, pray, the way into the town, and we shall deal kindly with you."
25 And he showed them the way into the town, and they struck the town
26 by the edge of the sword, but the man and his clan they sent off. And
    the man went to the land of the Hittites and built a town and called

---

18. *And Judah took Gaza and its territory*. This verse is another instance in
which the writer's location in a time when the Philistine coastal enclave had
long been subdued is retrojected to the period of the Judges. Here three of the
five towns of the Philistine pentopolis are said to be conquered by Judah. But
in the subsequent narrative, down to the time of David, the Philistines remain
autonomous and a potent military threat; and in Judges itself, in the Samson
story, Gaza is very much in the hands of the Philistines.

19. *was not able*. The Hebrew of the received text sounds odd at this point: "was
not able" occurs in Onkelos's Aramaic version.

20. *the three sons of the giant*. Though many interpreters prefer to understand
the last term here, *'anaq*, as a proper noun, it does mean "giant," and there is
a clear tradition reflected in Numbers, Deuteronomy, Joshua, and Judges that
some of the indigenous inhabitants of the land were giants.

22. *Bethel*. The report now moves to the north. Bethel was to become a central
cultic location in the northern kingdom of Israel after the split in the monarchy.

24. *the way into the town*. Yigal Yadin has cited archeological evidence that
some Canaanite towns had tunnels that provided secret access to them. That
sounds plausible here because the lookouts are surely not asking directions to
the main gate of the town.

its name Luz—that is its name to this day. And Manasseh did not take   27
possession of Beth-She'an and its hamlets nor Taanach and its hamlets
nor the inhabitants of Dor and its hamlets nor the inhabitants of Ibleam
and its hamlets nor the inhabitants of Megiddo and its hamlets, but the
Canaanite went on dwelling in this land. And it happened, when Israel   28
grew strong, that it put the Canaanite to forced labor, but it did not dispossess him. And Ephraim did not dispossess the Canaanite dwelling in   29
Gezer, and the Canaanite dwelled in his midst in Gezer. Zebulun did not   30
dispossess the inhabitants of Kitron, nor the inhabitants of Nahalal, and
the Canaanite dwelled in his midst and did forced labor. Asher did not   31
dispossess the inhabitants of Acco, nor the inhabitants of Sidon, Ahiab,
Achzib, Helbah, Aphek, and Rehob. And the Asherite dwelled in the   32
midst of the Canaanites, inhabitants of the land, for he did not dispossess them. Naphtali did not dispossess the inhabitants of Beth-Shemesh   33
and the inhabitants of Baal-Anath, and he dwelled amidst the Canaanites inhabitants of the land, and the inhabitants of Beth-Shemesh and
of Beth-Anath did forced labor for them. And the Amorites drove the   34
Danites into the high country, for they did not let them come down
into the valley. And the Amorite continued to dwell in Mount Heres, in   35
Ajalon, and in Shaalbim, but the hand of the house of Joseph lay heavy
upon them, and they did forced labor. And the territory of the Amorites   36
was from the Ascent of Akrabbim, from Sela on up.

---

28. *Israel . . . put the Canaanite to forced labor, but it did not dispossess him.*
Whether this subjugation of the Canaanite population to the Israelites was a
historical fact or is merely a face-saving formula for the failure of the conquest
is uncertain. In any case, the chapter from this point on spells out a theme of
incompletion that had fluctuated through the Book of Joshua. In the first half
of Joshua, the conquest of the land appears to be comprehensive; in the second
half, there are some indications that much remains to be conquered. Now we
have a whole catalogue of failed conquests, all attributed to the northern tribes
that would constitute the break-away kingdom of Israel.

31. *Acco . . . Sidon, Ahiab, Achzib.* These coastal towns bring us far to the north,
near present-day Haifa and beyond, with Sidon actually being a Phoenician city.

35. *upon them.* These words are merely implied in the Hebrew.

CHAPTER 2

1 And a messenger of the LORD came up from Gilgal to Bochim, and he said: "I have taken you up from Egypt and brought you to the land that I swore to your fathers, and I said, 'I will never break my covenant 2 with you.' As for you, you shall not seal a covenant with the inhabitants of this land—their altars you shall smash. And you did not heed 3 My voice. What is this you have done? And I also said, 'I will not drive them out before you, and they shall become thorns to you, and their 4 gods shall become a snare for you.'" And it happened, when the LORD's messenger spoke these words to the Israelites, that the people raised 5 their voices and wept. And they called the name of the place Bochim,

---

1. *Bochim*. The name, which means "weepers," is proleptic, and its origin will be explained in verses 5–6.

I have taken you up from Egypt. The LORD's messenger is not speaking in his own person but is serving as God's mouthpiece, quoting His words.

I said. This verb in Hebrew can also mean "I thought" (perhaps an ellipsis for "I said in my heart"), and it is not clear whether God actually addresses these words to Israel or merely thinks them. The same ambiguity hovers over "I also said" in verse 3.

2. *their altars you shall smash*. This is in keeping with the vehement anti-pagan agenda of Deuteronomy.

3. *thorns*. The Hebrew *tsidim* would appear to mean "sides." A common expression in contexts like this one is "thorns [*tsinim*] in your side." This might be an ellipsis here, or, more likely, the similarity of the two words might have led a scribe to inadvertently replace *tsinim* with *tsidim*.

and they sacrificed there to the LORD. And Joshua sent off the people, 6
and the Israelites went every man to his estate to take hold of the land.
And the people served the LORD all the days of Joshua and all the days 7
of the elders who outlived Joshua, who had seen the great acts of the
LORD that He did for Israel. And Joshua son of Nun servant of the LORD 8
died, a hundred ten years old. And they buried him in the territory of 9
his estate, in Timnath-Heres in the high country of Ephraim north of
Mount Gaash. And that whole generation as well was gathered to its 10
fathers, and another generation arose after them that did not know the
LORD or the acts He had done for Israel. And the Israelites did evil in 11
the eyes of the LORD, and they served the Baalim. And they forsook the 12
LORD God of their fathers Who had brought them out of the land of
Egypt, and they went after other gods, of the gods of the peoples that
were all around them, and they bowed to them and vexed the LORD.
And they forsook the LORD and served Baal and the Ashtoroth. And the 13,14

---

6. *And Joshua sent off the people*. The appearance of Joshua makes it clear that
this entire passage loops back chronologically to the end of the Book of Joshua
(Chapter 24), when Joshua addresses the people, perhaps not long before his
death.

7. *And the people served the LORD all the days of Joshua*. This entire verse repeats
verbatim Joshua 24:31, with the exception of "the people," which in Joshua is
"Israel."
    the great acts. The Hebrew uses a singular noun with collective force. The
same usage occurs in verse 10.

11. *they served the Baalim*. This is the plural form of Baal, the Canaanite
weather-god and probably the most widely worshipped deity in the Canaanite
pantheon. Many interpreters infer that the plural form indicates Baal and other
pagan gods.

13. *Baal and the Ashtoroth*. Here "Baal" is singular and "Ashtoroth" shows a
feminine plural ending (the singular in this traditional transliteration would
be "Ashtoreth"). Ashtoreth is the Canaanite fertility goddess, though in some
Ugaritic texts she appears also as a warrior-goddess. The plural form, as with
Baalim in verse 11, may suggest that a variety of pagan goddesses is meant.

Lord's wrath flared up against Israel, and He gave them into the hand of plunderers who plundered them, and He handed them over to their enemies all around, and they were no longer able to stand up against
15 their enemies. Whenever they sallied forth, the Lord's hand was against them for harm, as the Lord had spoken and as the Lord had vowed
16 to them, and they were in sore straits. And the Lord raised up judges
17 and rescued them from their plunderers. And their judges, too, they did not heed, for they went whoring after other gods and bowed to them, they swerved quickly from the way in which their fathers had gone to
18 heed the Lord's command. They did not do so. And when the Lord raised up judges for them, the Lord was with the judge and rescued them from the hand of their enemies all the days of the judge, for the Lord felt regret for their groaning because of their oppressors and their

---

15. *Whenever they sallied forth, the* Lord's *hand was against them for harm.* This whole passage articulates a clearcut theological explanation for Israel's failure to conquer the entire land: its swerve into idolatry enrages God and causes Him to bring about Israel's defeat by its enemies.

16. *judges.* The Hebrew verbal noun *shofet* means both one who judges and one who rules, and the latter sense is more prominent here and in all that follows in this book. As a result, some modern translations opt for "chieftain" or an equivalent term. The *shofet* was an ad-hoc military leader (in this regard, "chieftain," suggesting a fixed and perhaps hereditary political institution, is misleading). From the subsequent narratives in this book, the judge was seen by his followers—or, at any rate, by the writer—as a figure suddenly invested with a divine spirit that impelled him to action and enabled his success. It is precisely on the model of the biblical judges that Max Weber borrowed the term "charisma" from the Greek to indicate a purely personal political power.

18. *the* Lord *was with the judge and rescued them from the hand of their enemies all the days of the judge.* A theological reason is offered here for a continuing unstable military situation. The judges were basically guerilla commanders. A judge, exercising personal magnetism and military prowess, could for a certain amount of time harass and drive back enemy forces that were probably superior in numbers and weaponry, but such successes were bound to be temporary. This fluctuating pattern is explained in terms of cultic loyalty and backsliding: under the charismatic influence of the judge, the Israelites were faithful to their God; when the judge died, they reverted to their pagan practices. Verse 17 suggests that they did not heed their judges, or only temporarily.

harassers. And it happened, when the judge died, they went back and 19
acted more ruinously than their fathers, to go after other gods, to serve
them, to bow to them. They left off nothing of their actions and their
stubborn way. And the LORD's wrath flared up against Israel, and He 20
said, "Because this nation has transgressed My covenant that I charged
to their fathers and has not heeded My voice, I on my part will not 21
continue to dispossess before them any of the nations that Joshua left
when he died in order to test Israel through them, whether or not they 22
will keep the LORD's way to go in it." And the LORD had left aside these 23
nations, not dispossessing them quickly, and He had not given them into
the hand of Joshua.

---

19. *their actions.* The implication in context is "evil actions," though the Hebrew
noun used is not intrinsically negative.

21.–22. *the nations that Joshua left when he died in order to test Israel through
them.* Here a new theological explanation of the incompleteness of the conquest is introduced. Joshua, given his sweeping military successes reported in
Joshua 1–12, might well have conquered the entire land, but he left some of it
in Canaanite hands in order to see whether future generations of Israel would
be faithful to their God and thus be worthy of taking hold of the rest of the land.
God's words in these two verses affirm that the people has failed the test and
so will not be able to complete the conquest. The next verse then makes clear
that Joshua's leaving part of the land unconquered was actually God's devising.

CHAPTER 3

1   And these are the nations that the Lord left aside to test Israel through
2   them—all who knew not the wars of Canaan, only so that the genera-
    tions of Israel might know, to teach them warfare, which before they did
3   not know: the five overlords of the Philistines and all the Canaanites and
    the Sidonites and the Hivites dwelling in the high country of Lebanon
4   from Mount Baal Hermon to Lebo-Hamath. And they came to test Israel
    through them, to know whether they would heed the command of the
5   Lord with which He charged their fathers by Moses. And the Israelites
    dwelled in the midst of the Canaanites, the Hittites and the Amorites
6   and the Perizzites and the Jebusites. And they took their daughters for
    themselves as wives, and their own daughters they gave to their sons,

---

1. *all who knew not the wars of Canaan.* The translation mirrors the looseness
of the Hebrew syntax, though this clause clearly modifies "Israel."

2. *to teach them warfare, which before they did not know.* Here an entirely different reason for the incompleteness of the conquest is introduced: Israel had
to learn the skills of war in gradual stages through conflict with the Canaanites
before it was prepared to conquer them.

4. *to test Israel . . . to know whether they would heed the command of the* Lord.
Now the writer reverts to the theological explanation for the incompleteness of
the conquest put forth in 2:21–23.

and they served their gods. And the Israelites did evil in the eyes of the 7
LORD, and they forgot the LORD their God, and they served the Baalim
and the Asheroth. And the LORD's wrath flared up against Israel, and He 8
handed them over to Cushan Rishathaim king of Aram Naharaim, and
the Israelites served Cushan Rishathaim eight years. And the Israelites 9
cried out to the LORD, and the LORD raised up a rescuer for the Israelites, Othniel son of Kenaz, Caleb's young brother, who rescued them.
And the spirit of the LORD was upon him, and he led Israel and went 10
out to battle, and the LORD gave into his hand Cushan Rishathaim king
of Aram, and his hand was strong against Cushan Rishathaim. And the 11
land was quiet forty years, and Othniel son of Kenaz died.

And the Israelites continued to do evil in the eyes of the LORD, and 12
the LORD strengthened Eglon king of Moab over Israel because they
had done evil in the eyes of the LORD. And he gathered round him the 13
Ammonites and the Amalekites, and he struck Israel and they took hold
of the Town of Palms. And the Israelites served Eglon king of Moab 14

---

7. *the Asheroth.* In the plural feminine form, a different Canaanite goddess is
evoked, not Ashtoreth but Asherah, the consort of the sky-god El.

8. *Cushan Rishathaim king of Aram Naharaim.* There are two oddities in this
name and title. Rishathaim, which means "double-evil," sounds more like a
symbolic epithet than an actual name. Aram Naharaim is Mesopotamian Aram
(there were Arameans closer to the eastern border of Israel), which would be
a long distance from which to exert temporary dominance over any population
west of the Jordan.

9. *Othniel son of Kenaz, Caleb's young brother.* He has already figured in the
narrative both in this book and in Joshua as the conqueror of Hebron. In that
instance, however, his military prowess was not enabled by the descent of the
spirit upon him, according to the pattern of the judges. His appearance now
as the first judge is no doubt intended to establish a bridge between the period
of Joshua and the period of the judges. All the elements of the judge paradigm
are evident: Israel's defection, its subjugation, its crying out, God's response
in raising up a rescuer, the descent of the spirit, the ensuing victory. But only
the outline of the pattern appears—no details are offered of Othniel's exploits.

15 eighteen years. And the Israelites cried out to the LORD, and the LORD
    raised up a rescuer for them, Ehud son of Gera the Benjaminite, a left-
    handed man. And the Israelites sent tribute in his hand to Eglon king
16 of Moab. And Ehud made himself a double-edged sword, a *gomed* in
17 length, and strapped it under his garments on his right thigh. And he
    presented the tribute to Eglon king of Moab, and Eglon was a very fat
18 man. And it happened when he had finished presenting the tribute that
19 he sent away the people bearing the tribute. And he had come back
    from Pesilim, which is by Gilgal. And he said, "A secret word I have for
    you, king." And he said, "Silence!" And all those standing in attendance

---

15. *the Benjaminite*. The tribe of Benjamin, as the subsequent narrative will
affirm, was noted for its skill in battle.

    a left-handed man. The literal sense of the Hebrew idiom is "a man impaired
[or bound up] in his right hand." Ehud's left-handedness plays a crucial part in
his assassination of Eglon.

    in his hand. Though the idiom means "through his agency," with verse 18
making clear that there are at least several people physically bearing the considerable tribute, the use of "hand" picks up the appearance of the ominous left
hand in the previous verse and its lethal deployment in verse 21.

16. *a gomed*. This measure of length occurs only here, but it has an evident cognate, *garmida*, in rabbinic Aramaic, which is a cubit, about seventeen
inches. This would be short enough to conceal the weapon strapped to the
thigh. The double edge of the straight sword makes it a thrusting weapon.
Typical swords of this period were single-edged and sickle-shaped and were
wielded by slashing.

17. *Eglon was a very fat man*. The name Eglon strongly suggests *'egel*, "calf."
In this satiric view of the enemy, he is a gross fatted calf, ready for slaughter.

19. *Pesilim*. This appears to be a place-name, but it means "the idols" (there is
a definite article), and so it is probably a cultic site.

    Silence. The Hebrew *hass* is onomatopoeic, something like shsh! When
Ehud tells Eglon that he has a secret to convey, these words elicit exactly the
response intended by the assassin: the king doesn't want anyone else to hear,
so he tells Ehud to keep quiet and orders everyone else out of the chamber. It
should be noted that Ehud's words to the king are abrupt, lacking the language
of deference ("my lord the king") required when addressing a royal personage.
Eglon, in his eagerness to hear the secret, takes no note of this.

on him went out from his presence. When Ehud had come to him, he   20
was sitting alone in the cool upper chamber that he had. And Ehud said,
"A word of God I have for you." And he rose from the seat. And Ehud   21
reached with his left hand and took the sword from his right thigh and
thrust it into his belly. And the hilt, too, went in after the blade and the   22
fat closed over the blade, for he did not withdraw the sword from his
belly, and the filth came out. And Ehud went out to the vestibule and   23

---

20. *A word of God.* At first, Eglon might have thought that the secret word was
some piece of military intelligence that this supposed collaborator was offering
him. Now Ehud presents it as an oracle, something that would be especially
likely if Eglon is aware that he has arrived by way of Pesilim. (In this second
bit of dialogue, Ehud is even more abrupt, now omitting the title "king.") Eglon
rises either because this is the proper posture in which to receive an oracle or
because of his eagerness to hear the "word of God" up close. By standing, of
course, he makes himself a perfect target for the sword-thrust.

21. *Ehud reached with his left hand.* Because Eglon does not see this as the
weapon-hand, Ehud gains a decisive moment as he whips out the sword before
Eglon can make a move to evade it.

22. *the hilt, too, went in after the blade.* The image of the weapon entirely
encased in Eglon's corpulence is deliberately grotesque.
　the filth. The Hebrew *parshedonah* clearly shows the element *peresh*, excrement. The anomalous ending of the word may be a scribal duplication of the
ending of *misderonah,* "to the vestibule," which is the third word after this one
in the Hebrew text. The release of the anal sphincter in the death spasm adds
a scatological note to the representation of the killing of Eglon.

23. *Ehud went out to the vestibule.* The exact meaning of the Hebrew noun is
uncertain, and our knowledge of the floor-plan of Moabite palaces remains
imperfect in this regard, though one scholar, Baruch Halperin, has made a
heroic effort to reconstruct the architectural scene. But this would have to be
some sort of courtyard or rear chamber on the other side of the king's special
chamber from the anteroom in which his attendants await him. The closing and
locking of the doors, then, would be pluperfect: Ehud locks them from within
and goes out through another, unspecified, exit.

24 closed the doors of the upper chamber and locked them. He had just
gone out, when Eglon's courtiers came and saw, and, look, the doors
of the upper chamber were locked. And they said, "He must be reliev-
25 ing himself in the cool chamber." And they waited a long while, and,
look, no one was opening the doors of the upper chamber. And they
took the key and opened them, and, look, their master was fallen to
26 the ground, dead. And Ehud had escaped while they tarried, and he
27 passed Pesilim and escaped to Seirah. And it happened when he came,
that he blasted the ram's horn in the high country of Ephraim, and
the Israelites came down with him from the high country, and he was

---

24. *and, look, the doors of the upper chamber were locked.* The use of the presentative *hineh*, "look," to mark a shift to the characters' point of view is tactically
effective here and in what follows: the courtiers are confronted by locked doors,
and perplexed.

    He must be relieving himself. The scatological detail is comic here: they can
clearly smell the consequences of the released sphincter, and they use their
inference to explain both the locked doors and the long delay.

25. *they took the key and opened them.* These doors evidently can be locked or
unlocked from either side.

    and, look, their master was fallen to the ground, dead. The management of
narrative point of view is both eloquent and dramatic. They look and first make
out "their master" (which is how they would have silently referred to him), take
in the fact that he is sprawled on the floor, and then realize, at the very end of
the syntactic chain, that he is dead. (With the short sword entirely buried in
his belly, it is possible that no blood would be visible.)

26. *And Ehud had escaped while they tarried.* The courtiers' long wait while
they supposed their king was relieving himself gives the assassin ample time
to get away.

27. *he blasted the ram's horn.* It often happens in biblical narrative that two
juxtaposed scenes are linked by the repetition of a term, in a different sense.
The verb *taqa'* means "to stab" or "to thrust" and is used for Ehud's killing of
Eglon. But it also means "to blast" (on a ram's horn or trumpet), which is what
he does now as a signal to rally fighters around him.

before them. And he said to them, "Come down after me, for the L ORD 28
has given your enemies, Moab, in your hand." And they came down after
him and took the fords of the Jordan from Moab, and they did not let
anyone cross over. And at that time they struck down Moab, about ten 29
thousand men, every stout fellow and every valiant man, and not a man
escaped. And on that day Moab was laid low under the hand of Israel. 30
And the land was quiet eighty years.

And after him there was Shamgar son of Anath. And he struck down the 31
Philistines, six hundred men, with an ox-goad, and he, too, rescued Israel.

---

28. *Come down after me*. The received text says *ridfu 'aharay*, which means
"pursue me," an idiom that always suggests hostile intent. The Septuagint reads
redu, "come down," and it is very likely that the extra consonant, generating a
wrong meaning, was inadvertently introduced through scribal copying in the
Masoretic text.

29. *every stout fellow*. The Hebrew adjective *shamen* usually means "fat" but
here has the sense of "stalwart" or "strong," a double meaning also exhibited
by the English term "stout." Its use here, however, clearly plays back ironically
against the corpulence of Eglon.

30. *eighty years*. In this case, it is twice the formulaic forty.

31. *Shamgar son of Anath*. Anath is the Canaanite warrior-goddess. Some scholars think Shamgar may incorporate the name of the Hurrian sun-god. It is a
puzzle that this judge should sport two eminently pagan names. It is possible
that the folk-traditions on which the tales of the judges draw might actually
reflect a fluid and syncretic situation in this early period in which on occasion a
warrior of Canaanite lineage might have fought alongside some Israelite group.
    with an ox-goad. This unconventional weapon anticipates Samson's slaying
Philistines with the jaw-bone of a donkey. The very oddness of this detail—the
sole detail we are given about Shamgar's exploits—might suggest an actual
memory of a fighter who used an improvised destructive implement, though
the number of six hundred killed (six hundred is a set figure for military contingents) is unlikely.

CHAPTER 4

1   And the Israelites continued to do evil in the eyes of the Lord—
2 and Ehud had died. And the Lord handed them over to Jabin, king
   of Canaan, who reigned in Hazor, and the commander of his army
3 was Sisera, and he lived in Harosheth-Goiim. And the Israelites cried
   out to the Lord—for he had nine hundred iron chariots and he had
4 oppressed the Israelites mightily for twenty years. And Deborah, a
   prophet-woman, wife of Lappidoth, she it was who judged Israel at

---

1. *and Ehud had died*. The Hebrew indicates a pluperfect by placing the subject before the verb and using the suffix conjugation (*qatal*) of the verb: Ehud's death leaves a hiatus, and Israel reverts to its wayward behavior.

2. *Jabin, king of Canaan*. This designation is a kind of hyperbole because there was no single king of Canaan. Hazor, however, was an important city, and so its king would have exercised considerable power among the city-states of Canaan. Later in the chapter, Jabin is called "king of Hazor."

3. *iron chariots*. As elsewhere, this characterization is an exaggeration, perhaps meant to emphasize the fearsome power of the chariots, because in this era the chariots were wooden, with at most iron reinforcing elements.

4. *a prophet-woman*. The translation mirrors the structure of the Hebrew, which does not say *nevi'ah* ("prophetess") but *'ishah nevi'ah*. The introduction of the "woman" component, which is not strictly required by idiomatic usage, highlights the prominence of woman vis-à-vis man that is evident both in Deborah's relation to Barak and in the story of Jael and Sisera.
   she it was who judged Israel at that time. The figure of Deborah manifests the ambiguity of the role of "judge," *shofet*. She is called a prophet because she evidently has a direct line of intelligence about God's strategic plans for Israel. In this, she resembles the martial judges, who are invested with the spirit of God. She is not called a judge, perhaps because she herself, as a woman, does

that time. And she would sit under the Palm of Deborah between 5
Ramah and Bethel in the high country of Ephraim, and the Israelites
would come up to her for judgment. And she sent and called to Barak 6
son of Abinoam from Kedesh-Naphtali and said to him, "Has not the
LORD God of Israel charged you: 'Go, and draw around you on Mount
Tabor and take with you ten thousand men from the Naphtalites and
the Zebulunites. And I shall draw down to you at the Kishon wadi 7
Sisera, the commander of Jabin's army, and his chariots and his force,
and I shall give him into your hand.'" And Barak said to her, "If you go 8
with me, I will go, and if you do not go with me, I will not go." And 9
she said, "I will certainly go with you, but it will not be your glory on
the way that you are going, for in the hand of a woman the LORD will
deliver Sisera." And Deborah rose and went with Barak to Kedesh.
And Barak mustered Zebulun and Naphtali at Kedesh, and he brought 10
up at his heels ten thousand men, and Deborah went up with him.

---

not go out to the battlefield, but she is the subject of the verb "judge," a capacity
she exercises in the judicial sense, as becomes entirely clear in the next verse.

6. *Has not the LORD God of Israel charged you.* Deborah would know what God
commands Barak because she is a prophet.

draw around you. The Hebrew verb says merely "draw," though the evident
meaning in context is to muster or rally. This verb is pointedly repeated in God's
speech in the next verse: Barak is to draw fighters around him, and God will
then draw the enemy into a place where he will be defeated.

8. *If you go with me, I will go.* Barak's hesitancy makes it evident that the male
commander needs this woman behind him in order to go out to battle. Thus he
becomes a kind of proxy for Deborah, who is to all intents and purposes also a
"judge" in the military sense.

9. *for in the hand of a woman the LORD will deliver Sisera.* The sentence has
a double meaning. The woman in the first instance is the "prophet-woman"
Deborah, who can rightly take credit for the victory. It also turns out to be Jael,
whose actual hand, driving in the tent-peg, will finish off Sisera.

10. *Zebulun and Naphtali.* In this prose version, which is almost certainly later
than the poetic version in Chapter 5, there are only two tribes involved and not
an alliance of several tribes.

at his heels. The literal sense of the Hebrew is "at his feet."

11 And Heber the Kenite had separated from Kayin, from the sons of
Hobeb father-in-law of Moses, and he pitched his tent at Elon-in-
12 Zaananim, which is by Kedesh. And they told Sisera that Barak son
13 of Abinoam had gone up to Mount Tabor. And Sisera mustered all his
chariots, nine hundred iron chariots, and all the troops that were with
14 him, from Harosheth-Goiim to the Kishon wadi. And Deborah said to
Barak, "Arise, for this is the day that the LORD has given Sisera into
your hand. Has not the LORD sallied forth before you?" And Barak
15 came down from Mount Tabor, and ten thousand men after him. And
the LORD panicked Sisera and all the chariots and all the camp by
the edge of the sword before Barak, and Sisera got down from the
16 chariot and fled on foot. And Barak had pursued the chariots and
the camp as far as Harosheth-Goiim, and all the camp of Sisera fell
17 by the edge of the sword, not one remained. And Sisera had fled on
foot to the tent of Jael, wife of Heber the Kenite, for there was peace
18 between Jabin king of Hazor and the house of Heber the Kenite. And
Jael came out to meet Sisera and said to him, "Turn aside, my lord,
turn aside to me, do not fear." And he turned aside to her, to the tent,

---

11. *Kayin.* This name is conventionally represented as "Cain" but is here
spelled as it is to indicate that the ethnic group is the same as Heber's identifying ethnic tag, "the Kenite."

14. *Has not the* LORD *sallied forth before you?* In almost all the reports of battle
in the Deuteronomistic History, YHWH figures as the warrior-god who defeats
the enemy, and there is little representation of human acts of martial prowess
or strategic cunning. The next verse invokes a characteristic locution: the LORD
"panics" the enemy, thus causing his defeat.

15. *Sisera got down from the chariot.* The same Hebrew verb is used here as
when Barak "came down" from Mount Tabor: the first coming down is a rapid
descent in an attack, and the second is a flight on foot from an encumbered or
perhaps damaged chariot.

18. *Turn aside, my lord, turn aside to me.* Her words, with an alliteration of
sibilants in the Hebrew (*surah, 'adoni, surah'elay*), are soothingly reassuring,
almost seductive.

and she covered him with a blanket. And he said to her, "Give me,   19
pray, a bit of water to drink, for I am thirsty." And she opened the skin
of milk and gave him to drink and covered him. And he said to her,   20
"Stand at the opening of the tent, and then, should a man come and
ask you, 'Is there a man here?,' you shall say there is not." And Jael wife   21
of Heber took the tent-peg and put a mallet in her hand and came to
him stealthily and drove the peg through his temple and it sunk into
the ground—as for him, he had been asleep, exhausted—and he died.
And, look, Barak was pursuing Sisera, and Jael went out to meet him   22
and said to him, "Come, that I may show you the man you seek." And
he went inside, and, look, Sisera was fallen, dead, the peg in his temple.

---

19. *she opened the skin of milk and gave him to drink.* Sisera has asked for water;
Jael in a gesture of hospitality offers him milk. The detail picks up a line from
the poem (5:25), but whereas the poem, in an epic flourish, has her offering
the milk in a "princely bowl," the prose narrative turns this into the homey
realistic receptacle of a skin bag. It also highlights, as the poem does not, the
ironic suggestion of Jael's playing a maternal role toward the man she is about
to kill: first she covers him with a blanket, then she gives him milk to drink and
readjusts the blanket.

20. *should a man come and ask you, 'Is there a man here?'* The repetition of "man"
(*'ish*) plays against the previous repetitions of "woman" as the man speaking is
about to be undone by a woman.

21. *and it sunk into the ground.* This grisly detail indicates that Jael has driven
in the sharpened tent peg with terrific power.

22. *Come, that I may show you the man you seek.* She was instructed to answer
the question, "Is there a man here?" by saying "there is not." Meeting Barak
in front of her tent, she volunteers the information that there is a man within
before being asked, but she withholds the fact that it is a dead man.
    and, look, Sisera was fallen, dead, the peg in his temple. As with the report of
the courtiers seeing the dead Eglon in Chapter 3, the character's visual point
of view is marked by the presentative *hineh*, "look," and the sequence of details
follows his visual in-take: the identity of the man, Sisera; the fact that he is
lying on the ground; the fact that he is dead; the instrument of death thrust
through his temple.

23 And on that day God laid low Jabin king of Canaan before the Israel-
24 ites. And the hand of the Israelites came down ever harder upon Jabin
king of Canaan till they cut off Jabin king of Canaan.

---

23. *God laid low Jabin king of Canaan.* Jabin had not taken part in the battle. Now, after the defeat of his principal force and his armored corps under the command of Sisera, he and his kingdom are laid low by the Israelites.

24. *the hand of the Israelites came down ever harder.* The literal sense of the Hebrew is "the hand of the Israelites went ever harder."

CHAPTER 5

And Deborah sang, and Barak son of Abinoam with her on that day, 1
saying:

> When bonds were loosed in Israel, 2
> when the people answered the call, bless the LORD!
> Hear, O kings, give ear, O chiefs— 3
> I to the LORD, I shall sing.
> I shall hymn to the LORD, God of Israel.

---

1. *And Deborah sang, and Barak son of Abinoam with her.* The use of a singular verb (feminine) followed by a compound subject is an indication in biblical grammar that the first of the subjects named is the primary actor and the second one ancillary to the action. Deborah is introduced as singer of the victory song, but that is not a claim of authorship, and elsewhere in the poem she is addressed in the second person. In any case, the scholarly consensus is that this is one of the oldest texts in the Bible, perhaps composed not long after the battle it reports, around 1100 BCE. Its language abounds in archaisms, many of them uncertain in meaning and probably some of them scrambled in scribal transmission.

2. *When bonds were loosed in Israel.* The Hebrew verb can mean undoing hair or casting off restraints. In the context here, it might refer to a time of wildness in military crisis when the ordinary social and political order was in abeyance.
   when the people answered the call. The noun here (*'am*) and the verbal stem *n-d-b* often occur as joined terms. The verb suggests volunteering or answering the call, but is also particularly associated with noblemen, who would be the ones to fling themselves into the fray as leaders with the rest of the people following them.

4   O Lᴏʀᴅ, when You came forth from Seir,
          when You strode from the fields of Edom,
    the earth heaved, the very heavens dripped rain,
          the clouds, O they dripped water.

5   Mountains melted before the Lᴏʀᴅ—
          He of Sinai—
             before the Lᴏʀᴅ, God of Israel.

6   In the days of Shamgar son of Anath,
          in the days of Jael, the caravans ceased,
             and wayfarers walked on roundabout paths.

7   Unwalled cities ceased,
          in Israel, they ceased,
    till you arose, Deborah,
          till you arose, O mother in Israel.

---

4. *Seir . . . Edom.* These places mark the route of conquest from the southeast toward Canaan reported in Numbers and Deuteronomy. YHWH as warrior-God marches ahead of the people.

dripped rain. "Rain" is merely implied in the Hebrew.

6. *In the days of Shamgar . . . in the days of Jael, the caravans ceased.* Shamgar, the first of the judges, is represented as chronologically overlapping with Jael, the heroine of the poem. Israelite caravans, according to the poem, were unable to journey safely because of the danger from Canaanite warriors.

7. *Unwalled cities.* There are wildly different interpretations of the obscure Hebrew noun *perazon.* This translation links it to the verbal stem *p-r-ts*, "to breach," and understands it to indicate a town without walls. At a moment of grave military instability, Israelites could no longer live in such unprotected places.

ceased, / in Israel, they ceased. This pattern of incremental repetition (the increment here is "in Israel") strongly marks this poem and is a hallmark of its archaic character. Incremental repetition is the most explicit form of development or intensification from the first half of the line to the second, a pattern in which something is literally added in the second verset.

till you arose, Deborah, / till you arose, O mother in Israel. This is another line built on incremental repetition. Although the ending of the verbs looks, according to later normative grammar, like a first person singular, it is almost certainly an archaic second person feminine ending.

They chose new gods,   8
          then was there war at the gates.
No shield nor lance was seen
          amidst forty thousand of Israel.
My heart to the leaders of Israel,   9
          who answered the call for the people, bless the Lord!
Riders on pure-white she-asses,   10
          sitting on regal cloths.
                    O wayfarers, speak out,
louder than the sound of archers,   11
          by the watering places.
There let them retell the Lord's bounties,
          His bounties for unwalled cities in Israel.
                    Then the Lord's people went down to the gates.
Awake, awake, O Deborah,   12
          awake, awake, O speak the song.

---

8. *They chose new gods*. As in the prose narratives, cultic disloyalty leads to
military catastrophe—"then was there war at the gates."

9. *who answered the call for the people*. Here the association of the verbal stem
n-d-b with nobility is made explicit because these are "the leaders of Israel."
The martial ethos of noble warriors prepared to risk all has a certain affinity
with the Homeric poems.

10. *Riders on pure-white she-asses*. In this early period, these would be the
mounts of noblemen or princes.

11. *archers*. Although this is a common understanding of *meḥatsetsim*, linking it
to *ḥets*, "arrow," widely different interpretations have been proposed. If in fact
the word refers to archers, the sound would be the twanging of many bows and
the whizzing of arrows as volleys are shot.
     unwalled cities. This is the same word that is used in verse 6. God's "boun-
ties" would be in re-establishing a safe order for the tribes of Israel in which
they could once more live in unfortified towns.
     went down to the gates. Battle is often engaged before the gates of the city.

12. *speak the song*. Yairah Amit proposes that the choice of the verb "speak,"
dabri, is motivated by a pun on the name Deborah. The phrase here is the increment in still another incremental repetition.

Arise, Barak,

> take your captives, Abinoam's son!

13 Then the remnant of the mighty came down,

> the LORD's people came down from amidst
> the warriors.

14 From Ephraim, their roots in Amalek.

> After you, O Benjamin, with your forces!

From Machir the leaders came down,

> And from Zebulun, wielders of the baton.

15 And the commanders of Issachar with Deborah,

> and Issachar like Barak, in the valley ran free.

In the clans of Reuben,

> great were the heart's probings.

16 Why did you stay among the sheepfolds,

> listening to the piping for the flocks?

In the clans of Reuben,

> great were the heart's probings.

---

13. *came down.* The Masoretic vocalization *yerad* is anomalous and has led many interpreters to see an entirely different verb here. The most plausible construction, however, is to understand it as an archaic variant of *yarad,* "came down." Since battle is joined at a wadi and the Israelite forces assemble in the hills, "came down" seems appropriate.

14. *After you, O Benjamin, with your forces!* The tribe of Benjamin, known for its military prowess, would be a likely candidate to lead the allied tribes into the fray.

15. *great were the heart's probings.* The translation follows several variant manuscripts that show *ḥiqrey,* "probings," as in the next verse, instead of *ḥiqeqey,* "rulings" (?). Given that Reuben is denounced in the next line for not joining the assembled tribes in battle, this phrase is probably sarcastic: the Reubenites give themselves to indecisive thought and speculation instead of marshalling their forces for battle. This entire verse and the next one reflect a real situation a century before the monarchy in which there is no central governing force and not all the tribes can be counted on to "answer the call" in a time of crisis.

Gilead across the Jordan dwelled,   17
          and Dan, why did he linger by the ships?
Asher stayed by the shore of the sea,
          and by its inlets he dwelled.
Zebulun, a people that challenged death,   18
          and Naphtali on the heights of the field.
Kings came, did battle,   19
          then Canaan's kings did battle,
in Taanach, by the waters of Megiddo,
          no spoil of silver did they take.
From the heavens the stars did battle,   20
          from their course they did battle with Sisera.
The Kishon wadi swept them off,   21

---

17. *Dan, why did he linger by the ships?* The reference is puzzling because Dan did not occupy coastal territory either in its early phase east of the Philistines or in its later migration to the north.

18. *challenged death.* Literally, "exposed its life to death."

19. *Kings came, did battle, / then Canaan's kings did battle.* This is another fine flourish of incremental repetition. "Then" is repeated through the poem, marking its narrative momentum. Unlike the narrative version of this story in Chapter 4, which has only one enemy king, Jabin, the Canaanite forces here are led more plausibly by an alliance of kings.

    no spoil of silver did they take. This is the first clear indication that they are defeated. It also anticipates the self-deluding notion of the Canaanite noblewomen at the end of the poem that their men are about to bring home an abundance of spoils.

20. *From the heavens the stars did battle.* This is a characteristic move of Israelite war poetry: no feats of valor on the battlefield are reported, for the victory comes from divine intervention. The fact that in Hebrew idiom the clustered stars are referred to as the "army" or "host" (*tzava'*) of the heavens encourages this representation of the stars battling on behalf of Israel.

21. *The Kishon wadi swept them off.* Although the poem's narrative report here is highly elliptical, it looks as though there is an evocation of the victory at the Sea of Reeds: perhaps here, too, the chariots are disabled in the muck of the wadi, which might be the concrete manifestation of the stars' battling for Israel.

an ancient wadi the Kishon wadi.

March on, my being, in valor!

22   The hooves of the horses hammered,

from the gallop, the gallop of his steeds.

23   "Curse Meroz," said the LORD's messenger,

"Curse, O curse its dwellers,

for they did not come to the aid of the LORD,

to the aid of the LORD midst the warriors."

24   Blessed above women Jael,

wife of Heber the Kenite,

above women in tents be she blessed.

25   Water he asked for, milk did she give,

in a princely bowl she served him curds.

---

22. *The hooves of the horses hammered.* This pounding of hoofbeats steps up the "march" or "tread," of the preceding line. The entire line in Hebrew is strongly alliterative and onomatopoeic, an effect the translation seeks to emulate.

23. *Curse Meroz.* Nothing is known about this particular town other than its representation in the poem as a place of egregious failure to join the general effort of battle.

the aid of the LORD midst the warriors. In this incremental repetition, it is evident that YHWH needs His human warriors in order to be victorious. The poem wavers in this fashion between understanding victory as a miraculous event and as the accomplishment of heroic deeds by brave warriors. Jael at the end certainly needs no divine assistance.

24. *above women in tents be she blessed.* This incremental repetition, by introducing an ostensibly automatic epithet for women with their domestic sphere, "in tents," sets the scene for the killing with the tent peg.

25. *Water he asked for, milk did she give.* Unlike the prose narrative, there is no dialogue, with its delineation of interaction of characters, only a series of gestures and acts.

in a princely bowl she served him curds. This is an eloquent flourish and heightening of the giving of milk in the first verset. At the same time, the offering of the bowl to Sisera (who has not yet been named) focuses visual attention on the hands of the woman bearing the bowl, and in the next line those hands will be murderous.

Her hand for the tent peg reached out   26
       and her right hand for the workman's hammer.
And she hammered Sisera, cracked his head.
       She smashed and pierced his temple.
Between her legs he kneeled, fell, lay,   27
       between her legs he kneeled, he fell,
             where he kneeled he fell, destroyed.
Through the window she looked out, moaned,   28
       Sisera's mother, through the lattice:
"Why is his chariot so long in coming,
       why so late the clatter of his cars?

---

26. *Her hand for the tent peg reached out*. This would have to be her left hand. In the elliptical narrative report of the poem, we are not told that Sisera has fallen asleep, though the understanding of the prose story that this is the case sounds plausible. Alternatively, as he was drinking, his face deep in the bowl, she might have attacked him from behind, though he appears to be facing her when he falls.

    she hammered Sisera, cracked his head. / She smashed and pierced his temple. The noun "hammer" at the end of the previous line now becomes a verb. In a related way, the entire report of the killing uses sequences of overlapping verbs, like cinematic frames one after the other—here: hammered, cracked, smashed, pierced. The verb "hammered" was previously applied to hoofbeats.

27. *Between her legs he kneeled, fell, lay.* His death agony is a kind of grotesque parody and reversal of sexual assault, a common practice in warfare, as we are reminded at the beginning of verse 30. This triadic line is one of the most brilliant deployments of incremental repetition in the poem, culminating in the climactic increment "destroyed" at the end.

28. *Through the window she looked out.* In a maneuver akin to cinematic *faux raccord*, we do not yet know that the "she" is Sisera's mother, and for a moment we might even imagine that the poem is referring to Jael, though the window could not belong in a tent.

    moaned. The Hebrew verbal stem *y-b-b* appears only here in the biblical corpus, and so one must surmise from context that it is some sort of lament, moan, or complaint.

    window . . . lattice. It then becomes apparent that the scene has switched from the simple setting of a tent to a luxurious palace.

    the clatter of his cars. The term "clatter" is more literally "pounding" and thus picks up the hammering hoofbeats of verse 22.

29   The wisest of her ladies answer her,
                 she, too, replies on her own:
30   "Why, they will find and share out the spoils—
                 a damsel or two for every man.
      Spoil of dyed stuff for Sisera,
                 spoil of dyed stuff,
      dyed needlework,
                 needlework pairs for every neck."
31   Thus perish all Your enemies, O LORD!
                 And be His friends like the sun coming out in its might.

And the land was quiet forty years.

---

30. *they will find and share out the spoils*. The reason for the delayed return, they imagine, is that the victorious warriors are taking time to gather booty.

a damsel or two. The Hebrew *raham* is an archaic term, with a cognate that figures in Ugaritic texts, hence the choice of "damsel." But it is transparently linked with *rehem*, "womb," and so might conceivably be a coarser term for a captive woman. In this warrior culture, the women unquestionably assume that it is the prerogative of the men to bring back fresh bedmates for themselves—even two to a customer—from the conquered enemy.

spoil of dyed stuff. But the women can anticipate their own special share in the spoils—gorgeous embroidered cloth taken from the women of the enemy. If this is the raiment of the captive women, they will have no need of such finery as sex-slaves of their captors.

CHAPTER 6

A nd the Israelites did evil in the eyes of the LORD, and He gave them   1
into the hand of Midian seven years. And the hand of Midian was   2
strong over Israel. Because of Midian the Israelites made themselves
the dugouts that are in the mountains and the caves and the strongholds. And it happened when Israel planted, that Midian and Amalek   3
and the Easterners came up against them. And they encamped against   4
them and destroyed the yield of the land all the way to Gaza, and they
would not leave a source of livelihood in Israel, nor sheep nor ox nor
donkey. For they with their flocks and tents would come up, like locusts   5
in multitude, and they and their camels were beyond numbering, and
they came into the land to destroy it. And Israel was sorely impover-   6
ished because of Midian, and the Israelites cried out to the LORD. And   7

---

1. *Midian*. The Midianites, unlike the indigenous peoples of Canaan confronted
by Deborah and Barak, are nomads whose chief territory is east of the Jordan.

2. *the dugouts*. On the basis of an Arab cognate, the term probably refers to
some sort of man-made trench. In modern Hebrew, this word, *minharah*, is
used for "tunnel."
    strongholds. These would not be architectural structures but the tops of
crags that are adapted as fortifications.

4. *destroyed the yield of the land*. The Midianites are not an invading army but
ruthless marauders, and so they pillage the fields or use them for grazing and
confiscate the Israelites' livestock.

5. *camels*. These beasts, only recently domesticated toward the end of the
second millennium BCE, were the distinctive mounts of the desert-dwelling
Midianites. The Israelites for the most part used donkeys.

it happened, when the Israelites cried out to the LORD about Midian,
8 that the LORD sent a prophet-man to the Israelites, and he said to
them, "Thus said the LORD God of Israel; 'It is I Who brought you up
9 from Egypt and brought you out from the house of slaves. And I saved
you from the hand of Egypt and from the hand of all your oppressors,
10 and I drove them out before you and I gave you their land. And I said
to you—I am the LORD your God. You shall not revere the gods of the
Amorite in whose land you dwell. And you did not heed My voice.'"
11 And the LORD's messenger came and sat under the terebinth that is in
Ophrah, which belongs to Joash the Abiezerite, and Gideon his son was
12 threshing wheat in the winepress to conceal it from Midian. And the
LORD's messenger appeared to him and said, "The LORD is with you,
13 valiant warrior." And Gideon said to him, "Please, my lord, if the LORD
is with us, why has all this overtaken us, and where are all His wonders
of which our fathers told us, saying, 'Did not the LORD bring us up from
Egypt?' And now the LORD has abandoned us and given us into the grip
14 of Midian." And the LORD's messenger turned to him and said, "Go in
this power of yours and rescue Israel from the grip of Midian. Have I

---

11. *Gideon*. The name transparently derives from the verbal stem *g-d-ʻ*, which
means "to hack down." Since the name appears to be a consequence of his first
act in the story, one might guess that his original name was actually the pagan
name Jerubaal, which would mean, "Baal contends [for his loyal worshippers],"
and not, as verse 32 suggests, "Let Baal contend for himself," or perhaps, referring to Gideon, "he contends with Baal."

12. *the LORD's messenger*. The Masoretic text reads "the LORD," but some
Hebrew manuscripts have "the LORD's messenger." The same problem occurs
in verse 16. There are scholars who think "messenger" was piously added earlier
and later in the passage in order to avoid excessive anthropomorphism, but, on
the other hand, the image of God Himself poking at something with the tip of
a walking-stick (verse 21) would be anomalous, and so it seems wiser to assume
that the interlocutor throughout is a divine emissary, not the divinity.
    valiant warrior. He has not yet earned this epithet, which is thus predictive,
and, in fact, he seems, as Yairah Amit has observed, a rather fearful man.

14. *Go in this power of yours*. This phrase probably suggests that the LORD's
messenger is conferring power on Gideon.

not sent you?" And he said to him, "Please, my lord, how shall I rescue 15
Israel? Look, my clan is poor in Manasseh, and I am the youngest in my
father's house." And the Lᴏʀᴅ's messenger said to him, "For I shall be 16
with you, and you will strike down Midian as a single man." And he said 17
to him, "If, pray, I have found favor in your eyes, give me a sign that you
are speaking with me. Pray, do not move from here until I come to you 18
and bring out my offering and set it before you." And he said, "I shall
sit here until you return." And Gideon had gone and prepared a kid and 19
an ephah worth of flour of flatbread. He put the meat in a basket and
the broth in a pot, and he brought it out to him under the terebinth
and brought it forward. And God's messenger said to him, "Take the 20
meat and the flatbread, and set them on yonder crag, and pour out the
broth." And so he did. And the Lᴏʀᴅ's messenger reached out with the 21
tip of the walking-stick that was in his hand and touched the meat and
the flatbread, and fire went up from the rock and consumed the meat
and the flatbread. And the Lᴏʀᴅ's messenger went from his sight. And 22
Gideon saw that he was a messenger of the Lᴏʀᴅ. And Gideon said,
"Alas, Lᴏʀᴅ my Master, for I indeed have seen a messenger of the Lᴏʀᴅ
face to face." And the Lᴏʀᴅ said to him, "It is well with you. Do not 23

---

15. *my clan is poor . . . I am the youngest.* Such professions of inadequacy regularly occur in the call narratives of the prophets, and they are evident in Moses's call narrative. In fact, the possession of numerous servants (or, perhaps, slaves) indicates that Gideon's family is well-off.

20. *pour out the broth.* Though the liquid in question is not conventional in the cult, this looks like a libation.

21. *And the Lᴏʀᴅ's messenger went from his sight.* Given the fact that he has just miraculously ignited a fire on the rock, it is likely that his going away is equally miraculous—a sudden vanishing.

22. *Alas, Lᴏʀᴅ my Master.* Here the direct reference to God is appropriate because one would pray to God, not to a divine emissary. But Gideon fears that beholding even a messenger of God could mean death for him.

24 fear. You shall not die." And Gideon built there an altar to the LORD, and
    called it YHWH Shalom. To this day it is still in Ophrah of the Abiezeri-
25 tes. And it happened on that night that the LORD said to him, "Take the
    bull which is your father's and the second bull, seven years old, and you
    shall destroy the altar of Baal which is your father's, and the cultic pole
26 that is on it you shall cut down. And you shall build an altar to the LORD
    your God on top of this stronghold on the surface, and you shall take the
    second bull and offer it up as a burnt offering on the wood of the cultic
27 pole that you cut down. And Gideon took ten men of his servants and did
    as the LORD had spoken to him. And it happened as his father's house-
    hold and the men of the town feared to do it by day, that he did it at night.
28 And the men of the town rose early in the morning, and, look, the altar of
    Baal was shattered and the cultic pole that was on it was cut down, and
29 the second bull was offered up on the altar that had been built. And every
    man said to his fellow, "Who has done this thing?" And they inquired and
30 sought out, and they said, "Gideon son of Joash has done this thing." And
    the men of the town said to Joash, "Bring out your son that he may die,
    for he has shattered the altar of Baal and cut down the cultic pole that

---

24. *YHWH Shalom.* That is, "the LORD—it is well," the words God spoke to
Gideon.

25. *the second bull.* This second bull is a puzzle because nothing afterward is
done in the story with what appears to be a first bull. Some scholars solve the
problem by emending *sheini*, "second," to *shamen*, "fat," thus eliminating the
multiplicity of bulls.

26. *this stronghold.* See the comment on verse 3.
    on the surface. The Hebrew *ma'arakhah* is a little odd. It usually refers to
anything arrayed in a set order, like the items in a sacrifice or troops in an army.
Perhaps here it is a kind of metonymy, as Kimchi surmised, indicating the flat
surface of the rock on which the sacrifice is to be laid out.

27. *the men of the town feared to do it by day.* Here the fearful ones are Gideon's
subordinates, not Gideon himself. This nocturnal act is of a piece with the
clandestine threshing of wheat in a winepress. However, the people feared here
are not Midianite marauders but the Israelite inhabitants of the town, who have
made Baal worship the official cult there, as we see vividly in their resolution
to execute Gideon for having desecrated the altar of Baal.

was on it." And Joash said to all who stood round him, "Will you contend 31
for Baal, will you rescue him? Let he who would contend for him be put
to death by morning. If he is a god, he will contend for himself, for his
altar has been shattered." And he was called on that day Jerubaal, which 32
is to say, "Let him contend for himself, for his altar has been shattered."

And all of Midian and Amalek and the Easterners gathered together, 33
and they crossed over and camped in the Valley of Jezreel. And the 34
spirit of the LORD invested Gideon, and he blasted the ram's horn, and
Abiezer was mustered behind him. And he sent messengers through- 35
out Manasseh, and it, too, was mustered behind him. And he sent
messengers in Asher and in Zebulun and in Naphtali, and they went
up to meet them. And Gideon said to God, "If You are going to rescue 36
Israel by my hand as You have spoken, look, I am about to place a 37
fleece of wool on the threshing floor. If there is dew on the fleece alone
but on the ground it is dry, I shall know that You will rescue Israel by
my hand as You have spoken." And so it was: he rose early the next day 38
and squeezed the fleece and wrung out dew from the fleece, a bowlful

---

31. *Let he who would contend for him be put to death.* Joash shrewdly argues that
if Baal has real power as a god, he will fight his own battles and exact punishment from the person who violated his altar. If he does not do that, he is not
worthy of worship.

33. *crossed over.* The term indicates crossing the Jordan from their habitual
territory to the east.

34. *blasted the ram's horn.* As in the Ehud story, this is a call to arms.

37. *I am about to place a fleece of wool.* Moses, too, was given signs before the
beginning of his mission, but the apprehensive Gideon sets up an elaborate test
for a sign and then reverses its terms for a second test.

39 of water. And Gideon said to God, "Let Your wrath not flare up against me. I would speak just this one time more and I would make a trial, pray, just this one time more with the fleece. Let it be dry on the fleece

40 alone, and on the ground let there be dew." And, so God did on that night, and it was dry on the fleece alone and on all the ground there was dew.

---

39. *Let Your wrath not flare up.* Gideon obviously feels he is pushing matters with God, but he nevertheless requires an additional proof that God will be with him when he leads the insurrection against the powerful Midianites.

    Let it be dry on the fleece alone, and on the ground let there be dew. This is a more miraculous outcome than the first test because fleece would naturally absorb moisture that might well evaporate from the ground.

CHAPTER 7

$\mathcal{A}$nd Jerubaal, that is, Gideon, rose early, and all the troops that were 1
with him, and they camped by Ein Harod. And the camp of Midian
was north of Gibeath Hamoreh in the valley. And the LORD said to 2
Gideon, "The troops that are with you are too many for Me to give
Midian into their hand, lest Israel boast to Me saying, 'My own hand
made me victorious.' And, now, call out, pray, in the hearing of the 3
troops, saying: 'Whoever is fearful and trembling, let him turn round
from Mount Gilead.'" And twenty-two thousand turned back from the
troops, and ten thousand remained. And the LORD said to Gideon, "The 4
troops are still too many. Bring them down to the water and I shall sift
them out for you there. And so, of whom I say to you, 'This one shall go
with you,' he shall go with you, and all of whom I say, 'This one shall not
go with you,' he shall not go." And he brought the troops down to the 5
water. And the LORD said to Gideon, "Whoever laps the water with his
tongue, as a dog laps, set him apart, and whoever kneels on his knees
to drink, set him apart." And the number of those lapping from their 6

---

2. *The troops that are with you are too many*. One suspects that behind this tale
of a test that eliminates the vast majority of the fighting men there may lie a
historical memory of a small group of guerillas that defeated numerically superior Midianite forces in a surprise attack.

3. *turn round*. The verb *ts-p-r* is unusual and the meaning uncertain, but there
is a noun derived from this root that suggests going around.

5. *Whoever laps the water with his tongue, as a dog laps*. The point of the first
of the two winnowing procedures—sending home whoever is afraid—is self-
evident. This second elimination procedure is at first blush peculiar because

hand to their mouth came to three hundred men. And all the rest of
7 the troops kneeled on their knees to drink water. And the LORD said
to Gideon, "With the three hundred men who lapped I shall make you
victorious and give Midian into your hand, and let all the other troops
8 go each to his place. And they took the provisions of the troops in their
hand as well as their ram's horns, and he sent off all the men of Israel
each to his tent, and he held onto the three hundred men. And the
9 camp of Midian was below him in the valley. And it happened on that
night that the LORD said to him, "Arise. Go down into the camp, for I
10 have given it into your hand. And if you are afraid to go down, go down
11 both you and Purah your lad. And you shall listen to what they say, and
then your hands will be strengthened and you shall go down into the
camp." And he went down, and Purah his lad with him, to the edge of
12 the armed men who were in the camp. And Midian and Amalek and all
the Easterners lay along the valley, like locusts in multitude, and their
camels were beyond numbering, like the sand that is on the shore of the

---

similarity to a dog—in general a reviled animal in the biblical world—might not
appear to be a recommendation for a good soldier. The lapping of the water, as
the next verse clarifies, is not done by putting face to water-source but rather
by scooping up water in one's palm and then lapping it. The fighters who drink
in this way remain alert and ready for combat even as they drink, unlike those
who kneel to drink. Perhaps the feral and dangerous connotations of "dog" in
Hebrew usage are also invoked here.

8. *of the troops.* The troops in question would have to be those who were sent
back, leaving their provisions and ram's horns (which in this context serve as
battle horns) behind.

10. *if you are afraid to go down.* God has already experienced Gideon's hesitancy
in the two miraculous signs Gideon asked of Him.
    your lad. The all-purpose noun *na'ar* in this context clearly indicates a func-
tion like "attendant" or even "armor-bearer."

12. *like locusts in multitude . . . beyond numbering, like the sand that is on the
shore of the sea.* This repetition of the vastness of the Midianite forces is an
obvious counterpoint to the bare three hundred men whom Gideon now leads.
The Hebrew writer evinces a special fascination with the numerous camels,
the unfamiliar mounts of the Midianite marauders.

sea in multitude. And Gideon came, and, look, a man was recounting a 13
dream to his fellow, and he said, "Look, I dreamed a dream, and, look,
a loaf of barley bread was rolling over through the camp of Midian and
came up to the tent and struck it and overturned it and the tent fell."
And his fellow answered and said, "That could only be the sword of 14
Gideon son of Joash man of Israel. God has given into his hand Midian
and all its camp." And it happened, when Gideon heard the recounting 15
of the dream and its explanation, that he bowed down and went back
to the camp of Israel and said, "Arise, for the LORD has given into your
hand the camp of Midian." And he split the three hundred men into 16
three columns and put ram's horns in everyone's hand and empty pitchers with torches inside the pitchers. And he said to them, "Look to me 17
and do the same, and just when I come to the edge of the camp, so as

---

13. *loaf*. The meaning of the Hebrew *tselil* is disputed. Some interpreters link
it to the root *ts-l-l*, which means to make a ringing noise and thus understand it
to have a sense like "commotion" or "noise." Rolling noise, however, is a problematic notion. Many medieval Hebrew commentators derive it, plausibly, from
tseli, "roast," construing it as a term for a round flat loaf baked over coals, which
in fact is how Bedouin to this day make their *pittah*. It remains a puzzle as to
why bread, and specifically barley bread, is the instrument of destruction in the
dream, other than its being totally unexpected in this function, like Gideon's
strategy with the horns and the torches. It might be linked with the first image
of Gideon threshing grain.

15. *he bowed down*. This may be a gesture of obeisance to God, Who, as he now
confidently knows, is about to make him triumph.

16. *he split the three hundred men into three columns*. This move makes it
possible for Gideon's men to come down on the Midianite from three sides.
Perhaps four sides would have been even more strategically effective, but that
consideration is trumped by the numerical neatness of three hundred divided
by three.

17. *Look to me and do the same*. In the Hebrew, the force of this command is
underscored by a rhyme: *mimeni tir'u wekhein ta'asu*.

18 I do, do the same. And when I blast on the ram's horn, and all those by
    me, you too shall blast on the ram's horns all round the camp and say,
19 'For the LORD and for Gideon!'" And Gideon came, and the hundred
    men who were with him, to the edge of the camp, at the beginning of
    the middle watch—they had just then posted the watchmen—and they
    blasted on the ram's horns and smashed the pitchers that were in their
20 hands. And the three columns blasted on the ram's horns and broke the
    pitchers and held the torches with their left hand, and their right hand
    the ram's horns to blast on, and called out: "Sword for the LORD and for
21 Gideon!" And each one stood in his place all round the camp. And all

---

18. *and all those by me.* These would be the one hundred men in the column
headed by Gideon, as we see in the next verse.
   For the LORD and for Gideon! Some Hebrew manuscripts and two ancient
versions show "sword for the LORD," as in verse 20.

19. *at the beginning of the middle watch.* The night was divided into three
watches (which here neatly correspond to the tripartite division of Gideon's
fighters), so this would be something approaching midnight, when the Midianite troops were deep in slumber.
   they had just then posted the watchmen. Either they have not yet settled into
their positions of observation or they are not yet fully alert because they have
just been wakened to take up their watch.

20. *held the torches with their left hand, and their right hand the ram's horns.*
Presumably, their swords remained strapped to their sides as they rely entirely
on the effect of panic caused by the sudden blaring sound and the torch-light.

21. *each one stood in his place.* These are the horn-blowing, torch-wielding
Israelites.

the camp ran off and shouted and fled. And they blasted on the three 22
hundred ram's horns and the LORD set every man's sword against his
fellow throughout the camp, and the camp fled to Beth-Shittah, toward
Sererah, to the banks of the Meholah brook by Tabbath. And the men 23
of Israel rallied, from Naphtali and from Asher and from all Manasseh,
and they pursued Midian. And Gideon sent messengers throughout the 24
high country of Ephraim, saying, "Come down to meet Midian and take
from them the water-sources, as far as Beth-Barah, and the Jordan." And
all the men of Ephraim rallied and took the water-sources as far as Beth-
Barah, and the Jordan. And they took the two Midianite commanders, 25
Oreb and Zeeb, and they killed Oreb at the Rock of Oreb, and Zeeb
they killed in the Winepress of Zeeb, and they pursued Midian. And the
heads of Oreb and Zeeb they brought to Gideon from across the Jordan.

---

22. *the* LORD *set every man's sword against his fellow.* In other accounts of Israelite victories, we are told that the LORD "panicked" the enemy. Only here do we
get the mechanism of the panic, which in fact is a stratagem devised by Gideon
to terrorize the sleeping army.

   brook. Though most translations treat *'avel* as a proper noun ("Abel"), it
means "brook," being an alternate form of the more common *yuval.* Representing it as "brook" clarifies the meaning of "banks" (the Hebrew *sefat* is a singular
noun).

24. *Gideon sent messengers.* Having routed the large Midianite army with only
three hundred men, he now rallies behind him a much larger force to pursue
the fleeing enemy.

   took the water-sources. In the first instance. they take hold of brooks to the
west of the Jordan, where they can readily cut down the Midianites seeking to
ford the streams, and then they take hold of the fords of the Jordan itself. The
prominence of bodies of water in the destruction of the Midianites loops back
to the test of how the Israelite fighters drink water from a stream.

25. *Oreb and Zeeb.* The two names mean, respectively, raven and wolf. Animal
names were common among the Northwest Semites, including the Israelites.

   they brought to Gideon from across the Jordan. The fleeing Midianite commanders are overtaken and killed east of the Jordan, having eluded the Israelite
forces holding the fords. Gideon himself is still on the west side of the Jordan.
He will cross it in the next episode in pursuit of the enemy.

CHAPTER 8

1   And the men of Ephraim said to him, "What is this thing you have done to us, not to call us when you went to do battle with Midian?" And they
2   contended vehemently with him. And he said to them, "What have I done now to you? Are not the gleanings of Ephraim's grapes better than the
3   vintage of Abiezer? Into your hand God gave the commanders of Midian, Oreb and Zeeb, and what could I have done like you?" Then their anger
4   against him abated when he spoke this thing. And Gideon came to the Jordan, about to cross over, he and the three hundred men who were with
5   him, famished and in pursuit. And he said to the men of Succoth, "Give, pray, some loaves of bread to the troops that are at my heels, for they are famished, and I am pursuing Zebah and Zalmunna, the Midianite kings."
6   And the notables of Succoth said, "Is the palm of Zebah and Zalmunna

---

2. *What have I done now to you?* The received text says "like you," but many manuscripts show "to" (literally, "in" or "against"). An error in copying may have been triggered by "what could I have done like you" in verse 3.

Are not the gleanings of Ephraim's grapes better than the vintage of Abiezer? Gideon now exhibits a new skill as a leader—the shrewd use of persuasive rhetoric. The Ephraimites had been resentful because Gideon did not summon them to fight in the first stage of the conflict with Midian. He responds with a pointed aphorism that would have spoken to any viticulturist: Ephraim, having been responsible for the capture and execution of Oreb and Zeeb, is so much superior to Gideon's clan, Abiezer, that the stray grapes it leaves behind in the harvest are better than what Abiezer actually harvests in the vineyard.

5. *the Midianite kings.* It is improbable that Midian would have more than one king, so the term appears to be used loosely here to mean "leader."

6. *Is the palm of Zebah and Zalmunna already in your hand.* Given the extended period during which the Israelites were painfully vulnerable to the Midianites,

already in your hand that we should give bread to your army?" And 7
Gideon said, "Then when the LORD gives Zebah and Zalmunna into my
hand, I will harrow your flesh with the thorns and thistles of the wilderness!" And he went up from there to Penuel, and he spoke to them in 8
the same fashion, and the men of Penuel answered him as the men of
Succoth had answered. And he said as well to the men of Penuel, saying, 9
"When I come back safe and sound, I will smash this tower!" And Zebah 10
and Zalmunna were in Karkor and their camps with them, about fifteen
thousand, all who remained from all the Easterners, and their fallen
were a hundred fifty thousand sword-wielding men. And Gideon went 11
up on the road of the tent dwellers east of Nobah and Jogbahah, and
he struck the camp when the camp thought itself secure. And Zebah 12
and Zalmunna fled, and he pursued them and took the two Midianite
kings, Zebah and Zalmunna, and he made all the camp tremble. And 13
Gideon son of Joash came back from the battle at Heres Ascent. And 14
he caught a lad from the men of Succoth, and questioned him and the
lad wrote down for him the notables and the elders of Succoth, seventy-

---

the town elders don't really believe that Gideon will subdue this enemy, and
so, in fear of Midianite retribution, they do not want to offer him aid. Amit
proposes that the palm is mentioned because of a practice, attested among the
Egyptians, of slicing off the palms of a defeated enemy.

7. *I will harrow your flesh with the thorns.* This fierce declaration—the literal
sense of the Hebrew verb used is "thresh"—and of the matching one to the
elders of Penuel is less a matter of personal vengeance than of military justice:
the failure to give provisions to an army that is in desperate need is an act of
treason and will be punished as such.

11. *the road of the tent dwellers.* These would be encampments of nomads (still
evident in the Jordan Valley)—Gideon is heading into desert country.
   thought itself secure. "Thought itself" is merely implied in the Hebrew.

14. *the lad wrote down for him the notables and the elders of Succoth.* The captive boy is constrained to be an informer. Though it is likely that literacy at
this moment in the history of Israel was limited to a privileged elite, the writer
evidently assumed that it was sufficiently widespread that he could attribute
the skill of writing to a random lad seized by Gideon.

15 seven men. And he came to the men of Succoth and said, "Here are
Zebah and Zalmunna about whom you insulted me saying, 'Is the palm
of Zebah and Zalmunna already in your hand that we should give bread
16 to your famished men?'" And he took the elders of the town and the
thorns and the thistles of the wilderness and harrowed with them the
17 men of Succoth. And the tower of Penuel he smashed, and he killed
18 the men of the town. And he said to Zebah and Zalmunna, "Who are
the men whom you killed in Tabor?" And they said, "They were just
19 like you, like princes in their features." And he said, "They were my
brothers, my mother's sons. By the LORD, had you let them live, I would
20 not kill you." And he said to Jether his firstborn, "Rise, kill them!" And
the lad did not draw his sword, for he was afraid, for he was still a lad.

---

15. *give bread to your famished men.* Gideon, in his verbatim repetition of the
words of the notables, adds a single telling word, "famished," which was used
by the narrator but not by them, and changes "army" to "men." That is to say:
to famished fighting men you were brazen enough to deny food.

16. *harrowed with them the men of Succoth.* Given that he goes on to kill the
elders of Penuel, we may infer that the same fatal result is achieved at Succoth
by the harrowing—a slow and painful death. In the Masoretic text, the verb
used appears to mean "cause to know" (hence the bizarre King James Version,
in which Gideon "taught" the elders with thorns and thistle). The Septuagint
shows "harrowed" (a difference of one consonant in the Hebrew), which is the
likely reading.

18. *They were just like you, like princes in their features.* The Midianite kings
imagine that they are flattering Gideon, but in divulging the family resemblance, they pronounce their own death-sentence. By the ethic of family blood-
vengeance, he now feels obliged to kill them.

19. *my mother's sons.* And not the sons of any other of my father's wives. The
connection, then, with Gideon is a strong one because these were not merely
half-brothers.

20. *Jether his firstborn.* Blood-vengeance is a family affair, and so Gideon wants
his firstborn to carry out the sentence. He may also want to toughen him to
killing, which is, in a sense, the family business.
    he was afraid. He was afraid, of course, not of the captive (and probably fet-
tered) kings but of the act of stabbing them.

And Zebah and Zalmunna said, "You rise and stab us, for as the man, 21
so is his valor." And Gideon rose and killed Zebah and Zalmunna, and
he took the crescent ornaments that were on the necks of their camels.
And the men of Israel said, "Rule over us, you and also your son and 22
also your son's son, for you have rescued us from the hand of Midian."
And Gideon said to them, "I will not rule over you nor will my son rule 23
over you. The LORD will rule over you." And Gideon said to them, "Let 24
me ask something of you—give me, every man of you, his ring taken as
booty," for they had golden rings, as they were Ishmaelites. And they 25
said, "We will certainly give." And they spread out a cloak, and each man
flung there his ring taken as booty. And the weight of the golden rings 26
for which he had asked came to seventeen hundred shekels of gold,
besides the pendants and the garments of purple that had been on the
Midianite kings and besides the collars that were on the necks of their
camels. And Gideon made them into an ephod and set it out in his town, 27

---

21. *You rise and stab us, for as the man, so is his valor.* Killing is a grown man's
business for both sides in the martial code of this story. They also may assume
that a proven warrior like Gideon will finish them off with one swift blow.

    the crescent ornaments. This detail is proleptic of the agreement to which he
comes with his men.

23. *I will not rule over you nor will my son rule over you. The LORD will rule
over you.* This emphatic repetition of their proposal that he establish a dynasty
reflects an ideology circulating in pre-monarchic Israel, and which will still be
maintained by the prophet Samuel. The vehicle of the LORD's rule is the spirit,
or charisma, with which He invests the ad-hoc leaders of Israel.

24. *And Gideon said to them.* This repetition of the formula for introducing
dialogue without an intervening response from the second party in the dialogue
indicates that they are baffled, or perhaps even angered, by his refusal to accept
their offer of kingship. Gideon realizes that he now has to propose something to
placate or reassure them, but what he proposes proves to be disastrous.

    rings. These are earrings or nose-rings, not rings worn on the finger.

    as they were Ishmaelites. Ishmaelite and Midianite are often interchange-
able terms. These semi-nomadic folk were evidently known for wearing golden
ornaments.

27. *Gideon made them into an ephod.* The clear allusion in this episode is to
Aaron's fashioning the golden calf from the golden ornaments that he collects

in Ophrah, and all Israel went whoring after it there, and it became a
28 snare for Gideon and for his household. And Midian was laid low before
Israel, and they no longer lifted their heads, and the land was quiet forty
29,30 years. And Jerubaal son of Joash went and returned to his house. And
31 Gideon had seventy sons, issue of his loins, for he had many wives. And
his concubine who was in Shechem also bore him a son, and he named
32 him Abimelech. And Gideon son of Joash died in ripe old age and was
33 buried in the grave of Joash his father the Abiezerite in Ophrah. And it
happened when Gideon died that the Israelites again went whoring after
34 the Baalim, and they made Baal-Berith their god. And the Israelites did
not recall the Lord their God Who had saved them from the hand of all
35 their enemies round about. And they did not do kindness with the house
of Jerubaal-Gideon as all the good he had done for Israel.

---

from the Israelites. In other contexts, the ephod is a priestly breastplate or an
oracular device. The latter function may come into play here. In any case, the
declaration that Israel "went whoring after it" clearly indicates it was treated as
a sacred icon to be worshipped instead of God.

31. *Abimelech.* This name, which had some general currency (see Genesis 20),
incorporates the element *melekh*, "king," the very role that Gideon rejected
when it was offered but that this reprobate son will try to arrogate for himself.
Though Gideon himself dies in ripe old age, retribution, perhaps for making
the ephod, overtakes his offspring through the malefic agency of Abimelech.

CHAPTER 9

And Abimelech son of Jerubaal went to his mother's brothers and to 1 all the clan of his mother's patriarchal house, saying, "Speak, pray, in the 2 hearing of all the notables of Shechem: 'What is better for you, that seventy men should rule over you, all the sons of Jerubaal, or that one man should rule over you? And you should remember that I am your bone and your flesh.'" And his mother's brothers spoke about him all 3 these words in the hearing of the notables of Shechem and their heart was swayed to follow Abimelech, for they said, "He is our kinsman." And 4 they gave him seventy shekels of silver from the house of Baal-Berith, and Abimelech hired with them no-account reckless men, and they followed him. And he came to his father's house in Ophrah and killed his 5 brothers, the sons of Jerubaal, seventy men on one stone, and Jotham

---

1. *to his mother's brothers and to all the clan of his mother's patriarchal house.* The initial base of support that he enlists is his relatives—first his uncles and then the larger clan.

2. *that one man should rule over you.* His language takes us back to the proposal of Gideon's warriors that he rule over them, with the scoundrel Abimelech obviously assuming the opposite view from Gideon's about the advisability of monarchic rule.

4. *the house of Baal-Berith.* This is the local pagan temple. One should keep in mind throughout this story that the principal actors are Canaanites, not Israelites, and that Abimelech, though his father was an Israelite, shows no allegiance to the people or the God of Israel.

5. *on one stone.* This detail, which is repeated in the story, suggests an execution-style killing: first he captures and fetters his brothers, then murders them one by one, probably either by stabbing or beheading.

6 the youngest son of Jerubaal was left, for he had hidden. And all the notables of Shechem and all Beth-Millo gathered and proclaimed Abi-
7 melech king by the standing terebinth which is in Shechem. And they told Jotham, and he went and stood on the top of Mount Gerizim, and he raised his voice and called out and said to them: "Listen to me, O
8 notables of Shechem, that God may listen to you. Once upon a time the trees went to anoint a king over them. And they said to the olive tree,
9 'Reign over us.' And the olive tree said, 'Have I left off my rich oil, for which God and men honor me, that I should go sway over the trees?'
10,11 And the trees said to the fig tree, 'Go, you, reign over us.' And the fig tree said to them, 'Have I left off my sweetness and my goodly yield that
12 I should go sway over the trees?' And the trees said to the vine, 'Go, you,
13 reign over us.' And the vine said to them, 'Have I left off my new wine,
14 that gladdens God and men, that I should go sway over the trees?' And
15 all the trees said to the thornbush, 'Go, you, reign over us.' And the thornbush said to the trees, 'If you are really about to anoint me king over you, come shelter in my shade. And if not, a fire shall come out

---

6. *the standing terebinth*. Though this is a reasonable construction of the two Hebrew words, they look odd syntactically.

8. *Once upon a time*. The Hebrew formula *hayoh hayah* signals the beginning of a parable. The attempts of some scholars to scan it as formal verse are unconvincing, but its rhythmic character and its use of stylized repetition, with the three-plus-one folktale structure, set it apart formally from the surrounding narrative.

13. *gladdens God and men*. This might also justifiably be construed as "gladdens gods and men," reflecting a mythological background in which the gods, as in Greek tradition, quaff wine.

15. *come shelter in my shade*. This is, of course, sarcastic—the lowly thornbush gives no shade. The argument of the parable works both against Abimelech—a low and prickly character—and against the institution of kingship: only a nasty and unproductive type would aspire to the power of a king.
a fire shall come out. It is in the nature of kings to broadcast destruction, as Abimelech has already done in murdering his seventy brothers and as he will do much more extensively. In the last moments of his lethal career, he will in fact use fire as a weapon.

from the thornbush and consume the cedars of Lebanon.' And now, if 16
you have acted truly and honestly in making Abimelech king over you
and if you have acted well toward Jerubaal and his house and have acted
toward him as he deserves, for my father fought for you and risked his 17
life and saved you from the hand of Midian, yet you rose up against my 18
father's house today and killed seventy men on one stone and made
Abimelech the son of his slavegirl king over the notables of Shechem,
for he was your kinsman. And if you have acted truly and honestly 19
toward Jerubaal and toward his house on this day, rejoice in Abimelech
and let him, too, rejoice in you. And if not, let a fire come out from 20
Abimelech and consume the notables of Shechem and Beth-Millo, and
let a fire come out from the notables of Shechem and from Beth-Millo
and consume Abimelech." And Jotham fled and ran off and went to Beer 21
and stayed there because of Abimelech his brother. And Abimelech 22
lorded it over Israel three years. And God sent an evil spirit between 23
Abimelech and the notables of Shechem, and the notables of Shechem
betrayed Abimelech, that the outage of the seventy sons of Jerubaal and 24
their blood should come upon Abimelech their brother, who killed them,
and upon the notables of Shechem, who abetted him in killing his brothers. And the notables of Shechem laid ambushes for him on the moun- 25
tain tops, and they robbed whoever passed over them on the way. And it
was told to Abimelech. And Gaal son of Ebed came with his kinsmen 26
and passed through Shechem, and the notables of Shechem trusted

---

18. *the son of his slavegirl*. Jotham chooses a term of opprobrium for the concubine, just as Sarah does for Hagar in Genesis 21.

24. *abetted him*. Literally, "strengthened his hands."

25. *they robbed whoever passed*. Despoiling wayfarers is hardly required to
combat Abimelech, and so it is a sign that the notables of Shechem are as scurrilous as he, and both parties will come to a bad end. In fact, these depredations
may be what gives away to Abimelech their location on the heights.

26. *Gaal son of Ebed*. The patronymic means either "son of a slave" or Ebed is
a shortened form for "Obadiah," which means "slave/servant of God."

27 him. And they went out to the field and harvested their vineyards and
    trod the vintage and held a celebration and came to the house of their
28 god and ate and drank and reviled Abimelech. And Gaal son of Ebed
    said, "Who is Abimelech and who the men of Shechem that we should
    be subject to them? Were not the son of Jerubaal and Zebul his officer
    subject to the men of Hamor father of Shechem? So why should we be
29 subject to him? Would that this people were in my hands. I would
    remove Abimelech, and I would say to Abimelech, 'Muster the full
30 strength of your army and sally forth.'" And Zebul, the commander of
    the town, heard the words of Gaal son of Ebed, and his wrath flared.
31 And he sent messengers to Abimelech in Arumah, saying, "Look, Gaal
    son of Ebed and his kinsmen are coming to Shechem, and they are
32 about to turn the town against you. And now rise in the night, you and
33 the troops who are with you, and lie in ambush in the field. And so, in
    the morning, as the sun comes up, rise early and attack the town, and,
    look, he and the troops who are with him will be coming out toward you,
34 and you shall do whatever you are able." And Abimelech rose, and all
    the troops who were with him, in the night, and they lay in ambush
35 against Shechem in four columns. And Gaal son of Ebed came out and
    stood at the entrance of the gate of the town, and Abimelech and the

---

27. *held a celebration.* The vintage celebration involves drinking, and it is in a
state of drunkenness that Gaal can confidently incite the celebrants to rebel
against Abimelech, who is, after all, a ruthless killer and also, as will become
clear, a savvy military commander.

28. *Were not the son of Jerubaal and Zebul his officer subject to . . . Hamor father
of Shechem?* Abimelech is the son of an Israelite father who was not a native of
Shechem. As such, he has no legitimate claim to dominate the Shechemites.

29. *Muster the full strength of your army.* Literally, "multiply your army," the idea
being: show me all you have—I can handle it.

31. *Arumah.* The received text says Tormah, but Abimelech is in Arumah.

troops who were with him rose up from the ambush. And Gaal saw the 36
troops and said to Zebul, "Look, troops are coming down from the
mountain tops." And Zebul said to him, "You are seeing the shadows of
the mountains as though they were men." And Gaal spoke again and 37
said, "Look, troops are coming down from the heartland and one column
is coming from Elon Meonenim." And Zebul said to him, "Where then 38
is your big mouth that you should have said, 'Who is Abimelech that we
should be subject to him?' Are not these the troops whom you scorned?
Sally forth now, pray, and do battle with them." And Gaal sallied forth 39
before the notables of Shechem and did battle with Abimelech. And 40
Abimelech pursued him, and he fled from him, and many slain fell as far
as the entrance of the gate. And Abimelech stayed in Arumah, and Zebul 41
drove out Gaal and his kinsmen from dwelling in Shechem. And it hap- 42
pened the next day that the troops sallied forth to the field, and they told
Abimelech. And he took his troops and split them into three columns 43
and lay in ambush in the field. And he saw and, look, the troops were
sallying forth from the town, and he rose against them and struck them.

---

36. *the shadows of the mountains.* The Hebrew has a singular "shadow." Zebul's
canny strategem is to make Gaal think there is no army swooping down on him
until it is too late. Given that it is very early in the morning, mountains to the
east would cast long shadows.

37. *troops are coming down from the heartland.* Some time has elapsed, and Gaal
now can clearly see that these are troops, and that one column is headed toward
him from a particular place, Elon Meonenim (which means "Soothsayers' Terebinth"). The exact meaning of *tabor ha'arets,* translated here as "heartland," is
uncertain because *tabur* appears nowhere else. The Septuagint renders it as
"navel of the land," and in later Hebrew this was taken up as the word for "navel."

38. *your big mouth.* The Hebrew says only "your mouth," but a sarcastic sense
of this sort is strongly implied.

42. *the troops.* These troops are the armed men of Shechem.

44 And Abimelech and the column that was with him attacked and took a
    stance at the entrance of the town's gate, and the two columns attacked
45 whoever was in the field. And Abimelech did battle with the town all
    that day, and he took the town and killed the people who were in it and
46 smashed the town and sowed it with salt. And all the notables of
    Shechem Tower heard, and they went into the redoubt of the house of
47 El-Berith. And it was told to Abimelech that all the notables of Shechem
48 Tower had gathered together. And Abimelech went up Mount Zalmon,
    he and all the troops who were with him, and he took one of the axes in
    his hand and cut down a bough and lifted it up and put it on his shoul-
    der. And he said to the troops who were with him, "What you saw me
49 doing, quick, do as I do." And all the troops cut down each one his
    bough and followed Abimelech and put them against the redoubt and
    set fire with them to the redoubt. And all the people of Shechem Tower
50 died, about a thousand men and women. And Abimelech went to Thebez
51 and camped against Thebez and took it. And there was a tower strong-
    hold within the town, and all the men and women and all the notables
    of the town fled there and shut themselves in and went up on the roof
52 of the tower. And Abimelech came up to the tower and did battle against

---

44. *the column*. The Masoretic text shows a plural, but Abimelech would have
to be leading only one of the three columns, and the singular is reflected in one
version of the Septuagint.

45. *sowed it with salt*. Though there is some dispute about the meaning of this
gesture, sowing a field with salt would make it infertile, so the likely intention
is to mark the site as a place of eternal desolation.

46. *Shechem Tower*. In all likelihood this name indicates a place close to
Shechem but not part of it.
    the redoubt. The Hebrew *tsariaḥ* is a rare term, and its exact meaning is
uncertain. Its occurrence in 1 Samuel 13:6 suggests it was some sort of fortified
underground structure.
    the house of El-Berith. The god to which this temple is dedicated is probably
the same as Baal-Berith, mentioned in verse 4.

48. *one of the axes*. The received text reads "the axes," but the Septuagint
appears to have used a Hebrew text that showed "one of the axes."

it. And he approached the entrance of the tower to burn it in fire. And   53
a certain woman flung down an upper millstone on Abimelech's head
and shattered his skull. And he called quickly to the lad who was his   54
armor bearer and said to him, "Draw your sword and put me to death
lest they say, 'A woman killed him.'" And his lad ran him through and he
died. And the men of Israel saw that Abimelech had died and each man   55
went back to his place. And God turned back the evil of Abimelech that   56
he had done to his father to kill his seventy brothers. And all the evil of   57
the men of Shechem God turned back on their heads, and the curse of
Jotham son of Jerubaal came down upon them.

---

53. *a certain woman*. It is noteworthy that in this book based on a male warrior
culture, first Jael and now this anonymous woman of Thebez deliver death-
blows to an enemy. In a more seductive feminine mode, Delilah will bring down
the Israelite hero Samson.

    an upper millstone. This is the lighter of the two millstones and therefore
feasible for a woman to lift up and drop from the tower.

54. *lest they say, "A woman killed him."* In 2 Samuel 11:21, we learn from Joab's
words to the messenger that in fact Abimelech's death by the hand of a woman
had become proverbial. His last wish, then, is frustrated.

CHAPTER 10

1   And after Abimelech Tola son of Pua, son of Dodo, a man of Issachar, arose to rescue Israel, and he dwelled in Shamir in the high country of
2   Ephraim. And he led Israel twenty-three years, and he died and was
3   buried in Shamir. And after him Jair the Gileadite arose and led Israel
4   twenty-two years. And he had thirty sons who rode on thirty donkeys, and they had thirty towns. They call them Jair's Hamlets to this day,
5   which are in the land of Gilead. And Jair died and was buried in Camon.

6   And the Israelites once again did evil in the eyes of the LORD and served the Baalim and the Ashtaroth and the gods of Aram and the gods of Sidon and the gods of Moab and the gods of the Ammonites and the

---

1. *after Abimelech*. This is merely an indication of chronology since Abimelech was no rescuer of Israel.

Tola son of Pua, son of Dodo. The first five verses of this chapter are devoted to bare notices of two judges, Tola and Jair, with no accompanying narrative material. The number of years of their leadership, respectively, twenty-three and twenty-two, are not formulaic, which could conceivably mean that they record actual historical memory.

4. *he had thirty sons who rode on thirty donkeys*. In this period, donkeys, not horses, were the usual mounts for nobility. The number of sons, donkeys, and towns looks formulaic, but the detail about riding is odd enough that it might reflect a remembered historical fact.

6. *served the Baalim and the Ashtaroth and the gods of Aram*. The first two items are generic terms for pagan gods and goddesses, respectively; adding the gods of the five surrounding peoples mentioned here, one comes to the formulaic number seven.

gods of the Philistines. And they forsook the LORD and did not serve
Him. And the LORD's wrath flared against Israel, and He handed them 7
over to the Philistines and to the Ammonites. And they smashed and 8
shattered the Israelites in that year—eighteen years, all the Israelites
who were across the Jordan in the land of the Amorites which is in
Gilead. And the Ammonites crossed the Jordan to do battle as well with 9
Judah and Benjamin and the house of Ephraim, and Israel was sorely
distressed. And the Israelites cried out to the LORD, saying, "We have 10
offended against you and we have forsaken our God and served the
Baalim." And the LORD said to the Israelites, "Was it not from Egypt and 11
from the Amorites and from the Ammonites and from the Philistines,
and the Sidonites and Amalek and Maon—they oppressed you and you 12
cried out to me and I rescued you from their hand? But you forsook Me 13
and served other gods. Therefore I will no longer rescue you. Go, cry out 14
to the gods you have chosen. Let them rescue you in the hour of your
distress." And the Israelites said to the LORD, "We have offended. Do to 15
us whatever is good in Your eyes, but save us, pray, this day." And they 16

---

7. *to the Philistines and to the Ammonites.* These are enemies to the southwest
and to the northeast of the major concentration of Israelite population.

8. *in that year—eighteen years.* If the received text is correct (some manuscripts
of the Septuagint do not show "in that year"), this would mean that the Philistines and the Ammonites battered Israel in direct assaults for a year and
continued to dominate them for eighteen years.

11. *Was it not from Egypt.* The syntax is a little odd, but this is probably best
construed as a periodic sentence continuing to the end of verse 12 with the verb
"rescued" referring back to the chain of nations, most of which are preceded by
"from." Rashi neatly observes, "Seven rescues appear here corresponding to the
seven idolatries that they practiced."

15. *We have offended.* God's sarcastic invitation to Israel to turn for help to the
gods it has worshipped drives home to them the point that only He can save
them from their enemies.

Do to us whatever is good in Your eyes. The Hebrew uses an emphatic form,
literally, "You, do to us." What they are saying is that they are ready to submit
to punishment for their defection, but they nevertheless implore God to rescue
them from oppression, which is too unbearable a punishment.

removed the alien gods from their midst and served the Lord, and He
could not bear the misery of Israel.

17 And the Ammonites were mustered and camped in Gilead, and the
18 Israelites gathered and camped at Mizpah. And the troops, the commanders of Gilead, said to each other, "Whoever the man who begins to
do battle with the Ammonites, he shall become chief of all the inhabitants of Gilead."

---

17. *And the Ammonites were mustered.* A new unit begins here: the circumstances for the impending battle with the Ammonites are established, and the
need for a military leader sets the stage for the appearance of Jephthah.

18. *the troops, the commanders of Gilead.* Perhaps *'am* here means "people."
The appositional phrase "the commanders of Gilead" is awkward and might be
a scribal gloss.

   the man who begins to do battle. They scarcely permit themselves to imagine
victory but are prepared to proclaim as chief whoever will dare to fight the
Ammonites.

CHAPTER 11

Ａnd Jephthah the Gileadite was a valiant warrior, and he was the son   1
of a whore-woman, and Gilead had begotten Jephthah. And Gilead's wife   2
bore him sons, and the wife's sons grew up and they drove Jephthah out
and said to him, "You shall not inherit in our father's house, for you are
the son of another woman." And Jephthah fled from his brothers and   3
dwelled in the land of Tob, and no-account men drew round Jephthah
and sallied forth with him. And it happened after a time that the Ammon-   4

---

2. *Gilead's wife bore him sons*. The probable, though not inevitable, inference is
that the legitimate sons were born after Jephthah, he belonging to his father's
wild oats phase.

You shall not inherit in our father's house. This declaration, accompanied by
the banishment, appears to be a performative speech act with legal force.

for you are the son of another woman. They don't dare call his mother a whore
to his face, and so they use a euphemism. Their behavior toward him, however,
is brutal (in this regard, see the next comment here).

3. *And Jephthah fled from his brothers*. The fact that he has to flee suggests that
their driving him out was implemented with a threat of doing him bodily harm.

the land of Tob. This is a remote region in the northeastern sector of Gilead.

no-account men. The same term, *reiqim* (literally, "empty") is also used for
the mercenaries hired by Abimelech. It probably refers to men without property, on the margins of society, who have nothing to lose and readily join a band
of guerillas or bandits. The young David also puts together a private militia of
this sort when he flees from Saul.

5 ites did battle with Israel. And it happened when the Ammonites did
   battle with Israel, that the elders of Gilead went to take Jephthah from
6 the land of Tob. And they said to Jephthah, "Come, be our captain, that
7 we may do battle with the Ammonites." And Jephthah said to the elders
   of Gilead, "Did you not hate me and drive me out from my father's
8 house, and why do you come to me now when you are in distress?" And
   the elders of Gilead said to Jephthah, "Therefore now we have come
   back to you, and you shall go with us and do battle with the Ammonites,
9 and you shall become chief for us, for all the inhabitants of Gilead." And
   Jephthah said to the elders of Gilead, "If you bring me back to do battle
   with the Ammonites and the Lord gives them to me, it is I who will be

---

5. *the elders of Gilead went to take Jephthah from the land of Tob.* Their going to
seek him out in the badlands where he has located with his fighters obviously
reflects the dire straits in which they find themselves.

6. *Come, be our captain.* Their initial speech to him is brusque, devoid of deference or diplomatic gesture. The position they offer him is military commander,
qatsin.

7. *Did you not hate me and drive me out from my father's house.* We now learn
something new about the banishment: the brothers' harsh act either had the
tacit endorsement of the elders or was actively abetted by them.

8. *Therefore now we have come back to you.* The "therefore" amounts to a concession on their part: precisely because we were complicit in your banishment,
we now come to you to make amends. "Come back" or "bring back" is a thematic keyword in this story.
    chief. Now they up the political ante: he will not be merely a captain but
chief, or head, *ro'sh*, of the whole community.

9. *If you bring me back.* The man who was driven out now contemplates being
brought back, as the elders have "come back" to him. Instead of accepting the
immediate offer to be chief, he stipulates that he will assume that position only
if he is victorious in battle, but he would have to become captain in order to
undertake the battle.
    it is I. The Hebrew puts the pronoun "I," usually not needed, before the
conjugated verb in a structure of emphasis.

your chief." And the elders of Gilead said to Jephthah, "May the Lord   10
be witness between us that we will surely do according to your word."
And Jephthah went with the elders of Gilead, and the people set him   11
over them as chief and captain, and Jephthah spoke all his words before
the Lord at Mizpah.

And Jephthah sent messengers to the king of the Ammonites, saying,   12
"What is between you and me that you have come to do battle in my
land?" And the king of the Ammonites said to Jephthah's messengers,   13
"For Israel took my land when it came up from Egypt, from the Arnon to
the Jabbok and to the Jordan. And now, give them back in peace." And   14
Jephthah again sent messengers to the king of the Ammonites, and he   15
said to him, "Thus says Jephthah: Israel did not take the land of Moab
and the land of the Ammonites, but when it came up from Egypt, Israel   16
went in the wilderness as far as the Sea of Reeds and came to Kadesh.
And Israel sent messengers to the king of Edom, saying, 'Let me pass,   17
pray, through your land,' and the king of Edom did not listen. And to the
king of Moab, too, they sent and he would not agree. And Israel stayed
in Kadesh. And they went through the wilderness and swung round the   18
land of Edom and the land of Moab and came from the east of the land
of Moab and camped across the Arnon and did not come into the terri-

---

10. *May the Lord be witness.* Literally, "May the Lord listen."

11. *the people set him over them as chief and captain.* In the event, both positions
are conferred on him before the battle.
   Jephthah spoke all his words before the Lord. This is a prayer before the battle
or perhaps an inquiry of an oracle.

12. *And Jephthah sent messengers to the king of the Ammonites.* The scholarly
consensus is that this entire passage of attempted diplomatic negotiation has
been spliced in from another source. According to the account in Numbers
20 and 33, it is Moab, not Ammon, that refuses right of transit to Israel, and,
in fact, Moab is mentioned first here (verse 15) and more often, together with
Edom and the Amorites. "The land of the Ammonites" may well be an editorial
addition intended to link this passage with the surrounding narrative. Chemosh, the deity mentioned in verse 24, is the national god of the Moabites,
whereas the Ammonite god would be Milcom.

19 tory of Moab because the Arnon is the border of Moab. And Israel sent
messengers to Sihon king of the Amorites, king of Heshbon, and said to
20 him, 'Let us pass, pray, through your land to our place.' And Sihon did not
trust Israel to pass through his territory, and Sihon gathered all his troops,
21 and they camped at Jahaz and did battle with Israel. And the Lord God
of Israel gave Sihon and all his troops into the hand of Israel, and they
struck them down, and Israel took hold of all the land of the Amorites,
22 the inhabitants of that land. And they took hold of all the territory of the
Amorites from the Arnon to the Jabbok and from the wilderness to the
23 Jordan. And so, the Lord God of Israel dispossessed the Amorites before
24 His people Israel, and would you possess it? Do you not take possession
of what Chemosh your god gives you to possess? And all that the Lord
25 our God has given us to possess, of that we shall take possession. And
now, are you really better than Balak son of Zippor king of Moab? Did
26 he strive with Israel, did he do battle with them? When Israel dwelled
in Heshbon and in its hamlets and in Aroer and in its hamlets and in all
the towns that are along the Arnon three hundred years, why did you not
27 recover them in all that time? I on my part have committed no offense
against you, yet you are doing evil to battle with me. Let the Lord, who is
28 judge, judge today between the Israelites and the Moabites." But the king
of the Ammonites did not listen to Jephthah's words that he had sent him.

---

24. *Do you not take possession of what Chemosh your god gives you to possess?*
The theological assumption of this statement is perfectly characteristic of this
early period of Israelite history. Israel has its own God, YHWH ("the Lord"),
believed to be more powerful than other gods, but each nation has its guiding
deity, assumed to look after the national destiny.

25. *Did he strive with Israel, did he do battle with them?* In fact, he fought against
Israel, as is reported in Numbers 22, but to no avail, for YHWH caused him
to be defeated.

And the spirit of the LORD was upon Jephthah, and he passed through   29
Gilead and Manasseh and passed through Mizpeh Gilead, and from
Mizpeh Gilead he passed on to the Ammonites. And Jephthah made a   30
vow to the LORD and said, "If You indeed give the Ammonites into my
hand, it shall be that whatever comes out of the door of my house to   31
meet me when I return safe and sound from the Ammonites shall be the
LORD's, and I shall offer it up as a burnt offering." And Jephthah crossed   32
over to the Ammonites to do battle with them, and the LORD gave them
into his hand. And he struck them from Aroer to where you come to   33
Minnith, twenty towns, and to Abel Ceramim, a very great blow, and
the Ammonites were laid low before Israel. And Jephthah came to his   34
house at Mizpah, and, look, his daughter was coming out to meet him
with timbrels and with dances, and she was an only child—besides her,

---

29. *And the spirit of the* LORD *was upon Jephthah.* Only now, when Jephthah
actually leads his troops into battle, do we have the formula of the investment by
the divine spirit, the leader's charisma, that is used for most of the other judges.

31. *whatever comes out of the door of the house to meet me.* The Hebrew is ambiguous: it could mean "whatever" or "whoever." Some scholars have argued for the
latter because "to meet" seems to imply a person, but the Hebrew, which is in fact
a preposition and not a verb, has the sense of "toward," and it seems unlikely that
Jephthah would have deliberately envisaged human sacrifice from the start. In any
case, it is a rash vow: the Midrash Tanhuma shrewdly notes that the first creature
out of the house could have been a dog or a pig, animals unfit for sacrifice. The
vow focuses on the act of return to the house, but the killing of Jephthah's only
child will mean the destruction of his house in the extended sense of the term.

32. *the* LORD *gave them into his hand.* This is all we are provided by way of a
description of the battle.

34. *and, look.* As repeatedly used elsewhere, the presentative term marks the
switch to the visual point of view of the character.
   with timbrels and with dances. It was the role of the young women to celebrate the victory in this fashion. The dance of joy will immediately turn into
lamentation.

35 he had neither son nor daughter. And it happened when he saw her, that he rent his garments, and he said, "Alas, my daughter, you have indeed laid me low and you have joined ranks with my troublers, for I myself have opened my mouth to the LORD, and I cannot turn back."

36 And she said to him, "My father, you have opened your mouth to the LORD. Do to me as it came out from your mouth, after the LORD has wreaked vengeance for you from your enemies, from the Ammonites."

37 And she said to her father, "Let this thing be done for me: let me be for two months, that I may go and weep on the mountains and keen for my

---

35. *my daughter*. This is an affectionate form of address, like "child."

for I myself have opened my mouth to the LORD. The Hebrew incorporates a crucial pun. Jephthah's name, *yiftah*, means "he opens." The verb used here, *patsah*, is slightly different from the verb *patah* on which the name is based, but it is a close phonetic and semantic cousin. The belief shared by father and daughter is that vows to God are irrevocable and non-negotiable: what comes out of the mouth cannot be brought back ("I cannot turn back," a locution heavy with ironic resonances in light of Jephthah's attempt to come back to the house from which he was driven).

36. *Do to me as it came out from your mouth*. Neither she nor her father can bring themselves to mention explicitly the horrific content of the vow. She speaks almost as though the vow were an autonomous agent that came out of her father's mouth and cannot be called back.

37. *And she said to her father*. This is one of the most arresting instances of the convention of repeating the formula for the introduction of speech with no intervening answer in order to indicate a difficulty in responding on the part of the interlocutor in the dialogue. Jephthah, hearing his daughter's declaration that she is willing to become a burnt offering in fulfillment of the vow, is dumbfounded and doesn't know what to say. His daughter then goes on to add her special request to the affirmation of compliance she has just uttered.

weep. The Hebrew verb *weyaradti* in the form in which it appears would normally mean "and I shall go down," but going down upon mountains doesn't make much sense. The least strained solution is to assume it is a scrambling of *'arid*, which in Psalm 55:3 is a verb associated with weeping or complaint. Another possibility is to link the term here with the rare verbal stem *r-w-d*, which probably means something like "wander."

maidenhood, I and my companions." And he said, "Go." And he sent ₃₈
her off for two months, her and her companions, and she keened for
her maidenhood on the mountains. And it happened at the end of the ₃₉
two months, that she came back to her father, and he did to her as he
had vowed, and she had known no man. And it became a fixed practice
in Israel that each year the daughters of Israel would go to lament the ₄₀
daughter of Jephthah the Gileadite four days in the year.

---

38. *And he said, "Go."* Jephthah's extreme brevity of response suggests a man
choked with emotion, barely able to speak.

her and her companions. Here and in the previous verse, it is unambiguous
in the Hebrew that the companions are female—nubile young women like
Jephthah's daughter.

39. *he did to her as he had vowed.* The narrator, like father and daughter in the
dialogue, avoids spelling out the terrible act of child sacrifice. This whole story
has parallels elsewhere in the ancient Mediterranean world, the most obvious
being Agamemnon's sacrifice of his daughter Iphigenia in order to obtain favorable winds to sail to the Trojan war. The parallel episode within the Bible is
the Binding of Isaac, but here, in contrast to Genesis 22, the ending is tragic.

and she had known no man. This concluding note about her virginity underscores the point of keening for her maidenhood: she is cut off from the living
without ever having had the opportunity to enjoy the fulfillment that life has
in store for a woman.

40. *each year the daughters of Israel would go to lament the daughter of Jephthah.*
The long-standing scholarly hypothesis that this is an etiological tale to explain
an annual ritual still seems valid: one suspects a pagan practice in which young
women go off to mourn the descent into the underworld each year of a vegetation goddess, a virgin like themselves, roughly analogous to the Greek Perse-
phone and to the Mesopotamian male vegetation god, Tammuz.

CHAPTER 12

A
1   nd the men of Ephraim were mustered and they crossed over north-
    ward and said to Jephthah, "Why did you cross over to do battle with the
    Ammonites, but us you did not call to go with you? We will burn down
2   your house upon you." And Jephthah said to them, "I and my people
    were in strife and the Ammonites sorely afflicted me, and I summoned
3   you, but you did not rescue me from their hand. And I saw that you were
    not about to rescue me, and I put my life at risk and crossed over to the
    Ammonites, and the Lord gave them into my hand. And why have you
4   come up to me this day to do battle with me?" And Jephthah gathered all
    the men of Gilead and did battle with Ephraim, and the men of Gilead
    struck down Ephraim, for Ephraim's fugitives had said, "You, Gilead, are

---

1. *they crossed over.* This verb—Hebrew *'avar*—is a keyword in the episode.
In their challenge to Jephthah, they will say, "Why did you cross over?" These
occurrences prepare the way for the testing of the Ephraimite fugitives who
seek to cross over the Jordan at the fords (the Hebrew noun for "ford" derives
from this same verb *'avar*).

We will burn down your house. Jephthah, who was driven from his father's
house and whose familial house has been destroyed in the sacrifice of his
daughter, is now threatened with the destruction of his physical house.

2. *I and my people were in strife and the Ammonites sorely afflicted me.* The
received text is syntactically distorted here, reading: "I and my people were in
strife with the Ammonites very." The translation adopts a reading attested in
several versions of the Septuagint, which appear to have used a Hebrew text
that had one additional word, *'inuni*, "they afflicted me" before "very" (or "very
much").

4. *Ephraim's fugitives had said, "You, Gilead, are in the midst of Ephraim, in
the midst of Manasseh.* The obscure wording here has given rise to conflicting
interpretations. The one followed in this translation is Rashi's proposal: even

in the midst of Ephraim, in the midst of Manasseh." And Gilead took 5
the fords of the Jordan from Ephraim, and it happened when a fugitive
of Ephraim would say, "Let me cross over," the men of Gilead would
say to him, "Are you an Ephraimite?" and he would say "No." And they 6
would say to him, "Say, pray, shibboleth," and he would say "sibboleth,"
and he would not manage to pronounce it right, and they would seize
him and slaughter him at the fords of the Jordan. And at that time forty-
two thousand of Ephraim fell. And Jephthah led Israel six years, and 7
Jephthah the Gileadite died and was buried in his town, in Gilead.

And after him Ibzan from Bethlehem led Israel. And he had thirty sons, 8,9
and thirty daughters he sent outside, and thirty girls he brought for his
sons from outside. And he led Israel seven years. And Ibzan died and 10
was buried in Bethlehem. And after him Elon the Zebulunite led Israel 11
ten years. And Elon the Zebulunite died and was buried in Ajalon in the 12
land of Zebulun. And after him Abdon son of Hillel the Pirathonite led 13
Israel. And he had forty sons and thirty grandsons who rode on seventy 14
donkeys. And he led Israel eight years. And Abdon son of Hillel the
Pirathonite died and was buried in Pirathon in the land of Ephraim in
the high country of the Amalekite.

---

the least important, the fugitives, of Ephraim tell the Gileadites that they are
no more than a tolerated presence in the midst of Ephraim and its brother tribe,
Manasseh. In the denouement of the civil war, all the Ephraimite warriors will
become fugitives to be slaughtered at the fords of the Jordan.

6. *shibboleth . . . sibboleth.* In contrast to the English use of "shibboleth," here it
is a password. The necessary inference is that in the dialect of Hebrew spoken
by the Ephraimites, *sh* was pronounced as *s*. The Hebrew word can mean either
stream or stalk of grain, but, given the proximity to the Jordan, the former sense
is more likely. One might note that what comes out of the mouth of the fugitives
leads to death, as was the case with Jephthah's vow.
    forty-two thousand. As with numbers elsewhere, this is hardly realistic.

7. *in his town, in Gilead.* The Masoretic text reads "in the towns of Gilead," but
the Septuagint shows the reading adopted here.

9. *outside.* The probable meaning is "outside the clan."

14. *who rode on seventy donkeys.* See the comment on 10:4.

CHAPTER 13

And the Israelites once more did evil in the eyes of the Lord, and He gave them into the hand of the Philistines for forty years.

2 And there was a man from Zorah from the clan of the Danite, and his name was Manoah. And his woman was barren, she had borne no child.

3 And a messenger of the Lord appeared to the woman and said to her, "Look, pray, you are barren and have borne no child. But you shall con-

4 ceive and bear a son. And now, guard yourself, pray, and drink no wine

5 or strong drink and eat no unclean thing. For you are about to conceive and bear a son, and no razor shall touch his head, for the lad shall be a

---

2. *his woman was barren.* The Hebrew noun *'ishah*, like *femme* in French, can mean either "woman" or "wife." This translation renders it as "woman" through-out the chapter because it is a thematic keyword that sets the stage for the story of Samson and his involvement with women. Indeed, the reason that she is not given a name, in contrast to her husband, may be to enable the narrator to repeat the word "woman" again and again in this episode.

his woman was barren, she had borne no child. These words signal the incep-tion of the annunciation type-scene. Of all the judges, only Samson is accorded this scene, which, as we shall see, has several features that distinguish it from the other annunciations.

4. *strong drink.* The indication is verse 14 that specifically products of the vine are prohibited is evidence that this is liquor, *sheikhar*, derived from grapes, a form of grappa.

5. *touch his head.* Literally, "go up on his head."

nazirite of God from the womb. And he shall begin to rescue Israel from
the hand of the Philistines" And the woman came and said to her hus- 6
band, saying, "A man of God came to me, and his appearance was like
the appearance of a messenger of God, very fearsome. And I did not ask
him from where he was, and his name he did not tell me. And he said to 7
me, 'You are about to conceive and bear a son. And now, drink no wine
or strong drink and eat no unclean thing, for the lad shall be a nazirite
of God from the womb till his dying day.'" And Manoah entreated the 8
LORD and said, "Please, my Master, the man of God whom you sent, let
him, pray, come again to us and teach us what we should do for the lad
who is to be born." And God heeded Manoah's voice, and the messenger 9
of God came again to the woman, when she was sitting in the field and

---

nazirite. The nazirite (see Numbers 6) is a person who takes on himself
special vows of abstinence. The noun derives from a verbal stem that means to
be separated or set apart.

he shall begin to rescue Israel. The divine messenger chooses his words carefully: any victory Samson achieves over the Philistines will be incomplete.

6. *A man of God.* Since he appears to her in human form, however "fearsome,"
she has no reason to assume that he is a divine being, though he might seem
to resemble one.

7. *drink no wine or strong drink.* Since the fetus feeds from the mother, the clear
implication is that this prohibition, which begins in her pregnancy, will also be
obligatory for the future nazirite. Nazirites in general refrain from alcoholic
beverages. It is noteworthy that she says nothing about the ban on cutting the
hair, which is another general practice for nazirites.

till his dying day. For the divine messenger's "will begin to rescue Israel," she
substitutes this phrase, ominously introducing the idea of Samson's death into
the story before he is even conceived.

9. *And God heeded Manoah's voice, and the messenger of God came again to the
woman.* In fact, God does not send a response to the two of them ("come again
to us") as Manoah asked but only to the woman who is alone in the field. This
version of the annunciation-type scene systematically sidelines the man, who
really doesn't grasp what is going on.

10 Manoah her husband was not with her. And the woman hurried and ran
and told her husband and said to him, "Look, the man that came to me
11 during the day has appeared to me." And Manoah arose and went after
his wife and came to the man and said to him, "Are you the man who
12 spoke to the woman?" And he said, "I am." And Manoah said, "Now,
may your word come true! What shall be the conduct of the lad and his
13 acts?" And the LORD's messenger said to Manoah, "From all that I said
14 to the woman she must guard herself. From all that comes from the vine
she shall not eat, and wine and strong drink she shall not drink, and no
15 unclean thing shall she eat. All that I charged her she must keep." And
Manoah said to the LORD's messenger, "Let us detain you, pray, and we
16 shall prepare a kid for you." And the LORD's messenger said to Manoah,
"If you detain me, I cannot eat of your food, and if you prepare a burnt
offering, to the LORD you shall offer it up." For Manoah did not know

---

10. *during the day*. This slightly obscure phrase evidently refers to the day before.

12. *his acts*. The Hebrew uses a singular.

13. *From all that I said to the woman she must guard herself.* There is a little
note of annoyance in these words: after all, I already explained to your wife
what should be done about the child, and so why are you being so obtuse as to
ask me to repeat myself? As a matter of fact, the celestial messenger does not
directly answer Manoah's question about what will be the conduct of the child
because everything he says pertains to the restrictions that the future mother
must observe. It is probably implied that all these restrictions must be followed
by the son as well. The most striking aspect of this response to Manoah is a
crucial omission: no word is said about not cutting the hair, as though this were
a secret shared between the divine messenger and the woman that neither will
entrust to Manoah. In the ensuing story, it is the secret of Samson's indomitable
strength that, when revealed to a woman, brings about his downfall.

16. *I cannot eat of your food.* The word for "food" here is literally "bread," but
because the proffered meal is kid's meat, the literal translation could be confusing. The alimentary ground rules, one should note, for divine beings have
changed: in Genesis 18, God and His two supernatural companions partake of
the feast that Abraham prepares for them.
    For Manoah did not know. Even at this late point in the story, he still doesn't
get it. And thus he goes on to ask for the name of the mysterious stranger, so

that he was a messenger of the LORD. And Manoah said to the LORD's   17
messenger, "What is your name? When your word comes true, we shall
honor you." And the LORD's messenger said to him, "Why do you ask   18
my name when it is a mystery?" And Manoah took the kid and the grain   19
offering and offered them up on a rock to the LORD, and the other was
performing a wonder, with Manoah and his woman watching. And it   20
happened when the flame went up from the altar to the heavens, that
the LORD's messenger went up in the flame of the altar, with Manoah
and his woman watching, and they fell on their faces to the ground. And   21
the LORD's messenger appeared no more to Manoah and to his woman.
Then Manoah knew that he was a messenger of the LORD. And Manoah   22

---

that after the birth of the child he can find a way to pay honor to the bearer of
the good tidings.

18. *a mystery*. The Hebrew root of this term is the same as the verb for performing a wonder in the next verse.

19. *the other*. The Hebrew simply says "he." This translation is meant to avoid
the erroneous notion that it is Manoah who is performing the wonder.

20. *the LORD's messenger went up in the flame of the altar*. Of all the annunciation scenes, only here does the bringer of the annunciation disappear into the
heavens in a column of flame. That pyrotechnic exit of course points to the
supernatural character of the child to be born, but, even more strategically,
it announces the motif of fire that will recur in Samson's story. At the end,
even when fire is not present either literally or in the figurative language of the
story, it remains as a powerful analogue for Samson, the hero who blindly sows
destruction, like fire.

21. *And the LORD's messenger appeared no more*. This clause could equally mean
that he disappeared from their sight and that he did not again come to them.
    Then Manoah knew. It takes all this to get him finally to recognize the real
identity of the bearer of the tidings.

23 said to his woman, "We are doomed to die, for we have seen God." And
his woman said to him, "Had the Lord desired to put us to death, He
would not have taken from our hand burnt offering and grain offering,
nor would He have shown us all these things and at this time instructed
24 us in this manner." And the woman bore a son, and she called his name
25 Samson, and the lad grew up, and the Lord blessed him. And the spirit
of the Lord began to drive him in the camp of Dan between Zorah and
Eshtaol.

---

23. *Had the* Lord *desired to put us to death, He would not have taken from our
hand burnt offering and grain offering, nor would He have shown us all these
things.* As her husband quails in terror, she calmly points out to him with impeccable logic that God could scarcely have intended to kill them (for beholding a
divine creature) if He went to all the trouble of conveying to them instructions
about their promised son. The annunciation-type scene is fundamentally matri-
archal, the revelations being vouchsafed to the future mother, but here we are
given a virtually satiric version of the annunciation, highlighting male obtuse-
ness and the good sense of the woman. This scene thus becomes a perfect
prelude to the story of a brawny male hero whose lapses of judgment in regard
to women entangle him in repeated difficulties and ultimately destroy him.

24. *Samson.* Though the *–on* suffix of the Hebrew *Shimshon* is used for quite a
few biblical names, it could also be related to *'on,* "potency," making the name
suggest "sun of potency." Some scholars have conjectured that behind this
figure there might be traditions about a solar deity. In any case, the link with
the sun is another warrant for the fire motif. In terms of mythological patterns,
this figure also bears some resemblance to Hercules, a muscular hero who
performs arduous labors.

25. *drive him.* Now, at last, we get the descent of the spirit on the judge. But
the carefully chosen verb is unique to Samson: it means, more literally, "to
pound/pulsate" [within] him, and neatly adumbrates his career of intermittent
violent action.

CHAPTER 14

And Samson went down to Timnah and saw a woman in Timnah of   1
the daughters of the Philistines. And he went up and told his father and   2
his mother and said, "A woman I have seen in Timnah of the daughters
of the Philistines, and now, take her for me as a wife." And his father   3
and his mother said to him, "Is there no woman among your kinsmen's
daughters or in all my people that you should go to take a wife from the
uncircumcised Philistines?" And Samson said to his father, "Her take for
me because she pleases me." But his father and his mother did not know   4
that it was from the LORD, for He sought a pretext from the Philistines,

---

1. *Samson went down to Timnah and saw a woman.* The first common noun that
appears in the Samson narrative is "woman," a word that will be reiterated and
that picks up the repeated use of "woman" in the annunciation scene. "Woman"
is also the very first word of dialogue assigned to Samson (and for that reason,
this translation follows the syntactic order of the Hebrew).

3. *my people.* Some scholars emend this to "your people."
   the uncircumcised Philistines. This is a recurrent epithet for the Philistines,
a people of Hellenic origin, and is not used for the Canaanites, who in some
instances may have possibly practiced circumcision. The foreskin is an obvious
mark of difference but it also focuses a sense of sexual recoil: the Philistine
woman, whom Samson would have as a sexual partner, belongs to an uncircumcised people and was begotten by an uncircumcised male.
   because she pleases me. The literal sense is "because she is right in my eyes."
Since there is no indication that Samson has exchanged a single word with the
woman, we may infer that his only reason for wanting her as wife is physical
attraction—what he has seen.

4. *it was from the LORD.* The theological explanation is a little shaky: God knows
that the only way to get this particular hero to act against the Philistines is to

5 and at that time the Philistines were ruling over Israel. And Samson
went down, and his father and his mother with him, to Timnah, and they
came as far as the vineyards of Timnah, and, look, a young lion came
6 roaring at him. And the spirit of the LORD seized him, and he ripped
it apart as one would rip apart a kid, with nothing in his hand, and he
7 did not tell his father and his mother what he had done. And he went
8 down and spoke to the woman, and she pleased Samson. And he came
back after a time to marry her and turned aside to see the place where
the lion had fallen, and, look, there was a swarm of bees in the lion's
9 carcass, and honey. And he scooped it up into his palms and went off
eating as he went, and he went to his father and to his mother and gave
them, and they ate. And he did not tell them that he had scooped up the
10 honey from the lion's carcass. And his father went down to the woman,

---

involve him with a woman, which will lead to his being tricked by her countrymen, which then will provoke him to vengeance.

5. *and, look, a young lion came roaring at him.* The shift of perspective marked
by "look" is of course to Samson's viewpoint. At this moment, though he has
been accompanied by his parents, he is clearly separated from them, and they
do not witness the killing of the lion. Ehrlich proposes that Samson, as an
energetic young man, has bounded far ahead of his parents, who are walking
slowly on the path to Timnah.

6. *And the spirit of the LORD seized him.* In Samson's case, the divine afflatus
enables violent action by the hero and is not the charisma of an ad-hoc military
leader. All his heroic acts are performed by him alone.
    he did not tell his father and his mother. Samson has a penchant for secrets,
but he gets himself in trouble when he reveals his secrets to women.

7. *he went down and spoke to the woman.* The verb "spoke" here, as in some
other contexts, is probably a technical term for a proposal of marriage.

9. *And he scooped it up into his palms.* It should be noted that carcasses are
considered to be ritually unclean, so that by taking food from the lion's bones
Samson is violating one of the terms of the nazirite vow. The setting, moreover,
is a vineyard, though he does not touch the grapes.

and Samson made a feast there, for thus did the young men do. And it 11
happened when they saw him, that they took thirty companions to be
with him. And Samson said to them, "Let me pose you a riddle. If you 12
actually explain it to me during the seven days of the feast and find the
solution, I shall give you thirty fine cloths and thirty changes of garment.
And if you are not able to explain it to me, you shall give me thirty fine 13
cloths and thirty changes of garment." And they said to him, "Pose your
riddle, that we may hear it." And he said to them: 14

From the eater food came forth,
         and from the strong sweet came forth."

And they could not explain the riddle for three days. And it happened 15
on the fourth day that they said to Samson's wife, "Entice your husband
that he explain the riddle or we will burn you and your father's house in

---

11. *companions.* They are, in effect, designated companions for the bridegroom
during the seven days of the feast, though Samson has no personal relationship
with them.

12. *find the solution.* The Hebrew uses an ellipsis, merely the verb "find."
   I shall give you thirty fine cloths and thirty changes of garment. The confident
Samson takes on himself an indemnity in the bet thirty times that of each of
the Philistine men.

14. *From the eater food came forth.* The Hebrew uses cognate terms: from the
eater what-is-eaten came forth. The riddle, as is appropriate for riddles, is cast
in a line of verse. It is, of course, an unfair riddle (hence Samson's confidence)
because it depends on unique circumstances known only to the riddler, and
nothing in its formulation provides a clue to the solution.

15. *on the fourth day.* The translation follows the Septuagint; the Masoretic text
reads "on the seventh day," but it is not credible that they would have waited
until the very last moment, and this would also contradict the report that she
pestered him for the solution day after day. There remains some problem about
the number of days because in verse 17 she is said to have been weeping before
Samson seven days, not four.
   Entice. The Hebrew verb in context means something like "cajole" or "coax,"
but it also has a sexual connotation, "entice" or "seduce," and the Philistine men
are clearly suggesting that she use her feminine wiles on her husband.
   or we will burn you and your father's house in fire. Here the fire motif introduced in the annunciation scene enters the story proper. This is, of course, an
offer that the woman cannot refuse.

16 fire. Did the two of you call us here to beggar us?" And Samson's wife
    wept before him and said, "You only hate me and don't love me. You
    posed a riddle to my countrymen, but to me you did not explain it." And
    he said to her, "Look, to my father and my mother I did not explain it,
17 and shall I explain it to you?" And she wept before him the seven days
    that they had the feast, and it happened on the seventh day, that he
    explained it to her, for she had badgered him. And she explained the
18 riddle to her countrymen. And the townsmen said to him on the seventh
    day before the sun went down:

> "What is sweeter than honey,
>   and what is stronger than a lion?"

And he said to them:

> "Had you not plowed with my heifer,
>   you would not have solved my riddle."

Did the two of you call us here to beggar us? The Hebrew conjugates the verb
"call" (in the sense of "invite") in the plural, and the translation uses "the two
of you" to make that clear: in effect, they are angrily accusing the woman of
conspiring against them with her Israelite husband.

here. Reading *halom*, with the Septuagint, for the Masoretic *halo'*.

16. *You only hate me and don't love me.* Here the dialogue has a sharp edge of
realism: if you really loved me, you wouldn't keep secrets from me. And her
speech, moreover, is accompanied by tears. Samson tries to resist and hold on
to the secret, as we see in his immediate response, but in the end he succumbs
to her persistent tears and imploring.

18. *before the sun went down.* They wait till the last possible moment to spring
the answer on him, an effect perhaps highlighted here by the use of a quasi-
epic flourish *beterem yavo' haharsah* in which the word for sun, *harsah*, is archaic
and poetic instead of the standard *shemesh*.

Had you not plowed with my heifer, / you would not have solved my riddle. Their
statement of the solution to the riddle, like the riddle itself, is cast in a line of
verse with three accents in each verset. Samson's response is equally a 3/3 line,
though he also uses rhyme (an occasional occurrence in biblical poetry): *'eglati /
hidati.* The plowing image is obviously sexual: if you had not played around with

And the spirit of the Lord seized him, and he went down to Ashkelon   19
and struck down from among them thirty men and took their armor, and
he gave the changes of garment to the explainers of the riddle. And his
wrath flared, and he went up to his father's house. And Samson's wife   20
was given to one of his companions who had been in his company.

---

my wife, she would not have revealed the secret to you. Thus, Samson has no
notion that his wife acted under a death-threat but instead imagines that she has
been unfaithful to him—perhaps, with thirty different men! He therefore departs
enraged not only against the thirty "companions" but also against his wife.

19. *he went down to Ashkelon*. Timnah is a small Philistine town in the lowlands
(Shephelah), whereas Ashkelon is one of the five principal Philistine towns on
the Mediterranean coast.

their armor. From the one other biblical occurrence of this term *ḥalitsah* in 2
Samuel 2:21, it is clear that it refers to armor, not clothing in general. Samson,
then, chooses to confront and kill armed warriors. It is probably the armor that
he sends as "changes of garment" to the thirty men who were at his wedding:
this would be an act of defiance, demonstrating to them the bold and deadly
thing he has done. No mention is made of the fine cloths, perhaps because the
armor is far more than the equivalent in value of fine cloth and garment.

20. *Samson's wife was given to one of his companions*. The marriage is in effect
annulled, and the plowing with Samson's heifer takes place after the fact of his
mentioning it to the companions.

one of his companions who had been in his company. The Hebrew uses a
cognate noun and verb and literally says, "his companion." The subject and
object of the verb are ambiguous: it could be read either as "he [the companion]
befriended / was companion to him [Samson]" or "he [Samson] befriended /
was companion to him [the companion]."

CHAPTER 15

¹ And after a time, in the days of the wheat harvest, Samson visited his wife with a kid, and he said, "Let me come to my wife in the chamber," and her father would not let him come in. And her father said, "I surely thought that you altogether hated her, and I gave her to your companion. Is not her younger sister better than she? Let her be yours instead of her." And Samson said to them, "This time I am clear of the Philistines, for I am about to do harm to them." And Samson went and caught three hundred foxes and took torches and turned tail to

---

1. *Let me come to my wife in the chamber.* What he has in mind is obviously sex, and, in fact, the initial verb could also be construed as "let me come to bed with my wife."

2. *I surely thought that you altogether hated her.* He has two good reasons for thinking this: Samson's angry declaration that his wife has been unfaithful to him with the thirty companions (14:18) and his abrupt return to his own father's house.

3. *to them.* Evidently, he is addressing not only his father-in-law but other Philistines he views as complicit in wronging him.
   This time I am clear of the Philistines. I am clear of guilt for what I will do to them, seeing as how they have behaved toward me. The emphasis on "this time" returns later in the story.

4. *caught three hundred foxes.* Most of the numbers in the story are multiples of three. Samson, himself a feral hero, is repeatedly involved with animals: the lion, the foxes, and then the jawbone of a donkey. The foxes, running wild through the fields with fire at their tails, are an effective delivery system for spreading incendiary destruction.

tail and put one torch between each two tails. And he set fire to the 5
torches and sent them into the Philistines' standing grain and set fire
to the stacked grain and the standing grain and the vineyards and the
olive trees. And the Philistines said, "Who did this?" And they said, 6
"Samson, the son-in-law of the Timnite, for he took his wife and gave
her to his companion." And the Philistines came up and burned her
and her father in fire. And Samson said to them, "If this is what you 7
do, I will be avenged of you, and then I will stop." And he struck them 8
a great blow, hip on thigh, and went down and stayed in the crevice of
the rock of Eitam. And the Philistines came up and camped in Judah 9
and deployed at Lehi. And the men of Judah said, "Why have you come 10
up against us?" And they said, "We have come up to bind Samson, to do

---

5. *the stacked grain and the standing grain and the vineyards and the olive trees.*
These items cover most of the principal products of agriculture in this region,
and, moreover, the wheat harvest is just taking place, so the overall destruction
is devastating.

6. *burned her and her father in fire.* Many manuscripts and two ancient translations read "her and her father's house." Fire answers fire now, and it is in the
nature of fire uncontrolled to destroy everything in its path, much like Samson.

7. *If this is what you do, I will be avenged of you.* The Philistine retaliation leads
to a second round of vengeance for Samson.

8. *he struck them a great blow, hip on thigh.* The implication is that he battered
down a large throng of Philistines, though the number in this case is not specified. The word for "hip" actually means "leg" or "calf of the leg," but "hip on
thigh" is a fine old locution coined by the King James translators that effectively
conveys the intended sense of a murderous thrashing.

9. *Lehi.* As elsewhere, the name, which means "jawbone," is proleptic, and is
explained in verse 17.

10. *to bind Samson.* He is such a lethally powerful adversary that before they
can think of killing him, they have to imagine immobilizing him by trussing him
up. The notion of binding Samson will return in Delilah's dealings with him.

11 to him as he has done to us." And three thousand men of Judah went down to the crevice of the rock of Eitam and said to Samson, "Do you not know that the Philistines rule over us? And what have you done to us?" And he said to them, "As they did to me, so I have done to them." 12 And they said to him, "We have come down to bind you, to give you into the hand of the Philistines." And Samson said to them, "Vow to me 13 that you yourselves will not harm me." And they said to him, "No, for we will certainly bind you and give you into their hand, but we will not put you to death." And they bound him with two new ropes and brought 14 him up from the rock. He was coming up to Lehi when the Philistines shouted to greet him, and the spirit of the LORD seized him, and the ropes that were on his arms became like flax burning in fire, and his 15 bonds fell apart from upon his hands. And he found the fresh jawbone of a donkey and reached out his hand and took it, and he struck down 16 a thousand men with it. And Samson said:

---

11. *three thousand men.* This is still another multiple of three.

As they did to me, so I have done to them. This unbending code of vengeful retaliation is fully shared by Samson and the Philistines. Compare verse 10.

12. *Vow to me that you yourselves will not harm me.* He uses the emphatic pronoun before the conjugated verb to make sure that they are not the ones who intend to harm him. If they were, he would have to exert his power and wreak havoc among his countrymen, which he wants to avoid. On this condition, he allows himself to be bound.

14. *the ropes that were on his arms became like flax burning in fire.* The fire motif is continued here in a simile as it will be in Delilah's failed attempts to have him bound. New ropes also occur in the Delilah episode, the idea being that new ropes are in no way worn or frayed and so are very hard to break.

fell apart. Literally, "melted."

15. *the fresh jawbone of a donkey.* The skeletal remains of the beast are relatively new, and so the jawbone would not be dry and brittle. As before, Samson fights with an improvised and unconventional weapon. This is the second time he comes in contact with what is left of an animal carcass—an unclean object: the first time, he draws out something sweet; now, antithetically, he finds a weapon.

"With a donkey's jawbone,
　　　　mound upon mound,
With a donkey's jawbone,
　　　　I struck down a thousand men."

And it happened when he finished speaking, that he flung the jawbone 17
from his hand, and he called that place Ramath Lehi. And he was 18
very thirsty, and he called out to the LORD: "You Yourself gave a great
victory in the hand of your servant, and now should I die from thirst
and fall into the hand of the uncircumcised?" And God split open the 19
hollow that was in Lehi, and water came out of it, and he drank and
his spirit returned and he revived. Therefore has its name been called
Ein Hakkore to this day. And he led Israel in the days of the Philistines 20
twenty years.

---

16. *With a donkey's jawbone, / mound upon mound.* Samson seals his conquest,
like Lamech in Genesis 4, with an exulting poem of triumph. The meaning of
the second verset of this line is not certain. A long tradition of interpretation
understands it as "mounds"—perhaps, the mounds of bodies of the slain. In
that case, the two Hebrew words *ḥamor ḥamoratayim* would be a pun on *ḥamor,*
"donkey." But the word for "mound" requires different vowels, so it is possible
that the phrase is actually an incremental repetition of "donkey" in the first
verset and means "a donkey, a pair."

17. *Ramath Lehi.* The name means "casting of the jawbone."

19. *hollow.* The Hebrew *makhteish* means "mortar" (as in mortar and pestle)
and by extension a concave formation in rock.
　　Ein Hakkore. In this etiology of the name, it is understood to mean "the
spring of the one who calls out." But the Hebrew *qorei',* one who calls out, has
a homonym that means "partridge," and it is likely that a place originally called
Partridge Spring, because partridges frequented the area, was given this new
narrative explanation for its name.

20. *And he led Israel . . . twenty years.* This notice of the length of Samson's
career seems out of place because further episodes of his story follow. The
statement is repeated at the very end of his story, where we would expect it,
with the verb "led" (or "judged") in the pluperfect.

CHAPTER 16

1   And Samson went to Gaza, and he saw there a whore-woman and
2   came to bed with her. And it was told to the Gazites saying, "Samson
    has come here." And they lay in ambush for him all night long at the
    town gate, and they plotted together all night long, saying, "At morn-
3   ing's light, we shall kill him." And Samson lay till midnight, and he
    arose at midnight and seized the doors of the town's gate and the two
    doorposts and pulled them free with the bolt and put them on his
    shoulders and took them up to the top of the mountain that faces
    Hebron.

---

1. *he saw there a whore-woman.* This is a precise verbal echo of his first encounter with a Philistine woman, only the professional designation "whore" being
added. There is a certain parallel with the story of the two spies who came to
Jericho to Rahab the whore, but Samson comes only for his own pleasure, avails
himself of the woman's services, and does not have to hide or flee because he
can rely on his strength.

2. *And it was told.* Those words are added from the Septuagint.

3. *seized the doors of the town's gate.* In this provocative act, he not only asserts
his invulnerability but also leaves the town exposed.

And it happened afterward that he loved a woman in Nahal Sorek, and   4
her name was Delilah. And the Philistine overlords went up to her and   5
said to her, "Entice him and see in what his great power lies and with
what we can prevail against him and bind him to torture him. As for us,
each of us will give you eleven hundred silver shekels." And Delilah said   6
to Samson, "Tell me, pray, in what your great power lies, and with what
could you be bound to be tortured?" And Samson said, "If they were to   7
bind me with seven moist thongs that had not been dried out, I would
be weakened and become like any man." And the Philistine overlords   8
brought up to her seven moist thongs that had not been dried out, and

---

4. *he loved a woman in Nahal Sorek.* In this climactic episode in the series of
three women with whom Samson is involved, we are told that he actually loves
the woman, and of the three, only Delilah is given a name. Nahal Sorek (Wadi
of the Vine) is in Israelite territory, and Delilah may well be an Israelite woman.

5. *the Philistine overlords.* The term *seranim* always appears in the plural and is
the title of the rulers of the five towns that make up the Philistine pentapolis.
Many scholars think it is cognate with the Greek *tyrranos.* The fact that the
overlords themselves should come to make the appeal to Delilah reflects the
importance they attach to the capture of this deadly Israelite adversary.
    bind him to torture him. They are frank about their brutal intentions toward
Samson: instead of killing him on the spot, they want him rendered helpless so
that they can torment and abuse this despised enemy who has wreaked such
havoc among them.
    eleven hundred silver shekels. This is a vast sum—5,500 shekels all told—and
so more than enough to appeal to her mercenary impulses.

6. *with what could you be bound to be tortured.* In repeating the words of the
overlords, Delilah does not hesitate to speak openly of torture. Presumably, she
is putting this to Samson as a merely hypothetical condition, though the talk
of binding and torture also makes this sound like a perverse sex game they are
playing.

7. *moist thongs.* These are either animal tendons or cords plaited from leather—
in either case, still moist so that they are very hard to tear apart.

9 she bound him with them. And the ambush was laid out in her chamber. And she said to him, "Philistines are upon you, Samson!" And he
snapped the cords as the wick of tow snaps when it touches fire, and
10 the secret of his power was not known. And Delilah said to Samson,
"Look, you have mocked me and spoken lies to me. Now, tell me, pray,
11 with what could you be bound?" And he said to her, "If they make sure
to bind me with new ropes with which no task has been done, I would
12 be weakened and become like any man." And Delilah took new ropes
and bound him with them, and she said to him, "Philistines are upon
you, Samson!" And the ambush was laid out in the chamber. And he
13 snapped them from his arms like a thread. And Delilah said, "Until now
you have mocked me and spoken lies to me. Tell me, with what could
you be bound?" And he said to her, "If you weave my head's seven tresses
together with the web and drive them with a peg into the wall, I would
14 be weakened and become like any man." And she drove them with a peg
into the wall, and she said to him, "Philistines are upon you, Samson!"
And he awoke from his sleep and pulled free the peg and the loom

---

9. *when it touches fire*. The fire motif returns in the simile.

12. *Delilah took new ropes*. Here the aid of the Philistine overlords is not mentioned, though it may be implied.

13. *If you weave my head's seven tresses together with the web*. Only now do
we learn how Samson wears his uncut hair (and one should note the magical
number seven). In the third of his three false explanations, he edges toward
the real secret because his hair is involved. This version also comes close to his
actual predicament because it conjures up entanglement in a woman's instrument, the loom.
    *and drive them with a peg into the wall, I would be weakened and become
like any man*. Both these clauses are absent in the Masoretic text, which is
manifestly incomplete here, but they appear in the Septuagint, in the Targum
Yonatan, and in the Peshitta.

14. *And she drove them with a peg into the wall*. "Into the wall" is supplied
from the Septuagint. The driving of the peg recalls Jael and Sisera, but in this
instance the woman's deadly intent is not realized.

and the web. And she said to him, "You only say 'I love you,' but your   15
heart is not with me. Three times now you have mocked me and have
not told me in what lies your great power." And it happened when she   16
badgered him with her words day after day and beleaguered him, that
he was vexed unto the death. And he told her all that was in his heart,   17
and he said, "No razor has touched my head, for I have been a nazirite
of God from my mother's womb. Were I shaven, my power would turn
away from me and I would be weakened and become like any man."
And Delilah saw that he had told her all that was in his heart, and she   18
sent and called the Philistine overlords, saying, "Come up, for he has
told me all that is in his heart." And the Philistine overlords came up
to her and brought the silver in their hand. And she put him to sleep   19
on her knees and called the man and shaved his head's seven tresses,
and she began to torture him, and his power turned away from him.

---

15. *You only say 'I love you.'* She uses the same feminine argument as Samson's
first wife.

Three times now. The folktale pattern of three times—in this case, three
times with a fourth time that swerves to a new outcome—is made an object of
deliberate attention. The story as a whole is organized around threes—three
women, and the multiples of three killed by Samson.

17. *all that was in his heart.* Literally, "all his heart."

19. *she put him to sleep on her knees.* This is, of course, necessary so that his
hair can be cut, but it is also a powerful image of the seductive woman lulling
the mighty hero and reducing him to a baby in her lap.

called the man and shaved his head's seven tresses. The verb "shaved" is conjugated in the feminine. Some emend it to a masculine form; others claim, with
little philological warrant, that it means "caused him to be shaved." It makes
more sense to assume that Delilah, who can't very well move with Samson
asleep on her knees, calls the man to bring her a razor so that she can then
shave Samson's head. Her performance of the act herself is thematically and
psychologically apt: the seductress cuts away the source of Samson's potency.

she began to torture him. She is the very first to torment him in an appropriately sadistic move.

20 And she said, "Philistines are upon you, Samson!" And he awoke from
his sleep, and said, "I will go out as all the other times and shake myself
loose," but he did not know that the LORD had turned away from him.
21 And the Philistines seized him and gouged out his eyes. And they brought
him down to Gaza and bound him in fetters, and he was put to grinding
22 in the prison. And the hair of his head began to grow as soon as it was
23 shaven. And the Philistine overlords had gathered to offer a great sacrifice
to Dagon their god and to celebrate, and they said, "Our god has given
24 into our hand Samson our enemy." And the people saw him and praised
their god, for they said, "Our god has given into our hand our enemy, the
destroyer of our land, him who brought down many victims among us."
25 And it happened when they were merry that they said, "Call Samson,
that he may play for us." And they called Samson from the prison, and he
26 played before them, and they set him between the pillars. And Samson
said to the lad who was holding his hand, "Let me rest and feel the pillars
27 on which the temple stands, that I may lean on them." And the temple
was filled with men and women, and all the Philistine overlords were
there, and on the roof about three thousand men and women watching as

---

20. *as all the other times*. The times motif recurs here (the Hebrew, *kefa'am
befa'am*, doubles the word "time").

21. *gouged out his eyes*. A Freudian would see an upward displacement of castration in this act, but it should be noted that these were the eyes that saw the
women who led to all the trouble. Gouging out the eyes was also a punishment
for a rebellious vassal (compare the blinding of Zedekiah by the Babylonians,
2 Kings 25:7).

25. *that he may play for us*. The playing might be dancing or, more likely, blindly
stumbling about, while the audience laughs (the same Hebrew verb as "play").

26. *Let me rest*. This might also be construed to mean "lead me."

27. *all the Philistine overlords were there*. So that Samson's vengeance may be
complete, the rulers of the five Philistine towns, the very men who plotted his
blinding and captivity, are present.
    on the roof about three thousand men and women. Again, we have a multiple
of three. It is clearly implied that there are many more people in the main space
of the temple.

Samson played. And Samson called to the LORD and said "My Master,   28
LORD, recall me, pray, and strengthen me just this time, O God, that I
may avenge myself in one act of vengeance from the Philistines for my
two eyes." And Samson grasped the two central pillars on which the   29
temple stood and pushed against them, one with his right hand and
one with his left hand. And Samson said, "Let me die with the Philis-   30
tines!" and he pushed powerfully, and the temple fell on the overlords
and on all the people who were in it. And the dead that he killed in his
death were more than he had killed in his life. And his kinsmen and   31
all his father's household came down and bore him off and buried him
between Zorah and Eshtaol in the grave of Manoah his father. And he
had led Israel twenty years.

---

28. *just this time*. At the penultimate moment of the story, the thematically
fraught word *pa'am*, "time," appears again. It shows, pointedly, the same root
as the verb "drive" or "pound" in 13:25 that marks the beginning of Samson's
narrative.

    that I may avenge myself in one act of vengeance from the Philistines. It is true
that Samson in his last moment turns in prayer to God—perhaps feeling that
his great strength has returned but not being quite sure and in any case rec-
ognizing that its ultimate source is God. But even now, his motive is personal
vengeance: one sees why the messenger of the LORD prophesied that Samson
would no more than "begin" to rescue Israel from the Philistines.

30. *And the dead that he killed in his death were more than he had killed in
his life*. Samson's career as an Israelite champion ends in an act of wholesale
destruction in which he, too, dies, like fire that consumes everything in its path
and eventually itself as well.

CHAPTER 17

There was a man from the high country of Ephraim, and his name was
2 Micayhu. And he said to his mother, "The eleven hundred silver shekels
that were taken from you, and you yourself uttered a curse and even said
it in my hearing—look, the silver is with me, it is I who took it." And his
3 mother said, "Blessed are you, my son, to the LORD." And he gave back
the eleven hundred silver shekels to his mother, and his mother said,
"I had solemnly dedicated the silver to the LORD from my hand to my
son, to make a statue and molten image, and now I give it back to you."

---

1. *There was a man from the high country of Ephraim.* This formula signals
the beginning of a story that does not involve a judge. The two narratives that
unfold respectively in Chapters 17–18 and 19–21 constitute a kind of epilogue
to the Book of Judges, illustrating the general condition of moral and political
anarchy in the period before the monarchy.

Micayhu. Later in the story, the name appears without the theophoric ending
as "Micah."

2. *The eleven hundred silver shekels.* Rashi shrewdly observes that this is the precise amount that each of the Philistine overlords paid Delilah: "The episodes
are linked through the evil silver equal in amount, and in both cases it is a kind
of silver that leads to disaster."

you yourself uttered a curse. She pronounced a curse on whoever stole the
silver.

look, the silver is with me. He evidently is frightened by the curse and so is
ready to admit he has "taken" (he avoids saying "stolen") the silver and will now
give it back.

Blessed are you. Ehrlich suggests that by these words she seeks to reverse
the curse.

3. *to make a statue and molten image.* Amit argues that this is a hendyadis—a
statue that is a molten image, though in 18:20 they are separated syntactically

And he gave the silver to his mother, and his mother took two hundred 4
silver shekels and gave them to the silversmith, and he made out of it a
statue and molten image. And they were in the house of Micayhu. And 5
the man Micah had a house God, and he made an ephod and teraphim
and installed one of his sons, and he became a priest for him. In those 6
days there was no king in Israel, every man did what was right in his
eyes. And there was a lad from the town of Bethlehem in Judah from 7
the clan of Judah, and he was a Levite, and he sojourned there. And the 8

---

by ephod and teraphim. In any case, though the mother dedicates the silver to
the LORD, this expression has a strong association with idolatry.

and now I give it back to you. If the received text is correct, the silver passes
back and forth: he takes it from her, gives it back to her; she gives it to him; he
gives it back to her. This rapid exchange may be intentional: it is "hot" treasure,
first stolen by the son from his mother, then earmarked for a questionable end.

4. *two hundred silver shekels.* Either this is the payment for the silversmith's
work and the remaining nine hundred shekels are used to fashion the statue,
or she has quietly pocketed nine hundred, despite her pious vow.

5. *an ephod and teraphim.* These are both divinatory devices, the latter term
used elsewhere to designate household idols. Micah is clearly setting up shop
in his little house of God, probably with the intention of exacting payment for
rendering sundry cultic services.

6. *every man did what was right in his eyes.* The last phrase here is the same one
used in 14:3 by Samson in relation to the Philistine woman he sees in Timnah,
but there it is translated as "pleased me" because the character is referring to
a woman he finds attractive.

7. *Bethlehem in Judah.* There was another Bethlehem ("house of bread") in
Zebulun.

from the clan of Judah. This looks like a contradiction because he is a Levite.
It has been proposed that the story harks back to an early moment in Israelite
history when the Levites' tribal identity may not have crystallized and "Levite"
might be the designation of a cultic officiant.

sojourned. This is a term of temporary residence, and as the story unfolds, it
is evident that the Levite is an itinerant.

man went from the town, from Bethlehem in Judah, to sojourn wherever
he chanced, and he came to the high country of Ephraim to the house

9 of Micah, wending his way. And Micah said to him, "From where do
you come?" And the Levite said to him, "I am from Bethlehem in Judah,

10 and I go to sojourn wherever I chance." And Micah said to him, "Stay
with me, and be father and priest for me, and I on my part will give you
ten silver shekels a year and a set of clothing and your board." And the

11 Levite went, and the Levite agreed to stay with the man, and the lad

12 became for him like one of his sons. And Micah installed the Levite,

13 and the lad became a priest for him, and he was in Micah's house. And
Micah said, "Now I know that the LORD will deal well with me, for the
Levite has become my priest."

---

10. *father and priest.* "Father" here means someone in a position of authority. In
fact, the Levite is a "lad," a generation younger than Micah, as one may infer
from verse 12. Micah had already installed one of his sons to act as priest,
but he prefers to have the Levite because he is a cultic professional (whether
hereditary or not is unclear).

ten silver shekels a year. If this is a reasonable annual income, the amount of
eleven hundred shekels would have been enormous.

And the Levite went. This brief clause (two Hebrew words) seems extrane-
ous, and some textual critics propose deleting it.

12. *and he was in Micah's house.* The blandness of the verb "to be" here—not
"he dwelled/stayed" or "he sojourned"—introduces a hint of ambiguity about
his relation to Micah's house. In the event, he will betray Micah and move on.

CHAPTER 18

In those days there was no king in Israel. And in those days the tribe 1
of the Danites was seeking an estate for itself in which to dwell, for till
that day no estate had fallen to it in the midst of the tribes of Israel.
And the Danites sent out from their clans, from the pick of them, five 2
men who were valiant warriors from Zorah and from Eshtaol to spy
out the land and to search it, and they said to them, "Go, search the
land." And they came to the high country of Ephraim to Micah's house,
and they spent the night there. They were at Micah's house, and they 3
recognized the voice of the Levite lad and turned aside there and said
to him, "Who brought you here, and what are you doing in this place,
and what do you have here?" And he said to them, "Thus and so has 4
Micah done for me, and he has hired me, and I have become a priest

---

1. *till that day no estate had fallen to it in the midst of the tribes of Israel.* This
formulation gives the impression that no tribal territory was assigned to the
Danites. The actual case was that they were not able to hold their own against
their Philistine neighbors and the local Canaanites and so were driven to
migrate. The Philistine pressure on Dan is evident in the Samson narrative,
which immediately precedes this story.

3. *they recognized the voice of the Levite lad.* Given his itinerancy, they may have
actually run across him somewhere else in the south. Others conjecture that
they detect a Judean accent.

4. *Thus and so has Micah done for me.* This summarizing formula, which one
would not find in novelistic dialogue, is occasionally introduced into biblical
dialogue. "Thus and so" obviously refers to the Levite's appointment as priest
with the annual stipend.

5 for him." And they said to him, "Inquire, pray, of God, that we may
6 know whether our way on which we go will prosper." And the priest
said to them, "Go in peace—before the LORD is your way on which
7 you go." And the five men went and came to Laish, and they saw the
people within it dwelling secure in the manner of the Sidonians, quiet
and secure, and no one in the land troubled them, and there was no
heir to the throne, and they were far-off from the Sidonians, nor did
8 they have any dealings with other people. And they came back to their
kinsmen in Zorah and Eshtaol, and their kinsmen said to them, "How
9 is it with you?" And they said, "Arise, and let us go up against them, for
we have seen the land, and, look, it is very good, and you remain silent!
10 Do not be idle about going to come and take hold of the land. When
you come, you will come to a people that dwells secure, and the land
is spacious—why, God has given it into your hand!—a place in which
11 nothing on earth is lacking." And the six hundred men from the tribe
of the Danites, from Zorah and Eshtaol, girded in battle gear, journeyed

---

5. *Inquire, pray, of God.* This idiom indicates inquiry of an oracle; the probable
instrument would have been the ephod.

6. *before the* LORD *is your way on which you go.* Though the burden of this clause
is that God will favor their endeavor, the formulation is a bit vague and even
ambiguous: like oracles everywhere, the Levite is hedging his bets.

7. *dwelling secure in the manner of the Sidonians.* The inhabitants of the Phoenician city of Sidon, to the north on the Mediterranean coast, were evidently
thought to live relatively free of fear from foreign attacks.
    *they were far-off from the Sidonians, nor did they have any dealings with other
people.* Though the gist of these two clauses is that Laish was isolated and had
no allies on which to rely, the wording—especially of the second clause—is
somewhat obscure.

10. *a people that dwells secure.* As the use of this phrase in verse 7 makes clear,
the gist is that this people lives in a sense of security, not suspecting that they
will be attacked.

11. *six hundred men.* As the recurrence of this number in military contexts in
the Book of Samuel suggests, this is the fixed size of a combat unit, something
like a battalion.

from there. And they went up and camped at Kiriath-Jearim in Judah. 12
Therefore have they called that place the Camp of Dan to this day—
there it is, west of Kiriath-Jearim. And they passed on from there to 13
the high country of Ephraim and came to Micah's house. And the five 14
men who had gone to spy out the land of Laish spoke up and said to
their kinsmen, "Did you know that in these houses there are an ephod
and teraphim and a statue and molten image? And now, know what
you should do." And they turned aside there and came to the house 15
of the Levite lad, at Micah's house, and asked him how he fared. And 16
the six hundred men girded with their battle gear, who were from the
Danites, stationed themselves at the entrance of the gate. And the five 17
men who had gone to spy out the land came in there, took the statue
and the ephod and the teraphim and the molten image, and the priest
was stationed at the entrance to the gate, and the six hundred men
girded with battle gear. And the former group had come into Micah's 18
house and taken the statue and the ephod and the teraphim and the
molten image. And the priest said to them, "What are you doing?"
And they said to him, "Be quiet! Put your hand over your mouth and 19
go with us and be father and priest for us. Is it better for you to be

---

14. *these houses*. From the plural, one infers that Micah's house was part of a
small compound.

And now, know what you should do. Anticipating the conquest of Laish, they
want to acquire the paraphernalia to set up a cult there after they take the town.

16. *the six hundred men . . . stationed themselves at the entrance of the gate*. The
five spies, whom the Levite already knows, are sent in to parlay with him, while
the armed enforcers wait at the gate.

17. *took the statue and the ephod and the teraphim and the molten image*. They
immediately seize the cultic objects, not asking the Levite, who is in no position to resist.

18. *And the former group*. The Hebrew says merely "and these," but it has to
refer to the five spies in contradistinction to the six hundred men.

19. *Put your hand over your mouth and go with us and be father and priest for us*.
They follow an implied threat—shut up, if you know what is good for you—
with the inducement of an offered position.

priest for the house of one man or to be priest for a tribe and clan in
20 Israel?" And the priest was pleased, and he took the ephod and the
21 teraphim and the statue, and joined the troops. And they turned and
went, and they put before them the little ones and the cattle and the
22 heavy goods. They had gone a distance from Micah's house when the
people in the houses that were by Micah's house were mustered, and
23 they overtook the Danites. And they called out to the Danites, and they
turned round and said to Micah, "What's the matter with you that you
24 have mustered?" And he said, "My god that I made you have taken and
the priest, and you have gone off. And what else do I have, and how
25 is this you say to me, 'What's the matter with you'?" And the Danites
said to him, "Don't raise your voice to us, lest embittered men assault

---

20. *And the priest was pleased.* Nobody in this story, beginning with Micah and
his mother, has noble motives. The Levite immediately recognizes that this
new position, priest for a tribe, is a considerable advancement, no doubt with
a larger salary, and so he happily colludes in the theft of the cultic articles.

21. *they put before them the little ones and the cattle and the heavy goods.* Only
now do we learn that the six hundred warriors are not just a raiding party but
the first wave of a tribal migration, having brought with them their children
(and presumably their wives) and their possessions. They put all these in front
of them because the attack they anticipate would come from the rear, from a
pursuing party of Micah and his men.

24. *My god that I made.* His language here, in keeping with "statue" and "molten
image," is frankly pagan. No one in this story appears to be a serious monotheist. Though the narrative was composed late (see the comment on verse
30), the whole bizarre story appears to be an authentic reflection of an early
moment in pre-monotheistic Israelite history when the exclusive worship of
YHWH was not generally established.

25. *embittered men.* This is their condition because they have been displaced
from their tribal territory and are for the moment homeless.

you and you lose your life and the lives of your household." And the 26
Danites went on their way, and Micah saw that they were stronger than
he, and he turned and went back to his house. And they had taken what 27
Micah made and the priest that he had. And they came against Laish,
against a quiet and secure people, and they struck them down with the
sword, and the town they burned in fire. And there was none to save it, 28
for it was far-off from Sidon, nor did they have any dealings with other
people. And it was in the valley of Beth-Rehob. And they rebuilt the
town and dwelled in it. And they called the town Dan, like the name of 29
Dan their forefather who was born to Israel, but Laish was the name of

---

26. *Micah saw that they were stronger than he.* The story plays out through force.
Micah can scarcely contend with six hundred heavily armed ruthless men who
have just threatened to kill him and his whole household, and so he has to let
them keep the precious objects they have stolen from him, which he had fashioned with silver he originally stole from his mother.

27. *they struck them down with the sword.* No moral considerations are involved.
These people have attractive land; Dan needs land; the Danites slaughter the
inhabitants of Laish and build their own town there.

29. *like the name.* The Masoretic text reads "in the name," but many Hebrew
manuscripts show the standard idiom "like the name."
    who was born to Israel. The reference is to Jacob, not to the nation.

30 the town at first. And the Danites set up the statue for themselves, and
    Jonathan son of Gershom son of Moses, he and his sons were priests for
31 the tribe of the Danites till the day the land went into exile. And they
    set for themselves Micah's statue that he had made all the days that the
    house of God was in Shiloh.

---

30. *Jonathan son of Gershom son of Moses.* At the very end, we are given the
name and genealogy of the Levite. The Masoretic text inserts a superscript *nun*
in *Moshe*, Moses, turning it into *Menashe*, Manasseh, but this can't be right
because Gershom was the son of Moses and Manasseh is not a priestly tribe.
Rashi aptly explains the orthographic oddity: "Out of respect for Moses, a *nun*
is inscribed in order to change the name." The genealogy marks a steep decline:
Moses's own grandson is a base sacerdotal mercenary, officiating in a cult that
is at the very least semi-pagan. Placing the Levite just two generations after
Moses would mean that the whole story is supposed to take place very early,
at the beginning of the twelfth century BCE, a temporal location that has the
inconvenient consequence of putting the Danite migration before the time of
Samson, a Danite living in the south near the Philistines.

   till the day the land went into exile. The reference is to the exile of the northern kingdom of Israel by the Assyrians in 721 BCE, which means that the story,
at least in its final formulation, had to be composed after that date, unless this
final notation is a later editorial addition.

31. *all the days that the house of God was in Shiloh.* The anomalous introduction of this reference to the Shiloh sanctuary at the very end of the story is
in all likelihood, as Yair Zakovitch has argued, an editorial move to link the
material here with the beginning of the Book of Samuel, where Shiloh plays
a central role.

CHAPTER 19

And it happened in those days, when there was no king in Israel, that a Levite man was sojourning in the far reaches of the high country of Ephraim, and he took for himself a concubine-woman from Bethlehem in Judah. And his concubine played the whore against him and went away from him to her father's house in Bethlehem in Judah, and she was there for a while, four months. And her husband arose and went after her to speak to her heart to bring her back, and his lad was with him and a pair of donkeys. And she brought him into her father's house, and the young woman's father saw him and rejoiced to greet

---

1. *a Levite.* Though nothing further is made in the story of his status as Levite, and no reference is made to any sacerdotal function performed by him, there is an obvious link with the morally dubious Levite lad in the immediately preceding story. Hereditary connection with the cult is clearly no guarantee of character.

2. *played the whore against him.* Given that a man and his concubine are involved, this could refer to sexual infidelity, but the fact that she goes off to her father's house and that he wants her back argues for the metaphorical sense of this idiom: she pulled away from him, no longer wanted to remain with him.

3. *his lad was with him and a pair of donkeys.* Both servant and donkey will have a role to play as the story darkens.
   rejoiced to greet him. The rejoicing may be from the father's perception that his daughter and the Levite will now be reconciled, but there is an odd emphasis in the story that the father is somehow smitten with the Levite, to the exclusion of concern for his daughter.
   the young woman's. The fact that she is young, a *na'arah*, will make what ensues all the more painful.

4 him. And his father-in-law, the young woman's father, entreated him, and he stayed with him three days, and they ate and drank and lodged
5 there. And it happened on the fourth day that they rose early in the morning, and he got up to go, and the young woman's father said to his son-in-law, "Refresh yourself with a morsel of bread, and afterward you
6 may both go." And the two of them sat and ate together, and the young woman's father said to the man, "Consent, pray, to spend the night, that
7 you may enjoy good cheer." And the man got up to go, and his father-
8 in-law pressed him and he stayed and spent the night there. And he rose early in the morning on the fifth day to go, and the young woman's father said, "Refresh yourself, pray." And they lingered till the day was
9 waning, and the two of them ate. And the man got up to go, he and his concubine and his lad. And his father-in-law, the young woman's father, said to him, "Look, the day is declining toward evening. Spend the night, pray. Look, the day is gone. Spend the night here, that you may enjoy good cheer, and tomorrow you both will rise early on your
10 way, and you will go to your tent." But the man did not want to spend the night, and he arose and went and came opposite Jebus, which is to say, Jerusalem, and with him were the pair of saddled donkeys and
11 his concubine with him. They were by Jebus, and the day was very far spent, and his lad said to his master, "Come, pray, and let us turn aside

---

5. *a morsel of bread.* This is a polite understatement for a full meal.

6. *enjoy good cheer.* This mood idiom usually implies feasting and drinking.

7. *his father-in-law pressed him and he stayed.* In this story that turns on the refusal and then violation of hospitality, the father-in-law's importuning of his guest looks in its exaggeration like a grotesque parody of hospitality.

8. *the two of them ate.* The Levite and his father-in-law. The concubine is not part of the feast.

8.–9. *the day was waning . . . the day is declining toward evening.* This proliferation of expressions for the approach of night underscores the zone of danger into which the Levite and his concubine will enter as night falls.

10. *the pair of saddled donkeys.* At the end of the story, one of them will carry a grisly load on its back.

to this town of the Jebusites that we may spend the night there." And his   12
master said to him, "We shall not turn aside to a town of strangers who
are not of the Israelites. Let us pass on as far as Gibeah." And he said to   13
his lad, "Come and let us approach one of the places, and we shall spend
the night in Gibeah or in Ramah. And they passed on and went, and the   14
sun set on them by Gibeah, which is Benjamin's. And they turned aside   15
to come to spend the night, and he came and sat in the town square, but
there was no man to take them in to spend the night. And, look, an old   16
man was coming from his work in the field in the evening. And the man
was from the high country of Ephraim and he was sojourning in Gibeah,
but the people of the place were Benjaminites. And he raised his eyes   17
and saw the wayfaring man in the town square, and the old man said,
"Where are you going and from where do you come?" And he said to   18
him, "We are passing from Bethlehem in Judah to the far reaches of the
high country of Ephraim—I am from there, and I have gone to Bethlehem in Judah—and I am going to the house of the LORD, but no man is

---

12. *We shall not turn aside to a town of strangers.* In the event, this consideration
proves to be a bitter delusion because Israelites will behave more barbarically
to them than any strangers.

13. *And he said to his lad.* The repetition of the formula for introducing speech
indicates that the servant is perplexed or disturbed by what his master says but
has no way of answering him: why, he must be thinking, does he insist that we
move on when the only reasonable thing to do would be to seek refuge in this
nearby Jebusite town?

15. *but there was no man to take them in.* This is the first signal of the network
of allusions to the story of the visit of the two divine messengers to Sodom in
Genesis 19.

16. *the man was from the high country of Ephraim.* Pointedly, the sole person
in Gibeah prepared to honor the civilized obligation of hospitality is not a
Benjaminite.

18. *to the house of the LORD.* This is a little odd because there is no indication that he lives in a sanctuary back in the far reaches of the high country of
Ephraim. Also, instead of the preposition *'el,* "to," the text shows an accusative
particle, *'et.* Many, following the Septuagint, emend the two Hebrew words
here to read, "to my house."

19 taking me in. And there is even straw and provender for our donkeys,
   and there is even bread and wine for me and for your slave-girl and for
20 the lad who is with your servant. Nothing is lacking." And the old man
   said to him. "It is well with you. Only all your lack is upon me. Only do
21 not spend the night in the square." And he brought him into his house
   and mixed fodder for the donkeys, and they washed their feet and ate
22 and drank. They were making good cheer when, look, the men of the
   town, worthless men, drew round the house, pounding on the door, and
   they said to the old man who was master of the house, saying, "Bring
23 out the man that has come to your house that we may know him." And
   the man who was master of the house went out to them and said, "No,
   my brothers, no, pray, do no harm. Seeing that this man has come into
24 my house, do not do this scurrilous thing. Here are my virgin daughter

---

20. *Only all your lack is upon me.* The old man refuses the Levite's offer to bring
his own provisions into the house.

Only do not spend the night in the square. The old man knows how dangerous
it would be to spend the night outside exposed to the lubricious townsmen. The
parallel with the story of Lot and his two daughters begins to become explicit.

22. *They were making good cheer.* As before, this is a mood idiom associated
with eating and drinking.

worthless men. This judgmental phrase is added to the verbatim quotation
from Genesis 19.

Bring out the man . . . that we may know him. This is a direct quotation of
Genesis 19:5, except that there the plural "men" appears because there are two
of them. The gang-rapists' preference here is heterosexual since they would
probably have been aware that the stranger was traveling with a young woman.

23. *No, my brothers, no, pray, do no harm.* These words are quoted from Genesis
19:8.

scurrilous thing. The Hebrew *nevalah* is a term generally used for shameful
sexual acts.

24. *Here are my virgin daughter and his concubine.* This replicates Lot's offer
of his two virgin daughters to the rapists (Genesis 19:8). One does not know

and his concubine. Let me, pray, bring them out, and rape them and do
to them whatever you want. But to this man do not do this scurrilous
act." But the men did not want to listen to him, and the man seized his 25
concubine and brought her out to them. And they knew her and abused
her all night long till morning, and they let her go at daybreak. And the 26
woman came toward morning and fell at the entrance to the house of

---

which is the more outrageous proposal, offering his daughter to be gang-raped
or his guest's concubine, over whom he surely does not have jurisdiction.

rape them and do to them whatever you want. The parallel text in Genesis
19:8 lacks the brutally direct "rape" (or "abuse"). Its insertion makes us wonder
all the more what kind of father the old man is and what kind of host he is to
the young woman, whom he appears to regard as a piece of disposable property.

25. *the man seized his concubine and brought her out to them.* In the event, it is
the Levite, prepared to do anything to save his own skin, who thrusts his concubine into the clutches of the rapists. No action follows on the old man's offer
of his daughter to the rapists. Perhaps, seeing the Levite thrust his concubine
outside, he concludes that one victim will suffice.

And they knew her and abused her all night long till morning. The source story
in Genesis takes place in legendary times when there was supernatural intervention in human affairs. The two strangers, because they are divine beings,
blind the would-be rapists and secure the safety of those within the house. In
the latter-day era of the present story, there is no miraculous intervention—the
female victim is gang-raped all night long and dies at daybreak from the pro-
longed violent abuse.

26. *fell at the entrance to the house.* She expires in this liminal space, her arms
stretching out across the threshold of the house where she might have been
safe, her body sprawled on the ground before the house, which is the outside
zone of anarchic and destructive lust.

27 the man where her master was as the light was coming up. And her
master arose in the morning and opened the doors of the house and
went out to go on his way. And, look, the woman, his concubine, was
28 fallen at the entrance of the house, her hands on the threshold. And he
said to her, "Get up, and let us go." And there was no answer. And he
29 took her on his donkey, and the man arose and went to his place. And
he came into his house and took a cleaver and held his concubine and
cut her up limb by limb into twelve pieces, and he sent her through
30 all the territory of Israel. And so whoever saw her would say, "There
has not been nor has there been seen such a thing from the day the
Israelites came up from the land of Egypt to this day. Pay heed about
her, take counsel, and speak."

---

27. *her master.* Only at the end of the story is he called, repeatedly and almost
ironically, "her master."

arose . . . and opened the doors of the house and went out to go on his way. He
is all brisk business and seems unconcerned about the fate of his concubine.

And, look, the woman, his concubine. Only now does he look down and see
her brutalized body, identifying her first as a woman and then as his concubine.

28. *Get up, and let us go.* He at first does not realize that she is dead. This
brusque command reveals his utter moral callousness: he expects the woman,
after having been gang-raped hour after hour, to pick herself up quickly and
join him on the journey back.

he took her on his donkey. At first, we may think he means to give her a
decent burial near his home.

29. *took a cleaver and held his concubine and cut her up limb by limb into
twelve pieces.* Although the intention is to trigger outrage in all the tribes—the
number twelve is automatic, but it would actually be eleven, because Benjamin
is excluded—over the atrocity that has been perpetrated, the act itself is barbaric, and in biblical terms, it is a desecration of the human body. It should be
said, moreover, that the Levite until this point has himself been singularly lacking in outrage over the gang-rape of his concubine. In any case, the butchering
of her body completes the set of images of mutilation and other violence done
to the body that begins in the opening chapter of Judges with the chopping off
of the thumbs and big toes of the captured king Adoni-Bezek.

CHAPTER 20

$\mathcal{A}$nd all the Israelites went out, and the community assembled as one   1
man from Dan to Beersheba in the land of Gilead before the LORD at
Mizpah. And all the leaders of the people, all the tribes of Israel in   2
the assembly of God's people, took their stance, four hundred thousand sword-wielding foot soldiers. And the Benjaminites heard that   3
the Israelites had gone up to Mizpah. And the Israelites said, "Speak!
How did this evil come about?" And the Levite man, husband of the   4
murdered woman, answered and said, "I came with my concubine to

---

1. *as one man.* This phrase recurs in the story, emphasizing the solidarity of the
eleven tribes in their opposition to Benjamin.

2. *four hundred thousand sword-wielding foot soldiers.* Although military numbers
in all these stories are exaggerated, this figure is especially fantastic. At no time
in the history of ancient Israel could the nation have deployed this large an army.

4. *husband of the murdered woman.* Only now does the narrative spell out that
the night-long gang-rape is tantamount to murder.
   I came with my concubine. The Hebrew uses "I came" in the singular, followed by a second grammatical subject of the verb "my concubine," a form that
indicates that the first subject of the verb is primary. The Levite remains true
to character, making the woman ancillary to himself.

5 Gibeah to spend the night. And the notables of Gibeah rose against
me and surrounded the house upon me at night. Me they thought
6 to kill, and my concubine they raped, and she died. And I seized my
concubine and cut her up and sent her through all the lands of Israel's
7 estate, for they did a foul and scurrilous thing in Israel. Look, you are
8 all Israelites. Offer a word of counsel here." And the whole people
rose as one man, saying, "We will not go each to his tent and we will
9 not turn aside each to his home! And now, this is the thing we shall do
10 to Gibeah: we shall go up against it by lot. And we shall take ten men
out of a hundred from all the tribes of Israel and a hundred out of a
thousand and a thousand out of ten thousand to take provisions for
the troops, to do for those coming to Benjamin's Gibeah, according to
11 all the scurrilous thing they did in Israel." And all the men of Israel
12 gathered at the town, joined as one man. And the tribes of Israel sent
throughout the tribe of Benjamin, saying, "What is this evil that has
13 come about among you? And now, give over the worthless men who are
in Gibeah that we may put them to death and root out the evil from

---

5. *Me they thought to kill.* In fact, the men of Gibeah sought to have sex with
him, a detail the Levite prefers not to mention, substituting for it a purported
direct threat to his life.

    and my concubine they raped. He says nothing about the fact that he himself
thrust her out the door into the hands of the rapists.

6. *I seized my concubine and cut her up.* He has already said that she died, but
this way of putting it creates the macabre impression of his cutting up the
person, not the corpse.

7. *Offer a word of counsel here.* Obviously, the word he assumes his tale will
elicit is a resolution of vengeance.

10. *ten men out of a hundred.* Though it seems evident that 10 percent of
the assembled troops are to provide logistical support to the warriors, the
wording—ten out of a hundred, a hundred out of a thousand, a thousand out
of ten thousand—is a bit confusing.

    for those coming to Benjamin's Gibeah. The translation follows the reading
in the Septuagint. The Masoretic text looks garbled here. "for their coming."

12. *the tribe of Benjamin.* The received text shows, illogically, a plural, "tribes,"
but both the Septuagint and the Vulgate have a singular noun.

Israel." But the Benjaminites did not want to heed the voice of their
Israelite brothers. And the Benjaminites gathered from the towns at 14
Gibeah to go out to battle with the Israelites. And the Benjaminites 15
from the towns mustered on that day twenty-six thousand sword-
wielding men, besides the inhabitants of Gibeah who mustered seven
hundred picked men. From all these troops there were seven hundred 16
picked men, left-handers; every one of them could sling a stone at a
hair and not miss. And the men of Israel, except for Benjamin, mus- 17
tered four hundred thousand sword-wielding men, every one of them
a man of war. And they arose and went up to Bethel and inquired of 18
God, and the Israelites said, "Who shall go up first for us in battle
with the Benjaminites?" and the LORD said, "Judah first." And the 19
Israelites arose in the morning and encamped against Gibeah. And the 20
men of Israel went out to battle with Benjamin, and the men of Israel

---

13. *But the Benjaminites did not want to heed the voice of their Israelite brothers.*
The Israelites at first sought to punish only the perpetrators of the murderous
sex-crime. The refusal of the Benjaminites to hand them over then sets the
stage for the bloody civil war.

14. *gathered from the towns.* These would have to be the sundry towns besides
Gibeah that were in the tribal territory of Benjamin.

15. *twenty-six thousand sword-wielding men.* There is an unresolved discrepancy
between this number and verse 35, where the total number of Benjaminite
fighting men is given as 25,000.

16. *left-handers.* This might have been a genetic trait common among the
Benjaminites, or they might have trained themselves to use their left hand in
combat, like the great tennis player, Rafael Nadal. One recalls that the Benjaminite Ehud used his left-handed prowess to take Eglon by surprise.
    every one of them could sling a stone at a hair and not miss. Thus the Benjamin-
ites, though vastly outnumbered, are formidable warriors. The large casualties
they inflict on the first two days of battle may be because they can accurately
strike their enemies from a distance, with a weapon that has a greater range
than a spear and can be deployed more mobily than a bow.

18. *inquired of God.* It was standard procedure throughout the ancient Near
East to inquire of an oracle before battle.
    Judah first. The oracle is extremely terse, and it offers no guidance as to how
to conduct the battle.

21 were arrayed for battle with them at Gibeah. And the Benjaminites
    sallied forth from Gibeah, and they laid waste among Israel on that
22 day twenty-two thousand men. And the troops of the men of Israel
    summoned their strength and once again were arrayed for battle in the
23 place where they had been arrayed on the first day. And the Israelites
    went up and wept before the LORD till evening, and they inquired of
    the LORD, saying "Shall I once again join battle with my Benjaminite
24 brother?" And the LORD said, "Go up against him." And the Israelites
25 drew near to the Benjaminites on the second day. And Benjamin sal-
    lied forth to meet them from Gibeah on the second day, and they
    laid waste among the Israelites another eighteen thousand men, all
26 of them sword-wielding. And the Israelites and all the troops went up
    and came to Bethel and wept, and they sat there before the LORD and
    fasted on that day till evening, and they offered up burnt offerings and
27 well-being sacrifices before the LORD. And the Israelites inquired of
    the LORD—and in those days the Ark of God's Covenant was there,
28 and Phineas son of Eleazar son of Aaron was in attendance before Him
    in those days—saying, "Shall I once again sally forth in battle with
    my Benjaminite brother or shall I leave off?" And the LORD said, "Go
29 up, for tomorrow I shall give him into your hand." And Israel placed

---

21. *laid waste.* This is an unusual idiom for killing enemies in battle (the literal
sense is: "waste to the ground"). It is possible that the usage, repeated several
times in the story, is intended to evoke an association of cutting off progeny
because it is precisely the idiom used to describe Onan's practice of coitus
interruptus (Genesis 38:9). The question of progeny and the survival of Benjamin becomes urgent in the next chapter.

23. *Go up against him.* Again, the oracle offers no counsel or prediction about
the battle.

27. *in those days the Ark of God's Covenant was there.* This clause and the next,
which runs through the first half of verse 28, are an editorial interpolation
intended to explain to a later audience why the Israelites had come to Bethel
to inquire of the oracle.

28. *Go up, for tomorrow I shall give him into your hand.* Following the familiar
folktale pattern of three repetitions with a reversal the third time, God now

ambushers round about Gibeah. And the Israelites went up against 30
the Benjaminites on the third day and were arrayed against Gibeah
as on the times before. And the Benjaminites sallied forth to meet 31
the troops, they were drawn away from the town, and they began to
strike down from the troops, as on the times before, on the highways,
one going up to Bethel and one to Gibeah, about thirty men of Israel.
And the Benjaminites thought, "They are routed before us as before." 32
But the Israelites had said, "Let us flee and draw them away from the
town to the highways." And all the men of Israel had arisen from their 33
place and were arrayed in Baal-Tamar, and the Israelite ambush was
emerging from its place west of Gibeah. And ten thousand picked men 34
from all Israel came opposite Gibeah, and the battle was fierce, but the
Benjaminites did not know that harm was about to touch them. And 35
the LORD routed Benjamin before Israel, and the Israelites laid waste
among Benjamin on that day twenty-five thousand one hundred men,
all of them sword-wielding. And the Benjaminites saw that they were 36
routed. And the men of Israel gave ground before Benjamin, for they
trusted the ambush that they had set for Gibeah. And the ambushers 37
rushed out and assaulted Gibeah, and the ambushers drew together

---

assures the Israelites that this time they will be victorious. Some interpreters see a contradiction between God's granting the victory and its achieve-
ment through a military stratagem—the ambush and the false retreat—but
this account is actually in keeping with the system of dual causation one often
finds in biblical narrative: events are attributed to divine intervention but are
implemented by human initiative.

31. *the highways.* Unlike *derekh*, which is any kind of road or way, these *mesilot*
are paved roads.

about thirty men. In this third battle, the casualties they inflict before they
are trapped and overwhelmed are insignificant.

37. *the ambushers drew together and struck the whole town with the edge of the
sword.* The stratagem used here to capture and destroy the town is identical
with the one deployed by the Israelite forces against Ai in Joshua 8. Many
scholars think that the writer in Joshua drew on this story.

38 and struck the whole town with the edge of the sword. And the time
that had been set for the men of Israel with the ambushers was when
39 they sent up a column of smoke from the town, the men of Israel were
to turn round in the battle. And Benjamin had begun to strike down
among the men of Israel about thirty men, for they thought, "Why, he
40 is surely routed before us as in the first battle." And the column began
to go up from the town, a pillar of smoke, and Benjamin turned around
to its rear and, look, the entire town had gone up in smoke to the heav-
41 ens. And the men of Israel turned round, and the men of Benjamin
42 panicked, for they saw that harm had touched them. And they turned
from before the men of Israel to the wilderness road, but the battle
overtook both them and the ones from the town. They were laying
43 waste to them within it. They had encircled Benjamin, pursued him to
44 Menuhah, led him to a point over against Gibeah from the east. And
45 eighteen thousand men of Benjamin fell, all of them valiant men. And
they turned and fled to the wilderness to the Rock of Rimmon, but
they picked off five thousand men of them on the highways, and they

---

38. *the time that had been set for the men of Israel with the ambushers was when
they sent up a column of smoke.* In the parallel episode in Joshua, it is Joshua
who gives the signal by raising his javelin, as Moses raised his staff against
Amalek. Here we have the more likely military device of a signal-fire. The
Masoretic text has an anomalous word *herev* ("much"?) after "the ambushers,"
but this is in all likelihood a dittography for *ha'orev*, "the ambushers," and so it
has been deleted in the translation.

39. *And Benjamin had begun to strike down among the men of Israel about thirty
men.* This duplicates verse 31 and may reflect an editorial glitch.

41. *they saw that harm had touched them.* They now realize that they are caught
in a pincer move between the ambushers and the main Israelite force.

42. *They were laying waste to them within it.* The wording of the Hebrew is
somewhat crabbed, and this trait is reflected in the translation.

overtook them at Gidom and struck down two thousand men of them.
And all those who fell of Benjamin on that day came to twenty-five 46
thousand sword-wielding men, all of them valiant men. And six hun- 47
dred men turned and fled to the wilderness to the Rock of Rimmon
and stayed at the Rock of Rimmon four months. And the men of Israel 48
had turned back against the Benjaminites, and they struck them by
the edge of the sword from the town, from man to beast, whatever was
there. All the towns, too, that were there they set on fire.

---

47. *six hundred men . . . stayed at the Rock of Rimmon.* It seems unlikely that
this wilderness crag was either impregnable or invisible to the pursuing army,
so the Israelites may have made a decision to spare some remnant of the Benjaminite fighting men.

48. *they struck them by the edge of the sword from the town, from man to beast.*
This formulation would seem to suggest that Gibeah and the other Benjaminite towns were put under the ban, the ḥerem. For the phrase "from man to
beast," the translation, following some manuscripts and two ancient versions,
reads *mimetim* (literally, "from people") rather than the Masoretic *metom*
("unwounded spot").

CHAPTER 21

1 And the men of Israel had vowed at Mizpah, saying, "No man of
2 us will give his daughter as wife to Benjamin. And the people came
to Bethel and stayed there till evening before God, and they raised
3 their voice and wept bitterly. And they said, "Why, O Lord God of
Israel, has this come about in Israel, that today one tribe should be
4 missing from Israel?" And it happened on the next day that the people
rose early and built an altar there and offered up burnt offerings and
5 well-being offerings. And the Israelites said, "Who has not come up
in the assembly to the Lord from all the tribes of Israel?"—for great
was the vow concerning whoever had not gone up to the Lord at
6 Mizpah, saying, "He is doomed to die." And the Israelites were regret-
ful about Benjamin their brother, and they said, "Today one tribe has
7 been cut off from Israel. What shall we do for wives for those who
remain, as we have vowed to the Lord not to give our daughters to

---

1. *the men of Israel had vowed at Mizpah.* The Hebrew indicates a pluperfect because this solemn vow was taken before the beginning of the war with
Benjamin.

3. *Why . . . has this come about in Israel.* Now, after the victory, the people are
confronted with a dilemma because of their binding vow, for its consequence
will be the elimination of one of the twelve tribes of Israel.

5. *for great was the vow.* This second vow, to destroy whoever held back from joining in the war against Benjamin, will be used to find a way out of the first vow.

6. *cut off.* The Hebrew uses a rather violent verb, *nigda'* (literally, "hacked off")
instead of the usual *nikhrat.* Some scholars prefer to read *nigra',* "is taken away,"
which would be in keeping with "missing" in verse 3.

them as wives?" And they said, "Which is the one of the tribes of 8
Israel that did not come up to the LORD at Mizpah?" And, look, not
a man had come to the camp from Jabesh-Gilead to the assembly.
And the troops were mustered, and, look, there was no man there 9
from the inhabitants of Jabesh-Gilead. And the community sent there 10
twelve thousand of the valiant men and charged them, saying, "Go
and strike down the inhabitants of Jabesh-Gilead by the edge of the
sword, and the women and the little ones. And this is the thing that 11
you shall do: every male and every woman who has lain with a male
you shall put under the ban." And they found among the inhabitants 12
of Jabesh-Gilead four hundred young virgin women who had not lain
with a male, and they brought them to the camp at Shiloh, which is
in the land of Canaan. And all the community sent and spoke to the 13
Benjaminites who were at the Rock of Rimmon, and they declared

---

8. *Jabesh-Gilead.* This northern territory to the east of the Jordan was allied with
Benjamin, as will be clear in the story of Saul in 1 Samuel. Many have inferred
that the whole story of the civil war and of the place of Jabesh-Gilead in its
aftermath is meant to discredit Benjamin, Saul's tribe.

10. *Go and strike down the inhabitants of Jabesh-Gilead.* Jabesh-Gilead is to be
put under the ban, all its population except for female virgins to be massacred.
It is historically unlikely that the *herem* was practiced by one set of Israelites on
another, and as Amit points out, it would have been a singularly bad solution to
the dilemma of Benjamin's survival to achieve it by wiping out a whole group
of Israelites, men, women, and children.

12. *they brought them to the camp at Shiloh.* The setting now shifts from Bethel
to Shiloh, laying the ground for the opening chapters of the Book of Samuel,
which are centered in Shiloh.

14 peace with them. And Benjamin came back at that time, and they gave
    them the women that they had kept alive from the women of Jabesh-
15 Gilead, but they did not find enough for them. And the people had
    become regretful concerning Benjamin, for the LORD had made a breach
16 in the tribes of Israel. And the elders of the community said, "What shall
    we do for wives for those left, for the women of Benjamin have been
17 destroyed?" And they said, "How will a remnant be left for Benjamin,
18 that a tribe not be wiped out from Israel, and we cannot give them wives
    from our daughters, for the Israelites vowed, saying, 'Cursed be he who
19 gives a wife to Benjamin'?" And they said, "Look, there is a festival to
    the LORD every year in Shiloh, which is north of Bethel, east of the
    highway that goes up from Bethel to Shechem and south of Lebonah."
20 And they charged the Benjaminites, saying, "Go and lie in wait in the
21 vineyards. And when you see that, look, the daughters of Shiloh come
    out to dance, you shall snatch each of you his wife from the daughters

---

14. *but they did not find enough for them.* There are six hundred Benjaminites at
the Rock of Rimmon, so the shortfall in brides is two hundred. But in all likelihood, the story of the delivery of the four hundred young women from Jabesh-
Gilead and the story of the snatching of the dancing girls in the vineyards are
two different versions of how the surviving Benjaminites got their brides that
have been edited together, with the numerical deficiency introduced in the first
story so that it can be made up in the second.

19. *there is a festival to the LORD every year in Shiloh.* The name and nature
of the festival are unspecified. The fact that it is said to be in Shiloh might
encourage the inference that it was a special local celebration at Shiloh. On
the other hand, the Mishnah (Ta'anit 4:8) reports a practice on the fifteenth of
Av and on Yom Kippur in which the nubile young women went out dancing in
the vineyards in borrowed white garments to be chosen as wives by the young
men of the community.

21. *you shall snatch each of you his wife from the daughters of Shiloh.* What is
involved is a kind of abduction, not rape, or, if the report in the Mishnah is
historically grounded, a collective mating ceremony. This odd tale of snatching
brides during the celebration of a festival has parallels in Herodotus (where it
is a festival honoring Artemis) and in Livy's well-known story of the abduction
of the Sabine women (where the festival is dedicated to Neptune). In any case,
the Book of Judges, which begins in violence and is dominated by violence,
ends here on an upbeat note with dancing girls and the taking of brides.

of Shiloh, and you shall go to the land of Benjamin. And should their 22
fathers or their brothers come in dispute to us, we shall say to them, 'We
showed mercy to them, for no man of them took his wife in battle, for it
was not you who gave to them. Now should you bear guilt?'" And thus 23
the Benjaminites did, and they took wives according to their number
from the dancing girls whom they stole away, and they returned to their
estate and rebuilt the towns and dwelled within them. And the Israelites 24
went off from there at that time each man to his tribe and to his clan,
and they went out from there each man to his estate.

In those days there was no king in Israel. Every man did what was right 25
in his own eyes.

---

22. *We showed mercy to them, for no man of them took his wife in battle.* This
whole speech is somewhat garbled (and the verb that means "show mercy"
is conjugated in an untenable way in the Masoretic text). The received text
has "we took," but three ancient versions read "they took." The sense one can
extract, without entirely rewriting the verse, is: The Benjaminites did not take
these young women as war captives; we showed mercy to them and arranged
for the taking of brides; you yourselves did not give the girls as brides, for the
vow against doing that was incumbent on you. Now why should you oppose our
proper procedure and incur guilt?

23. *stole away.* The Hebrew verb *gazal*, it should be said, generally indicates the
illicit appropriation of someone else's possessions.

25. *In those days there was no king in Israel. Every man did what was right in his
own eyes.* This refrain is now inserted at the end as a kind of epilogue to the
Book of Judges. The state of political anarchy has been especially manifest in
the story of the concubine at Gibeah and the civil war it triggers, and perhaps
in the war's aftermath as well. The refrain sets the stage for the Book of Samuel,
which will move in swift steps to the founding of the monarchy.

SAMUEL

TO THE READER

THE MAJOR SEQUENCE that runs, according to the conventional book and chapter divisions of later editorial traditions, from 1 Samuel 1 to 1 Kings 2 is one of the most astounding pieces of narrative that has come down to us from the ancient world. The story of David is probably the greatest single narrative representation in antiquity of a human life evolving by slow stages through time, shaped and altered by the pressures of political life, public institutions, family, the impulses of body and spirit, the eventual sad decay of the flesh. It also provides the most unflinching insight into the cruel processes of history and into human behavior warped by the pursuit of power. And nowhere is the Bible's astringent narrative economy, its ability to define characters and etch revelatory dialogue in a few telling strokes, more brilliantly deployed.

It must also be said, after nearly two centuries of excavative scholarship, that the precise literary history and authorship of this great narrative remain beyond recovery. To specialists who have exercised painstaking analysis in order to expose an intricate patchwork of sources and historical layers in the book as a whole and in most of its episodes, it may seem a provocation or an expression of ignorance to speak at all of the story of Samuel, Saul, and David. Even a reader looking for unity must concede that certain passages are not of a piece with the rest. The most salient of these is the coda placed just before the end of the David story (2 Samuel: 21–24), which comprises material from four different sources, none of them reflecting the style or perspective of the David story proper. It may be unwise to think of these disparate passages as intrusions because creating a purposeful collage of sources was demonstrably a standard literary procedure in ancient Israel. In any case, the architectonic cohesion of the narrative from the birth of Samuel to the

death of David has been made increasingly clear by the innovative literary commentary of the past three decades, and much of the richness
and complexity of the story is lost by those who imagine this book as a
stringing together of virtually independent sources: a prophetic Samuel
narrative, a cycle of Saul stories, a history of the rise of David, a succession narrative, and so forth.

Readers should not be confused by the conventional division into
books. The entities 1 and 2 Samuel are purely an artifact of ancient
manuscript production. Scrolls used by scribes were roughly the same
length, and when the Hebrew Bible was translated into Greek in the
third century BCE, a single scroll was not long enough to encompass
the whole book, so it was divided into two parts in no way intrinsic
to the original composition. (The Talmud speaks of a single Book of
Samuel.) It is also demonstrable that the first two chapters of 1 Kings,
as I shall try to show in my commentary, are the real conclusion of the
book, subtly echoing earlier moments in the story and evincing the same
distinctive literary mastery. Later redactors placed these two episodes
at the beginning of Kings so that they could serve as a preface to the
story of Solomon.

But if the ancient editors passed this material down to posterity as
a book, what are we to make of its composite nature? Two fundamental issues are involved: the presence of the so-called Deuteronomist
in the book, and the introduction of purportedly independent narratives. In regard to the second of these two considerations, the base-
line for modern scholarly discussion was set in a 1926 monograph by
the German scholar Leonhard Rost. He concentrated on what he saw
as two independent narratives—an Ark Narrative (1 Samuel 4–7:1,
plus 2 Samuel 6) and a Succession Narrative (2 Samuel 9–20 and 1
Kings 1–2). The argument for an originally independent Ark Narrative
has a good deal of plausibility: there are some stylistic differences in
this segment; human agents, at the center of the surrounding narrative, are marginal; miraculous intervention by God, not in evidence
elsewhere, is decisive; and the figure of Samuel with which the story
began temporarily disappears. The Ark Narrative is often thought to
be the oldest component of the Book of Samuel, perhaps actually pre-
Davidic, because it does not envisage a royal cult in Jerusalem and
has no interest in the more political concerns of the larger story. Even

in this case, however, the narrative in question has to be read in the context of the comprehensive literary structure into which it has been integrated, whether by editorial ingenuity or by the allusive artistry of the author of the David story. Thus, the old priest Eli, sitting at the gate awaiting the news of disaster from the battlefield (news that will include the death of his sons), generates a haunting avatar in the aging David at Mahanaim, sitting between the two gates of the walled city, anxiously awaiting the messenger from the battlefield who will tell him of the death of his son. A second scene of receiving catastrophic tidings is tied in with Eli: the old priest hears an uproar in the town, asks what it means, and then a messenger arrives to give him a breathless report of the terrible defeat, just as the usurper Adonijah, at the end of the David story, will hear an uproar in the town and then a breathless report from an eyewitness of the developments that have destroyed his hopes for the throne.

The argument for an independent Succession Narrative, long embraced by scholarly consensus, is shakier. Rost's contention that it is stylistically distinct from the preceding text is unconvincing, and his notions of style are extremely vague. One may question whether the succession to the throne is actually the central concern of this sequence of episodes, which are more powerfully focused on David's sin and the consequent theme of the unfolding of the prophet's curse on the house of David. (This theme has a certain affinity with Greek tragedy, as Faulkner, ultimately a better reader of the David story than Rost, keenly understood in *Absalom, Absalom!*) The powerful imaginative continuities in the representation of David from agile youth to decrepit old age speak for themselves. To read, for example, David's grim response to the death of his infant son by Bathsheba (2 Samuel 12) as part of an independent Succession Narrative, unrelated to his previous public utterances and acts in a purported History of the Rise of David, is to do palpable violence to the beautiful integrity of the story as the probing representation of a human life. Over the past three decades, admirable work has been done by scholars from different points on the geographical and methodological map to illuminate the fine and complex interconnections among the various phases of the story of David, Saul, and Samuel. The most notable contributions are those of the Dutch scholar J. P. Fokkelman, the North American

Robert Polzin, and the Israeli Shimon Bar-Efrat, and I shall frequently follow their precedent or build on their insights in my comments on the text.

The other pervasive question about the stratification of this book involves its Deuteronomistic editing. No one knows with certainty when the main part of the original narrative was written, though there is good reason to place it, as a recurrent scholarly view does, quite close to David's own time, in the first half of the tenth century BCE. (Gerhard von Rad proposed the court of Solomon as the setting for the composition of the story.) Samuel is set into the larger history that runs from Joshua to the end of 2 Kings and that scholarly usage designates as the Deuteronomistic History. The book was probably edited at the time of King Josiah's cultic and theological reforms in the late seventh century BCE, though it may well have undergone a secondary Deuteronomistic redaction in the Babylonian Exile, during the sixth century BCE. But to what extent is Samuel a product of the work of the Deuteronomist? The bulk of the story shows no traces of the peculiar brand of nationalist pietism that marks the Deuteronomistic movement—its emphasis on the purity and the centralization of the cult, its insistence on a direct causal link between Israelite defection from its covenant with God and national catastrophe, and its distinctive and strikingly formulaic vocabulary for expressing this outlook. The compelling conclusion is that the Deuteronomistic editors did no more with the inherited narrative than to provide some minimal editorial framing and transition (far less than in the Book of Judges) and to interpolate a few brief passages. Thus I strenuously disagree with Robert Polzin, one of the most finely perceptive readers of this book (in his two volumes *Samuel and the Deuteronomist* and *David and the Deuteronomist*). Exercising great ingenuity, Polzin sees the historical perspective of the Deuteronomist manifested in all the minute details of the story.

Let me recall a signal instance I mentioned in my general introduction where the Deuteronomist has patently inserted a bit of dialogue of his own contrivance into the story that probably antedates his editing by more than three centuries, for the contrast with what immediately follows vividly illustrates the kind of world that defines David, Joab, Saul, Abner, and all these memorable figures steeped in the bitter juices of politics and history. Here, full quotation with commentary may be help-

ful. On his deathbed, David summons Solomon in order to convey to
him an oral last will and testament (1 Kings 2):

> I am going on the way of all the earth. And you must be strong, and
> be a man. *And keep what the* LORD *your God enjoins, to walk in His*
> *ways, to keep His statues, His commands, and His dictates and His*
> *admonitions, as it is written in the Teaching of Moses, so that you may*
> *prosper in everything you do and in everything to which you turn. So*
> *that the* LORD *may fulfill His word that He spoke unto me, saying, 'If*
> *your sons keep their way to walk before Me in truth with their whole*
> *heart and with their whole being, saying, no man of yours will be cut*
> *off from the throne of Israel.'* And, what's more, you yourself know
> what Joab son of Zeruiah did to me, what he did to the two com-
> manders of the armies of Israel, Abner son of Ner and Amasa son
> of Jether—he killed them and spilled the blood of war in peace,
> and put the blood of war on his belt that was round his waist and
> on his sandals that were on his feet. And you must act in your
> wisdom, and do not let his gray head go down in peace to Sheol.

Every word in the italicized section of the passage shows the finger-
prints of the Deuteronomist. The phraseology is almost identical with
recurrent phraseology in the Book of Deuteronomy: the heavy stress on
"keeping" and "commands," whole strings of terms such as "walk in His
ways," "His statutes, His commands, and His laws and His dictates," "so
that you may prosper in everything you do," "to walk before me in truth
with their whole heart and with their whole being." The very mention
of the "Teaching [*torah*] of Moses" is a Deuteronomistic rallying point
that would scarcely have been invoked in the tenth century. Stylistically, moreover, these long-winded sentences loaded with didactically
insistent synonyms are nothing like the sentences spoken by characters
in the David story.

  Why did the Deuteronomist interpolate these lines of dialogue? The
most plausible inference is that, given his brand of pious monotheism,
he was uncomfortable with the vengeful way the founding king of the
divinely elected dynasty speaks on his deathbed. David and Joab go
back together half a century. David has been repeatedly dependent on
Joab's resourcefulness and ruthlessness as his principal strong man,

but he also feels himself to have been terribly wronged by his henchman—above all, in Joab's self-interested and treacherous murders of
two army commanders whom David had embraced (and also in his killing of Absalom, against the king's explicit orders, which David refrains
from mentioning). The image of Joab splashed in blood from waist
to feet strongly recalls the narrative report of his butchering Amasa
with a stealthy sword-thrust to the belly, and invokes the recurrence
of spilled blood as material substance and moral symbol throughout
the story. When David enjoins the proverbially wise Solomon to act in
his wisdom, the quality in question is not the wisdom of the Torah of
Moses but rather the wisdom of a Talleyrand. Soon after David's death,
Solomon will show how adept he is in exercising that faculty of wary
calculation. The Deuteronomistic editor could not delete this material,
but he sought to provide a counterweight to its unblinking realism by
first having David on his deathbed speak in a high moral tone. In fact,
nobody in the David story talks like this. The dialogues show nothing of
this hortatory style, nothing of this unalloyed didacticism. It is not that
the writer is devoid of any ideological viewpoint: he believes in a morally
imperative covenantal relationship between God and Israel; he believes
in the authority of prophecy; and he believes in the divine election of
the Davidic line. But one must hasten to say that he believes in all these
things only with enormous dialectic complication, an order of complication so probing that at times it borders on subversion.

The dialectic complication of national ideology is a phenomenon
worth explaining, for it brings us to the heart of the greatness of the
David story. Biblical scholarship by and large has badly underread this
book by imagining that ideological strands can be identified like so many
varieties of potatoes and understood as simple expressions of advocacy.
In this fashion, it is repeatedly claimed in the critical literature that
one component of the book is prophetic, promoting the interests of
prophetic circles; that another is "Saulide"; that a third is basically a narrative apologetic for the Davidic dynasty; and so forth. All of this strikes
me as badly misconceived, and it is blind to the complexity of vision of
this extraordinary writer.

The representation of the prophet Samuel is instructive in this connection. It has been conjecture that a "prophetic" writer, active perhaps
a century or two after the reported events, is responsible for this por-

tion of the book as well as for the ones in which Nathan the prophet figures. But there is scant evidence in the text for the construction of this hypothetical entity. It is rather like assuming that Shakespeare must have been a "royalist," or perhaps even royal, writer in order to have written *Henry IV*. What, in fact, is the writer's attitude toward Samuel? There is no question that he is shown to be a prophet confirmed in his vocation by God Himself, as the dedication scene, in which God calls to him in the night at the Shiloh sanctuary (1 Samuel 3) makes clear. It is concomitantly stressed that Samuel has been chosen to exercise a spiritual authority that will displace the priestly authority of the house of Eli, on which an irrevocable curse is pronounced soon after the report of Samuel's birth. The entire people becomes subservient to Samuel, and they feel that only through the initiative of the prophet (however grudging) can they get the king they want. In all this, one could claim that the story is confirming a prophetic ideology by reinforcing the notion of the indispensability of prophetic authority to Israelite national life.

Yet as in the case of Saul, David, and all the principal figures around them, Samuel is a densely imagined character, and, it must be said, in many respects a rather unattractive one. The Israeli poet Yehuda Amichai neatly catches the dubiety of the mature Samuel in a wry little poem: "When Samuel was born, she said words of Torah, / 'For this lad I prayed.' / When he grew up and did the deeds of his life, / she asked, 'For this lad I prayed?'" The prophet Samuel may have God on his side, but he is also an implacable, irascible man, and often a palpably self-interested one as well. His resistance to the establishment of the monarchy may express a commitment to the noble ideal of the direct kingship of God over Israel, but it is also motivated by resentment that he must surrender authority, and the second of his two antimonarchic speeches is informed by belligerent self-defensiveness about his own career as national leader. When he chooses Saul, he wants to play him as his puppet, dictating elaborate scenarios to the neophyte king, even setting him up for failure by arriving at an arranged rendezvous at the last possible moment. He is proud, imperious, histrionic—until the very end, when he is conjured up by Saul as a ghost on the eve of the fatal battle at Mount Gilboa.

It would be misleading, I think, to imagine that any of this is intended to discredit the idea of prophetic authority. Samuel is invested with prophetic power by an act of God. But the writer understands that he is also a man, all too human, and that any kind of power, including spiritual power, can lead to abuse. Samuel toys with the idea of creating a kind of prophetic dynasty through his two sons, even though they are just as corrupt as the two sons of Eli, whose immoral behavior seals the doom of their father's priestly line. Is Samuel's choice of Saul really dictated by God, or rather by his own human preconceptions? (He is on the point of making the same mistake twice when he is ready to anoint David's eldest brother Eliab, another strapping young man who seems to stand out from the crowd.) When he insists it is God's will that the entire population and all the livestock of Amalek should be slaughtered, and then offers King Agag as a kind of human sacrifice to the Lord, does he act with divinely authorized prophetic rightness, or, as Martin Buber thought, is he confusing his own human impulses with God's will? The story of Samuel, then, far from being a simple promotion of prophetic ideology, enormously complicates the notion of prophecy by concretely imagining what may become of the imperfect stuff of humanity when the mantle of prophecy is cast over it.

The representation of David is another instance, far more complex and compelling, of the complication of ideology through the imaginative reconstruction of historical figures and events. Before I try to explain how that process is played out in the David story, a few words are in order about the relation of this entire narrative to history.

As with almost every major issue of biblical studies, there have been sharp differences among scholars on this particular question. On the one hand, Gerhard von Rad in the 1940s and others after him have seen the David story as the beginning of history writing in the Western tradition. On the other hand, one group of contemporary scholars, sometimes known as minimalists, is skeptical about whether there ever was a King David and likes to say that this narrative has about the same relation to historical events as do the British legends about King Arthur. The gritty historical realism of the story—what Hans Frei shrewdly identified as its "history-like" character—surely argues against the notion that it is simply legendary. Were David an invention of much later national tradition, he would be the most peculiar of legendary founding kings: a figure who early on is shown as a collaborator with the archenemies of Israel, the Philistines; who compounds adultery with murder; who more than once exposes himself to humiliation, is repeatedly seen in his weakness, and oscillates from nobility of sentiment and act to harsh vindictiveness on his very deathbed. (On this last point, the editorial intervention of the Deuteronomist that we observed suggests that he had inherited not a legendary account but a historical report that made him squirm.) If, moreover, the bulk of the story was actually composed within a generation or two, or perhaps three, after the reported actions, it is hard to imagine how such encompassing national events as a civil war between the house of Saul and the house of David, the Davidic campaigns of conquest east of the Jordan, and the usurpation of the throne by Absalom with the consequent military struggle, could have been invented out of whole cloth.

This narrative nevertheless has many signs of what we would call fictional shaping—interior monologues, dialogues between the historical personages in circumstances where there could have been no witness to what was said, pointed allusions in the turns of the dialogue as well as in the narrative details to Genesis, Joshua, and Judges. What we have in this great story, as I have proposed elsewhere, is not merely a report of history but an imagining of history that is analogous to what Shakespeare did with historical figures and events in his history plays. That is, the known general contours of the historical events and of the principal players are not tampered with, but the writer brings to bear the resources of his literary art in order to imagine deeply, and critically, the concrete moral and emotional predicaments of living in history, in the political realm. To this end, the writer feels free to invent an inner language for the characters, to give their dialogues revelatory shape, to weave together episodes and characters with a fine mesh of recurrent motifs and phrases and analogies of incident, and to define the meaning of the events through allusion, metaphor, and symbol. The writer does all this not to fabricate history but in order to understand it.

In this elaborately wrought literary vehicle, David turns out to be one of the most unfathomable figures of ancient literature. He begins as the fair-haired boy of Israel—if the term "red" or "ruddy" in his initial description refers to hair color, it might be something like auburn. Everyone seems to love him. He is beautiful, he is musical, and he is brave and brilliantly resourceful on the battlefield. He is also, from the start, quite calculating, and it can scarcely be an accident that until the midpoint of his story every one of his utterances, without exception, is made on a public occasion and arguably is contrived to serve his political interests. The narrative repeatedly reveals to us the churning fears and confusions within Saul while blocking access to David's inner world. Beset by mortal dangers, David is constantly prepared to do almost anything in order to survive: with the help of his devoted wife, Michal, wordlessly fleeing Saul's assassins; playing the drooling madman before the Philistine king Achish; serving as vassal to the Philistines, massacring whole towns in order to keep his real actions unknown to his overlords; profiting politically from the chain of violent deaths in the house of Saul while vehemently dissociating himself from each of the killings. He is, in sum, the first full-length portrait of a Machiavellian prince in Western literature. The Book of Samuel is one of those rare masterworks that, like Stendhal's *Charterhouse of Parma,* evinces an unblinking and abidingly instructive knowingness about man as a political animal in all his contradictions and venality and in all his susceptibility to the brutalization and the seductions of exercising power.

And yet, David is more than a probing representation of the ambiguities of political power. He is also an affecting and troubling image of human destiny as husband and father and as a man moving from youth to prime to the decrepitude of old age. The great pivotal moment of the whole story in this regard is when he turns to his perplexed courtiers, after putting aside the trappings of mourning he had assumed for his ailing infant son, now dead, and says, "I am going to him. He will not come back to me." These are the very first words David pronounces that have no conceivable political motive, that give us a glimpse into his inwardness, revealing his sense of naked vulnerability to the inexorable mortality that is the fate of all humankind. For the rest of the story, we shall see David's weakness and his bonds of intimate attachment in fluctuating conflict with the imperatives of power that drive him as a king surrounded by potential enemies and betrayers.

The story of David, in turn, cannot be separated from the story of the man he displaces, Saul. (The moral and psychological complication with which both men are imagined argues powerfully against the simplification of sorting out the book into "Davidide" and "Saulide" narratives.) As a number of observers have proposed—perhaps most vividly, in a series of ballads, the early twentieth-century Hebrew poet Saul Tchernichovsky—Saul is the closest approximation of a tragic hero in the Hebrew Bible. A farm boy from Benjamin seeking his father's lost donkeys, he is overtaken by a destiny of kingship of which he had not dreamed and that at first he tries to escape. Ambivalence and oscillation are the hallmarks of the story of Saul, and the writer may have been led to mirror this condition in his abundant use of paired or even tripled episodes: three different coronation scenes are required for the reluctant Saul; two tales of Saul among the prophets, the first elevating him at the beginning of his career and the second devastating him at the end; two incidents of Saul's hurling his spear at David; two encounters with the fugitive David, who spares his life and receives a pledge of love and a kind of endorsement from Saul, still not to be trusted by David as the older man veers wildly between opposed feelings.

The stories of Saul and David interlock antithetically on the theme of knowledge. Saul, from first to last, is a man deprived of the knowledge he desperately seeks. At the outset, he has to turn to the seer Samuel in order to find his father's asses. In subsequent episodes, he has no luck with oracles and divination in guiding him on his military way, and he tries to coerce fate by imposing a rash vow of fasting on his troops in the midst of battle. He seizes on the report of informers in his pursuit of David, but David continues to elude him. At the very end, on the eve of his last battle, he tries oracle and prophecy and dreams in order to find out what the impending future will be, but all fail, and he is compelled to resort to the very art of necromancy that he himself had made a capital crime. The knowledge he then receives from the implacable ghost of Samuel is nothing but the news of his own imminent doom.

David, on the other hand, at first seems peculiarly favored with knowledge. The position that he is brought to the court to fill is for a man "skilled in playing" (the literal meaning of the Hebrew is "*knowing to play*") and "prudent in speech." In what follows, David demonstrates impressive prudence and agile resourcefulness. It also emerges that once he has become a fugitive, he is rapidly equipped with an oracular ephod and a priest to use it and so, in contrast to Saul, has a direct line of communication with God in making his key decisions. Much later in the story, when things have begun to fall apart, the wise woman from Tekoa will tell David, "My lord is wise as with the wisdom of a

messenger of God, to know everything in the land" (2 Samuel 14:20).
By this point, however, it has become painfully evident that her words
are a gesture of deference to the king that is ironically contradicted by
fact. The knowing David of the earlier part of the narrative has become
the king isolated in his palace. He must even send intermediaries to
discover the identity of the naked beauty bathing on the rooftop in view
of his palace, though she seems to be the daughter of one of the members of his own elite guard. He is singularly unaware of his son Amnon's
lust for his half sister Tamar, then of Absalom's plot to murder Amnon
in revenge, then of Absalom's scheme to usurp the throne. The pitiful
image of the shivering, bedridden David, ignorant of the grand feast of
self-coronation arranged by his son Adonijah, then reminded or perhaps
rather persuaded by Bathsheba and Nathan that he has promised the
throne to Solomon, is the ultimate representation of the painful decline
of knowledge in this once perspicacious figure, the brilliant successor
to the purblind Saul.

Who could have written a story like this, and what could his motives
have been? The way this question is typically posed in biblical studies is to ask what interests the writer could have been serving, but it
seems to me that framing the issue in those terms involves a certain
reductionism that harks back to the historical positivism of the nineteenth century. Although it is safe to assume that no biblical author
wrote merely to entertain his audiences, and although there is no evidence of a class of professional storytellers in ancient Israel analogous
to the bards of Greece, the social location and political aims of the biblical writer remain unclear. (The prophets, who sometimes incorporated
autobiographical passages in their writing, and who stand out sharply as
critics of society and often of the royal establishment, are the one clear
exception to this rule.) Scholars of the Bible often speak of "schools" or
"circles" of biblical writing (prophetic, priestly, Wisdom, Davidic, and so
forth), but in fact we have no direct knowledge of such groups as cultural institutions. The one school or movement for which a very strong
case can be made is the Deuteronomistic movement. In this instance,
a comprehensive, uncompromising reform of cultic practice, theology,
and law was instituted during the reign of Josiah, around 621 BCE. The
Book of Deuteronomy was composed, with abundant satellite literature
to come after it, as a forceful literary instrument of the reform. In the

great speeches of Deuteronomy, literature has patently been marshaled to inculcate an ideological program. Yet the very contrast we observed in 1 Kings 2 between the didacticism of the Deuteronomist and the worldly realism of the author of the David story argues for the idea that the latter had very different aims in mind from the simple promotion of a political program.

My guess is that the author of the David story thought of himself as a historian. But even if he frequented the court in Jerusalem, a plausible but not at all necessary supposition, he was by no means a writer of court annals or chronicles of the kings of Judea, and, as I have argued, he was far from being an apologist for the Davidic dynasty. I would imagine that he was impelled to write out of a desire to convey to his contemporaries and to posterity a true account of the significant events involved in the founding of the monarchy that governed the nation. It is conceivable that he had some written reports of these events at his disposal or at any rate drew on oral accounts of the events. Perhaps he had spoken with old-timers who were actual participants, or, if one places him very early, he himself might have been an observer of some of what he reports. He also did not hesitate to exploit etiological tales (Saul among the prophets) and folk tales (David slaying the giant Goliath) in order to flesh out his historical account and dramatize its meanings. Though committed to telling the truth about history, his notion of historical factuality was decidedly different from modern ones. His conception of history writing involved not merely registering what had happened and who had been the principal actors but also reflecting on the shifting interplay between character and historical act, on the way social and political institutions shape and distort individual lives, on the human costs of particular political choices.

The author of the David story was in all likelihood firmly committed to the legitimacy of the Davidic line. In the book he wrote, after all, God explicitly elects David once Saul has been rejected and later promises that the throne of David will remain unshaken for all time. But the author approaches the David story as an imaginative writer, giving play to that dialectic fullness of conception that leads the greatest writers (Shakespeare, Stendhal, Balzac, Tolstoy, Proust, to name a few apposite instances) to transcend the limitations of their own ideological points of departure. Even though the vocational identity of "imaginative writer" was not socially defined in ancient Israel as it would be in later cultures, the accomplished facts of literary art in many cultures, ancient and modern, suggest that the impulse of literary creation, with the breadth of vision that at its best it encourages, is universal.

The person who wrote this story is not only a formidably shrewd observer of politics and human nature but also someone who manifestly delights in the writerly pleasures of his craft and is sometimes led to surprising insights by his exploration of those pleasures. He has an ear for dialogue, and for the contrastive treatment of the two interlocutors in particular dialogues, that Joyce might have envied. Though both narrator and characters are sparing in figurative language, the metaphors he gives them are telling, and sometimes set up electrically charged links between one moment of the story and another. This writer has a keen sense of the thematic uses of analogy between one episode and another, as when he gives us Amnon lying in a pretended sickbed so that he can summon his sister Tamar to serve his violent lust, right after the story of David's rising from his siesta bed to see the bathing Bathsheba and then summon her to the palace for his illicit pleasure. (Both prohibited sexual acts lead to murder and political disarray.) Like most of the great masters of narrative art, the author of the David story is constantly asking himself what it must be like concretely—emotionally, psychologically, morally, even physically—to be one or another of these characters in a particular predicament, and it is this salutary imaginative habit that generates many of the dialectic complications of the historical account. Saul on the last night of his life is not merely represented as fearful of the Philistine foe but driven by desperation into the necromancer's den. This last gesture of grasping for knowledge denied makes the fate of the defeated king seem wrenching, indeed, tragic. David's flight from Absalom is not merely a story of political intrigue and opposing interests but also a tale of anguished conflict between father and king in the same man, culminating in David's horrendous stutter of grief over Absalom's death and followed by Joab's harsh rebuke to him for his behavior.

One of the hallmarks of this whole writerly relation to the historical material is the freighted imagining of the detail not strictly necessary to the historical account. Let me offer one brief instance that may stand for all the others. David's first wife Michal, it will be recalled, is married off by her father Saul to a man named Paltiel son of Laish after David's flight from his father-in-law's assassins. We know nothing about Paltiel except his name, and nothing about Michal's feelings concerning the union with him imposed by her father. When Abner, the commander of the forces of the house of Saul, comes to transfer his fealty to David and end the civil war, David stipulates that Michal daughter of Saul must first be sent back to him. (Presumably, his motive is strictly political.) Michal is duly removed by Abner's decree from Paltiel, with no word or emotion of hers reported by the writer. What he does give us are these few, indelible words: "And her husband went with her, weeping as he went after her, as far as Bahurim. And Abner said to him, 'Go back!' And he went back." (2 Samuel 3:16). To a sober historian, this moment might well seem superfluous. To a great imaginative writer like the author of this story, such moments are the heart of the matter. Paltiel never even speaks in the story, but his weeping speaks volumes. He is a loving husband caught between the hard and unyielding men who wield power in the world—Abner, Saul's tough field commander, and his adversary turned ally, David, who insists on the return of the woman he has acquired with a bloody bride price because he calculates that as Saul's daughter she will bolster his claim to be Saul's legitimate successor. The tearful Paltiel walking after the wife who is being taken from him, then driven back by the peremptory word of the strongman with whom he cannot hope to contend, is a poignant image of the human price of political power. If history, in the hackneyed aphorism, is the story told by the victors, this narrative achieves something closer to the aim that Walter Benjamin defined as the task of the historical materialist, "to brush history against the grain." Lacking all but the scantiest extrahistorical evidence, we shall probably never know precisely what happened in Jerusalem and Judea and the high country of Benjamin around the turn of the first millennium BCE, when the Davidic dynasty was established. What matters is that the anonymous Hebrew writer, drawing on what he knew or thought he knew of the portentous historical events, has created this most searching story of men and women in the rapid and dangerous current of history that still speaks to us, floundering in history and the dilemmas of political life, three thousand years later.

1 Samuel

CHAPTER 1

Λnd there was a man from Ramathaim-Zophim, from the high country 1
of Ephraim, and his name was Elkanah son of Jeroham son of Elihu
son of Tohu son of Zuph, an Ephraimite. And he had two wives; the 2
name of the one was Hannah and the name of the other, Peninnah.

The story of Hannah provides an instructive illustration of the conventions
of narrative exposition that govern a large number of biblical stories. First the
main character, or characters, are identified by name, pedigree, and geographical location. The only verb used is "to be" (verses 1–2). In this instance the
standard biblical story beginning, "there was a man," is in part a false lead
because the real protagonist of the story is Elkanah's wife Hannah. Then there
is a series of reported actions in the iterative tense—that is, an indication of
habitually repeated actions (verses 3–7). (In all this, compare Job 1.) The narrative then zooms in to a particular moment, one of those annually repeated
events of Hannah's frustration at Shiloh, by way of Elkanah's dialogue (verse 8),
which could not plausibly be an iterative event. At this point, we have moved
from prelude to story proper. The writer himself seems quite conscious of this
play between recurring units of time and specific moments in time: the word
yamim, "days," but often as in verse 3 with the sense of "annual cycle," is used
five times, together with the singular *yom*, in an iterative sense, at the beginning
of verse 4. (These recurrences are complemented by "year after year," *shanah
beshanah*, in verse 7.)

2. *And he had two wives.* The reference to two wives, one childbearing, the other
childless, immediately alerts the audience to the unfolding of the familiar annunciation type-scene. The expected sequence of narrative motifs of the annunciation scene is the report of the wife's barrenness (amplified by the optional motif
of the fertile co-wife less loved by the husband than is the childless wife); the
promise, through oracle or divine messenger or man of God, of the birth of a son;
cohabitation resulting in conception and birth. As we shall see, the middle motif
is articulated in a way that is distinctive to the concerns of the Samuel story.

3 And Peninnah had children but Hannah had no children. And this man
would go up from his town year after year to worship and to sacrifice
to the LORD of Armies at Shiloh, and there the two sons of Eli, Hophni
4 and Phineas, were priests to the LORD. And when the day came round,
Elkanah would sacrifice and give portions to Peninnah his wife and to all
5 her sons and her daughters. And to Hannah he would give one double
portion, for Hannah he loved, and the LORD had closed her womb.
6 And her rival would torment her sorely so as to provoke her because
7 the LORD had closed up her womb. And thus was it done year after
year—when she would go up to the house of the LORD, the other would
torment her and she would weep and would not eat.

8 And Elkanah her husband said to her, "Hannah, why do you weep and
why do you not eat and why is your heart afflicted? Am I not better to you

---

3. *the two sons of Eli.* The reference is initially puzzling but points forward to
the focus on proper and improper heirs to the priesthood in Samuel's story.

5. *And to Hannah he would give one double portion.* The Hebrew phrase, which
occurs only here, means literally "one portion [for the?] face," and has perplexed commentators. The conclusion of several modern translators that the
phrase means "only a single portion" makes nonsense out of the following words
that the allotment was an expression of Elkanah's special love. It seems wisest
to follow a long tradition of commentators who take a cue from the doublative
ending of *'apayim*, the word for "face" (perhaps even a textual corruption for
another word meaning "double") and to construe this as a double portion to
Hannah who, alas, unlike Peninnah, has no children.

7. *And thus was it done.* The Hebrew is literally "thus did he do," but the impersonal masculine active singular is often used in this kind of passive sense.
  the other. The Hebrew simply says "she," but the antecedent is clearly
Peninnah.

8. *Am I not better to you than ten sons?* The double-edged poignancy of these
words is that they at once express Elkanah's deep and solicitous love for Hannah
and his inability to understand how inconsolable she feels about her affliction
of barrenness. All the annunciation stories must be understood in light of the
prevalent ancient Near Eastern view that a woman's one great avenue to fulfillment in life was through the bearing of sons. It is noteworthy that Hannah does
not respond to Elkanah. When she does at last speak, it is to God.

than ten sons?" And Hannah arose after the eating in Shiloh and after 9
the drinking, while Eli the priest was sitting in a chair by the doorpost
of the Lord's temple. And she was deeply embittered, and she prayed to 10
the Lord, weeping all the while. And she vowed a vow and said, "Lord 11
of Armies, if you really will look on your servant's woe and remember
me, and forget not your servant and give your servant male seed, I will
give him to the Lord all the days of his life, no razor shall touch his
head." And it happened as she went on with her prayer before the Lord, 12
with Eli watching her mouth, as Hannah was speaking in her heart, her 13
lips alone moving and her voice not heard, Eli thought she was drunk.
And Eli said to her, 14

"How long will you go on drunk?
    Rid yourself of your wine!"

---

11. *I will give him to the Lord.* Hannah's prayer exhibits a directness of style,
without ornament or conventional liturgical phrasing, and an almost naive simplicity: if you give him to me, I will give him to you. This canceling out of the
two givings is reconciled by the introduction of another verb at the end of the
story: Hannah "lends" to God the child He has given her.

no razor shall touch his head. As an expression of her dedication of the prayed-
for child, Hannah vows that he will be a nazirite (like Samson), a person specially
dedicated to God who took a vow of abstinence from certain activities. (The
literal meaning of the Hebrew is "no razor will go up on his head.") The nazirites
also refrained from wine, which throws an ironic backlight on Eli's subsequent
accusation that Hannah is drunk. A few biblical texts link nazirite and prophet.

14. *How long will you go on drunk?* The central annunciation motif of the type-
scene is purposefully distorted. Since Hannah receives no direct response from
God—she prays rather than inquires of an oracle—Eli the priest should be playing the role of man of God or divine intermediary. But at first he gets it all wrong,
mistaking her silent prayer for drunken mumbling, and denouncing her in a
poetic line (marked by semantic and rhythmic parallelism) of quasi-prophetic
verse. When in verse 17 he accepts her protestation of innocent suffering, he
piously prays or predicts—the Hebrew verb could be construed either way—that
her petition will be granted, but he doesn't have a clue about the content of the
petition. The uncomprehending Eli is thus virtually a parody of the annunciating
figure of the conventional type-scene—an apt introduction to a story in which the
claim to authority of the house of Eli will be rejected, and ultimately, sacerdotal
guidance will be displaced by prophetic guidance in the person of Samuel, who
begins as a temple acolyte but then exercises a very different kind of leadership.

15 And Hannah answered and said, "No, my lord! A bleak-spirited woman
am I. Neither wine nor hard drink have I drunk, but I have poured out
16 my heart to the LORD. Think not your servant a worthless girl, for out of
17 my great trouble and torment I have spoken till now." And Eli answered
and said, "Go in peace, and may the God of Israel grant your petition
18 which you asked of Him." And she said, "May your servant but find favor
in your eyes." And the woman went on her way, and she ate, and her face
19 was no longer downcast. And they rose early in the morning and bowed
before the LORD and returned and came to their home in Ramah. And
20 Elkanah knew Hannah his wife and the LORD remembered her. And it
happened at the turn of the year that Hannah conceived and bore a son,
and she called his name Samuel, "For from the LORD I asked for him."

21 And the man Elkanah with all his household went up to offer to the
22 LORD the yearly sacrifice and his votive pledge. But Hannah did not

15. *bleak-spirited*. The Hebrew, which occurs only here as a collocation, is
literally "hard-spirited."

20. *she called his name Samuel*. There is a small puzzlement in the Hebrew
because it is the name Saul, *Sha'ul*, not Samuel, *Shmu'el*, that means "asked"
(or "lent"). This has led some modern scholars to speculate that a story originally composed to explain the birth of Saul was transferred to Samuel—perhaps
because Saul's eventual unworthiness to reign made it questionable that he
should merit a proper annunciation scene. But it must be said that the only
evidence for this speculation is the seeming slippage of names here. That could
easily be explained, as by the thirteenth-century Hebrew commentator David
Kimchi, if we assume Hannah is playing on two Hebrew words, *sha'ul me'el*,
"asked of God." In any case, biblical writers allowed themselves considerable
license in etymologizing names.

21. *the yearly sacrifice*. The annual cycle of iterative actions invoked at the
beginning is seemingly resumed, but everything is different now that Hannah
has borne a son, and she herself introduces a change in the repeated pattern.
   votive pledge. Although this is the same Hebrew term, *neder*, that is used
for Hannah's vow at the beginning of verse 11, its most likely referent here is
a vowed thanksgiving offering on the part of the husband for his wife's safe
delivery of a son.

go up, for she had said to her husband, "Till the lad is weaned! Then I will bring him and we will see the LORD's presence, and he shall stay there always." And Elkanah her husband said to her, "Do what is right 23 in your eyes. Stay till you wean him, only may the LORD fulfill what your mouth has uttered." And the woman stayed and nursed her son till she weaned him. And she took him up with her when she weaned him, with 24 a three-year-old bull and one *ephah* of flour and a jar of wine, and she

---

22. *Till the lad is weaned.* The word for "lad," *na' ar*, is quite often a tender designation of a young son. Though it typically refers to an adolescent, or even to a young man at the height of his powers (David uses it for the usurper Absalom), it evidently can also be used for an infant. Nursing and weaning (compare the end of this verse and the beginning of the next verse) are insisted on here with a peculiar weight of repetition and literalness. This usage surely intimates the powerful biological bond between Hannah and the longed-for baby and thus points to the pain of separation she must accept, whatever the postponement, according to the terms of her own vow. In the Ark Narrative that follows, there will be a surprising recurrence of this image of nursing mothers yearning for their young. At this point, the only other indication of her feelings about the child is the term "lad" that she uses for him.

we will see the LORD's presence. Or, even more concretely, "the LORD's face." The anthropomorphism of this ancient idiom troubled the later transmitters of tradition sufficiently so that when vowel points were added to the consonantal text, roughly a millennium after the biblical period, the verb "we will see" (*nir'eh*) was revocalized as *nir'ah* ("he will be seen"), yielding a more chastely monotheistic "he will appear in the LORD's presence."

23. *what your mouth has uttered.* The Masoretic text has "His word." But a fragment of Samuel found in Cave 4 at Qumran reads "what your mouth has uttered," which, referring directly to Hannah's vow at Shiloh, makes much better sense since God, after all, has made no promises.

24. *a three-year-old bull.* This is again the reading of the Qumran Samuel text. The Masoretic text has "three bulls," but only one bull is sacrificed in the next verse, and three-year-old beasts were often designated for sacrifice.

25 brought him to the house of the LORD, and the lad was but a lad. And
26 they slaughtered the bull and they brought the lad to Eli. And she said,
"Please, my lord, by your life, my lord, I am the woman who was poised
27 by you here praying to the LORD. For this lad I prayed, and the LORD
28 granted me my petition that I asked of Him. And I on my part granted
him for the asking to the LORD; all his days he is lent to the LORD." And
she bowed there to the LORD.

---

25. *they slaughtered the bull . . . they brought the lad.* The plural subject of these
verbs is evidently Elkanah and Hannah. The simple parallelism of the brief
clauses is eloquent: both the bull and the child are offerings to the LORD, and
Samuel's dedication to the sanctuary is, surely for the parents, a kind of sacrifice. It may be relevant that the term "lad," *na 'ar,* is precisely the one used for
Isaac when he is on the point of being sacrificed and for Ishmael when he is
on the brink of perishing in the wilderness. Perhaps that background of usage
also explains the odd insistence on "the lad was but a lad" at the end of the
preceding verse. Given the late weaning time in the ancient world, and given
Hannah's likely impulse to postpone that difficult moment, one might imagine
the child Samuel to be around the age of four or five.

26. *Please, my lord.* As in their previous encounter, Hannah's speech is full of
deference and diffidence in addressing the priest—a reverence, we may already
suspect, that he does not entirely deserve.

27. *For this lad I prayed.* She spells out the act of petition and its precise fulfillment, insisting twice on the root *sh-'-l,* "to ask." The Hebrew is literally: "my
asking that I asked of Him."

28. *granted him for the asking to the LORD; all his days he is lent to the LORD.* The
English here is forced to walk around an elegant pun in the Hebrew: in the *qal*
conjugation, *sh-'-l* means to ask or petition; in the *hiph'il* conjugation the same
root means to lend; and the passive form of the verb, *sha'ul,* can mean either
"lent" or "asked."
    And she bowed. The translation again follows the reading of the Samuel frag-
ment discovered at Qumran. The Masoretic text reads "and he bowed" (a difference of one initial consonant in the Hebrew), but it is Hannah, not Elkanah,
who has been speaking for the last two verses.

CHAPTER 2

And Hannah prayed and she said:
"My heart rejoiced through the L ORD,
my horn is raised high through the L ORD.

According to the standard collagelike convention of biblical narrative composition, Hannah's psalm has been set into the story at a later stage in the editorial process than the original tale, and it gives evidence of having been taken from a familiar repertory of thanksgiving or victory psalms. The reference to the anointed king at the end of the poem assumes the institution of the monarchy, not established until two generations after the moment when Hannah is said to have pronounced this prayer. It is clearly the invocation in verse 5 of the barren woman who bears seven that encouraged the introduction here of this particular text. But the larger thematic assertion in the poem of God's power to reverse fortunes, plunging the high to the depths and exalting the lowly, is a fitting introduction to the whole Saul-David history. This psalm (verses 1–10) and David's victory psalm (2 Samuel 22) echo each other and act as formal "bookends" to the extended narrative sequence that includes the stories of Samuel, Saul, and David.

1. *my horn is raised high.* This archaic Hebrew animal imagery is worth preserving literally in English, as did Tyndale and the King James Version. The idea seems to be that the animal's horn is its glory and power, held high, perhaps in triumph after goring an enemy into submission. There is a sequence of body parts at the beginning of the first three versets of the poem, two literal and the middle one metaphorical: "my heart," "my horn," "my mouth." The raising high of the horn is crucial to the thematic unfolding of the poem, which reiterates a pattern of vertical movement, elevation and descent, that manifests God's power to reverse the fortunes of humankind. The upraised horn at the beginning returns in the envelope structure of the last line, a prayer that the L ORD "raise high His anointed's horn." That final image, in turn, involves a hidden pun, because the Hebrew "horn" (*qeren,* actually one of the rare Semitic terms cognate with Indo-European—*cornu/horn*) is also the receptacle containing the oil with which the king is anointed.

My mouth is wide to bolt down my foes;
> for I was gladdened by Your rescue.

2 There is no one holy like the LORD,
> for there is no one beside You,
>> and there is no bastion like our God.

3 Do not go on talking high and mighty—
> arrogance slips from your mouth—
for a God all-knowing is the LORD,
> and His is the measure of actions.

4 The warriors' bow is shattered
> and stumblers gird up strength.

5 The sated are hired for bread
> and the hungry cease evermore.
The barren woman bears seven
> and the many-sonned woman is bleak.

6 The LORD deals death and grants life,
> brings down to Sheol and lifts up.

7 The LORD impoverishes and bestows wealth,
> plunges down and also exalts.

8 He raises the poor from the dust,
> from the dungheaps the wretched He lifts
to seat among princes,

My mouth is wide to bolt down my foes. The Hebrew does not express but implies "bolt down." The conventional rendering of this idiom as "gloated" is an evasion of its intimation of predatory violence.

4. *shattered.* The verb used is restricted to poetry; a noun derived from it means "rubble" or "tiny broken fragments," hence the sense seems to be more extreme than the standard term "to break."

5. *the hungry cease evermore.* The Masoretic text is rather cryptic. This translation revocalizes the last Hebrew word of the line 'ad ("until," or, by a long conjectural stretch, "prey") as 'od, an adverb indicating persistence through time. The Masoretes attached the word to the beginning of the next clause, where, however, its semantic function is equally unclear.

8. *to seat among princes.* The language here might anticipate the monarchic flourish at the end of the poem. "Throne" (kis'ei) in the next line can mean

a throne of honor He bequeaths them.
For the LORD's are the pillars of earth,
    upon them He founded the world.
The steps of His faithful he watches,   9
    and the wicked in darkness turn dumb,
        for not by might will a man prevail.
The LORD shatters his adversaries,   10
    against them in the heavens He thunders.
The LORD judges the ends of the earth:
    may He grant strength to His king
        and raise high His anointed's horn."

And Elkanah went to Ramah to his home while the lad was ministering 11
to the LORD in the presence of Eli the priest. And the sons of Eli were 12
worthless fellows; they did not know the LORD. And this was the priest's 13
practice with the people: each man would offer his sacrifice, and the
priest's lad would come when the meat was boiling, a three-pronged fork
in his hand. And he would thrust into the cauldron or the pot or the vat 14
or the kettle, whatever the fork would pick up, the priest would take

---

either throne or chair. Robert Polzin has made an elaborate argument for seeing
not only Hannah's prayer but all the early chapters of 1 Samuel as a grand foreshadowing of the fate of the monarchy with the old and failing Eli, who will die
falling off his chair or throne, as a stand-in for the Davidic kings.

9. *the wicked in darkness turn dumb*. The verb obviously refers to death—the
underworld in other psalms is sometimes called *dumah*, the realm of silence
or speechlessness, a noun cognate with the verb *yidamu* used here. Those who
talked high and mighty, their mouths spewing arrogance (verse 3), are now
forever silenced.

10. *The LORD shatters his adversaries*. The Masoretic text reads, "LORD, Your
adversaries are shattered." But the Samuel fragment from Qumran has God as
the subject of a verb in the singular (a difference of only one letter) with the
adversaries as the object. This makes better syntactic sense, especially since
it is God who is thundering against the enemies in the second half of the line.
The verb *shatter* is the same one used for the warriors' bow in verse 4.

14. *the cauldron or the pot or the vat or the kettle*. This catalogue of implements
is quite untypical of biblical narrative (and in fact the precise identification of

away with it. Thus they would do to all the Israelites who came there, to
15 Shiloh. Even before they had burned off the fat, the priest's lad would
come and say to the man who was sacrificing, "Hand over meat to roast
16 for the priest, for he won't take boiled meat from you, only raw." And
the man would say, "Let them burn off the fat now and then take for
yourself whatever you want," and he would say, "No! For you shall hand
17 it over now, and if not, I will take it by force." And the lads' offense was
18 very great before the LORD, for they scorned the LORD's offering. And
Samuel was ministering in the presence of the LORD, a lad girt in linen
19 ephod. And a little cloak would his mother make him and would bring
up to him year after year when she came up with her husband to offer
20 the yearly sacrifice. And Eli would bless Elkanah and his wife and would
say, "May the LORD bestow on you seed from this woman in place of the
loan she has lent to the LORD," and they would go back to their place.
21 For the LORD singled out Hannah and she conceived and bore three
sons and two daughters. And the lad Samuel grew up with the LORD.

---

the sundry cooking receptacles is unsure). The unusual specification serves a
satiric purpose: Eli's sons are represented in a kind of frenzy of gluttony poking
their three-pronged forks into every imaginable sort of pot and pan. This sense
is then heightened in the aggressiveness of the dialogue that follows, in which
Eli's sons insist on snatching the meat uncooked from the worshippers, not
allowing them, as was customary, first to burn away the fat.

18. *ephod.* A short garment, chiefly of linen, worn by priests. The Hebrew term
has a second meaning, a device for divination manipulated by the officiating
priests, and that is the evident sense of ephod when it recurs in verse 28.

19. *And a little cloak would his mother make him.* This is a poignant instance of
the expressive reticence of biblical narrative. We have been told nothing about
Hannah's feelings as a mother after her separation from the child for whom
she so fervently prayed. This minimal notation of Hannah's annual gesture of
making a little cloak for the son she has "lent" to the LORD beautifully intimates
the love she preserves for him. The garment, fashioned as a gift of maternal
love, stands in contrast to the ephod, the acolyte's official garb for his cultic
office. Moreover, the robe (*me'il*) will continue to figure importantly in Samuel's
life, and even in his afterlife, as we shall have occasion to see.
    year after year. The phrase takes us back to the iterative tense of the begin-
ning of the story.

And Eli was very old. And he heard of all that his sons did to all the Isra- 22
elites, and that they lay with the women who flocked to the entrance of
the Tent of Assembly. And he said to them, "Why do you do such things 23
of which I hear—evil things about you from all these people? No, my 24
sons! For it is not good, what I hear that the LORD's people are spreading
about. If a man offends against man, God may intercede for him, but 25
if against the LORD a man should offend, who can intercede for him?"
And they did not heed their father's voice, for the LORD wanted to put
them to death. And the lad Samuel was growing in goodness with both 26
the LORD and with men.

And a man of God came to Eli and said to him, "Thus says the LORD! 27
Did I not reveal myself to your father's house when they were in Egypt,
slaves to Pharaoh's house? And did I not choose him from all the tribes 28
of Israel as a priest for me, to go up to My altar, to burn incense, to carry
an ephod before Me? And I gave to your father's house all the Israelites'
burnt offerings. Why do you trample on My sacrifice and My offering 29

---

22. *and that they lay with the women*. This whole clause is missing in the
Qumran scroll and in one version of the Septuagint; in fact, sexual exploitation
was not mentioned in the initial narrative report of the sons' misdeeds. There
is, however, a consonance between their appetitive impulse in snatching the
meat and grabbing the women, perhaps reinforced by the satiric, and phallic,
image of thrusting forks into bubbling pots.
    flocked. The Hebrew verb might also mean "ministered."

27. *a man of God came to Eli*. This enunciation of a curse on the house of Eli,
at the very beginning of the Samuel story, is introduced at precisely the corresponding place in the narrative as the denunciation and admonition of the
divine messenger at the beginning of Judges (Chapter 2). An analogous curse
will be pronounced by Nathan the prophet on the house of David (2 Samuel
12) and will be enacted in the subsequent narrative.
    slaves to Pharaoh's house. The Masoretic text lacks "slaves to" but it is attested
in the Qumran Samuel scroll, in the Septuagint, and in the Targum of Yonatan
ben Uziel.

29. *My sacrifice and My offering which I have commanded*. The Masoretic text
reads "which I commanded [as a?] habitation [*ma'on*]." Since that makes no
sense, and all attempts to rescue a meaning seem forced, I have assumed that

which I have commanded, and you honor your sons more than Me, to batten upon the first portions of each offering of Israel My people?
30 Therefore, says the LORD God of Israel, I indeed said, 'Your house and your father's house will walk before Me forever,' but now, says the LORD, God forbid I should do it! For those who honor Me will I honor, and my
31 spurners shall be dishonored. Look, a time is coming when I will cut down your seed and the seed of your father's house, and there shall be
32 no elder in your house. And you shall look with a jaundiced eye at all the bounty bestowed upon Israel, and there will be no elder in your house
33 for all time. Yet no man of you will I cut off from My altar, to make your eyes waste away and your spirit ache, and the increase of your house
34 shall fall by the sword of men. And this is the sign for you—that which comes upon your two sons, Hophni and Phineas, on a single day the

---

ma'on is an excrescence, perhaps inadvertently transposed by a scribe from verse 32, where it also occurs rather enigmatically. Several points in the curse pronounced by the man of God look textually defective.

30. *will walk before Me.* The biblical idiom suggests dedicated service of a deity.
  honor . . . dishonored. The Hebrew terms mean, etymologically, "heavy" and "light" (that is, "weighty" and "worthless"). These antonyms will recur at strategic moments in the Ark Narrative and in the story of David.

32. *look with a jaundiced eye.* The received text at this point is very doubtful, yielding, literally, a nonsense chain: "you will look narrow habitation." This translation adopts an emendation that has considerable scholarly currency: *'ayin* instead of *ma 'on* (a difference of one consonant in the Hebrew). That yields the idiom *tsar- 'ayin,* "jealously" or "with a jaundiced eye." But the Qumran text and one version of the Septuagint lack the entire clause.

33. *no man of you will I cut off.* The usual understanding of these words is that God will leave them alive to witness in pain the destruction of the family. This interpretation seems a bit strained because in the next verse God promises to destroy both of Eli's sons on a single day. Perhaps the clause originally read, "every man of you will I cut off," though this phrasing is not reflected in any of the ancient versions.
  fall by the sword of men. Again, both the Qumran fragment and Version B of the Septuagint confirm this reading, which seems much likelier than the Masoretic text's cryptic "shall die [as?] men."

two of them shall die! And I will set up for Myself a stalwart priest, 35
according to my heart and my spirit he shall act, and I will build him a
stalwart house and he shall walk before My anointed for all time. And 36
it will happen that whoever remains from your house shall come to bow
before him for a bit of silver and a loaf of bread, and he shall say, "Add
me on, pray, to one of the priestly details for a crust of bread to eat."

---

35. *a stalwart priest . . . a stalwart house*. The Hebrew *ne'eman* in the first
instance means "faithful" or "trustworthy," in the second instance, "well-
founded," "enduring." The present translation draws on an older sense of "stalwart," which can be applied to structures and inanimate objects as well as to
people. The probable referent of the prophecy is the house of Zadok, which
was to become the priestly line in the Davidic monarchy.

before My anointed. Like Hannah's psalm, this whole passage of prophecy
appears to presuppose a historical context in which the monarchy was an established fact.

CHAPTER 3

1   And the lad Samuel was ministering to the LORD in Eli's presence,
    and the word of the LORD was rare in those days, vision was not spread
2   about. And it happened on that day that Eli was lying in his place, his
3   eyes had begun to grow bleary, he could not see. The lamp of God had
    not yet gone out, and Samuel was lying in the temple of the LORD, in
4   which was the Ark of God. And the LORD called to Samuel, and he said,
5   "Here I am." And he ran to Eli and he said, "Here I am, for you called

---

1. *the word of the* LORD *was rare . . . vision was not spread about.* The "word of
the LORD" is often a technical term referring to oracular message. Inquiring of
the oracle would have been a priestly function, and so there is an intimation
here of some sort of breakdown in the professional performance of the house
of Eli. But the same phrase also is used to announce prophecy, and "vision" is
a prophetic term: the whole episode concerns the transition from priestly to
prophetic authority.

2. *he could not see.* Eli's blindness not only reflects his decrepitude but his
incapacity for vision in the sense of the previous verse. He is immersed in permanent darkness while the lad Samuel has God's lamp burning by his bedside.

3. *The lamp of God had not yet gone out.* Since the sanctuary lamp would have
burned through most of the night, this may be an indication, as Kyle McCarter,
Jr. has proposed, that the scene occurs close to dawn. But the symbolic over-
tones of the image should not be neglected: though vision has become rare,
God's lamp has not yet gone out, and the young ministrant will be the one to
make it burn bright again (see verses 19–21, plus 4:1a). The actual lamp would
have been a concave earthenware vessel filled with oil.

5. *he ran to Eli and he said, "Here I am."* These words make clear that the previous "Here I am" is not a direct response to God but rather the boy's calling out

me," and he said, "I did not call. Go back, lie down." And he went and lay down. And the Lord called once again, "Samuel!" And Samuel rose 6 and went to Eli and said, "Here I am, for you called me." And he said, "I did not call, my son. Go back, lie down." And Samuel did not yet 7 know the Lord, and the word of the Lord had not yet been revealed to him. And the Lord called still again to Samuel, a third time, and he 8 rose and went to Eli and said, "Here I am, for you called me." And Eli understood that the Lord was calling the lad. And Eli said to Samuel, 9 "Go lie down, and should someone call to you, say, 'Speak, Lord, for Your servant is listening.'" And Samuel went and lay down in his place. And the Lord came and stood poised and called as on each time before, 10 "Samuel, Samuel!" And Samuel said, "Speak, for Your servant is listening." And the Lord said to Samuel, "I am about to do such a thing in 11 Israel that whoever hears of it, both his ears will ring. On that day I 12 will fulfill against Eli all that I have spoken concerning his house, from

---

from the inner chamber of the sanctuary to Eli in the outer room, thinking that it is Eli who called him. Samuel's thrice-repeated error in this regard reflects not only his youthful inexperience but, as the sixteenth-century Hebrew exegete Yosef Karo has proposed, the general fact that "the word of the Lord was rare," revelation an unfamiliar phenomenon.

6. *"Samuel!"* In an intensifying pattern, as the folk-tale structure of three repetitions with a final reversal unfolds, God's address is now represented more immediately in dialogue instead of indirectly as in verse 4. The third time, God will say, "Samuel, Samuel!"

"I did not call, my son." Until this point, we have been told nothing about Eli's relationship with Samuel. The introduction of this single term of affection, "my son," reveals the fondness of the blind and doomed Eli for his young assistant. His own biological sons have of course utterly betrayed his trust.

9. *"Speak, Lord, for Your servant is listening."* This is virtually a formula of deferential response to superior authority. When Samuel repeats these words in verse 10, he omits "Lord," perhaps, as Shimon Bar-Efrat has suggested, in diffidence about addressing God.

12. *all that I have spoken concerning his house.* This clause, and the one beginning "I have told him" in the next verse, refer back to the prophecy of doom pronounced by the man of God in Chapter 2.

13 beginning to end. And I have told him that I was passing judgment
    on his house for all time because of the sin of which he knew, for his
14 sons have been scorning God and he did not restrain them. Therefore
    I have sworn against the house of Eli, that the sin of the house of Eli
15 will not be atoned by sacrifice and offering for all time." And Samuel lay
    until morning, and he opened the doors of the house of the LORD, and
16 Samuel was afraid to tell the vision to Eli. And Eli called to Samuel and

---

13. *his sons have been scorning God.* The Masoretic text reads, "his sons have
been scorning for themselves [*lahem*]," but the last Hebrew word has long been
recognized as a *tiqun sofrim*, a scribal euphemism for *'elohim*, God—that is, the
scribes were loath to write out so sacrilegious a phrase as scorning, or cursing,
God. The verb here is commonly used in the sense of "to damn" or "to express
contempt." In this case, the sons' contempt would have been expressed by their
snatching of choice portions from the sacrificial meat.

he did not restrain them. The Hebrew *kihah* occurs only here as a transitive
verb in the *pi'el* conjugation, though it is fairly common as an intransitive verb
in the *qal* conjugation, meaning "to grow weak," "to become dark," or, as with
the eyes of Eli in verse 2, bleary. The transitive sense of the verb would then
be something like "to incapacitate," to prevent someone from doing something.
Its unusual usage in this sentence is obviously meant to align Eli's failing in
parental authority with the failing of his sight.

11.–13. It is noteworthy that God's first message to Samuel is a prophecy of
doom. Its content not only indicates the overthrow of the priestly authority
of the house of Eli and the implicit move to a different sort of authority to be
embodied by the prophet Samuel, but it also adumbrates the rather dour and
dire role Samuel will play as leader, in relation to both Israel and to Saul.

15. *And Samuel lay until morning.* The verb does not necessarily imply that
he fell asleep again after this riveting revelation, and if in fact the whole scene
takes place close to dawn, there would be little time before the first light roused
him.

he opened the doors of the house of the LORD. He resumes his usual business as faithful temple ministrant, almost as though he wanted to shrug off
the divine revelation that implied a more portentous role for him than that of
priestly acolyte.

Samuel was afraid to tell the vision. The divine message is called a vision
though it was conveyed through words rather than images. The term used here,
mar'eh, is different from *ḥazon*, the word that occurs in verse 1, though both
refer to sight, the faculty Eli lacks.

said, "Samuel, my son," and he said, "Here I am." And he said, "What 17
is the thing He spoke to you? Pray, do not conceal it from me. Thus
and more may God do to you if you conceal from me anything of all the
things He spoke to you." And Samuel told him all the things and he did 18
not conceal from him, and he said, "He is the LORD. What is good in
His eyes let Him do."

And Samuel grew up and the LORD was with him, and He let not fall 19
to the ground any of his words. And all Israel, from Dan to Beersheba, 20
knew that Samuel was stalwart as a prophet to the LORD. And the LORD 21
continued to appear in Shiloh, for the LORD was revealed to Samuel in
Shiloh through the word of the LORD, and Samuel's word was upon all 4:1a
Israel.

---

17. *Thus and more may God do to you.* This is a set idiom for abjuration: may
terrible things befall you if you fail to perform what I require of you.

18. *What is good in His eyes let Him do.* Old Eli's response is pious resignation
to the prophecy of doom. He of course is aware of his sons' misdeeds and of his
own failure to intervene successfully.

19. *He let not fall to the ground any of his words.* The antecedent of "his" is
ambiguous, but since the point of the narrative report is to confirm Samuel's
prophetic authority, the more likely reading is that God did not allow any of
Samuel's words to go awry but fulfilled all of His prophet's predictions.

20. *from Dan to Beersheba.* That is, from the far north, near Phoenician territory,
to the Negeb in the south.
  stalwart. Or, "faithful." That is, Samuel's authority as prophet was recognized
by all Israel.

21. *And the LORD continued to appear . . . the LORD was revealed.* This emphatic
indication is an obvious counterpoint to the first verse of the chapter: instead
of being withheld, divine communication is now regular and repeated through
the person of Samuel.

4:1a. Although the conventional chapter division attaches this brief clause to the
next episode, it is clear that it is actually a final summary of Samuel's new authority at the end of his dedication story. The next words of the text (Chapter 4:1b)
in fact refer to a military initiative undertaken by the Israelites without Samuel's
authorization.

CHAPTER 4

1b A̲nd Israel went out in battle against the Philistines, and they encamped by Eben-Ezer, while the Philistines were encamped at 2 Aphek. And the Philistines drew up their lines against Israel, and the battle forces were deployed, and Israel was routed by the Philistines, and they struck down in the lines in the field about four thousand men.

1b. *the Philistines*. The Philistines were part of the general incursion of the so-called Sea Peoples from the Aegean—the prophet Amos names Crete as their land of origin—into the eastern Mediterranean region perhaps less than a century before the early eleventh-century setting of our story. (There is some evidence that they first migrated to Anatolia, then moved southward.) They established a powerful presence in Canaan on the coastal plain, concentrated in the region a little south of present-day Tel Aviv. They were intrepid warriors (note the martial exhortation of verse 9) and also exercised a mastery of military science and military technology. In the coastal plain, they were able to deploy iron chariots (which seem to have been lacking among the Israelites) as well as infantry. Perhaps their failure to extend their mini-kingdom of five allied cities more than a dozen or so miles eastward from the coast was related to a loss of the strategic advantage of chariots as they went up into the high country.

2. *the Philistines drew up their lines . . . and the battle forces were deployed.* Interestingly, the language of strategic deployment is attached only to the Philistines. "Battle forces" is, literally, "battle." Although the precise indications of these terms are unclear, their use elsewhere in the Bible makes it evident that they had a technical military application.

the lines. The Hebrew, *ma'arakhah,* is a singular, with the sense of "battle formation" or "front line."

And the troops came into the camp, and the elders of Israel said, "Why   3
has the L ORD routed us today before the Philistines? Let us take to us
from Shiloh the Ark of the Covenant of the L ORD, that it may come
into our midst and rescue us from the hands of our enemies." And the   4
troops sent to Shiloh and they bore from there the Ark of the Covenant
of the L ORD of Armies enthroned on the cherubim, and there the two
sons of Eli were with the Ark of the Covenant of God—Hophni and
Phineas. And when the Ark of the Covenant of the L ORD came into   5
the camp, all Israel let out a great shout, and the earth resounded. And   6
the Philistines heard the sound of the shouting and said, "What is the
sound of this great shouting in the camp of the Hebrews?" And they

---

3. *Let us take to us.* The addition of this seemingly superfluous personal pronoun suggests how the elders arrogate to themselves a sacred object for their
own purposes, conceiving the Ark magically or fetishistically as a vehicle of
power that they can manipulate for military ends.

  the Ark of the Covenant of the L ORD. This would have been a large case made
of acacia wood, with carved cherubim on its top, containing the stone tablets
of the Law given at Sinai. As the material residue of the defining encounter
between God and Israel, these tablets were viewed as the most sacrosanct possession of the nation. Hence the horror at the end of this episode over the news
that the Ark has been captured by the Philistines.

4. *troops.* The Hebrew has a collective noun, *'am,* "people," which in military
contexts refers to the ordinary soldiers.

  the Ark of the Covenant of the L ORD of Armies enthroned on the cherubim.
This extravagantly full title is a kind of epic flourish reflecting the power that
the elders of Israel attribute to the Ark. "Armies" ("hosts" in older translations)
underscores the L ORD's martial nature. The cherubim are fierce winged beasts
imagined as God's celestial steeds, and so the carved cherubim on the Ark are
conceived as the earthly "throne" of the invisible deity.

  Hophni and Phineas. In an odd stylistic tie, each time the two sons are mentioned in this chapter, their proper names are stuck on at the very end of the
sentence, as though their precise identity were being isolated for opprobrium.

6. *the camp of the Hebrews.* "Hebrews" is generally the designation of the Israelites when they are named by other peoples.

7 knew that the Ark of the LORD had come into the camp. And the Philistines were afraid, for they thought, "God has come into the camp."
8 And they said, "Woe to us! For it was never so in times gone by. Woe to us! Who will save us from the hands of these mighty gods? They are the very gods who struck Egypt with every blow in the wilderness.
9 Muster strength and be men, O Philistines, lest you become slaves to
10 the Hebrews as they were slaves to you. Be men and do battle!" And the Philistines did battle and Israel was routed, and every man fled to his tent and the blow was very great, thirty thousand foot soldiers of
11 Israel fell. And the Ark of the LORD was taken, and the two sons of Eli
12 died—Hophni and Phineas. And a man of Benjamin ran from the lines and came to Shiloh that day, his garments torn and earth on his head.
13 He came, and, look, Eli was seated in a chair by the road on the look-

---

7. *God has come into the camp.* Here *'elohim* is the subject of a verb in the singular, but in verse 8, in proper polytheistic fashion, the Philistines use the same term but construe it grammatically as a plural, "gods."

8. *every blow.* The Hebrew *makah* also means "plague," an obviously appropriate sense here, but it is important that the writer uses the same word in verse 10, though with a military meaning, for a theological irony is intended in the pun: they feared the might of the LORD Who struck such terrible blows against Egypt, and then they themselves strike a blow against Israel, which actually does not have God in its midst, only His sacred paraphernalia. Here as elsewhere in the Bible, the national fiction is maintained that all the peoples of Canaan were intimately familiar with the Exodus story and deeply impressed by it.

9. *Muster strength and be men.* There may be a pointed antithesis in their speech between "gods" and "men." In any case, they summon stirring rhetoric to rouse themselves from their fear of a supernatural adversary and to go out to do battle.

12. *his garments torn and earth on his head.* This disheveled appearance is not because of the fighting but reflects the customary signs of mourning.

13. *Eli was seated in a chair by the road.* Similarly, in Chapter 1, he was seated in a chair in the temple—in both instances a token of his infirmity, his passivity or incapacity as leader. The Hebrew phrase behind "by the road" is textually problematic, as is the related phrase attached to the word "gate" in verse 18.

out, for his heart was trembling over the Ark of God, and the man had
come to tell in the town and the whole town cried out, and Eli heard 14
the sound of the outcry and said, "What is this sound of uproar?" The
man had hurried, and he came and told Eli. And Eli was ninety-eight 15
years old, his eyes were rigid and he could not see. And the man said 16
to Eli, "I am the one who has come from the lines, I from the lines fled
today." And he said, "What happened, my son?" And the bearer of tid- 17
ings answered and said, "Israel fled before the Philistines, and what's

---

Scholarly opinion differs as to whether Eli is sitting by the road, by the gate,
or, like David in 2 Samuel 18, above the gate. The last of these possibilities
would best explain his breaking his neck when he falls, but it is by no means
the inevitable meaning of the Hebrew, and the Hebrew preposition in verse 18
actually indicates *through* the gate.

    his heart was trembling over the Ark of God. Apprehension over the fate of his
scurrilous sons is not mentioned.

14. *What is this sound of uproar?* Eli's question pointedly, and ironically, parallels
the question asked by the Philistines in verse 6 about the jubilant uproar from
the Israelite camp. At the very end of the David story (1 Kings 1), the usurper
Adonijah will ask virtually the same question about an uproar that spells disaster for him and his followers.

15. *his eyes were rigid*. The idiom for Eli's blindness has a stark finality here
that it does not have in 3:2. Presumably a good deal of time has elapsed since
that moment of the young Samuel's dedication as prophet, and the process of
blindness is now complete. It is because Eli can see nothing that he must ask
with particular urgency about the reason for all the shouting.

16. *I am the one who has come from the lines, I from the lines fled today.* This
odd repetition may reflect a stammer of nervousness or confusion, as Shimon
Bar-Efrat has proposed.

17. The report of the battle moves from a general indication of the defeat, to
the admission of a rout, to the death of Eli's two sons, and, finally, to what is
assumed to be the worst catastrophe, the capture of the Ark. It should be noted
that 1 and 2 Samuel are in part organized around a series of inter-echoing
scenes in which a messenger brings ill tidings. The bearer of ill tidings to Adonijah at the very end of this long narrative also nervously repeats *wegam*, "what's
more" as he recounts the catastrophe.

more, there was a great rout among the troops, and what's more, your two sons died—Hophni and Phineas—and the Ark of God was taken."

18 And the moment he mentioned the Ark of God, Eli fell backward from his chair through the gate and his neckbone was broken and he died, for the man was old and heavy. And he had judged Israel forty years.

19 And his daughter-in-law, Phineas's wife, was big with child, and when she heard the report about the taking of the Ark, and that her father-in-law and her husband were dead, she crouched down and gave birth,

20 for her birth pangs overwhelmed her. And as she was on the point of death, her attendant women spoke up, "Fear not, for you have borne

21 a son." And she did not answer or pay heed. And she called the boy Ichabod, which is to say, "Glory is exiled from Israel"—for the taking of

22 the Ark and for her father-in-law and her husband. And she said, "Glory is exiled from Israel, for the Ark of God is taken."

---

18. *And he had judged Israel forty years.* This notice, with its use of the formulaic forty years, is odd because Eli certainly has not been a judge, either in the military-charismatic or the juridical sense. This sentence could be an attempt to establish a carry-over from the Book of Judges, or it could be an inadvertent editorial repetition of the Judges formula.

19. *big with child.* The Hebrew says literally "was pregnant to give birth."
   she crouched down. In the ancient Near East, women generally gave birth in a kneeling position, leaning on a special birthing stone—examples have been uncovered by archeologists—called in Hebrew a *mashber*.

21. *Ichabod . . . Glory is exiled.* The Hebrew name is conventionally construed to mean "Inglorious," though Kyle McCarter, Jr., has argued that the more probable meaning is "Where is glory?" or "Alas for glory!" In any case, it is a most peculiar name—the dying mother, overcome by the loss of the Ark (which affects her much more than her husband's demise), inscribing the national catastrophe in her son's name. Where one must agree unhesitatingly with McCarter is that the verb in this verse and the next should be rendered as "exiled" and not, as it is customarily translated, as "departed." Exile is what it clearly denotes, and it is surely significant that this whole large sequence of stories that will provide an account of the founding of Israel's dynasty and the crystallization of its national power begins with a refrain of glory exiled from Israel. It is also noteworthy that the term for "glory," *kavod*, is transparently cognate with *kaved*, "heavy," the adjective used to explain Eli's lethal tumble from his chair—the leader who might be supposed to represent Israel's glory exhibits only deadly heaviness.

CHAPTER 5

And the Philistines had taken the Ark of God and brought it from Eben- 1
Ezer to Ashdod. And the Philistines took the Ark of God and brought it to 2
the house of Dagon and set it up alongside Dagon. And the Ashdodites 3
arose on the next day and, look, Dagon was fallen forward to the ground

---

The Ark Narrative at this point leaves behind the house of Eli, Samuel, and
the paramount question of Israel's leadership in order to tell a bizarre satiric
story of a battle between cult objects—the potent Ark of the Covenant, which
is conceived as the conduit for the cosmic power of the God of Israel, and the
idol of Dagon, vainly believed to be a real deity by the Philistines. The dominant
tone of the story is a kind of monotheistic triumphalism; accordingly, themes
from the story of the plagues of Egypt are replayed, though in a virtually scatological key.

1. *from Eben-Ezer to Ashdod.* The Ark is carried down from Eben-Ezer, in the
western part of the territory of Ephraim (roughly ten miles from the coast and
just a little to the north of present-day Tel Aviv) to Ashdod, on the Mediterranean, in the heart of Philistine territory.

2. *Dagon.* This god is now generally thought to be a vegetation or fertility god,
its name cognate with the Hebrew *dagan*, "grain" (and not, as was once widely
imagined, with the Hebrew *dag*, "fish").
   set it up alongside Dagon. Either to amplify the power of their own deity or
to express the subservience of the God of Israel to Dagon.

3. *and, look, Dagon was fallen forward to the ground.* This clause and the parallel
one in the next verse reflect the visual perspective of the Ashdodites when they
come into the temple early in the morning and make their shocking discovery.
Tyndale's translation gets into the spirit of the scene, though with a certain
creative license, by rendering this, "lay grovelling upon the ground."

before the Ark of the LORD. And they took Dagon and set him back in
4 his place. And they arose the next morning and, look, Dagon was fallen
forward to the ground before the Ark of the LORD, and Dagon's head and
both his hands were chopped off upon the threshold—his trunk alone
5 remained on him. Therefore the priests of Dagon, and all who enter the
house of Dagon, do not tread on the threshold of the house of Dagon
6 to this day. And the hand of the LORD was heavy upon the Ashdodites
and He devastated them, and He struck them with tumors, Ashdod and

---

4. *his trunk alone remained on him.* The Masoretic text has cryptically, "Dagon
alone remained on him," but several of the ancient translations appear to have
used a version which read *geivo,* "his trunk," instead of *Dagon.* Dagon's first
downfall might be attributed to a natural, accidental cause—the idol's somehow slipping from its pedestal. This second incident, in which the hands and
head of the idol have been chopped off, offers to the Philistines clear proof of
divine intervention. Hacking the hands and feet off war prisoners was a well-
known barbaric practice in the ancient Near East, and similar acts of mutilation
are attested in the Book of Judges.

5. *Therefore.* This is the introductory formula for etiological explanations. An
observed Philistine practice of skipping over the sanctuary threshold, as a special measure for entering sacred space, is reinterpreted as a reminiscence of
the victory of Israel's God over Dagon.

6. *the hand of the LORD was heavy upon the Ashdodites.* The word *kaved,* previously associated with Eli's corpulence and linked by root with *kavod,* "glory,"
recurs here in a clause that introduces the first of several echoes of the plagues
against Egypt.
    tumors. Many translations render this as "hemorrhoids," and there is a little
confusion in the Masoretic text: the consonantal written version (*ketiv*) has
"tumors," but the tradition for reciting the text (*qeri*) indicates "hemorrhoids."
This confusion is compounded because the Septuagint, seconded by Josephus,
includes a plague of mice not in evidence in the Masoretic version, and the
golden mice of the next chapter look very much like a response to just such a
plague. The fact, moreover, that hemorrhoids are a humiliating but not lethal
disorder and are not spread by epidemic, whereas the Philistines protest that
they are dying, gives support to an interpretation at least as old as Rashi: the
plague in question is bubonic plague, carried by rats (metamorphosed in this
story into mice, and associated with the epidemic but perhaps not clearly
understood as the bearers of the disease); the tumors are the *buboes* of bubonic
plague, which might especially afflict the lower body, including the rectal area.

all its territories. And the people of Ashdod saw that it was so, and they 7
said, "Let not the Ark of the God of Israel stay among us, for His hand
is hard upon us and upon Dagon our god." And they sent and gathered 8
to them all the Philistine overlords and they said, "What shall we do
with the Ark of the God of Israel?" And they said, "To Gath let the Ark
of the God of Israel be brought round." And they brought round the Ark
of the God of Israel. And it happened after they had brought it round 9
that the hand of the LORD was against the town—a great panic. And
He struck the people of the town, young and old, and they had tumors
in their secret parts. And they sent the Ark of God on to Ekron, and it 10
happened when the Ark of God came to Ekron that the Ekronites cried
out, saying, "They have brought round to me the Ark of the God of Israel
to bring death to me and my people." And they sent and gathered all the 11
Philistine overlords and they said, "Send the Ark of the God of Israel
back to its place, and let it not bring death to me and my people." For
there was death panic throughout the city, the hand of God was very
heavy there. And the people who did not die were struck with tumors, 12
and the town's outcry rose to the heavens.

---

8. *overlords.* The Hebrew term *seranim* is a Philistine loanword and is applied
only to Philistines as a touch of local color (like calling Spanish aristocrats "gran-
dees"). Some scholars have linked the word with the Greek *tyrranos.* Since there
is only one *seren* for each Philistine city, they are clearly more than just "lords."

   Gath. The Ark is carried around to three of the five Philistine cities. The
other two are Gaza and Ashkelon.

9. *the hand of the LORD was against the town—a great panic.* This apposition
reflects the Hebrew syntax, which sounds a little peculiar, but there is not
convincing evidence of a defective text here.

   they had tumors in their secret parts. The verb *yisatru* is peculiar. This translation follows Rashi, Kimchi, and the King James Version in linking it with *seter,*
secret place.

12. *the town's outcry rose to the heavens.* This clause balances on the edge of an
ambiguity. "The heavens" (*hashamayim*) can be simply the sky or the abode of
God. Is God, Who has been present in the story through His acts, His heavy
hand—but not, as it were, in person—listening to the anguished cries of the
Philistines, or is this merely an image of the shrieks of the afflicted Philistines
echoing under the silent vault of the heavens?

CHAPTER 6

1,2 And the Ark of the LORD was in Philistine country seven months. And
the Philistines called to the priests and the soothsayers, saying, "What
shall we do with the Ark of the LORD? Tell us, how shall we send it back
3 to its place." And they said, "If you are about to send back the Ark of
the God of Israel, do not send it back empty-handed, for you must give
back to Him a guilt offering. Then you will be healed and there will be
4 atonement for you. Why should His hand not relent from you?" And
they said, "What guilt offering should we give back to Him?" And they

---

This chapter—the episode actually ends in the first verse of Chapter 7—which
concludes the Ark Narrative, also brings to a climax the traits that set it off from
the larger narrative of Samuel, Saul, and David in which it is placed. Instead of
the sharply etched individual characters of the surrounding narrative, we have
only collective speakers and agents. Instead of the political perspective with its
human system of causation, the perspective is theological and the culminating events of the story are frankly miraculous. God, Who does not speak in
this narrative, manifests His power over Philistines and Israelites alike through
supernatural acts in the material realm, as the strange tale of the cart and the
golden images vividly demonstrates.

3. *send it back*. The Hebrew *meshalhim* is the same verb repeatedly used for
Pharaoh's sending Israel out of Egypt and thus sustains the network of allusions
to the Exodus story. In Exodus, the Israelites, too, were told that they would
not leave Egypt "empty-handed" but would take with them golden ornaments
despoiled from the Egyptians.
there will be atonement for you. The Masoretic text has "it will become
known to you" (*wenod'a lakhem*), but the reading of both the Qumran Samuel
scroll and the Septuagint, *wenikaper lakhem*, "and it will be atoned for you,"
makes far better sense.

said, "The number of the Philistine overlords is five. Five golden tumors and five golden mice. For a single plague is upon all of you and upon your overlords. And you shall make images of your tumors and images of 5 your mice that are ravaging the land, and you shall give glory to the God of Israel—perhaps He will lighten His hand from upon you and from upon your god and your land. And why should you harden your hearts 6 as Egypt and Pharaoh hardened their hearts? After He made sport of them, did they not let the Hebrews go, and off they went? And so, fetch 7 and make one new cart, and two milch cows that no yoke has touched, and harness the cows to the cart, but bring their calves back inside.

---

5. *you shall give glory to the God of Israel—perhaps He will lighten His hand.* Once again, the writer harks back to the play of antonyms, *kavod/kaved* (glory/ heavy) and *qal* (light, and in other contexts, worthless). Glory has been exiled from Israel with the capture of the Ark: now, with the restitution of the Ark together with an indemnity payment of golden images, glory will be restored. This process helps explain the insistence on the term "give back" associated with the guilt offering.

6. *harden your hearts.* This phrase is not only an explicit link with the Exodus story, but it also continues the play on glory/heaviness because the literal Hebrew idiom is "make your heart heavy" (the verb *kabed*).

   let the Hebrews go. The Hebrew says "let them go," but the lack of antecedent for the pronoun would be confusing in English.

7. *one new cart.* It is to be an undefiled instrument made specifically for this ritual purpose.

   that no yoke has touched. The cows, too, are uncompromised by use in ordinary labor, though the more important point is that they are entirely devoid of experience as draft animals, so that their ability to pull the cart straight to Beth-Shemesh would have to be a manifestation of God's intervention, or of the intrinsic power of the Ark.

   their calves back inside. This, of course, is the crux of the test: the milking cows will have to go against nature in plodding forward into Israelite territory with their calves behind them, shut up in the manger and waiting to be fed.

8   And you shall fetch the Ark of the LORD and set it on the cart, and
the golden objects that you give back to Him as a guilt offering you
shall place in a chest at its side, and you shall send it away and off it
9   will go. And you will see—if on the road to its own territory, to Beth-
Shemesh, it will go up, He it was Who did this great evil to us, and
if not, we shall know that it was not His hand that afflicted us but
10 chance that came upon us." And so the men did: they took two milch
cows and harnessed them to the cart, but their calves they shut up
11 inside. And they placed the Ark of the LORD on the cart and the chest
12 and the golden mice and the images of their tumors. And the cows
went straight on the way, on the way to Beth-Shemesh, on a single road
they went, lowing as they went, and they veered neither right nor left,

---

8. *chest*. The Hebrew *'argaz* appears only here. Postbiblical Hebrew consistently understood it as "chest," though some scholars, on the basis of Semitic
cognates, have argued for the meaning of "pouch." It may be more plausible
that precious objects would be placed in orderly fashion in a chest rather than
piled up in a pouch.

11. *the Ark of the LORD . . . and the chest and the golden mice and the images of
their tumors*. This whole scene has a certain grotesquely comic and incongruous
effect: Israel's most sacred cult object drawn in a cart by two cows with swollen
udders, and alongside the Ark golden images of vermin and tumors.

12. *straight on the way, on the way to Beth-Shemesh, on a single road they went . . .
and they veered neither right nor left*. Against the spareness and swift efficiency
of normal Hebrew narrative style, the writer here lavishes synonyms and repetitions in order to highlight the perfect geometry of the miracle: against all
conceivable distractions of biology or sheer animal unknowingness, the cows
pursue an arrow-straight northwest trajectory from Ekron to Beth-Shemesh.
   lowing as they went. This small but vivid descriptive detail is an even more
striking exception to the stringent economy that governs biblical narrative. The
last thing one would expect in a biblical story, where there is scant report of the
gestures of the human actors, is a specification of sounds made by draft animals.
The point, however, is that the milch cows—more driven by the Ark than hauling
it—are going strenuously against nature: their udders full of milk for the calves
they have been forced to leave behind, they mark with maternal lowing their distress over the journey they cannot resist. There is a peculiar resonance between
this episode and Hannah's story in Chapter 1. There, too, a nursing mother does

with the Philistine overlords walking after them to the border of Beth-Shemesh. And the men of Beth-Shemesh were harvesting the wheat 13 harvest in the valley, and they raised their eyes and saw the Ark, and they rejoiced at the sight. And the cart had come to the field of Joshua the 14 Beth-Shemeshite and it came to rest there, and a great stone was there, and they split the wood of the cart, and the cows they offered up as a burnt offering to the LORD. And the Levites had brought down the Ark 15 of the LORD and the chest that was with it, in which were the golden objects, and they placed them on the great stone, and the men of Beth-Shemesh offered up burnt offerings and sacrificed sacrifices on that day to the LORD. The five Philistine overlords saw, and they returned to 16 Ekron on that day. And these are the golden tumors that the Philistines 17 gave back as guilt offering to the LORD: for Ashdod, one; for Gaza, one;

---

not want to be separated from her young, and, as we noted, special emphasis is placed on the physical acts of nursing and weaning. (The connection between the two episodes is underscored in the Hebrew, which literally calls the cows' young their "sons," not their calves.) In both stories, sacrifice is offered after mother and young are separated. Here, of course, the mothers become the objects of the sacrifice; in Hannah's story, it is a bull, and, in symbolic rather than literal fashion, the son as well. Though all these correspondences seem too pointed to be coincidental, it is unclear whether they represent the literary artifact of the redactor, or an allusion by the author of the Samuel story to the Ark Narrative.

1 3. *the men of Beth-Shemesh were harvesting*. The Hebrew uses an ellipsis: "Beth-Shemesh were harvesting."

1 4. *the cows they offered up*. One connection between the Ark Narrative, with its concern for sanctity, and the Samuel-Saul-David cycle, with its preoccupation with politics, is a kind of brooding sense of the cruel price exacted for dedication to the higher cause. The milch cows are burned on the improvised altar; Hannah and her son Samuel must be separated in *his* dedication to the sanctuary; and later both Saul and David will pay terrible costs in their personal lives for their adhesion to power.

1 7. *And these are the golden tumors*. The introductory formula suggests a kind of ritual or epic catalogue, so that we know there is in fact one golden image corresponding to each of the five Philistine towns, just as the soothsayers had stipulated.

18 for Ashkelon, one; for Gath, one; for Ekron, one. And the golden mice were the number of all the Philistine towns, from the fortified cities to the unwalled villages. And the great stone on which they set the Ark of the LORD is to this day in the field of Joshua the Beth-Shemeshite. 19 And He struck down men of Beth-Shemesh, for they had looked into the Ark of the LORD, and he struck down from the people seventy men [fifty thousand men], and the people mourned, for the LORD had struck 20 down the people with a great blow. And the people of Beth-Shemesh

---

18. *the golden mice were the number of all the Philistine towns.* This appears to contradict the explicit directions in verse 4, that there should be exactly five golden mice. Kimchi resolves the discrepancy by proposing that, in the event, as added insurance for all the villages (since the mice had overrun the fields), the Philistines went beyond their instructions and fashioned multiple images of the mice.

And the great stone. The Masoretic text reads *'avel* (brook or meadow) instead of *'even* (stone), but both the Septuagint and the Qumran scroll have the latter reading. The Masoretic text also has "and to" (*we'ad*) preceding this word, but that is probably an inadvertent scribal duplication of the preposition that occurs twice before in the verse.

19. *fifty thousand men.* This figure makes no sense because Beth-Shemesh was a small agricultural village. It appears in all the ancient versions, but Josephus seems to have possessed a text in which only the much more plausible number seventy appeared. The fact that the Hebrew has no indication of "and" between "seventy" and "fifty thousand" is further evidence that the latter number is an intrusion in the text.

a great blow. As in 4:8, the Hebrew for "blow" can also mean "plague." If there is a historical kernel to this whole story, an epidemic ravaging the Philistines could have easily spread to the bordering Israelites, perhaps even through the agency of the cart and the Ark.

said, "Who can stand before this holy Lord God, and to whom will He go up away from us?" And they sent messengers to the inhabitants of 21 Kiriath-Jearim, saying, "The Philistines have brought back the Ark of the Lord. Come down and carry it up to you." And the men of Kiriath- 7:1 Jearim came and carried up the Ark of the Lord and brought it to the house of Abinadab on the hill, and Eleazar his son they consecrated to watch over the Ark of the Lord.

---

20. *Who can stand before this holy Lord God.* Throughout the Ark Narrative, including what may be its epilogue in 2 Samuel 7, runs an archaic sense of God's sacred objects as material precipitates of an awesome and dangerous power. This notion led Leonhard Rost, one of the earliest scholars to argue for an entirely distinct Ark Narrative, to assume that the author must have been a priest, though that is hardly an inevitable inference, as these attitudes were widely held in ancient Near Eastern cultures. The phrase "stand before" means idiomatically "to serve."

will He go up. The Hebrew could equally be construed as "will it go up," referring to the Ark. From the point of view of the terrified speakers, it may amount to the same thing.

21. *And they sent messengers to the inhabitants of Kiriath-Jearim.* There seems to be no question of sending the Ark back to Shiloh, which has led to the scholarly inference that the Shiloh sanctuary was destroyed in the wake of the defeat at Aphek. The destruction of Shiloh is in fact attested in other sources.

CHAPTER 7

2 And it happened from the day the Ark dwelled in Kiriath-Jearim that the days grew many and became twenty years, and the whole house of
3 Israel was drawn after the LORD. And Samuel said to the whole house of Israel, saying, "If with your whole heart you now return to the LORD, put away the alien gods from your midst and the Ashtaroth, and set your

---

This chapter, which offers a summary account of Israel's religious reformation and military ascendancy under Samuel's rule, serves as a bridge between the Ark Narrative and the great narrative of the founding of the monarchy that will occupy the rest of 1 and 2 Samuel and the first two chapters of 1 Kings.

2. *twenty years*. This is half the formulaic figure of forty years that recurs so frequently in the Book of Judges. The period of twenty years could refer to the time until David brings the Ark up to Jerusalem, though given the immediate narrative context, the more likely reference is the time until Samuel assembles the tribes at Mizpah. During this period, the presence of the Ark at Kiriath-Jearim inspires the people to cultic loyalty to God.

was drawn after. The Hebrew *yinahu* is anomalous. The usual meaning of this verbal root, to weep, makes little sense here (though it was followed by the King James translators). The present translation adopts the proposal of Rashi, who may simply have been interpreting from context. The Hebrew could also be a scribal error for *yinharu*, which clearly means "to be drawn after."

3. *with your whole heart*. This phrase, and Samuel's language here in general, is notably Deuteronomistic, and the narrative line in this chapter follows the Deuteronomistic theological assumption that cultic faithfulness leads to military success. Neither this language nor this assumption is much in evidence in the main body of the Samuel-Saul-David narrative.

Ashtaroth. The form is a feminine plural of Ashtoreth (Astarte), the Canaanite fertility goddess. The plural either indicates a plurality of goddesses or—more likely—the multiple icons of Astarte.

heart firm for the Lord and serve Him alone, that He may rescue you from the hand of the Philistines." And the Israelites put away the Baalim 4 and the Ashtaroth and they served the Lord alone.

And Samuel said, "Assemble all Israel at Mizpah that I may intercede for 5 you before the Lord. And they assembled at Mizpah and they drew water 6 and spilled it before the Lord and they fasted on that day and there they said, "We have offended the Lord." And Samuel judged Israel at Mizpah. And the Philistines heard that the Israelites had assembled at Mizpah, and 7 the Philistine overlords came up against Israel, and the Israelites heard and were afraid of the Philistines. And the Israelites said to Samuel, "Do not hold 8 still from crying out for us to the Lord our God, that He rescue us from the hand of the Philistines." And Samuel took one suckling lamb and offered it 9

---

4. *Baalim.* This is the masculine plural of Baal, the principal Canaanite male deity.

5. *Mizpah.* Mizpah appears as a point of tribal assembly at two significant junctures in the Book of Judges. The name means "lookout" and in the Hebrew has a definite article.

6. *they drew water and spilled it before the Lord.* This act is a small puzzle because a water-drawing ritual is otherwise known only from the late Second Temple period (through Mishnaic sources), and there it is associated with fertility and the fall festival of Sukkot. The context makes clear that in this instance it must be a rite of penitence or purification. Rashi puts it succinctly: "It can only be a symbol of abnegation, that is, 'Behold we are in your presence like this water spilled forth.'"

7. *the Philistines heard that the Israelites had assembled.* Either the Philistines assumed that the assembly was a mustering of the tribes for war, which might not have been far off the mark (compare the assembly at Mizpah at the end of Judges 10), or they decided to seize this opportunity of the gathering of Israel for cultic purposes in order to attack the assembled tribes.

9. *one suckling lamb.* The Hebrew is literally "milk lamb" (*teleh ḥalav*). The choice of the sacrificial animal strikes an odd little echo with the two milch cows sacrificed at the end of the Ark Narrative and with the emphasis on nursing and weaning in Samuel's own infancy.

up whole as a burnt offering to the LORD, and Samuel cried out to the LORD
10   on behalf of Israel, and the LORD answered him. And just as Samuel was
offering up the offering, the Philistines drew near to do battle with Israel,
and the LORD thundered with a great sound on that day upon the Philistines
11   and panicked them, and they were routed before Israel. And the men of
Israel sallied forth from Mizpah and pursued the Philistines and struck them
12   down as far as below Beth-Car. And Samuel took a single stone and set it up
between Mizpah and Shen, and he called its name Eben-Ezer and he said,
13   "As far as here has the LORD helped us." And the Philistines were brought
low and they no longer came into Israelite country, and the hand of the LORD

---

10. *the LORD thundered . . . and panicked them.* The key terms restate a recurrent
pattern in 1 Samuel: God's hand, or God's voice (the thunder), comes down on
the enemy, and the enemy is smitten with "panic" (*mehumah*). Compare, also,
the end of Hannah's poem: "the LORD shatters His adversaries, / against them
in the heavens He thunders." Essentially, it is God Who does battle, with the
Israelite foot soldiers merely mopping up after His celestial bombardment. This
Deuteronomistic view will fade from the Saul and David narratives.

12. *Shen.* If the Masoretic text is correct (the Septuagint reflects a different
place-name), this name means "cliff" and, like Mizpah, it is preceded by a
definite article.
    Eben-Ezer. The name means "stone of help," with "help" bearing a particu-
larly martial implication. This place may not be the same as the one where
the Ark was captured. In any case, the recurring name is meant to signify the
righting of old wrongs.
    As far as here. The Hebrew phrase could be either temporal ("up till now")
or spatial, but the placing of a stone as a marker makes the latter more likely:
as far as this point the LORD granted us victory.

13. *the hand of the LORD was against the Philistines all the days of Samuel.* Since
under Saul's kingship the Philistines remained a dominant military power, "all
the days of Samuel" could refer only to the period of Samuel's actual leadership.
In any case, there are later indications that even under Samuel the Philistines
remained powerful.

was against the Philistines all the days of Samuel. And the towns that the 14
Philistines had taken from Israel were returned to Israel, from Ekron as far
as Gath, and their territories Israel retrieved from the hand of the Philistines.
And there was peace between Israel and the Amorite. And Samuel judged 15
Israel all the days of his life. And he would go about from year to year and 16
come round Bethel and Gilgal and Mizpah and would judge Israel in all
these places. And his point of return was Ramah, for there his home was, 17
and there he judged Israel. And he built there an altar to the LORD.

---

14. *peace between Israel and the Amorite.* This seemingly incongruous notice
actually throws light, as Shmuel Avramsky has proposed, on Israel's military-
political situation. The Amorites—a designation often used loosely by the biblical writers for the indigenous Canaanite peoples—had also been dominated
by the Philistine invaders, and Israel's success against the Philistines may
have been facilitated by an alliance, or at least a nonaggression pact, with the
Amorites.

15. *And Samuel judged Israel.* The precise nature of his leadership is left ambiguous, as befits this transitional figure in Israel's political evolution. Some of the
"judging" may actually be performance of a judicial function, as the next verse
indicates that Samuel operated as a kind of circuit judge, though he may well
have carried out cultic or priestly duties as well (the towns at which he stopped
are all cultic sites). He is also judge in the sense of "chieftain" or political leader,
though he plays this role not as a warrior, according to the model of the Book of
Judges, but as exhorter and intercessor. He is also, as we shall see in the Saul
story, a seer and a reprover-prophet.

16. *from year to year.* This locution for iterative annual peregrination takes us
back to Hannah and Elkanah at the very beginning of the Samuel story.

17. *his point of return was Ramah.* The Hebrew says literally "his return was
Ramah." This is evidently the same place as Ramathaim Zofim, where his parents lived. Samuel's circuit is an uneven ellipsis roughly twenty miles across in
the northern part of the territory of Benjamin (Saul's tribe) and the southern
part of the territory of Ephraim, in north-central Israel. It is far from encompassing all the tribal territories.

CHAPTER 8

₁ And it happened when Samuel grew old that he set his sons up as
₂ judges for Israel. And the name of his firstborn son was Joel and the
₃ name of his secondborn was Abijah—judges in Beersheba. But his sons
did not go in his ways and they were bent on gain and took bribes and
twisted justice.

₄ And all the elders of Israel assembled and came to Samuel at Ramah.
₅ And they said to him, "Look, you yourself have grown old and your
sons have not gone in your ways. So now, set over us a king to rule

---

1. *he set his sons up as judges for Israel.* It is a signal expression of the ambiguity
of Samuel's role as leader that he oversteps his mandate as judge (*shofet*—both
judicial authority and ad hoc political leader) by attempting to inaugurate a kind
of dynastic arrangement. The two sons who betray their trust of office are a nice
parallel to Eli's two corrupt sons, who essentially were displaced by Samuel.

2. *judges in Beersheba.* It is a little puzzling that Samuel should send both his
sons from north-central Israel to this city in the south. Josephus evidently was
familiar with a tradition in which one son was sent to Bethel in the north and
the other to Beersheba, a more plausible deployment.

3. *bent on gain . . . twisted justice.* The two verbs are different conjugations of
the same root, *n-t-h*, which means to bend off from the straight and narrow.

us, like all the nations." And the thing was evil in Samuel's eyes when 6
they said, "Give us a king to rule us." And Samuel prayed to the LORD.
And the LORD said to Samuel, "Heed the voice of the people in all that 7
they say to you, for it is not you they have cast aside but Me they have
cast aside from reigning over them. Like all the deeds they have done 8
from the day I brought them up from Egypt to this day, forsaking Me
and serving other gods, even so they do as well to you. So now, heed 9
their voice, though you must solemnly warn them and tell them the
practice of the king that will reign over them." And Samuel said all 10
the words of the LORD to the people who were asking of him a king.

---

6. *the thing was evil in Samuel's eyes.* Samuel is ideologically opposed to the
monarchy because he is committed to the old idea of the ad hoc inspired leader,
shofet, who is a kind of direct implementation of God's rule through the divine
spirit over the unique nation of Israel. God appears to agree with him but yields
to political necessity. It is noteworthy that when the elders' words are replayed
in this verse from Samuel's point of view, the very phrase rejecting covenantal
status that must especially gall him, "like all the nations," is suppressed.

8. *forsaking Me and serving other gods.* Both the locutions used and the preoccupation with cultic loyalty are notably Deuteronomistic, and the coupling of
the shift in style with this theme leads one to suspect a seventh-century interpolation here, since there has been no question of idolatry in the immediate
context. The elders' expressed concern has been rather with the breakdown
of the institution of the judge in Samuel's corrupt sons. The grounds for the
argument for and against monarchy will shift once again in Samuel's speech
(verses 11–18).

10. *asking of him a king.* The Hebrew participle *sho'alim* takes us back to the
verb of asking used in Samuel's naming and points forward to *Sha'ul,* Saul.

11 And he said, "This will be the practice of the king who will reign over you: Your sons he will take and set for himself in his chariots and in his cavalry,
12 and some will run before his chariots. He will set for himself captains of thousands and captains of fifties, to plow his ground and reap his harvest

---

11. *the practice of the king.* This whole episode turns repeatedly on an untranslatable pun. *Mishpat* means "justice," the very thing that Samuel's sons have twisted by taking payoffs. *Mishpat* also means "habitual behavior," "mode of operation," or "practice." As a verb the same root means either "to judge" or "to rule": it is used (in a verbal noun) in the former sense in verses 1 and 2, in the latter sense in verses 5 and 6. The recurrent scholarly assumption that this whole attack on the encroachments of the monarchy reflects a knowledge of Solomon's reign or of later Davidic kings is by no means inevitable: all the practices enumerated—military conscription, the corvée, expropriation of lands, taxation of the agricultural output—could easily have been familiar to an early writer from observing the Canaanite city-states or the larger imperial regimes to the east and the south.

who will reign over you. The people had spoken of the king ruling/judging them (the verb *shafat*); Samuel unambiguously speaks of reigning (*malakh*, the cognate verb of *melekh*, king).

Your sons he will take. Samuel's speech is solidly constructed as a hammering piece of anti-monarchic rhetoric. All the cherished possessions to be expropriated by the king are placed emphatically at the beginning of each clause, followed by the verb of which they are objects. "He will take" (one word in the Hebrew, *yiqah*) is insisted on with anaphoric force. The speech moves systematically from the expropriation of sons and daughters to land and produce to slaves and beasts of burden, ending with the climactic "you will become his slaves." A modern American reader might easily be reminded of the rhetoric of a radical libertarian inveighing against the evils of big government and the encroachments of its bureaucracies and taxation. In no part of his pragmatic argument does Samuel mention the Deuteronomistic themes of abandoning the LORD or betraying His direct kingship.

11.–12. *chariots . . . cavalry . . . captains.* The first item in the indictment of monarchy is military conscription. As is clear in the response of the people (verse 20), the consolidation of national military power under the king is precisely what attracts them to monarchy. All this leads one to suspect that the domination over the Philistines was by no means so comprehensive as claimed by the narrator in Chapter 7.

12. *to plow his ground and reap his harvest.* The Hebrew is literally "to plow his plowing and harvest his harvest."

and to make his implements of war and the implements of his chariots. And your daughters he will take as confectioners and cooks and 13
bakers. And your best fields and your vineyards and your olive trees 14
he will take and give to his servants. And your seed crops and your 15
vineyards he will tithe and give to his eunuchs and to his servants. And 16
your best male and female slaves and your cattle and your donkeys he
will take and use for his tasks. Your flocks he will tithe, and as for you, 17
you will become his slaves. And you will cry out on that day before 18
your king whom you chose for yourselves and he will not answer you

---

to make his implements. After conscripting men to fight and men to perform
agricultural service, the king will also draft the artisan class for his purpose—
ironsmiths, carpenters, wheelwrights, and so forth.

his chariots. Samuel's emphasis from the start on chariots signals the political shift he envisions, for chariots were the instruments of the monarchies with
which Israel contended, whereas the Israelites in this early stage did not have
this sort of military technology at their disposal, at least according to the Book
of Judges.

14. *give to his servants.* "Servants" in a royal context would be the functionaries
of the royal bureaucracy, whose service to the king was in fact often rewarded
by land grants.

16. *your cattle.* The Masoretic text has "your young men" (*baḥureikhem*), but
the reading of the Septuagint, *beqarkhem*, "your cattle," is much more likely,
given the fact that the sons and daughters have already been mentioned and
that the next term is "your donkeys."

18. *you will cry out . . . and he will not answer you.* The language used here in
relation to the king is precisely the language used elsewhere in relation to God
(compare 7:9, where the people implore Samuel to "cry out" on their behalf to
God). Cries to *this* power will not be answered.

19 on that day." And the people refused to heed Samuel's voice and they
20 said, "No! A king there shall be over us! And we, too, will be like all
the nations and our king shall rule us and sally forth before us and fight
21 our battles." And Samuel listened to all the words of the people and
22 he spoke them in the LORD's hearing. And the LORD said to Samuel,
"Heed their voice and make them a king." And Samuel said to the men
of Israel, "Go every man to his town."

---

19. *A king there shall be over us.* They do not say, "We will have a king" but "A
king shall be over us."

20. *rule us.* Again, the people use the ambiguous key verb, *shafat*, "to rule/
judge."
   sally forth before us. This phrase reflects a specific military idiom—the full
version of it is, literally, "to go out and come in before us," that is, to lead in
battle, to execute maneuvers. The military power that can accrue to the nation
through the king is what is uppermost in the minds of the people.

22. *Go every man to his town.* Though God has just instructed Samuel to comply
with the people's demand for a monarchy, Samuel's immediate response instead
is to send them back to their homes. His acquiescence remains grudging: he
appears to be buying time, perhaps with the claim that he needs to find a suitable candidate. The reluctance will persist, and grow, after he has encountered
Saul and anointed him.

CHAPTER 9

And there was a man of Benjamin whose name was Kish son of Abiel 1
son of Zeror son of Bechorath son of Aphiah, a Benjaminite, a man of
great means. And he had a son whose name was Saul, a fine and goodly 2
young fellow, and no man of the Israelites was goodlier than he, head
and shoulders taller than all the people. And some asses belonging to 3
Kish, Saul's father, were lost, and Kish said to Saul his son, "Take, pray,
with you one of the lads, and rise, go seek the asses." And he passed 4
through the high country of Ephraim and he passed through the region
of Shalishah, but they did not find them. And they passed through
the region of Shaalim, and there was nothing there, and they passed
through the region of Benjamin, but they did not find them. They were 5
just coming into the region of Zuf when Saul said to his lad who was

---

1. *And there was a man of Benjamin whose name was Kish.* The formulaic
phrasing—"there was a man," followed by name, home region, and genealogy—signals to the audience that we are beginning a discrete new story within
the larger narrative. (Compare the beginning of Hannah's story in 1:1–2.)

2. *head and shoulders taller than all the people.* The Hebrew says literally "from his
shoulders taller than all the people." Saul's looming size, together with his good
looks, seems to be an outward token of his capacity for leadership, but as the
story unfolds with David displacing Saul, his physical stature becomes associated with a basic human misperception of what constitutes fitness to command.

5. *They were just coming . . . when.* This relatively infrequent indication of
simultaneous actions occurs four times in this single episode. The writer seems
to want to highlight a crucial series of temporal intersections and concatena-
tions as Saul moves unwitting toward his destiny as king.
  Zuf. This is, of course, Samuel's home region.

with him, "Come, let us turn back, lest my father cease worrying about
6 the asses and worry about us." And he said to him, "Look, pray, there
is a man of God in this town, and the man is esteemed—whatever he
says will surely come to pass. Now then, let us go there. Perhaps he
7 will tell us of our way on which we have gone." And Saul said to his
lad, "But look, if we are to go, what shall we bring to the man? For the

---

Come, let us turn back. According to the general principle of biblical narrative that the first reported speech of a character is a defining moment of
characterization, Saul's first utterance reveals him as a young man uncertain
about pursuing his way, and quite concerned about his father. This concern,
especially in light of the attention devoted to tense relations between fathers
and sons in the ensuing narrative, is touching, and suggests that the young
Saul is a sensitive person—an attribute that will be woefully submerged by
his experience of political power. But as this first dialogue unfolds, it is Saul's
uncertainty that comes to the fore because at every step he has to be prodded
and directed by his own servant.

6. *there is a man of God in this town . . . whatever he says will surely come to pass.*
The fact that neither Saul nor his servant seems to have heard of Samuel by
name (and the town, too, is left unnamed) has led many scholars to conclude
that this story comes from a different source. But, as Robert Polzin has vigorously argued, the palpable shift between Chapter 8 and Chapter 9 may rather
reflect "the varying play of perspectives (between narrator and reader, between
reader and character, and between character and character) that forms the stuff
of sophisticated narrative." Saul's entire story, until the night before his death
on the battlefield, is a story about the futile quest for knowledge of an invet-
erately ignorant man. Samuel may have been presented before as the spiritual
leader of all the tribes, but this particular Benjaminite farm boy knows nothing
of him, and Saul's servant, who presumably has also spent all his time on the
farm, has picked up merely a local rumor of his activity but not his name. From
the rural-popular perspective of both, and in keeping with the themes of knowledge and prediction of this story, Samuel is not a judge and political leader but
a "man of God" and a "seer" (compare verse 9) who can predict the future.

he will tell us of our way on which we have gone. The Hebrew verb clearly indicates some sort of past action and not, as one might expect, "on which we should
go." Perhaps they feel so lost that they need the seer to tell them where they
have been heading. In the event, it is toward a kingdom, not toward lost asses.

7. *But look, if we are to go, what shall we bring.* The diffident Saul is on the
point of quitting before the encounter. He needs the counsel, and the provident

bread is gone from our kits and there is no gift to bring to the man of God. What do we have?" And the lad answered Saul once again and he said, "Look, I happen to have at hand a quarter of a shekel of silver that I can give to the man of God, that he may tell us our way." In former times in Israel, thus would a man say when he went to inquire of God, "Come, let us go to the seer." For the prophet today was called in former times the seer. And Saul said to his lad, "What you say is good. Come, let us go." And they went on to the town in which the man of God was. They were just coming up the ascent to the town when they met some young women going out to draw water, and they

---

quarter-shekel, of his servant in order to move forward and make the portentous connection with Samuel.

bread. As in general biblical usage, this is a synecdoche for "food."

9. In former times in Israel. This terminological notice simultaneously alerts the audience to the gap between the time of the story (the eleventh century BCE) and the audience's own time (at the very least, two or three generations later) and underscores the ambiguity of Samuel's transitional role as leader: he is variously called judge, man of God, seer, and prophet, and he also performs priestly functions.

to inquire of God. The idiom means to inquire of an oracle.

10. What you say is good. Saul the future leader follows someone else's lead—here, a slave's.

11. they met some young women going out to draw water. The wells would have typically been outside the walls of the city. The encounter between a young man in foreign territory with young women (ne'arot) drawing water seems to signal the beginning of a betrothal type-scene (compare Rebekah, Rachel, and Zipporah at their respective wells). But the betrothal scene is aborted. Instead of a betrothal feast, there will be a sacrificial feast that adumbrates a rite of coronation. The destiny of kingship to which Saul proceeds will lead to grimmer consequences than those that follow in the repeated story of a hero who finds this future bride at a well.

12 said to them, "Is there a seer hereabouts?" And they answered them and said, "There is. Look, he is straight ahead of you. Hurry now, for today he has come to town, for the people have a sacrifice today on the

13 high place. As soon as you come into town, you will find him before he goes up on the high place to eat. For the people will not eat till he comes, as he will bless the sacrifice and then the guests will eat. So go

14 up, for today you will find him." And they went up to the town. They were just coming into the town when Samuel came out toward them

15 to go up to the high place. And the LORD had disclosed to Samuel the

16 day before Saul's arrival, saying, "At this time tomorrow I will send to you a man from the region of Benjamin and you shall anoint him prince

---

12.–13. The reply of the young women is notable for its garrulousness. One talmudic sage sought to explain this trait with a simple misogynistic formula: "women are talkative" (*Berakhot* 48 b), whereas, more amusingly, the Midrash proposes that the young women kept repeating themselves because they were so smitten by Saul's beauty. The clues in the immediately preceding narrative context suggest a less fanciful explanation: seeing the evident signs of confusion and incomprehension in Saul's face, the women take elaborate measures to spell out where Samuel is to be found and what Saul should do in order to be sure not to miss him. In all this, it is noteworthy, as Polzin has observed, that Samuel, having agreed to find a king for Israel, has made no move whatever toward that purpose. Instead, the future king "finds" him.

the high place. The *bamah* was an elevated place, a kind of open-air natural altar, perhaps sometimes with a structure erected alongside it (see the "hall" in verse 22), where sacrifices were generally offered in the period before the centralization of the cult in Jerusalem. The kind of sacrifice involved here is one in which parts of the animal would be burned on the altar and the rest eaten in a ceremonial feast.

16. *prince.* The Hebrew *nagid* is not used to refer to leaders before this moment in Israelite history and is used only rarely after the very early years of the monarchy. It is a term that suggests the exercise of political power in a designated role of leadership rather than in the manner of the ad hoc charismatic leadership of the *shofet*, or judge. But God, in keeping with this transitional moment and perhaps even in deference to Samuel's keen resentment of the monarchy, pointedly does not use the word "king."

over My people Israel and he shall rescue My people from the hand of the Philistines. For I have seen the plight of My people, yes, their outcry has reached Me." And Samuel saw Saul, and the LORD answered 17 him, "Here is that man of whom I said to you, 'This one will govern My people.'" And Saul approached Samuel in the gateway and said, "Tell 18 me, pray, where is the house of the seer?" And Samuel answered Saul 19 and said, "I am the seer. Go up before me to the high place, and you will eat with me today, and I shall send you off in the morning, and whatever is in your heart I shall tell you. And as to the asses that have been lost to 20 you now three days, pay them no heed, for they have been found. And whose is all the treasure of Israel? Is it not for you and all your father's

---

he shall rescue My people. Again, the previously reported ascendancy over the Philistines seems to have vanished, and God endorses military effectiveness as the rationale for the monarchy.

the plight of My people. The Masoretic text lacks "the plight of," though the phrase appears to have been in the version used by the Septuagint translators. It is conceivable that what we have here is not an inadvertent scribal omission but an ellipsis.

17. *And Samuel saw Saul*. The seer sees the divinely designated object of his sight, and God immediately confirms that this is the man. Or, in the light of subsequent developments, Samuel is persuaded that he has received direct instruction from God. All the knowledge is on Samuel's side rather than on Saul's.

18. *where is the house of the seer?* Addressing the very seer himself, Saul picks up no clues that Samuel is anything but an ordinary passerby. He also assumes that the seer has a house in the town, though the young women have said that the seer has come to town for the sacrifice. (The scholarly assumption that the unnamed town must be Samuel's hometown, Ramah, is not entirely compelling.)

20. *as to the asses*. It is at this point that Samuel reveals his access to supernatural knowledge: no one has told him that Saul was looking for asses, but Samuel knows both of the lost animals and where to find them.

whose is all the treasure of Israel? This is a deliberately oblique reference to kingship: if all the choice possessions of Israel are to be yours, why worry about a few asses? Although the Hebrew term *hemdah* can mean "desire," it more often has the sense of "desired, or valued, thing," as in the common idiom, *kley hemdah*, "precious objects."

21 house?" And Saul answered and said, "Am I not a Benjaminite, from the
    smallest of the tribes of Israel, and my clan is the least of all the tribe of
22 Benjamin? So why have you spoken to me in this fashion?" And Samuel
    took Saul and his lad and brought them into the hall, and he gave them
23 a place at the head of the guests, about thirty men. And Samuel said
    to the cook, "Bring the portion that I gave to you, about which I said,
24 'Set it aside.'" And the cook lifted up the thigh and put it before Saul.
    And Samuel said, "Here is what is left. Put it before you and eat, for it
    has been kept for you for the appointed time as I said to the people I

---

21. *a Benjaminite, from the smallest of the tribes of Israel.* The young Saul is no
doubt overcome by Samuel's hint of a throne, but the language is also part of an
etiquette of deference. In fact, Benjamin was one of the most powerful tribes,
and given Kish's affluence, his clan would scarcely have been so humble.

   all the tribe of Benjamin. The Masoretic text has "tribes" but the Septuagint
reflects the more logical singular. The plural form is in all likelihood a scribal
replication of the plural in "tribes of Israel" at the beginning of the verse.

22. *a place at the head of the guests.* Samuel offers no explanation to the assembled company as to why this signal honor is accorded to the strangers.

23. *Set it aside.* The Hebrew reads literally "Put it by you."

24. The text here seems clearly defective at two different points. The phrase
"lifted up the thigh" is followed by an anomalously ungrammatical form of "and
that which is on it" (*wehe'aleyha*). It seems best to delete this word, as does the
Septuagint. The phrase "as I said to the people" is no more than an interpretive
guess about an asyntactic chain of three words in the Hebrew, which literally
are "saying the-people I-invited.

invited." And Saul ate with Samuel on that day. And they came down 25
from the high place into the town, and they made a bed for Saul on the
roof, and he slept. And as dawn was breaking, Samuel called out to Saul 26
on the roof, saying, "Arise and I shall send you off." And Saul arose, and
the two of them, he and Samuel, went outside. They were just going 27
down past the edge of the town when Samuel said to Saul, "Tell the lad
to pass on before us." And he passed on. "As for you, stand now, that I
may let you hear the word of God."

---

25. *they made a bed for Saul on the roof, and he slept.* The Masoretic text has
"he spoke with Saul on the roof and they rose early." The present translation
follows the far more plausible reading of the Septuagint: the report of speech
on the roof is odd because no content or explanation for it is given, and the
rising early is contradicted by the fact that in the next phrase Samuel calls up
to Saul on the roof in order to rouse him. Evidently, a scribe substituted the
common word *wayidaber*, "he spoke," for the more unusual word *wayirbedu*,
"they made a bed" (the same consonants with the order reversed). *Wayishkav*,
"and he slept," differs from *wayashkimu*, "and they rose early," by one consonant
in the unvocalized text.

   the roof. Presumably, the encounter takes place during the warm season, and
the roof would be a cool sleeping place.

27. *Tell the lad to pass on before us.* Every step that Samuel takes here in conferring the kingship on Saul is clandestine. He speaks to him only after they have
reached the outskirts of the town, and he is sure first to get Saul's servant out
of earshot. This course of action is rather puzzling because the people, after
all, have already publicly declared to the prophet that they want him to choose
a king for them. Samuel's need to proceed in secrecy may reflect his persistent
sense that the monarchy is the wrong path for the people, or it might be an
expression of doubt as to whether this strapping young Benjaminite is really
the right man for the job, despite the unambiguous indication that the prophet
has just received from God.

CHAPTER 10

A nd Samuel took the cruse of oil and poured it over his head and
kissed him, and he said, "Has not the Lord anointed you over His
inheritance as prince? When you go away from me today you shall
find two men by Rachel's Tomb in the region of Benjamin at Zelzah,
and they will say to you, 'The asses that you went off to seek have
been found, and, look, your father has put aside the matter of the
asses and is worrying about you, saying, What shall I do about my

---

1. Anointment is the biblical ritual of conferring kingship, like coronation in the
later European tradition. Samuel carries out this act secretly, on the outskirts of
the town, conferring on Saul, in keeping with the term God has used, the title
nagid, "prince," rather than "king."

2. *When you go away from me today.* This elaborate set of instructions and
predictions is, as Robert Polzin has argued, a strategy for asserting continued
control over the man Samuel has just anointed. Every predictive step manifests
Samuel's superior knowledge as prophet, and all the instructions reduce the
new king to Samuel's puppet.
   Rachel's Tomb. The burial site of the mother of Benjamin, the eponymous
founder of the tribe, underscores Saul's own tribal affiliation.
   at Zelzah. This otherwise unattested name may not be a place-name but an
error in transcription in the Masoretic text.
   your father has put aside the matter of the asses and is worrying about you.
According to the fixed procedure of verbal recycling in biblical narrative, the
predicted words of the two men are nearly identical with Saul's first words to
his servant. One should note that in the scenario Samuel lays out for him, Saul
has no opportunity to respond to his father's concern for his absence: on the
contrary, his new regal obligations rush him onward toward a daunting rite of
initiation.

son?' And you shall slip onward from there and you shall come to the 3
Terebinth of Tabor, and there three men will find you who are going up
to God at Bethel, one bearing three kids and one bearing three loaves
of bread and one bearing a jug of wine. And they will greet you and give 4
you two loaves of bread, and you shall take from their hand. Afterward 5
you shall come to Gibeath-Elohim, where the Philistine prefect is. And
as you come into town there, you shall encounter a band of prophets
coming down from the high place, preceded by lute and drum and flute

---

3. *slip onward*. The Hebrew verb *ḥalaf* suggests passing through a medium and
may well indicate the clandestine nature of Saul's movements.

   the Terebinth of Tabor. Evidently, a cultic site.

   three men . . . three kids . . . three loaves of bread. The triple three is a folktale
pattern. It also manifests a mysterious design clearly grasped by Samuel, who
annunciates this whole prediction, and into which Saul is thrust unwitting.
The three men bear meat (or animals that can be turned into meat), bread,
and wine—the three symbolic staffs of life. They will offer Saul the primary of
the three, bread (in counterpoint to the "worthless fellows" at the end of the
episode who give the new king no tribute).

5. *Gibeath-Elohim*. The name means Hill of God, but it would seem to be the
same as the Gibeah of Judges 19, in which the Benjaminites perpetrate a lethal
gang rape, and is also known as Gibeath-Benjamin and Gibeath-Saul.

   the Philistine prefect. This glancing reference to a Philistine garrison deep
within Benjaminite territory is still another indication of the Philistines' military
ascendancy. That might be another reason for keeping the anointment secret,
at least until the new king can consolidate military force around him. The
Masoretic text has a plural "prefects," but three different ancient translations
reflect a singular.

   a band of prophets. These are professional ecstatics who would whip themselves into a frenzy with the insistent rhythms of the musical instruments mentioned—a phenomenon familiar in enthusiastic religious sects worldwide—and
then would "prophesy," become caught up in ecstatic behavior, which could
involve glossolalia ("speaking in tongues"), dancing, writhing, and the like. The
chief connection between these figures and the later literary prophets is the
idea that both are involuntarily inhabited by an overpowering divine spirit.

   lute. The Hebrew word for this instrument, *nevel*, is identical with the word
for "jug" used at the end of verse 3 (the homonymity may be explained by a
perceived lyre shape in the jug). It is a fairly common procedure in biblical
narrative to link segments in immediate sequence by using this sort of pun as a
linchpin. Here it has the effect of intimating an uncanny link between the first
and second stages of the script Samuel is designing for Saul.

6 and lyre, and they will be speaking in ecstasy. And the spirit of the LORD
shall seize you, and you shall go into ecstasy with them and you shall
7 turn into another man. And when these signs come upon you, do what
8 your hand finds to do, for God is with you. And you shall go down before
me to Gilgal, and, look, I shall be coming down to you to offer burnt
offerings and to sacrifice well-being sacrifices. Seven days shall you wait
9 until I come to you, and I shall inform you what you must do." And it
happened as he turned his back to go off from Samuel, that God gave
him another heart and all these signs came to pass on that day.

---

6. *you shall turn into another man.* The drastic nature of this process is surely
meant by Samuel to be startling: nothing less will do in order to transform this
diffident farmer's son into a king than to be devastated by the divine spirit,
violently compelled to radical metamorphosis. This whole story of Saul among
the prophets is repeated, with very significant changes, in Chapter 19, near the
end of his tortuous career. As we shall have occasion to see, the seeming repetition, far from being a regrettable "doublet" produced in redaction, is entirely
purposeful: the same etiological tale is rotated 180 degrees to show us first Saul
being invested with the spirit, and with the monarchy, and then divested of the
monarchy by the spirit.

7. *do what your hand finds.* The biblical idiom means do whatever is within
your power.

8. *you shall go down before me to Gilgal . . . Seven days shall you wait.* The third
stage in the set of predictions/instructions that Samuel announces to Saul is in
fact not carried out till much later. Saul's divergence from the prophet's script
adumbrates his future failures of obedience in relation to Samuel. Robert Polzin
has made the shrewd argument that the unfulfilled prediction also reflects
Samuel's failure as a prophet, and that he has actually placed Saul in a double
bind by telling him that he may do whatever he wants because God is with him
and yet "has paradoxically commanded strict royal dependence upon prophetic
direction." Samuel, in other words, seems to want both a king and a puppet.

9. *as he turned his back.* The Hebrew *shekhem* is also the word for "shoulder," and
so reminds us of Saul's regal stature, head and shoulders above all the people.
  God gave him another heart and all these signs came to pass. These words are
a kind of proleptic headnote for the narrative report that follows, and it is not
implied that the transformation and the signs occurred the very moment Saul
turned to go.

And they came there to Gibeah, and look, a band of prophets was   10
coming toward him, and the spirit of the LORD seized him and he went
into ecstasy in their midst. And so, whoever knew him from times gone   11
by, saw, and, look, with the prophets he spoke in ecstasy, and each would
say to his fellow,

"What has befallen the son of Kish?
Is Saul, too, among the prophets?"

---

10. *And they came there to Gibeah.* There is no report of the first of Samuel's
predicted encounters, with the three men bearing kids, bread, and wine. It is
unclear whether this reflects merely a narrative ellipsis or whether this, too,
is an unfulfilled prophecy. The report of the meeting with the two men who
announce that the asses have been found is also omitted. In any case, the
transformative meeting with the band of ecstatics is obviously the chief focus
of the writer's attention.

the spirit of the LORD seized him. This same phrase, or a slight variant of
it, is repeatedly used in the Book of Judges to indicate the inception of the
judge's enterprise as charismatic military leader. There is some overlap with
Saul's taking on the kingship, which will also involve military leadership, but
the report of ecstasy or "prophesying" is a new element, with its more radical
implication that the new leader must become "another man."

11. *Is Saul, too, among the prophets?* This evidently proverbial question, its full
origins scarcely remembered, is the perplexity that generates the etiological
tale. The question seems to be proverbial of a case of extreme incongruity (like
the English "bull in a china shop")—what on earth is a man like Saul doing
among the prophets? The tale then comes to explain how the saying arose.
But the etiological tale, together with its antithetical counterpart in Chapter 19, figures significantly in the literary design of the Saul story. Even the
characterizing theme of Saul's repeated exclusion from predictive knowledge
is inscribed in the question, "Is Saul, too, among the prophets?" The people
ask their question about Saul in a line of poetry (consisting of two parallel
versets). The verse form explains why Saul is first referred to as "son of Kish"
because in poetry based on parallelism, it is the fixed procedure for treating
proper names to use the given name in one verset and, in lieu of a synonym,
the patronymic in the other. Thus, the claim made by some scholars that "son
of Kish" is derogatory has no basis.

12 And one man from there would answer and say, "And who is their father?"
13 Therefore it became a proverb, "Is Saul, too, among the prophets?" And
14 he ceased from his ecstasy and came to the high place. And Saul's uncle
said to him and to his lad, "Where did you go?" And he said, "To seek the
15 asses. And we saw that they were nowhere and we came to Samuel." And
16 Saul's uncle said, "Tell me, pray, what did Samuel say to you?" And Saul
said to his uncle, "He indeed told us that the asses had been found." But
the matter of the kingship of which Samuel had spoken he told him not.

17,18 And Samuel mustered the people to the LORD at Mizpah. And he said to
the Israelites, "Thus said the LORD God of Israel: 'I brought Israel up out

---

12. *who is their father?* The reference is obscure. The least convoluted explanation makes the prophets the antecedent of "their." The meaning then would be that unlike Saul, whose father is Kish, a landholder and a man of substance, the ecstatics are a breed apart, with no father anyone can name (the leader of a band of prophets was called idiomatically their father). The prevalent attitude toward such prophets was ambivalent: they were at once viewed as vehicles of a powerful and dangerous divine spirit, and as crazies (compare Hosea 9:7).

14. *Saul's uncle.* The appearance, without introduction, of an uncle (and not Saul's father, who after his brief initial appearance is never brought into the narrative proper) is puzzling. It has been proposed that this uncle is Ner the father of Abner, who will become Saul's commander in chief, but if that is the case, why is he left unnamed here?

16. *But the matter of the kingship . . . he told him not.* Saul's studied reticence confirms the clandestine character of his anointment.

17. *And Samuel mustered the people.* This national assembly is the second of three episodes that inaugurate Saul's kingship. One should not leap too quickly to the conclusion that these are merely a stitching together of variant sources. From the writer's viewpoint, the institution of the monarchy, with Saul as first king, is both a difficult and a dubious process, and it cannot happen all at once. First there is the clandestine anointment, followed by an initiatory experience, under the nose of the Philistine prefect. Then there is a public proclamation of the king, at which time sufficient forces can be marshaled to bolster him against the Philistines.

18. *Thus said the LORD God of Israel.* Samuel begins his speech with the so-called messenger formula, which is used to initiate prophetic messages. His

of Egypt and I rescued you from the hand of Egypt and from the hand
of all the kingdoms that have oppressed you.' And you on your part have   19
cast aside your God Who rescues you from all your ills and troubles,
and you have said, 'No! A king you shall put over us!' And so, stand forth
before the Lord by your tribes and your clans." And Samuel brought   20
forward all the tribes of Israel and the lot fell to the tribe of Benjamin.
And he brought forward the tribe of Benjamin by its clans and the lot   21
fell to the Matrite clan, and the lot fell to Saul son of Kish, and they
sought him but he was not to be found. And they inquired again of the   22
Lord: "Has a man come here?" And the Lord said, "Look, he is hidden
among the gear." And they ran and fetched him from there, and he stood   23
forth amidst the people, and he was head and shoulders taller than all
the people. And Samuel said to all the people, "Have you seen whom   24
the Lord has chosen? For there is none like him in all the people." And

---

speech is in fact a kind of prophetic denunciation of the people for having
"cast aside" God in demanding a king and so is a reprise of his antimonarchic
harangue in Chapter 8, even as he implements the choice of a king.

20. *the lot fell.* The Hebrew verb *lakad* that is used for the drawing of lots
means to be caught or trapped. As both Polzin and McCarter note, the only
other biblical instances of such drawing of lots among the tribes are in order
to discover a culprit, and so Samuel has chosen a mechanism associated with
incrimination and punishment.

22. *Has a man come here?* This translation reads *'ad halom* instead of the Masoretic *'od halom*, which would mean "again here."
   Look, he is hidden among the gear. This detail is virtually a parody of the
recurring motif of the prophet-leader's unwillingness to accept his mission.
Saul the diffident farm boy had expressed a sense of unworthiness for the high
office Samuel conferred on him. Now, confronted by the assembled tribes and
"trapped" by the process of lot drawing, he tries to flee the onus of kingship,
farcically hiding in the baggage.

24. *there is none like him in all the people.* Perhaps especially because Saul
has been hauled out from the midst of saddle packs and sundry impedimenta,
Samuel now executes a gesture of public relations: look at this strapping, handsome fellow—there is none in Israel who can match him. In the event, he
proves wrong about Saul's fitness for the throne, and one may even wonder
whether Samuel's proclamation that this is the one God has chosen (con-

25 all the people shouted and said, "Long live the king!" And Samuel spoke
out to the people the practice of kingship and wrote it on a scroll and
placed it before the LORD. And Samuel sent all the people away to their
26 homes. And Saul, too, had gone to his home in Gibeah, and the stalwart
27 fellows whose hearts God had touched went with him. And worthless
fellows had said, "How will this one rescue us?" And they spurned him
and brought him no tribute, but he pretended to keep his peace.

---

firmed by the narrator's previous report) is not a misperception to justify his
own (erring) choice.

Long live the king. The people's proclamation does not use *nagid* (prince)
but the unambiguous *melekh* (king).

25. *the practice of kingship.* The phrase here, *mishpat hamelukhah*, is close
enough to *mishpat hamelekh*, the term used in Chapter 8, and so the reasonable inference is that the content of the speech is a reiteration of the dangers
of encroachment of individual rights by the king that Samuel warned of in the
assembly at Ramah.

26. *stalwart fellows.* The translation follows the Qumran Samuel text and the
Septuagint in reading *giborey hahayil* instead of the Masoretic *hahayil*, "the
troop." The phrase, as many commentators have noted, is an obvious antithesis
to "worthless fellows" in the next sentence.

27. *How will this one rescue us?* "This one" (*zeh*) is contemptuous.

but he pretended to keep his peace. The Masoretic text has two Hebrew
words here, *wayehi kemaharish*, which bear this meaning and have the attraction of indicating the inception of court intrigues and calculations at the very
beginning of Saul's reign—he is aware of political dissidence but chooses for
the moment not to react. It must be said, however, that the Qumran Samuel
fragment, supported by allied readings in the Septuagint and Josephus, has
wayehi kemehodesh (the graphemes for r and d are quite similar), "And it happened after about a month," affixing these two words at the beginning of the
next episode rather than at the end of this one.

CHAPTER 11

And Nahash the Ammonite came up and encamped against Jabesh- 1
Gilead. And all the men of Jabesh said to Nahash, "Make a pact with

---

1. *Nahash the Ammonite*. During this period, the Ammonite kingdom, in the region to the east of the Jordan, was the second great military threat to the Israelites, after the Philistines to the west. David would later besiege the Ammonite capital, Rabbath Ammon (near the site of present-day Amman). This episode, marking the inception of Saul's military activity, has several details that will be echoed later in the David story.

Jabesh-Gilead. This Israelite settlement, in the tribal territory of Manasseh, was located several miles east of the Jordan and hence was exposed to Ammonite attack. In the story of the concubine at Gibeah—Saul's hometown—the men of Jabesh-Gilead refuse to fight in the civil war against Benjamin, and so some special kinship between them and Saul's tribe is inferable. The Samuel scroll found in Cave 4 at Qumran reports a general campaign by Nahash against the trans-Jordanian Israelites. Here are the verses from the Qumran version (brackets indicate reconstructed letters or words, where there are gaps in the scroll): "[and Na]hash king of the Ammonites oppressed the Gadites and the Reubenites mightily and gouged out the right eye of e[very] one of them and imposed fe[ar and terror] on [I]srael, and there remained not a man of the Israelites be[yond] the Jordan [who]se right eye Nah[ash king of] the Ammonites did n[ot] [gou]ge out. Only seven thousand men [fled from] the Ammonites and came to [J]abesh-Gilead. And after about a month"—the words that follow are identical with verse 1 in the Masoretic text.

2   us, and we shall be subject to you." And Nahash the Ammonite said
    to them, "This is how I shall make a pact with you—with the gouging
    out of the right eye of every one of you, and I shall make it a disgrace
3   for all Israel." And the elders of Jabesh said to him, "Leave us alone
    for seven days, that we may send messengers through all the territory
    of Israel, and if there is none to rescue us, we shall come out to you."
4   And the messengers came to Gibeath-Saul and spoke the words in the
    hearing of the people, and all the people raised their voices and wept.
5   And, look, Saul was coming in behind the oxen from the field, and Saul
    said, "What is the matter with the people that they are weeping?" And
6   they recounted to him the words of the men of Jabesh. And the spirit
    of God seized Saul when he heard these words, and he was greatly

---

2. *the gouging out of the right eye.* Mutilation of captives was a fairly common
practice. Josephus explains that the blinding of the right eye would have
impaired the ability to fight because the left eye was largely covered by the
shield in battle. In any case, submitting to this ghastly mutilation was a mark
of great humiliation, or "disgrace" (*ḥerpah*).

3. *Leave us alone for seven days.* Nahash's seemingly surprising agreement to
this condition is by no means a sign of generosity but must be understood
from his viewpoint as an additional opportunity to humiliate the Israelites: he
scarcely imagines that the disunited tribes will produce a "rescuer," and thus
the impotent tribes will all be forced to witness helplessly the mutilation of
their trans-Jordanian kinsmen.

4. *the messengers came to Gibeath-Saul.* The men of Jabesh-Gilead have told
Nahash they would search through "all the territory of Israel." But perhaps
they know something he does not—that Israel already has a tribally acclaimed
ruler and military leader who resides in Gibeah, but who has not yet begun to
act. The scholarly assumption that this entire story blatantly contradicts the
previous account of Saul's election as king and hence must derive from an
independent source is by no means necessary.

6. *the spirit of God seized Saul.* As many commentators have noted, the story
here explicitly follows the model of the inception of the charismatic leader's
career in Judges, when a kind of berserker spirit enters him and ignites him
with eagerness to do battle. Saul's coming in from the field behind the oxen is
also reminiscent of the pattern in Judges in which an agriculturalist (compare
Gideon) is transformed by an access of the spirit into a warrior. Given the

incensed. And he took a yoke of oxen and hacked them to pieces and   7
sent them through all the territory of Israel by the hand of messengers,
saying, "Whoever does not come out after Saul and after Samuel, thus
will be done to his oxen!" And the fear of the LORD fell on the people,
and they came out as one man. And Saul marshaled them in Bazek, and   8
there were three hundred thousand Israelites and thirty thousand men

---

uncertainty about the new monarchic dispensation, it is quite possible that
Saul, after having been proclaimed king at Mizpah, might have returned to his
work in the field, awaiting the occasion when he would begin to act on his new
royal authority. The archetypal tale of the farmer who steps forward to save the
nation in time of crisis will recur in Roman tradition in the story of Cincinnatus
at the plow.

7. *he took a yoke of oxen and hacked them to pieces.* This violent symbolism
doubly distinguishes Saul from the model of the ad hoc warrior-leader in
Judges. The dismemberment of the oxen is an explicit repetition of the dismemberment of the concubine at the end of Judges 19 after she has been
gang raped to death by the men of Gibeah (later the home of Saul). In Judges,
too, the bloody members were used to assemble all the tribes of Israel to war,
though the person who hacked the body to pieces was not a judge but rather
the morally dubious Levite, husband of the dead woman. The allusion here is
exquisitely ambiguous. Is this an act of restitution, a setting right of the ghastly
civil war caused by the atrocity at Gibeah, or does it inaugurate the narrative
of Saul's public actions under the shadow of an earlier act of turpitude? Saul
also differs from the judges in behaving like a king, for he prepares for war by
instituting a kind of military conscription binding on all the tribes (the judges
depended on volunteers and worked locally). Kings, like mafia capos, operate
through coercion: Saul, in sending the hacked-up oxen parts to his fellow Israelites with the threat, "Whoever does not come out . . . thus will be done to his
oxen," is presenting them with an offer they cannot refuse.

   after Saul and after Samuel. The medieval Hebrew commentator Kimchi
offers a shrewd explanation for Saul's adding Samuel to his exhortation. "Since
not all of them had accepted him as king, he said 'after Samuel.'"

   the fear of the LORD. This seemingly pious phrase might also mean "a terrible
fear," and it is, after all, Saul's frightening threat conveyed by the bloody oxen
parts that moves the people.

8. *three hundred thousand.* As usual, the inflated figure does not reflect historical reality. The ten-to-one ratio between Israel and Judah does mirror the ratio
of ten tribes to one.

9 of Judah. And he said to the messengers who had come, "Thus shall you say to the men of Jabesh-Gilead: 'Tomorrow victory will be yours as the sun grows hot.'" And the messengers came and told the men of Jabesh
10 and they rejoiced. And the men of Jabesh said [to the Ammonites], "Tomorrow we shall come out to you and you may do to us whatever is
11 good in your eyes." And it happened on the next day that Saul set the troops in three columns. And they came into the camp in the morning watch and struck down Ammon till the heat of the day, and so those who remained were scattered and not two of them remained together.
12 And the people said to Saul, "Whoever said, 'Saul shall not be king over
13 us,' give us these men and we shall put them to death." And Saul said, "No man shall be put to death this day, for today the LORD has wrought victory in Israel."

---

10. *Tomorrow we shall come out to you.* These words are intended to lull the Ammonites into a false sense of security before Saul's surprise attack in the last hours before dawn ("the morning watch").

12. *Saul shall not be king over us.* The "not" appears in some variant manuscripts. The Masoretic text as it stands is usually construed as a question: "Saul will be king over us?" Robert Polzin tries to save the simple declarative sense of the Masoretic text by proposing that after Saul has just powerfully acted like one of the old-time judges, the people, with the implicit endorsement of Saul, are inclined to retract their own insistence on monarchy and return to the institution of judgeship. This reading is ingenious, but may create more problems than it solves. The report of continuing dissidence about Saul's claim to the throne, as at the end of the previous chapter, in fact sets the stage for much that will follow.

13. *No man shall be put to death this day.* Saul's magnaminity, after his demonstration of coercion and military effectiveness, strikes a positive note at the beginning of his reign, though he will later prove to be utterly ruthless against subjects he suspects of disloyalty.

And Samuel said to the people, "Come, let us go to Gilgal and we shall   14
renew there the kingship." And all the people went to Gilgal and they   15
made Saul king there before the Lord at Gilgal, and they sacrificed their
well-being sacrifices before the Lord, and Saul rejoiced there, and all
the men of Israel with him, very greatly.

---

14. *we shall renew there the kingship.* This clause helps make sense of the triple
story of Saul's dedication as king. First there was the clandestine anointment,
with no publicly visible consequences. Then there was the tribal assembly at
Mizpah in which a reluctant Saul was chosen by lot and proclaimed king. After
that event, however, he appears to have returned for the time being to private
life. Now, following his signal success in mustering the tribes and defeating
Ammon, Samuel calls for a new assembly to reconfirm Saul's standing as king,
which will then be seen in subsequent episodes manifested in the institutions
and power of a regular court.

CHAPTER 12

¹ And Samuel said to all Israel, "Look, I have heeded your voice in all
² that you said to me and have set a king over you. And so now the king
walks before you and I have grown old and gray, and my sons, they are
here with you, and I have walked before you from my youth till this

---

1. *And Samuel said to all Israel.* It is not clear whether Samuel's farewell speech
takes place at Gilgal on the ceremony of "renewing the kingship" mentioned at
the end of the preceding chapter, or whether this is a separate occasion. It does
seem in character for Samuel that he would end up converting the coronation
assembly into still another diatribe against the monarchy and an apologia for
his own authority as prophet-judge.

I have heeded your voice. The phrase takes us back to the tribal convocation
in Chapter 8, when the grudging Samuel was enjoined by God to heed the
people's voice and make them a king.

2. *the king walks before you.* As we have had occasion to note earlier, this idiom
means to serve or act as a functionary.

my sons, they are here with you. This slightly odd reference to Samuel's sons is
in all likelihood a final verbal gesture toward the dynasty he has failed to create:
Samuel's crooked sons have already disqualified themselves from assuming his
mantle, but here he appears to take a last wistful look at that prospect—my
sons are here among you, but you insist instead on a king.

day. Here I am! Witness against me before the LORD and before His ₃
anointed. Whose ox have I taken and whose donkey have I taken, whom
have I wronged and whom have I abused, and from whose hand have I
taken a bribe to avert my eyes from him? I shall return it to you!" And ₄
they said, "You have not wronged us and you have not abused us, and
you have not taken a thing from any man." And he said to them, "The ₅
LORD is witness against you, and His anointed is witness this day, that
you have found not a thing in my hand." And they said, "He is witness."
And Samuel said to the people, "Witness is the LORD, Who appointed ₆
Moses and Aaron and Who brought up your fathers from the land of
Egypt! And now, stand forth, that I may seek judgment with you before ₇
the LORD, and I shall tell you all the LORD's bounties that He did for
you and for your fathers. When Jacob came into Egypt, and your fathers ₈
cried out to the LORD, the LORD sent Moses and Aaron, and they brought
your fathers out of Egypt and settled them in this place. And they forgot ₉

---

3. *Whose ox have I taken and whose donkey have I taken.* Samuel's profession of
innocence, as Kyle McCarter, Jr., has aptly noted, picks up antithetically his
admonition against the "practice of the king" in Chapter 8. There he warned
repeatedly that the king would "take" all the people's cherished possessions.
Here he proclaims that he, the prophet-judge, has taken nothing. In both
instances, he shows himself a master of rhetoric.
   abused. The Hebrew verb means etymologically to crush or smash.

6. *Witness is the LORD.* The Masoretic text lacks "Witness" (*'ed*), which is supplied by the Septuagint. (The next clause also looks textually problematic
because the verb rendered here as "appointed," *'asah*, actually means "made"
and is not idiomatic.) It is noteworthy that Samuel sets up his entire speech as
a legal disputation between him and the people in which all the evidence, as
they are compelled to admit, stands in his favor.

7. *and I shall tell you.* The Masoretic text lacks these words, but the next phrase,
"all the LORD's bounties," preceded by the accusative particle *'et*, clearly requires
a verb, and the appropriate verb is reflected in the Septuagint.

8. *When Jacob came into Egypt, and your fathers cried out.* The Septuagint
inserts between these two clauses the words "the Egyptians oppressed them."
But the Greek translators may have simply filled out a narrative ellipsis in the
original Hebrew text.

the Lord your God, and He delivered them into the hand of Sisera commander of Hazor, and into the hand of the Philistines, and into the
10 hand of the king of Moab, and they fought against them. And they cried out to the Lord and said, 'We have offended, for we have abandoned the Lord and served the Baalim and the Ashtaroth. And now, rescue us
11 from the hand of our enemies, and we shall serve You.' And the Lord sent Jerubaal and Bedan and Jephthah and Samuel, and He rescued you from the hand of your enemies all around, and you dwelled in safety.
12 And you saw that Nahash king of the Ammonites had come against you

---

10. *we have abandoned the* Lord *and served the Baalim and the Ashtaroth*. Samuel's speech seems to be an intertwining of an early story with a Deuteronomistic (seventh-century or sixth-century) editorial recasting. The vehement opposition to the monarchy would be original, perhaps even going back to the historical figure of Samuel. The Deuteronomistic school on its part was by no means anti-monarchic, though it wanted to limit the monarch with the rules of the Book of God's Teaching (the Torah). On the other hand, the sin of idolatry is not an issue in the Samuel story, but it is a Deuteronomistic preoccupation. It is at this point in the speech that we encounter clusters of Deuteronomistic verbal formulas: "abandoned the Lord and served the Baalim," "delivered [literally, sold] into the hand of," "fear the Lord and serve Him and heed His voice," "serve Him truly with all your heart."

11. *Bedan*. The name of this judge is otherwise unknown, but since there is no reason to assume that the list in the Book of Judges is exhaustive, it seems prudent not to emend this into a familiar name.

and Samuel. It makes sense that Samuel would refer to himself by name rather than with the first-person pronoun because he wants to set himself as a matter of official record in the great roll call of judges.

12. *Nahash king of the Ammonites*. Since there had been no question of Nahash in the original demand for a king in Chapter 8, many scholars have inferred that the present episode reflects a different tradition, in which the call for monarchy is specifically linked with the Ammonite incursion reported in Chapter 11. But Moshe Garsiel proposes an interesting political reading that preserves the unity of the text. The original request for a king stresses the need for a military leader but mentions no particular enemy, perhaps because the people fear to name the dominant Philistines. Saul would have initially been installed in the ceremony at Mizpah as a sort of vassal king (or, alternatively, leader of an underground movement), for the Philistines had garrisons in the territory of Benjamin. Now, after Saul's military success against the Ammonites, Samuel explicitly associ-

and you said to me, 'No! A king shall reign over us,' though the LORD
your God was your king. And now, here is the king you have chosen, for   13
whom you have asked, and here the LORD has put over you a king. If you   14
fear the LORD and serve Him and heed His voice and rebel not against
the LORD's words, and if both you and the king who reigns over you will
follow the LORD your God, He will rescue you. But if you heed not the   15
voice of the LORD and you rebel against the LORD's words, the hand of
the LORD will be against you and against your king to destroy you. Even   16
now, take your stance and see this great thing that the LORD is about to
do before your eyes. Is it not wheat harvest today? I shall call unto the   17

---

ates the call for a monarchy with Nahash's assault on Israel. This meeting at
Gilgal would also have been an occasion to enlist the allegiance to Saul of the
trans-Jordanian tribes.

13. *the king you have chosen, for whom you have asked.* Several times Samuel
plays sardonically on "asked" (*sha'al*) and "Saul" (*Sha'ul*). Moshe Garsiel also
suggests a pun as well in "chosen" (*baḥar*) and the introductory designation of
Saul as a "fine fellow" (*baḥur*, literally "chosen one"). Although the story of the
institution of the monarchy indicates that God does the choosing, there is no
real contradiction—Samuel, in his acute discomfort with the monarchy that
has displaced his own authority, readily imputes the choosing to the people,
despite his awareness that God has supposedly chosen. God on His part no
more than acquiesces in the people's stubborn insistence on a king. The ambiguity of Saul's divine election will continue to be manifested in the narrative.

14. *rebel not against the LORD's words.* The Hebrew says literally "against the
LORD's mouth," but the same verb (root *m-r-h*) appears elsewhere with "words"
as object, and the two formulations are variants of the same idiom.
    He will rescue you. The Masoretic text lacks a clause stating what will happen
if Israel remains faithful to God. These words (which would reflect a single verb
with its suffix in the Hebrew) are supplied from the Septuagint.

15. *against your king to destroy you.* The Masoretic text reads "against your
fathers" (without "to destroy you"). This makes no sense because it is a prediction of future catastrophe. Some ancient and medieval interpreters construe
the word "as against your fathers," but the Septuagint's reading, reflected in this
translation, is more likely because Samuel repeatedly brackets "you and your
king" sarcastically in this speech.

17. *wheat harvest.* That is, early summer, when no rain falls in Israel.

LORD and He will send thunder and rain, and mark and see, that the
evil you have done is great in the eyes of the LORD, to ask for yourselves
18 a king." And Samuel called unto the LORD, and the LORD sent thunder
and rain on that day, and all the people feared the LORD greatly, and they
19 feared Samuel as well. And all the people said to Samuel, "Intercede on
behalf of your servants with the LORD your God, that we may not die,
for we have added to our offenses an evil thing to ask for ourselves a
20 king." And Samuel said to the people, "Fear not. You have done all this
evil, but swerve not from following the LORD and serve the LORD with
21 all your heart. And swerve not after mere emptiness that will not avail
22 or rescue, for they are mere emptiness. For the LORD will not desert His
people for the sake of His great name, as the LORD has undertaken to
23 make you His people. I on my part, too, far be it from me to offend the
LORD by ceasing to intercede on your behalf. I shall instruct you in the
24 good and straight way. Only fear the LORD and serve Him truly with all
25 your heart, for see the great things He has done for you. And if indeed
you do evil, both you and your king will be swept away."

---

19. *an evil thing to ask for ourselves a king.* Through the pressure of Samuel's
oration, this "renewal of the kingship" most peculiarly turns into a collective
confession of the sin of having wanted a king.

21. *swerve not after mere emptiness.* "Swerve" is once again Deuteronomistic
terminology—to veer off from the straight and narrow path of the LORD. The
Masoretic text inserts "that" (*ki*) after this verb, creating a small problem of
syntax, but the Septuagint deletes the word. The present translation adds the
adjective "mere" to "emptiness" (*tohu*) in order to convey the full pejorative
sense of the noun, which in many contexts suggests futility and is associated
with the emptiness of the desert (compare the *tohu wabohu,* "welter and waste,"
of the beginning of Genesis).

23. *far be it from me to offend the LORD by ceasing to intercede on your behalf.*
One should note how deftly Samuel upstages the king whom he has just helped
the people to confirm in office. It is true, his argument runs, that you have made
the sinful error of choosing yourself a king. (Samuel of course makes no allow-
ance for God's role in the choice, which might express grudging divine recognition of a new political necessity.) That cannot be reversed, but never fear—I
will still be here to act as the intercessor you will desperately continue to need.

CHAPTER 13

Saul was [] years old when he became king, and [-] two years he   1
reigned over Israel.

And Saul chose for himself three thousand from Israel, and two thou-   2
sand were with Saul at Michmash and in the Bethel high country, and a
thousand were with Jonathan at Gibeath-Benjamin, and the rest of the
people he sent away each man to his tent.

And Jonathan struck down the Philistine prefect who was in Gibeah   3
and the Philistines heard of it. And Saul blew the ram's horn through-

---

1. *Saul was [] years old . . . and [-] two years he reigned.* The Masoretic text,
notoriously defective at this point, says "Saul was a year old . . . and two years
he reigned." This whole sentence is absent from the Septuagint, leading one
to suspect that the redactor here stitched into the narrative a textual fragment
in which there were lacunae in the numbers that he did not presume to fill in.

3. *Jonathan struck down the Philistine prefect.* Though the Hebrew uses the
standard idiom for killing someone in battle, the context of Israel's subservience to the Philistines suggests that this was an act of assassination, intended
to trigger general rebellion. Jonathan enters the narrative without introduction. The neophyte king had himself seemed a rather young man, but with the
casualness about chronology characteristic of the biblical storyteller, Saul now
has a grown son.
   in Gibeah. The text reads "Geba," but the two names, which continue to
alternate, appear to be variants of the same name.
   Saul blew the ram's horn . . . saying, "Let the Hebrews hear!" The ram's horn,
which produces shrill, piercing sounds, was often used for a call to arms. The
"hearing" of the Israelites is counterpointed to the just-reported "hearing" of the
Philistines. "Hebrews" is usually the term used by foreigners for the Israelites.

4 out the land, saying, "Let the Hebrews hear!" And all Israel heard, saying, "Saul has struck down the Philistine prefect, and, indeed, Israel has become repugnant to the Philistines." And the people rallied round

5 Saul at Gilgal. And the Philistines had assembled to do battle against Israel—thirty thousand chariots and six thousand horsemen and troops multitudinous as the sand on the shore of the sea. And they came up

6 and encamped at Michmash, east of Beth-Aven. And the men of Israel saw that they were in straits, for the troops were hard pressed, and the troops hid in caves and among thorns and among rocks and in dugouts

7 and in pits. And Hebrews had crossed the Jordan into the territory of Gad and Gilead, while Saul was still at Gilgal, and all the troops were

---

As J. P. Fokkelman has observed, Saul invokes "a name used in contempt by enemies such as Pharaoh and the Philistines . . . in order to arouse his people's pride and fortify their will to resist."

4. *Saul has struck down*. Though Jonathan was the assassin, Saul, as political leader of the rebel forces, is credited with responsibility for the act.

Israel has become repugnant. The literal meaning of the Hebrew idiom is very much like "to be in bad odor with," but that antiquated English idiom has a certain Victorian fussiness not suitable to this narrator.

5. *thirty thousand chariots*. This inflated figure is reduced to three thousand in the Septuagint.

6. *in dugouts*. The Hebrew term *tsariaḥ* appears only here and in Judges 9. Though the context in Judges has led some interpreters to construe it as a tower, extrabiblical evidence from Late Antiquity argues for a chamber, or sepulcher, hewn out of rock.

7. *And Hebrews had crossed*. Here the narrator's use of "Hebrews" may have been encouraged by the attraction of a folk-etymological pun: *'ivrim* (Hebrews) *'avru* (had crossed).

Saul was still at Gilgal. This cultic site is, according to a common identification, near Jericho in the Jordan Valley. The "Hebrews"—perhaps the general population and not the army—who cross the Jordan appear to be fleeing the Philistines to the relative safety of the territory of Gad and Gilead to the northeast.

trembling behind him. And he waited seven days for the fixed time   8
Samuel had set, and Samuel did not come, and the troops began to slip
away from him. And Saul said, "Bring forth to me the burnt offering and   9
the well-being sacrifice," and he offered up the burnt offering. And it   10
happened as he finished offering the burnt offering that, look, Samuel
was coming, and Saul went out toward him to greet him. And Samuel   11
said, "What have you done?" And Saul said, "For I saw that the troops
were slipping away from me, and you on your part had not come at the
fixed time, and the Philistines were assembling at Michmash. And I   12
thought, 'Now the Philistines will come down on me at Gilgal, without
my having entreated the Lord's favor.' And I took hold of myself and

---

8. *the fixed time Samuel had set.* The words "had set" (one word in the Hebrew)
are lacking in the Masoretic text but are supplied by two of the ancient versions. The fact that the Hebrew word in question, *sam*, has the same consonants as the first two consonants of Samuel's name may have led to the scribal
error. The entire story of Samuel's fixing a period of seven days for Saul to await
him at Gilgal before the offering of sacrifices goes back to 10:8. The fulfillment
of that initial instruction to the new king has been interrupted by the election
of Saul by lottery, his campaign against the Ammonites, and the renewal of the
kingship at Gilgal. One must assume either that the order to await Samuel at
Gilgal was for an eventual meeting at an unspecified future time or that one
literary strand of the Saul story has been interrupted by the splicing in of other
strands (Chapters 11–12).

    the troops began to slip away from him. Battle could not be engaged without
first entreating the favorable disposition of the deity through sacrifice (compare
Saul's words of explanation in verse 12). Saul's men are beginning to give up
hope and to desert; so he feels, with good reason, that he can afford to wait
no longer.

10. *as he finished offering the burnt offering that, look, Samuel was coming.*
The timing gives the distinct appearance of a cat-and-mouse game played
by Samuel. He is not absolutely late, but he has waited till the last possible
moment—sometime well into the seventh day (or it might even be the eighth
day), by which time Saul has been obliged to take matters into his own hands.

12. *I took hold of myself.* The Hebrew verb *hit'apeq* means to force yourself to
do, or to refrain from doing, something. The same verb is used when the tearful Joseph "could not hold himself in check" in the presence of his brothers
(Genesis 45:1).

13 offered up the burnt offering." And Samuel said to Saul, "You have played the fool! Had you but kept the command of the LORD your God that He commended you, now the LORD would have made your kingdom over

14 Israel unshaken forever. But now, your kingdom shall not stand. The LORD has already sought out for Himself a man after His own heart, and the LORD has appointed him prince to his people, for you have not

---

13. *Had you but kept the command of the* LORD. The Masoretic text has a declarative, "you have not kept," but the structure of the whole sentence argues strongly for emending *lo'* ("not") to *lu* ("if" introducing a clause contrary to fact). Samuel flatly assumes that his own commands and the commandments of the LORD are entirely equivalent. In fact, it is he, not God, who has given Saul the elaborate instructions about waiting seven days at Gilgal. In a kind of prophet's tantrum, Samuel insists again and again in this speech on the words "commanded" and "command." (In verse 14, "appointed him prince" is literally "commanded him prince.")

   made your kingdom . . . unshaken forever. The Hebrew verb *hekhin* means both to establish and to keep on a firm foundation (*makhon*), and so it is misleading to translate it only as the initiating "to establish."

14. *your kingdom shall not stand.* Samuel's rage over the fact that Saul has offered the sacrifice derives from his construing that act as a usurpation of his own prerogatives as master of the cult (though there are other biblical instances of kings who offer sacrifices). One suspects that Samuel has set up Saul for this "failure," and that he would have been content only with a puppet king.

   The LORD *has already sought out for Himself a man after His own heart.* Though this would have to be a veiled prediction of the advent of David, in naturalistic terms, the incensed Samuel is in a way bluffing: fed up with Saul, he announces to the king that God has already chosen a successor—about whom Samuel himself as yet knows nothing whatever, nor has he even had time for a communication from God that there will be a successor.

   appointed him prince to his people. As Polzin shrewdly notes, David will later use these very words (2 Samuel 6:21) when he angrily tells Saul's daughter Michal that it is he who has been divinely elected to replace her father.

kept what the LORD commanded you." And Samuel arose and went 15
up from Gilgal to Gibeath-Benjamin. And Saul mustered the troops
remaining with him, about six hundred men. And Saul and Jonathan 16
his son and the troops remaining with them were staying at Gibeath-
Benjamin, and the Philistines had encamped at Michmash. And a 17
raiding party sallied forth from the Philistine camp in three columns—
one column turned toward the road to Ophrah, to the Shual region, and 18
one column turned toward the road to Beth-Horon, and one column
turned toward the border road that looks out over the Zeboim Valley,
toward the desert. And no smith could be found in all the land of Israel, 19
for the Philistines had said, "Lest the Hebrews make sword or spear!"
And all Israel would go down to the Philistines for every man to put 20
an edge on his plowshare and his mattock and his ax and his sickle.

---

15. *to Gibeath-Benjamin.* It looks improbable that Samuel would now go off
after this confrontation to Gibeah, which is Saul's hometown. The text at this
point in the Septuagint has him going "on the way," leaving the more likely
outcome that he abandons Saul and his small handful of man at Gibeah to
tackle the Philistines.

    about six hundred men. By this point, 1,400 have "slipped away."

17. *the Shual region.* The name literally means "Foxland."

18. *Zeboim Valley.* Or, Jackal Valley.

19. *no smith could be found in all the land of Israel.* This bit of background
notation vividly reflects the abject status of the Israelites under Philistine domination. Ironsmiths are banned among them to prevent their developing the
weaponry needed for rebellion.

20. *his sickle.* The reading used here is, as in the Septuagint, *ḥermesho*, instead
of the Masoretic *maḥareshato*, "his plowshare," which repeats the first term in
the list.

21 And the price of the sharpening was a *pim* for the plowshares and the
mattocks and the three-pronged forks and the axes, and for setting the
22 goads. And so it was, on the day of battle, that no sword nor spear was
found in the hands of all the troops who were with Saul and Jonathan,
23 but in the hands of Saul and Jonathan his son. And the Philistine garrison sallied forth to the pass of Michmash.

---

2 1. *the price of the sharpening was a* pim. The italicized term occurs only here in
the Bible, but the archeologists have found stone weights marked *pim*, which
is two-thirds of a shekel (here, evidently, a silver shekel). The Philistines, then,
not only deprive the Israelites of the technology for making weapons but also
reap a profit from their smithless vassals for the maintenance of the agricultural
tools they need for their livelihood.

    the three-pronged forks. A commonly proposed emendation yields "a third of
a shekel for the forks and the axes and for the setting of the goads." This change
would make sense if in fact the sharpening of these implements were half the
work of sharpening plowshares and mattocks, but that is not entirely clear.

CHAPTER 14

$\mathbb{A}$nd when the day came round, Jonathan son of Saul said to the lad 1
bearing his armor, "Come, let us cross over to the Philistine garrison
which is on the other side there," but his father he did not tell. And Saul 2
was sitting at the outskirts of Gibeah under the pomegranate tree which
is at Migron, and the troops that were with him were about six hundred
men. And Ahijah son of Ahitub brother of Ichabod son of Phineas son 3
of Eli priest of the LORD at Shiloh was bearer of the ephod, and the
troops did not know that Jonathan had gone. And in the pass through 4
which Jonathan sought to cross over to the Philistine garrison there was

---

1. *but his father he did not tell.* One assumes that his father would have forbidden him to go out on so dangerous a mission, but there is also an implicit
contrast between Saul, sitting under the pomegranate tree, hesitant to act in
the face of the superior forces of the enemy, and Jonathan, prepared to execute
a daring commando raid.

3. *Ahijah son of Ahitub brother of Ichabod.* The genealogy here casts a certain
suspect light on Saul: the priest who accompanies him to the battlefield, and on
whose prognostication he relies, belongs to the blighted—and rejected—house
of Eli.
    bearer of the ephod. The title, *nose' ephod*, is formally parallel to "armor
bearer," *nose' kelim*, and so suggests a contrast between Saul, who relies on
divination, and Jonathan, who relies on his weapons.

4. *the pass through which Jonathan sought to cross over.* The Philistines and the
Israelites are encamped on the tops of two steep hills facing each other, with a
deep gully, or wadi, running between them. Jonathan and his armor bearer are
able to make their way down the slope unseen by taking cover among the crags
and under overhangs. But Jonathan realizes that there will be a moment of truth
in this tactic, for when they reach the floor of the gully, they will be "exposed"
(verse 8) to the Philistine outpost.

a rocky crag on one side and on the other side, and the name of the one
5   was Bozez and the name of the other Seneh. The one crag loomed to
the north facing Michmash and the other to the south facing Gibeah.
6   And Jonathan said to the lad bearing his armor, "Come, let us cross over
to the garrison of these uncircumcised! Perhaps the LORD will act for
us, for nothing holds the LORD back from rescue, whether by many or
7   by few." And his armor bearer said to him, "Do you whatever your heart
8   inclines—here I am with you, my heart as yours." And Jonathan said,
"Look, we are about to cross over to the men and we shall be exposed
9   to them. If thus they say, 'Stand still until we get to you,' we shall stand
10 where we are and not go up to them. And if thus they say, 'Come up to
us,' we shall go up, for the LORD will have given them in our hand, and
11 that will be the sign for us." And the two of them were exposed to the
Philistine garrison, and the Philistines said, "Look, Hebrews are coming

---

5. *loomed*. The Hebrew *mutsaq* means literally "column." It might conceivably
be a scrambled scribal repetition of the next Hebrew word in the text, *mitsafon*,
"from the north."

6. *these uncircumcised*. This designation for the Philistines is of course contemptuous. Its spirit is precisely reflected, from the other side of the ethnic barrier, in Othello's reference to a Turk he killed in battle as a "circumcised dog."

7. *Do whatever your heart inclines—here I am with you, my heart as yours*. The
translation follows the reading of the Septuagint. The Masoretic text conveys
the same general idea, though a bit less coherently: "Do whatever is in your
heart, incline you—here I am with you as your heart."

10. *that will be the sign for us*. Readers from the Talmud to our own times have
construed this as a kind of divination. It is far more likely that a further contrast
is implied between Saul, who depends on divination, and Jonathan, who is
thinking in pragmatic military terms: if they invite us to come up to them, that
will be our great opportunity; if they order us to await their descent, we may
have no recourse (except, perhaps, flight at the last moment).

11. *Look, Hebrews are coming out of the holes where they've been hiding*. These
words accord perfectly with the report in 13:6 of the Israelites hiding in every
nook and cranny, and also vividly express the contempt of the Philistines for the
Hebrews, whom they depict as so many vermin. The contempt is extended in
the taunting challenge to Jonathan and his lad in the next verse.

out of the holes where they've been hiding." And the men of the garrison 12
spoke out to Jonathan and his armor bearer and said, "Come up to us,
and we'll teach you something!" And Jonathan said to his armor bearer,
"Come up behind me, for the LORD has given them into the hand of
Israel." And Jonathan climbed up on his hands and knees with his armor 13
bearer behind him, and they fell before Jonathan with his armor bearer
finishing them off behind him. And the first toll of dead that Jonathan 14
with his armor bearer struck down was about twenty men, with arrows
and rocks of the field. And terror shook the camp in the field and all 15
the troops. The garrison and the raiding party were also shaken, and the
earth trembled, and it became dire terror. And the lookouts attached 16
to Saul at Gibeath-Benjamin saw and, look, the multitude was melting
away and going off yonder. And Saul said to the troops who were with 17
him, "Call the roll, pray, and see who has gone from us," and they called

---

13. *Jonathan climbed up on his hands and knees.* Although it is not easy to
reconstruct the exact tactic of surprise, this notation makes clear that instead
of walking up the slope directly to the Philistine outpost, Jonathan and his
armor bearer manage to slip off to one side and make their way up the slope by
a circuitous route, crouching and crawling in order to take shelter among the
rocks, and thus come upon the outpost undetected.

14. *the first toll of dead.* The literal meaning of the Hebrew is "the first blow."
  with arrows and rocks of the field. The translation adopts the reading of the
Septuagint. The Masoretic text has here, "within about half a furrow long, an
acre [?] of field," but that sequence of Hebrew words looks scrambled.

15. *terror shook.* The Hebrew *ḥaradah* means both terror and shaking.
  dire terror. The Hebrew is literally "terror of God," but the latter word,
'elohim, serves as an intensifier. In any case, the idiom functions as a kind of
pun—dire terror is terror caused by God.

16. *going off yonder.* The translation presupposes *halom* ("yonder"), a repeated
word in this episode, instead of the Masoretic *wahalom*, which could mean
either, asyntactically, "and yonder," or "and hitting" (that is, the Philistines were
going on, hitting each other).

18   the roll and, look, Jonathan and his armor bearer were absent. And Saul
     said to Ahijah, "Bring forth the ephod." For on that day he was bear-
19   ing the ephod before the Israelites. And it happened that as Saul was
     speaking to the priest, the tumult in the Philistine camp was growing
     greater and greater. And Saul said to the priest, "Pull back your hand."
20   And Saul and all the troops who were with him rallied and entered into
     the fighting, and, look, every man's sword was against his fellow—a very
21   great panic. And there were Hebrews who were previously with the
     Philistines, who had come up with them into the camp, and they, too,
22   turned round to be with Israel under Saul and Jonathan. And all the
     men of Israel who were hiding out in the high country of Ephraim had

---

18. *Bring forth the ephod.* The Masoretic text, both in this clause and the next, has "Ark of God" instead of "ephod," but the reading of the Septuagint, *ephod*, is compelling on several grounds. We have been informed earlier that the Ark of God was left, not to be moved for the foreseeable future, at Kiriath-Jearim. The Ark was not an instrument of divination, like the ephod, and what Saul wants Ahijah to do here is to divine. It is possible that Ahijah's lineal connection with the keepers of the Ark at Shiloh led some early transmitter of the text to align this episode with the earlier story in which the Ark—quite misguidedly—was brought out from Shiloh to the battlefield. The Masoretic text also reads, asyntactically, "for the Ark of God on that day was, and the Israelites," whereas the Septuagint, far more coherently, has "for on that day he was bearing the ephod before the Israelites."

19. *Pull back your hand.* That is, desist from the act of divination you have begun—it is no longer necessary, for the auditory evidence of the Philistine rout has reached our ears.

20. *and, look, every man's sword was against his fellow.* This spectacle of total, self-mutilating panic (*mehumah*)in the camp of the enemy is a recurrent motif that goes back to Judges (compare the effect of Gideon's surprise attack on the Midianite camp), and is a kind of narrative realization of God's direct intervention in battle to grant victory to Israel. The foundational instance of this motif is the victory at the Sea of Reeds in Exodus.

21. *Hebrews who were previously with the Philistines.* Given the subject status of the Israelites, it is not surprising that some of them would have been conscripted by the Philistines, either as soldiers or to perform menial tasks for the troops. They are referred to here as "Hebrews" because that is how their Philistine masters would have referred to them.

heard that the Philistines were fleeing, and they, too, gave chase after them in the fighting. And the LORD delivered Israel on that day.   23a

And the fighting moved on past Beth-Aven. And the men of Israel were   23b,24
hard pressed on that day. And Saul made the troops take an oath, saying, "Cursed be the man who eats food until evening, until I take vengeance upon my enemies!" And all the troops tasted no food. And the whole   25
country came into the forest, and there was honey on the ground. And   26
the troops entered the forest and, look, there was a flow of honey, but

---

24. *And the men of Israel were hard pressed.* The explanation for being hard pressed is not certain. The Hebrew term, *nigas*, most naturally refers to being at a military disadvantage, but here the Israelites appear to have the upper hand. The other possibility is that the men are weak from hunger, not having had the opportunity to eat in their hot pursuit of the Philistines. The oath Saul exacts would then compound this predicament. It should be said that the Septuagint reflects a different text for this entire clause: "And Saul committed a great blunder on that day."

Cursed be the man who eats food. As we shall have occasion to see later in the David narrative, it was a fairly common practice (though by no means an automatic one) for fighting men to take on themselves a vow of abstinence from food, in order to enter the battle in what amounted to a state of dedicated ritual purity. But Saul in this instance makes a miscalculation, imposing a fast on hungry men, in an effort to force the hand of divinity. (Thus the Septuagint's version of the first clause of this verse might be regarded as an interpretive gloss on the lapidary formulation of the received text.)

25. *And the whole country came into the forest.* This sounds as odd in the Hebrew as in translation because "country" (*ha'arets*) is not an idiomatic term for "people." Extensive textual surgery yields this conjectural reconstruction of an original clause: "and there was honeycomb on the ground." An additional difficulty in this passage is that the common Hebrew term *ya'ar*, forest, has a rare homonym that means honeycomb. (In verse 27, the term that occurs is *ya'arah*, which is unambiguous both because with the feminine suffix it can refer only to honeycomb and because it is joined with *devash*, honey.) But the received text in our verse has the preposition "into" (*b^e*), which presumes that *ya'ar* means "forest" and not "honeycomb."

27 none touched his hand to his mouth, for the troops feared the vow. But Jonathan had not heard when his father made the troops swear, and he reached with the tip of the staff that was in his hand and dipped it into the honeycomb and brought his hand back to his mouth, and his

28 eyes lit up. And a man from the troops spoke up and said, "Your father made the troops solemnly swear, saying, 'Cursed be the man who eats

29 food today.' And so the troops were famished." And Jonathan said, "My father has stirred up trouble for the land. See, pray, that my eyes have

30 lit up because I tasted a bit of this honey. How much better still if the troops had really eaten today from the booty of their enemies that they found, for then the toll of Philistines would have been all the greater."

31 And they struck down the Philistines on that day from Michmash to

32 Ajalon, and the troops were very famished. And the troops pounced on

---

27. *his eyes lit up.* The idiom used for the refreshing effect of a taste of food is a pointed one because, as Shimon Bar-Efrat has noted, the verb "to light up" (the Hebrew verb *'or*) plays antithetically on Saul's "cursed (*'arur*) be the man."

29. *My father has stirred up trouble.* The verb *'akhar* that is used here is doubly important. Etymologically, it means "to muddy," as in stirring up muck in a pond. Thus, it is an antithesis to the lighting up of the eyes Jonathan has just experienced through partaking of food. It is also the verb Jephthah invokes when he sees it is his daughter who has come out to greet him: "and you have been among those who stir up trouble for me" (Judges 11:35). The echo sets up a network of intertextual links with the Jephthah story: here, too, a father who is a military leader seeks to influence the outcome of the battle by a rash vow that is an unwitting death sentence on his own child.

31. *And they struck down the Philistines.* Although the form of the two verbs does not indicate it, the narrative logic of the scene compels us to construe this sentence as a pluperfect summary of the day's action, responding to Jonathan's reference to the "toll" (literally, "blow") exacted from the Philistines.

32. *the troops pounced on the booty . . . ate them together with the blood.* The first verb here has pejorative force, being generally used for birds of prey descending on their victims. Biblical law repeatedly prohibits the consumption of meat together with the blood because the blood is regarded as the sacred stuff of life. The slaughtering on the ground here would make it more difficult to allow the blood to drain off, as would have been done in slaughtering on a stone platform or altar. (Note Saul's correction of the practice in verses 33–34.) Jonathan's

the booty and took sheep and cattle and calves and slaughtered them on the ground, and the troops ate them together with the blood. And they 33 told Saul, saying, "Look, the troops are offending the LORD by eating together with the blood!" And he said, "You have acted treacherously. Roll a big stone over to me now." And Saul said, "Spread out among 34 the troops, and say to them, 'Every man bring forth to me his ox and his sheep and slaughter them here and eat, and you shall not offend the LORD by eating together with the blood.'" And all the troops brought forth each man what he had in hand that night and they slaughtered it there. And Saul built an altar to the LORD, it was the first altar he built 35 to the LORD.

And Saul said, "Let us go down after the Philistines by night and 36 despoil them till daybreak, and we shall not leave a man among them." And they said, "Whatever is good in your eyes, do." And the priest said, "Let us approach God yonder." And Saul inquired of God, "Shall I go 37 down after the Philistines? Will You give them in the hand of Israel?" And He did not answer him on that day. And Saul said, "Draw near, 38 all you chiefs of the troops, mark and see, wherein is this offense

---

tasting a bit of honey thus leads to an orgy of gluttonous consumption of meat with blood. This consequence attaches an association of violation of sacred law to Jonathan's act, but the ultimate fault lies with Saul, who by imposing a fast on already famished men has set them up to abandon all restraint the moment the taboo against eating is broken.

34. *what he had in hand*. This accords with the Septuagint, *'asher beyado*, against the Masoretic, "his bull in his hand," *shoro beyado*.

37. *And Saul inquired of God . . . And He did not answer him*. Although it was extremely common for military leaders everywhere in the ancient Near East to consult an oracle before going into battle, Saul's failed inquiry here participates in a larger pattern in his story: he is constantly seeking knowledge of what is about to happen (as in his quest for a seer to help him locate the asses at the very beginning), but this knowledge is repeatedly withheld from him.

38. *wherein is this offense*. Saul assumes that the oracle did not respond because someone among his troops committed some "offense." The narrator does not necessarily endorse this assumption.

39 today? For as the LORD lives Who delivers Israel, were it in Jonathan my son, he would be doomed to die!" And none answered him from all
40 the troops. And he said to all Israel, "You will be on one side and I and Jonathan my son on the other side." And the troops said to Saul, "What
41 is good in your eyes, do." And Saul said, "LORD, God of Israel! Why did You not answer Your servant today? If there is guilt in me or in Jonathan my son, O LORD God of Israel, show Urim, and if it is in Your people Israel, show Thummim." And the lot fell on Jonathan and Saul, and the
42 troops came out clear. And Saul said, "Cast between me and Jonathan

---

39. *were it in Jonathan my son.* "It" refers to the just mentioned "offense." Is this a flourish of rhetorical emphasis, or, as J. P. Fokkelman has suggested, does it open the possibility that Saul has Jonathan in mind? In the immediately preceding episode, after all, Jonathan has gone out on a military operation without permission. Jonathan now is brought forth as the possible perpetrator of some further, not yet specified offense, which will prove to be the tasting of the honey. In any case, there seems to be some deep ambivalence between father and son well before the appearance of David at court.

41. *LORD, God of Israel! Why did You not answer Your servant today? If there is guilt in me or in Jonathan my son . . . show Urim, and if it is in Your people Israel, show Thummim.* This version comes from the Septuagint. The Masoretic text here has the short and cryptic "Show Thammim [sic]." Saul's frustrated reference to his failure to receive an answer from the oracle makes a great deal of narrative sense (see the comment on verse 37). The Septuagint version also makes intelligible the process of oracular lottery. The Urim and Thummim were two divinatory objects attached to the ephod, probably in a special compartment. They may have been in the form of stones or tokens with lettering on them. They provided indication of binary oppositions: thus the question addressed to the oracle had to take the form of yes or no, x or y. The opposition may have been underscored by the fact that Urim and Thummim begin, respectively, with the first and last letter of the Hebrew alphabet. More speculatively, Urim might be linked with *'aror,* "to curse," and Thummim with the root *t-m-m,* whole or innocent.

the lot fell on Jonathan and Saul. The same idiom of being "caught" by the lot that was used for Saul's election recurs here in the devolution of the curse on Jonathan.

42. *Cast between me and Jonathan.* Since the Urim and Thummim can provide only binary responses, it is necessary to divide again into two alternatives in order to get an answer.

my son." And the lot fell on Jonathan. And Saul said, "Tell me, what have   43
you done?" And Jonathan told him and said, "I indeed tasted from the
tip of the staff that was in my hand a bit of honey. Here I am, ready to
die!" And Saul said, "So may God do to me, and even more, for Jonathan   44
is doomed to die!" And the troops said to Saul, "Will Jonathan die, who   45
has performed this great rescue in Israel? Heaven forbid, as the LORD
lives, that a single hair of his head should fall to the ground! For with
God has he wrought this day." And the troops saved Jonathan, and he
did not die. And Saul went away from pursuing the Philistines and the   46
Philistines went back to their place.

And Saul had taken hold of the kingship over Israel, and he did battle   47
round about with all his enemies, with Moab and with the Ammonites

---

43. *indeed tasted . . . a bit of honey.* Jonathan begins by clearly and emphatically
admitting responsibility, using the infinitive absolute followed by the verb (literally, "taste I have tasted"). But he chooses, with precision, the minimal verb
"taste" rather than "eat" and holds back its minimal object, "a bit of honey," for
the very end of the sentence.

45. *And the troops said to Saul, "Will Jonathan die . . .?"* As several commentators have observed, this is a precise reversal of the incident after Saul's victory
over Nahash, in which the troops sought to kill dissidents and Saul saved their
lives. Now he has become the severe autocrat, and his son's well-earned popularity with the troops saves the prince.

47. *Saul had taken hold of the kingship.* The verb used, *lakad*, is the same one
just invoked for the process of being caught, trapped, taken hold of, in the
divine lottery. Saul himself was "caught" for kingship. Now, through conquest,
he catches, or secures, the kingship. There is thus surely an undertone of ambiguity in this report of his success as monarch.
   he would inflict punishment. The Hebrew *yarshi'a* usually means to condemn someone as guilty in a court of justice. But a related idiom, "to do justice," *'asot shephatim,* also means to carry out punitive acts against an enemy.
The Masoretic version is to be preferred to the Septuagint's *yoshi'a,* "he would
rescue," because in this narrative, God, not Saul, is represented as the rescuer.
Apparently, the implication is that he carried out punishing expeditions against
Israel's enemies to the east of the Jordan without actually conquering them, as
David was to do.

and with Edom and with the kings of Zobah and with the Philistines, and
48 wherever he turned he would inflict punishment. And he triumphed and
struck down Amalek and rescued Israel from the hand of its plunderers.

49 And Saul's sons were Jonathan and Ishvi and Malkishua, and the names
of his two daughters were Merab the firstborn and Michal the younger.
50 And the name of Saul's wife was Ahinoam daughter of Ahimaaz. And
51 the name of his commander was Abiner son of Ner, Saul's uncle. And
52 Kish, Saul's father, and Ner, Abner's father, were sons of Abiel. And the
fighting against the Philistines was fierce all the days of Saul, and when
Saul saw any warrior or valiant fellow, he would gather him to himself.

---

49. *And Saul's sons.* This entire notice of Saul's family and of his conquests is
placed as a formal marker of conclusion to the body of the Saul story. What
follows is the episode that will definitively disqualify him for the throne in
Samuel's eyes, and then David will enter the scene. The episode in which Saul
pronounces a death sentence on his son and heir heralds the climactic encounter with Samuel over Amalek in which the prophet will pronounce the end
of Saul's incipient dynasty. Eventually, Saul and Jonathan, the parties jointly
indicated by the first cast of the Urim, will perish in battle on the same day.

50. *Abiner.* A variant vocalization of Abner.

52. *And the fighting against the Philistines.* Saul has greater success on the
eastern front, but he is unable to subdue the Philistines. In the end, they will
destroy him in their victory at Gilboa.
    when Saul saw any warrior . . . he would gather him to himself. This report of
constant military conscription indicates the institutionalization of the monarchy and also accords with Samuel's warning about the burden of conscription
that the king would impose.

CHAPTER 15

And Samuel said to Saul, "Me has the Lᴏʀᴅ sent to anoint you as ₁ king over His people Israel. And now, heed the voice of the words of the Lᴏʀᴅ. Thus says the Lᴏʀᴅ of Armies, 'I have made reckoning of ₂ what Amalek did to Israel, that he set against him on the way as he

---

1. *Me has the* Lᴏʀᴅ *sent*. Samuel, by placing the accusative first-person pronoun at the beginning of his speech (normal Hebrew usage would simply attach an accusative suffix to the verb), once again highlights his own centrality to this whole process: it is only because he, as God's unique delegate, has anointed Saul that Saul can claim to be king. In this way, Samuel sets the stage rhetorically for the prerogative of canceling Saul's kingship that he will exercise later in this episode.

heed the voice of the words of the Lᴏʀᴅ. This redundant phrasing is a little odd, but it is dictated by the pressure of the thematically fraught key phrase, "heed [or listen to] the voice," that defines the entire episode. Saul fails to listen as he fails to see.

2. *reckoning of what Amalek did to Israel*. After Amalek massacred the Israelite stragglers (see Deuteronomy 25:18), Israel was commanded to destroy all remnants of the Amalekites.

set against him. This phrase may be an ellipsis for "set ambushes against him."

3 was coming up from Egypt. Now, go and strike down Amalek, and put
   under the ban everything that he has, you shall not spare him, and you
   shall put to death man and woman, infant and suckling, ox and sheep,
   camel and donkey.'"

4 And Saul summoned the troops and assembled them at Telaim, two
5 hundred thousand foot soldiers and ten thousand men of Judah. And
6 Saul came up to the city of Amalek and lay in wait in the ravine. And
   Saul said to the Kenite, "Go, turn away, come down from amidst the
   Amalekite, lest I sweep you away together with him, for you did kindness to all the Israelites when they came up from Egypt." And the Kenite
7 turned away from the midst of Amalek. And Saul struck down Amalek
8 from Havilah till you come to Shur, which is before Egypt. And he

---

3. *put under the ban everything that he has.* The verb here is in the plural, evidently including the troops together with Saul, though the subsequent verbs in
this verse are in the singular. The "ban" (*ḥerem*), one of the cruelest practices
of ancient Near Eastern warfare, is an injunction of total destruction—of all
living things—of the enemy. Amalek is, of course, the archetypal implacable
enemy of Israel, but it should be said that here, as throughout the Samuel story,
there is at least some margin of ambiguity as to whether the real source of this
ferocious imperative is God or the prophet who claims to speak on His behalf.
    you shall not spare him. The Hebrew verb *ḥamal* straddles two senses, to feel
mercy for and to allow to survive, and the ambiguity between the emotional and
the pragmatic sense is exploited throughout the story.

4. *summoned the troops.* The word for "summoned" (there are several more
common terms for mustering troops in the Bible) is quite rare, and literally
means "made them listen." The same verb as "to listen" in a different conjugation, it continues to call attention to this thematically weighted activity.
    two hundred thousand foot soldiers and ten thousand men of Judah. The troops
from Judah are presumably also foot soldiers, and so an ellipsis is probable:
"and another ten thousand foot soldiers from the men of Judah."

6. *Go, turn away, come down from amidst.* These overlapping imperative verbs
are obviously meant to underscore the urgency of the command. The Kenites
appear to have been a tribe of migratory metalsmiths (the meaning of their
name) somehow allied with Israel (compare Judges 4–5), though the nature of
the "kindness" they did for Israel is not known.

caught Agag king of Amalek alive, and all the people he put under the
ban with the edge of the sword. And Saul, and the troops with him, 9
spared Agag and the best of the sheep and the cattle, the fat ones and
the young ones, everything good, and they did not want to put them
under the ban. But all the vile and worthless possessions, these they
put under the ban.

And the word of the LORD came to Samuel, saying, "I repent that I made 10,11
Saul king, for he has turned back from Me, and My words he has not fulfilled." And Samuel was incensed and he cried out to the LORD all night
long. And Samuel rose early in the morning to meet Saul, and it was told 12
to Samuel, saying, "Saul has gone to Carmel and, look, he has put up a
monument for himself, and has turned about and passed onward, and
gone down to Gilgal." And Samuel came to Saul, and Saul said to him, 13

---

9. *And Saul, and the troops with him, spared Agag.* The Hebrew says simply
"Saul and the troops spared Agag," but because a singular verb is used with the
plural subject, it signals to the audience that Saul is the principal actor and the
troops only accessories. (This highlighting of the first-mentioned agent through
a singular verb for a plural subject is a general feature of biblical usage.) When
confronted by Samuel, Saul will turn the responsibility for the action on its
head. "Spared" momentarily sounds as though it could mean "had mercy on,"
but then it is also attached to cattle and sheep. There is a morally scandalous
pairing in the selective massacre Saul and his troops perpetrate: they kill all
the defective animals and every man, woman, child, and infant, while sparing
the good, edible animals and the king (perhaps with the idea that some further
profit can be extracted from him).

the fat ones. The Masoretic text has *mishnim* (two-year-olds?), but, in a reversal of consonants, the Syriac and the Targum reflect *shmenim*, fat ones.

11. *Samuel was incensed.* The reasons for his rage are wonderfully unspecified,
or perhaps overdetermined. He may well be incensed with Saul, or with the
people who coerced him into this whole distasteful monarchic business in the
first place, or even with God for making him heed the people.

12. *Carmel.* This is not the Carmel near Haifa but a town in the tribal territory
of Judah, in the general vicinity of Hebron.

he has put up a monument for himself. This would be a victory marker, probably in the form of a stele.

14 "Blessed be you to the LORD! I have fulfilled the word of the LORD." And
Samuel said, "And what is this sound of sheep in my ears, and the sound
15 of cattle that I hear?" And Saul said, "From the Amalekite they have
brought them, for the troops spared the best of the sheep and the cattle
in order to sacrifice to the LORD your God, and the rest we put under
16 the ban." And Samuel said, "Hold off, that I may tell you what the LORD
17 spoke to me this night." And he said, "Speak." And Samuel said, "Though
you may be small in your own eyes, you are the head of the tribes of
18 Israel, and the LORD has anointed you king over Israel. And the LORD
sent you on a mission and said to you, 'You shall put under the ban the
offenders, Amalek, and do battle against them till you destroy them all.'

---

14. *this sound of sheep . . . and the sound of cattle.* "Sound" and "voice" are
the same word in Hebrew (*qol*), and so the thematic key word of the episode
comes to the fore: Saul had been enjoined to listen to the voice of the LORD;
now Samuel tells him that all that can be heard (the same verb as "listen" in
Hebrew) is the bleating and mooing "voice" of the very flocks which, according
to God's word, should have been destroyed.

15. *they have brought them.* Saul first uses a vague third-person plural, entirely
shifting the responsibility to unnamed others who have done the bringing.
   the troops spared the best of the sheep and the cattle. In verse 9, of course, it was
expressly reported that Saul, with the troops as accessories, spared the flocks.
   in order to sacrifice to the LORD your God. This pious justification for the act
was nowhere in evidence in the narrator's initial account of it (verses 8–9).
Although it is common enough in biblical usage when addressing a holy man
to say "the LORD your God," that locution, invoked twice in this story by Saul,
stresses the distance between him and God and his sense that it is Samuel who
has proprietary claims on the divinity.

17. *Though you may be small in your own eyes.* Samuel is obviously harking back
to Saul's initial expression of unworthiness for the throne ("from the smallest
of the tribes of Israel," 9:21), as if to say, Well, you may not really amount to
much, as you yourself said at the outset, but you nevertheless have taken upon
yourself the solemn responsibility of king.

18. *mission.* Literally, "a way."
   till you destroy them all. The Masoretic text, illogically, has "till they destroy
them all," but the second-person suffix is supplied in some of the ancient versions.

And why did you not heed the voice of the LORD, for you pounced on the   19
booty and did evil in the eyes of the LORD?" And Saul said to Samuel,   20
"But I heeded the voice of the LORD and went on the way the LORD sent
me, and I brought back Agag king of Amalek, but Amalek I put under
the ban. And the troops took from the booty sheep and cattle, the pick   21
of the banned things, to sacrifice to the LORD your God at Gilgal." And   22
Samuel said,

> "Does the LORD take delight in burnt offerings and sacrifices
>   as in heeding the voice of the LORD?
> For heeding is better than sacrifice,
>   hearkening, than the fat of rams.
> For the diviner's offense is rebellion,   23

---

19. *why did you not heed the voice of the* LORD. Samuel hammers home the thematic point of the whole confrontation: Saul, actually the initiator, proclaims
he has listened to the voice of the people (verse 24)—as, ironically, Samuel
himself was enjoined by God to do in Chapter 8—instead of to the voice of
God. This antithesis is more pointed in the Hebrew because the more general
meaning of the word for "troops," *'am*, is "people."

you pounced on the booty. Samuel uses the same verb for greedy predation
that was used to describe the orgy of meat-eating after the breaking of the vow
of fasting in Chapter 14.

21. *the troops took.* Once again, Saul shifts the responsibility for the act from
himself to his troops.

22. *Does the* LORD *take delight in burnt offerings.* Samuel caps his prophetic
denunciation with the declamation of a prophetic poem. The theme that
God requires obedience, not rote performance of the cult, is a common one
among the later "literary" prophets, though in their poetry, obedience to God
means refraining from acts of exploitation rather than carrying out a program
of extermination.

heeding the voice of the LORD. The thematic phrase is now placed in the fore-
ground of the prophetic poem, reinforced by "heeding [or listening] is better
than sacrifice" and "hearkening" in the next lines.

23. *the diviner's offense is rebellion.* That is, rebellion is as great a sin as divination or sorcery. The choice of the comparison is not accidental, considering
Saul's repeated futile attempts to divine the future.

the transgression of idols—defiance.
Since you have cast off the word of the LORD,
He has cast you aside as king."

24 And Saul said to Samuel, "I have offended, for I have transgressed
the utterance of the LORD, and your word, for I feared the troops and
25 listened to their voice. Now then, forgive, pray, my offense, and turn
26 back with me, that I may bow down before the LORD." And Samuel
said to Saul, "I will not turn back with you, for you have cast aside
the word of the LORD and He has cast you aside from being king over
27 Israel." And Samuel turned round to go, and Saul grasped the skirt of
28 his cloak, and it tore. And Samuel said to him, "The LORD has torn
away the kingship of Israel from you this day and given it to your fel-
29 lowman who is better than you. And, what's more, Israel's Eternal
does not deceive and does not repent, for He is no human to repent."

---

the transgression of idols—defiance. The first phrase in the Hebrew is literally
"transgression and idols," but is readily construed as a hendyadis (two words
for a single concept) without emending the text. The gist of this parallel verset:
defiance is as great a sin as the worship of idols (*teraphim*).

24. *I have transgressed the utterance of the LORD, and your word.* The Hebrew is
literally "the mouth of the LORD." There is a kind of hesitation in Saul's words: I
have violated God's command, and yours as well. Is there a difference between
the two? Though there may well be, Saul is in no position to argue that Samuel's
words are not God's.

25. *turn back with me, that I may bow down.* It would have been Samuel's function to offer the sacrifice. For Samuel not to accompany Saul to the altar would
be a manifest public humiliation, a gesture of abandonment.

27. *Saul grasped the skirt of his cloak, and it tore.* The "little cloak" that Hannah
would bring each year for the child Samuel has now become the prophet's flowing robe. Samuel, who never misses a cue to express his implacability toward
Saul, immediately converts the tearing of the cloak into a dramatic symbol of
Saul's lost kingdom. The Saul story, as we shall see, will return to cloaks and to
their torn or cut skirts.

29. *Israel's Eternal does not deceive and does not repent.* Samuel's use of the
verb "repent" strikes a peculiar dissonance. We in fact have been told that God

And Saul said, "I have offended. Now show me honor, pray, before the 30
elders of my people and before Israel, and turn back with me, that I
may bow to the LORD your God. And Samuel turned back from Saul, 31
and Saul bowed to the LORD. And Samuel said, "Bring forth to me 32
Agag king of Amalek!" And Agag went to him with mincing steps, and
he thought, "Ah, death's bitterness is turned away!" And Samuel said, 33

> "As your sword has bereaved women,
>> more bereaved than all women your mother!"

---

repented that He made Saul king. What Samuel says here is that God will not
change His mind about changing His mind. But might not this verbal contradiction cast some doubt on Samuel's reliability as a source for what God does
and doesn't want? There even remains a shadow of a doubt as to whether the
election of Saul in the first place was God's, or whether it was merely Samuel's
all-too-human mistake.

30. *show me honor.* Saul reverts to the recurrent term *kabed*—"honor" or "glory"
(as in "glory is exiled from Israel"). Knowing that Samuel has rejected him, he
implores the prophet at least to help him save face in offering the sacrifice.

31. *Samuel turned back from Saul.* All English versions render this, erroneously,
to indicate that Samuel nevertheless accompanied Saul to the sacrifice. But
the expression "turn back with" (*shuv 'im*), as in verse 30, and "turn back from
[literally, after]" (*shuv 'aharei*) are antonyms, the latter meaning unambiguously
"to abandon." (It is precisely the latter idiom that we see in God's condemnation
of Saul in verse 11.) Samuel is completing his rejection of Saul here by refusing
to accompany him in the cult, shaming him by forcing him to offer the sacrifice
without the officiating of the man of God.

32. *with mincing steps.* The Hebrew adverbial term *ma'adanot* is much disputed. Some interpret it as "stumbling," others, by a reversal of consonants,
read it as "in fetters." But the root of the word seems to point with the least
strain to '-d-n—"pleasure," "delicate thing." That makes sense if one construes
Agag's words (the meaning of which is also in dispute) as the expression of a
last illusion: I have been spared in the general massacre, and now I am brought
to parlay with the chief holy man of the Hebrews for some important purpose;
so surely they will not kill me.

34 And Samuel cut him apart before the Lord at Gilgal. And Samuel went to Ramah, while Saul went up to his home in Gibeath-Saul.

35 And Samuel saw Saul no more till his dying day, for Samuel was grieved about Saul, and the Lord had repented making Saul king over Israel.

---

33. *Samuel cut him apart before the* Lord. There is a long-standing consensus that the unique verb used here means something to this effect. The ghastly idea seems to be a kind of ritual butchering.

34. *Ramah . . . Gibeath-Saul.* Each returns to his hometown. Their relationship is to all intents and purposes finished.

35. *Samuel was grieved about Saul.* Or is it over the fact that he made the mistake of first choosing Saul? As J. P. Fokkelman notes, this sentence includes both death (*mot*) and grieving or mourning (*'abel*), though Saul is still alive: "we realize that Saul as king is dead; no stronger expression of the termination of his monarchy can be imagined."

CHAPTER 16

And the LORD said to Samuel, "How long are you going to grieve about   1
Saul when I have cast him aside from reigning over Israel? Fill your horn
with oil and go. I am sending you to Jesse the Bethlehemite, for I have
seen Me among his sons a king." And Samuel said, "How can I go? For   2
should Saul hear, he will kill me." And the LORD said, "Take a heifer with

---

1. *And the* LORD *said to Samuel.* In the preceding episodes, the typical form
of divine communication was Samuel's report of what God had said, although
at Samuel's first sighting of Saul, a brief direct message from God is offered.
As we have observed, these reports open up a certain margin of doubt as to
whether the purported divine injunctions are really God's or Samuel's. The
present episode unfolds systematically through repeated dialogue between God
and Samuel, and so God's judgments are rendered with perfect, authoritative
transparency. Evidently, the writer (or redactor) felt that the initial election of
David had to be entirely unambiguous. As the story continues, God will no
longer play this role of direct intervention.

I have seen Me among his sons a king. The verb "to see" (*ra'ah*) followed by
the preposition *l^e* has the idiomatic sense of "to provide," but it is essential to
preserve the literal meaning because this entire episode is built on the repetition of the thematically weighted word "to see," just as the previous episode
turned on "to listen."

2. *For should Saul hear, he will kill me.* Suddenly, a whole new political perspective is thrown on the estrangement between Samuel and Saul. The prophet may
claim the higher ground of divine authority, but it is the king who has the armed
divisions, and who might be ready to use them if Samuel should take any active
steps to replace him. At this point, Samuel's "grieving" over Saul begins to look
like grieving over the mistake he made in first choosing him. God, understanding Samuel's political predicament, suggests to him a cover story for his trip
from Ramah to Bethlehem, in the tribal territory of Judah.

3 you, and you will say, "To sacrifice to the LORD I have come.' And you
   will invite Jesse to the sacrifice. And I Myself shall let you know what
4 you must do, and you will anoint for Me the one that I say to you." And
   Samuel did what the LORD had spoken, and he came to Bethlehem, and
   the elders of the town came trembling to meet him and they said, "Do you
5 come in peace?" And he said, "In peace! To sacrifice to the LORD I have
   come. Purify yourselves and come with me to the sacrifice." And Jesse
6 purified his sons and invited them to the sacrifice. And it happened when
   they came that he saw Eliab and he said, "Ah yes! Before the LORD stands
7 His anointed." And the LORD said to Samuel, "Look not to his appearance
   and to his lofty stature, for I have cast him aside. For not as man sees does
   God see. For man sees with the eyes and the LORD sees with the heart."

---

3. *invite Jesse to the sacrifice.* The kind of sacrifice in question, *zevaḥ*, involves
both the ritual act and a feast made of the substantial parts of the animal not
burned on the altar.

4. *came trembling.* Their reaction is another reflection of the dangerous political
situation: the estrangement between Samuel and Saul appears to be generally
known, and the elders are terrified at the idea that Samuel may have come to
designate a new king, or otherwise subvert the reigning monarch, which could
bring royal retribution down on Bethlehem.
   and they said, "Do you come in peace?" The Masoretic text has "he said," but
both the Septuagint and the Qumran Samuel scroll show the plural. Both also
add "O seer" to the question of the elders.

6. *he saw Eliab.* Nothing could illustrate more vividly Samuel's persistent unre-
liability as seer (*ro'eh*). Having made a fatal mistake by electing Saul, "head
and shoulders taller than all the people," convinced he was directed by God,
Samuel is poised to repeat his error in being impressed by the "appearance" and
"lofty stature" of Jesse's firstborn. This whole story is also a heightened and stylized playing out of the theme of the reversal of primogeniture that dominates
Genesis. Instead of an elder and a younger son, Jesse has the formulaic seven
sons, plus an eighth, the youngest of all, who will be chosen.

7. *for I have cast him aside.* The language of rejection links the strapping Eliab
with the lofty Saul.
   does God see. These words, absent from the Masoretic text, are supplied by
the Septuagint.
   the LORD sees with the heart. Some construe this as "into the heart." In any
case, the heart is the seat of understanding, or insight, in biblical physiology.

And Jesse called Abinadab and made him pass before Samuel, and he   8
said, "This one, too, the LORD has not chosen." And Jesse made Sham-   9
mah pass by, and he said, "This one, too, the LORD has not chosen." And   10
Jesse made his seven sons pass before Samuel, and Samuel said to Jesse,
"The LORD has not chosen these." And Samuel said to Jesse, "Are there   11
no more lads?" And he said, "The youngest still is left, and, look, he is
tending the flock." And Samuel said to Jesse, "Send and fetch him, for
we shall not sit to eat until he comes here." And he sent and brought   12
him. And he was ruddy, with fine eyes and goodly to look on. And the
LORD said, "Arise, anoint him, for this is the one." And Samuel took the   13
horn of oil and anointed him in the midst of his brothers. And the spirit
of the LORD gripped David from that day onward. And Samuel rose and
went to Ramah.

8.–9. The verbatim repetition reflects the stylization of the episode, which is
set off from the surrounding narrative by its formal symmetries. After the first
three named sons, the rest pass by in summary by invocation of a narrative "et
cetera" principle, with the formulaic wrap-up at the end of verse 10, "The LORD
has not chosen these."

11. *he is tending the flock.* By his sheer youth, he has been excluded from
consideration, as a kind of male Cinderella left to his domestic chores instead
of being invited to the party. But the tending of flocks will have a symbolic
implication for the future leader of Israel, and, in the Goliath story, it will also
prove to have provided him with skills useful in combat.

12. *he was ruddy, with fine eyes and goodly to look on.* David's good looks will
play a crucial role in the magnetic effect he is to have on women and men. But
he is not big, like his brother Eliab, and Samuel has no opportunity to make a
judgment on his appearance, for David is brought from the flock sight unseen,
and then God immediately informs Samuel, "this is the one."

13. *anointed him in the midst of his brothers.* The anointment takes place within
the family circle and is a clandestine act.

14 And the spirit of the LORD had turned away from Saul, and an evil spirit
15 from the LORD had struck terror in him. And Saul's servants said to
16 him, "Look, pray, an evil spirit from God has stricken terror in you. Let
our lord, pray, speak. Your servants are before you—we shall seek out
a man skilled in playing the lyre, and so, when the evil spirit of God is
17 upon you, he will play and it will be well with you." And Saul said to
his servants, "See for me, pray, a man who plays well, and bring him to
18 me." And one of the lads answered and said, "Look, I have seen a son
of Jesse the Bethlehemite, skilled in playing, a valiant fellow, a warrior,

---

14. *And the spirit of the* LORD *had turned away from Saul.* In the transfer of
election of monarchs, one gets the picture of a kind of spiritual seesaw. As the
spirit of the LORD descends on and seizes David, it departs from Saul. That
vacuum is promptly filled by "an evil spirit from the LORD." In the theopsychol-
ogy of ancient Israel, extraordinary states were explained as investments by a
divine spirit. The charisma of leadership, now passed to David, was a descent
of the spirit. Saul's psychosis—evidently, fits of depression later manifested as
paranoia—is possession by another kind of spirit from the LORD.

15. *Saul's servants.* These would be his court officials or attendants.

16. *we shall seek out a man.* The Hebrew is literally "they will seek out a man."
 a man skilled in playing the lyre. In modern terms, what they have in mind
is a kind of music therapist. But David's mastery of the lyre evinces both his
power over the realm of the spirit (or of spirits) and his future association with
song and poetry.

17.–18. *See for me . . . I have seen.* The insistence on this verb picks up the key word
of the preceding episode. Saul first uses it in the sense God did in verse 1, "provide."

18. *Look, I have seen a son of Jesse.* This volunteered information is a bit peculiar
because, before any real search is undertaken, one of the young men in court
already has a candidate, and from a different tribal region. Is it possible that
word of David's clandestine anointment has circulated among limited groups,
and that the anonymous "lad" may be a kind of pro-David mole in the court
of Saul? It is also noteworthy that, just as at the beginning of his story, in his
quest for the lost asses, Saul did not know what to do and was dependent on
the counsel of his "lad" (*na'ar*); here one of his lads (*ne'arim*) offers the needed
advice for dealing with his melancholia.
 a valiant fellow, a warrior. These details of the characterization are surprising, for all that should be known about David is that he is a handsome shepherd

prudent in speech, a good-looking man, and the LORD is with him." And 19
Saul sent messengers to Jesse and said, "Send me David your son, who is
with the flock." And Jesse took a donkey laden with bread and a skin of 20
wine, and a kid, and he sent them by the hand of David his son to Saul.
And David came to Saul and stood in his presence, and Saul loved him 21
greatly, and he became his armor bearer. And Saul sent to Jesse, saying, 22
"Let him stand, pray, in my presence, for he has found favor in my eyes."
And so, when the spirit of God was upon Saul, David would take up the 23
lyre and play, and Saul would find relief, and it would be well with him,
and the evil spirit would turn away from him.

---

boy with musical skills. The influence of the subsequent narrative has clearly
made itself felt here, and these epithets may even be an editorial maneuver
to harmonize this episode with the next one, in which David makes his debut
before Saul not as a lyre player but as a military hero.

20. *a donkey laden with bread.* The Hebrew uses what appears to be an ellipsis
"a donkey of bread."

bread . . . a skin of wine . . . a kid. As Polzin has shrewdly observed, these
items replicate the items that Samuel told Saul would be carried by the three
men he was to encounter (10:3). David, then, is beginning anew the process
on which Saul launched.

21. *and Saul loved him greatly.* As Fokkelman has noted, Saul is the first of many
people in this narrative reported to love David—the very man he will come to
think of as his bitter enemy.

he became his armor bearer. This is not the position proposed by Saul's courtiers. Perhaps there was no set position of court lyre player, and so Saul gives
David an appointment that will ensure his constant proximity.

22. *Let him stand . . . in my presence.* The Hebrew idiom means to be in someone's service, though it also can suggest being presented to a dignitary, its evident meaning in verse 21.

23. *would find relief.* The Hebrew employs an untranslatable pun: the verb
"would find relief," *rawaḥ*, is a transparent cognate of *ruaḥ*, "spirit."

the evil spirit would turn away from him. In an elegant verbal symmetry the
episode that began with the (good) spirit of the LORD turning away from Saul
concludes with the evil spirit turning away from him, thanks to David's musical
mastery over the domain of spirits.

CHAPTER 17

₁ And the Philistines gathered their camps for battle, and they gathered at Socoh, which is in Judah, and they encamped between Socoh and ₂ Azekah, at Ephes-Dammim. And Saul and the men of Israel had gathered and encamped in the Valley of the Terebinth and they deployed to ₃ do battle against the Philistines. The Philistines took their stand on the hill on one side and Israel took its stand on the hill on the other side, ₄ with the ravine between them. And the champion sallied forth from the Philistine camps, Goliath was his name, from Gath, his height was six ₅ cubits and a span. A bronze helmet he had on his head, and in armor

---

3. *the hill on one side . . . the hill on the other . . . the ravine between them.* As we have seen before, this positioning of the opposing armies on opposite hilltops was a characteristic procedure of warfare in the hilly terrain of central Israel. But the opening verses also set up the strong spatial perspective through which this episode is organized. The perspective of the previous story was implicitly vertical: from God above to Samuel below, in the household of Jesse in Bethlehem. Here, by contrast, is a richly elaborated horizontal deployment of troops and individuals. God is out of the picture, except for the invocation through David's words.

4. *the champion.* The literal meaning of the Hebrew is "the man between"— that is, the man who goes out between the opposed battle lines to fight a counterpart. That particular Hebrew term thus reinforces the spatial definition of the story.
   six cubits and a span. This would make him over eight feet tall.

5.–6. *A bronze helmet . . . armor of mail . . . greaves of bronze . . . a spear of bronze.* This "Homeric" enumeration of armor and weapons is quite untypical of the Hebrew Bible. The thematic effect is clear: Goliath is represented as a hulking man of material military impedimenta—everything is given gargantuan

of mail he was dressed, and the weight of the armor was five thousand bronze shekels. And greaves of bronze were on his legs and a spear 6 of bronze between his shoulder blades. The shaft of his spear like a 7 weaver's beam, and the blade of his spear six hundred iron shekels. And his shield bearer went before him. And he stood and called out to the 8 Israelite lines and said to them, "Why should you come forth to deploy for battle? Am I not the Philistine, and you are slaves to Saul? Choose you a man and let him come down to me! If he prevail in battle against 9 me and strike me down, we shall be slaves to you, but if I prevail and strike him down, you will be slaves to us and serve us." And the Phi- 10 listine said, "I am the one who has insulted the Israelite lines this day! Give me a man and let us do battle together!" And Saul heard, and all 11

---

size or weight, again with untypical specification. All this will be counterposed to David's declaration on the battlefield that "not by sword nor spear does the LORD deliver."

five thousand bronze shekels. The armor alone is about 125 pounds.

7. *his shield bearer went before him.* For this reason the shield is not included in the catalogue of Goliath's armor. The gargantuan proportions of his dependence on the material implements of warfare are reinforced by the fact that he enters the battlefield with a man walking before him carrying his (presumably massive) shield.

8. *Am I not the Philistine.* Most often in the body of the story he is referred to as "the Philistine" and not by the name Goliath. This has led many scholars to infer that a tradition about Goliath was superimposed on an original story featuring an archetypal "Philistine."

9. *we shall be slaves to you.* In the event, this condition is not fulfilled: the Philistines retreat in disarray, but will later regroup to continue their war against the Israelites.

10. *I am the one who has insulted the Israelite lines.* Nearly all the English versions render the verb here as "defied," which is one end of the semantic range of the Hebrew *ḥeref*. But the verb is transparently linked with the noun *ḥerpah*—insult, disgrace, shame. By his taunting words, Goliath has laid an insult on Israel that only a victorious champion can "take away" (see verse 26)

11. *And Saul heard . . . and they were dismayed.* Saul, as the man head and shoulders taller than all the people, might be thought to be the one Israelite

Israel with him, these words of the Philistine, and they were dismayed and very frightened.

12 And David was the son of this Ephrathite man from Bethlehem in Judah named Jesse, and he had eight sons, and the man in the days
13 of Saul was old, advanced in years. And the three oldest sons of Jesse went after Saul to the war. And the names of his three sons who went to the war were Eliab the firstborn and the secondborn Abinadab and
14 the third Shammah. As for David, he was the youngest, and the three
15 oldest had gone after Saul. And David would go back and forth from
16 Saul's side to tend his father's flock in Bethlehem. And the Philistine
17 came forward morning and evening and took his stand, forty days. And Jesse said to David his son, "Take, pray, to your brothers this ephah of

---

fighter who stands a chance against Goliath. Instead, he leads his own troops in fearfulness: the stage is set for his deplacement by David.

12. *David was the son of this Ephrathite man.* The use of the demonstrative pronoun "this" is peculiar. It seems to be the first of several attempts (presumably, by the redactor) to harmonize this account of David's debut in Saul's court with the previous one, by referring to Jesse as someone already mentioned. Polzin has noted that demonstrative pronouns are unusually prominent in this whole episode: in many instances, they express contempt ("this Philistine"), but they are also sometimes necessary pointers in the emphatically spatial organization of the story.

15. *And David would go back and forth from Saul's side.* The last phrase has a sense close to "from Saul's presence" and is another strategem for harmonizing the two episodes. It invites us to suppose that David divided his time between playing the lyre for Saul and tending his father's flocks. The implicit assumption, however, of the story that unfolds is that David is unknown in the court of Saul, and that any to-and-fro movement between Bethlehem and the front would be to bring provisions to his older brothers.

17. *Take, pray, to your brothers.* If Saul has organized a standing army, it seems that his quartermaster corps still leaves something to be desired, and whatever rations may be provided for the troops need to be supplemented. In the same connection of skimpy provisions, Jesse sends a gift of ten wedges of cheese to his sons' commander.

parched grain and these ten loaves of bread and rush them to the camp to your brothers. And these ten wedges of cheese you shall bring to 18 the captain of the thousand and you shall see if your brothers are well, and you shall take their token. And Saul and they and all the men of 19 Israel are in the Valley of the Terebinth fighting with the Philistines." And David rose early in the morning and left the flock with a keeper 20 and bore [the provisions] and went off as Jesse had charged him. And when he came to the staging ground, the army going out to the lines was shouting the battle cry. And Israel and the Philistines deployed line 21 against line. And David left the gear that was on him with the keeper 22 of the gear and he ran to the lines and came and asked his brothers if they were well. As he was speaking to them, look, the champion was 23 coming up from the Philistine lines, Goliath the Philistine from Gath was his name, and he spoke words to the same effect, and David heard. And all the men of Israel, when they saw the man, fled from him and 24 were very frightened. And a man of Israel said, "Have you seen this 25 man coming up? Why, to insult Israel he comes up! And the man who strikes him down the king will enrich with a great fortune, and his daughter he will give him, and his father's household he will make free

---

18. *take their token.* Jesse expects his sons to send back some object with David as assurance that they are alive and well.

20. *the staging ground.* The Hebrew is literally "the circle," but the context (and a few allied ones elsewhere in the Bible) suggests a technical military sense.

22. *David left the gear that was on him with the keeper.* The phrase used precisely echoes his leaving the flock with a keeper. The narrative invokes a series of divestments by David of impediments for which he has been made responsible—flock, provisions, and then Saul's armor.

25. *the man who strikes him down the king will enrich . . . and his daughter he will give him.* It is at this point that the folkloric background of the second story of David's debut becomes particularly clear. The folktale pattern is one that is very familiar from later European tradition: a community is threatened by a giant, or ogre, or dragon that nobody can face. The king offers great wealth, and the hand of his daughter, to the man who can slay the giant. A young man from the provinces then appears on the scene, who in his youth and slight stature seems quite unfit for the daunting challenge, but by wit and resourcefulness,

26 of levies in Israel." And David said to the men who were standing with him, "What will be done for the man who strikes down yonder Philistine and takes away insult from Israel? For who is this uncircumcised
27 Philistine that he should insult the battle lines of the living God?" And the troops said to him to the same effect, "Thus will be done for the
28 man who strikes him down." And Eliab his oldest brother heard when he spoke with the men, and Eliab was incensed with David and he said, "Why is it you have come down, and with whom have you left that bit of flock in the wilderness? I'm the one who knows your impudence and

---

using unexpected means, he conquers the ogre. The appeal of this archetypal folktale no doubt made it attractive for inclusion in the David narrative. What must be emphasized, however, is that the folkloric materials have been historicized and even to an extent psychologized. The slaying of the giant becomes an emblem for Israel's prevailing over the numerically superior forces all around it as well as for the resourcefulness of its first dynastic king in securing power. The dialogue between David and his oldest brother vividly evokes a thick background of sibling jealousies. And David appears here—in the first scene in which he is assigned speech in the narrative—as a poised master of rhetoric, who knows how to use publicly enunciated words to achieve political ends.

26. *And David said . . . , "What will be done for the man . . . ?"* These are David's first recorded words in the narrative—usually, in biblical narrative convention, a defining moment of characterization. His first words express his wanting to know what will be gained—implicitly, in political terms—by the man who defeats Goliath. The inquiry about personal profit is then immediately balanced (or covered up) by the patriotic pronouncement, "who is this uncircumcised Philistine that he should insult the battle lines of the living God?" David has, of course, just heard one of the troops stipulate the reward for vanquishing the Philistine, but he wants to be perfectly sure before he makes his move, and so he asks for the details to be repeated. One sees how the folktale has been artfully historicized, subtly drawn into the realm of politics and individualized character.

28. *that bit of flock.* Eliab prefixes a term of diminution, *me'at*, to "flock" to express his contempt for David. The demonstrative pronoun, as elsewhere in the chapter, is also contemptuous, even as it points to the spatial distance between the battlefield and the pastureland around Bethlehem.
      I'm the one who knows. The relative clause here reflects the special emphasis of the Hebrew first-person pronoun *'ani*, which ordinarily would not be used

your wicked impulses, for it's to see the battle that you've come." And 29
David said, "What now have I done? It was only talk." And he turned 30
away from him toward someone else, and he spoke to the same effect,
and the troops answered him with words like the ones before. And the 31
words David had spoken were heard, and they told them to Saul, and
he fetched him. And David said to Saul, "Let no man's heart fail him! 32
Your servant will go and do battle with this Philistine." And Saul said to 33
David, "You cannot go against this Philistine to do battle with him, for
you are a lad and he is a man of war from his youth." And David said to 34
Saul, "A shepherd has your servant been for his father with the flock.
When the lion or the bear would come and carry off a sheep from the
herd, I would go out after him and strike him down and rescue it from 35
his clutches. And if he would rise against me, I would seize his beard

---

because the verb that follows it, *yad'ati*, has a first-person ending. The same
structure occurs in Goliath's boasting speech in verse 10.
   your wicked impulses. The literal meaning of the Hebrew is "the wickedness
of your heart," the heart being in biblical language the seat of understanding
and the place where plans or desires are shaped.

29. *It was only talk.* The translation follows an interpretation that goes back to
the Aramaic Targum of Late Antiquity and to Rashi in the Middle Ages. But the
Hebrew—literally, "Is it not a word?"—is gnomic. The ambiguity is compounded
because *davar* can mean "word," "message," "matter," "thing," "mission," and more.

30. *And he turned away from him toward someone else.* Ignoring his brother's
rebuke, David wants to hear the details of the reward a third time.

32. *Let no man's heart fail him.* The Septuagint has "Let not my lord's heart fail
him," but this could easily be an explanatory gloss. David uses a generalizing
phrase because he doesn't want to come out and say directly what all can see,
that the king's heart is failing him (literally, "falling").

34. *A shepherd has your servant been.* David's carefully contrived speech proclaims his tested courage and strength but, interestingly, is silent about the
shepherd's weapon—the slingshot—that he intends to use against Goliath.

35. *from his clutches.* The Hebrew says literally, "from his mouth."
   I would seize his beard. This of course refers only to the lion, not to the bear,
but this sort of focusing of the narrative report on one of its two instances is

36 and strike him and kill him. Both lion and bear your servant has struck down, and this uncircumcised Philistine will be like one of them,

37 for he has insulted the battle lines of the living God." And David said, "The LORD who has rescued me from the lion and the bear will rescue me from the hand of this Philistine." And Saul said to David,

38 "Go, and may the LORD be with you." And Saul clothed David in his own battle garb and put a bronze helmet on his head and clothed him

39 in armor. AndDavid girded his sword over his garments, but he was unable to walk, for he was unused to it, and David said to Saul, "I cannot walk in these, for I am unused to it." And David removed them.

---

perfectly natural in biblical usage, and no emendation of the word for "beard" is called for.

37. *And David said.* This is a particularly striking instance of the biblical convention that can be schematized as: And X said to Y; [no response from Y]; and X said to Y, with the intervening silence being dramatically significant. Saul is nonplussed by these extravagant claims on the part of the young shepherd from Bethlehem, and he doesn't know what to say. David, observing the skepticism of his interlocutor, now invokes God by way of explanation ("the LORD who has rescued me from the lion and the bear"). This theological argument persuades Saul. For another instance of the X said to Y, X said to Y convention, compare Goliath's boast and Israel's silence in verses 8–10.

38. *his own battle garb.* The Hebrew *madim* is not the ordinary term for "garment" but is most often used either for the special garments worn by men in battle or by priests in the cult (hence the present translation adds "battle"). The fact that this word is related etymologically to *midah*, proportion or measure, is relevant to the incident as it unfolds, since David is clothed in battle gear too big for him.

39. *he was unable to walk.* The translation, with the Septuagint, reads *wayil'e*, instead of the Masoretic *wayo'el* (a simple reversal of letters in the consonantal text), which would yield "he undertook to walk."
    I cannot walk in these, for I am unused to it. David states the obvious fact that, as a shepherd boy, he is not used to marching about in heavy armor, with a big sword. What he chooses not to mention is that since this is the armor of the hulking Saul, it is in any case far too big for him. Thematically, heroic fitness will be seen to reside in something other than being head and shoulders taller than all the people, or six cubits tall, like Goliath.

And he took his stick in his hand and chose five smooth stones from   40
the creek and put them in the shepherd's pouch he had, in the satchel,
and his slingshot was in his hand, and he came forward toward the Philistine. And the Philistine was drawing near to David, the man bearing   41
the shield before him. And the Philistine looked and saw David, and   42
he despised him, for he was a lad, and ruddy, with good looks. And the   43
Philistine said to David, "Am I a dog that you should come to me with
sticks?" And the Philistine cursed David by his gods. And the Philistine   44
said, "Come to me, that I may give your flesh to the birds of the heavens
and the beasts of the field!" And David said to the Philistine, "You come   45
to me with sword and spear and javelin, and I come to you with the name
of the LORD of Armies, God of the battle lines of Israel that you have

---

40. *he took his stick.* That is, his shepherd's staff, which he is used to carrying.
David evidently does this as a decoy, encouraging Goliath to imagine he will
use cudgel against sword (compare verse 43) and thus camouflaging the lethal
slingshot.

    he came forward toward the Philistine . . . the Philistine was drawing near.
The spatial realization of the whole episode is nearing its climax: on the two
hilltops, the opposing camps; in front of them, the battle lines; between the
hostile lines, David and the Philistine "man between" approaching each other.
In a moment, they will be close enough to exchange insults. Goliath will invite
David to take the last few steps forward so that they can engage in hand-to-
hand combat—"Come to me, that I may give your flesh to the birds of the heavens. . . ." Instead of traversing this final interval of space, David will surprise
his adversary by taking him down with a slung stone, accurately aimed at the
exposed forehead beneath his huge bronze helmet.

45. *You come to me with sword and spear and javelin.* This short list of weapons
harks back to the epic catalogue of weapons and armor that introduced Goliath
to the story. David's rejoinder to the Philistine is couched in impeccable terms
of standard Israelite belief: as in the Psalms, it is not sword or might that gives
victory but the LORD. David speaks almost as though he expects to prevail
through a miracle of divine intervention ("all the earth shall know that Israel
has a God!"), but in fact his victory depends on his resourcefulness in exploiting
an unconventional weapon, one which he would have learned to use skillfully
as a shepherd.

46 insulted. This day shall the LORD give you over into my hand and I will
strike you down and take off your head, and I will give your corpse and
the corpses of the Philistine camp this day to the birds of the heavens
and the beasts of the earth, and all the earth shall know that Israel has
47 a God! And all this assembly shall know that not by sword nor by spear
does the LORD rescue, for the LORD's is the battle and he shall give you
48 into our hand!" And it happened as the Philistine arose and was drawing
near David that David hastened and ran out from the lines toward the
49 Philistine. And he reached his hand into the pouch and took from there
a stone and slung it and struck the Philistine in his forehead, and the
50 stone sank into his forehead and he fell on his face to the ground. And
David bested the Philistine with sling and stone, and he struck down the
51 Philistine and killed him, and no sword was in David's hand. And David
ran up and stood over the Philistine and took the sword from him and
pulled it out of its sheath and finished him off and cut off his head with
52 it. And the Philistines saw that their warrior was dead, and they fled.
And the men of Israel and Judah rose and shouted and gave chase to
the Philistines until you come to the ravine and until the gates of Ekron,
and the Philistine dead fell on the way to Shaaraim and as far as Gath and
53 Ekron. And the Israelites came back from pursuing the Philistines and

---

46. *Your corpse and the corpses.* This is the reading of the Septuagint. The Masoretic text lacks "your corpse."

48. *David hastened and ran out from the lines toward the Philistine.* This last
gesture would encourage the Philistine to think David was rushing up for the
awaited hand-to-hand combat. In fact, David is darting in close enough to get
a good shot with his sling. To do this (verse 49), he will break his charge, stop,
and let fly with the sling.

51. *took the sword . . . and finished him off.* The gigantic Philistine is stunned
but perhaps not dead, and so David completes his kill with the sword he takes
from the prostrate Goliath.

52. *to the ravine.* The Septuagint corrects *gay'* to *Gath,* with the end of this
verse in mind. But there is a ravine between the two hills on which the armies
are encamped, and what the narrator may be saying is that the Philistines fled
westward by way of the ravine to their own territory.

looted their camps. And David took the Philistine's head and brought it 54
to Jerusalem, but his weapons he put in his tent.

And when Saul saw David sallying forth toward the Philistine, he said 55
to Abner the commander, "Whose son is the lad, Abner?" And Abner

---

54. *brought it to Jerusalem*. This notation is problematic because Jerusalem at
this point is still a Jebusite city. The report is either proleptic, or simply out
of place chronologically. David's bringing the sword into his tent may also be
questionable because, as someone who has not been a member of the army, he
would have no tent. Some scholars, influenced by the fact that Goliath's sword
later appears in the sanctuary at Nob, have proposed reading here "in the tent
of the LORD."

55. *Whose son is the lad, Abner?* It is at this point that the evident contradiction
between the two stories of David's debut is most striking. If David had been
attending Saul in court as his personal music therapist, with Saul having explicitly sent a communication to Jesse regarding David's entering his service, how
could he, and Abner as well, now be ignorant of David's identity? Efforts to harmonize the two stories in terms of the logic of later conventions of realism seem
unconvincing (for example, amnesia has been proposed as a symptom of Saul's
mental illness, and Abner pretends not to recognize David in deference to the
ailing king). The prevalent scholarly view that Chapters 16 and 17 represent
two different traditions about David's beginnings is persuasive. (To complicate
matters, most scholars detect two different strands in Chapter 17.) What we
need to ask, however, is why the redactor set these two stories in immediate
sequence, despite the contradictions that must have been as evident to him
as to us. A reasonable conclusion is that for the ancient audience, and for the
redactor, these contradictions would have been inconsequential in comparison
with the advantage gained in providing a double perspective on David. In the
Greek tradition, there were competing versions of the same myths, but never in
a single text. Modern Western narrative generally insists on verisimilar consistency. In the Bible, however, the variants of a single story are sometimes placed
in a kind of implicit dialogue with one another (compare the two accounts of
creation at the beginning of Genesis). Here, in the first, vertically oriented
story, with its explicit instructions from God to man, David is emphatically
elected by God, is associated with the spirit and with song, and gains entrée in
the court of Saul by using song to master the spirit. In the second story, with
its horizontal deployment in space, David makes his way into Saul's presence
through martial prowess, exhibiting shrewdness, calculation, and rhetorical

56 said, "By your life, king, I do not know." And the king said, "Ask you,
57 pray, whose son is the youth?" And when David returned from striking
down the Philistine, Abner took him and brought him before Saul, the
58 Philistine's head in his hand. And Saul said, "Whose son are you, lad?"
And David said, "The son of your servant Jesse the Bethlehemite."

---

skill. Interestingly, it is this folktale version of David's debut rather than the
theological one that will lead directly into the historical (or at least, history-
like) narrative of David's rise and David's reign. But the redactor must surely
have felt that both the "spiritual" and the political-military sides of the figure of
David had to be represented in the account of his origins. It is also noteworthy
that this whole episode, which launches David on his trajectory to the throne,
ends with Saul once more in a state of ignorance, compelled to ask twice about
David's identity, and getting no answer until David himself speaks out.

CHAPTER 18

And it happened as he finished speaking with Saul, that Jonathan's 1
very self became bound up with David's, and Jonathan loved him as
himself. And Saul took him on that day and did not let him go back to 2
his father's house. And Jonathan, and David with him, sealed a pact 3
because he loved him like himself. And Jonathan took off the cloak 4

---

1. *as he finished speaking with Saul.* The speech referred to is the exchange
between David and Saul after the vanquishing of Goliath. This is a clear
instance in which the (late medieval) chapter division actually interrupts a
narrative unit.

Jonathan loved him as himself. No reason is given, so one may infer that
Jonathan was smitten by David's personal charm and perhaps by the sheer
glamour of his victory, which exceeded even Jonathan's own military exploits. It
is noteworthy that throughout this narrative David is repeatedly the object but
never the subject of the verb "to love"—in this chapter, Jonathan, the people,
and Michal are all said to love David.

3. *And Jonathan, and David with him, sealed a pact.* This is one of the most
significant instances of the expressive grammatical pattern in which there is a
plural subject with a singular verb, making the first member of the plural subject the principal agent: the initiative for the pact of friendship is Jonathan's,
and David goes along with it.

4. *Jonathan took off the cloak.* This gesture strongly invites comparison with
Saul's failed effort to dress David in his battle gear in the previous episode.
This time David accepts the proffered garments and weapons: practically, they
are presumably his own size, but he also is now ready to assume a regular role
in the army. The first item Jonathan offers is his cloak, *me'il*, the very piece of
clothing Samuel associated symbolically with kingship. Bearing that in mind,
J. P. Fokkelman has proposed that "with his cloak Jonathan is conveying to

that was on him and gave it to David, and his battle garb, and even his
5 sword and his bow and his belt. And David would sally forth, wherever
Saul sent him he would succeed. And Saul set him over the men of war,
and it was good in the eyes of the troops and also in the eyes of Saul's
6 servants. And it happened when they came, when David returned from
striking down the Philistine, that the women came out from all the
towns of Israel in song and dance, to greet Saul the king with timbrels
7 and jubilation and lutes. And the celebrant women called out and said,

> "Saul has struck down his thousands
> and David his tens of thousands!"

8 And Saul was very incensed, and this thing was evil in his eyes, and
he said, "To David they have given tens of thousands and to me they
have given the thousands. The next thing he'll have is the kingship."

David the crown prince's rights and claims to the throne." Perhaps one should
say that he is conveying these subliminally or proleptically rather than as a fully
conscious act.

5. *Saul set him over the men of war*. The designation for fighting men is also the
one Saul uses for Goliath. Moshe Garsiel has suggested that this may be a term
for elite troops, and that later, when Saul appoints David captain of a thousand
(verse 13), he is in effect transferring him to the position of an ordinary officer.

6. *lutes*. As is often the case with ancient musical instruments, the precise
identification of the term is in doubt. The Hebrew *shalishim* derives from *she-
loshah*, three, but it could refer either to a three-stringed lute, which was fairly
common in the ancient Near East, or perhaps to a triangle.

8. *To David . . . tens of thousands and to me . . . the thousands*. It is a fixed rule
in biblical poetry that when a number occurs in the first verset, it must be
increased in the parallel verset, often, as here, by going up one decimal place.
Saul shows himself a good reader of biblical poetry: he understands perfectly
well that the convention is a vehicle of meaning, and that the intensification or
magnification characteristic of the second verset is used to set David's triumphs
above his own. Saul, who earlier had made the mistake of listening to the voice
of the people, now is enraged by the people's words.

And Saul kept a suspicious eye on David from that day hence. And on 9,10 the next day, an evil spirit of God seized Saul and he went into a frenzy within the house when David was playing as he was wont to, and the spear was in Saul's hand. And Saul cast the spear, thinking, "Let me 11 strike through David into the wall." And David eluded him twice. And 12 Saul was afraid of David, for the Lord was with him, but from Saul He had turned away. And Saul removed him from his presence and 13 set him as captain of a thousand, and he led the troops into the fray. And David succeeded in all his ways, and the Lord was with him. 14

---

10. *went into a frenzy*. The verb here is the same one that refers to "speaking in ecstasy" or "prophesying" in the episode of Saul among the prophets, but in the present context only the connotation of raving and not that of revelation is relevant.

when David was playing as he was wont to. The present version of the story at this point seeks to integrate the account of David as victor over Goliath with the preceding report of David as Saul's personal lyre player. Evidently, when he is not playing the lyre, he is sent out intermittently at the head of the elite troops. After this incident, Saul removes him entirely from the court by making him a regular commander. The one thing Saul cannot afford to do is to dispense with David's brilliant services as a military leader. In the Hebrew, "was playing" is literally "was playing with his hand," which sets up a neat antithesis to the spear in Saul's hand ("with" and "in" are represented by the same particle, *be* in Hebrew).

11. *Let me strike through David*. Saul picks up the verb of striking from the song of the celebrant women that so galled him.

12. *for the Lord was with him*. This emphatic refrain-like phrase recalls the Joseph story (see especially Genesis 39), another tale of a handsome shepherd boy who ascends to regal grandeur. Like Joseph, David is repeatedly said to "succeed" (though different verbs are used in the two stories.) Allusions to the Joseph story will turn from this initial consonance to ironic dissonance.

15,16 And Saul saw that he was very successful, and he dreaded him. But all Israel and Judah loved David, for he led them into the fray.

17 And Saul said to David, "Here is my eldest daughter, Merab. Her shall I give you as wife, only be a valiant fellow for me and fight the battles of the LORD." And Saul had thought, "Let not my hand be against him 18 but let the hand of the Philistines be against him." And David said to Saul, "Who am I and who are my kin, my father's clan in Israel, that I

---

15. *Saul saw . . . and he dreaded him.* Throughout this pivotal episode, Saul's feelings and motives remain perfectly transparent—here, through the narrator's report of his emotions, and in the next scene, through interior monologue. At the same time, David is pointedly left opaque. No word of his is reported when Jonathan gives him his cloak and battle gear. We know that Saul is afraid of David but not whether David is afraid of Saul, who, after all, has tried to kill him. And when David speaks in the next scene, it will be manifestly a speech framed for a public occasion, which leaves his real motives uncertain.

16. *led them into the fray.* The Hebrew says literally, "was going out and coming in before them," an idiom that means to lead in battle.

17. *Here is my eldest daughter, Merab.* Only now is the promise of the hand of the king's daughter for the vanquisher of Goliath implemented. But the fulfillment of that promise, as it turns out, is part of a plan to destroy David.
   Let not my hand be against him. The interior monologue leaves no doubt about Saul's intentions. Could it be that his very transparency as a political schemer, manifested in the means of narrative presentation, is a reflection of his incapacity in the harsh realm of politics? David, by contrast, knows how to veil his motives and intentions—a veiling replicated in the narrative strategies used to present him.

18. *Who am I and who are my kin.* The translation adopts a scholarly proposal of considerable currency to revocalize the Masoretic ḥayai, "my life" as ḥayi, "my kin," a conjectured term based on the Arabic. David's protestation of unworthiness recalls Saul's when Samuel hinted he was going to confer the kingship on him. Perhaps these words are dictated by court etiquette, the commoner obliged to profess unworthiness when offered the honor of a royal connection. Perhaps the young David may actually feel unworthy of the honor. But it is also clearly in his interest to conceal from the jealous king any desire he may harbor to marry the king's daughter, for such an alliance could be converted into an implicit claim to be successor to the throne.

should be the king's son-in-law?" And it happened at the time for giving ₁₉ Merab the daughter of Saul to David, that she was given to Adriel the Meholathite as wife. And Michal the daughter of Saul loved David, and ₂₀ they told Saul, and the thing was pleasing in his eyes. And Saul thought, ₂₁ "I shall give her to him, that she may be a snare to him, and that the hand of the Philistines may be against him." And Saul said to David, "Through the second one you can be my son-in-law now." And Saul ₂₂ charged his servants: "Speak to David discreetly, saying, 'Look, the king desires you, and all his servants love you, and now, then, become son-in-law to the king.'" And Saul's servants spoke these words in David's ₂₃ hearing and David said, "Is it a light thing in your eyes to become son-in-law to the king, and I am a poor man, and lightly esteemed?" And ₂₄ Saul's servants told him, saying, "Words of this sort David has spoken."

---

20. *And Michal the daughter of Saul loved David.* Not only is she the third party in this chapter said to love David, but she is also the only woman in the entire Hebrew Bible explicitly reported to love a man. Nothing is said, by contrast, about what David feels toward Michal, and as the story of their relationship sinuously unfolds, his feelings toward her will continue to be left in question.

21. *Through the second one.* The Hebrew is quite cryptic, and the text might be defective here. Literally, it says, "through two" (*beshtayim*). This has variously been interpreted to mean: through two daughters (if not one, then the other); through two conditions (vanquishing the Philistines and bringing back their foreskins?); for two reasons (perhaps, "the king desires you" and "all his servants love you").

22. *discreetly.* The root of the Hebrew adverb refers to covering up, but the usual translation of "secretly" is misleading. This is not a clandestine communication but one in which the servants—that is, Saul's court attendants—must be careful to cover up their master's real intentions.

24. *Words of this sort David has spoken.* Saul may well have counted on the fact that David would initially demur, perhaps because he was the youngest son of eight and thus lacked a suitable bride price for a princess. This refusal would then set the stage for Saul's extravagant proposal, which he assumed would be a fatal one, of a hundred dead Philistines.

25 And Saul said, "Thus shall you say to David: 'The king has no desire for any bride price except a hundred Philistine foreskins, to take vengeance against the king's enemies.'" And Saul had devised to make David fall

26 by the hand of the Philistines. And Saul's servants told these words to David, and the thing was pleasing in David's eyes, to become son-in-law

27 to the king. And the time was not done, when David arose and went, he and his men, and he struck down among the Philistines two hundred men, and David brought their foreskins and made a full count to the king, to become son-in-law to the king, and Saul gave him Michal his

---

25. *The king has no desire for any bride price except a hundred Philistine foreskins.* The language Saul directs to David through his attendants—note that he now has begun to communicate with David only through intermediaries—makes it sound as though this were a small thing instead of an enormous thing. Beyond this story, there is no indication that the Israelites had a custom of collecting the foreskins of the uncircumcised Philistines like scalps. Fokkelman shrewdly notes that the foreskins are associated with (impure) sexuality and conjectures that "by this condition Saul really wants to contaminate David"—just as Saul is using his own daughter's sexuality as a lure to destroy David. "He thinks," Fokkelman goes on to observe, "that this rival has outdone him amongst the women and now uses woman as a trap."

Saul had devised to make David fall. The narrator continues his systematic effort to make Saul's intentions transparent.

27. *And the time was not done.* Literally, "the days were not filled." The presumable reference is to a period fixed by Saul during which David was to go out and bring back the grisly trophies. Moshe Garsiel has interestingly proposed that the idiom here deliberately echoes a phrase used in the Jacob story (Genesis 29:21) and signals a whole network of allusions to the Jacob narrative: in both stories the young man is a candidate to marry two sisters and gets the one not at first intended; in both stories he must provide a bride price he cannot pay for from material resources; in both stories he must "count out" (literally "fill") payment to a devious father-in-law; eventually each man flees his father-in-law, aided and abetted by his wife; and in each instance, as we shall see, household idols (*teraphim*) are involved. Later in the David story, other kinds of parallels with Jacob will be invoked.

daughter as wife. And Saul saw and marked that the LORD was with 28
David, and Michal the daughter of Saul loved him. And Saul was all the 29
more afraid of David, and Saul became David's constant enemy. And 30
the Philistine captains sallied forth, and whenever they sallied forth,
David succeeded more than all Saul's servants, and his name became
greatly esteemed.

28.–30. These verses constitute a formal concluding frame to the whole episode, much like the concluding verses in Genesis 39, which mirror the opening
ones. Once again, in a pointed repetition of phrases, the following is brought
to our attention: David's success, the fact that the LORD is with him, Saul's fear
of David, Michal's love of David, and David's great reputation. The concluding words of the chapter, "his name became greatly esteemed," are a pointed
antithesis to his protestation of unworthiness, "I am a poor man, and lightly
esteemed."

CHAPTER 19

¹ And Saul spoke to Jonathan his son and to all his servants to put David ² to death, but Jonathan the son of Saul was very fond of David, and Jonathan told David, saying, "Saul my father seeks to put you to death, and so now, be on the watch, pray, in the morning, and stay in a secret ³ place and hide. And I on my part shall come out and stand by my father in the field where you are, and I shall speak of you to my father. And ⁴ if I see something, I shall tell you." And Jonathan spoke well of David to Saul his father and said to him, "Let not the king offend against his servant David, for he has not offended you, and his deeds have been ⁵ very good toward you. He took his life in his hands and struck down the Philistine, and the LORD made a great victory for all Israel. You saw and rejoiced, and why should you offend with innocent blood to put David to ⁶ death for no cause?" And Saul heeded Jonathan's voice, and Saul swore,

---

1. *Jonathan his son . . . Jonathan the son of Saul.* In keeping with the biblical practice of using relational epithets to underscore a thematic point, Jonathan is identified as Saul's son at the very moment when he takes David's part against his father.

4. *Let not the king offend.* Saul's royal power is palpable in the dialogue, for his own son is careful to address him by title in the deferential third person.

6. *Saul heeded Jonathan's voice, and . . . swore.* Saul's paranoia and uncontrolled outbursts manifest themselves in an intermittent cycle. He is amenable to the voice of reason and conscience, and vows in presumably good faith not to harm David, but further evidence of David's military brilliance will unleash another round of violent impulses. In consequence, through this sequence of the narrative David oscillates between being a proscribed person and someone Saul expects to be a faithful member of his court.

"As the LORD lives, he shall not be put to death." And Jonathan called ⁊
to David, and Jonathan told him all these things. And Jonathan brought
David to Saul, and he served him as in times gone by.

And there was still more fighting, and David sallied forth and did battle 8
with the Philistines and struck a great blow against them, and they fled
before him. And an evil spirit of the LORD came upon Saul as he was 9
sitting in his house, his spear in his hand and David playing. And Saul 10
sought to strike the spear through David into the wall, but he slipped
away from Saul, and Saul struck the spear into the wall. Then David fled
and escaped on that night. And Saul sent messengers to David's house to 11
keep watch over him and to put him to death in the morning. And Michal
his wife told David, saying, "If you do not get yourself away tonight,
tomorrow you'll be dead." And Michal let David down from the window, 12

---

9. *his spear in his hand and David playing.* As in the previous incident of the
spear cast at David, the Hebrew exhibits the pointed antithesis of "his spear
in his hand [*beyado*]" and David "playing by hand [*beyad*]." Conventional biblical scholarship explains the repetition of incident, and the other doublets in
this narrative, as an inclusion of two versions of the same event from different
sources. It is at least as plausible to assume that the author of the Saul and
David narrative had a fondness for paired incidents that could be used to good
literary effect. Saul's mental disturbance involves compulsive repetition. He
does his best to be reconciled with David, his soothing lyre player and indispensable military leader, but the recurrent flashes of jealousy drive him again
to the same lethal action. After the second occurrence of spear throwing, David
realizes he must flee the court, but he does not imagine that Saul will send
assassins to surround his house.

10. *Saul struck . . . David fled.* As several interpreters have noted, these are
the very two verbs used in verse 8 to report David's military triumph over the
Philistines: as David battles Israel's enemies, the distraught king battles David.

11. *Michal his wife.* This is another pointed familial identification. Previously,
she was referred to as Saul's daughter.
    If you do not get yourself away tonight, tomorrow you'll be dead. It is striking
that we are given Michal's urgent dialogue here but not a word of response
from David, only the chain of his rapid actions after she lets him down (by
an improvised rope?) from the window—"he went off and fled and got away."
Perhaps this asymmetrical presentation of the two characters is meant to sug-

13 and he went off and fled and got away. And Michal took the household
gods and put them in the bed, and the twist of goat's hair she put at its
14 head, and covered them with a cloth. And Saul sent messengers to take
15 David, and she said, "He is ill." And Saul sent messengers to see David,
saying, "Bring him up to me in the bed, that he may be put to death."
16 And the messengers came, and, look, the household gods were in the bed
17 and the twist of goat's hair at its head! And Saul said to Michal, "Why
have you thus deceived me, and let my enemy go, and he got away?" And
Michal said to Saul, "He said to me: 'Let me go. Why should I kill you?'"

---

gest David's breathless flight, with no time for conversation. In any case, it
continues the pattern of occluding David's inner responses that we observed in
Chapter 18. Michal is risking a great deal in order to save David. We have no
idea about his feelings toward her as she does this.

13. *Michal took the household gods . . . and the twist of goat's hair . . . and covered
them with a cloth.* She adopts the familiar trick used by prisoners round the
world of concocting a dummy to mask an escape. But the means she chooses
introduce another elaborate allusion to the Jacob story. The household gods
(*teraphim*) are what Rachel stole and hid from her father when Jacob fled from
him. Like Rachel, who pleads her period and does not get up from the cushions
under which the *teraphim* are hidden, Michal also invokes "illness" (verse 14) to
put off the searchers. Both stories feature a daughter loyal to her husband and
rebelling against a hostile father. Michal puts goat's hair at the head of the bed
because, being black or dark brown, it would look like a man's hair, but goats
(and the color of their hair) are also prominent in the Jacob story. Finally, the
cloth or garment (*beged*) used to cover the dummy recalls the repeated association of garments with deception in the Jacob story. Laban, of course, never
finds his *teraphim*, whereas Saul's emissaries, to their chagrin, find the *teraphim*
instead of the man they are looking for.

15. *Bring him up to me in the bed.* If Michal claims David is ill, Saul will have
him brought up bed and all.

17. *Why have you thus deceived me . . . ?* These words are close to the ones
spoken by the outraged Laban to Jacob (Genesis 31:26).
Why should I kill you? This purported death threat by David is of course
pure invention by Michal in order to make it seem that she was forced to help
David flee.

And David had fled and gotten away and had come to Samuel at Ramah 18
and told him all that Saul had done to him. And he, and Samuel with
him, went and stayed at Naioth. And it was told to Saul, saying, "Look, 19
David is at Naioth in Ramah." And Saul sent messengers to take David, 20
and they saw a band of prophets in ecstasy with Samuel standing poised
over them, and the spirit of God came upon Saul's messengers and they,
too, went into ecstasy. And they told Saul, and he sent other messen- 21
gers, and they, too, went into ecstasy. And Saul still again sent a third
set of messengers, and they, too, went into ecstasy. And he himself went 22
to Ramah, and he came as far as the great cistern which is in Secu, and
he asked and said, "Where are Samuel and David?" And someone said, 23
"Here, at Naioth in Ramah." And he went there, to Naioth in Ramah,
and the spirit of God came upon him, too, and he walked along speaking

---

18. *David had fled and gotten away and had come to Samuel.* The twice-repeated
verbs of safe flight are reiterated once more. David takes refuge with the man
who anointed him, though it is not entirely clear whether the prophet's authority will really protect him, or the prophet.

Naioth. Some have claimed this is not a place-name but a common noun,
nawot, "oases" (according to one suggestion, a collection of huts where the
prophets resided). But then one would expect a definite article, which does not
occur. Naioth is most plausibly construed as a little village or place of temporary
residence in the vicinity of the town Ramah.

20. *Samuel standing poised over them.* The image is implicitly military: the term
for "poised" (*nitsav*) is cognate with the terms for garrison and prefect. Samuel,
like the pope, commands no divisions, but the band of ecstatics are his troops,
and the infectious spirit of God that inhabits them and devastates Saul's emissaries acts as a defensive perimeter.

22. *And he himself went.* Again, we have the folktale symmetry of three identical
repetitions, then a fourth repetition with a crucial change.

Where are Samuel and David? Once more, Saul (*Sha'ul*) has to ask (*sha'al*).
This particular question recalls his initial question in Chapter 9 about where
the seer was.

24 in ecstasy until he came to Naioth in Ramah. And he, too, stripped off
his clothes, and he, too, went into ecstasy before Samuel and lay naked
all that day and all that night. Therefore do they say, "Is Saul, too, among
the prophets?"

---

24. *he . . . stripped off his clothes . . . and lay naked.* In the clash between
Saul and Samuel that marked their final estrangement, Samuel had explicitly
associated garment with kingship. Now the frenzy that seizes Saul drives him
to strip off his garments—implicitly, to divest himself of the kingship, just as
the first episode of Saul among the prophets was an investment with kingship. Polzin brilliantly links this moment with Michal's use of a garment and
the contrasting narrative presentations of David and Saul: "Whereas Michal
covers David's bed with his clothes (verse 13) Saul strips off his clothes and
lies naked all day and night (verse 24)—a graphic picture of how the narrator
hides David and bares Saul throughout the last two chapters."

Therefore do they say, "Is Saul, too, among the prophets?" This is the same
etiological tag as at the end of the first story of Saul among the prophets in
Chapter 10. The doublet, far from being a stammer of transmission or inept
or automatically inclusive redaction, is vividly purposeful, providing a strong
frame for Saul's painful story. Fokkelman states the effect nicely: "The same
faculty for the numinous and the same sensitivity for suddenly being lifted into
a higher state of consciousness which occurred there [in Chapter 10] under the
positive sign of election, appear here under the negative sign of being rejected,
and now bring Saul into a lower state of consciousness, a kind of delirium." The
conventions of verisimilitude of a later literary tradition would lead one to conclude that this encounter would have to have occurred either at the beginning
of Saul's career or at the end, but not twice. To the ancient audience, however,
the recurrence would not have seemed a contradiction, and the conflicting
valences given to the explanation of the proverbial saying add to the richness
of the portrait of Saul, formally framing it at beginning and end.

CHAPTER 20

And David fled from Naioth in Ramah and came and said before Jona- 1
than: "What have I done? What is my crime and what my offense before
your father that he should seek my life?" And he said to him, "Heaven 2
forbid! You shall not die! Look, my father will do nothing, whether great
or small, without revealing it to me, and why should my father hide
this thing from me? It cannot be!" And David swore again and said, 3

---

1. *David . . . said before Jonathan.* The seeming awkwardness of the preposition
is actually strategically calculated. The normal usage would be "said *to*" (*'el*).
"Before" (*lifney*) is a preposition that commonly designates approach to the
presence of regal or seigniorial authority. (Compare its occurrence in David's
words, "What my offense *before* your father.") This speech is a remarkable
instance of the pattern of occluding the personal side of David that we have
been following. Quite strikingly, these are David's first reported words to Jonathan, though Jonathan's devotion to David and one speech to David (19:2–3)
have been duly recorded. It is noteworthy that this is not a personal communication to Jonathan but a kind of political statement—a protestation of
innocence cast in patently rhetorical language ("What have I done? What is
my crime . . .?"). David speaks to Jonathan less as an intimate friend than as
a courtier, later in the dialogue even invoking the deferential self-reference of
"your servant."

2. *why should my father hide this thing from me?* If one considers Saul's previous behavior and his relationship with Jonathan, this faith in his father's openness with him seems singularly misplaced. Throughout, Jonathan remains well
meaning and naive, over against the wary, calculating David.

3. *David swore again.* It is ill advised to emend the verb here, as some scholars
have proposed. In fact, David's first speech ("before" Jonathan) was a kind of
oath of innocence, and now he continues to swear, rather than simply speaking.

"Your father surely knows that I have found favor in your eyes, and he
will think, 'Let not Jonathan know this, lest he be pained.' And indeed,
as the LORD lives and as you live, there is but a step between me and
4 death." And Jonathan said, "Whatever you desire, I shall do for you."
5 And David said to Jonathan, "Look, it is the new moon tomorrow, and
I am supposed to sit with the king to eat. Let me go and I shall hide in
6 the field till the evening of the day after tomorrow. Should your father
in fact mark my absence, you shall say, 'David has urgently asked of me
that he run to Bethlehem his town, for the seasonal sacrifice is to take
7 place there for the whole clan.' If thus he says, 'Good!' it is well with
your servant. But if in fact he is incensed, know that the evil has been
8 resolved by him. And you shall keep faith with your servant, for into a
pact of the LORD you have brought your servant with you. And if there

---

there is but a step between me and death. This vivid image surely is meant to
recall the quick dodging step that twice enabled David to elude Saul's hurled
spear.

5. *the new moon.* In early biblical times, this was an important festival. Sacrifices were offered, ceremonial feasts were held, and ordinary business was not
transacted.
    the day after tomorrow. The Masoretic text has "the third evening," treating
hashelishit as an adjective modifying "evening," though it has the wrong gender
suffix. It is more likely a noun meaning the day after tomorrow (the day on
which one speaks being day one in the sequence of three). One should then
read *'erev hashelishit* instead of the Masoretic *ha 'erev hashelishit.* In any case,
the number three will play an important role as the episode develops.

7. *If thus he says, 'Good!' it is well with your servant.* After Saul's attempts on
David's life by the "hand of the Philistines," by the spear in his own hand, and
by a team of assassins, can David really believe that any statement by the king
of favorable disposition means it will be well with him? Polzin has shrewdly
suggested that David's real intention is "to provoke Saul to an angry outburst
that would remove Jonathan's misconceptions, not his own."

8. *faith.* The two parties to a pact, contract, or other binding agreement owe
each other *hesed,* faithful performance of their covenantal obligations.
    into a pact of the LORD you have brought your servant with you. David's formu-
lation of the arrangement is pointed and quite accurate: it was Jonathan who
initiated the pledge of mutual fealty out of his love for David, and who drew
David into the commitment.

be any crime in me, put me to death yourself, for why should you bring me to your father?" And Jonathan said, "Heaven forbid you say it! If in 9 fact I learn that the evil has been resolved by my father, would I not tell it to you?" And David said to Jonathan, "Who will tell me if your father 10 answers you harshly?" And Jonathan said, "Come, let us go out to the 11 field." And the two of them went out to the field. And Jonathan said to 12 David, "Witness the LORD God of Israel, that I will sound out my father at this hour tomorrow, [or] the day after, and whether he is well disposed to David or not, I will send to you and reveal to you. Thus may the LORD 13 do to Jonathan, and even more, if it seems good to my father [to bring] the evil upon you, I will reveal it to you and I will send you off and you shall go safely and the LORD shall be with you as He was with my father. Would that while I am still alive you may keep the LORD's faith with 14 me, that I not die, and that you do not cut off your faithfulness from my 15 house for all time, not even when the LORD cuts off all David's enemies

---

9. *Heaven forbid you say it*. The Hebrew has, elliptically, "Heaven forbid you."

10. *Who will tell me . . . ?* David is not questioning Jonathan's good faith but registering a practical difficulty: if Saul is in fact determined to kill him, how will Jonathan be able to get word to him?

12. *Witness the LORD*. The word "witness" (*'ed*) is absent in the Masoretic text but is reflected in Josephus and the Peshitta.
   tomorrow, [or] the day after. Again, the time reference in the Hebrew is somewhat confusing. The text reads literally "tomorrow the third day" or even "the morrow of the third day."

13. *if it seems good to my father [to bring] the evil*. The ironic antithesis of good and evil is patent. All ancient versions lack "to bring," which seems required by the context. The word may have been inadvertently deleted by a scribe because it closely resembles the preceding word in the text—*'avi* (my father), *lehavi'* (to bring).
   the LORD shall be with you as He was with my father. Here Jonathan explicitly recognizes that the persecuted David is to displace Saul, his father.

14. *Would that*. This translation treats the Hebrew consonants as *welu* instead of the Masoretic *welo'* ("and not").

16 from the face of the earth. For Jonathan has sealed a pact with the house
17 of David and the LORD shall requite it from the hand of David." And
Jonathan once again swore to David in his love for him, for he loved
18 him as he loved himself. And Jonathan said to him, "Tomorrow is the
new moon, and your absence will be marked because your place will be
19 vacant. The day after tomorrow you will go all the way down and come
to the place where you hid on the day of the deed and stay by the Ezel
20 stone. As for me, I shall shoot three arrows to the side of it, as though
21 I were aiming at a target. And look, I shall send the lad, 'Go, find the
arrows!' If I expressly say to the lad, 'Look, the arrows are on this side of
you, fetch them,' come, for it will be well with you, and nothing will be
22 the matter, as the LORD lives. But if thus I say to the youth, 'Look, the
arrows are on the far side of you,' go, for the LORD will have sent you
23 away. And as for the matter of which you and I have spoken, look, the
LORD is witness between you and me for all time."

---

16. *Jonathan has sealed a pact.* The Hebrew idiom is literally "cut" (with "pact"
implied) and so picks up the play of the two different occurrences of "cut off"
in the previous sentence (the same verb in a different conjugation). Jonathan's
insistence that David not cut off Jonathan's descendants once he gains power
will have prominent ramifications later in the story.
  requite it from the hand of David. The Masoretic text has "from the hand
of the enemies of David," but the substitution of a person's "enemies" for the
person himself is a common Hebrew scribal euphemism (here, so as not to say
something negative about David), as both Rashi and David Kimchi recognized
in the Middle Ages.

19. *The day after tomorrow.* The Masoretic vocalization *weshilashta* treats this
as a verb (to do something a third time or in a third instance), but it is more
plausible to vocalize it as a noun, *ushelishit,* "and on the third day." (See the
comment on verse 5.)
  you will go all the way down. The Hebrew, literally "you will go down very
much" (or, "you will wander very much"), is problematic.
  the place where you hid on the day of the deed. The meaning has been disputed, but the most likely reference is to David's hiding, and Jonathan's speaking in his defense, in 19:1–7.

23. *the LORD is witness.* Again, "witness" is absent from the Masoretic text but
supplied by the Septuagint.

And David hid in the field, and it was the new moon, and the king sat 24
down to table to eat. And the king sat in his place as he was wont to do, 25
in the seat by the wall, and Jonathan preceded him, and Abner sat by
Saul's side, and David's place was vacant. And Saul spoke no word on 26
that day, for he thought, "It is a mischance. He is unclean and has not
been cleansed." And it happened on the day after the new moon, the 27
second day, that David's place was still vacant. And Saul said to Jonathan
his son, "Why has not the son of Jesse come to the feast either yesterday
or today?" And Jonathan said to Saul, "David has urgently asked of me 28
to go to Bethlehem. And he said to me, 'Let me go, pray, for we have 29
a clan sacrifice in the town, and my brother has summoned me to it.

---

24. *to table.* The Hebrew is literally "to the bread."

25. *Jonathan preceded him.* This translation reads *weyiqdam* instead of the
Masoretic *wayaqom* ("and he rose"). The seating arrangement remains a little
obscure, but the verb *qadam* cannot mean "to sit opposite," as some scholars
have claimed.

26. *He is unclean.* Since on the new moon celebrants partook of a sacrificial
feast, they would have to be in a state of ritual purity. (A seminal emission, for
example, which might be hinted at in the Hebrew term for "mischance," would
render a person impure until the evening of the day on which he cleansed
himself by ablution.)

27. *the son of Jesse.* At the end of the Goliath episode, Saul wanted to know
whose son David was. Now he refers to him repeatedly only by patronymic,
which is dismissive, rather like our using a person's last name only. David's
status in Saul's eyes is a constant reflex of Saul's acute ambivalence: the king
wants him at court as a royal intimate, or, alternately, as someone under surveillance; yet he makes him flee the court as persona non grata.

29. *my brother has summoned me.* Jonathan, in playing out the scenario David
has dictated to him, improvises one element—that David has gone off to his
hometown at the express urging of his brother, and in order to be with his brothers. His evident intention is to provide a palliative to David's absence: he had
to go to Bethlehem because of family pressure. But Saul's outraged response
suggests that Jonathan's invention has the opposite effect. Saul concludes that
David's loyalty to his clan takes precedence over his loyalty to his king, and he

And so, if I have found favor in your eyes, let me, pray, get away that I may see my brothers.' Therefore has he not come to the king's table."
30 And Saul was incensed with Jonathan and he said to him, "O, son of a perverse wayward woman! Don't I know you have chosen the son of Jesse to your own shame and the shame of your mother's nakedness?
31 For as long as the son of Jesse lives on the earth, you and your kingship will not be unshaken! And now, send and fetch him to me, for he is a
32 dead man!" And Jonathan answered Saul his father and said to him,
33 "Why should he be put to death? What has he done?" And Saul cast the spear at him to strike him down, and Jonathan knew that it was

---

may even suspect that David means to use his clan as a power base to challenge the throne.

let me . . . get away. Jonathan inadvertently substitutes for "run" in David's instructions the very verb of escape repeatedly used when David fled Saul's assassins.

30. *O, son of a perverse wayward woman.* All English translations have treated the last Hebrew term here, *mardut*, as "rebellion," deriving it from the root *m-r-d*, "to rebel." But this form (with the *ut* suffix of abstraction) would be anomalous in the Hebrew, whereas the vocalization in the received text yields a Hebrew word well known in rabbinic Hebrew and meaning "discipline." (The verbal root is *r-d-h*, "to rule sternly.") She is "perverse against discipline"— hence "wayward" in this translation.

the shame of your mother's nakedness. This is quite violent. "Nakedness" refers to the sexual part (as in the idiom for taboo intercourse, "uncovering the nakedness of"), and so, it has virtually the force of "your mother's cunt," though the language is not obscene.

31. *he is a dead man.* The Hebrew is literally "son of death," thus playing back on "son of Jesse."

32. *Why should he be put to death? What has he done?* These two questions are four compact words in the Hebrew.

33. *Saul cast the spear at him to strike him down.* Saul's madness is vividly reflected in his attempt to kill his own son in the same way that he tried to kill David—just after he has been urging Jonathan to protect the security of his own future kingship. The act thus expresses his blind destructive impulse toward his own dynasty.

resolved by his father to put David to death. And Jonathan rose from 34
the table in burning anger, and he ate no food on the second day of the
new moon because he was pained for David and because his father had
humiliated him.

And it happened in the morning that Jonathan went out to the field for 35
the fixed meeting with David, and a young lad was with him. And he 36
said to his lad, "Run, find, pray, the arrows that I shoot." The lad ran,
and he shot the arrow beyond him. And the lad came to the place of 37
the arrow that Jonathan had shot, and Jonathan called after the lad and
said, "Look, the arrow is on the far side of you." And Jonathan called 38
after the lad, "Quick, hurry, don't stand still!" And Jonathan's lad gathered up the arrows and came to his master. And the lad knew nothing, 39

---

34. *because he was pained for David and because his father had humiliated him.*
The Hebrew text does not have "and" but it is clearly implied.

35. *And it happened in the morning.* On the third day there are three figures in
the field and three arrows will be shot. The triangle of two knowing persons and
one ignorant one is an ironic replication of the David-Jonathan-Saul triangle.
The lad's running after the arrows may also pick up David's (fictitious) "running" to Bethlehem.

36. *the arrow.* Some scholars, bothered by the switch from three arrows to one,
have emended the text to reduce all plurals of arrow to a singular. The maneuver is misconceived because, as we have seen before, Hebrew narrative readily
switches from multiple instances to a particular case.

37. *Jonathan called after the lad.* Again, the use of the preposition is quite precise because the lad has run on ahead of Jonathan.

38. *gathered up the arrows.* The Masoretic text has "arrow" in the singular at this
point, but the verb "to gather up" (*laqet*) accords much better with collecting
several objects, and Jonathan's having shot all three of the arrows earlier mentioned would require more time on the part of the lad and hence would give
Jonathan and David more of an opportunity to talk in confidence.

40 but Jonathan and David knew the matter. And Jonathan gave his gear to
41 his lad and said to him, "Go, bring them to town." Just as the lad came,
David arose from by the mound and fell on his face to the ground and
bowed three times, and each man kissed the other and each wept for
42 the other, though David the longer. And Jonathan said to David, "Go in
peace, for the two of us have sworn in the name of the LORD, saying,
'The LORD is witness between me and you, and between my seed and
21:1 your seed, for all time.'" And Jonathan arose and came to the town.

---

40. *Jonathan gave his gear to his lad.* Fokkelman reminds us that Jonathan earlier
gave his armor and weapons to David, and now "the successor to the throne
indicated by Saul . . . devotes himself defenselessly to the intimate contact with
the man who, according to his father, is his rival."

41. *arose from by the mound.* This follows the Septuagint. The Masoretic text
has "arose from the south."

42. *The LORD is witness.* As in the previous occurrences in Samuel of this formula
of vow taking, the Masoretic text lacks "witness," but that word is reflected in
the Septuagint. It may well be an idiomatic ellipsis in the original Hebrew version, but the problem with leaving it that way in the English is that it could
sound as though Jonathan were saying that the LORD will intervene between
him and David ("the LORD will be between me and you"). Polzin contends that
the double meaning is intended, but that reading seems a little strained.

CHAPTER 21

And David came to Nob, to Ahimelech the priest, and Ahimelech trem- 2
bled to meet David and said to him, "Why are you alone and no one is with
you?" And David said to Ahimelech the priest, "The king has charged me 3
with a mission, and said to me, 'Let no one know a thing of the mission
on which I send you and with which I charge you.' And the lads I have
directed to such and such a place. And now, what do you have at hand, 4
five loaves of bread? Give them to me, or whatever there is." And the 5
priest answered David and said, "I have no common bread at hand, solely
consecrated bread, if only the lads have kept themselves from women."

---

2. *Nob.* This is the very beginning of David's flight after the exchange with
Jonathan in the field, and Nob is less than three miles south of Gibeah, his
approximate point of departure.

Why are you alone and no one is with you? The doubling of the question (in
a pattern that is reminiscent of the parallelism of verse) reflects Ahimelech's
astonishment: a prominent commander in Saul's army would not ordinarily go
about without his retinue. From his first sight of David, Ahimelech suspects
that he may be a fugitive, which is why he "trembles" to meet him—fear of the
powerful king's retribution stalks the land.

4. *five loaves of bread.* The number five is sometimes used idiomatically in biblical Hebrew to mean "a few."

5. *if only the lads have kept themselves from women.* Ordinarily, consecrated
bread would be eaten only by the priests. Ahimelech is willing to stretch the
point if David's "lads"—his fighting men—are not in a state of ritual impurity
through sexual intercourse.

6 And David answered the priest and said to him, "Why, women were taboo to us as in times gone by when I sallied forth, and the lads' gear was consecrated, even if it was a common journey, and how much
7 more so now the gear should be consecrated." And the priest gave him what was consecrated, for there was no bread there except the Bread of the Presence that had been removed from before the LORD
8 to be replaced with warm bread when it was taken away. And there a man of Saul's servants that day was detained before the LORD, and his name was Doeg the Edomite, chief of the herdsmen who were Saul's.
9 And David said to Ahimelech, "Don't you have here at hand a spear or a sword? For neither my sword nor my gear have I taken with me, for the

---

6. *women were taboo to us.* This is the second reference in this narrative to a general practice of refraining from sexual activity during periods of combat.

the lads' gear was consecrated. The term for "gear," the all-purpose *kelim*, could equally refer to weapons, clothing, and vessels for containing food. There are no grounds for restricting the meaning here to the last of these three items, as some interpreters have done.

7. *the Bread of the Presence.* This would be twelve loaves laid out in display on a table in the sanctuary. When they were replaced with fresh loaves, the old loaves could be eaten by the priests. Polzin proposes a link between the eating of forbidden food here and in the story of Jonathan and the honey. Death will ensue, though not for the eater.

8. *And there a man of Saul's servants.* This seemingly intrusive notation is a piece of ominous foreshadowing. For the moment, all we can pick up is a certain dissonance in the presence of a foreigner in the sanctuary and the nearness of a high official of Saul's to the fugitive David. The ghastly consequences of David's visit to Nob (Chapter 22) will pivot on Doeg's fatal presence. His identity as Edomite reflects the enlistment of foreign mercenaries in the new royal bureaucracy. It also marks him as a man who will have no inhibitions in what he does to Israelites, even Israelite priests.

detained before the LORD. The verb is derived from the same root ('-*ts*-*r*) as the one used for "taboo" in verse 6, but it is unclear whether the reference is to being detained at the sanctuary for some unspecified reason or being detained from participation in the cult.

9. *For neither my sword nor my gear have I taken.* David, of course, has fled weaponless from his encounter with Jonathan in the field. Now he uses the supposed urgency of his royal mission to explain his lack of arms and to ask for a weapon.

king's mission was urgent." And the priest said, "The sword of Goliath 10
the Philistine whom you struck down in the Valley of the Terebinth, here
it is, wrapped in a cloak behind the ephod. If this you would take for
yourself, take it, for there is none other but it here-abouts." And David
said, "There's none like it. Give it to me."

And David rose on that day and fled from Saul and he came to Achish 11
king of Gath. And the servants of Achish said to him, "Is not this David 12
king of the land? Is it not he for whom they call out in dance, saying,

   'Saul has struck down his thousands
       and David his tens of thousands.'"

---

10. *If this you would take for yourself, take it, for there is none other but it here-abouts.* The last exchange between Ahimelech and David is a vivid instance of the biblical use of contrastive dialogue. The priest's language is a wordy hesitation dance of repetitions and synonymous expressions. David responds with the most imperative succinctness (just four words in the Hebrew): "There's none like it. Give it to me." The fact that this huge sword might be too big for David is submerged by the symbolic notion that it is the weapon of the Philistine champion he vanquished which he now takes up. In any case, David is no longer a raw shepherd lad but a battle-hardened warrior.

11. *he came to Achish king of Gath.* David flees to the southwest to the one place where he imagines he will be safe from Saul's pursuit—enemy territory. Such a crossing over to the enemy is a familiar enough move on the part of political refugees. Gath was the hometown of Goliath, and so one must assume that David planned to enter the city incognito, as an anonymous Hebrew fugitive. He would clearly have had to hide the telltale sword before coming into town.

12. *David king of the land.* The Philistine courtiers, unfortunately, immediately identify David and can even quote the song sung by the Israelite women after his victories. Their characterization of him as "king of the land" is no doubt a tribute to his preeminence on the battlefield but also is an inadvertent confirmation of his clandestine election, of his displacing Saul. Appropriately, though, as Fokkelman notes, they use a somewhat vague designation instead of the more official "king of Israel."

13 And David took these words to heart, and he was very afraid of
14 Achish king of Gath. And he altered his good sense in their eyes and
played the lunatic before them, and he scrabbled on the doors of
15 the gate and drooled onto his beard. And Achish said to his servants,
"Look, do you see this man is raving mad! Why would you bring him
to me? Do I lack madmen that you should bring this one to rave for
me? Should this one come into my house?"

---

13. *he was very afraid of Achish.* He has come unarmed and, evidently, alone,
and now he realizes he has been recognized.

15. *Do I lack madmen that you should bring this one to rave for me?* Achish's
words are a mirror of outrage and disgust. As Shimon Bar-Efrat has nicely
observed, Achish three times uses the root for raving mad (*meshuga'*), three
times the first person pronoun, and three times the root *b-w-'* ("to bring" or
"to come"). Thus David has succeeded in making himself so revolting that he
arouses in Achish a primitive revulsion from the spectacle of the insane, so that
the king simply wants to get David out of sight rather than have him killed. This
is an extraordinary moment in the story of the founding king of Israel: David,
the glamorous young hero of the preceding episodes, is prepared to do whatever
is necessary in order to survive, even if it means making himself appear to be
the most repulsive of humankind. It is an even lowlier disguise than Odysseus's
as beggar, and it is also not the last experience of humiliation into which David
in adversity will willingly plunge. It is noteworthy that David feigns madness in
order to survive and eventually become king, in contrast to Saul, whose genuine
madness reflects his loss of control over the kingdom.

CHAPTER 22

And David went from there and got away to the Cave of Adullam, and 1
his brothers heard, as well as all his father's household, and they came
down to him there. And every man in straits and every man in debt and 2
every man who was embittered gathered round him, and he became
their captain, and there were about four hundred men with him. And 3
David went from there to Mizpeh of Moab. And he said to the king of

---

1. *Adullam.* The location is in the hilly terrain at the western edge of the tribal
territory of Judah, near the Philistine region.

his brothers . . . all his father's household. Saul's rage over the notion that
David would have neglected the new moon festivity at the palace to join his
brothers in Bethlehem is given an after-the-fact political confirmation here:
David's brothers and clansmen rally round him, forming a kind of family militia.
But there is a push as well as a pull in their going out to David in the badlands:
if they remained in Bethlehem, they would be subject to retribution by Saul's
soldiery. David's decision to move his parents across the border to Moab (verse
3) is another reflection of fear of royal vengeance against the family. Jesse, earlier characterized as very aged, would have been too old to join the fighting men.

2. *every man in straits . . . in debt . . . embittered.* David's guerilla band has a core
drawn from his clan and a rank and file of the dispossessed and malcontent—
men with nothing to lose who have been oppressed by the established order.
David's social base as guerilla chieftain is strongly reminiscent of Jephthah's
(Judges 11).

3. *Mizpeh of Moab.* The word *mizpeh* (or in some places, *mizpah*) means "outlook" or "vista," and so this particular Mizpeh must be identified as the one
in Moab, east of the Jordan. If the Book of Ruth provides reliable genealogy,
David's great-grandmother Ruth was a Moabite, and so David here may be calling on a family connection in requesting asylum for his parents.

Moab, "Pray, let my father and my mother come out with you until I
4 know what God will do with me." And he led them into the presence of
the king of Moab and they stayed with him all the time that David was
5 in the stronghold. And Gad the prophet said to David, "You must not
stay in the stronghold. Go, and come you to the territory of Judah." And
David went and came to the forest of Hereth.

6 And Saul heard that David was discovered, and the men who were
with him, and Saul was sitting in Gibeah under the tamarisk on the
height, his spear in his hand and all his servants poised in attendance
7 upon him. And Saul said to his servants poised in attendance upon
him, "Listen, pray, you Benjaminites: will the son of Jesse give every

---

4. *all the time that David was in the stronghold.* The identity of the stronghold
has puzzled interpreters, especially because David is said to have set up headquarters in a cave. Some have argued that the two terms refer to the same place,
but the Hebrew for "stronghold," *metsudah,* usually refers to a height. Others
read "cave," *me'arah,* for *metsudah.* That proposal is problematic because Adullam is in the territory of Judah, and in verse 5 David is enjoined to leave the
stronghold and head for the territory of Judah. The most reasonable inference
is that after the parlay with the king of Moab, David moves his fighting men
from Adullam at the western border of the territory of Judah to an unspecified
stronghold, probably in the craggy border region between Moab and Israel.

5. *Gad the prophet.* This figure appears in the story without introduction or
explanation. What is important is that we see David with an open line of communication with the divinity, in sharp contrast to Saul.

6. *Saul heard that David was discovered.* From this point onward, the narrative
will switch back and forth deftly between David and Saul. It now turns to an
ominous piece of unfinished business—Saul's response to the priest of Nob
who helped David in his flight. The specific reference of Saul's hearing "that
David was discovered" could well be intelligence that places David's hideout at
the stronghold. That would explain why Gad urges David to move on from the
stronghold to a forest in Judahite territory.
   his spear in his hand. The same spear in hand with which he sought to kill
David, and then Jonathan. This small detail thus foreshadows the massacre of
an entire town that Saul will order.

7. *you Benjaminites.* Evidently, the inner circle at the court is enlisted from
his own tribe. The tribal affiliation helps explain the sarcasm of his rhetorical

one of you fields and vineyards, will he make every one of you captains
of thousands and captains of hundreds, that all of you should have   8
conspired against me and none revealed to me when my son made a
pact with the son of Jesse, and none of you was troubled for my sake
to reveal to me that my son has set up my servant to lie in wait against
me as on this very day?" And Doeg the Edomite, who was poised in   9
attendance with Saul's servants, spoke out and said, "I saw the son of
Jesse coming to Nob to Ahimelech the son of Ahitub. And he inquired   10
of the LORD, and provisions he gave him, and the sword of Goliath the
Philistine he gave him." And the king sent to summon Ahimelech the   11
son of Ahitub and all his father's household, the priests who were in
Nob, and they all came to the king. And Saul said, "Listen, pray, son of   12
Ahitub." And he said, "Here I am, my lord." And Saul said, "Why did   13
you conspire against me, you and the son of Jesse, giving him bread
and sword and inquiring of God for him, so that he set up to lie in

---

questions: could they really expect someone from the tribe of Judah to bestow
all these bounties on them?

fields . . . vineyards . . . captains. As Moshe Garsiel has aptly noted, Saul's
paranoid outburst picks up key terms from Samuel's warning about the "practice of the king" in Chapter 8. It is also noteworthy that Saul's distraught speech
takes the form of one lone onrushing sentence (all the way to the end of verse
8). Once again, Saul refers to David contemptuously solely by patronymic, as
"the son of Jesse."

8. *none revealed to me.* Once again, Saul's problem, which is also the symptom
of his paranoia, is that he feels essential knowledge is denied him.

10. *he inquired of the LORD.* There was no report in Chapter 21 of Ahimelech's
inquiring of the oracle for David, and it seems unlikely that so essential a fact
would have been simply elided by the narrator. The first item, then, in Doeg's
denunciation of Ahimelech looks like a fabrication—and one that would especially enrage Saul, who has repeatedly had access to divine knowledge blocked.

12. *son of Ahitub.* It is a shocking piece of rudeness for Saul to address someone
invested with the authority of priesthood merely by patronymic.

14 wait against me on this very day?" And Ahimelech answered the king and said, "And who of all your servants is like David, loyal and the king's son-in-law and captain of your palace guard and honored in your house?
15 Did I this day for the first time inquire for him of God? Far be it from me! Let not the king impute anything to his servant or to all my father's house, for your servant knew nothing of all this, neither great nor small."
16 And the king said, "You are doomed to die, Ahimelech, you and all your
17 father's house!" And the king said to the sentries poised in attendance on him, "Turn round and put to death the priests of the LORD, for their hand, too, is with David, for they knew he was fleeing and did not reveal it to me!" And the king's servants did not want to reach out their hand to stab

---

14. *who of all your servants is like David.* Ahimelech may still be laboring under the delusion that the fugitive David was embarked on a special secret mission for Saul. His testimony to David's loyalty and eminence will of course stoke Saul's already blazing anger.

15. *Did I this day for the first time inquire for him of God?* Some interpreters read this as a declarative sentence, but the context compels one to construe it as a question: I never previously consulted the oracle for David, and why on earth would I do it now? (Perhaps he is suggesting that consultation of the oracle is a service to be offered only to the king.) He is silent, however, about providing bread and sword, which in fact he has done.

16. *you and all your father's house.* Ahimelech is the great-grandson of Eli. The slaughter of the entire clan of priests here is the grim fulfillment of the curse on the house of Eli first enunciated by the man of God in 2:27–36.

17. *for their hand, too, is with David.* The Hebrew adverb *gam*, often a general term of emphasis, surely has the force of "too" here: the paranoid Saul sees conspirators on all sides—his son, his Benjaminite court attendants, and now the priests of Nob.
the king's servants did not want to reach out. Beyond any moral considerations and any concern for the king's sanity, it would be a violation of a taboo to murder the priests of the LORD.
to stab. The core meaning of the Hebrew verb *paga'* is the meeting or intersection of two material bodies or human agencies. It can mean "to encounter," "to accost," and, by extension, "to entreat," but in contexts of violent action, it refers to the "encounter" between forged blade and flesh. The verb "to strike down" (*hikah*, as in verse 19) indicates the consummated act of killing. In verse 21, the narrator uses *harag*, the unadorned verb that means "to kill."

the priests of the Lord. And the king said to Doeg, "You, then, turn 18 round and stab the priests," and Doeg the Edomite turned round and he it was who stabbed the priests and he put to death on that day eighty-five men who wore the linen ephod. And he struck down Nob the priests' 19 town with the edge of the sword, man and woman, infant and suckling, ox and donkey and sheep, all by the edge of the sword.

And one son of Ahimelech the son of Ahitub got away, and his name 20 was Abiathar, and he fled after David. And Abiathar told David that Saul 21 had killed the priests of the Lord. And David said to Abiathar, "I knew 22 on that day that Doeg the Edomite was there, that he would surely tell Saul. I am the one who caused the loss of all the lives of your father's house. Stay with me. Do not fear, for whoever seeks my life seeks your 23 life, so you are under my guard."

---

18. *You, then.* Saul emphatically adds the second person pronoun *'atah* to the imperative verb: if none of my Israelite subjects will kill the priests, you, then, as an Edomite, may carry out my orders.

who wore the linen ephod. This is a kind of epic epithet for priests.

19. *man and woman, infant and suckling.* Saul, with the Edomite Doeg as his cat's-paw, flings himself into an orgy of mass murder, killing not only the adult priests but every living creature in Nob. Now he is carrying out the ban he executed only imperfectly against Amalek (the terms used are virtually identical), but the massacre is directed at his own innocent people. Saul's madness has become sinister and lethal, like that of Macbeth, who also becomes a murderer of children—the well-meaning farmer's son who became king has turned into a bloody tyrant.

all by the edge of the sword. "All" catches the force of the Hebrew preposition *'ad* ("even" or "as far as") reiterated before each term in the catalogue of the massacre.

20. *And one son of Ahimelech . . . got away.* This sole survivor (his name means "my father remains") will then be able to provide David with priestly services, including access to the oracle.

22. *I am the one who caused the loss of all the lives.* The Hebrew uses an ellipsis, "caused all the lives," but the sense is clearly loss of life.

CHAPTER 23

1   And they told David, saying, "Look, the Philistines are fighting against
2   Keilah and they are looting the threshing floors." And David inquired
    of the LORD, saying, "Shall I go and strike down these Philistines?"
    And the LORD said to David, "Go and strike down the Philistines and
3   rescue Keilah." And David's men said to him, "Look, we're afraid here
    in Judah, and how much more so if we go to Keilah against the Phi-
4   listine lines!" And David again inquired of the LORD, and the LORD
    answered him and said, "Rise, go down to Keilah, for I am about to
5   give the Philistines into your hand." And David, and his men with him,
    went to Keilah and did battle with the Philistines, and he drove off
    their cattle and struck them a great blow, and David rescued the inhab-

---

1. *Keilah.* Keilah is a town on the western perimeter of the territory of Judah,
facing the Philistine border. Its vulnerability to Philistine incursions is thus
understandable. David's men (verse 3) speak as though Keilah were not part of
Judah because as a border town it seems to them much more dangerous than
their location deep within their own tribal territory. Some scholars have specu-
lated that Keilah was an independent town without tribal affiliation.

2. *David inquired of the LORD.* The means of inquiry are not specified, but since
his questions invite the usual yes-or-no response, it seems likely he is using the
ephod and not, as some interpreters have claimed, a more immediate mode of
communication with God. The information, then, in verse 6 that the fugitive
priest Abiathar has arrived from Nob with the ephod is probably retrospective.
The phrase "at Keilah" (one word in Hebrew) in that verse perhaps should
be deleted as an inadvertent scribal duplication of "Keilah" at the end of the
preceding verse—by the testimony of Chapter 22, Abiathar fled to David when
David was in the forest of Hereth in Judah, before he undertook the rescue
mission to Keilah.

itants of Keilah. And it happened when Abiathar the son of Ahimelech 6
fled to David at Keilah, that the ephod came down in his hand.

And it was told to Saul that David had come to Keilah, and Saul said, 7
"God has given him in my hand, for he is closed inside a town with
double gate and bolt." And Saul summoned all the troops for battle to 8
go down to Keilah to lay seige against David and his men. And David 9
knew that Saul was scheming evil against him and he said to Abiathar
the priest, "Bring forth the ephod." And David said, "LORD, God of 10
Israel, Your servant has indeed heard that Saul seeks to come to Keilah
to destroy the town on my count. Will the notables of Keilah hand me 11
over to him? Will Saul come down, as Your servant has heard? LORD,
God of Israel, tell, pray, Your servant." And the LORD said, "He will come
down." And David said, "Will the notables of Keilah hand me over, and 12
my men, to Saul?" And the LORD said, "They will hand you over." And 13

---

6. *the ephod came down in his hand*. From the viewpoint of the ancient audience,
the ephod would have been indispensable as an instrument of what we would
call military intelligence. An ephod, we should recall, is also a priestly garment.
At Nob, Saul slaughtered eighty-five priests "who wore the linen ephod." Fokkelman perceptively describes the appearance of the oracular ephod in David's
camp as a "countermove by God"—"Saul may bloody the 85 linen priestly garments called the ephod, but the one ephod which acts as a medium for the
decisive word of God turns up at the place of the alternative anointed one."

7. *given him in my hand*. The Masoretic text has *nikar*, "made a stranger," but
the Septuagint reflects a verb meaning "sold" or "handed over."

11. *Will the notables . . . hand me over . . . ? Will Saul come down?* Since the
binary device of the ephod can give only one answer of yes or no, David receives
an answer only to the second question and then is obliged to repeat the first
question (verse 12) in order to get a response to it.

12. *They will hand you over*. It may seem base ingratitude on the part of the
Keilah notables to betray the man who has just rescued their town from the
Philistines. But they must fear Saul's retribution should they collaborate with
David at least as much as they fear the Philistines. The political paradox of
the situation that has evolved is evident: David has achieved a victory against
Israel's principal enemy; Saul now moves to destroy that victor, enlisting the
aid of the people David saved.

David arose, and his men with him, about six hundred men, and they came out from Keilah and moved about wherever they could, and to Saul it was told that David had gotten away from Keilah, and he ceased going out.

14   And David stayed in the wilderness in strongholds, and he stayed in the high country in the wilderness of Ziph. And Saul sought him all the
15   while but God did not give him into his hand. And David saw that Saul had come out to seek his life, and David was in the wilderness of Ziph in
16   the forest. And Jonathan the son of Saul arose and went to David in the
17   forest and bade him take heart in the LORD. And he said to him, "Do not fear, for the hand of Saul my father shall not find you, and it is you who shall be king over Israel, and I on my part will be your viceroy, and even

---

14. *in the wilderness in strongholds.* Since the Hebrew term for strongholds (*metsadah* or *metsudah*—attempts to distinguish the two being questionable) generally occurs in wilderness settings, it seems likely that these are not built-up structures but rather natural formations that afforded effective defensive positions, such as promontories surrounded by outcroppings of rock.

in the wilderness of Ziph. The location is in the tribal territory of Judah, about five miles southeast of Hebron and about ten miles southeast of Keilah, where David has just fought the Philistines.

16. *bade him take heart in the LORD.* The literal meaning of the Hebrew idiom used is "strengthened his hand in the LORD." The Hebrew thus is able to pick up the word "hand" at the beginning of Jonathan's speech, "the hand of my father Saul shall not find you."

17. *I on my part will be your viceroy.* For the second time, Jonathan makes a pact with David in which he concedes that it is David who will inherit the throne. There is a pattern of incremental repetition here: only now does Jonathan specify that he will be David's viceroy (literally "second," *mishneh*, but this is an ellipses for *mishneh lamelekh*, "second to the king"). The faithful Jonathan persists in his naivete, imagining that he will be able to serve as viceroy to his dear friend, who is also the man destined to displace the dynasty Saul would have established. As an alleged doublet, this episode has narrative plausibility: Jonathan first confirmed a pact with David when he told him he must flee from Saul; now, no doubt at some risk to himself, he is impelled to seek out the fugitive and beleaguered David in order to assure him of his continuing loyalty and encourage him in his adversity. Once again, characteristically, David's response to Jonathan is not reported.

Saul my father knows it." And the two of them sealed a pact before the 18
LORD, and David stayed in the forest but Jonathan went to his house.

And Ziphites came up to Saul at Gibeah, saying, "Is not David hiding 19
out among us in the strongholds in the forest on the hill of Hachilah to
the south of the wasteland? And so whenever you may desire, O king, 20
to come down, come down, and ours is the part to deliver him into the
hand of the king." And Saul said, "Blessed are you to the LORD, for you 21
have shown pity on me. Go, pray, make certain, and mark and see the 22
place where his foot treads, and who has seen him there, for it has been
said to me that he is very cunning. See and mark all the hideouts where 23

---

19. *Ziphites.* Since no definite article is used, this appears to be one group
of Ziphites and not a delegation representing the entire clan. The motive for
betraying David could equally be desire for a reward and fear of retribution
should Saul discover that they had allowed David to hide out in their territory:
the ruthless massacre at Nob would have been a grim object lesson duly noted
throughout the Israelite populace.

*in the strongholds in the forest on the hill of Hachilah to the south of the
wasteland.* The Ziphite informers want to make their identification of David's
whereabouts as precise as possible, hence the unusual string of geographical indications. As it emerges, the intelligence they provide is still not precise
enough for the frustrated Saul, as his response ("make certain . . . when you are
certain") clearly shows. It should be said that most translators have treated the
last geographical term used by the Ziphites, "the wasteland," as a proper noun
(*yeshimon*), but because it bears a definite article, and because *yeshimon* is a
well-attested common noun, it is preferable not to construe it as a place-name.
This episode uses three different terms for uninhabited terrain—wilderness,
wasteland, and desert (or four, if one adds forest)—which has the cumulative effect of emphasizing how David is constrained to take refuge beyond the
populated areas of Israel.

21. *you have shown pity on me.* Saul uses the same verb for pity or "sparing"
that was prominently deployed in the Amalek story. The idea that the poor king,
thwarted by a cunning and malicious David, needs to be shown pity is surely
another manifestation of his paranoia—we might say, of its maudlin side.

22. *where his foot treads.* The Hebrew says literally "where his foot is." The focus
on David's foot reflects the eye of the pursuer on the track of his elusive prey.

for it has been said to me. The Hebrew reads literally, "for he has said to me,"
but there is no need to emend the text because biblical Hebrew sometimes uses

he may take cover there and come back to me when you are certain
and I shall go with you. And if indeed he is in the land, I shall search
24 for him among all the clans of Judah." And they arose and went to Ziph
ahead of Saul, and David and his men were in the wilderness of Maon
25 in the desert south of the wasteland. And Saul went, and his men with
him, to seek David. And it was told to David, and he went down to the
crag and stayed in the wilderness of Maon, and Saul heard, and pursued
26 David into the wilderness of Maon. And Saul went on one side of the
mountain and David and his men on the other side of the mountain, and
David made haste to go off from before Saul, while Saul and his men
27 were circling the mountain after David and his men to catch them. Just
then a messenger came to Saul, saying, "Hurry, and go, for the Philis-

---

a third person masculine singular verb with no specified grammatical subject
to perform the function of the passive. Notice that Saul claims someone has
told him David is very cunning—not, which is the case, that Saul himself has
decided that his "enemy" is cunning.

24. *Maon.* This would be roughly three miles due south of the wilderness of
Ziph.

26. *Saul and his men were circling the mountain.* Kyle McCarter, Jr., has made
the plausible suggestion that what is indicated in this language is a pincer
movement: Saul's forces are moving around the circumference of the mountain
on two sides in order to trap David between them, who is on the far side of the
mountain. He, evidently realizing the nature of Saul's maneuver, scrambles to
flee—"David made haste to go off from before Saul"—before the pincer snaps
shut.

27. *Hurry, and go, for the Philistines have invaded the land.* This last-minute
diversion of course has the effect of rescuing David from Saul, but it also
points up the madness of his obsessive pursuit of David: at a time when Israel's
major national enemy is repeatedly sending troops against the territory Saul is
supposed to be governing and protecting, he is devoting his attention, and his
troops, to the pursuit of David.

tines have invaded the land!" And Saul turned back from pursuing David 28
and went to meet the Philistines. Therefore do they call that place the
Crag of the Divide.

And David went up from there and stayed in the strongholds of Ein-Gedi. 24:1

---

28. *the Crag of the Divide*. This etiological notice explains the place-name,
sela' hamaḥleqot, as deriving from the "divide" between Saul's forces, which
went one way, and David's, which went another. Several commentators have
proposed that the name derived not from *maḥloqet*, "division," but from *ḥalaq*,
"smooth," and so the original meaning would have been Slippery Crag, or
Unforested Crag.

24:1. *the strongholds of Ein-Gedi*. David now flees eastward from the forest area
of Ziph, south of Hebron in the central region of Judah's territory, to Ein-Gedi,
in the rocky heights overlooking the Dead Sea. He would have felt safer in this
remote region with its forbidding terrain. But Ein-Gedi is an oasis, which would
have provided a water supply and vegetation for him and his troops

CHAPTER 24

And it happened when Saul turned back from the Philistines that they
told him, saying, "Look, David is in the wilderness of Ein-Gedi." And
Saul took three thousand picked men from all Israel and he went to seek
David over the rocks of the wild goats. And he came to the sheep-folds
along the way, and there was a cave there, and Saul went in to relieve
himself, while David and his men were sitting in the far end of the cave.
And David's men said to him, "Here is the day that the LORD said to you,
'Look, I am about to give your enemy into your hands, and you may do to
him whatever seems good in your eyes.'" And David rose and stealthily

---

3. *three thousand picked men.* David, it should be recalled, commands a guerilla
band of about six hundred men; so he is outnumbered five to one and is facing
elite troops.

4. *Saul went in to relieve himself . . . David and his men . . . in the far end of
the cave.* The topography is quite realistic, for the cliffs overlooking the Dead
Sea in the region of En-Gedi are honeycombed with caves. Power and power-
lessness are precariously balanced in this episode. David and his men are in
all likelihood hiding in the far end of the cave from Saul's search party. Had a
contingent of soldiers entered the cave, they would have been trapped. Instead,
Saul comes in alone, and he is in a double sense exposed to David and his men.

5. *Here is the day that the LORD said to you.* David's eager men exhibit a certain
theological presumptuousness. They surely know that their leader has been
secretly anointed to be king, but nothing in the preceding narrative indicates a
divine promise that God would deliver Saul into David's hands.
   do to him whatever seems good in your eyes. They carefully avoid the plain
word "kill."

cut off the skirt of the cloak that was Saul's. And it happened then that 6
David was smitten with remorse because he had cut off the skirt of the
cloak that was Saul's. And he said to his men, "The LORD forbid me, 7
that I should have done this thing to my master, the LORD's anointed,
to reach out my hand against him, for he is the LORD's anointed." And 8
David held back his men with words and did not let them rise against
Saul, and Saul rose from the cave and went on the way. And David then 9
rose and came out of the cave and called after Saul, saying, "My lord

6. *David was smitten with remorse.* The Hebrew is literally "David's heart
smote him."

he had cut off the skirt of the cloak that was Saul's. Clearly, what David feels
is that he has perpetrated a kind of symbolic mutilation of the king by cutting
off the corner of his garment—not with anything like a scissors, of course, but
surely with his sword, his instrument for killing his enemies. The cloak (*me'il*)
has already been linked emblematically with kingship in the final estrangement
between Samuel and Saul, and so David is in symbolic effect "cutting away"
Saul's kingship. For all the remorse he feels, he will continue to make double
use of the corner of the cloak, as we shall see.

7. *that I should have done this thing to my master, the LORD's anointed.* Some
interpreters have read this whole episode as an apology for David's innocence and piety in relation to Saul. But the very gesture of piety is also self-
interested—David, after all, is conscious that he, too, is the LORD's anointed,
and it is surely in his long-term interest that the reigning king's person should
be held sacred by all his subjects.

8. *David held back his men.* The meaning of the verb *shisa'* is disputed, but it
is most plausibly linked with the noun *shesa'*, a split or cleft. The sense here
would then be: he "split off" his men from Saul, using his words to interpose a
kind of barrier between them and the king. In any case, the first clause of this
verse appears to respond to the men's initial inclination to kill Saul (verse 5)
rather than following from David's remorse over the cutting of the garment—a
chronological displacement noted as early as Rashi.

9. *David . . . came out of the cave and called after Saul.* David is taking a calculated risk. Saul could, after all, order his troops to attack David and the men
behind him in the cave. David first throws Saul off his guard by paying obeisance to him as king and prostrating himself—hardly what one would expect
of a fugitive or rebel. He then counts on the persuasive power of his own
rhetoric, and on the telltale scrap of the king's cloak that he clutches, to deflect

the king!" And Saul looked behind him, and David knelt, his face to
10 the ground, and bowed down. And David said to Saul, "Why should
you listen to people's words, saying, 'Look, David seeks to harm you'?
11 Look, this day your eyes have seen that the LORD has given you into
my hand in the cave, and they meant to kill you, and I had pity for
you and said, 'I will not reach out my hand against my master, for he
12 is the LORD's anointed.' And, my father, see, yes, see the skirt of your
cloak in my hand, for when I cut off the skirt of your cloak and did not
kill you, mark and see that there was no evil or crime in my hand and
13 I did not offend you, yet you stalk me to take my life. Let the LORD
judge between me and you, and the LORD will avenge me of you, but
14 my hand will not be against you. As the proverb of the ancients says,

---

Saul from his lethal intentions. David is cannily self-protective but he is also
a gambler.

10.–11. *Why should you listen to people's words . . . ? . . . this day your eyes have
seen.* Instead of rumor heard about David's harmful intentions, here is ocular
evidence of his innocence—and of God's having devised to give David the
upper hand over Saul.

11. *and they meant to kill you.* The Masoretic text has "he meant," which may
be either corrected to a plural, as some of the ancient versions do, or construed
as "someone said."

12. *my father see, yes, see the skirt of your cloak in my hand.* It is, appropriately,
ambiguous whether "my father" is a form of respectful address to an authority
or an attempt to reach back to the moment of affectionate intimacy in their
relationship. We may note that David, for all the remorse he felt over having
cut off the skirt of Saul's garment, makes great display of it now as evidence
of having had Saul entirely at his mercy. The proof of his innocence is thus
inseparable from the reminder of the power he had over his rival.

13. *Let the LORD judge between me and you . . . the LORD will avenge me of you.*
David's great protestation of innocence and his purported gesture of reconciliation move toward a barely veiled threat: you are the one who has wronged me,
and vengeance will be exacted, but by God, not by me.

14. *the proverb of the ancients.* The Masoretic text has "ancient," in the singular,
but the Qumran Samuel scroll, more plausibly, shows the plural form.

'From wicked men does wickedness come forth,' but my hand will not be
against you. After whom has the king of Israel come forth, after whom are 15
you chasing? After a dead dog, after a single flea? The LORD will be arbi- 16
ter and judge between me and you, that He may see and plead my case
and judge me against you." And it happened when David had finished 17
speaking these words to Saul, that Saul said, "Is this your voice, my son,

---

From wicked men does wickedness come forth. The gnomic saying—only three
words in the Hebrew!—that David chooses to cite is archly double-edged:
Wicked acts are perpetrated only by the wicked, so I won't be the one to touch
you. But there is also the distinct hint that the wicked person in question could
be Saul himself. Though David cannot know this, Saul will die by his own hand.

but my hand will not be against you. The words that the writer attributes to
David ironically echo the words of Saul's first murderous plot against David,
conveyed in interior monologue, when Saul said, "Let not my hand be against
him but let the hand of the Philistines be against him" (18:17).

15. *has the king of Israel come forth.* The very verb attached to the wicked in
the proverb!

After a dead dog, after a single flea. In his peroration, David outdoes himself
in professing his humble station. A dead dog was proverbial in ancient Israel as
a contemptible, worthless thing, but David goes the idiom one better by saying
he is scarcely more important than a single flea on the dead dog's carcass, a
brilliant adaptation to prose of the logic of intensification of biblical poetry,
in which a term introduced in the first part of the line is raised to the second
power semantically in the parallel second half.

16. *judge me against you.* The Hebrew is literally "judge me from your hand,"
that is, judge me favorably and rescue me from your hand. The term thus picks
up the insistence on "hand" throughout David's speech.

17. *Is this your voice, my son, David?* These first words of Saul's response to
David are one of the most breathtaking instances of the biblical technique
of contrastive dialogue. David's speech had been, by biblical standards, quite
lengthy, and very much a speech—a beautifully crafted piece of rhetoric, with
complex political aims in mind. Saul responds with four choked Hebrew words,
haqolkha zeh beni Dawid? His designation of David as "my son" is free of the
ambiguity attached to David's calling him "my father." This is one of those
extraordinary reversals that make biblical narrative such a probing representation of the oscillations and the unpredictability of human nature: David's words
have cut to the quick of the king's conscience, and suddenly the obsessive

18 David?" And Saul raised his voice and wept. And he said to David, "You are more in the right than I, for it is you who requited me good whereas

19 I requited you evil. And you told today how you wrought good with me, when the LORD delivered me into your hand and you did not kill me.

20 For if a man finds his enemy, does he send him off on a good way? The LORD will repay you with good for what you have done for me this day.

21 And so, look, I know that you will surely be king and that the kingship

22 of Israel will stay in your hands. And now, swear to me by the LORD that you shall not cut off my seed after me and that you shall not blot out my

23 name from my father's house." And David swore to Saul, and Saul went home while David and his men went up to the stronghold.

---

pursuer feels an access of paternal affection, intertwined with remorse, for his imagined enemy. Saul asks his question because he has to shake himself to believe his enemy is his friend, because he stands at a certain distance from David (who has called out "after" Saul), and also because his eyes are blinded with tears. He is thus reminiscent of the blind father Isaac, who was able to make out the voice, but not the identity, of his son Jacob, and from whom a blessing was wrested.

18. *You are more in the right than I.* These words echo the ones pronounced by Judah, referring to his vindicated daughter-in-law Tamar, who will become the progenitrix of David's line.

you who requited me good . . . I requited you evil. The antithesis of good and evil is played on through the next three verses and should not be sacrificed in the English for the sake of imagined idiomatic fluency.

21. *I know that you will surely be king.* This marks Saul's first open admission that David is the "fellowman who is better than you" of whom Samuel spoke. He has been doubly convinced—by God's having put him at David's mercy and by David's refusal to harm him, a kingly act and not the act of a rebel and usurper.

CHAPTER 25

And Samuel died, and all Israel gathered and mourned him, and they 1
buried him at his home in Ramah. And David arose and went down to
the wilderness of Paran.

And there was a man in Maon, whose stock was in Carmel, and the 2
man was very great; he had three thousand sheep and a thousand
goats. And it happened when he was shearing his sheep in Carmel—
and the man's name was Nabal and his wife's name was Abigail, and 3
the woman had a good mind and lovely looks, but the man was hard

---

1. *the wilderness of Paran.* This geographical indication is puzzling because,
unless there is some other place called Paran, it would refer to the Sinai desert,
where it would make no sense for David to go and where he could scarcely be
if he and his men are engaged with Nabal's shepherds in Judea. The Septuagint
reads "wilderness of Maon."

2. *Maon . . . Carmel.* Both places are in the tribal territory of Judah, in the vicinity of Hebron, and just a few miles apart.

3. *the man's name was Nabal.* On the face of it, this is an improbable name
because *nabal* in Hebrew plainly means "base fellow," "churl," or "fool," as Abigail
(verse 25) will point out. It is at least conceivable that the name is not originally
Hebrew, and various meanings drawn from other ancient Near Eastern languages
have been proposed for it, such as "archer" and "chosen one of the god."
   a good mind and lovely looks. As yet, we do not know why this characterization will be important. Her shrewd intelligence will be vividly demonstrated
in her brilliant speech to David, and her physical attractiveness will stir his
matrimonial interest in her.

4 and evil in deeds, and a Calebite—David heard in the wilderness that
5 Nabal was shearing his sheep. And David sent ten lads, and David said to
   the lads, "Go up to Carmel, and come to Nabal and ask him in my name
6 how he fares. And say, 'Thus may it be this time next year, that you fare
7 well, and your house fare well, and all that is yours fare well. And so, I
   have heard that they are doing your shearing. Now, the shepherds who
   belong to you were with us—we did not humiliate them and nothing of
8 theirs was missing the whole time they were at Carmel. Ask your lads
   and they will tell you! And may our lads find favor in your eyes, for we
   have come on a festive day. Give, pray, whatever you can to your servants

---

and a Calebite. The Calebites were non-Israelites who in effect joined the
tribe of Judah. Several medieval Hebrew commentators detected a double
meaning because *kalibi* could also be construed as "doglike."

6. *Thus may it be this time next year.* The compact Hebrew phrase *koh leḥay*
occurs only here, and its meaning has been disputed. This translation adopts an
interpretation that goes back to Rashi, which is based on the similarity to a well-
known idiom, *ka'et ḥayah*.That would make sense in terms of the narrative situation: the prosperous Nabal is obviously "faring well" at the moment, and David's
greeting of peace (to fare well in the Hebrew idiom is to possess *shalom*) contains
a veiled threat—let us hope that you continue to fare well a year from now.

7. *we did not humiliate them.* This is the same verb used for Jonathan's sense of
his father's treatment of him (20:34), though here it has the meaning of "molest."
   nothing of theirs was missing. The message is that David's men did not permit
themselves to take any of Nabal's flock, and perhaps also that as armed men
they defended Nabal's people against marauders (compare verse 16, "They
were a wall around us both night and day"). But there is a certain ambiguity as
to whether David was providing protection out of sheer good will or conducting
a protection racket in order to get the necessary provisions for his guerilla band.

8. *our lads.* The Hebrew says "the lads"—"our" is added for the sake of clarity,
to distinguish David's retainers from Nabal's.
   for we have come on a festive day. The time of sheep shearing was a sort of
holiday, with feasting and drinking. Nabal's own feast back home at Maon
(verse 36) may have been encouraged by the festivities in which he joined with
his shearers out in the field.
   Give, pray, whatever you can to your servants. The request for a payoff is
politely worded, and no quantities are specified.

and to your son, to David.'" And David's lads came and spoke to Nabal   9
all these words in David's name, and they paused. And Nabal answered   10
David's servants and said, "Who is David and who is the son of Jesse?
These days many are the slaves breaking away from their masters. And   11
shall I take my bread and my water and my meat that I slaughtered for
my shearers and give it to men who come from I know not where?" And   12
David's lads whirled round on their way and went back and told him all
these words. And David said to his men, "Every man, gird his sword!"
And every man girded his sword, and David, too, girded his sword. And   13
about four hundred men went up after David, while two hundred stayed
with the gear.

---

to your son, to David. This is an expression of deference or humility to the
powerful and presumably older Nabal. It also strikes an ironic note of correspondence with the language of David's encounter with Saul at the cave near
Ein-Gedi in the previous episode. There, David addressed Saul as "my father,"
and the king, in an access of feeling, called David "my son."

10. *Who is David and who is the son of Jesse?* This sarcastic question, in verse-
like parallelism, picks up another ironic correspondence with Saul, who after
the vanquishing of Goliath asked whose son this was. In Nabal's case, of
course, the question expresses the contempt of a rich landowner for David and
his ragtag band of dispossessed men and malcontents ("men who come from I
know not where").

many are the slaves breaking away from their masters. On the surface, these
words reflect the disdain of a propertied man (who would also be a slave-
holder) for all landless rebels who threaten the established social hierarchy. But
there is also a barbed hint that David himself is a slave or subject (the same
word in Hebrew) who has rebelled against his master, Saul.

11. *shall I take my bread and my water.* The Septuagint has "wine" instead of
"water." In any case, Nabal's harsh and contemptuous response to David's men
vividly illustrates that he is a "hard" man, and a churlish one. His outrage over
the notion of parting with any of his possessions is nicely indicated, as Shimon
Bar-Efrat has noted, by the fact that there are eight grammatical expressions of
the first person singular in this one sentence.

12. *Every man, gird his sword!* The angry David wastes no words: he merely gives
the urgent command to take up weapons and move out for the kill.

14 And to Abigail the wife of Nabal one of the lads told, saying, "Look, David sent messengers from the wilderness to greet our master, and
15 he pounced on them. And the men have been very good to us and we were not humiliated and we missed nothing the whole time we went
16 about with them when we were out in the field. They were a wall around us both night and day the whole time we were with them tending the
17 sheep. And now, mark and see what you must do, for the evil is resolved against our master and against all his house, and he is such a scoundrel
18 no one can speak to him." And Abigail hurried and fetched two hundred loaves of bread and two jugs of wine and five dressed sheep and five seahs of parched grain and a hundred raisin cakes and two hundred fig
19 cakes, and she put them on the donkeys. And she said to her lads, "Pass on ahead of me and I'll be coming right after you." But her husband she
20 did not tell. And so she was riding on the donkey coming down under the cover of the mountain and, look, David and his men were coming
21 down toward her, and she met them. And David had said, "All in vain did I guard everything that belonged to this fellow in the wilderness, and nothing was missing from all that was his, and he paid me back evil for

---

15. *And the men have been very good to us.* In keeping with the general practice of biblical dialogue, the servant recycles the language of David's message to Nabal—"we were not humiliated and we missed nothing the whole time"—but amplifies it by adding this clause as well as the image in the next verse, "They were a wall around us both night and day." He thus makes emphatically clear that David's men really provided protection faithfully, whether in the simple sense or in the racketeering sense.

17. *And now, mark and see what you must do.* Unlike the "lads" who address Saul, this one offers no specific advice to Abigail, for she is more than clever enough to figure out what steps she must immediately take.

20. *And so she was riding on the donkey coming down under the cover of the mountain and, look, David and his men were coming.* The two parties moving toward each other introduce a moment of suspense, for David, after all, as the next verse (with a pluperfect verb) makes utterly clear, is armed and angry. The "look" (*hineh*) is used in characteristic fashion to indicate Abigail's visual perspective: he at first doesn't see her because she is coming down the sheltered slope of the mountain, but she sees him and his men with their swords girded ready for battle.

good! Thus may God do to David and even more, if I leave from all that   22
is his until morning a single pisser against the wall!" And Abigail saw   23
David and hurried and got down from the donkey and flung herself on
her face before David and bowed to the ground. And she flung herself   24
at his feet and said, "Mine, my lord, is the blame! But let your servant
speak in your ears, and hear the words of your servant. Pray, let not my   25
lord pay mind to this scoundrel of a man, to Nabal, for just like his name
he is, his name means Base and baseness is with him. And as for me,

---

22. *a single pisser against the wall.* The literal meaning of the Hebrew is properly followed in the King James Version, as it is in this translation. The phrase,
of course, is a rough and vivid epithet for "male," and one that occurs only in
curses. Its edge of vulgarity seems perfectly right for David's anger.

23.–24. *flung herself on her face . . . bowed to the ground . . . flung herself at
his feet.* In a world where an angry king could massacre every man, woman,
and child in Nob, Abigail has no way of knowing whether David will have an
impulse to kill her on the spot. (She has not heard the words that limit the
threat of slaughter to the males.) Thus, her first move in this highly dangerous
situation, before she speaks a word, is to demonstrate her absolute submission
to David through these extravagant gestures of obeisance.

24. *Mine.* The shrewdness of her extraordinary speech begins with the very first
syllable she utters. She immediately takes all the blame on herself, though in
the next breath she will be sure to transfer it heartily to her contemptible husband. At the same time, she exploits a momentary pun, for the word *bi* ("mine,"
"in me") in other contexts can mean "I beseech you," so she initiates her address
to David with what sounds like a term of imploring.

25. *this scoundrel of a man . . . his name means Base . . . And as for me.* It is
hard to think of another instance in literature in which a wife so quickly and
so devastatingly interposes distance between herself and her husband. She
rapidly denounces her spouse and then counterposes herself ("And as for me,"
wa'ani) as a person who had no part in the rude rejection of David's emissaries.
Abigail of course wants to save her own neck, but she clearly has been chafing
over her marriage with a boorish, unpleasant, and probably older man, and she
sees an opportunity here.

26 your servant, I never saw my lord's lads whom you sent. And now, my
lord, as the LORD lives and as you live—the LORD Who kept you from
coming into blood guilt with your own hand rescuing you—and now, like
27 Nabal may your enemies be who seek evil against my lord. And now, this
blessing that your servant has brought to my lord, let it be given to the
28 lads who go about in the footsteps of my lord. Forgive, pray, the crime of
your servant, for the LORD will surely make for my lord a stalwart house,
for my lord fights the battles of the LORD and no evil will be found in you
29 all your days. And when a person rises to pursue you, to seek your life,

---

26. *Who kept you from coming into blood guilt.* Abigail is no doubt speaking in
general, but the reader can scarcely forget the immediately preceding episode,
in which David refused to harm Saul when he had him in his power.

27. *this blessing that your servant has brought.* The obvious sense of "blessing"
(*berakhah*) in context is "gift," but the primary meaning of the word is worth
preserving for two reasons. First, it is clearly intended to answer to David's reiterated use of "blessed" in his response to Abigail. Then, as Moshe Garsiel has
aptly observed, it is a key term in a network of allusions to the moment in Genesis 33 when Jacob is reunited with his brother Esau: Esau, too, approaches
dauntingly with four hundred armed men; Jacob, like Abigail, prostrates himself before the figure he fears; and he, too, has brought with him generous
tribute to be offered in conciliation, which he refers to not as a "gift" (*minhah*)
but as a "blessing." And in Genesis 33, that term plays back against the fraught
meanings of "blessing" in the larger Jacob-Esau narrative.

28. *Forgive, pray, the crime of your servant.* "Servant" is in the feminine, but the
conventional "handmaiden" sounds too fussy. By way of deference, Abigail once
again speaks as though the fault were hers, though she has made it quite clear
that her husband alone is the guilty one.
    a stalwart house. A stalwart, or enduring, house is precisely what was prom-
ised the priestly line that was to replace the house of Eli (2:35).
    no evil will be found in you all your days. Abigail exploits the temporal ambi-
guity of the Hebrew imperfective verb to make a statement that is both descriptive of the way David has conducted himself and predictive of the way he will,
or should, conduct himself.

29. *when a person rises to pursue you.* The generality of "a person" (*'adam*) picks
up David's use of the same word in the preceding episode when he addresses
Saul ("Why should you listen to people's words" [*divrey 'adam*]), and, even more
pointedly, recalls his very first speech to Saul in 17:32, "Let no man's heart [*lev'*

my lord's life will be bound in the bundle of the living with the LORD your
God, and the lives of your enemies He will sling from the hollow of the
sling. And so, when the LORD does for my lord all the good that He has   30
spoken about you and He appoints you prince over Israel, this will not   31
be a stumbling and a trepidation of the heart to my lord, to have shed
blood for no cause and for my lord to have carried out his own rescue,
then will the LORD do well with my lord, and you will remember your

---

adam] fail him," where the term seems to refer to Saul himself, who may be
the hidden referent here.

bound in the bundle of the living. Although Kyle McCarter, Jr., following
Tur-Sinai, has claimed that "bundle" (*tsror*) actually means document or book,
a more plausible identification is the pouch in which little stones keeping a
tally of live sheep were placed. Thus both this positive image and the negative
one of the slingshot would be associated with sheepherding. And as Shimon
Bar-Efrat had nicely observed, *tsror* in biblical Hebrew also means "stone," the
object that would normally be placed in the hollow of the sling; so there is a
punning cross-link between the two images.

will sling from the hollow of the sling. Instead of being bound up and safely
kept, their lives will be flung out into the void of extinction. (The literal sense of
the preposition attached to "hollow" in the Hebrew is "in.") Abigail has chosen
her metaphor shrewdly because it would be general knowledge that David used
his sling to destroy a formidable enemy.

30.–31. *when the* LORD *. . . appoints you prince over Israel, this will not be a
stumbling and a trepidation of the heart to my lord*. Abigail deftly pitches her
argument to David's political self-interest. Once he makes the move from guerilla chieftain to monarch, he will not want his record stained by blood he has
spilled. It is therefore more prudent to let God take care of his enemies—"the
LORD" in biblical parlance being the piously proper way to talk about the course
of events, but its pragmatic equivalent being "other people" or "circumstances."

31. *and you will remember your servant*. These final words of Abigail's lengthy
and carefully calculated speech are strategically chosen, and discreet. What,
in fact, does she have in mind? The Israeli novelist, Meir Shalev, in a perceptive and lively essay on this story, makes a bold and, to my mind, persuasive
proposal. Abigail has matrimony in view, once her cantankerous old husband
is out of the way, but why does she think she will deserve so signal an honor,
or reward, from David? Shalev argues that when Abigail dissuades David from
killing Nabal, repeatedly assuring him that the LORD will pay off David's scores
against him, she is really suggesting herself as the agency for "the LORD." She is,
in other words, proposing to David that she carry out a kind of contract killing

32 servant." And David said to Abigail, "Blessed is the LORD, God of Israel,
33 Who has sent you this day to meet me. And blessed is your good sense
and blessed are you, for this day you held me back from coming into
34 blood guilt with my own hand rescuing me. And yet, as the LORD, God
of Israel, lives, Who kept me from harming you, had you not hurried and
come to meet me, there would not have been left to Nabal by morning's
35 light a single pisser against the wall!" And David took from her hand
what she had brought him, and to her he said, "Go up in peace to your
house. See, I have heeded your voice and granted your petition."

36 And Abigail came to Nabal, and, look, he was having himself a feast in
his house like a king's feast, and Nabal's heart was of good cheer, and
he was exceedingly drunk. And she told him nothing, neither great nor
37 small. And it happened in the morning when the wine was gone out of
Nabal that his wife told him these things and his heart died within him

---

of her husband, with the payoff that she will become the wife of the handsome
young warrior and future king.

32.–34. David, though persuaded by Abigail's prudent advice, cannot resist one
last reminder that he was indeed about to cut down every pisser against the
wall in the house of Nabal.

36. *And she told him nothing*. Abigail again makes a careful calculation: she does not
want to convey the scary news to him while he is enveloped in an alcoholic haze.

37. *in the morning when the wine was gone out of Nabal*. She catches him cold
sober, and perhaps even with a painful hangover.
 his heart died within him and he became like a stone. The terrifying information that David had been on his way—or did she say, was still on his way?—with
four hundred armed men intent on mayhem triggers a paralyzing heart attack
or, perhaps, a stroke (the biblical understanding of physiology not being ours).
Abigail gives the distinct appearance of counting on her husband's cowardice
and on a bad heart she might have been aware of from previous manifestations
of ill health. If this assumption is correct, she would be using her knowledge of
his physical frailty to carry out the tacit contract on his life—bloodlessly, with
God Himself left to do the deed (compare the end of verse 38). Polzin perceptively notes that the figurative use of the stone for paralysis cinches a circle of
images: the enemies flung from the hollow of the sling and the smooth stone
with which David killed Goliath.

and he became like a stone. And it happened after about ten days that 38 the LORD smote Nabal and he died.

And David heard that Nabal had died, and he said, "Blessed is the LORD 39 Who has taken up my cause of insult against Nabal, and His servant He has withheld from evil, and Nabal's evil the LORD has brought down on his own head." And David sent and spoke out for Abigail to take her as wife. And David's servants came to Abigail at Carmel and spoke to her, 40 saying, "David sent us to you to take you to him as wife." And she arose 41 and bowed, her face to the ground, and said, "Look, your servant is but a slavegirl to wash the feet of my lord's servants." And Abigail hurried 42 and rose and rode on the donkey, her five young women walking behind her, and she went after David's messengers, and she became his wife. And Ahinoam David had taken from Jezreel, and both of them became 43 his wives. And Saul had given Michal his daughter, David's wife, to Palti 44 son of Laish, who was from Gallim.

---

39. *David . . . spoke out for Abigail.* In biblical idiom, the verb "to speak" followed by the preposition b^e instead of the usual *'el* ("to") means to enter into discussion about a betrothal. David, losing no time, has certainly grasped the veiled implication of Abigail's last words to him.

41. *your servant is but a slavegirl to wash the feet of my lord's servants.* In one last flourish of the etiquette of humility, she professes herself unworthy of so great an honor as to become David's wife. But perhaps this is just what she has been aiming to become, and so, once again "hurrying," she sets off to join her new husband. She then vanishes from the subsequent narrative.

44. *And Saul had given Michal his daughter, David's wife, to Palti.* The legality of this act is questionable. David's having taken two wives—of Ahinoam all we know is her place of origin—while hiding out from Saul is no justification because, given the practice of polygamy, he could have done that even if he were living under the same roof with Michal. Saul's motive is political, to deprive David of one claim to the throne by removing the connection through marriage with the royal family. But that connection has already been established, as the narrator's identification of Michal as "David's wife" is meant to remind us. We can only guess what Michal, who we know loved David, feels about being passed around in this fashion, or what she feels about the man her father has imposed on her. Later, we will be accorded a brief but unforgettable glimpse into Palti's feelings for Michal.

CHAPTER 26

1   And the Ziphites came to Saul at Gibeah, saying, "Is not David
2   hiding out at the hill of Hachilah facing the wasteland?" And Saul
arose and went down to the wilderness of Ziph, and with him three
thousand picked men of Israel, to seek David in the wilderness of

---

1. *And the Ziphites came to Saul at Gibeah.* This verse, echoing much of the
language of 23:19, announces the beginning of the last of the elaborately
paired episodes that structure the story of David and Saul. Scholarly consensus
assumes that these doublets reflect different sources or traditions bearing on
the same events, though the possibility cannot be rejected out of hand that the
original writer may have deliberately composed his story with paired incidents.
In any case, the pairings need to be read as part of the purposeful compositional
design of the redacted version of the narrative that we have. As the Russian
Formalist critic Viktor Shklovsky observed long ago, every parallelism in a literary text serves to point up a certain semantic difference. Here, we note at
the outset that the elaborately detailed intelligence about David's whereabouts
provided by the Ziphites in 23:19 is largely absent from this briefer account:
this story will prove to be an *inversion* of the earlier one, David discovering
Saul instead of the other way around. Another indication that the doublet is
manipulated as an element of purposeful design is the fact that this episode
simultaneously repeats *two different* previous episodes—not only the earlier
story of Saul's pursuit of David into the wilderness of Ziph but also the encounter between David and Saul at the cave near Ein-Gedi (Chapter 24). There,
just as here, David refused to kill Saul when he, or one of his men, could have
done so, and there he professed his innocence to a remorseful Saul who called
him as he does here, "my son, David."

Ziph. And Saul camped at the hill of Hachilah which is facing the ₃
wasteland, along the way; and David was staying in the wilderness, and
he saw that Saul had come after him into the wilderness. And David ₄
sent spies and he knew with certainty that Saul had come. And David ₅
arose and came to the place where Saul had camped. And David saw
the place where Saul lay, and Abner son of Ner and Saul were lying
within the staging ground, and the troops were encamped around him.
And David spoke up and said to Ahimelech the Hittite and to Abishai ₆
son of Zeruiah, saying, "Who will come down with me to Saul, to the
camp?" And Abishai said, "I on my part shall go down with you." And ₇
David came, and Abishai, to the troops by night, and, look, Saul was

---

3. *he saw that Saul had come after him.* The placement of this second account
of pursuit in the wilderness of Ziph after Saul's solemn pledge in Chapter 24
not to harm David underlines the compulsive character of his obsession with
David. Whatever his avowed good intentions, Saul cannot restrain his impulse
to destroy his rival. There is thus strong narrative logic in the recurrence: after
this last encounter with Saul, David will sensibly conclude that he can no
longer trust the king's professions of good faith, and he will take flight beyond
the borders of Israel.

4. *David sent spies and he knew with certainty.* In contrast to the episode in
Chapter 23, it is David here who commands military intelligence. The writer
makes this point neatly by using the same (relatively unusual) phrase, *'el
nakhon,* "with certainty," which in Chapter 23 was spoken by Saul, referring to
the information about David he expected to get from the Ziphites.

6. *Ahimelech the Hittite.* In biblical usage, "Hittite" is a loose designation for
Canaanite peoples and does not necessarily refer to the Indo-European group
that originated in Anatolia. The presence of a foreigner in David's inner circle
of warriors suggests an openness of his band of disaffected men to adven-
ture seekers, freebooters, and other mobile types in the Canaanite population.
Ahimelech is nowhere else mentioned in the biblical record, which has led
some scholars to infer that the mention of this foreigner may be an authentic
early notice of a historical personage. The name itself is Hebrew.
    Abishai son of Zeruiah. If the report in Chronicles is reliable, Zeruiah was
David's sister—hence the unusual matronymic instead of a patronymic. David
the warrior chieftain is surrounded by his three nephews, the three bloody-
minded sons of Zeruiah: two of them impetuous (Abishai and Asahel), the
third, who is David's commander, ruthlessly calculating (Joab).

lying asleep within the staging ground, his spear thrust into the ground
8 at his head, and Abner and the troops were lying around him. And
Abishai said to David, "God has this day delivered your enemy into
your hand, and now, let me, pray, strike him through with the spear
9 into the ground just once, I will need no second blow." And David said
to Abishai, "Do no violence to him! For who can reach out his hand
10 against the LORD's anointed and be guiltless?" And David said, "As the
LORD lives, the LORD will smite him, or his day will come and he will
11 die, or in battle he will go down and perish. The LORD forbid that I
should reach out my hand against the LORD's anointed! And so now,
take, pray, the spear which is at his head and the water jug and let

---

8. *God has this day delivered your enemy into your hand.* These words explicitly
echo the words of David's men when they discover Saul unawares in the cave.
    strike him through with the spear . . . just once, I will need no second blow.
This bit of warrior's bravado helps us make an important connection, as J. P.
Fokkelman has nicely observed: twice Saul hurled this same spear at David,
who eluded him. Abishai on his part vows he will deliver one swift, lethal blow.

9. *And David said.* Abishai, dumbfounded, offers no response to David's forbidding him to harm this archenemy, and so David has to explain that God will
settle accounts with Saul in His own good time.

10. *Do no violence to him.* Instead of one of three expected verbs, "to strike
down," "to kill," "to put to death," David uses the verb *hishḥit*, which basically
means "to destroy," but which can carry the association, as Kyle McCarter, Jr.,
rightly observes, of mutilation or defacement, the taboo acts that should not be
perpetrated on the person of the king.

11. *take . . . the spear.* In the episode at the cave, David carried away the cut-off
corner of Saul's garment, which had been symbolically linked with kingship.
The spear is an alternative image of kingship, obviously more directly associated with martial potency, and so this version conveys a greater sense that
David is depriving Saul of something essential in the token of kingship he bears
off. Again, the placement of this version of the paired episodes is telling, for the
next time we see Saul in the narrative he will be undone on the battlefield by
the Philistines and will turn his own weapon against himself.
    and the water jug. The spear protects life by destroying; the water jug sus-
tains life for the warrior in battle under the hot sun.

us go off." And David took the spear and the water jug at Saul's head,   12
and they went off, with no one seeing and no one knowing and no one
waking, for they were all asleep, for the LORD's deep slumber had fallen
upon them. And David crossed over to the opposite slope and stood on   13
the mountaintop from afar, great was the distance between them. And   14
David called out to the troops and to Abner son of Ner, saying, "Will
you not answer, Abner?" And Abner answered and said, "Who are you,
that you have called out to the king?" And David said to Abner, "Are you   15
not a man, and who is like you in Israel, and why have you not guarded
your lord the king? For one of the troops has come to do violence to the
king your lord. It is not good, this thing that you have done, as the LORD   16
lives, for you all deserve death, because you did not guard your master,
the LORD's anointed. And now, see, where are the king's spear and the

---

12. *And David took the spear and the water jug.* David takes them himself, after
having ordered Abishai to do it. The medieval Hebrew exegete David Kimchi
offers a shrewd explanation: "He changed his mind and didn't want Abishai to
approach the king, lest he prove unable to restrain himself and kill Saul."

14. *Who are you, that you have called out to the king?* Some ancient versions
omit "to the king" because David has called out to Abner, not to Saul. David's
shouting from the prominence, however, occurs in the middle of the night,
and it clearly has awakened Saul, which seems to be what is bothering Abner.
David has chosen Saul's commander as his first interlocutor in order to stress
the sacred responsibility of those around the king to protect his person. His
noble words are not devoid of self-interest because David is clearly conscious
of the fact that he is the future king.

15. *one of the troops has come to do violence to the king.* Although this could
refer to Abishai, the essential referent is David himself—something he does not
want to say in so many words.

16. *you all deserve death.* "All" is supplied in the translation in order to convey
the fact that here the pronoun "you" is a plural in the Hebrew. This death sentence pronounced on Saul's entire entourage is extravagant, but Abner at least
will die a violent death.

17 water jug that were at his head?" And Saul recognized David's voice and
he said, "Is this your voice, my son, David?" And David said, "It is my

18 voice, my lord the king." And he said, "Why is it that my lord chases
after his servant, for what have I done, and what evil is in my hand?

19 And now, let my lord the king hear, pray, the words of his servant. If the
LORD has incited you against me, let Him be appeased by an offering,
and if it be men, cursed are they before the LORD, for they have banished me today from joining the LORD's inheritance, saying, 'Go, serve

20 other gods.' And now, let not my blood fall to the ground away from the
LORD's presence, for the king of Israel has come forth to seek a single

21 flea, as he would chase a partridge in the mountains." And Saul said, "I

---

17. *Is this your voice, my son, David?* These are the identical words he pronounces outside the cave near Ein-Gedi. Here, he "recognizes" the voice—as,
symbolically, in this remission of his madness, he recognizes his paternal bond
with David—but he is not entirely sure because of the darkness, and so he asks.

18. *what evil is in my hand?* As elsewhere, "hand" and "in my hand" have multiple
valences. What David literally has in his hand as he speaks is the king's spear!

19. *If the LORD has incited . . . if it be men.* These two alternatives are a kind of
diplomatic maneuver. David doesn't want to put the blame squarely on Saul,
so he proposes that the king either was "incited" by God for some mysterious
reason or by malicious people.
    let Him be appeased by an offering. The Hebrew says literally, "let Him smell
[the fragrant odor of] an offering."
    banished me . . . from . . . the LORD's inheritance. The LORD's inheritance
clearly refers to the land of Israel. Since every national region had its own cult,
David is saying that to be excluded from his own national borders is tantamount
to being obliged to worship other gods. In fact, his flight from Saul has been
mostly within Israelite territory, but he seems to be anticipating that his next
move, for his own safety, will have to be into Philistine country.

20. *to seek a single flea, as he would chase a partridge in the mountains.* The
language of the entire clause recycles the words David used to conclude his
speech outside the cave. But the dead dog has been deleted and a partridge has
been introduced instead. This image is less forceful, but its attraction in the
Hebrew, as several commentators have noted, is a witty pun: partridge (*qore'*) is
a homonym for "he who calls out." David (verse 14) was identified by Abner as
the one who called out to the king—a caller out on the mountain, a partridge
pursued on the mountains.

have offended. Come back, my son, David, for I will not harm you again in as much as my life was precious in your eyes this day. I have played the fool and have erred gravely." And David answered and said, "Here is 22 the king's spear. Let one of the lads cross over and take it. And the LORD 23 will pay back to a man his right actions and his loyalty, for the LORD gave you today into my hand and I did not want to reach out my hand against the LORD's anointed. And, look, just as I valued your life highly 24 today, may the LORD value my life highly and may He save me from every strait." And Saul said to David, "Blessed are you, my son, David. 25 You shall surely do much and you shall surely win out." And David went on his way, but Saul returned to his place.

---

22. *And David answered and said, "Here is the king's spear."* It is noteworthy that David does not immediately respond to Saul's renewed profession of regret and good faith. (The Masoretic consonantal text, the *ketiv*, tries to rescue this lapse by representing these words as a vocative, "Here is the spear, king," but the *qeri*, or pronounced Masoretic version, properly renders it as *ḥanit hamelekh*, "the king's spear.") In the encounter at the cave, David vowed he would not harm Saul's descendants, though his actual words were not reported. Here, he first gives an impersonal order to have the spear brought back to Saul. It is only when he goes on to recapitulate his profession of innocence that he again addresses Saul. By this point, he no longer trusts any promises Saul may make not to harm him but hopes that God will note his own proper conduct and therefore protect him (verse 24).

24. *I valued your life highly.* The literal Hebrew idiom is "your life was great in my eyes."

25. *Blessed are you, my son, David.* These words of fatherly blessing are the last ones Saul speaks to David: the two never meet again. It is notable that in their previous encounter, Saul explicitly conceded that David would replace him as king, whereas here he merely says in general language, "You shall surely do much and you shall surely win out."
David went on his way, but Saul returned to his place. This is a biblical formula for marking the end of a narrative unit, but it also nicely distinguishes between the two men: David continues on the move while Saul goes back to his set place of residence.

CHAPTER 27

1   And David said in his heart, "Now, I shall perish one day by the hand of Saul. There is nothing better for me than to make certain I get away to Philistine country. Then Saul will despair of seeking me anymore 2 through all the territory of Israel, and I shall get away from him." And David arose, and he crossed over, he and the six hundred men who were 3 with him, to Achish son of Maoch, king of Gath. And David stayed with Achish in Gath, he and his men, each man with his household, David

---

1. *And David said in his heart.* This is the first actual interior monologue given for David. The decision to "cross over" (verse 2) to the enemy is a momentous one, and the writer wants to make it perfectly clear that David had definitely realized Saul was bound to kill him sooner or later ("I shall perish one day by the hand of Saul") unless he moved to the safety of enemy territory.

2. *he crossed over . . . to Achish . . . king of Gath.* For those scholars who have argued that David is no more a historical figure than King Arthur, this whole episode constitutes a problem: why would a much later, legendary, and supposedly glorifying tradition attribute this act of national treachery to David? (It would be rather like the invention of a story that Winston Churchill spent 1914–1918 in Berlin, currying the favor of the kaiser.) The compelling inference is that the writer had authentic knowledge of a period when David collaborated with the Philistines; he was unwilling to omit this uncomfortable information, though he did try to mitigate it.

3. *David stayed with Achish in Gath . . . each man with his household.* The circumstances have changed drastically since David arrived in Gath alone and was obliged to play the madman. Now he comes with six hundred men under his command, a fighting unit that could be of great use to Achish, and essentially offers to become Achish's vassal. The notice about the households sets the stage for the Amalekite raid on Ziklag in Chapter 29, for we now become aware that David's guerilla band carries in its train a sizable group of wives and children.

with his two wives, Ahinoam the Jezreelite and Abigail wife of Nabal
the Carmelite. And it was told to Saul that David had fled to Gath, and ₄
he no longer sought after him. And David said to Achish, "If, pray, I ₅
have found favor in your eyes, let them give me a place in one of the
outlying towns that I may dwell there. For why should your servant
dwell in the royal town with you?" And Achish gave him Ziklag on that ₆
day. Therefore has Ziklag belonged to the kings of Judah until this day.
And the span of time that David dwelled in Philistine country was a ₇
year and four months. And David went up, and his men with him, and ₈
they raided the Geshurite and the Gerizite and the Amalekite, for they
were the inhabitants of the land of old, till you come to Shur and to
the land of Egypt. And David struck the land, and he left not a man or ₉
woman alive, and he took sheep and cattle and donkeys and camels and

---

5. *For why should your servant dwell in the royal town with you?* On his part,
David would like to establish his own headquarters and enjoy much greater
freedom of movement. But given that his six hundred men with multiple
wives and children could easily have made up a group of two or three thousand people, they would have in fact been a rather burdensome presence in a
modest-sized Philistine city.

6. *Ziklag.* The best archeological guess is that this is a site a few miles to the
northwest of Beersheba, in an area under Philistine jurisdiction but facing the
border with Israel.
   Therefore has Ziklag belonged to the kings of Judah. This seemingly technical
geopolitical notice serves a function of historical foreshadowing, as Fokkelman
observes: David, the Philistine vassal and fugitive from Saul, is destined to
found a lasting dynasty, "the kings of Judah."

8. *for they were the inhabitants of the land of old, till you come to Shur.* There
might be a textual distortion here: several versions of the Septuagint read "the
inhabited land from Telem to Shur." But the Masoretic version has a certain
logic: what David sets out to do is to attack the age-old inhabitants of the land,
who are Israel's staunch enemies, throughout this southern region. In doing
this, he is also serving Achish's purposes, for these peoples are equally hostile
to the Philistines (like the Israelites, latecomer interlopers in Canaan).

9. *he left not a man or woman alive.* The narrator offers no indication of whether
he thinks these massacres are morally objectionable or merely what Israel's traditional enemies deserve. A pragmatic reason for the butchery will be given in
verse 11. It should be noted that David is not carrying out a total "ban" (*ḥerem*)

10 clothes, and he returned and came to Achish. And Achish said, "Where were you raiding now?" And David said, "The Negeb of Judah and the
11 Negeb of the Jerahmeelite and the Negeb of the Kenite." And neither man nor woman did David leave alive to bring to Gath, thinking, "Lest they tell about us, saying, 'Thus did David do.'" And such was his prac-
12 tice all the time he dwelled in Philistine country. And Achish trusted David, saying, "He has surely become repugnant to Israel and he will be my perpetual vassal."

---

against these groups because he keeps all the livestock as booty, thus palpably building up a base of wealth for himself and his followers.

10. *Where were you raiding now?* Achish of course wants to know about the military activities of his vassal. David answers with a flat lie, claiming he has been conducting raids against his own tribe, Judah, and against two ethnic groups more or less attached to Judah. In fact, he has been attacking only non-Israelite groups.
    The Negeb. The term Negeb means "dry land" and refers to the desert stretching across southern Israel from near the Dead Sea to near the coastal plain. Its subregions are then identified by the tribe or ethnic group that inhabits each.

11. *Lest they tell about us, saying, 'Thus did David do.'* David wipes out all these populations because he wants no one surviving to bring word back to Gath that he has restricted his attacks entirely to Canaanite and related peoples, and also that he has been enriching himself with more booty than he has been sharing with Achish his overlord by way of tribute. David is clearly a man who will do anything to survive. His words here will come back in a surprising new context in his elegy for Saul and Jonathan, when he says, "Tell it not in Gath."

12. *Achish trusted David.* He believes the lie, or so it seems.
    my perpetual vassal. The Hebrew *'eved* has the general meaning of "slave" or "servant," but the present episode makes the sense of "vassal" compelling.

And it happened at that time that the Philistines had gathered their 28:1
ranks for the army to do battle with Israel, and Achish said to David,
"You surely know that with me you must sally forth in the ranks, both
you and your men." And David said, "Then you yourself know what your 2
servant will do." And Achish said to David, "Then I shall make you my
bodyguard for life."

28:1 *You surely know that with me you must sally forth.* Despite the just reported
"trust" in David, Achish appears to harbor a lingering doubt (hence the coer-
cive edge of "you surely know") as to whether David will actually fight against
his fellow Israelites, something that, to Achish's knowledge, David has only
claimed to do (27:10).

2. *you yourself know what your servant will do.* This is an artful dodge: it could
be construed, as David means it to be construed, as "yes, of course, I'll do it,"
but the language evasively does not repeat Achish's words about sallying forth
(against Israel).

I shall make you my bodyguard for life. As befits a ruler addressing a former
enemy with whom he is in uneasy alliance, Achish's gesture is a studied ambiguity—either he is rewarding David for his loyalty by making him a permanent
bodyguard, or he is seeking to maintain surveillance over David by an appointment that would keep him close to the court.

CHAPTER 28

3   And Samuel had died, and all Israel mourned him, and they buried him in Ramah, in his town. And Saul had taken away the ghosts and the familiar spirits from the land.

4   And the Philistines gathered and came and camped at Shunem. And
5   Saul gathered all Israel and they camped at Gilboa. And Saul saw the

---

3. *And Samuel had died.* This second obituary notice for Samuel, with a pluperfect verb, is introduced in order to set the stage for the conjuration of Samuel's ghost.

Saul had taken away the ghosts and the familiar spirits from the land. The two Hebrew terms, *'ovot* and *yid'onim*, are generally paired, and both refer to the spirits of the dead. (The latter is derived from the verbal root *y-d-'* "to know," and so prepares the way for the reappearance of the theme of [withheld] knowledge that has been stalking Saul from the beginning of his story.) The ghosts and familiar spirits are linked metonymically with the necromancers who call them up—it is the latter who of course would have been the actual object of Saul's purge—but the terms themselves primarily designate the spirits. Biblical views about post-mortem existence tend to fluctuate. Often, the dead are thought to be swallowed up in "the Pit" (*she'ol*) where they are simply silenced, extinguished forever. Sometimes, the dead are imagined as continuing a kind of shadowy afterlife in the underworld, rather like the spirits of the dead in Book 11 of the Odyssey. Following on this latter view, necromancy in the ancient Hebrew world is conceived not as mere hocus-pocus but as a potentially efficacious technology of the realm of spirits, which, however, has been prohibited by God, Who wants no human experts interfering in this realm. Saul, then, has been properly upholding monotheistic law—reflected in Leviticus—in proscribing necromancy, but in his desperation, he is now about to violate his own prohibition.

Philistine camp, and he was afraid, and his heart trembled greatly. And 6
Saul inquired of the LORD, and the LORD did not answer him, neither by
dreams nor by the Urim nor by prophets. And Saul said to his servants, 7
"Seek me out a ghostwife, that I may go to her and inquire through her."
And his servants said to him, "There is a ghostwife at Ein-Dor." And 8
Saul disguised himself and put on different clothes, and he went—he
together with two men—and they came to the woman by night, and he
said, "Conjure me, pray, a ghost, and summon up the one I say to you."
And the woman said to him, "Look, you yourself know what Saul did, 9
that he cut off the ghosts and the familiar spirits from the land, and why
do you entrap me to have me put to death?" And Saul swore to her by 10
the LORD, saying, "As the LORD lives, no blame will befall you through

---

6. *the LORD did not answer*. One last time, Saul is excluded from divine knowledge, all the accepted channels for its conveyance, being enumerated here—
dream interpretation, oracular device, prophecy.

8. *Saul disguised himself and put on different clothes*. The narrative motivation is
obvious: as the very ruler who has made necromancy a capital crime (see verse
9), Saul can scarcely come to engage the services of a necromancer unless he
is disguised as a commoner. But his disguise also is the penultimate instance
of the motif of royal divestment. As we have seen, clothing is associated with
Saul's kingship—the torn or cut garment is the tearing of his kingship, and
among the ecstatics surrounding Samuel, Saul stripped himself naked. Now, in
an unwitting symbolic gesture, he divests himself of his royal garments before
going to learn of his own impending death.

9. *you yourself know*. An ironically emphatic use of "to know" to the man who
never knows what he needs to.
   he cut off the ghosts. In place of the more abstract term, "to take away," used
by the narrator in verse 3, she, from her perspective as a threatened practitio-
ner, chooses the violent verb, "to cut off."
   why do you entrap me. She uses the verb of entrapment with neat precision,
for she fears that the stranger who has come to her may be an undercover agent
for Saul's necromancy enforcement authority.

10. *Saul swore to her by the LORD*. The irony of Saul's doing this in a negotiation
with a conjurer of spirits is vividly caught by the Midrash: "Whom did Saul
resemble at that moment? A woman who is with her lover and swears by the
life of her husband" (Yalkut Shimoni 2:247:139).

11 this thing." And the woman said, "Whom shall I summon up for you?"
12 And he said, "Samuel summon up for me." And the woman saw Samuel
and she screamed in a loud voice, and the woman said to Saul, "Why
13 did you deceive me, when you are Saul?" And the king said to her, "Do
not fear. But what do you see?" And the woman said to Saul, "A god do

---

12. *the woman saw Samuel and she screamed in a loud voice*. What terrifies
her is not the apparition of Samuel but the sudden realization of the identity
of her nocturnal visitor. How does she know it is Saul? The most persuasive
explanation has been offered by Moshe Garsiel. As other biblical references to
conjuration of the dead suggest, the usual method would be for the necromancer to listen to and interpret the supposed "chirping" (*tsiftsuf*) or murmuring
sounds made by shadows or wispy wraiths believed to be the presences of the
dead. (There is scant biblical evidence for the claim that the necromancer was
a medium from whose throat the ghost spoke.) In this case, however, the spirit
appears not as a murmuring wisp or shadow but as the distinctly defined image
of Samuel, in his prophet's cloak (see verses 13–14), and the woman of Ein-Dor
immediately realizes that it is only for the king that the prophet Samuel would
have thus risen from the underworld in full-body image. It is noteworthy that
the narrator is discreetly silent about the actual mechanics of the conjuration
procedure, perhaps out of a kind of monotheistic reticence.

13. *Do not fear. But what do you see?* Saul assures her that even though he is the
very king who prohibited necromancy, he will stand by his vow that no blame
will be attached to her. What he urgently wants to know is the identity of the
conjured presences—she can see the spirit, but he cannot, so once more Saul
needs some mediation for the knowledge he seeks.
A god do I see rising up from the earth. The Hebrew balances precariously
on a linguistic ambiguity that has no happy English equivalent. The word for
"god" here is *'elohim*, which when treated grammatically as a singular (it has
a plural ending) usually means God. In the plural, it often refers to "gods" in
the polytheistic sense. It also occasionally means "angel" or "divine being," and
some have argued, unconvincingly, that it sometimes means "judge." A further
complication here is that the ghostwife uses *'elohim* with a plural participle
(and hence the King James Version renders it as "gods"). It seems likely that
the grammatical crossover we have just reviewed encouraged a fluidity of usage
in which the plural might sometimes be employed with a singular sense, even
when the referent was not the one God. In the immediately following question
and response between Saul and the woman, it is presupposed that she has seen
only one male figure, and the narrator has already told us she has seen Samuel.
When she says she sees *'elohim* rising up, she probably means an imposing
figure like unto a god or an angel, or perhaps she is using it as a term for "spirit."

I see rising up from the earth." And he said to her, "What does he look 14
like?" And she said, "An old man rises up, and he is wrapped in a cloak."
And Saul knew that it was Samuel, and he bowed to the ground and did
obeisance. And Samuel said, "Why have you troubled me to summon 15
me up?" And Saul said, "I am in dire straits, and the Philistines are
fighting against me and God has turned away from me and no longer
answers me, neither through prophets nor dreams, and I called to you
to let me know what I should do." And Samuel said, "And why do you 16
ask me, when the LORD has turned away from you and become your
foe? And the LORD has done to you as He spoke through me, and the 17
LORD has torn the kingship from your hand and given it to your fellow-

---

14. *wrapped in a cloak.* It is the cloak, *me'il,* that clinches the identification
for Saul—the same prophet's cloak that he clung to and tore. From childhood,
when Samuel's mother would make him a new *me'il* each year, to the grave,
Samuel is associated with this garment.

15. *Why have you troubled me . . . ?* In perfect character, Samuel begins by
addressing an angry question to Saul, using a verb that refers to disturbing a
person from sleep, or from the sleep of death. In divergence from the usual
necromantic procedure, the ghost of Samuel speaks directly to Saul, who in
turn questions Samuel himself. In fact, the ghostwife appears to have absented
herself at this point, for the indication in verse 21, "And the woman came to
Saul and saw that he was very distraught," is that she is returning to the room
after having left it.

*I am in dire straits, and the Philistines are fighting . . . and God has turned
away . . . and I called to you.* The desperate Saul spills out all the causes for his
desperation in one breathless run-on sentence, which this translation tries to
reproduce.

neither through prophets nor dreams. Addressing a prophet, Saul makes
prophecy the first item. He deletes the Urim—perhaps, it has been suggested,
because of his guilty recollection of his massacre of the priests at Nob.

16. *why do you ask me . . . ?* Once again, in this case sardonically, there is a play
on Saul's name (*Sha'ul*) and the verb "to ask" (*sha'al*).

17. *the LORD has torn the kingship from your hand.* As this particular clause highlights, Samuel's entire speech is a recapitulation of the denunciatory speech
he made to Saul at the end of the Amalek episode (Chapter 15). The tearing
of the kingship "from your hand" visually recalls Saul's hand grasping the torn

18 man, to David. In as much as you did not heed the voice of the LORD
and you did not carry out His burning wrath against Amalek, therefore
19 has the LORD done this thing to you this day! And the LORD shall give
Israel, too, together with you, into the hands of the Philistines. And
tomorrow—you and your sons are with me. The camp of Israel, too,
20 shall the LORD give into the hand of the Philistines." And Saul hastened
and flung himself full length on the ground and was very frightened by

---

skirt of Samuel's cloak. There, Samuel had said God would give the throne to
"your fellowman, who is better than you." Now, of course, he can spell out the
name David.

18. *you did not heed the voice of the LORD.* The phrasal motif of "heeding the
voice" from Chapter 15 is again invoked. After Samuel's return to the underworld, the woman of Ein-Dor, on a purely mundane plane, will speak twice
about heeding voices (verses 21–22).

19. *And tomorrow—you and your sons are with me.* Saul, having come to seek
advice on the eve of a great battle, is given a denunciation concluding with a
death sentence, conveyed in these words with spooky immediacy, as the ghost
of Samuel beckons Saul and his sons down into the underworld. This entire
scene is conceivably one of the inspirations for Macbeth's encounter with the
three witches, though the biblical writer, in contrast to Shakespeare, places it
at the penultimate moment of his doomed king's story.
   The camp of Israel, too . . . There is no need to perform textual surgery on
this sentence simply because it repeats the burden of the first sentence of the
verse. It would be perfectly in character for Samuel to rub in the news of the
imminent catastrophe: not only will you and your sons perish, but, as I have
said, all your forces will be defeated by the Philistines, your kingship ending
in wholesale failure.

20. *Saul hastened and flung himself full length on the ground.* Most translators
have interpreted the second verb here as an involuntary one ("fell"). But the
verb "to hasten" (*miher*) is generally part of a sequence of voluntary actions,
as its use in verse 24 ("and she hastened and butchered it and took") neatly
illustrates. Saul, in his terror and despair, flings himself to the ground, and
then scarcely has the strength to get up. The Hebrew for "full length" includes
the component *qomah*, "stature," and so is a reminder that the man of majestic
stature is now cast to the ground in final defeat.

Samuel's words. Neither did he have strength, for he had eaten no food all day and all night. And the woman came to Saul and saw that he was 21 very distraught, and she said to him, "Look, your servant has heeded your voice, and I took my life in my hands and heeded your words that you spoke to me. And now, you on your part, pray heed the voice of your 22 servant, and I shall put before you a morsel of bread, and eat, that you may have strength when you go on the way." And he refused and said, 23 "I will not eat." And his servants pressed him, and the woman as well, and he heeded their voice and arose from the ground and sat upon the couch. And the woman had a stall-fed calf in the house. And she has- 24 tened and butchered it and took flour and kneaded it and baked it into flatbread, and set it before Saul and before his servants, and they ate, 25 and they arose and went off on that night.

---

for he had eaten no food. There is no convincing evidence to support the claim of some scholars that a person had to fast before seeing a necromancer. Perhaps Saul's fasting is a reflex of his distraught condition, but he may well be fasting because he is about to enter into battle. (It appears that his two bodyguards have also not eaten.) This would invite a connection, which has been made by both Fokkelman and Garsiel, with the vow of abstinence from food that Saul earlier imposed on his troops (Chapter 15). There, he was ready to put Jonathan to death for having tasted a bit of honey; here, he will end by partaking of a feast.

22. *a morsel of bread.* She says this to play down what she will serve him, which is a hearty dinner, with a main course of veal.

24. *the woman had a stall-fed calf.* It would have taken several hours to accomplish this slaughtering and cooking and baking. One must imagine Saul sitting in the house at En-Dor, brooding or darkly baffled or perhaps a little catatonic. It is an odd and eerie juncture of the story. David has already twice been saved, from death and then from blood guilt, by women. Saul is now given sustaining nurture by a woman—but only to regain the strength needed to go out to the battlefield where he will die.

CHAPTER 29

And the Philistines gathered all their camps at Aphek, while Israel was
2   encamped by the spring in Jezreel. And the Philistine overlords were
    advancing with hundreds and with thousands, and David and his men
3   were advancing at the rear with Achish. And the Philistine captains said,

---

1. *the Philistines gathered all their camps at Aphek.* The "all" stresses that this is a
massing of the entire Philistine army, not merely a division or two, for a decisive
confrontation with the Israelites. As Polzin notes, the first major clash with the
Philistines in 1 Samuel began with the Philistines' camping at Aphek (4:1), so
the mention of their encampment here at the same site creates a kind of symmetrical frame for the book. Aphek is roughly forty miles south of Jezreel, not
far from Philistine territory, and would have served as a general staging ground.
The Philistine army then advances northward to camp at Shunem (27:4), just
opposite Saul's forces at the spring of Jezreel and near Mount Gilboa.

2. *David and his men were advancing at the rear with Achish.* Given David's
double role as Achish's vassal and as his special bodyguard, his position in battle
should have been alongside Achish. Until this mention of David, we might have
imagined that the report of the deployment of forces was a direct continuation
of the account of Saul's seance at Ein-Dor on the night before the battle. Now
it rapidly becomes clear that the narrative has again switched tracks from Saul
to David, suspending the fulfillment of Saul's dire fate in order to follow the
movement of his successor, who approaches the very same battlefield as part
of the enemy forces, only to be turned away. The switch in narrative focus
also involves backtracking in time: we left Saul in the dark of the night (also a
symbolic darkness for him); the deployment of armies and the Philistine dialogues take place on the previous day; David's early departure, "just when it is
brightening" (an antithesis to Saul in the dark, as Fokkelman notes), will be on
the morning of the battle.

3. *the Philistine captains.* These are the military commanders, *sarim*, and they
should not be thought of as synonymous with the overlords (*seranim*) of the

"Who are these Hebrews?" And Achish said to the Philistine captains, "Is this not David, servant of Saul king of Israel, who has been with me these many days or years, and I have found nothing amiss in him from the day he fell in with me until this day?" And the Philistine captains 4 were furious with him, and the Philistine captains said to him, "Send the man back and let him go back to his place that you set aside for him there, and let him not come down with us into battle, so that he become not our adversary in battle. For how would this fellow be reconciled with his master—would it not be with the heads of our men? Is this not David 5 for whom they sing out in the dances, saying,

'Saul has struck down his thousands,
and David his tens of thousands'?"

---

five Philistine cities. It is the military men who, understandably, fear a serious security risk in the presence of a Hebrew contingent in their ranks.

Who are these Hebrews? The Hebrew is literally "What are these Hebrews?", which many translations interpret as "What are these Hebrews doing here?" Again, "Hebrews" is the term used by foreigners for the Israelites.

David, servant of Saul king of Israel. Achish means to stress that Saul's former courtier and commander has defected to the Philistine side, but his choice of words inadvertently reminds the Philistine captains that David may still be loyal to Saul.

these many days or years. Some scholars suspect that these two terms reflect a conflated text, and that one should simply read "these many days." It could, however, make sense for Achish to be a little vague about the time and to exaggerate it in order to emphasize David's loyalty—in fact, David has been with him one year and two months.

fell in with me. Kyle McCarter, Jr., proposes that the verb has the sense of "to defect."

4. *would it not be with the heads of our men?* They actually use a euphemism, "the heads of these men," in order to avoid pronouncing a terrible fate on themselves. Perhaps another euphemism is involved, through upward displacement, since in Chapter 18 it was a different part of the anatomy of the slain Philistines that David brought back to Saul.

6 And Achish called to David and said to him, "As the LORD lives, you
are upright, and your going into the fray with the camp has been good
in my eyes, for I have found no evil in you from the day you came to
me until this day. But in the eyes of the Philistine overlords you are not
7 good. And so now, return, and go in peace, and you shall do no evil in the
8 eyes of the Philistine overlords." And David said to Achish, "But what
have I done, and what have you found in your servant from the day I
appeared in your presence until this day, that I should not come and do

---

6. *As the* LORD *lives*. It is curious that a Philistine should be swearing by the
LORD, unless, as has been argued, he is leaning over backward to adopt David's
perspective.

you are upright. In fact, David has been lying to Achish about the object of
his raids (27:8–11).

good in my eyes . . . I have found no evil in you. This entire exchange turns
on the neat antithesis between good and evil, rather like the exchange between
Saul and David outside the cave near Ein-Gedi. Achish will go on to say, quite
extravagantly, that David is "as good in my eyes as a messenger of God" (verse
9). The reader, however, may well wonder whether David is in fact so unambiguously good.

in the eyes of the Philistine overlords you are not good. Some scholars, following the Septuagint, read here "you are good," contending that Achish claims a
difference of opinion between the overlords and the captains. It makes better
sense simply to assume that he is referring the negative view of David to the
highest echelon of authority, though in fact the complaint came from the field
commanders.

8. *what have I done . . . that I should not . . . do battle with the enemies of
my lord the king?* Continuing to play the role of the perfect Philistine vassal,
David protests his eagerness to fight the Israelites, though in point of fact he
must be immensely relieved to escape from the intolerable position of battling against his own people. As several interpreters have noticed, the words he
archly chooses have a double edge because "my lord the king" could be a covert
reference to Saul, in which case the "enemies" would be the armies of Achish
and his confederates. Whether David, lacking this providential way out, would
really have pitted himself against his own people is another imponderable in
the character of this elusive figure.

from the day I appeared in your presence. The idiomatic force of the phrase
is, "from the day I entered your service." Achish had simply said, "from the day
you came to me."

battle with the enemies of my lord the king?" And Achish answered and 9
said to David, "I know that you are as good in my eyes as a messenger of
God. But the Philistine captains have said, 'He shall not go up with us
to battle.' And so now, rise early in the morning, you and the servants of 10
your lord who have come with you, and rise early in the morning when
it is just brightening for you, and go." And David rose early, he and his 11
men, to go in the morning to return to Philistine country, while the Philistines went up to Jezreel.

---

10. *you and the servants of your lord*. The translation follows the reading in the
Septuagint. The Masoretic text, a little less coherently, lacks "you."

11. *to Philistine country*. They are in fact headed to the place Achish has "set
aside" for them at the eastern border of Philistine country—the town of Ziklag.
Disaster awaits them there.

CHAPTER 30

₁ And it happened when David and his men came to Ziklag on the third
day that the Amalekites had raided the Negeb, and Ziklag, and they
₂ had struck Ziklag and burned it in fire. And they had taken the women
captive, from the youngest to the oldest, they put no one to death. And

---

1. *on the third day*. If, as seems plausible, David and his men were sent away
from the Philistine ranks just before the engagement with the Israelites, the
battle, ending in the catastrophic defeat of Saul's forces, took place while David
was traveling southward. The writer, it seems, wants to get David as far away
as he can from the battlefield in the Valley of Jezreel, perhaps to remove him
from any possible implication in Saul's death. But an indirect question lurks
in the margin of the narrative, for we are left to wonder what would have been
the outcome of the battle had David turned against his Philistine allies, as their
field commanders feared he would.

the Amalekites had raided the Negeb, and Ziklag. David must initially confront a military disaster on his own home front that mirrors the disaster which,
unknown to him, has unfolded in the north. His habitual enemies, the Amalekites, have of course exploited the absence of the fighting men at Ziklag.

burned it in fire. It is possible , though not entirely certain, that the idiomatic
force of this seemingly redundant idiom, which occurs frequently, is "utterly
consumed," "burned to the ground."

2. *they put no one to death*. At first blush this notice casts a favorable light on
the Amalekites in comparison to David, whose practice as a raider has been
general massacre of the conquered population. What becomes clear, however,
is that the Amalekites (who do not have David's motive of secrecy) consider the
women and children to be part of the booty and have carried them off in order
to exploit them as slaves. The appearance of the Egyptian man (verse 11) serves
as a reminder of the Amalekites' role as slaveholders, and of how inhumanely
they treat their slaves.

they drove them off and went on their way. And David, and his men with   3
him, came to the town, and, look, it was burned in fire, and their wives
and their sons and their daughters were taken captive. And David, and   4
the troops who were with him, raised their voices and wept until there
was no strength left in them to weep. And David's two wives were taken   5
captive, Ahinoam the Jezreelite and Abigail wife of Nabal the Carmelite.
And David was in dire straits, for the troops thought to stone him, for all   6
the troops were embittered, every man over his sons and his daughters.
And David took strength in the Lord his God. And David said to Abiathar   7
the priest, son of Ahimelech, "Bring forth, pray, the ephod." And Abiathar brought forth the ephod to David. And David inquired of the Lord,   8
saying, "Shall I pursue this raiding party? Shall I overtake it?" And He
said, "Pursue, for you will surely overtake it, and you will surely rescue."

---

they drove them off. This rather brutal verb is typically used for driving animals as in verse 20, and so highlights the rapaciousness of the Amalekites.

6. *And David was in dire straits, for the troops thought to stone him.* The initial
phrase might momentarily be construed as referring to David's feelings ("and
he felt very distressed"), but it is immediately made clear that the reference
is to the practical predicament in which he suddenly finds himself in relation
to his men. As before, David's real emotions remain opaque—we know only
of his participation in the public orgy of weeping. This moment is also a vivid
reminder, as are others in the Saul-David story, of how precarious political
power is: David, the charismatic and brilliant commander who has led his men
through a host of dangers, suddenly discovers that these hard-bitten warriors
are ready to kill him because of the disastrous turn of events. It was he, after all,
who drew them to the north with the Philistine army, leaving Ziklag exposed.
    David took strength in the Lord his God. He finds encouragement in the face
of mortal despair—specifically, as the next verse explains, by calling for the
oracle. In this fashion, he staves off the assault his men are contemplating by
dramatically showing that they still have means of redress against the Amalekites, and that he has a special channel of communication with God.

7. *Bring forth, pray, the ephod.* As several interpreters have observed, there is an
antithetical contrast here between David, who has priest and ephod to convey
to him God's oracular counsel, and Saul, who, frustrated in all his attempts to
discover God's intentions, resorts to forbidden necromancy.

8. *you will surely rescue.* The ephod, as we have noted before, can yield only a
binary yes-or-no answer, so the gist of the oracle is that David should pursue the

9 And David went, he and the six hundred men who were with him, and
10 they came to the Wadi Besor, and those to be left stayed behind. And
     David continued the pursuit, he and four hundred men, and the two
     hundred men who were too exhausted to cross the Wadi Besor stayed
11 behind. And they found an Egyptian man in the field and took him to
     David, and they gave him bread and he ate, and they gave him water.
12 And they gave him a slice of pressed figs and two raisin cakes. And he
     ate, and his spirits revived, for he had eaten no bread and drunk no

---

raiding party. But rescuing the captives, which is surely paramount in the minds
of the embittered guerilla fighters, was not an explicit part of David's inquiry of
the oracle—perhaps because he was afraid to presume so much. The "yes" from
the oracle is now taken to imply that David and his men will both overtake the
raiders and rescue their dear ones.

9. *those to be left stayed behind.* The first phrase (literally, "the ones being left")
has bothered some commentators, but it is in keeping with occasional biblical
usage to introduce this sort of proleptic reference, creating what from a modern
point of view is a redundancy between the first and second phrases.

10. *were . . . exhausted.* The verb *piger* may be related to the noun *peger*, corpse,
and so would have the sense of "dead tired." It should be kept in mind that
David and his men had been traveling three days from the Philistine camp,
and now they have had to continue on into the desert at top speed in order to
overtake the raiding party.

11. *they found an Egyptian man in the field.* This is the first of three memorable
instances in the David story in which a foreigner brings intelligence of a dire
event, although in this case the subject of the intelligence is not the event itself
but the whereabouts of the perpetrators.

12. *for he had eaten no bread and drunk no water.* The act of abandoning a sick
slave in the desert to perish of thirst and hunger dispels any illusions we may
have harbored about the humanity of the Amalekites. Fokkelman has proposed
a correspondence (in his calculation, also a synchronicity) between the starving
Egyptian and the fasting Saul at Ein-Dor.

water three days and three nights. And David said to him, "To whom do 13
you belong, and where are you from?" And he said, "I am an Egyptian
lad, the slave of an Amalekite man, and my master abandoned me, for I
have been sick now three days. We on our part had raided the Negeb of 14
the Cherethites and that of Judah and the Negeb of Caleb, and Ziklag
we burned in fire." And David said to him, "Will you lead me down to 15
this raiding party?" And he said, "Swear to me by God that you will not
put me to death and that you will not hand me over to my master. Then
I shall lead you down to this raiding party." And he led him down, and, 16
look, they were sprawled out all over the ground eating and drinking and
reveling with all the vast booty they had taken from the land of the Philistines and the land of Judah. And David struck them from daybreak till 17
the evening of the next day, and not a man of them got away except for
four hundred lads who rode off on camels and fled. And David rescued 18
all that the Amalekites had taken, and his own two wives David rescued.
And nothing of theirs was missing, from the youngest to the oldest, from 19
sons to daughters to booty, all that they had taken for themselves, David

---

13. *I am an Egyptian lad.* The term "lad" (*na'ar*) does not necessarily indicate
chronological age here but rather subservient status, a decorous synonym for
"slave," which the Egyptian proceeds to use.

16. *and, look, they were sprawled out.* The presentative "look" (*hineh*) as an indicator of transition from the narrator's overview to the character's point of view
has particular tactical importance here. The Amalekites, as we can infer from
the fact that four hundred escape the general slaughter, must number well over
a thousand. David arrives with only four hundred men. But he finds the raiders
entirely vulnerable to a surprise attack—drunk, sated, and sleeping (rather like
the Hessian mercenaries whom Washington caught unawares by the Delaware
after their Christmas feast). The term rendered as "sprawled out" (*netushim*)
derives from a verbal root that means to abandon or cast away, and so in this
context suggests some kind of dissipation. The people who left the Egyptian
to starve to death in the desert are now exposed to destruction through their
unrestrained indulgence in food and drink.

17. *four hundred lads.* Again, the versatile *na'ar* is not an indication of chronological age but is used in its military sense, which appears to be something like
"elite troops," or perhaps simply "fighting men."

20 restored it all. And David took all the sheep and the cattle. They drove before them that livestock and said, "This is David's booty."

21 And David came to the two hundred men who had been too exhausted to go with David, so he had them stay at the Wadi Besor. And they came out to greet David and to greet the troops who were with him, and David
22 approached with the troops and asked how they fared. And every wicked and worthless man of the men who had gone with David spoke up and said, "In as much as they did not go with us, we will give them nothing from the booty that we rescued, only each man his wife and his children,
23 that they may drive them off and go." And David said, "You must not do so, my brothers, with what the LORD has given us. For He has guarded us and has given into our hands the raiding party that came against us.

---

20. *They drove before them that livestock.* The Masoretic text has the syntactically problematic "before that livestock" (*lifney hamiqneh hahu'*). This translation is based on a small emendation, *lifneyhem* ("before them"), assuming a haplography—an inadvertent scribal deletion of repeated letters, since the last two letters of *lifneyhem* (*heh* and *mem*) are also the first two letters of *hamiqneh*.

This is David's booty. Since the Amalekites had been raiding throughout the Negeb, both in Judahite and Philistine territory, they would have assembled a very large collection of plundered flocks. Thus David has abundant livestock to distribute as "gifts"—the word also means "blessing" or "greeting"—to the sundry elders of Judah.

21. *he had them stay.* The Masoretic text has "they had them stay" (a difference of one vowel). The Septuagint has the singular subject.

22. *that they may drive them off.* The coarseness of the ill-spirited men is reflected in the verb they use for taking away the wives and children, *nahag*, which, as we have noted, usually means to drive cattle. (Compare the irate Lot's use of the same verb in reference to Jacob's treatment of Rachel and Leah, Genesis 31:26.)

23. *with what the LORD has given us.* The syntactical link of this clause with what precedes is not entirely clear. Given the ideology of victory that David assumes—all triumph and all spoils of war come from God—it is best to construe the particle *'et* that introduces the clause not as a sign of the accusative but as "with."

And who would listen to you in this matter? Rather, as the share of him 24
who goes down into battle is the share of him who stays with the gear,
together shall they share." And so from that day hence it became a set 25
practice in Israel until this day. And David came to Ziklag and he sent 26
from the booty to the elders of Judah, to his friends, saying, "Here is a
gift for you from the booty of the LORD's enemies," to those in Bethel, 27
and to those in Ramoth-Negeb, and to those in Jattir, and to those in 28
Aroer, and to those in Siphmoth, and to those in Eshtamoa, and to those 29
in Racal, and to those in the towns of the Jerahmeelite, and to those in
the towns of the Kenite, and to those in Hormah, and to those in Bor- 30
Ashan, and to those in Athach, and to those in Hebron and in all the 31
places where David, with his men, had moved about.

---

24. *who stays with the gear.* There is an implicit rationale for giving an equal
share to those who remain behind—beyond the consideration of exhaustion,
they have played a role in guarding the gear, thus enabling the other fighting
men to proceed to battle with a lightened load. It is for this reason that David
"had them stay" (or "posted them") at the ford of the wadi. In all respects, this
episode is meant to demonstrate David's attributes as leader: he finds strength
in the face of disaster, consults God's oracle, intrepidly leads his troops in a
counterattack, and now makes the most equitable arrangement for the division
of spoils.

26. *he sent from the booty to the elders of Judah, to his friends.* This act shows
David the consummate political man, shoring up support among the sundry
leaders of his home tribe of Judah (hence the catalogue of place-names), and
preparing for himself a base in Hebron (at the end of the catalogue), the principal town of Judah, where he will soon be proclaimed king. Some scholars
have been troubled by "to his friends" (*lerei'eihu*, which would normally mean
"to his friend") and have sought to emend it. Kimchi, however, persuasively
argues that the ostensibly singular noun can be legitimately read as a plural on
the basis of other biblical precedents, and that the reference to "friends" makes
good political sense: these are the same elders of Judah who provided cover for
David during the period when he was hiding out from Saul in his own tribal
territory. The verb "move about" (*hithalekh*) in the wrap-up verse of this section
is an allusion to precisely this period, for it recalls David's flight with his men
from Saul at Keilah in 23:13—"and they moved about wherever they could."

CHAPTER 31

1   And meanwhile the Philistines were battling against Israel, and the men of Israel fled before the Philistines, and they fell slain on Mount 2 Gilboa. And the Philistines followed hard upon Saul and his sons, and the Philistines struck down Jonathan and Abinadab and Malkishua, the 3 sons of Saul. And the battle went heavy against Saul, and the archers, the bowmen, found him, and he quaked with fear of the archers.

---

1. *And meanwhile the Philistines were battling.* The Hebrew does not explicitly say "meanwhile," but it is implied by the unusual use of the participial form of the verb (literally, "are battling") to begin the narrative unit. Rashi neatly catches the effect: "As when a person says, 'Let us return to the previous subject.'"

3. *the archers, the bowmen.* It has been argued that the duplication reflects a conflation of two textual variants, but it may be that the writer intended to highlight the use of the bow, in contrast to other weapons. In characteristics biblical fashion, the narrative offers no details of the battle, but the following broad outline can be reconstructed: The major engagement of forces takes place in the Jezreel Valley, to the northwest of Mount Gilboa. The level ground of the valley would have given the Philistines the opportunity to deploy their iron chariots, one of their great strategic advantages over the Israelites. In the rout of the Israelites that ensues, Saul's forces retreat to the high ground of Mount Gilboa, where the Philistine chariots would have greater difficulty maneuvering. But the Philistines send contingents of archers—the bow being the ideal weapon to use against an army in flight—who exact heavy casualties from the Israelite forces.
   he quaked with fear. A revocalization of the verb favored by many scholars yields "he was badly wounded." But there is much to be said for the Masoretic vocalization: Saul's fear has been a recurring theme in the narrative; here it would be matched by the armor bearer's great fear of violating the king; and it is far from clear that Saul is seriously wounded when he decides to commit suicide (if he were, would he have the strength to fling himself on his sword?).

And Saul said to his armor bearer, "Draw your sword and run me through with it, lest these uncircumcised come and run me through and abuse me." But the armor bearer did not want to do it because he was very frightened, and Saul took the sword and fell upon it. And the armor bearer saw that Saul was dead, and he, too, fell upon his sword, and he died with him. And Saul died, and his three sons and his armor bearer, and all his men as well, together on that day. And the men of Israel who were on the other side of the valley and on the other side of the Jordan saw that the men of Israel had fled and that Saul and his sons were dead, and they abandoned the towns and fled, and the Philistines came and occupied them.

And it happened the next day that the Philistines came to strip the slain, and they found Saul and his three sons fallen on Mount Gilboa. And they cut off his head and stripped him of his armor, and they sent

4. *and abuse me.* Like the urgent request of the dying Abimelech in Judges 9, with whom the dying Saul has sometimes been compared, Saul's last wish will be denied him—the Philistines, though deprived of the opportunity to kill him, will decapitate his body and defile it by hammering it up on the wall of Beth-Shan.

6. *and all his men as well.* The parallel texts in both 1 Chronicles 10 and in the Septuagint lack this phrase. The argument for it is that it reinforces the image of martial solidarity in defeat: Saul, his sons, his armor bearer, his men, all perish "together" (*yaḥdaw*).

7. *they abandoned the towns . . . and the Philistines came and occupied them.* After this major victory, the Philistines manage to cut the Israelite settlement in two by establishing a sedentary presence across the lower Galilee from the coastal plain to the Jordan, separating the tribes in the far north from Benjamin and Judah to the south.

9. *they cut off his head and stripped him of his armor.* Saul's successor David had marked his entry on the scene by cutting off the head of a Philistine; now they cut off Saul's head. The stripping of the armor—and the all-purpose Hebrew *kelim* could also include his clothing—is the final divestment of Saul, who is stripped before the prophets, stripped of his royal garments at Ein-Dor, and now lies naked on the battlefield in ultimate defeat.
    they sent throughout the Philistine country. There is some grammatical ambiguity as to whether they simply sent tidings, or Saul's armor as visible token of the victory. The parallel verse in Chronicles lacks "temples of."

throughout the Philistine country to bring the tidings to the temples of
10 their idols and to the people. And they put his armor in the temple of
11 Ashtaroth, and his body they impaled on the wall of Beth-Shan. And
the inhabitants of Jabesh-Gilead heard what the Philistines had done
12 to Saul. And every valiant fellow arose, and they went all night long,
and they took Saul's corpse, and the corpses of his sons from the wall of
13 Beth-Shan, and they came back to Jabesh and burned them there. And
they took their bones and buried them under the tamarisk in Jabesh,
and they fasted seven days.

---

10. *his body they impaled on the wall of Beth-Shan.* Throughout the ancient
Mediterranean world, there was a horror about leaving a corpse unburied (compare, for example, the potency of this question in Sophocles' *Antigone*). Saul's
corpse, moreover, is disfigured through decapitation. Beth-Shan (or, Beth-
She'an) is a town about eleven miles to the southwest of Mount Gilboa, near
the Jordan.

11. *the inhabitants of Jabesh-Gilead.* This settlement is roughly another twelve
miles to the southeast of Beth-Shan, on the eastern side of the Jordan, and
hence just beyond the perimeter of the new Philistine occupation. It was
Jabesh-Gilead that Saul rescued from Nahash the Ammonite (Chapter 11) to
inaugurate his career as king and general, and there are kinship bonds between
Jabesh-Gilead and Saul's tribe of Benjamin.

12. *every valiant fellow arose.* It would have been a very dangerous exploit to
sneak into the territory now controlled by the Philistines and, under the cover
of night, to make off with the corpses.
the corpses of his sons. This is an amplification of the Philistine atrocity, since
we were not previously informed that the bodies of the sons were impaled along
with Saul's.
and burned them there. Cremation was not the usual Israelite practice, but
it may be, as Kimchi has proposed, that in this case the bodies were burned
because the flesh had already begun to rot.

13. *and they fasted seven days.* This, too, is an unusual practice as a mourning rite. Perhaps it merely reflects the grievousness of the loss that the men
of Jabesh-Gilead have experienced, though Fokkelman makes the interesting
proposal that the seven days of fasting are a counterpart to the seven days
Nahash the Ammonite allowed Jabesh-Gilead for a deliverer (who turned out
to be Saul) to appear.

2 Samuel

CHAPTER 1

Ａnd it happened after the death of Saul, when David had returned 1
from striking down Amalek, that David stayed in Ziklag two days. And it 2
happened on the third day that, look, a man was coming from the camp,
from Saul, his garments torn and earth on his head. And it happened
when he came to David, that he fell to the ground and did obeisance.
And David said to him, "From where do you come?" And he said, "From 3
the camp of Israel I have gotten away." And David said to him "What has 4
happened? Pray, tell me." And he said, "The troops fled from the battle,
and also many of the troops have fallen and died, and also Saul and
Jonathan his son died." And David said to the lad who was telling him, 5

---

1. *after the death of Saul . . . David had returned from striking down Amalek.*
As the story unfolds, an odd symmetry emerges: David has just struck down
Amalek; an Amalekite says he has struck down Saul; David has this Amalekite
put to death.

2. *look, a man was coming . . . his garments torn and earth on his head.* The "look"
signals the visual perspective of David and his entourage: what they see is a
man who has adopted the most visible signs of conventional mourning. The
Amalekite wants to make it clear that he regards Saul's death, and the defeat,
as a catastrophe, though, as we shall see, he really has another purpose in mind.

4. *What has happened?* The words he uses, *meh hayah hadavar,* are identical
with those spoken to the messenger who brings the news of the disastrous
defeat to Eli in 1 Samuel 4:16. There are several other echoes here of that
earlier scene.

5. *the lad who was telling him.* The triple repetition of this phrase, as Fokkelman
has noted, calls attention to the act of telling and by underlining that act may
make us wonder whether this is an authentic report or a fabrication.

6 "How do you know that Saul died, and Jonathan his son?" And the lad
who was telling him said, "I just chanced to be on Mount Gilboa, and,
look, Saul was leaning on his spear, and, look, chariots and horsemen
7 had overtaken him. And he turned round behind him and saw me and
8 called to me, and I said, 'Here I am.' And he said to me, 'Who are you?'
9 And I said to him, 'I am an Amalekite.' And he said to me, 'Pray, stand
over me and finish me off, for the fainting spell has seized me, for while
10 life is still within me. . . .' And I stood over him and finished him off,

---

6. *I just chanced to be on Mount Gilboa.* Does one accidentally stumble onto a
battlefield while the killing is still going on? A more likely scenario is that the
Amalekite came onto the battlefield immediately after the fighting as a scav-
enger, found Saul's corpse before the Philistines did, and removed the regalia.

  Saul was leaning on his spear. From Saul's words in verse 9, what this means
is not that he was resting but that he was entirely spent, barely able to stand.

8. *I am an Amalekite.* Only now, in the middle of the story, is the national identity of the messenger revealed. The fact that he was an Amalekite means he
would have felt no recoil of taboo about doing violence to the king of Israel—
something Saul appears to grasp at once. (Compare Doeg the Edomite's slaughter of the priests of Nob in 1 Samuel 22.) But there is also dramatic irony here:
Saul lost his hold on the kingship when he failed to kill the Amalekite king; now
he begs an Amalekite to kill him, the king of Israel.

9. *Pray, stand over me and finish me off.* "Stand over" suggests that Saul himself
is barely standing, that he is collapsed against the support of his spear—the
very spear that has been associated with his kingship and with his outbursts of
rage. "Finish me off" is somewhat inelegant as English diction, but the nuance
of the Hebrew (the *polel* conjugation of the verbal stem that means "to die") is
essential to the story: Saul feels he is dying, and he asks the Amalekite lad not
to kill him but to finish him off before the Philistines can get to him. The Amalekite and David concur in this indication of what the Amalekite does to Saul.

  the fainting spell. The Hebrew noun appears only here. It may be related to
a root that suggests "confusion," or, alternately, "weakness."

  for while life is still within me. This clause, which has vexed some critics and
has led to emendations, is most simply construed as a broken-off sentence that
the failing Saul does not have the strength to complete.

10. *I stood over him and finished him off.* This whole story obviously contradicts
the account of Saul's death by his own hand in 1 Samuel 31. Predictably, this

for I knew that he could not live after having fallen. And I took the diadem that was on his head and the band that was on his arm, and I have brought them here to my lord." And David took hold of his gar- 11 ments and tore them, and all the men who were with him did so, too. And they keened and they wept and they fasted till evening for Saul 12 and for Jonathan his son and for the LORD's people and for the house of Israel because they had fallen by the sword. And David said to the lad 13 who had told him, "From where are you?" And he said, "The son of an Amalekite sojourner am I." And David said to him, "How were you not 14 afraid to reach out your hand to do violence to the LORD's anointed?" And 15 David called to one of the lads and said, "Come forward, stab him." And he struck him down, and he died. And David said to him, "Your blood 16 is on your own head, for your mouth bore witness against you, saying, 'I

---

has led many critics to imagine two conflicting "sources." It is reassuring that more recent scholarly consensus has come to the sensible conclusion that the Amalekite lad is lying. Having come upon Saul's body, he sees a great opportunity for himself: he will bring Saul's regalia to David, claim personally to have finished off the man known to be David's archenemy and rival, and thereby overcome his marginality as resident alien ("sojourner," *ger*) by receiving a benefaction from the new king—perhaps a portion of land at David's disposal. Fokkelman shrewdly notes that the Amalekite, instead of removing the diadem and armband from Saul's body, might better have buried the body or dragged it off and so saved it from desecration by the Philistines.

for I knew that he could not live after having fallen. The Amalekite sees Saul's condition "leaning" on his spear to be equivalent to having fallen ("for the fainting spell has seized me") and assumes, as does Saul himself in this account, that in any case the king will not survive.

14. *How were you not afraid . . . to do violence to the LORD's anointed?* Though the Israelite piety of David's statement is noteworthy, his words, as in the previous episodes in which he warned against harming Saul, are also politically self-interested because he, too, is the LORD's anointed. In fact, now with Saul's death, he alone is the LORD's anointed.

16. *your mouth bore witness against you.* There is no way of knowing whether David actually believes the Amalekite's story, but it is certainly convenient for him to be able to point an accusing finger at someone with whom he has had nothing to do as the person responsible for Saul's death, and then to order immediate punishment.

17 was the one who finished off the LORD's anointed.'" And David sang this
18 lament for Saul and for Jonathan, and he said to teach hard things to the
    sons of Judah—look, it is written down in the Book of Jashar:

19   "The splendor, O Israel, on your heights lies slain,
                    how have the warriors fallen!
20   Tell it not in Gath,
                    proclaim not in Ashkelon's streets.
        Lest the Philistine daughters rejoice,

---

the LORD's anointed. At the end of the episode, David makes a point of using
the epithet of divinely grounded royal status instead of simply calling his predecessor "Saul," as the Amalekite (who never even refers to him as "king") had done.

17. And David sang this lament. We have been aware since 1 Samuel 16 of
David's gift as a lyre player and (presumably) as a singer. Only now do we hear
him in action as a singer-poet. This grandly resonant lament, cast in archaic
epic diction, marks a great moment of transition in the larger narrative, as the
David-Saul story becomes the David story. It is also another public utterance of
David's that beautifully serves his political purposes, celebrating his dead rival
as it mourns his loss and thus testifying that David could never have desired
Saul's death.

18. to teach hard things. The Masoretic text has "to teach the bow"—a problematic reading because the lament scarcely provides instruction in the arts of
war. Some critics delete "bow" (*qeshet*), following the Septuagint. The present
translation revocalizes as *qeshet* as *qashot*, with Fokkelman.
    look, it is written down in the Book of Jashar. This lost work, mentioned else-
where in the Bible, was obviously familiar to the ancient audience. The title
probably means "Book of the Upright," though another reading of *yashar*, as a
verb rather than as a noun, yields "Book of Songs." (This, however, requires
revocalizing the word.) It might have been an anthology of archaic Hebrew
poems.

20. Tell it not in Gath. There is an ironic echo here of the account of David's
activities as vassal to the king of Gath, activities that he did not want told in
Gath (see 1 Samuel 27:11).
    Lest the Philistine daughters rejoice. In this martial culture, the young
women had the role of celebrating the victors ("Saul has struck down his thousands. . . ."), gloating over the defeated enemy, and enjoying the spoils the men
brought back from their conquest (compare verse 24).

> lest the daughters of the uncircumcised gloat.
> O hills of Gilboa—no dew!
> and no rain upon you, O lofty fields.
> For there the warriors' shield was besmirched,
> the shield of Saul unburnished with oil.
> From the blood of the slain,
> from the warriors' fat—
> Jonathan's bow did not retreat,
> and the sword of Saul never turned away empty.
> Saul and Jonathan, beloved and dear,
> in their life and their death they were not parted.
> They were swifter than eagles,
> and stronger than lions.

21

22

23

---

21. *O hills of Gilboa.* As Shimon Bar-Efrat has observed, apostrophe is the dominant form of address throughout the elegy. David first turns, in a plural verb, to Israel at large ("Tell it not in Gath"), then to the hills of Gilboa, then to Saul and Jonathan, then to the daughters of Israel, then to Jonathan alone. The apostrophe is a form of address that underscores the actual absence of the person or object addressed and so is especially apt for an elegy.

lofty fields. The Hebrew *usedeh terumot* is a little obscure. The simplest solution is to treat the initial particle *u* as an excrescence and to read the phrase as a poetic inversion of the similar *meromey sadeh* in Judges 5:18. In the parallelism here, "lofty fields" would be an epithet for "hills of Gilboa."

unburnished with oil. The shields were made of leather, often studded with metal plates. Rubbing them with oil before battle would have made their outer surface slippery and thus would have enhanced their effectiveness in deflecting weapons. But the Hebrew for "unburnished," *beli mashiaḥ*, is a pun—it means "unanointed" or "messiah-less," a haunting intimation that the LORD's anointed is no more. Clearly, the image of the royal shield lying befouled in the dust is a powerful metonymy for Saul himself.

22. *Jonathan's bow . . . the sword of Saul.* After the image of the implement of defense, the shield, lying cast aside, we get a retrospective picture of these two offensive weapons destroying the enemy. The idea of the sword or the bow consuming flesh and blood is conventional in ancient Near Eastern martial poetry.

23. *in their life and their death they were not parted.* This is, of course, an extravagant idealization on the part of the elegist since father and son were almost estranged and twice Saul was on the point of killing Jonathan.

24   O daughters of Israel, weep over Saul,
         who clothed you in scarlet and bangles,
            who studded your garments with jewelry of gold.
25   How have the warriors fallen
         in the midst of the battle.
     Jonathan, upon your heights slain!
26   I grieve for you, my brother, Jonathan.
         Very dear you were to me.
     More wondrous your love to me
         than the love of women.
27   How have the warriors fallen,
         and the gear of battle is lost."

---

24. *O daughters of Israel, weep.* The invocation of the daughters of Israel to weep over the king who brought them precious booty is a symmetrical antithesis to the initial warning to keep the news away from the daughters of the Philistines, who would rejoice.

26. *I grieve for you, my brother, Jonathan.* Jonathan several times proclaimed his love for David. It is only in Jonathan's death, and at the distance of apostrophe, that David calls him "my brother" and says that Jonathan was dear to him.
     More wondrous . . . than the love of women. Repeated, unconvincing attempts have been made to read a homoerotic implication into these words. The reported details of the David story suggest that his various attachments to women are motivated by pragmatic rather than emotional concerns—and in one instance, by lust. This disposition, however, tells us little about David's sexual orientation. The bond between men in this warrior culture could easily be stronger than the bond between men and women.

27. *How have the warriors fallen, / and the gear of battle is lost.* The first clause here echoes the second verset of the opening line of the poem and so closes the elegy in a ringing envelope structure. The second clause beautifully picks up the image of the castoff shield lying in the dust, and of the relentless bow and sword that will never more be borne into battle. It is misguided to render the verb at the end as "perished" (King James Version, New Jewish Publication Society) because that presupposes that "gear of battle" is actually an epithet for Saul and Jonathan. Far more effectively, the lament concludes with a concrete image of shield and sword and bow abandoned, and by a simple process of metonymy we vividly understand the fate of the two men who once wielded them.

CHAPTER 2

And it happened afterward that David inquired of the Lord, saying, 1
"Shall I go up into one of the towns of Judah?" And the Lord said to
him, "Go up." And David said, "Where shall I go up?" And He said, "To
Hebron." And David went up there, and his two wives as well, Ahinoam 2
the Jezreelite and Abigail wife of Nabal the Carmelite. And his men 3
who were with him David brought up, each man and his household, and
they settled in Hebron. And the men of Judah came and anointed David 4a
there as king over the house of Judah.

---

1. *David inquired of the Lord.* In keeping with the repeated emphasis of the
preceding narrative, David, at each crucial juncture, solicits guidance from
God's oracle before he makes his move.

go up into one of the towns of Judah. The preposition is used with precision: David does not want to "go up to one of the towns" but "into one of the
towns"—that is, to set up headquarters in the town, leaving Ziklag at the edge
of Philistine territory.

Where shall I go up? Given the binary character of the oracle's response, the
actual form of the question would have been, "Shall I go up to Hebron?" But
the question is recast in its present form to emphasize that God has picked out
Hebron from all the towns of Judah.

4a. *king over the house of Judah.* It is a little odd for a single tribe to have a "king,"
but the act is deliberately presumptive on David's part—first the king of Judah,
eventually of all the tribes. Saul's son Ish-Bosheth, by contrast, becomes king
of an alliance of northern tribes. The text is silent on the Philistines' view of
David's move to kingship in Hebron, but one can assume they countenanced
it as a reasonable act on the part of their vassal opposing the house of Saul.

4b And they told David, saying, "It was the men of Jabesh-Gilead who
5 buried Saul." And David sent messengers to the men of Jabesh-Gilead
    and said to them, "Blessed are you to the LORD, that you have done
6 this kindness with your lord, with Saul, and have buried him. And now,
    may the LORD show faithful kindness to you, and I on my part as well
7 shall do this bounty for you because you have done this thing. And now,
    may your hands be strengthened and be you men of valor, for your lord
    Saul is dead, and it is I whom the house of Judah has anointed as king
    over them."

8 And Abner son of Ner commander of Saul's army had taken Ish-Bosheth
9 son of Saul and brought him over to Mahanaim and made him king over
    Gilead and over the Asherite and over Jezreel and over Ephraim and over

---

5. *David sent messengers to the men of Jabesh-Gilead.* This is another shrewd
political maneuver. The men of Jabesh-Gilead had been closely allied with
Saul. David, seizing the occasion of their act of bravery, summons them, praises
their burying of Saul, and offers them an unspecified "bounty" (or "benefice"—
literally, "good thing").

7. *for your lord Saul is dead, and it is I whom the house of Judah has anointed as
king over them.* David finesses Saul's hostility toward him and presents himself as the legitimate successor: just as the men of Jabesh-Gilead have been
valorous in burying Saul, they should now show valor in following the newly
anointed David.

8. *Abner . . . had taken Ish-Bosheth.* Abner the commander in chief is clearly the
real power here, and this surviving son of Saul is little more than a puppet king.
The original name (reflected in Chronicles) was Ish-Baal, with the "baal" component being a general epithet for God (or god), not necessarily referring to the
Canaanite deity. But because of its pagan associations, the sternly monotheistic
later editors systematically substituted *boshet* for *ba'al, boshet* meaning "shame."
    Mahanaim. The location is to the east of the Jordan and hence outside the
new area of Philistine conquest.

9. *Asherite.* The Masoretic text reads "Ashurite," which would be, implausibly, a
non-Israelite people. Some critics emend to "Geshurite," but that is a Canaanite group, and so the emendation perpetuates the problem. It is simplest to read
this word as a reference to the northern tribe of Asher.

Benjamin and over Israel altogether. Forty years old was Ish-Bosheth   10
when he became king over Israel, and two years did he reign. But the
house of Judah followed David. And the span of time that David was   11
king in Hebron over the house of Judah was seven years and six months.

And Abner son of Ner with the servants of Ish-Bosheth sallied forth   12
from Mahanaim to Gibeon. And Joab son of Zeruiah and the servants of   13
David had sallied forth, and they met each other by the pool of Gibeon,
and they took up their positions on either side of the pool. And Abner   14
said to Joab, "Pray, let the lads arise and play before us." And Joab said,

---

and over Israel altogether. Shimon Bar-Efrat has made the plausible proposal
that this final phrase is not a summary of the preceding list but the last stage
in a chronological process: Ish-Bosheth extended his rule gradually, beginning
with Gilead in trans-Jordan and moving westward into the territory the Philistines had conquered. It was only after a time that he actually ruled "over Israel
altogether."

10. *two years did he reign.* At first thought, his reign should have been nearly as
long as David's seven and a half years in Hebron. But if it took him five years
to consolidate his control over the northern tribes, the reign of two years would
make perfect sense.

12. *Abner . . . sallied forth from Mahanaim to Gibeon.* The reason for this expedition may have been David's attaching the men of Jabesh-Gilead, who had
clearly been in Saul's camp, to himself. Gibeon is in the territory of Benjamin,
just a few miles northwest of Jerusalem.

14. *let the lads arise and play before us.* The "lads" (*ne 'arim*) are elite warriors.
The verb "play" clearly indicates gladiatorial, or representative, combat. (Goliath calling for an Israelite champion to fight him is another instance of combat
through designated representative.) It is, however, deadly combat and not just
a form of jousting, as the details of the fighting make clear.

15 "Let them arise." And they arose and crossed over—twelve in number for Benjamin and for Ish-Bosheth son of Saul and twelve from the ser-
16 vants of David. And each man grasped the head of the other with his sword at the side of the other, and they fell together. And they called
17 that place the Field of Flints, which is in Gibeon. And the fighting was very fierce on that day, and Abner with the men of Israel were routed
18 by the servants of David. And the three sons of Zeruiah were there, Joab and Abishai and Asahel. And Asahel was as swift-footed as one of
19 the gazelles of the open field. And Asahel chased after Abner, and he

---

15. *twelve in number.* Throughout this strange episode, as Polzin has aptly observed, there is an "extended ritualization of action as it is described through extensive stylization of language." The ritual combat is virtually an allegory of the civil war that it inaugurates. (Polzin reads it as an allegory of Israelite monarchy.) The twelve champions on each side recall the twelve tribes of Israel—an image of a nation destructively divided against itself. (The number of fallen soldiers on Abner's side will be 360—thirty times twelve—and on Joab's side twenty, an eighteenth part of the other side's casualties.) The implausibility of the account of combat, then, would have been overridden for the writer by the neatness of its symbolic function.

16. *each man grasped the head of the other with his sword at the side of the other.* The evidence of artifacts from the ancient world suggests that precisely this mode of ritualized combat was quite widespread. A bas-relief found in Syria, roughly contemporaneous with our story, an Egyptian carving, archaic Greek vase paintings, and a Roman sculpture all show warriors in precisely this posture.
they fell together. All twenty-four warriors were killed—hardly a surprising outcome if each man was free to wield a sword against his adversary's side. Because there can be no decisive outcome in this encompassing mutual slaughter, general fighting then breaks out.
the Field of Flints. It is not clear whether they were fighting with flint weapons (perhaps because these were archaic and part of the ritualized combat), or whether the old term had become a general designation for knives or swords.

17. *Abner with the men of Israel were routed.* Given the relatively low number of casualties, it seems likely that less than a thousand on each side were engaged. In such limited combat, the veterans of David's battle-hardened guerilla band of six hundred might have had a distinct advantage.

swerved not to the right or left in going after Abner. And Abner turned 20
round and said, "Are you Asahel?" And he said, "I am." And Abner said 21
to him, "Swerve you to your right or your left and seize for yourself one
of the lads, and take you his armor." But Asahel did not want to turn
away from him. And Abner once more said to Asahel, "Turn you away 22
from me. Why should I strike you to the ground, and how would I show
my face to Joab your brother?" And he refused to turn aside, and Abner 23
struck him in the belly with the butt of the spear and the spear came
out behind him, and he fell there and died on the spot. And it happened
that whoever came to the place where Asahel fell and died, stood still.

---

20. *Are you Asahel?* Abner, who surely would not have had any compunction
about killing some other Judahite, realizes, quite accurately, that it will mean
trouble for him to kill one of the sons of Zeruiah. Asahel, the ace sprinter,
sounds very much like the youngest of the three, although we are not told
specifically about the order of their birth.

21. *his armor.* This noun, *ḥalitsah*, appears only here and in the Samson story. It
is rendered in modern translations, erroneously, as "tunic," "garment," or even
"belt," but as we know from the *Iliad*, it is rather armor that a warrior takes from
a slain foe on the battlefield. (The King James Version actually gets it right here
but not in the Samson story.) The word is related to *ḥaluts*, vanguard, and the
vanguard fighters would surely have worn armor.

22. *Why should I strike you to the ground . . . ?* Abner, the seasoned warrior, is
coolly confident that if necessary he has the skill and the combat experience to
kill this impetuous young man.
    how would I show my face to Joab your brother? The literal wording of the
Hebrew is "lift up my face." What is at stake here is not merely a question
of diplomatic relations with the opposing commander but vendetta justice
(Hebrew, *ge'ulat hadam*, "redemption of the blood"): if Abner sheds the blood
of Joab's brother, Joab will feel honor-bound to shed the blood of the killer in
return.

23. *struck him in the belly with the butt of the spear.* Asahel is pursuing Abner at
top speed. Abner, to save his own life, uses an old soldier's trick: he suddenly
stops short and thrusts his spear backward, under his pursuer's shield (if Asahel
is carrying one) and into the soft belly. The momentum of Asahel's rapid running would have contributed to the penetrating force of the spear's butt.

24 And Joab and Abishai chased after Abner, and as the sun was setting,
they had come to the hill of Ammah, which faces Giah on the way to
25 the wilderness of Gibeon. And the Benjaminites gathered behind Abner
and formed a single band, and they took a stance on the top of a certain
26 hill. And Abner called out to Joab and said, "Must the sword devour
forever? You surely know that it will be bitterness in the end. And how
long will you not say to the troops to turn back from their brothers?"
27 And Joab said, "As God lives, had you but spoken, from this morning
28 the troops would have given up pursuit of their brothers." And Joab
sounded the ram's horn, and all the troops halted, and they no longer
29 chased after Israel, and they fought no more. And Abner and his men
went all that night through the Arabah, and they crossed the Jordan and
30 went all the way through the ravine and came to Mahanaim. And Joab

---

24. *Ammah . . . Giah.* The first name means "conduit," the second "gushing,"
and so both may be related to an aqueduct system linked to the pool at Gibeon.

26. *You surely know that it will be bitterness in the end.* This grim prognostication
hovers over not only the continuing civil war but over the entire David story.
In the previous verse, Abner's forces were reported regrouping and taking up
a defensive position on the hilltop, so they are now, after the rout, in a state
to inflict serious casualties on their adversaries if Joab persists. Therefore he
agrees to the truce, though he surely has vendetta on his mind.

27. *had you but spoken.* The Masoretic text has "had you not spoken." This has
led some interpreters to construe "morning" as "tomorrow morning" (that is, the
troops would have gone on pursuing you all night long had you not spoken up
now). But this is strained because the Hebrew *'az mehaboker* (literally, "then
from the morning") idiomatically refers to the morning of the day on which one
is speaking. One should either emend "had not" (*lulei'*) to "had" (*lu*) or, as Rashi
proposed long ago, construe the former in the sense of the latter.

29. *the Arabah.* This is a north-south depression running from the Sea of Galilee all the way to the Gulf of Aqabah.
  the ravine. The Hebrew term *bitron* might conceivably be a place-name. The
root means to cleave or split and occurs in the Song of Songs collocated with
"mountains," yielding something like "mountains of the divide." The scholarly proposal that this word means "middle of the morning" has no warrant in
ancient Hebrew usage.

had turned back from pursuing Abner, and he gathered together all the troops, and nineteen of David's servants were missing, and Asahel. And 31 David's servants had struck down from Benjamin and from Abner's men three hundred and sixty men. And they bore off Asahel and buried him 32 in his father's grave, which is in Bethlehem, and Joab and his men went all night long, and day brightened for them in Hebron.

---

32. *all night long*. Perhaps the reason for this forced march through the night is that Joab's troops want to get safely out of Benjaminite territory, not entirely trusting the truce.

CHAPTER 3

¹ And the fighting between the house of Saul and the house of David went on a long time, and David grew stronger and the house of Saul weaker and weaker.

^{2,3} And sons were born to David in Hebron. And his firstborn was Amnon, by Ahinoam the Jezreelite. And the second was Chileab, by Abigail wife of Nabal the Carmelite. And the third was Absalom son of Maacah ⁴ daughter of Talmai king of Geshur. And the fourth was Adonijah son of

---

1. *And the fighting*. This summary notice at the head of the chapter follows directly from the story of the battle at Gibeon that precedes it: the truce on that day is only temporary, and a drawn-out civil war ensues.

2. *And sons were born to David*. The insertion of this genealogical list here may be motivated by the fact that the northern tribes, brought round by Abner, are about to cast their lot with David, making him monarch of the entire nation and thus a properly dynastic king. But succession to the throne is not simple, and the list bristles with future disasters: Amnon, who will rape his half sister and will be murdered by her brother; Absalom, who will usurp the throne; Adonijah, who will proclaim himself king while the infirm, aged David lies in bed unawares.

3. *Chileab*. The Septuagint and the Qumran Samuel fragment have a different name, Daluiah. In any case, this son plays no role in the ensuing narrative, nor do Shephatiah and Ithream.
   Maacah daughter of Talmai king of Geshur. Geshur is a small trans-Jordanian kingdom at the foot of the Golan. The marriage is clearly a political act through which David establishes an alliance in the north, outflanking the house of Saul. It is conceivable that Absalom's later aspiration to the throne may be influenced by his awareness that, alone of David's sons, he is grandson of a king. After the killing of Amnon, he will take refuge in Geshur.

Haggith. And the fifth was Shephatiah son of Abital. And the sixth was 5
Ithream, by Eglah wife of David. These were born to David in Hebron. 6

And it happened during the fighting between the house of Saul and the
house of David that Abner kept growing in strength in the house of Saul.
And Saul had a concubine named Rizpah daughter of Aiah. And Ish- 7
Bosheth said to Abner, "Why did you come to bed with my father's concubine?" And Abner was very incensed over the words of Ish-Bosheth, 8
and he said, "Am I a dog's head attached to Judah? Today I have kept
faith with the house of Saul your father, with his kinsmen and his com-

---

5. *Eglah wife of David*. It is a little odd that only she is so designated. This might
be because she stands at the end of the list, or because there was knowledge
of another Eglah who was not David's wife. In all this, one notes that David
the guerilla leader with his two wives has now become David the king with a
whole royal harem.

6. *Abner kept growing in strength*. This is the same verb, in a different conjugation, as in the opening verse of the chapter, which reported David's growing
strength and the weakening of the house of Saul. As the Saulide forces are
progressively harder pressed in the continuing war, the nominal king becomes
more and more dependent on his military commander; and Abner, while not
actually pretending to the throne, arrogates more and more power to himself.

7. *Why did you come to bed with my father's concubine?* This crucial act is elided
in the narrative report and revealed only in Ish-Bosheth's indignant question.
To take sexual possession of a king's consort was to make an implicit claim to
the power he exercised, as we shall see again when Absalom publicly cohabits
with David's concubines. "To come to bed with"—literally, "to come into"—is
an idiom for sexual intercourse that generally indicates sexual possession of
a woman with whom a man has not been previously intimate. (I explain the
semantic logic of the idiom in my commentary on Genesis. *The Five Books of
Moses*, page 39).

8. *Am I a dog's head attached to Judah?* The dog in biblical idiom regularly figures as a contemptible beast—the antonym of the fierce and regal lion. The
phrase "attached to Judah" is lacking in the Septuagint, and some critics have
inferred that it is a scribal interpolation. It might make sense, however, as a
compounding of the insult because Judah is the despised enemy of Benjamin,
the tribe of Saul.

panions, in not handing you over to David, and you dare reproach me
9 with guilt over the woman today? Thus may God do to Abner, and even
10 more, for as the LORD has sworn to David, just so will I do for him—to
transfer the kingship from the house of Saul and to set up the throne of
11 David over Israel and over Judah from Dan to Beersheba!" And he could
say back not a word more to Abner in his fear of him.

12 And Abner sent messengers to David in his stead, saying, "To whom
should the land belong? Make a pact with me and, look, my hand will
13 be with you to bring round to you all Israel." And he said, "Good. I shall
make a pact with you. But one thing do I ask of you, namely, you shall
not see my face until you bring Michal daughter of Saul when you come

---

you dare reproach me with guilt over the woman. Abner's angry protest has
a nice double edge. You are entirely dependent on my loyal support, he tells
Ish-Bosheth, so how could you dare object to so trivial a thing as my taking a
particular woman as sexual partner? Alternately, the implication could be: you
are entirely dependent on me, so how could you object to my taking possession
of this sexual symbol of political power? You should have been content that I
left you nominally on the throne.

9. *for as the LORD has sworn to David.* Ish-Bosheth's protest about Rizpah drives
Abner, David's military adversary, to embrace the notion that God has promised
the throne to David. Rather than continue to serve a carping, pusillanimous man
like Ish-Bosheth, who neither fully accepts Abner's power nor knows how to
exercise power on his own, Abner now is ready to throw his weight with a truly
kingly leader and to help him become king over all the nation's tribes (verse 10).

11. *he could say back not a word.* The contrast between the angry Abner and
the quaking Ish-Bosheth is all the stronger because the puppet king's fearful
silence is set against what is by biblical standards a rather long speech—one
continuous outburst.

13. *see my face.* An idiom used for coming into the presence of royalty.
Michal daughter of Saul. The first marriage buttresses David's claim to reign
over all Israel, including the tribe of Benjamin. That is why he identifies Michal
to Abner as Saul's daughter. There is no indication that he has a personal motive
of affection as well as a political one in wanting Michal back.

to see my face." And David sent messengers to Ish-Bosheth son of Saul,   14
saying, "Give back my wife Michal, whom I betrothed with a hundred
Philistine foreskins." And Ish-Bosheth sent and took her from her hus-   15
band, from Paltiel son of Laish. And her husband went with her, weeping   16
as he went after her, as far as Bahurim. And Abner said to him, "Go back!"
And he went back.

And Abner parlayed with the elders of Israel, saying, "Time and again in   17
the past you sought to have David become king over you. And now, act,   18

---

14. *sent messengers to Ish-Bosheth.* It is to be inferred that Abner has made clear
to Ish-Bosheth that he must accede to this demand.
     my wife Michal, whom I betrothed with a hundred Philistine foreskins. In turn-
ing to the man who has jurisdiction over Michal (and her second husband), David
makes clear now that she is his wife, whom he legitimately acquired by providing
the bride price of a hundred Philistine foreskins stipulated by her father, Saul.

15. *from her husband.* The Masoretic text has "a husband" (or, "a man"), but the
possessive pronoun is supplied in the Septuagint and the Vulgate as well as in
at least two Hebrew manuscripts.

16. *weeping as he went.* There is scarcely a more striking instance of the evoca-
tive compactness of biblical narrative. We know almost nothing about Paltiel.
He speaks not a word of dialogue. Yet his walking after Michal, weeping all the
while, intimates a devoted love that stands in contrast to David's relationship
with her. Paltiel is a man whose fate is imposed on him. Michal was given to
him by Saul, evidently without his initiative. He came to love her. Now he must
give her up, and confronted by Saul's strongman with the peremptory order to
go back, he has no choice but to go back.

17. *Time and again in the past.* The idiom for "times gone by," *temol shilshom*
(literally, "yesterday and the day before") is reinforced by the emphatic adverb
gam, repeated before each of the two components of the idiom, probably as
an indication of repeated acts in times past. Most commentators refer the idea
of Israel's wanting David as king to his immense popularity during his early
military successes (1 Samuel 18). But there was no intimation then that the
people wanted to replace Saul with David on the throne. The suggestion of
repeated popular support for David's claims might well point to an otherwise
unreported undercurrent of dissatisfaction with the house of Saul and an interest in going over to David as a result of the losing civil war, if it is not Abner's
own diplomatic invention.

for the LORD has said, 'By the hand of David My servant will I rescue
My people Israel from the hand of the Philistines and from the hand of
19 all their enemies.'" And Abner spoke as well in the hearing of Benjamin,
and Abner went as well to speak in David's hearing in Hebron all that was
20 good in the eyes of Israel and in the eyes of Benjamin. And Abner came to
David in Hebron, and with him were twenty men. And David made a feast
21 for Abner and for the men who were with him. And Abner said to David,
"Let me rise and go and gather to my lord the king all Israel, that they may
make a pact with you, and you shall reign over all your heart desires." And
22 David sent Abner off, and he went in peace. And look, David's servants
and Joab had come from a raid, and abundant booty they brought with
them, and Abner was not with David in Hebron, for he had sent him off,
23 and he went in peace. And Joab and all the force that was with him had
come, and they told Joab, saying, "Abner son of Ner has come to the king,
24 and he sent him off, and he went in peace." And Joab came to the king
and said, "What have you done? Look, Abner has come to you! Why did

---

21. *And David sent Abner off, and he went in peace.* The going in peace befits the
feast of reconciliation and the agreed-on pact. The writer contrives to repeat
this sentence verbatim three times (here, verse 22, verse 23). But when Joab
refers to this very same departure of Abner from Hebron in verse 24, he substitutes for "in peace" (*beshalom*) the emphatic infinitive *halokh* ("going off").
This ominous substitution, as I put it in *The Art of Biblical Narrative*, "falls like
the clatter of a dagger after the ringing of bells"—especially because "to go"
sometimes occurs in the Bible as a euphemism for dying (see Job 27:21 and
Jeremiah 22:10). Polzin has noted that this entire episode is a crowded juncture
of comings and goings. The least complicated inference to be drawn from that
fact is that this is a crucial moment of transition in the David story: the house
of Saul comes to treat with the house of David; the long conflict with Saul,
culminating in civil war, comes to an end; David is about to become king of the
whole Israelite nation; a new line of division now emerges between David and
his chief henchman, Joab. All this flurry of transition and realignment is nicely
caught in the multiple comings and goings of Abner and Joab and the troops.

24. *Look, Abner has come to you.* The simple idiom for arrival (*ba' 'el*) ironically
echoes Ish-Bosheth's use of the very same idiom in its sexual sense ("come
into," "come to bed with") in his complaint to Abner. The sexual undertone is
sustained in the next verse because the prominent verb "to dupe" (*pitah*) has
the primary meaning of "seduce."

you send him off, and he went, going off? You know that Abner son of   25
Ner to dupe you has come and to learn your comings and goings and to
learn all that you do." And Joab went out from David's presence and sent   26
messengers after Abner, and they brought him back from the cistern of
Sirah, and David did not know. And Abner came back to Hebron, and   27
Joab drew him aside into the gate to speak with him deceptively, and he
struck him there in the belly, and he died for the blood of Asahel, Joab's
brother. And David heard afterward and said, "Innocent am I, and my   28
kingship, before the LORD for all time of the blood of Abner son of Ner!

---

26. *the cistern of Sirah.* The actual location has not been identified, but it would
have to be in the general vicinity of Hebron.

and David did not know. The narrator takes pains to underscore David's
innocence of involvement in Joab's scheme of murder. David on his part will
take extravagant steps to declare his innocence.

27. *deceptively.* The Hebrew adverb *basheli* occurs only here. It derives either
from the root *sh-l-h,* "to delude," or from the root *sh-l-w,* "to be quiet." Those
who favor the latter root render it, with a small leap of semantic inference, as
"privately."

he struck him there in the belly. Although this is the same part of the body in
which the now avenged Asahel received his fatal wound from Abner, there is a
world of difference between the two killings. Abner struck down Asahel in a deft
maneuver as Asahel was pursuing him on the battlefield with intent to kill. Joab
draws Abner aside into the gate under the pretence of speaking confidentially
with him, and, catching him unawares, stabs him in the belly.

for the blood of Asahel. Joab's vendetta is accomplished. But it has not
escaped notice that he is also eliminating a rival for the position of commander
in the new united monarchy.

28. *Innocent am I.* David's first eminently political reflex is to dissociate himself
categorically from the killing.

of the blood of Abner son of Ner. The Qumran Samuel text puts a full stop
after "before the LORD for all time," then makes this phrase the subject of the
next clause: "May the blood of Abner son of Ner come down on the head of
Joab." The Masoretic text has simply "May it come down on the head of Joab,"
and this translation supplies "blood guilt" (plural of *dam,* blood) for the sake
of clarity.

29 May the blood guilt come down on the head of Joab and all his father's
house, and may there never lack in the house of Joab a sufferer of discharge from his member and running sores on his skin and a man clutching the woman's spindle, and one falling by the sword and one wanting
30 for bread!" And Joab and Abishai his brother had lain in wait for Abner
because he put to death Asahel their brother in Gibeon in the fighting.
31 And David said to Joab and to all the troops who were with him, "Tear
your garments and gird on sackcloth and keen for Abner." And King
32 David was walking behind the bier. And they buried Abner in Hebron.
And the king raised his voice and wept over the grave of Abner, and all
33 the people wept. And the king lamented over Abner and said,

---

29. *discharge from his member.* The single Hebrew word *zav* refers to a man
suffering from diseased discharge from the male organ.

running sores on his skin. This is again one word in the Hebrew, *metsor'a*,
rendered as "leper" in the older translations but now generally thought to indicate a different skin disease.

a man clutching the woman's spindle. Some prefer to interpret the Hebrew
term as "crutch," thus linking it with the two preceding images of disease. This
noun, *pelekh*, occurs quite infrequently, but there is scant indication in the
biblical corpus that as a wooden implement it meant anything but "spindle."
The word "woman's" is added in the translation to catch the nuance of scorn
in a man's being reduced to woman's work. All in all, David puts together a
first-class curse to emphasize the distance between him and Abner's killer. This
blood guilt, many times compounded, will indeed come down on Joab's head,
but not till the end of David's life.

30. *had lain in wait for Abner.* The Masoretic text reads "had killed Abner"
(*hargu le'avner*). There are two problems with that reading. It is a flat repetition of what has already been reported more vividly (only adding the information that Abishai was complicit in the act), and the use of the particle *l^e* (as a
preposition, it means "to" or "for") to indicate the direct object of a verb is an
Aramaicism generally restricted to late biblical Hebrew. The Qumran Samuel
scroll has a different verb, evidently (the first consonant is not visible on the
parchment) *tsafnu*, "to lie in wait," "to hide."

33. *lamented.* This is David's second poetic lament (*qinah*) in quick sequence in
the text. It is much briefer than the lament over Jonathan and Saul and derives
its power from the lapidary character of its language.

"Like the death of the base
should Abner have died?
Your hands—never bound,   34
your feet never placed in fetters!
As one falls before scoundrels you fell."

And all the people continued to weep over him. And all the people 35
came to give David bread to eat while it was still day, and David swore,
saying, "Thus and more may God do to me, if before the sun sets I taste
bread or anything at all." And all the people took note and it was good in 36
their eyes, all that the king had done was good in the eyes of the people.
And all the people and all Israel knew on that day that it had not been 37
from the king to put to death Abner son of Ner. And the king said to 38
his servants, "You must know that a commander and a great man has

---

the death of the base. The term for "base fellow," *naval*, is the one encountered
in 1 Samuel 25 as an explanation for the name of Nabal, Abigail's husband. A
naval is someone who, as Kyle McCarter, Jr., rightly observes, perpetrates *nevalah*, a contemptible or scandalous act. It is an outrage, David says, that a noble
figure such as Abner should have been cut down in stealth as some scoundrel
might perish at the hands of hired assassins.

34. *Your hands—never bound, / your feet never placed in fetters!* The elliptical
nature of the language has led to some dispute over interpretation. It is most
plausibly understood as a brief retrospection on Abner's glory days as a martial
hero: no one ever succeeded in taking him captive, in putting him in a prisoner's
humiliating fetters.
As one falls before scoundrels you fell. But now the noble Abner has been
undone by treachery. In all the grandeur of the poetry, the sharp rebuke to the
sons of Zeruiah, who figure as vulgar cutthroats, is clear.

37.–38. The vehemence with which David here is repeatedly dissociated from
the killing of Abner leads one to suspect that, beyond his desire to exculpate
himself on the spot, there may have been a lingering shadow of suspicion that
he ordered the killing, a suspicion that the writer takes pains to dispel.

39 fallen this day in Israel. And I am gentle, and just anointed king, and these sons of Zeruiah are too hard for me. May the Lord pay back the evildoer according to his evil!"

---

39. *I am gentle, and just anointed king.* David's plight as a self-proclaimed "gentle" or "tender" man (*rakh*) vis-à-vis the "hard" sons of Zeruiah will continue to play a crucial role in the story. But though he dissociates himself from Joab and Abishai and goes so far as to pronounce a scathing curse on them and their descendants, he makes no move to get rid of them, and continues to depend on their activity as strongmen. And what of Joab's reaction to all this bitter denunciation? Is it possible that he prudently understands it is politic for the king to dissociate himself from the killing by denouncing the killers in poetry and prose? There is also a question here about the relation between the two phrases David uses. Many translations explain the link as "though anointed king." That construction is possible, though it would be an unusual use of the Hebrew particle *we* ("and"). The present translation adds "just," on the assumption that David is dramatizing his predicament as a gentle person on whom the kingship has been newly thrust and who must contend with these hard sons of Zeruiah. In point of fact, he was anointed in Hebron several years earlier, but this might be either rhetorical exaggeration or a reference to his brand-new condition of king of the nation, not just of the tribe of Judah.

CHAPTER 4

And the son of Saul heard that Abner had died in Hebron, and he was 1
utterly shaken, and all Israel was dismayed. And the son of Saul had two 2
men, commanders of raiding parties, the name of the one was Baanah
and of the other Rechab, sons of Rimmon the Beerothite, who was of the
Benjaminites, for Beeroth, too, was reckoned with Benjamin. And the 3
Beerothites fled to Gittaim and have been sojourners there till this day.

---

1. *the son of Saul*. The son in question is Ish-Bosheth. Both the Septuagint
and the Qumran Samuel scroll read, erroneously, "Mephibosheth." It has been
surmised that scribes deleted the mistaken name without replacing it with the
correct one.

was utterly shaken. The Hebrew says literally "his hands grew weak," the
hands being an idiomatic token of strength or courage. The force of the idiom
is a little like the colloquial English "lost his grip."

2. *sons of Rimmon the Beerothite, who was of the Benjaminites*. The Beerothites
are an originally non-Israelite group who have become what we might call naturalized Benjaminites. The two brothers are considered sufficiently Benjaminite
to have been entrusted with positions as the commanders of raiding parties—
also making them experienced killers—and so we are meant to understand that
the pusillanimous Ish-Bosheth is betrayed by his own tribesmen. At the same
time, the foreign origin of Baanah and Rechab participates in the recurring
pattern of the foreign messenger bringing news of a disaster to David. Finally,
the treacherous killing of the king by two brothers echoes the immediately
preceding episode, in which two brothers, Joab and Abishai, are said to lie in
wait for and kill Abner.

4   And Jonathan son of Saul had a lame son, five years old he was when the
    news of Saul and Jonathan came from Jezreel. And his nurse bore him
    off and fled, and it happened in her haste to flee that he fell and was
5   crippled. And his name was Mephibosheth. And the sons of Rimmon
    the Beerothite, Rechab and Baanah went and came in the heat of the
6   day to the house of Ish-Bosheth as he was taking his midday rest. And,
    look, the woman who kept the gate had been gleaning wheat, and
7   nodded and fell asleep. And they came into the house as he was lying
    in his bed in his bedchamber, and they struck him and killed him and
    cut off his head and took his head and went off through the Arabah all
8   night long. And they brought Ish-Bosheth's head to David in Hebron
    and said to the king, "Here is the head of Ish-Bosheth son of Saul your

---

4. *Jonathan . . . had a lame son.* The notice is inserted here to make clear that
after the murder of Ish-Bosheth, there will be no fit heir left from the house of
Saul, for Saul's one surviving grandson is crippled.

   Mephibosheth. As with Ish-Bosheth / Ish-Baal, the original form of the name
was Mephibaal, a component meaning "shame" substituted for the theophoric
ba'al with its pagan associations.

6. *And, look, the woman who kept the gate.* The translation of this entire verse
follows the text reflected in the Septuagint, out of a sense that the received text
at this point is simply not viable. The Masoretic text is problematic as idiomatic
Hebrew usage, includes one entirely unintelligible phrase, and is redundant
with the narrative report of the next verse. It reads: "and they [feminine pronoun!] came into the midst of the house, taking wheat [?], and they struck him
in the belly, and Rechab and Baanah his brother got away."

   gleaning wheat. This odd little domestic detail suggests that Ish-Bosheth
does not inhabit a grand palace with royal guards but lives in modest homey
circumstances.

   nodded and fell asleep. Both the king and the gatekeeper are asleep when the
assassins arrive, so they can slip by her and easily dispatch him.

7. *as he was lying in his bed in his bedchamber.* This twice-asserted detail underlines the scurrilousness of the act of assassination. The next time we encounter
a king taking his siesta, it will be David before he rises to behold Bathsheba.
Again, murder will ensue, though the king himself will be the perpetrator.

8. *Ish-Bosheth son of Saul your enemy, who sought your life.* The two sons of
Rimmon make exactly the same misguided calculation as the Amalekite messen-

enemy, who sought your life. The LORD has granted my lord the king
vengeance this day against Saul and his seed." And David answered 9
Rechab and Baanah his brother, the sons of Rimmon the Beerothite,
and he said to them, "As the LORD lives, Who saved my life from every
strait, he who told me, saying 'Look, Saul is dead,' and thought he was 10
a bearer of good tidings, I seized him and killed him in Ziklag instead of
giving him something for his tidings. How much more so when wicked 11
men have killed an innocent man in his bed in his house, and so, will
I not requite his blood from you and rid the land of you?" And David 12
commanded the lads, and they killed them and chopped off their hands
and feet and hung them by the pool in Hebron. And Ish-Bosheth's head
they took and buried in the grave of Abner in Hebron.

---

ger in Chapter 1, imagining that David will be delighted to hear of the destruction of anyone associated with Saul and will reward the bearers of the news.

11. *when wicked men have killed an innocent man in his bed in his house.* Either
this detail has been elided in the dialogue reported for Baanah and Rechab
when they come before David, or he has received advance word of the killing
and its circumstances from another source. In all this, the common scholarly
view is that the narrative is framed as an apology for David, taking pains to
clear him of any complicity in the deaths, first of Saul, then of Abner, and now
of Ish-Bosheth. But it is still more plausible that the writer is continuing his
representation of David as the consummately politic man: whether he really
feels moral revulsion against these assassins we have no way of knowing, but
he surely is aware, as he was after the murder of Abner, that it is in his political
interest to put the greatest possible distance between himself and the killers
of Saul's son, and what better way to do this than to have them executed on
the spot? David is nevertheless a beneficiary of the murder, for now there is no
claimant to the throne whom the northern tribes might follow instead of him.

12. *chopped off their hands and feet.* The dismembering of malefactors or prisoners was a common ancient Near Eastern practice, as we have seen before
(and compare the first chapter of Judges). Here the corpses are defiled by cutting off the hands that did the killing and the feet that carried the killers into
the victim's bedchamber. The whole episode ends in a strange image cluster
of detached body parts: the hands and feet of the two executed assassins and
the head of their victim. Even as David is about to assume control of a united
monarchy, we have an intimation of mayhem and dismemberment that is an
apt thematic prelude to the story of David's reign.

CHAPTER 5

1   And all the tribes of Israel came to David in Hebron, and they said,
2   "Here we are, your bone and your flesh are we. Time and again in the
    past when Saul was king over us you were the one who led Israel into
    the fray, and the LORD said to you,

    'It is you who will shepherd My people Israel
            and it is you who will be prince over Israel.'"

3   And all the elders of Israel came to the king in Hebron, and King David
    made a pact with them in Hebron before the LORD and they anointed

---

1. *all the tribes of Israel came to David*. "The tribes of Israel," in keeping with the
consistent usage of the preceding narrative, refers to the northern tribes that
had been loyal to the house of Saul. With the assassination of Abner and then
of Ish-Bosheth, they understandably now turn to David.

2. *you were the one . . . It is you*. The language of the tribal representatives puts
considerable emphasis on the second-person pronoun: you are the one that we,
and God, have chosen. The divine declaration of David's legitimacy as ruler,
quoted by the tribal spokesmen, is appropriately given the elevated status of
poetry.

3. *all the elders of Israel came to the king*. This is not a duplication of the report
in verse 1 from another source, as is often claimed. The convention used here is
the well-attested one of "resumptive repetition": when an interrupted narrative
strand is resumed, a phrase from the point of interruption is repeated verbatim
to mark the return to the main line. Here, the move to confirm David as king of
Israel, with which the episode began, after the insertion of the tribes' dialogue
(verses 1 and 2), is carried forward. It is the role of the tribal rank and file to
proclaim fealty, but of the elders to sign a pact and anoint David, and so "elders"

David as king over Israel. Thirty years old was David when he became 4
king, forty years he was king. In Hebron he was king over Judah seven 5
years and six months, and in Jerusalem he was king thirty-three years
over all Israel and Judah.

And the king went, and his men with him, to Jerusalem, to the Jebusite, 6
the inhabitant of the land, and he said to David, saying, "You shall not
enter here unless you can remove the blind and the lame," which is to

---

is now strategically substituted for "tribes" of the first verse. One should note
that the tribes come "to David" whereas the elders come "to the king," for they
are about to consummate the official business of kingmaking.

4. *forty years he was king.* In biblical usage, this is a formulaic number—in
Judges often used to indicate a full term of governing. But the specificity of
"seven years and six months" in Hebron has the look of a real number, whether
or not it is historically precise.

6. *the king went . . . to Jerusalem.* The chronological link between this action
and what precedes, as well as the chronology of the subsequent events in the
chapter, is not clear. The principle of organization appears to be thematic or
ideological rather than temporal. What we have here is a catalogue of salient
actions by which David consolidates his new monarchy: the conquest of a capital city in the center of the north-south axis of the country that does not belong
to any tribal territory (the same logic that led to the creation of Washington as
capital in the District of Columbia, not part of any state); the construction of
a palace with the assistance of a Phoenician alliance; the begetting of many
offspring, including the future heir to the throne, Solomon; the defeat of the
Philistines. The birth of Solomon is the clearest indication that these notices
do not follow the chronology of the preceding narrative.
   the blind and the lame. This puzzling phrase, together with its even more
enigmatic occurrence in verse 8, is a notorious crux. The most disparate theo-
ries have been proposed for how to read the words of the text and how to
reconstruct what is said to go on in the conquest of the city. The Qumran
Samuel scroll for this verse reads: "You shall not enter here, for the blind and
the lame have incited [*hesitu* for Masoretic *hesirkha*], saying, 'David shall not
enter here.'" This variant has the advantage of fluency, but one suspects it may
have been invented to make a difficult traditional text more intelligible. The
explanation proposed by Yigal Yadin is probably the most plausible: he points to
a Hittite text for the swearing in of troops in which a blind woman and a lame
man are set before the men with the monitory imprecation that their fate will be

7 say, "David shall not enter here!" And David captured the stronghold of
8 Zion, which is the City of David. And David said on that day, "Whoever
strikes down the Jebusite and reaches the conduit and the lame and the
blind utterly despised by David . . ." Therefore do they say, "No blind
9 man nor lame shall enter the House." And David stayed in the stronghold and called it the City of David, and David built round the rampart
10 and within. And David grew greater and greater, and the LORD God of
Armies was with him.

---

like that of those wretches if they fail in their duty. The Jebusites, then, might
have displayed the lame and the blind on the ramparts with an analogous curse
against those who would presume to attack the city. This taunting curse would
explain why these maimed figures are "despised by David."

8. *Whoever strikes down the Jebusite and reaches the conduit.* These words are
the other salient element of the crux, with debate still raging over the meaning
of "conduit" (*tsinor*). Some scholars have claimed it refers here to the windpipe,
or a lower part of the anatomy, of the Jebusites who are to be struck down, but
there is no Hebrew evidence for *tsinor* as anything but a water channel or tube,
and the argument from the analogy of shape is a weak one. Moreover, the verb
used here, *naga'*, means primarily "to touch," and in some biblical contexts, "to
reach" or "take charge of" but not "to strike." The most likely reference, then, is
to a daring route of surprise access into the city. A frequently proposed candidate is Warren's Shaft, discovered in 1867, an underground tunnel feeding in
from the Gihon Spring on a slope outside the wall to the east. Though everything about this report remains uncertain, David may be saying that whoever
manages to crawl through the tunnel, make his way up the vertical shaft that
transects it, and cut down the Jebusites within the town together with their
loathsome display of lame and blind will be given a great reward. (The reward
clause is missing; one is supplied in the parallel verse in Chronicles—"will
become a chief and commander.")

No blind man nor lame shall enter the House. The story is thus given an
etiological turn as an explanation for a known taboo, evidently pertaining to
the temple but perhaps to David's "house" (that is, the palace). One wonders
whether there is an invitation here to think of Jonathan's lame son—which
would be another gesture for denying the Saulides all future claim to the throne.

And Hiram king of Tyre sent messengers to David with cedar wood and ¹¹
carpenters and stonemasons, and they built a house for David. And ¹²
David knew that the LORD had set him up unshaken as king over Israel
and had exalted his kingship for the sake of His people Israel.

And David took other concubines and wives from Jerusalem after coming ¹³
from Hebron, and other sons and daughters were born to David. And ¹⁴
these are the names of those born to him in Jerusalem: Shammua and
Shobab and Nathan and Solomon, and Ibhar and Elishua and Nepheg ¹⁵
and Japhia, and Elishama and Eliada and Eliphelet. ¹⁶

And the Philistines heard that David had been anointed as king over ¹⁷
Israel, and all the Philistines came up to seek David. And David heard and
went down to the stronghold. The Philistines had come and deployed in ¹⁸
the Valley of Rephaim. And David inquired of the LORD, saying, "Shall I ¹⁹
go up against the Philistines? Will you give them into my hand?" And the
LORD said, "Go up, for I will surely give the Philistines into your hand."

---

11. *Hiram king of Tyre.* Hiram as a provider of timber and artisans points forward to Solomon's construction of the temple. If this is the Hiram with whom Solomon had dealings, David's palace building would have been undertaken rather late in his own reign in order to coincide with Hiram's regnal span.

13. *from Jerusalem.* Some Septuagint versions read "in Jerusalem."

17. *the Philistines heard.* David's assumption of the throne of all the tribes of Israel means that he has decisively cast aside his vassal status, and so the Philistines, who all along have been warring with the northern tribes, assemble their united forces ("all the Philistines") to suppress the new monarchy.
   the stronghold. The claim often made that this refers to the stronghold at Adullam (compare 1 Samuel 22) is unlikely because the battle here is entirely in the immediate vicinity of Jerusalem. This would have to be the stronghold within the city, referred to in verse 9. David can "go down" to it because his residence in Jerusalem could be topographically above the stronghold.

18. *the Valley of Rephaim.* The location is outside the walls of the Jebusite city, a couple of miles to the west.

20 And David came into Baal-Perazim, and David struck them down there, and he said, "The LORD has burst through my enemies before me like a bursting of water!" Therefore did he call the name of that place Baal-
21 Perazim. And they abandoned their idols there, and David with his men
22 bore them off. And once more the Philistines came up and deployed in
23 the Valley of Rephaim. And David inquired of the LORD, and He said, "You shall not go up. Turn around behind them and come at them from
24 opposite the willows. And as soon as you hear the sound of marching in the tops of the willows, then you must move boldly, for then shall the
25 LORD go out before you to strike down the camp of the Philistines." And David did just as the LORD had commanded him, and he struck down the Philistines from Geba till you come to Gezer.

---

20. *burst through my enemies . . . like a bursting of water*. The existing place-name is etiologically reinscribed to fit the military victory. Baal-Perazim may mean "god of earthquakes." The image of bursting through—the Hebrew term means "breach"—could suggest that David's forces have succeeded in punching a hole in the Philistine lines rather than in producing a general rout.

23. *opposite the willows*. The Hebrew *bekha'im* resists botanic identification—mulberry tree, pear tree, mastic bush, and others have been proposed. Some think it is a place-name, but the next verse makes that unlikely.

24. *the sound of marching in the tops of the willows*. Presumably, this is the wind. But it gives a sense that mysterious unseen agents of the LORD are advancing against the Philistines. More practically, some interpreters have proposed that the sound of the wind in the branches provided a cover for the sound of David's troops stealthily advancing for their surprise attack from the rear.

25. *from Geba till you come to Gezer*. Unlike the first victory, David now inflicts a general defeat on the Philistine forces, driving them back from the territory in central Canaan that they had occupied after triumphing over Saul at Gilboa. David has now completed the consolidation of his rule over all the land, and his real troubles are about to begin.

CHAPTER 6

And David gathered again all the picked men of Israel, thirty thou- 1
sand. And David arose and went, and all the troops who were with him, 2
to Baalah in Judah to bring up from there the Ark of God, over which
the name of the LORD of Armies enthroned on the cherubim is called.
And they mounted the Ark of God on a new cart and carried it off from 3
the house of Abinadab, which is on the Hill, and Uzzah and Ahio, the
sons of Abinadab, were driving the cart, and Ahio was walking before 4

---

1. *thirty thousand.* Some modern commentators understand *'alafim*, "thousands," as "military contingents," and thus reduce the number of troops to a
few hundred elite soldiers. But *'alafim* in a non-numerical sense refers to clans,
not military units; and as we have abundantly seen, exaggerated numbers are
common in these stories. Polzin, moreover, has aptly observed that thirty thousand is precisely the number of Israelites slain when the Ark was captured by
the Philistines (1 Samuel 4).

2. *to Baalah in Judah.* This place-name is a synonym for the Kiriath-Jearim of
1 Samuel 7:1—see, for example, Joshua 15:9. The Qumran Samuel scroll in
fact reads here: "Baalah, which is Kiriath-Jearim in Judah." The Masoretic text
reads *ba'aley yehudah*. Because this erroneous phrase was construed to mean
"the notables of Judah," a *mem* prefix ("from") was added to it to yield "from the
notables of Judah." But David is clearly going *to* the place Baalah.

3. *a new cart.* The new cart is a vehicle unpolluted by any previous secular use.

4. The Masoretic text begins this verse with a whole clause that is a scribal
duplication (dittography) of the first half of verse 3: "And they carried it off
from the house of Abinadab which is on the Hill." This clause is not present in
the Qumran Samuel, in the Septuagint, or in the parallel verse in 1 Chronicles
13:7. The Masoretic text also repeats the adjective "new" (*ḥadashah*) at the end
of verse 3, a repetition not reflected in the other ancient versions.

5 the Ark. And David and the whole house of Israel were playing before the LORD with all their might in song on lyres and tambourines and
6 castanets and cymbals. And they came to the threshing floor of Nacon, and Uzzah reached out to the Ark of God and took hold of it, for the
7 oxen had slipped. And the LORD's wrath flared up against Uzzah, and God struck him down there for reaching out his hand to the Ark, and
8 he died there by the Ark of God. And David was incensed because the LORD had burst out against Uzzah. And that place has been called Perez-
9 Uzzah to this day. And David was afraid of the LORD on that day and he
10 said, "How can the Ark of the LORD come to me?" And David did not want to remove the Ark of the LORD to himself in the City of David, and

---

5. *with all their might in song*. The translation reads here *bekhol 'oz uveshirim* with 1 Chronicles 13:8. The Masoretic text has *bekhol 'atsey beroshim*, "with all cypress woods," which only by a long interpretive stretch has been made to refer to percussion instruments.

6. *the threshing floor of Nacon*. The proper name here is in question. The Qumran Samuel reads "Nadon."

7. *the LORD's wrath flared up . . . and God struck him down*. This is an archaic story that defies later ethical categories: The Ark, as God's terrestrial throne, is invested with awesome divine power (compare 1 Samuel 6). To touch it, even in an effort to keep it from slipping off the cart, is to risk being consumed by its indwelling mana, as when one comes in contact with a high-voltage electric core. God's wrath against Uzzah triggers an answering wrath (the same verb in the Hebrew) on the part of David, frustrated in his purposes and now wondering whether he will ever manage to bring this symbol and earthly focus of God's power to his newly conquered capital.
for reaching out his hand to the Ark. The translation follows the parallel version in 1 Chronicles 13:10. The Masoretic text here has a single incomprehensible word, *shal*, which might be simply two consonants from the initial words of the lost clause recorded in Chronicles.

8. *Perez-Uzzah*. The Hebrew is construed to mean "bursting out against Uzzah." The naming story forms an antithetical symmetry with the story in 2 Samuel 5 of Baal-Perazim, there associated with God's "bursting through" the Philistine ranks.

David had it turned aside to the house of Obed-Edom the Gittite. And 11
the Ark of the Lord remained in the house of Obed-Edom three months
and the Lord blessed Obed-Edom and all his house. And it was told to 12
King David, saying, "The Lord has blessed the house of Obed-Edom
and all that he has on account of the Ark of God." And David went and
brought up the Ark of God from the house of Obed-Edom to the City
of David with rejoicing.

And it happened when the bearers of the Ark of the Lord had taken 13
six steps that he sacrificed a fatted bull. And David was whirling with 14
all his might before the Lord, girt in a linen ephod. And David and the 15
whole house of Israel were bringing up the Ark of the Lord in shouts
and with the sound of the ram's horn. And as the Ark of the Lord came 16
into the City of David, Michal daughter of Saul looked out through the

---

11. *Obed-Edom the Gittite.* He is a foreigner, perhaps (though this is not certain) from Philistine Gath—conceivably someone who had attached himself to
David during his sojourn there.

13. *when the bearers of the Ark of the Lord had taken six steps.* Some construe
this as an imperfect verb: with every six steps David would sacrifice a bull.
Apart from the difficulty that these constant sacrifices would make the procession interminable and require scores of thousands of bulls, the imperfect would
require the verb "to be" at the beginning of the sentence to appear in the suffix
conjugation *wehayah*, instead of the way it is, in the prefix conjugation, *wayehi*,
which implies a singulative, not an iterative, tense for the verb.

14. *girt in a linen ephod.* The wearing of the ephod surely underscores the fact
that in the procession of the Ark into Jerusalem, David is playing the roles of
both priest and king—a double service not unknown in the ancient Near East
(compare Melchisedek in Genesis 14). The ephod was probably a short garment tied around the hips or waist, and so David whirling and leaping might
easily have exposed himself, as Michal will bitterly observe.

16. *Michal daughter of Saul looked out through the window and saw King David.*
The preceding verse reports the shouts of jubilation and the shrill blasts of the
ram's horn: first she hears the procession approaching from the distance, then
she looks out and sees David dancing. Strategically, her repeated epithet in this
episode of final estrangement is "daughter of Saul," not "wife of David," and the
figure she sees is not "David her husband" but "King David." Shimon Bar-Efrat

window and saw King David leaping and whirling before the LORD, and
17 she scorned him in her heart. And they brought the Ark of the LORD
and set it up in its place within the tent that David had pitched for it,
and David offered up burnt offerings before the LORD and well-being
18 sacrifices. And David finished offering up the burnt offerings and the
well-being sacrifices, and he blessed the people in the name of the LORD
19 of Hosts. And he shared out to all the people, to all the multitude of
Israel, every man and woman, one loaf of bread and one date cake and
one raisin cake, and every one of the people went to his home.

20 And David turned back to bless his house. And Michal daughter of Saul
came out to meet David, and she said, "How honored today is the king

---

neatly observes that at the beginning of their story a loving Michal helped David
escape "through the window" from her father's henchmen while now she looks
at him from a distance "through the window," in seething contempt.

17.–20. Instead of proceeding directly to the confrontation between Michal
and David, as we might expect, the narrative lingers for a long moment over
David's cultic ministrations and royal benefactions to the people. One can
imagine that Michal continues to watch David from the window, performing
his role as the people's darling, and that she continues to simmer.

19. *date cake.* The Hebrew *'eshpar* appears nowhere else and so it is only a guess
as to what sort of delicacy it might be. Some traditional commentators construe
it as a portion of meat.

20. *How honored today is the king of Israel.* Astoundingly, until this climactic
moment, there has been no dialogue between Michal and David—only her
urgent instructions for him to flee in 1 Samuel 19 and his silent flight. We
can only guess what she may have felt all those years he was away from her,
acquiring power and wives, or during the civil war with her father's family. We
are equally ignorant of her feelings toward her devoted second husband, Paltiel
son of Laish. Now the royal couple are finally represented meeting, and when
Michal speaks out, it is in an explosion of angry sarcasm. Her first significant
word "honored" (balanced in David's rejoinder by two antonyms, "dishonored"
and "debased") is a complex satellite to the story of the grand entry of the Ark
with which it is linked. When the Ark was lost to the Philistines (1 Samuel 4),
the great cry was that "glory [or, honor, *kavod*—the same verbal root Michal
uses here] was exiled from Israel." Now glory/honor splendidly returns to Israel,

of Israel who has exposed himself today to the eyes of his servants' slavegirls as some scurrilous fellow would expose himself!" And David said   21
to Michal, "Before the LORD, Who chose me instead of your father and

---

but the actual invocation of the term is a sarcastic one, bitterly directed at
David, who will then hurl back two antonyms and try to redefine both honor
and dishonor to his wife. The logic of the larger story's moral and historical
realism requires that no triumph should be simple and unambiguous, that strife
and accusation pursue even the fulfillment of national destiny. One should also
note here that Michal speaks to her husband in the third person, not deferentially but angrily, and refers to him by public title, not in any personal relation
to her.

    who has exposed himself today to the eyes of his servants' slavegirls. The verb
"to expose" is clearly used in the sexual sense. The proud Michal's reference to
the lowly slavegirls' enjoying the sight of David's nakedness probably suggests
an edge of sexual jealousy as well as political resentment in her rage against
him. He has, after all, assembled a harem during their years apart, and there
is no indication that he has resumed sexual relations with her after having her
brought back to him forcibly for obviously political motives.

    as some scurrilous fellow would expose himself. The social thrust of the com-
parison is evident: she is a king's daughter, whereas he has now demonstrated
that he is no more than riffraff.

21. *Before the* LORD. Isaac Abravanel, the Hebrew commentator who was also
Ferdinand and Isabella's financial advisor until the expulsion of 1492, aptly
explains this: "Had he danced before some person to honor him, it would have
been a contemptible act, for his status was higher than any other person's. But
in his leaping before the LORD there is no cause for contempt." Thus David
can go on to say that he will perform ostensibly debasing acts, even debasing
in his own eyes (emending this to "His eyes" only clouds matters), acts that in
paradoxical fact are the opposite of debasement.

instead of all his house, to appoint me prince over the LORD's people,
22 over Israel, I will play before the LORD! And I will be dishonored still
more than this and will be debased in my own eyes! But with the slave-
23 girls about whom you spoke, with them let me be honored!" And Michal
daughter of Saul had no child till her dying day.

---

22. *with the slavegirls . . . with them let me be honored.* David flings back
Michal's sarcastic "how honored," suggesting that, unlike Michal, the simple
slavegirls will understand that his gyrations before the Ark are an act of reverence and will honor him for it. And there may also be a sexual edge in his
rejoinder: I will display myself to whomever I please, and it is I who will decide
whether it is honorable or not.

23. *And Michal daughter of Saul had no child till her dying day.* The whole story
of David and Michal concludes on a poised ambiguity through the suppression
of causal explanation: Is this a punishment from God, or simply a refusal by
David to share her bed, or is the latter to be understood as the agency for the
former?

CHAPTER 7

And it happened when the king was dwelling in his house and the Lord had granted him respite all around from his enemies, that the king said to Nathan the prophet, "See, pray, I dwell in a cedarwood house

---

1. *And it happened when the king was dwelling in his house.* This transitional note establishes a link with the previous episode, in which David brought the Ark into Jerusalem and had his final confrontation with Michal, which in a sense was the final blow to the house of Saul. What follows is a major caesura in the David story—a long pause marked by ideological reflections on the future, before David must deal once again with external enemies and then be engulfed by internecine strife in his court. The language of both Nathan's night vision and David's prayer is strikingly different from that of the surrounding narrative—more hortatory, more formulaic, more reminiscent of the Deuteronomistic school that would come to dominate Israel's national literature nearly four centuries after the reign of David. The literary archeology that has been performed on these two long passages remains in contention, some scholars claiming these are late compositions of a Deuteronomistic writer, others arguing that two or more authentically old literary strata have been joined together and framed by a later editor. These are not issues that it will be useful to attempt to resolve here. What is worth noting is the deliberate structural separation effected by these two passages between everything that precedes the ensconcing of throne and Ark in Jerusalem and everything that follows.

respite . . . from his enemies. The respite is partial, and temporary, because the subsequent chapters report further military campaigns.

2. *Nathan the prophet.* Not previously mentioned, and of unspecified background, he will play an important role in what follows.

a cedarwood house. The palace would have been a stone structure with cedar paneling within. Cedar was an expensive import item brought from Lebanon. (See 5:11.)

3 while the Ark of God dwells within curtains." And Nathan said to the
4 king, "Whatever is in your heart, go, do, for the LORD is with you." And
   it happened on that night, that the word of the LORD came to Nathan,
5 saying, "Go, say to My servant, to David, 'Thus says the LORD: Is it you
6 who would build Me a house for Me to dwell in? For I have dwelt in
   no house from the day I brought up the Israelites out of Egypt until
7 this day, but I have gone about in tent and tabernacle. Wherever I went
   about among all the Israelites, did I speak a word with any of the tribal
   chiefs of Israel whom I charged to shepherd My people Israel, saying,
8 Why did you not build me a cedarwood house? And now, thus shall you

---

curtains. The term is an obvious synecdoche for tent (compare 6:17).

3. *Whatever is in your heart, go, do.* Nathan's response to the brilliantly successful king, who has demonstrated through his triumphs that God is with him, is
perfectly reasonable. But in the night vision God will give different directions.

5. *Thus says the LORD.* The "messenger formula" signals the beginning of explicit
prophetic discourse. God's address to Nathan as a whole emphasizes the act
of speech, being constructed as an elaborate nesting of quoted speech within
quoted speech.

6. *I have dwelt in no house.* This is not, as some interpreters have claimed, the
expression of a pre-Solomonic antitemple ideology. The author of this episode
is faced with the difficulty of explaining a historical fact, that David did not
build the temple, as we might have expected, but rather it was his son Solomon who carried out the construction. The probable historical reason was that
David was too preoccupied with the struggles within his own court and family.
In Chronicles, the reason given is that he had shed blood. Here, the argument
God makes is that it is an act of presumption for a mere mortal to build a temple
for the unhoused God of Israelite history. But this line of reasoning actually
enhances the theological importance of Solomon's temple, for it suggests that
God Himself will build a house when He is good and ready, using the human
agency He chooses. Thus the temple that is to be raised up by David's seed will
have a more than human importance, being at once a token of God's indwelling among His people Israel and a divine underwriting of the Davidic dynasty.
   in tent and tabernacle. The latter was a portable shrine made of boards and
curtains. Presumably, local sanctuaries such as the one at Shiloh are assimilated into the archetype of tabernacle, being neither cultic centers for the
entire nation nor grand edifices like the Solomonic temple.

say to My servant, to David, Thus says the LORD of Hosts: I Myself took
you from the pasture, from following the flocks, to be prince over My
people, over Israel. And I have been with you wherever you have gone, 9
and I have cut down your enemies before you. And I will make you a
great name, like the name of the great of the earth. And I will set aside 10
a place for My people, for Israel, and plant them, and they shall abide
there and no longer quake, and the wicked shall no more afflict them as
before, from the day that I appointed judges over My people Israel. And 11
I will grant you respite from all your enemies, and the LORD declares
that it is He Who will make you a house. When your days are full and 12
you lie with your fathers, I will raise up your seed after you, who will
issue from your loins, and I will make his kingship unshaken. He it is 13
who will build a house for My name, and I will make the throne of his
kingship unshaken forever. I will be a father to him and he will be a son 14
to me, so should he do wrong, I will chastise him with the rod men use
and with the afflictions of humankind. But My loyalty shall not swerve 15
from him as I made it swerve from Saul whom I removed from before
you. And your house and your kingship shall be steadfast forever, your 16

10.–11. *no more afflict them as before, from the day that I appointed judges.*
Though the judges succeeded in temporarily driving off Israel's sundry oppressors, the period as a whole was one of instability and recurrent harassment by
enemy peoples.

11. *it is He Who will make you a house.* Both in this prophecy and in David's
prayer the double meaning of "house" is repeatedly exploited. God will grant
David a house—that is, a continuing dynasty, and then will have David's son
build Him a house—that is, a temple. The house in which David dwells in the
opening verse of this chapter is of course his palace in Jerusalem.

14. *the rod men use . . . the afflictions of humankind.* God will discipline the
future king as a father disciplines his son, and with familiar human tribulations,
not with supernatural bolts from the heavens.

15. *My loyalty.* The Hebrew *hesed* is the faithfulness and goodwill that one party
of a pact owes to the other.
  whom I removed. The Hebrew uses the same verb that is rendered here in
the immediately preceding phrase as "made it swerve."

17 throne unshaken forever.'" In accordance with all these words and in accordance with all this vision, so did Nathan speak to David.

18 And King David came and sat before the LORD and said, "Who am I, LORD God, and what is my house, that you have brought me this

19 far? And even this is too little in Your eyes, LORD God, for You have also spoken of Your servant's house in distant time, and this is a man's

20 instruction, LORD God. And how can David speak more to You, when

21 You know Your servant, LORD God? For the sake of Your word, and according to Your heart You have done all these great things, to make

22 known to Your servant. Therefore are You great, O LORD God, for there is none like You and there is no god beside You, in all we have heard

---

18. *David came and sat before the* LORD. David comes into the tent in which the Ark has been placed. The verb "sat," *yashav*, is identical with the verb at the beginning of the chapter that also means "dwell," and thus establishes a structural parallel between the passage on the postponed building of the temple and David's prayer.

19. *You have also spoken of Your servant's house in distant time.* These words refer directly to the prophecy conveyed to Nathan in verses 12–16, and thus undermine the claim of some scholars that David's prayer was originally part of the story of the introduction of the Ark to Jerusalem (Chapter 6), from which it was supposedly separated by the insertion of Nathan's prophecy.
this is a man's instruction. That is, he would scarcely think himself worthy of all this divine bounty about which God has just instructed him. But this is no more than an interpretive guess, for the meaning of the Hebrew—*zo't torat ha'adam*—is obscure.

22. *Therefore are You great, O* LORD *God.* Although the thread of piety in David's complex and contradictory character could be perfectly authentic, he does not elsewhere speak in this elevated, liturgical, celebratory style, and so the inference of the presence of another writer in this passage is plausible. Yet it is at least conceivable that the original writer has introduced this celebratory rhetoric to punctuate David's moment of respite in the story.

with our own ears. And who is like Your people Israel, a unique nation 23
upon earth, whom a god has gone out to redeem as a people to make
Him a name and to do great and awesome things for them, to drive out
from before Your people whom You redeemed from Egypt, nations with
their gods? And you made Your own people Israel unshaken forever, 24
and You, O LORD, became their God. And now LORD God, the word 25
that You have spoken to Your servant concerning his house—make it
stand forever and do as You have spoken. And may Your name be great 26
forever, so it be said, 'The LORD of Armies is God over Israel, and the
house of David Your servant shall be unshaken before You.' For You, O 27
LORD of Armies, God of Israel, have revealed to Your servant, saying, 'A
house will I build you.' Therefore has Your servant found the heart to
pray to you this prayer. And now, O LORD God, You are God and Your 28
words must be truth, You have spoken of this bounty to Your servant.
And now, have the goodness to bless the house of Your servant to be 29
before You forever, for it is You, LORD God, Who have spoken, and with
Your blessings may Your servant's house be blessed forever."

---

23. *for them.* The Masoretic text, at several points in these verses problematic, has "for you" (plural). The Qumran Samuel and the Septuagint have no
pronoun.

    to drive out. The Masoretic text is syntactically odd and semantically obscure.
The parallel verse in Chronicles omits "for your land" and adds "to drive out,"
as does this translation.

25. *the word that You have spoken to Your servant concerning his house.* This word
has just been conveyed to David through Nathan as God's intermediary. It is
humanly understandable that David should now fervently pray to God that the
grand promise of the night vision be fulfilled in time to come.

29. *it is You, LORD God, Who have spoken, and with Your blessings may Your
servant's house be blessed forever.* The fondness of biblical prose for thematic
key words is especially prominent in the grand theological performance that
is David's prayer, in which the key words function as formal rhetorical motifs.
The salient repeated terms are "speak" (the act of God's promise and continuing revelation), "house" (dynasty and palace but, in this speech, not temple),
"blessing" (in the final sentence it occurs three times in three different forms),
and "forever" (the adverbial index of the permanence of God's promise).

CHAPTER 8

1 And it happened thereafter that David struck down the Philistines and
subjugated them, and David took Metheg-Ammah from the hand of the
2 Philistines. And he struck down Moab, and measured them out with
a line, making them lie on the ground, and he measured two lengths
of a line to put to death and one full length to keep alive. And Moab

---

1. *And it happened thereafter*. This characteristically vague temporal reference
actually reflects the achronological arrangement of the narrative material at this
point. Chapter 7 was a long pause in the progress of the larger story that was
devoted to the theological grounds for the postponement of building a temple
and to the promise of a perpetual Davidic dynasty. Chapter 8 offers a summary
of David's conquests (which in historical fact would have spanned at least several years) resulting in the establishment of a small empire. We then revert to
the intimate story of David.

David struck down the Philistines and subjugated them. Neither the Hebrew
terms of the text nor the scant extrabiblical evidence allow one to conclude
whether David actually occupied the Philistine cities on the coastal plain or
merely reduced them to vassal status. In any case, he put an end to the Philistine military threat and was free to turn his attention to adversaries east of
the Jordan.

Metheg-Ammah. There are differences of opinion as to whether this is an
otherwise unknown place-name or the designation of some precious trophy
(*meteg* is an equestrian bit, *'amah* is a watercourse) taken from the Philistines.

2. *Moab*. It should be recalled that Moab, with whom David is linked by ances-
try, provided refuge for his parents from Saul. Perhaps now that David has
consolidated an Israelite monarchy, each side views the other as a threat. Or
perhaps Moab has been compelled by proximity to join forces with the anti-
Israelite kingdoms east of the Jordan.

and measured them out with a line. This procedure is not otherwise known.

became tribute-bearing vassals to David. And David struck down Hada- 3
dezer son of Rehob, king of Zobah as he went to restore his monument
by the Euphrates River. And David captured from him one thousand 4
seven hundred horsemen and twenty thousand foot soldiers, and David
hamstrung all the chariot horses, leaving aside a hundred of them. And 5
the Arameans of Damascus came to aid Hadadezer, king of Zobah, and
David struck down twenty-two thousand men from among the Arameans. And David set up prefects in Aram-Damascus, and the Arameans 6
became tribute-bearing vassals to David, and the LORD made David victorious wherever he went. And David took the golden quivers that had 7
belonged to the servants of Hadadezer and brought them to Jerusalem.
And from Betah and from Berothai, the towns of Hadadezer, King David 8
took a great abundance of bronze.

---

3. *Zobah*. Aram-Zobah was at this point the large dominant kingdom of Mesopotamia, to the north and east of biblical Israel.

   as he went to restore his monument. Presumably, the absence of the king from
the Aramean heartland exposed it to David's attack. The term *yad* here (usually "hand") is construed in its occasional sense of monument or stele, though
the idiom *heshiv yad* (literally, "to bring back the hand") also has the sense of
"strike." Were that the case here, however, one would probably expect an object
to the striking ("brought his hand back against X.").

4. *one thousand seven hundred horsemen*. The numbers reflected in Chronicles
and in the Septuagint as well as in the Qumran Samuel scroll are "one thousand
chariots and seven thousand horsemen."

   David hamstrung all the chariot horses. The most likely explanation for this
cruel act is that the Israelites, who initially fought on mountainous terrain, as
yet made no significant use of cavalry, and so David's only concern would be
to disable the horses in order that they could not be used against him in the
future. The hundred horses left unmaimed might perhaps be for use as a small
experiment with cavalry, or as draft animals.

7. *the golden quivers*. The relatively rare Hebrew term *shelatim* has often been
understood as "shields," but most of the other biblical occurrences encourage
the notion of something that contains arrows, as Rashi observed, and this sense
is supported by cognates in Babylonian and Aramaic.

9 And Toi king of Hammath heard that David had struck down all the
10 forces of Hadadezer. And Toi sent Joram his son to King David to ask
   after his well-being and to salute him for having done battle with Hadadezer and for striking him down, as Hadadezer was Toi's adversary. And
   in Joram's hand there were vessels of silver and vessels of gold and vessels
11 of bronze. These, too, did King David consecrate to the Lord, together
   with the silver and the gold that he consecrated from all the nations
12 he had conquered: from Edom and from Moab and from the Ammonites and from the Philistines and from Amalek and from the plunder of
13 Hadadezer son of Rehob, king of Zobah. And David made a name when
   he came back from striking down the Edomites in the Valley of Salt—
14 eighteen thousand of them. And he set up prefects in Edom, throughout
   Edom he set up prefects, and all Edom became vassals to David, and the
   Lord made David victorious wherever he went.

---

9. *Toi king of Hammath*. Hammath lay to the northwest of the kingdom of
Aram-Zobah, in present-day Syria. It was a neo-Hittite state.

10. *And Toi sent Joram his son to King David*. Sending the prince as emissary
is a token of the importance that the king attaches to the mission. The vessels
of precious metals are a peace offering to David or, from another perspective,
an advance payment of tribute. Toi, as a king who has been threatened by the
Arameans, has good reason to pledge fealty to David, but he surely also wants
to ward off any possible military thrust of the expansionist Israelites against his
own kingdom.

12. *from Edom*. The Masoretic text has "from Aram," but Chronicles, the Septuagint, and the Peshitta all have Edom, a kingdom contiguous with Moab,
which immediately follows. Aram (Zobah) is mentioned at the end of the verse.

13. *from striking down the Edomites*. Again, the Masoretic text has "Aram" in
contradiction to several other ancient versions. Since the Valley of Salt was
most probably in the vicinity of the Dead Sea, it would have been Edomite,
not Aramean, territory.

And David was king over all Israel, and it was David's practice to mete ₁₅
out true justice to all his people. And Joab son of Zeruiah was over the ₁₆
army, and Jehoshaphat son of Ahilud was recorder. And Zadok son of ₁₇
Ahitub and Abiathar son of Ahimelech were priests, and Seraiah was
scribe. And Benaiah son of Jehoida was over the Cherethites and the ₁₈
Pelethites, and David's sons served as priests.

---

15. *And David was king over all Israel.* The chronicle of David's conquests is
followed by a kind of epilogue—a notice of the royal bureaucracy.

16. *recorder.* The Hebrew term *mazkir* could also be represented as "remem-
brancer." It is not entirely clear what his duties were, though they obviously
went far beyond being a mere clerk. He may have been in control of the royal
archives. It has been proposed that he was also chief of protocol in the palace.

17. *Abiathar son of Ahimelech.* The Masoretic text makes Ahimelech the son
and Abiathar the father, in flat contradiction to the occurrences of these two
figures both earlier and later in the narrative.

  scribe. As with "recorder," the responsibilities were more than those of an
amanuensis. They might have included diplomatic translation and even coun-
seling in affairs of state.

18. *the Cherethites and the Pelethites.* There is debate over the national identity
of the latter, but the consensus is that the former are people of Cretan origins,
part of the wave of so-called Sea Peoples who immigrated to Canaan from the
Aegean toward the beginning of the eleventh century. David has taken care to
set up a special palace guard of foreign mercenaries on whose loyalty he can
rely, in contrast to Israelites who might have motives of tribal allegiance or support for some pretender to the throne in an attempt to displace him.

  and David's sons served as priests. This curious detail is probably parallel to
the report of a palace guard of foreign origins: just as David creates an elite
military contingent outside the framework of the Israelite troops, he invests
his own sons with sacerdotal duties within the circle of the court, outside the
framework of the hereditary priesthood that controlled the public cult.

CHAPTER 9

And David said "Is there anyone who is still left from the house of Saul, that I may keep faith with him for the sake of Jonathan?" And there was a servant of the house of Saul named Ziba, and they called him to David, and the king said to him, "Are you Ziba?" And he said, "Your servant." And the king said, "Is there anyone at all left from the house of Saul, that I might keep God's faith with him?" And Ziba said to the king,

---

1. *And David said.* We are immediately alerted to the fact that we are returning from the chronicle summary of Chapter 8 (where there is no dialogue) and from the long set speeches of Chapter 7 to the main body of the David story because once again the narrative is carried forward to a large extent by dialogue. We are again plunged into a world of personal and political transactions engaged through exchanges of spoken language.

Is there anyone who is still left from the house of Saul? The added emphasis of "still," 'od (compare the analogous emphatic phrase in verse 3), reflects David's genuine uncertainty as to whether, after all the deaths of the Saulides previously reported, there are in fact any surviving descendants of Saul. The courtiers who are queried evidently don't know, so they propose summoning a retainer of Saul's in order to put the question to him. The fact that David is later complicit in the execution of seven men of the house of Saul (Chapter 21) has led many analysts to conclude that the original place of that episode was before the present chapter. Polzin, on the other hand, argues that the postponement of the report in Chapter 21 is deliberately delayed exposition, meant to reveal another troubling facet of David near the end of his story.

3. *keep God's faith.* The "faith" in question (*ḥesed*) is not credal but faithful performance of one's obligation in a covenant, a term that also has the connotation of "kindness." "God" here has the force of an intensifier. The covenant that is explicitly alluded to is the one between Jonathan and David (1 Samuel 20:42). That tight link is one of several arguments against the view widely held ever

"There is yet a son of Jonathan's, who is crippled." And the king said, 4
"Where is he?" And Ziba said, "Why, he is in the house of Machir son of
Amiel from Lo-Debar." And King David sent and fetched him from the 5
house of Machir son of Amiel from Lo-Debar. And Mephibosheth son 6
of Jonathan son of Saul came to David and flung himself on his face and
prostrated himself. And David said, "Mephibosheth!" And he said, "Your 7
servant here." And David said to him, "Fear not, for I will surely keep
faith with you for the sake of Jonathan your father, and I will give back
to you all the land of Saul your grandfather, and as for you, you shall eat
bread at my table always." And he prostrated himself and said, "What is 8

---

since the 1926 study of Leonhard Rost that this episode marks the beginning
of a wholly independent Succession Narrative, which continues till 1 Kings 2.

   who is crippled. Ziba's mention of the surviving Saulide's handicap is probably intended to assure David that Mephibosheth will not pose any challenge
to the throne.

4. *Lo-Debar.* Mephibosheth was evidently taken to this northern trans-Jordanian town because it was a place of refuge. It is in the general vicinity of
Jabesh-Gilead, the town inhabited by Saul's allies and perhaps kinsmen.
Mephibosheth, it will be recalled, was five years old when he was dropped by
his nurse and crippled in the flight after the defeat at Gilboa. Since it seems
implausible that more than fifteen or so years would have passed since that
moment, one may surmise that he is now a man in his twenties.

6. *Mephibosheth . . . flung himself on his face and prostrated himself.* These
gestures of abasement may have been standard etiquette in approaching a
monarch, but Ziba is not reported making them. Mephibosheth is clearly terrified that the king may have summoned him in order to have him put to
death—David's possible complicity in the deaths of other figures associated
with the house of Saul might well have been a matter of continuing speculation in Benjaminite circles. As Fokkelman aptly notes, it would have been a
particularly painful business for a man crippled in both legs to fling himself
down in this fashion.

7. *I will give back to you all the land of Saul.* With the descendants of Saul fled
or dead, the king had expropriated Saul's ancestral land around Gibeah.

9 your servant that you should have turned to a dead dog like me?" And
   the king called to Ziba, Saul's lad, and said to him, "All that was Saul's
10 and his whole household's I give to your master's son. And you shall
   work the soil for him, you and your sons and your slaves, and you shall
   bring food to your master's house and they will eat. But Mephibosheth
   will always eat bread at my table." And Ziba had fifteen sons and twenty
11 slaves. And Ziba said to the king, "Whatever my lord the king commands his servant, thus will his servant do." And Mephibosheth ate at
12 David's table like one of the king's sons. And Mephibosheth had a little

---

9. *Saul's lad*. The Hebrew *na'ar* denotes subservience, but it is unclear whether,
as some have claimed, it indicates Ziba's role as majordomo (the philological
grounds for that construction are shaky) or rather his subaltern status in the
house of Saul.

10. *your slaves*. The Hebrew term *'eved* straddles the sense of freeborn under-
ling and slave. Ziba evidently belongs to the former category, and so the designation *'eved* is rendered as "servant" when it is attached to him. It seems likely
that the underlings of a prosperous servant would be slaves. Polzin has noted
that different forms of this verbal stem occur ten times in the chapter, which is
all about establishing lines of dominance and subservience.
   and you shall bring food for your master's house and they will eat. The translation here follows the text of the Septuagint. The Masoretic text reads: "and
you shall bring and it will be food for your master's son and he will eat it." That
version can be maintained only with strain, for the very next clause informs us
that Mephibosheth was not dependent on the yield of his own land but resided
in Jerusalem, sustained at the royal table.

11. *And Mephibosheth ate at David's table*. Again, the translation follows the
Septuagint. The Masoretic text has "And Mephibosheth is eating at my table,"
but the Bible never gives reported speech without an explicit introduction ("and
David said").

son named Micah, and all who dwelled in Ziba's house were servants
to Mephibosheth. And Mephibosheth dwelled in Jerusalem, for at the   13
king's table he would always eat. And he was lame in both his feet.

---

13. *for at the king's table he would always eat.* The refrainlike repetition of this
clause should give us pause. David is indeed treating Jonathan's crippled son
like one of his own sons, "keeping faith" or "showing kindness" to the offspring
of his dead comrade, as he had pledged. He surely means his benefaction to
be publicly perceived. At the same time, it is clearly in David's interest to keep
the only conceivable Saulide pretender to the throne close at hand, under easy
scrutiny. Mephibosheth's condition is ostensibly that of an unofficially adopted
son, but with an uneasy suspicion that it is really a kind of luxurious house
arrest.

And he was lame in both his feet. This emphatic concluding reiteration of his
physical impairment might be intended, as some commentators have proposed,
to explain why he could not travel back and forth between his estate and Jerusalem. But it surely also strikes a plaintive note at the end, underscoring the
vulnerability of Mephibosheth, whether cosseted or held under surveillance in
the Jerusalem court. As the court becomes more and more the arena of plots
and murderous conflict, Mephibosheth will be victimized by someone close to
him. This notice at the end about Mephibosheth's lameness also underscores
the continuing antithesis between the fates of the house of Saul and the house
of David: King David came into Jerusalem whirling and dancing before the
Lord; the surviving Saulide limps into Jerusalem, crippled in both legs

CHAPTER 10

1 And it happened thereafter that the king of the Ammonites died and
2 Hanun his son was king in his stead. And David said, "Let me keep faith
   with Hanun son of Nahash as his father kept faith with me." And David
   sent his servants in order to console him for his father, and David's ser-
3 vants came to the land of the Ammonites. And the Ammonite commanders said to Hanun their lord, "Do you imagine David is honoring your
   father in sending you consolers? Is it not in order to search out the city

---

1. *And it happened thereafter.* Once again this vague temporal formula reflects
the achronological ordering of the text. Since the Aramean king Hadadezer
is reported in 8:3–7 to have been decisively defeated by David and to have
become David's vassal, the campaign that is represented here, in which Hadadezer musters Aramean forces east of the Euphrates in order to confront David,
must have taken place as part of David's victorious struggle with Aram Zobah
registered in the summary of Chapter 8. This whole account of military opera-
tions—given its rather dry technical style, it may well have been drawn from
Davidic annals—is meant to establish the facts of continuing armed conflict
with the Ammonites, which is the crucial background for the story of David and
Bathsheba in the next chapter.

2. *Let me keep faith with Hanun son of Nahash as his father kept faith with me.* This
chapter, like the preceding one, opens with a declaration of David's desire to keep
faith with, or do kindness to, the son of a father toward whom he feels some prior
obligation. There is no notice in the previous narrative of Nahash's having done
favors for David, but several scholars have surmised that Nahash's enmity toward
Saul (see 1 Samuel:11) might have led him to provide refuge or logistical support
to David and his men when they were being hunted down by Saul.

3. *to search out the city.* As Moshe Garsiel notes, the walled cities of the ancient
Near East often had tunnels, underground conduits, or other points of vulner-

and to spy on it and to overthrow it that David has sent his servants to you?" And Hanun took David's servants and shaved off half the beard of   4
each and cut off half their diplomat's garb down to their buttocks, and sent them off. And they told David, and he sent to meet them, for the   5
men were very humiliated, and the king said, "Stay here in Jericho until your beards grow back and you can return."

And the Ammonites saw that they had become repugnant to David, and   6
the Ammonites sent and hired Arameans from Beth-Rehob and Arame-ans from Zobah, twenty thousand foot soldiers, and King Maacah with

---

ability that could provide access to the enemy in a siege. David's forces may have broken into Jerusalem in this fashion. (See the comment on 5:8.)

4. *shaved off half the beard of each and cut off half their diplomats' garb*. Shaving the beard is an insult to the masculinity of the ambassadors, all the more so because it is done in a disfiguring way, with half the beard left uncut. The exposure of one buttock, by cutting away half the garment vertically, is similarly shaming, perhaps sexually shaming. The garments in question, moreover, are not ordinary clothes, *begadim*, but *madim*, garb worn in the performance of an official function (compare the "battle garb," *madim*, that Saul gives to David in 1:17:38). The Ammonites thus are not merely insulting the ambassadors personally but provocatively violating their diplomatic privilege. In all this, we observe an extravagant reflection of the symbolic violation of Saul by David when he cut off a corner of the king's robe.

5. *Stay here in Jericho*. The town of Jericho is in the Jordan Valley just west of the Jordan, and is plausibly the first place of habitation that the ambassadors would come to on crossing back from Ammonite territory.

6. *And the Ammonites saw*. Shimon Bar-Efrat observes that this narrative sequence is formally structured by the "seeing" of David's trans-Jordanian adversaries (here, verse 14, verse 15, verse 19), in counterpoint to David's "hearing." The latter implies receiving word at a distance, as does the associ-ated locution, "it was told to David," whereas the former signifies immediate observation. Thus Joab, making out the deployment of hostile forces on the battlefield, is also said to see.

7 a thousand men, and the men of Tob, twelve thousand men. And David
8 heard and sent out Joab together with the whole army of warriors. And
   the Ammonites sallied forth and drew up for battle at the entrance to
   the gate, and Aram Zobah and Rehob and the men of Tob were apart
9 in the field. And Joab saw that there was a battle line against him in
   front and behind, and he chose from all the picked men of Israel and
10 drew them up to meet the Arameans. And the rest of the troops he gave
   into the hand of Abishai his brother, and he drew them up to meet the
11 Ammonites. And he said, "If the Arameans prove too strong for me, you
   will rescue me, and if the Ammonites prove too strong for you, I shall

---

7. *David heard and sent out Joab.* Throughout this chapter and the next, the verb
"to send" is repeatedly linked with David: for the first time, he plays the role not of
martial leader but of sedentary king, delegating the military task to his commander.
This new state of affairs will have major implications in the Bathsheba story.
    the whole army of warriors. This is a slight variant, supported by three ancient
versions, of the Masoretic text, which reads "the whole army, the warriors."

9. *there was a battle line against him in front and behind.* The Israelite forces
are in danger of being caught in the pincer movement between the Aramean
mercenaries advancing on them from the northeast and the Ammonites, presumably to the south. Joab rapidly improvises a counterstrategy, selecting a corp
of elite troops to assault the larger force of Arameans and sending his brother
Abishai with the rest of the troops against the Ammonites. Such attention to
military detail is quite untypical of biblical narrative, as is the rousing battlefield
exhortation (verse 12) with which Joab concludes his instructions. The point
of such detail is surely to show Joab as a superbly competent and resolute field
commander, just before the great pivotal episode in the next chapter in which
Joab maintains the siege against Rabbath Ammon while his commander in
chief slumbers, and lusts, in Jerusalem.

10. *the rest of the troops he gave.* Polzin observes, with puzzlement, that this
story proceeds by dividing things in half: beards, clothing, anti-Israelite forces,
Israelite troops. One wonders whether this narrative dynamic of mitosis, even
though it is a saving strategy in Joab's case, might be a thematic introduction to
all the inner divisions in court and nation, the fractures in the house of David,
that take up the rest of the narrative.

come to rescue you. Be strong, and let us find strength for the sake of 12
our people and for the sake of the towns of our God, and the LORD will
do what is good in His eyes!" And Joab advanced, and the troops who 13
were with him, to battle against the Arameans, and they fled before
him. And the Ammonites saw that the Arameans had fled, and they fled 14
from Abishai and went into the town, and Joab turned back from the
Ammonites and came to Jerusalem.

And the Arameans saw that they had been routed by Israel, and they 15
reassembled. And Hadadezer sent and brought out the Arameans who 16
were beyond the Euphrates, and their forces came with Shobach the
commander of Hadadezer's army at their head. And it was told to David, 17
and he gathered all Israel and crossed the Jordan, and they came to
Helam. And the Arameans drew up their lines against David and did 18
battle with him. And the Arameans fled before Israel, and David killed
seven hundred charioteers of the Arameans and forty thousand horsemen, and Shobach, the commander of their army, he struck down, and

---

14. *and went into the town*. The town into which they withdraw under pressure
from Abishai's troops is not named. It could be the capital, Rabbath Ammon
(present-day Amman), though some analysts have wondered whether Hanun
would be so unwise as to wait till the Israelites were at the gates of his own
city before taking a decisive stand. Another candidate that has been proposed
is Medbah, an Ammonite town considerably farther to the south.

15. *they reassembled*. This major regrouping for a second campaign against the
Israelites involves the enlisting of greater numbers of troops from the Arameans
east of the Euphrates, ethnic kin and in all likelihood political vassals to the
people of Aram Zobah.

17. *he gathered all Israel*. Alerted to the augmented size of the trans-Jordanian
forces, David musters his entire national army and this time elects to command
it himself.

19 he died there. And all the kings who were vassals to Hadadezer saw
that they had been routed by Israel, and they made peace with Israel
and became its vassals, and the Arameans were afraid to rescue the
Ammonites again.

---

19. *And all the kings who were vassals . . . made peace with Israel.* Seeing who has
the military upper hand, they take a small and logical step in exchanging vassal
status under Hadadezer for vassal status under David. It should be noted that
this whole annalistic prelude to the story of David and Bathsheba concludes
with an invocation of "all the kings." The immediately following episode begins
by mentioning "the time the kings sally forth"—though, as we shall see, the
noun itself there is pointedly ambiguous—and the tale that unfolds will powerfully raise the question of what constitutes kingly behavior.

CHAPTER 11

And it happened at the turn of the year, at the time the kings sally   1
forth, that David sent out Joab and his servants with him and all Israel,

Chapters 11 and 12, the story of David and Bathsheba and its immediate aftermath, are the great turning point of the whole David story, as both Sternberg
and Polzin have duly observed; and it seems as though the writer has pulled
out all the stops of his remarkable narrative art in order to achieve a brilliant
realization of this crucially pivotal episode. The deployment of thematic key
words, the shifting play of dialogue, the intricate relation between instructions
and their execution, the cultivated ambiguities of motive, are orchestrated with
a richness that scarcely has an equal in ancient narrative. Though the analytic
scholars have variously sought to break up these chapters into editorial frame
and Succession Narrative, Prophetic composition and old source, emending
patches of the text as they proceed, such efforts are best passed over in silence,
for the powerful literary integrity of the text speaks for itself.

1. *at the turn of the year*. The most plausible meaning is the beginning of the
spring, when the end of the heavy winter rains makes military action feasible.
    at the time the kings sally forth. There is a cunning ambiguity here in the
Hebrew text. The received consonantal text reads *mal'akhim*, "messengers,"
though many manuscripts show *melakhim*, "kings." As Polzin observes, the verb
"to sally forth" (or, in nonmilitary contexts, "to go forth") is often attached to
kings and never to messengers, so "kings" is definitely the more likely reading,
though the ghost of "messengers" shows through in the letters of the text. Polzin
beautifully describes this double take: "the verse clearly doubles back on itself
in a marvelous display of narrative virtuosity: at a time when kings go forth,
David did not, making it a time, therefore, when messengers must go forth; at
a time when messengers go forth, David, remaining in Jerusalem, sent Joab,
his servants and all Israel to ravage Ammon." What some see here as a scribal
error may well be a deliberate orthographic pun
    David sent out Joab. The verb "to send"—the right verb for "messengers"—
occurs eleven times in this chapter, framing the beginning and the end. This

and they ravaged the Ammonites and besieged Rabbah. And David was
sitting in Jerusalem.

2 And it happened at eventide that David arose from his bed and walked
about on the roof of the king's house, and he saw from the roof a woman
3 bathing, and the woman was very beautiful. And David sent and inquired
after the woman, and the one he sent said, "Why, this is Bathsheba

---

episode is not a moral parable but a story anchored in the realities of political
history. It is concerned with the institutionalization of the monarchy. David,
now a sedentary king removed from the field of action and endowed with a
dangerous amount of leisure, is seen constantly operating through the agency
of others, sending messengers within Jerusalem and out to Ammonite territory.
Working through intermediaries, as the story will abundantly show, creates a
whole new order of complications and unanticipated consequences.

And David was sitting in Jerusalem. The verb for "sitting" also means "to stay"
(compare verse 12), but it is best to preserve the literal sense here because of
the pointed sequence: sitting, lying, rising, and because in biblical usage "to sit"
is also an antonym of "to go out" (or sally forth).

2. *at eventide.* The Hebrew term *'et'erev* echoes ironically with the phrase *'et
tse't*, "at the time of sallying forth" in the previous verse. A siesta on a hot spring
day would begin not long after noon, so this recumbent king has been in bed
an inordinately long time.

he saw from the roof. The palace is situated on a height, so David can look
down on the naked Bathsheba bathing, presumably on her own rooftop. This
situation of the palace also explains why David tells Uriah to "go down" to his
house. Later in the story, archers deal destruction from the heights of the city
wall, the Hebrew using the same preposition, *me'al*, to convey the sense of
"from above."

3. *the one he sent said.* The Hebrew uses an unspecified "he said."

Bathsheba daughter of Eliam wife of Uriah the Hittite. It is unusual to identify
a woman by both father and husband. The reason may be, as Bar-Efrat suggests, that both men are members of David's elite corps of warriors. Although
Uriah's designation as Hittite has led some interpreters to think of him as a
foreign mercenary, the fact that he has a pious Israelite name ("the LORD is my
light") suggests that he is rather a native or at least a naturalized Israelite of
Hittite extraction. In any case, there is obvious irony in the fact that the man of
foreign origins is the perfect Good Soldier of Israel, whereas the Israelite king
betrays and murders him.

daughter of Eliam wife of Uriah the Hittite." And David sent messengers 4
and fetched her and she came to him and he lay with her, she having just
cleansed herself of her impurity, and she returned to her house. And the 5
woman became pregnant and sent and told David and said, "I am pregnant." And David sent to Joab: "Send me Uriah the Hittite." And Joab 6
sent Uriah the Hittite to David.

And Uriah came to him, and David asked how Joab fared and how the 7
troops fared and how the fighting fared. And David said to Uriah, "Go 8
down to your house and bathe your feet." And Uriah went out from the

---

4. *David sent . . . and fetched her and she came to him and he lay with her.* It
is not uncommon for biblical narrative to use a chain of verbs in this fashion to indicate rapid, single-minded action. What is unusual is that one verb
in the middle of this sequence switches grammatical subject—from David to
Bathsheba. When the verb "come to" or "come into" has a masculine subject
and "into" is followed by a feminine object, it designates a first act of sexual
intercourse. One wonders whether the writer is boldly toying with this double
meaning, intimating an element of active participation by Bathsheba in David's
sexual summons. The text is otherwise entirely silent on her feelings, giving the
impression that she is passive as others act on her. But her later behavior in the
matter of her son's succession to the throne (1 Kings 1–2) suggests a woman
who has her eye on the main chance, and it is possible that opportunism, not
merely passive submission, explains her behavior here as well. In all of this,
David's sending messengers first to ask about Bathsheba and then to call her
to his bed means that the adultery can scarcely be a secret within the court.

 cleansed herself of her impurity. The reference is to the ritually required bath
after the end of menstruation. This explains Bathsheba's bathing on the roof
and also makes it clear that she could not be pregnant by her husband.

5. *I am pregnant.* Astonishingly, these are the only words Bathsheba speaks in
this story. In keeping with the stringent efficiency of biblical narrative, the story
leaps forward from the sexual act to the discovery of pregnancy.

8. *Go down to your house and bathe your feet.* Some interpreters have made this
more heavy-handed than it is by construing the final phrase as a euphemism
for sex (because "feet" in the Bible is occasionally a euphemism for the male
genitals). But in the biblical world, bathing the feet is something travelers regularly do when they come from the dusty road. This bathing of the feet stands
in a kind of synecdochic relation to Bathsheba's bathing of her whole body,

9 king's house and the king's provisions came out after him. And Uriah lay
at the entrance to the king's house with all the servants of his master,
10 and he went not down to his house. And they told David, saying, "Uriah
did not go down to his house." And David said to Uriah, "Look, you have
11 come from a journey. Why have you not gone down to your house?" And
Uriah said to David, "The Ark and Israel and Judah are sitting in huts,
and my master Joab and my master's servants are encamped in the open
field, and shall I then come to my house to eat and to drink and to lie

---

discreetly suggesting that after the bathing of the feet, other refreshments of
the body will ensue.

the king's provisions. David has not explicitly mentioned food or wine, but he
sends a kind of catered dinner after Uriah, hoping that the feast with Bathsheba
will get husband and wife into the desired amorous mood.

9. *And Uriah lay at the entrance of the king's house.* The verb "to lie," according
to David's expectations, should have been followed by "with his wife." Instead,
we have not sex but a soldier's sleeping with his comrades, who are guarding the
king. It should be remembered (compare 1 Samuel 21) that soldiers in combat
generally practiced sexual abstinence.

11. *sitting in huts.* Some construe *sukot,* "huts," as a place-name, the city of
Succoth a little east of the Jordan. But if the Ark is sent out of Jerusalem to
the front, it would make no sense to detain it at a logistics center only halfway
to the battlefield, and Uriah's point is that neither the Ark nor the troops enjoy
proper shelter (while David is "sitting in Jerusalem").

shall I then come to my house to eat and to drink and to lie with my wife?
Uriah now spells out all that David left unsaid when he urged him to go down
to his house. The crucial detail of sleeping with Bathsheba comes at the very
end. Menakhem Perry and Meir Sternberg, in a pioneering Hebrew article in
1968 (revised by Sternberg for his English book of 1985), raised the provocative
issue of deliberate ambiguity (comparing the strategy of this story with the two
mutually exclusive readings possible for Henry James's short story "The Turn
of the Screw"). In their view, there are two equally viable readings. If Uriah
does *not* know that David has cuckolded him, he is the instrument of dramatic
irony—the perfect soldier vis-à-vis the treacherous king who is desperately
trying to manipulate him so that the husband will unwittingly cover the traces
of his wife's sexual betrayal. If Uriah *does* know of the adultery, he is a rather different character—not naive but shrewdly aware, playing a dangerous game of
hints in which he deliberately pricks the conscience of the king, cognizant, and
perhaps not caring, that his own life may soon be forfeit. More recently, Moshe

with my wife? By your life, by your very life, I will not do this thing."
And David said to Uriah, "Stay here today as well, and tomorrow I shall   12
send you off." And Uriah stayed in Jerusalem that day and the next. And   13
David called him, and he ate before him and drank, and David made
him drunk. And he went out in the evening to lie in the place where
he lay with the servants of his master, but to his house he did not go
down. And it happened in the morning that David wrote a letter to Joab   14
and sent it by the hand of Uriah. And he wrote in the letter, saying,   15
"Put Uriah in the face of the fiercest battling and draw back, so that
he will be struck down and die." And it happened, as Joab was keeping   16
watch on the town, that he placed Uriah in the place where he knew

---

Garsiel has proposed a reconciliation of these two readings: when Uriah first
arrives from the front, he is unaware of what has occurred; after the first night
with his comrades at the palace gate, he has been duly informed of the sexual
betrayal, so that in his second dialogue with the king, he cultivates a rhetoric
of implicit accusation. Garsiel observes that when Uriah swears emphatically
by David's life (verse 11), he does not add the deferential "my lord the king."

13. *David called him.* The verb here has the idiomatic sense of "invite."
   he ate before him. The preposition is an indication of hierarchical distance
between subject and king.
   David made him drunk. "David" has been added for clarity. The Hebrew says
only "he made him drunk." Plying Uriah with wine is a last desperate attempt,
and a rather crude one, to get him to have sex with his wife.

14. *sent it by the hand of Uriah.* The letter would be in the form of a small scroll
with either a seal or threads around it. David is counting on the fact that Uriah
as a loyal soldier will not dream of opening the letter. If he does not know of the
adultery, he has in any case no personal motive to look at the letter. If he does
know, he is accepting his fate with grim resignation, bitterly conscious that his
wife has betrayed him and that the king is too powerful for him to contend with.

15. *so that he will be struck down and die.* With no possibility of making Uriah
seem responsible for Bathsheba's pregnancy, David now gravely compounds
the original crime of adultery by plotting to get Uriah out of the way entirely by
having him killed. What follows in the story makes it clear that bloodshed, far
more than adultery, is David's indelible transgression.

17 there were valiant men. And the men of the town sallied forth and did battle with Joab, and some of the troops, some of David's servants, fell,
18 and Uriah the Hittite also died. And Joab sent and told David all the
19 details of the battle. And Joab charged the messenger, saying, "When
20 you finish reporting all the details of the battle to the king, if it should happen that the king's wrath is roused and he says to you, 'Why did you approach the town to fight? Did you not know they would shoot from
21 the wall? Who struck down Abimelech son of Jerubbesheth? Did not a woman fling down on him an upper millstone from the wall, and he died in Thebez? Why did you approach the wall?' Then shall you say,
22 'Your servant Uriah the Hittite also died.'" And the messenger went and

---

17. *some of the troops . . . fell, and Uriah the Hittite also died.* As Perry and Sternberg have keenly observed, one of the salient features of this story is the repeated alteration of instructions by those who carry them out. It is, indeed, a vivid demonstration of the ambiguous effecting of ends through the agency of others, which is one of the great political themes of the story. The canny Joab immediately sees that David's orders are impossibly clumsy (perhaps an indication that the Machiavellian David has suddenly lost his manipulative coolness): if the men around Uriah were to draw back all at once, leaving him alone exposed, it would be entirely transparent that there was a plot to get him killed. Joab, then, coldly recognizes that in order to give David's plan some credibility, it will be necessary to send a whole contingent into a dangerous place and for many others beside Uriah to die. In this fashion, the circle of lethal consequences of David's initial act spreads wider and wider.

21. *Did not a woman fling down on him an upper millstone . . . ?* The specificity of the prospective dialogue that Joab invents for a wrathful David may at first seem surprising. The story of the ignominious death of Abimelech at the hand of a woman (Judges 9:52–54) may have become a kind of object lesson in siege strategy for professional soldiers—when you are laying siege against a city, above all beware of coming too close to the wall. One suspects also that Joab's emphasis on a woman's dealing death to the warrior—Abimelech had asked his armor bearer to run him through so that it would *not* be said he was killed by a woman!—points back to Bathsheba as the ultimate source of this chain of disasters. (This would be Joab's soldierly judgment, not necessarily the author's.)

Your servant Uriah the Hittite also died. Joab obviously knows that this is the message for which David is waiting. By placing it in the anticipatory "script" that he dictates to the messenger, he is of course giving away the secret, more or

came and told David all that Joab had sent him for. And the messenger 23
said to David, "The men overpowered us and sallied forth against us
into the field, and then we were upon them back to the entrance of
the gate. And they shot at your servants from the wall, and some of the 24
king's servants died, and your servant Uriah the Hittite also died." And 25
the king said to the messenger, "Thus shall you say to Joab, 'Let this
thing not seem evil in your eyes, for the sword devours sometimes one
way and sometimes another. Battle all the more fiercely against the city
and destroy it. And so rouse his spirits.'"

---

less, to the messenger. Might this, too, be calculated, as an oblique dissemina-
tion of David's complicity in Uriah's death, perhaps to be used at some future
point by Joab against the king? In any case, given David's track record in killing
messengers who bear tidings not to his liking, Joab may want to be sure that
this messenger has the means to fend off any violent reaction from the king,
who would not have been expecting a report of multiple casualties.

23. *and then we were upon them back to the entrance of the gate*. The astute messenger offers a circumstantial account that justifies the mistake of approaching
too close to the wall: the Ammonites came out after the Israelites in hot pursuit; then the Israelites, turning the tide of battle, were drawn after the fleeing
Ammonites and so were tricked into coming right up to the gates of the city.

24. *and your servant Uriah the Hittite also died*. The messenger has divined the
real point of Joab's instructions all too well. He realizes that what David above
all wants to hear is the news of Uriah's death, and rather than risk the whole
outburst, indicated by the prospective dialogue invented by Joab with the reference to the woman who killed Abimelech, the messenger hastens to conclude
his report, before the king can react, by mentioning Uriah's death. Thus the
narrative makes palpable the inexorable public knowledge of David's crime.

25. *the sword devours sometimes one way and sometimes another*. The king
responds by directing to Joab what sounds like an old soldier's cliché (on the
order of "every bullet has its billet"). These vapid words of consolation to the
field commander are an implicit admission that Joab's revision of David's orders
was necessary: David concedes that many a good man had to die in order to
cover up his murder by proxy of Uriah.

Battle all the more fiercely. The Hebrew is literally "make fierce [or,
strengthen] your battle." The phrase is an emphatic formal echo of "the fiercest battling" in verse 15.

And so rouse his spirits. Literally, "and strengthen him"—that is, Joab.

26 And Uriah's wife heard that Uriah her man was dead, and she keened
27 over her husband. And when the mourning was over, David sent and
gathered her into his house and she became his wife. And she bore him
a son, and the thing that David had done was evil in the eyes of the
LORD.

---

27. *when the mourning was over*. Normally, the mourning period would be seven
days. Bathsheba, then, is even more precipitous than Gertrude after the death
of Hamlet the elder in hastening to the bed of a new husband. She does, of
course, want to become David's wife before her big belly shows.

David sent and gathered her into his house and she became his wife. Throughout this story, David is never seen anywhere but in his house. This sentence at
the end strongly echoes verse 4: "David sent . . . and fetched her and she came
to him and he lay with her."

the thing that David had done was evil in the eyes of the LORD. Only now, after
the adultery, the murder, the remarriage, and the birth of the son, does the
narrator make an explicit moral judgment of David's actions. The invocation of
God's judgment is the introduction to the appearance of Nathan the prophet,
delivering first a moral parable "wherein to catch the conscience of the king"
and then God's grim curse on David and his house.

CHAPTER 12

And the LORD sent Nathan to David, and he came to him and said to   1
him: "Two men there were in a single town, one was rich and the other

---

1. *And the* LORD *sent*. The second stage of the story of David and Bathsheba—
the phase of accusation and retribution—begins with a virtual pun on a prominent thematic word of the first half of the story. David was seen repeatedly
"sending" messengers, arranging for the satisfaction of his lust and the murder
of his mistress's husband through the agency of others. By contrast, God here
"sends" his prophet to David—not an act of bureaucratic manipulation but the
use of a human vehicle to convey a divine message of conscience.

Two men there were. Nathan's parable, from its very first syllables, makes
clear its own status as a traditional tale and a poetic construction. The way one
begins a storyteller's tale in the Bible is with the formula "there was a man"—
compare the beginning of Job, or the beginning of the story of Hannah and
Elkanah in 1 Samuel 1. The Hebrew prose of the parable also is set off strongly
from the language of the surrounding narrative by its emphatically rhythmic
character, with a fondness for parallel pairs of terms—an effect this translation
tries to reproduce. The vocabulary, moreover, includes several terms that are
relatively rare in biblical prose narrative: *kivsah* (ewe), *ra'sh* (poor), *helekh* (wayfarer), *'oreaḥ* (wayfarer). Finally the two "men" of the opening formula are at the
end separated out into "rich man," "poor man," and "the man who had come" (in
each of these cases, Hebrew *'ish* is used). This formal repetition prepares the
way, almost musically, for Nathan's two-word accusatory explosion, *'atah ha'ish*,
"You are the man!" Given the patently literary character of Nathan's tale, which
would have been transparent to anyone native to ancient Hebrew culture, it is
a little puzzling that David should so precipitously take the tale as a report of
fact requiring judicial action. Nathan may be counting on the possibility that
the obverse side of guilty conscience in a man like David is the anxious desire
to do the right thing. As king, his first obligation is to protect his subjects and to
dispense justice, especially to the disadvantaged. In the affair of Bathsheba and
Uriah, he has done precisely the opposite. Now, as he listens to Nathan's tale,

2 poor. The rich man had sheep and cattle, in great abundance. And the
3 poor man had nothing save one little ewe that he had bought. And he
nurtured her and raised her with him together with his sons. From his
crust she would eat and from his cup she would drink and in his lap she
4 would lie, and she was to him like a daughter. And a wayfarer came to
the rich man, and it seemed a pity to him to take from his own sheep and
cattle to prepare for the traveler who had come to him, and he took the
5 poor man's ewe and prepared it for the man who had come to him." And
David's anger flared hot against the man, and he said to Nathan, "As the
6 LORD lives, doomed is the man who has done this! And the poor man's

---

David's compensatory zeal to be a champion of justice overrides any awareness
he might have of the evident artifice of the story.

3. *eat . . . drink . . . lie.* As Polzin observes, these terms effect full contact with
the story of David and Bathsheba, being the three activities David sought to
engage Uriah in with his wife (compare Uriah's words in 11:11). The parable
begins to become a little fantastic here in the interest of drawing close to the
relationships of conjugal intimacy and adultery to which it refers: the little lamb
eats from her master's crust, drinks from his cup, and lies in his lap ("lap" as
a biblical idiom has connotations not merely of parental sheltering but also of
sexual intimacy: compare verse 8, "I gave . . . your master's wives in your lap").

4. *it seemed a pity to him.* The Hebrew uses an active verb, "he pitied," preparing for a literal ironic reversal in verse 6, "he had no pity"—or, "he did not pity."
    to prepare. The Hebrew is literally "to do" or "to make." When the verb has
as its direct object a live edible animal, it means to slaughter and cook.

5. *David's anger flared hot against the man.* Nathan's rhetorical trap has now
snapped shut. David, by his access of anger, condemns himself, and he becomes
the helpless target of the denunciation that Nathan will unleash.
    doomed is the man. Actually, according to biblical law someone who has
illegally taken another's property would be subject to fourfold restitution (verse
6), not to the death penalty. (The Hebrew phrase is literally "son of death"—
that is, deserving death, just as in 1 Samuel 26:16.) David pronounces this
death sentence in his outburst of moral indignation, but it also reflects the way
that the parable conflates the sexual "taking" of Bathsheba with the murder of
Uriah: the addition of Bathsheba to the royal harem could have been intimated
simply by the rich man's placing the ewe in his flock, but as the parable is told,
the ewe must be slaughtered, blood must be shed. David himself will not be
condemned to die, but death will hang over his house. As the Talmud (Yoma

ewe he shall pay back fourfold, in as much as he has done this thing, and because he had no pity!" And Nathan said to David, "You are the man! 7 Thus says the LORD God of Israel. 'It is I who anointed you king over Israel, and it is I Who saved you from the hand of Saul. And I gave you 8 your master's house and your master's wives in your lap, and I gave you the house of Israel and of Judah. And if that be too little, I would give you even as much again. Why did you despise the word of the LORD, 9 to do what is evil in His eyes? Uriah the Hittite you struck down with the sword, and his wife you took for yourself as wife, and him you have killed by the sword of the Ammonites! And so now, the sword shall not 10 swerve from your house evermore, seeing as you have despised Me and

---

22B) notes, the fourfold retribution for Uriah's death will be worked out in the death or violent fate of four of David's children: the unnamed infant son of Bathsheba, Tamar, Amnon, and Absalom.

7. *Thus says the LORD God of Israel.* After the direct knife thrust of "You are the man!", Nathan hastens to produce the prophetic messenger formula in its extended form, in this way proclaiming divine authorization for the dire imprecation he pronounces against David and his house.

7.–8. *It is I who anointed you. . . . And if that be too little, I would give you even as much again.* In the first part of this speech, there are several ironic echoes of David's prayer in Chapter 7, in which David thanks God for all His benefactions and professes himself unworthy of them.

8. *and your master's wives in your lap.* At least in the account passed down to us, there is no mention elsewhere of David's having taken sexual possession of his predecessor's consorts, though this was a practice useful for its symbolic force in a transfer of power, as Absalom will later realize.

9. *Uriah the Hittite you struck down with the sword.* The obliquity of working through agents at a distance, as David did in contriving the murder of Uriah, is exploded by the brutal directness of the language: it is as though David himself had wielded the sword. Only at the end of the sentence are we given the explanatory qualification "by the sword of the Ammonites."

10. *the sword shall not swerve from your house evermore.* As Bar-Efrat notes, David's rather callous message to Joab, "the sword sometimes consumes one way and sometimes another," is now thrown back in his face. The story of David's sons, not to speak of his descendants in later generations, will in fact

11 have taken the wife of Uriah the Hittite to be your wife.' Thus says the Lord, 'I am about to raise up evil against you from your own house, and I will take your wives before your eyes and give them to your fellowman,

12 and he shall lie with your wives in the sight of this sun. For you did it in

13 secret but I will do this thing before all Israel and before the sun.'" And David said to Nathan, "I have offended against the Lord." And Nathan said to David, "The Lord has also remitted your offense—you shall not

14 die. But since you surely spurned the Lord in this thing, the son born to you is doomed to die."

15 And Nathan went to his house, and the Lord afflicted the child whom Bathsheba wife of Uriah the Hittite had borne David, and he fell gravely

---

turn out to be a long tale of conspiracy, internecine struggle, and murder. One of the most extraordinary features of the whole David narrative is that this story of the founding of the great dynasty of Judah is, paradoxically, already a tale of the fall of the house of David. Once again, no one has grasped this tragic paradox more profoundly than William Faulkner in his recasting of the story in *Absalom, Absalom!* The author of the David story continually exercises an unblinking vision of David and the institution of the monarchy that exposes their terrible flaws even as he accepts their divinely authorized legitimacy.

11. *I am about to raise up evil against you from your own house.* As befits a predictive curse, the agents of the evil are left unnamed. The disaster announced is clearly the rebellion of Absalom—as the reference to public cohabitation with David's wives makes clear—and the rape of Tamar and the murder of Amnon that lead up to it. But further "evil" from the house of David will persist to his deathbed, as Absalom's rebellion is followed by Adonijah's usurpation.

12. *For you did it in secret but I will do this thing before all Israel.* The calamitous misjudgments that defined David's dealings with Bathsheba and Uriah were a chain of bungled efforts at concealment. Now, in the retribution, all his crimes are to be revealed.

14. *spurned the Lord.* The Masoretic text has "spurned the enemies of the Lord," a scribal euphemism to avoid making God the object of a harsh negative verb.

15. *Bathsheba wife of Uriah the Hittite.* At this point, she is still identified as wife of the husband she betrayed in conceiving this child.

ill. And David implored God for the sake of the lad, and David fasted, 16
and he came and spent the night lying on the ground. And the elders of 17
his house rose over him to rouse him up from the ground, but he would
not, nor did he partake of food with them. And it happened on the sev- 18
enth day that the child died, and David's servants were afraid to tell him
that the child was dead, for they said, "Look, while the child was alive,
we spoke to him and he did not heed our voice, and how can we say to
him, the child is dead? He will do some harm." And David saw that his 19
servants were whispering to each other and David understood that the
child was dead. And David said to his servants, "Is the child dead?" And
they said, "He is dead." And David rose from the ground and bathed 20
and rubbed himself with oil and changed his garments and came into
the house of the LORD and worshiped and came back to his house and
asked that food be set out for him, and he ate. And his servants said to 21

---

17. *fasted . . . and spent the night lying on the ground.* David's acts pointedly
replicate those of the man he murdered, who refused to go home and eat but
instead spent the night lying on the ground with the palace guard.

18. *on the seventh day.* Seven days were the customary period of mourning. In
this instance, David enacts a regimen of mourning, in an effort to placate God,
before the fact of death.

He will do some harm. Presumably, the courtiers fear that David will do harm
to himself in a frenzy of grief.

19. *He is dead.* In Hebrew, this is a single syllable, *met*, "dead"—a response
corresponding to idiomatic usage because there is no word for "yes" in biblical
Hebrew, and so the person questioned must respond by affirming the key term
of the question. It should be noted, however, that the writer has contrived to
repeat "dead" five times, together with one use of the verb "died," in these two
verses: the ineluctable bleak fact of death is hammered home to us, just before
David's grim acceptance of it.

20. *David rose . . . bathed . . . rubbed himself with oil . . . changed his garments
. . . worshiped . . . ate.* This uninterrupted chain of verbs signifies David's brisk
resumption of the activities of normal life, evidently without speech and certainly without explanation, as the courtiers' puzzlement makes clear. The entire
episode powerfully manifests that human capacity for surprise, and for paradoxical behavior, that is one of the hallmarks of the great biblical characters.
David here acts in a way that neither his courtiers nor the audience of the story
could have anticipated.

him, "What is this thing that you have done? For the sake of the living child you fasted and wept, and when the child was dead, you arose and 22 ate food?" And he said, "While the child was still alive I fasted and wept, for I thought, 'Who knows, the LORD may favor me and the child will 23 live.' And now that he is dead, why should I fast? Can I bring him back again? I am going to him and he will not come back to me."

24 And David consoled Bathsheba his wife, and he came to her and lay with her, and she bore a son and called his name Solomon, and the 25 LORD loved him. And He sent by the hand of Nathan the prophet and called his name Jedidiah, by the grace of the LORD.

---

23. *Can I bring him back again? I am going to him and he will not come back to me.* If the episode of Bathsheba and Uriah is the great turning point of the David story, these haunting words are the pivotal moment in the turning point. As we have repeatedly seen, every instance of David's speech in the preceding narrative has been crafted to serve political ends, much of it evincing elaborately artful rhetoric. Now, after the dire curse pronounced by Nathan, the first stage of which is fulfilled in the death of the child, David speaks for the first time not out of political need but in his existential nakedness. The words he utters have a stark simplicity—there are no elegies now—and his recognition of the irreversibility of his son's death also makes him think of his own mortality. In place of David the seeker and wielder of power, we now see a vulnerable David, and this is how he will chiefly appear through the last half of his story.

24. *David consoled Bathsheba his wife.* Now, after the terrible price of the child's life has been paid for the murder of her husband, the narrator refers to her as David's wife, not Uriah's. A specific lapse of time is not mentioned, but one must assume that at least two or three months have passed, during which she recovers from the first childbirth.

    she . . . called his name Solomon, and the LORD loved him. As a rule, it was the mother who exercised the privilege of naming the child. Despite some scholarly efforts to construe the name differently, its most plausible etymology remains the one that links it with the word for "peace" (the Hebrew term *Shelomoh* might simply mean "His peace"). The LORD's loving Solomon, who will disappear from the narrative until the struggle for the throne in 1 Kings 1, foreshadows his eventual destiny, and also harmonizes this name giving with the child's second name, Jedidiah, which means "God's friend."

25. *Jedidiah, by the grace of the LORD.* For the last phrase, this translation adopts a proposal by Kyle McCarter, Jr. The usual meaning of the preposition used,

And Joab battled against Rabbah of the Ammonites and he captured the 26
royal town. And Joab sent messengers to David and said, 27

"I have battled against Rabbah.
 Yes, I captured the Citadel of Waters.

And so now, assemble the rest of the troops and encamp against the city 28
and capture it, lest it be I who capture the city and my name be called
upon it." And David assembled all the troops and went to Rabbah and 29
battled against it and captured it. And he took the crown of their king 30
from his head, and its weight was a talent of gold, with precious stones,
and it was set on David's head. And the booty of the city he brought

---

ba'avur, is "for the sake of." It remains something of a puzzlement that the child
should be given two names, one by his mother and the other by God through
His prophet. One common suggestion is that Jedidiah was Solomon's official
throne name. But perhaps the second name, indicating special access to divine
favor, reflects a political calculation on the part of Nathan: he is already aligning
himself with Solomon (and with Bathsheba), figuring that in the long run it will
be best to have a successor to David under some obligation to him. In the event,
Nathan's intervention will prove crucial in securing the throne for Solomon.

26. *Joab battled against Rabbah.* It is possible, as many scholars have claimed,
that the conquest of Rabbah, in the siege of which Uriah had perished, in fact
occurs before the birth of Solomon, though sieges lasting two or more years
were not unknown in the ancient world.

27. *I have battled against Rabbah.* Joab is actually sending David a double message. As dutiful field commander, he urges David (verse 28) to hasten to the
front so that the conquest of the Ammonite capital will be attributed to him.
And yet, he proclaims the conquest in the triumphal formality of a little victory
poem (one line, two parallel versets) in which it is he who figures unambiguously as conqueror. This coy and dangerous game Joab plays with David about
who has the real power will persist in the story.
 the Citadel of Waters. The reference is not entirely clear, but the narrative
context indicates that Joab has occupied one vital part of the town—evidently,
where the water supply is—while the rest of the town has not yet been taken.

30. *the crown of their king.* The Septuagint reads "Milcom" (the Ammonite
deity) instead of *malkam,* "their king."

31 out in great abundance. And the people who were in it he brought out
and set them to work with saws and iron threshing boards and iron axes
and he put them to the brick mold. Thus did he do to all the Ammonite
towns. And David, and all the troops with him, returned to Jerusalem.

---

31. *set them to work with saws and iron threshing boards and iron axes.* The
meaning of this entire sentence is a little uncertain, but the most plausible
reading is that David impressed the male Ammonites into corvée labor. Some
have suggested that the Ammonites were forced to tear down the walls of their
own cities with the cutting tools listed in the catalogue here, though the reference to the brick mold at the end indicates some sort of construction, not just
demolition.

CHAPTER 13

And it happened thereafter—Absalom, David's son, had a beautiful 1
sister named Tamar, and Amnon, David's son, loved her. And Amnon 2
was so distressed that he fell sick over Tamar his sister, for she was a
virgin and it seemed beyond Amnon to do anything to her. And Amnon 3
had a companion named Jonadab son of Shimeah brother of David,

---

1. *a beautiful sister*. The catastrophic turn in David's fortune began when he saw
a beautiful woman and lusted after her. Now, the curse pronounced by Nathan
on the house of David begins to unfold through the very same mechanism:
a sexual transgression within the royal quarters resulting in an act of murder
elsewhere. Several important terms and gestures here reinforce this link with
the story of David and Bathsheba.

Amnon . . . loved her. The love in question will be revealed by the ensuing
events as an erotic obsession—what the early rabbis aptly characterized as "love
dependent upon a [material] thing."

2. *she was a virgin and it seemed beyond Amnon to do anything to her*. The last
phrase here has a definite negative connotation (rather like the British "to inter-
fere with her") and makes clear the narrow carnal nature of Amnon's "love" for
Tamar. Sexual tampering with a virgin had particularly stringent consequences
in biblical law.

3. *companion*. The Hebrew *rea'* could simply indicate a friend, though in royal
contexts it is also the title of someone who played an official role as the king's, or
the prince's, companion and counselor. The emphasis on Jonadab's "wisdom"—
in biblical usage, often a morally neutral term suggesting mastery of know-how
in a particular activity—makes the technical sense of counselor more likely,
though one role does not exclude the other.

4 and Jonadab was a very wise man. And he said to him, "Why are you
   so poorly, prince, morning after morning? Will you not tell me?" And
   Amnon said to him, "Tamar the sister of Absalom my brother I do love."
5 And Jonadab said to him, "Lie in your bed and play sick, and when your
   father comes to see you, say to him, 'Let Tamar my sister, pray, come and
   nourish me with food and prepare the nourishment before my eyes, so
6 that I may see and eat from her hand.'" And Amnon lay down and played

---

4. *And he said to him.* Shimon Bar-Efrat has aptly observed that the whole story
of the rape of Tamar is constructed out of seven interlocking scenes with two
characters in each, one of whom appears in the next scene. (The story of the
stealing of Isaac's blessing in Genesis 27 has the same structure.) The sequence
is: (1) Jonadab-Amnon, (2) Amnon-David, (3) David-Tamar, (4) Tamar-Amnon,
(5) Amnon-attendant, (6) attendant-Tamar, (7) Tamar-Absalom. J. P. Fokkelman adds to this observation that the spatial and structural center of this design
is the bed in Amnon's inner chamber (4), where the rape is perpetrated.

Tamar the sister of Absalom my brother. Kyle McCarter, Jr., vividly notes that
Amnon's speech with its alliterated initial aspirants in the Hebrew "is a series
of gasping sighs" (*'et-tamar' ahot 'avshalom 'ahi 'ani 'ohev*).

5. *Lie in your bed and play sick.* David at the beginning of the Bathsheba story
was first seen lying in bed, and then he arranged to have the desired woman
brought to his chamber. Jonadab on his part observes that Amnon already looks
ill (verse 2) and so suggests that he play up this condition by pretending to be
dangerously ill and in need of special ministrations.

nourish me. The Hebrew verbal root *b-r-h* and the cognate noun *biryah*
("nourishment") denote not eating in general but the kind of eating that is sustaining or restoring to a person who is weak or fasting. When you eat a *biryah*
you become *bari*, healthy or fat, the opposite of "poorly," *dal*. The distinction
is crucial to this story.

so that I may see and eat from her hand. Perhaps Amnon is encouraged to
say this because, as a person supposed to be gravely ill, he would want to see
with his own eyes that the vital nourishment is prepared exactly as it should
be. The writer is clearly playing with the equivalence between eating and sex,
but it remains ambiguous whether Jonadab has in mind the facilitating of a
rape, or merely creating the possibility of an intimate meeting between Amnon
and Tamar.

sick, and the king came to see him, and Amnon said to the king, "Let Tamar my sister, pray, come, and shape a couple of heart-shaped dumplings before my eyes, that I may take nourishment from her hand." And David sent to Tamar at home, saying, "Go, pray, to the house of Amnon your brother, and prepare nourishment for him." And Tamar went to the house of Amnon her brother—he lying down—and she took the dough and kneaded it and shaped it into hearts before his eyes and cooked the dumplings. And she took the pan and set it before him, but he refused to eat. And Amnon said, "Clear out everyone around me!" and everyone around him cleared out. And Amnon said to Tamar, "Bring the nourishment into the inner chamber, that I may take nourishment from your hand." And Tamar took the dumplings that she had made

7

8

9

10

---

6. *the king came to see him.* In Jonadab's original scenario, it was to be Absalom who played this role. As the events work out, David, who sinned through lust, inadvertently acts as Amnon's pimp for his own daughter.

shape a couple of heart-shaped dumplings. The verb and its object are both transparently cognate with *lev* (or *levav*), "heart." The term could refer to the shape of the dumplings, or to their function of "strengthening the heart" (idiomatic in biblical Hebrew for sustaining or encouraging). In the Song of Songs, this same verb is associated with the idea of sexual arousal.

9. *Clear out everyone around me!* The identical words are pronounced by another princelike figure, Joseph, just before he reveals his true identity to his brothers (Genesis 45:1). In Genesis, these words preface the great moment of reconciliation between long-estranged brothers. Here they are a prelude to a tale of fraternal rape that leads to fratricide. The story of the rape of Tamar continues to allude to the Joseph story, in reverse chronological order and with pointed thematic reversal. The moment before the rape echoes the encounter between Joseph and Potiphar's wife (Genesis 39) in the middle of the Joseph story, and the attention drawn to the ornamented tunic that the violated Tamar tears takes us back to Joseph's ornamented tunic at the beginning of his story (Genesis 37). From such purposeful deployment of allusion, the inference is inevitable that the author of the David story was familiar at least with the J strand of the Joseph story in a textual version very like the one that has come down to us.

11 and brought them to Amnon her brother within the chamber. And she
offered them to him to eat, and he seized her and said to her, "Come
12 lie with me, my sister." And she said to him, "Don't, my brother, don't
abuse me, for it should not be done thus in Israel, don't do this scur-
13 rilous thing. And I, where would I carry my shame? And you, you would
be like one of the scurrilous fellows in Israel. And so, speak, pray, to the

---

11. *Come lie with me, my sister.* The core of this abrupt command is a citation
of the words of Potiphar's wife to Joseph, "Lie with me." Perhaps, as some have
suggested, "Come" has a slight softening effect. The addition of "my sister" of
course highlights the fact that this sexual assault is also incestuous.

12. *Don't, my brother.* Tamar's response constitutes a structural allusion to
Joseph and Potiphar's wife, for he, when confronted by the sexual brusqueness
of her terse "lie with me," also responds, in contrastive dialogue, with a nervous
volubility in a relatively lengthy series of breathless objections.
  it should not be done thus in Israel . . . this scurrilous thing. The language
here echoes that of another sexual episode in Genesis, the rape of Dinah (Genesis 34). Again, the divergence in the parallel is significant, for Dinah's rapist
comes to love her after violating her and wants to make things good by marriage, whereas Amnon despises Tamar after he possesses her, and drives her
away. The rape in both stories leads to murderous fraternal vengeance. But
our writer's brilliant game of literary allusion does not end here, for, as Robert
Polzin has pointed out, Tamar's words are also a precise echo of the plea of the
Ephraimite in Gibeah to the mob of rapists: "Don't, my brothers . . . don't do
this scurrilous thing" (Judges 19:23). That story ended in the woman's being
gang-raped to death, an act that in turn led to bloody civil war—as Tamar's rape
will lead to fratricide and, eventually, rebellion and civil war.

13. *speak, pray, to the king, for he will not withhold me from you.* Marriage
between a half brother and a half sister is explicitly banned by biblical law.
Perhaps, it has been suggested, this prohibition was not yet held to be binding
in the early tenth century, or in the royal circle in Jerusalem. But it is at least
as plausible that the desperate Tamar is grasping at any possibility to buy time.
and deflect her sexual assailant: why do this vile thing and take me by force
when you can enjoy me legitimately?

king, for he will not withhold me from you." And Amnon did not want   14
to heed her voice, and he overpowered her and abused her and bedded
her. And Amnon hated her with a very great hatred, for greater was the   15
hatred with which he hated her than the love with which he had loved
her. And Amnon said, "Get up, go!" And she said to him, "Don't!—this   16
wrong is greater than the other you did me, to send me away now." And

---

14. *he overpowered her and abused her and bedded her*. The three transitive verbs
in quick sequence reflect the single-minded assertion of male physical force.
In the analogous story of Joseph and the Egyptian woman, because the gender
roles are reversed, the sexually assaulted male is strong enough to break free
from the woman's grasp and flee. Here, the assaulted woman cannot break her
assailant's grip (verse 11), and so she now succumbs to brute force. The verb
represented as "bedded" (*shakhav*) is the same one used by Jonadab in verse 5
("Lie in your bed," *shekhav 'al-mishkavkha*) and in Amnon's "lie with me." But
when it has a direct feminine object (instead of "lie *with*"), it suggests sexual
violation, and a transitive verb is called for in the English.

15. *greater was the hatred with which he hated her than the love with which he
had loved her*. The psychological insight of this writer is remarkable throughout
the story. Amnon has fulfilled his desire for this beautiful young woman—or,
given the fact that she is a bitterly resistant virgin, perhaps it has hardly been
the fulfillment he dreamed of. In any case, he now has to face the possibly dire
consequences to himself from her brother Absalom, or from David. The result
is an access of revulsion against Tamar, a blaming of the victim for luring him
with her charms into all this trouble.

   Get up, go! The brutality of these imperative verbs is evident. They are
also, as Bar-Efrat neatly observes, exact antonyms, in reverse order, of the two
imperative verbs of sexual invitation he used before, "Come, lie."

16. *Don't!—this wrong is greater*. There is a textual problem here in the Hebrew,
which seems to say, "Don't—about this wrong . . ." (*'al-'odot hara'ah*). Some versions of the Septuagint read here, "Don't, my brother" (*'al 'aḥi*), as in verse 12,
but this could reflect an attempt to straighten out a difficult text rather than a
better Hebrew version used by the ancient Greek translators.

   to send me away now. "Now" is added in the translation in order to remove
an ambiguity as to when the sending away is done. "Sending away" is an idiom
that also has the sense of "divorce"—precisely what the rapist of a virgin is not
allowed to do in biblical law. If some modern readers may wonder why being
banished seems to Tamar worse than being raped, one must say that for biblical women the social consequence of pariah status, when the law offered the

17 he did not want to heed her. And he called his lad, his attendant, and said, "Send this creature, pray, away from me and bolt the door behind
18 her!" And she had on an ornamented tunic, for the virgin princesses did wear such robes. And his attendant took her outside and bolted the
19 door behind her. And Tamar put ashes on her head, and the ornamented tunic that she had on she tore, and she put her hand on her head and
20 walked away screaming as she went. And Absalom her brother said to her, "Has Amnon your brother been with you? For now, my sister, hold

---

remedy of marriage to the rapist, might well seem even more horrible than the physical violation. Rape was a dire fate, but one that could be compensated for by marriage, whereas the violated virgin rejected and abandoned by her violator was an unmarriageable outcast, condemned to a lifetime of "desolation" (verse 20).

17. *Send this creature, pray, away from me.* "This creature" reflects the stingingly contemptuous monosyllabic feminine demonstrative pronoun, *zo't* ("this one"). Note that at the same time that Amnon speaks brutally to Tamar, he is polite to his servant, using the particle of entreaty *na'* ("pray").
    and bolt the door behind her. Having devised such an elaborate strategy for drawing Tamar into the inner chamber where he can have his way with her, he now has her thrust out into the open square, with the door bolted against her as though she were some insatiable, clinging thing against which he had to set up a barricade.

18. *ornamented tunic.* The translation for this term follows a suggestion of E. A. Speiser. (The famous King James Version rendering in Genesis is "coat of many colors.") Others interpret this as a garment reaching the ankles. In any case, Tamar and Joseph are the only two figures in the Bible said to wear this particular garment. Joseph's, too, will be torn, by his brothers, after they strip him of it and toss him into the pit, and they will then soak it in kid's blood. Tamar's ornamented tunic may well be blood-stained, too, if one considers what has just been done to her as a virgin.

19. *put her hand on her head.* This is a conventional gesture of mourning, like the rending of the garment and the sprinkling of ashes on the head.

20. *Has Amnon your brother been with you?* Absalom, addressing his screaming, tear-stained, disheveled sister, exercises a kind of delicacy of feeling in using this oblique euphemism for rape.

your peace. He is your brother. Do not take this matter to heart." And
Tamar stayed, desolate, in the house of Absalom her brother. And King 21
David had heard all these things, and he was greatly incensed. And 22
Absalom did not speak with Amnon either evil or good, for Absalom
hated Amnon for having abused Tamar his sister.

And it happened after two years that Absalom had a sheep shearing at 23
Baal-Hazor, which is near Ephraim, and Absalom invited all the king's

---

He is your brother. This identification, which plays back against the heavily
fraught, often ironic uses of "brother" and "sister" throughout the story, would
hardly be a consolation. What Absalom may be suggesting is that, were it any
other man, I would avenge your honor at once, but since he is your brother, and
mine, I must bide my time ("*For now,* my sister, hold your peace.")

Do not take this matter to heart. The idiom he uses echoes ironically against
the making of heart-shaped dumplings to which Amnon enjoined her.

21. *King David had heard all these things, and he was greatly incensed.* The
Qumran Samuel and the Septuagint add here: "but he did not vex the spirit of
Amnon his son, for he loved him, since he was his firstborn." But this looks suspiciously like an explanatory gloss, an effort to make sense of David's silence.
That imponderable silence is the key to the mounting avalanche of disaster in
the house of David. Where we might expect some after-the-fact defense of his
violated daughter, some rebuke or punishment of his rapist son, he hears, is
angry, but says nothing and does nothing, leaving the field open for Absalom's
murder of his brother. In all this, the rape of Tamar plays exactly the same pivotal role in the story of David as does the rape of Dinah in the story of Jacob.
Jacob, too, "hears" of the violation and does nothing, setting the stage for the
bloody act of vengeance carried out by his sons Simeon and Levi. By the end of
the episode, Jacob is seen at the mercy of his intransigent sons, and that is how
this once-powerful figure will appear through the rest of his story. An analogous
fate, as we shall abundantly see, awaits David from this moment on.

23. *a sheep shearing.* The sheep shearing is a grand occasion for feasting and
drinking (compare 1 Samuel 25:2–8), and so it is proper to speak of "having" a
sheep shearing as one would have a celebration.

24 sons. And Absalom came to the king and said, "Look, pray, your servant
has a sheep shearing. Let the king, pray, go, and his servants, with your
25 servant." And the king said to Absalom, "No, my son, we shall not all of
us go, and we shall not burden you." And he pressed him but he did not
26 want to go, and he bade him farewell. And Absalom said to him, "If not,
pray, let Amnon my brother go with us." And the king said to him, "Why
27 should he go with you?" And Absalom pressed him, and he sent Amnon
28 with him, together with all the king's sons. And Absalom charged his
lads, saying, "See, pray, when Amnon's heart is merry with wine and I
say to you, 'Strike down Amnon,' you shall put him to death, fear not,
29 for is it not I who charge you? Be strong, and act as valiant men." And
Absalom's lads did to Amnon as Absalom had charged them, and all the
30 king's sons arose and rode away each on his mule and fled. And as they
were on the way, the rumor reached David, saying, "Absalom has struck

---

24. *Let the king, pray, go.* Given David's increasingly sedentary habits, Absalom
appears to count on the fact that his father will refuse the invitation, and this
refusal will then give greater urgency to his invitation of Amnon. Had Absalom
begun by asking David to help him persuade Amnon to go the festivities, David
might have been suspicious about Absalom's motives, since the grudge he bore
his half brother would scarcely have been a secret. In any case, Absalom is
making David his go-between to lure Amnon to his death, just as Amnon made
David his go-between to lure Tamar to her violation.

27. *with all the king's sons.* This phrase recurs like a refrain from this point
on: David is haunted by the specter of the ultimate catastrophe, that "all the
king's sons" have perished, a specter that will cast a shadow over the subsequent events of the story as well. The man promised an everlasting house is
threatened with the prospect (like his avatar, Faulkner's Sutpen, in *Absalom,
Absalom!*) of being cut off without surviving progeny.

28. *when Amnon's heart is merry with wine.* The heart that lusted after Tamar
and asked her to make heart-shaped dumplings will now be befuddled with
wine to set up the murder.

29. *each on his mule.* In this period in ancient Israel, the mule was the customary mount for royal personages.

down all the king's sons, and not one of them remains." And the king 31
arose and tore his garments and lay on the ground, with all his servants
standing in attendance in torn garments. And Jonadab son of Shimeah 32
brother of David spoke up and said, "Let not my lord think, 'All the lads,
the king's sons, they have put to death, for Amnon alone is dead, for it
was fixed upon by Absalom from the day he abused Tamar his sister.
And now, let not my lord the king take the matter to heart, saying, 'All 33
the king's sons have died,' but Amnon alone is dead."

And Absalom fled. And the lookout lad raised his eyes and saw and, 34
look, a great crowd was going round the side of the mountain from the
road behind it. And Jonadab said to the king, "Look, the king's sons have 35

---

31. *the king arose and tore his garments and lay on the ground.* These acts of
mourning are reminiscent of Tamar's and of David's own when his infant son
by Bathsheba was deathly ill. Again there is a resemblance to Jacob, who flings
himself into extravagant mourning over a son supposed to be dead who is actually alive (Genesis 37).

32. *they have put to death.* Jonadab, exercising his "wisdom," is careful not to
condemn Absalom immediately, but instead first uses a plural verb with an
unspecified agent. Then he introduces Absalom as the source of the determination to kill Amnon, choosing a verb, "abused," that concedes the crime of rape.
Whether or not this was a possibility he had in mind when he offered counsel
to Amnon, he now implicity distances himself from Amnon's act.

33. *let not my lord the king take the matter to heart.* This is virtually the same
idiom Absalom used to Tamar in consoling her after the rape.

34. *going round the side of the mountain from the road behind it.* The Hebrew
has "the road behind it" before "the side of the mountain," such proleptic use of
pronominal reference sometimes occurring in biblical Hebrew. The Septuagint
reads "from the Horonim road" (*miderekh ḥoronim*) instead of "from the road
behind it" (*miderekh aḥaraw*).

36 come, as your servant has spoken, so it has come about." And just as
he finished speaking, look, the king's sons came, and they raised their
voices and wept, and the king, too, and all his servants wept very griev-
37 ously. And Absalom had fled, and he went to Talmai son of Amihur king
38 of Geshur. And David mourned for his son all the while. And Absalom
39 had fled and gone to Geshur, and he was there three years. And David's
urge to sally forth against Absalom was spent, for he was consoled over
Amnon, who was dead.

---

36. *wept very grievously.* The literal Hebrew phrasing is "wept a very great
weeping."

37. *Talmi son of Amihur king of Geshur.* Absalom takes refuge in the court of
his maternal grandfather in Geshur, to the north and east of the Jordan, outside
David's jurisdiction.
   David mourned for his son all the while. As verse 39, which will mark the
beginning of a new narrative episode, makes clear, the son he is mourning is
the dead Amnon, not the absent Absalom.

39. *David's urge to sally forth against Absalom was spent.* The received text is
either defective or elliptical at this point. The verb *watekhal* is feminine, though
there is no feminine noun in the clause. Many have construed it as the predicate of an omitted noun, *nefesh*, which coupled with this verb would yield idiomatically "David pined after Absalom." Such paternal longings scarcely accord
with David's refusal to see his son once he has returned to Jerusalem, or with
the very necessity of elaborate manipulation in order to get him to agree to
rescind Absalom's banishment. The Qumran Samuel scroll, though incomplete
at this point, appears to have the feminine noun—*ruaḥ*—"spirit," "impulse,"
"urge"—as the subject of the verb. An abatement of hostility against Absalom
rather than a longing for him makes much more sense in terms of what follows.

CHAPTER 14

And Joab son of Zeruiah knew that the king's mind was on Absalom. And   1, 2
Joab sent to Tekoa and fetched a wise woman from there and said to her,
"Take up mourning, pray, and, pray, don mourning garments, and do not
rub yourself with oil, and you shall be like a woman a long while mourning over a dead one. And you shall come to the king and speak to him in   3

---

1. *the king's mind was on Absalom.* The preposition *'al is* ambiguous, and it could
also mean "against."

2. *Joab sent to Tekoa.* Tekoa is a village about ten miles north of Jerusalem.
Why does Joab contrive to make David agree to Absalom's return? Given his
relentlessly political character, it seems likely that Joab perceives Absalom's
continuing banishment as a potential source of rebellion against the throne,
and concludes that the safest course is to reconcile the king with his son. This
calculation will prove to be gravely misguided because Joab does not reckon
with David's ambivalence toward his fratricidal son (see verse 24) or with the
impulse to usurpation that the ambivalence will encourage in Absalom.
   a wise woman. It should be noted that the whole David story, seemingly
dominated by powerful martial men, pivots at several crucial junctures on the
intervention of enterprising "wise women." The first of these is Abigail, though,
unlike two of the others, she is not assigned the epithet "wise woman" as a kind
of professional title. Later, a resourceful woman hides the two spies who are
bringing intelligence of Absalom to David in trans-Jordan. In the subsequent
rebellion of Sheba son of Bichri, another wise woman prevents Joab's massacre
of the besieged town of Abel of Beth-Maacah.
   like a woman a long while mourning over a dead one. The phrasing here pointedly echoes "David mourned for his son all the while" in 13:37.

4 this manner—" and Joab put the words in her mouth. And the Tekoite
woman said to the king, and she flung herself on her face to the ground
5 and bowed down, and she said, "Rescue, O king!" And the king said to
her, "What troubles you?" And she said, "Alas, I am a widow-woman,
6 my husband died. And your servant had two sons, and they quarreled in
the field, and there was no one to part them, and one struck down the
7 other and caused his death. And, look, the whole clan rose against your
servant and said, 'Give over the one who struck down his brother, that
we may put him to death for the life of his brother whom he killed, and
let us destroy the heir as well. And they would have quenched my last
remaining ember, leaving my husband no name or remnant on the face

---

3. *Joab put the words in her mouth.* As Polzin observes, the entire episode turns
on manipulation of people through language, with abundant repetition of the
verb "speak." In contrast to the common practice elsewhere in biblical narrative, we are not given the actual script that Joab dictates to the woman, which
she will then repeat to David. This omission heightens the sense that, using a
general outline provided by Joab, the woman is in fact brilliantly improvising—
which in some ways she would have to do, given the fact that she is not reciting
an uninterrupted speech but responding to David's declarations, picking up
clues from the way he reacts.

4. *Rescue, O king!* This is a formulaic plea used by petitioners for royal justice.

6. *they quarreled in the field . . . and one struck down the other.* As several commentators have noted, her formulation aligns the story with the archetypal
tale of Cain and Abel. The fratricidal Cain is banished, but also given a sign to
protect him from blood vengeance.

7. *and let us destroy the heir as well.* Although it is unlikely that the clansmen
would have actually said these words, there is no need to tamper with the text.
The wise woman, in reporting the dialogue, insinuates her own anxious maternal perspective into this last clause. The implication is that the members of
the clan would like to kill the remaining son not only to execute justice but in
order to get his inheritance.

of the earth." And the king said to the woman, "Go to your house and I   8
myself shall issue a charge concerning you. And the Tekoite woman said   9
to the king, "Upon me, my lord the king, and upon my father's house,
let the guilt be, and the king and his throne shall be blameless." And   10
the king said, "The man who dares speak to you I will have brought to
me, and he will not touch you any more." And she said, "May the king,   11
pray, keep in mind the LORD your God, that the blood avenger should
not savage this much and let them not destroy my son." And he said, "As
the LORD lives, not a single hair of your son's shall fall to the ground!"

---

8. *I myself shall issue a charge concerning you.* Although David emphatically
announces (by adding the first-person pronoun *'ani*) that he himself will take
up the case, his language remains vague ("issue a charge"), and the Tekoite
woman's response in the next verse clearly indicates that she requires something further of him.

9. *Upon me . . . the guilt . . . and the king and his throne shall be blameless.* The
legal issue involved is blood guilt. From David's vagueness, she infers that he
is loath to intervene on behalf of the fratricide because by so doing he, and his
throne, would take on the guilt of allowing the killing to go unavenged.

10. *The man who dares speak to you I will have brought to me.* Her declaration
that she and her father's house will bear the guilt for allowing the killer to
live—evidently construed by David as a performative speech act, efficacious
once uttered—encourages the king to declare that he will absolutely protect
her against the vengeful kinsmen who are seeking out her son.

11. *let them not destroy my son.* The woman is still not satisfied, for David's
pledge to safeguard her did not mention her son: she wants to extract an explicit
declaration from David that he will protect the life of her son.
    not a single hair of your son's shall fall to the ground. Now she has what she
has been after, with David's hyperbolic declaration about guarding the well-
being of the fratricidal son, she is prepared to snap shut the trap of the fiction,
linking it to David's life, just as Nathan did with the parable of the poor man's
ewe. We should note that not a single hair of the fictitious son is to fall to the
ground, whereas the extravagantly abundant hair of his real-life referent, Absalom, will be cut annually in a kind of public ceremony.

12 And the woman said, "Let your servant, pray, speak a word to my lord the
13 king." And he said, "Speak." And the woman said, "Why did you devise
    in this fashion against God's people? And in speaking this thing, the
    king is as though guilty for the king's not having brought back his own
14 banished one. For we surely will die, like water spilled to the ground,
    which cannot be gathered again. And God will not bear off the life of

---

12. *Let your servant, pray, speak*. She uses these words of entreaty to preface the
transition to the real subject, David and Absalom.

13. *against God's people*. The implicit key concept here is "inheritance," which
links her fiction to the national political situation. She may be hinting that
Absalom is the appropriate heir to the throne. In any case, his banishment is
potentially divisive to the kingdom.
     in speaking this thing, the king is as though guilty. The Hebrew of this whole
sentence is rather crabbed, an effect reproduced in the translation. Rather than
reflecting difficulties in textual transmission, her language probably expresses
her sense of awkwardness in virtually indicting the king: he is "as though guilty,"
for "in speaking this thing," in declaring his resolution to protect the fratricidal
son, he has condemned his own antithetical behavior in the case of Absalom.
But the woman is careful not to mention Absalom explicitly by name—she
struggles verbally in the crossover from fiction to life, knowing she is treading
on dangerous ground.

14. *we surely will die, like water spilled to the ground*. Moving beyond Absalom
to a wise woman's pronouncement on human fate, she breaks free of her verbal
stumbling and becomes eloquent. The spilled water as an image of irreversible
mortality is an obvious and effective counterpoint to her previous image of
the ember that should not be quenched. It also picks up thematically David's
own bleak reflection on the irreversibility of death after his infant son expires
(Chapter 12).
     God will not bear off the life of him who devises that no one of his be banished.
As the wise woman switches back from philosophic statement to the juridical
issue confronting David, her language again becomes knotty and oblique. What
she is saying is that God will scarcely want to punish the father who brings back
his banished son, even though blood guilt remains unavenged.

him who devises that no one of his be banished. And so now, the reason 15
I have come to speak this thing to the king my lord is that the people
have made me afraid, and your servant thought, 'Let me but speak to
the king. Perhaps the king will do what his servant asks. For the king 16
would pay heed to save his servant from the hand of the person bent
on destroying me and my son together from God's heritage.' And your 17
servant thought, 'May the word of my lord the king, pray, be a respite,
for like a messenger of God, so is my lord the king, understanding good
and evil.' And may the LORD your God be with you." And the king said 18
to the woman, "Pray, do not conceal from me the thing that I ask you."
And the woman said, "Let my lord the king speak, pray." And the king 19
said, "Is the hand of Joab with you in all this?" And the woman answered
and said, "By your life, my lord the king, there is no turning right or left
from all that my lord the king has spoken! For your servant Joab, he it

---

15. *the reason I have come to speak this thing to the king.* The Tekoite woman,
having nervously broached the issue of David and Absalom, now hastily retreats
to the relative safety of her invented story about two sons, as though that were
the real reason for her appearance before the king. The dramatic and psychological logic of this entire speech argues against scholarly attempts to make it
more "coherent" by moving around whole swatches of it.

17. *respite.* The king's word will give her respite from her persecutors, the
would-be killers of her son. The Hebrew term *menuḥah* also points to a bound
locution, *menuḥah wenaḥalah*, "respite and inheritance," the very thing the
kinsmen would take from her.

19. *Is the hand of Joab with you in all this?* David rightly infers that a village wise
woman would have no motive of her own for undertaking this elaborate stratagem, and so someone in court with political aims must be behind her. Polzin
shrewdly proposes that Joab may actually have wanted David to detect him at
the bottom of the scheme: "The woman's eventual admission that she has been
sent by Joab (vv. 19–20) may itself be part of Joab's indirect message to David—
something like, 'Bring Absalom back or I may side with him against you.'"
   there is no turning right or left from all that my lord the king has spoken. She
is saying two things at once—that the king has hit the target in saying that
Joab is behind her, and that, having committed himself by his own speech to
protect the fratricidal son, he cannot now permit himself to continue Absalom's
banishment.

was who charged me, and he it was who put in your servant's mouth all
20 these words. In order to turn the thing round your servant Joab has done
this thing. And my lord is wise, as with the wisdom of a messenger of
21 God, to know everything in the land." And the king said to Joab, "Look,
22 pray, I have done this thing. Go and bring back the lad Absalom." And
Joab flung himself on his face to the ground and bowed down. And he
blessed the king, and Joab said, "Your servant knows that I have found
favor in the eyes of my lord the king, for the king has done what his ser-
23 vant asked." And Joab rose and went to Geshur and he brought Absalom
24 to Jerusalem. And the king said, "Let him turn round to his house, and
my face he shall not see." And Absalom turned round to his house, and
the king's face he did not see.

25 And there was no man so highly praised for beauty as Absalom in all
Israel—from the sole of his foot to the crown of his head, there was
26 no blemish in him. And when he cut his hair, for from one year's end
till the next he would cut it, as it grew heavy upon him, he would
weigh the hair of his head, two hundred shekels by the royal weight.

---

20. *my lord is wise, as with the wisdom of a messenger of God.* It is of course she
who has been demonstrably wise. David will soon show unwisdom by bringing
Absalom back while resisting real reconciliation, and his subsequent blindness
to Absalom's demagogic activities within a stone's throw of the court indicates
that there is much in the land about which he knows nothing.

21. *bring back the lad Absalom.* Momentarily, David refers to Absalom by a
term (*na'ar*) that is generally an expression of paternal affection. He will use
the same word repeatedly during Absalom's rebellion to stress his concern for
Absalom's safety.

25. *there was no man so highly praised for beauty.* Both Absalom and his sister
Tamar are remarkable for their beauty (as was the young David). For Absalom,
this will become an asset he trades on in his appeal for popular support.

26. *when he cut his hair . . . he would weigh the hair of his head.* There is clearly
something narcissistic about this preoccupation with his luxuriant hair. It is of
course a foreshadowing of the bizarre circumstances of Absalom's death (Chapter 18:9–15). Beyond that, the spectacular growth of hair invokes a comparison
with Samson, who never cut his hair until the cutting of the hair against his

And three sons were born to Absalom and a daughter named Tamar, she   27
was a beautiful woman. And Absalom lived in Jerusalem two years, but   28
the king's face he did not see. And Absalom sent to Joab in order to send   29
him to the king, but he did not want to come to him, and he sent still a
second time, but he did not want to come. And he said to his servants,   30
"See Joab's field next to mine, in which he has barley—go set it on fire!"
And Absalom's servants set fire to the field. And Joab rose and came to   31
Absalom's house and said to him, "Why did your servants set fire to the

---

will led to his undoing. The parallel with Samson is extended in the burning
of Joab's field, which recalls the foxes with torches tied to their tails used by
Samson to set fire to the fields of the Philistines. Perhaps the parallel with
Samson is meant to foreshadow Absalom's fate as a powerful leader whose
imprudence brings him to an early death.

27. *And three sons were born to Absalom and a daughter named Tamar, she was
a beautiful woman.* Later, we are informed (18:18) that Absalom was childless.
The two reports can be harmonized only with considerable strain, and it is best
to view them as contradictory traditions incorporated in the final text. But it is
noteworthy that, against patriarchal practice, the sons are left unnamed here,
and only the daughter, named after Absalom's raped sister, is not anonymous.
It is unnecessary to assume that this second beautiful Tamar was born after
the violation of her aunt by Amnon: here she is represented as a woman, and it
seems unlikely that so many years would have passed from the time of Tamar's
rape until Absalom's resumption of residence in Jerusalem.

29. *he did not want to come.* Throughout this story, there is a precarious game
of power going on. Joab has manipulated David to effect Absalom's return, but
seeing that the king remains estranged from Absalom, Joab does not want to
push his luck by interceding at court on Absalom's behalf. The power of the
king may be qualified, but he remains the king.

30. *set it on fire.* Absalom's Samson-like burning of the field is a strong indication that he is a man prepared to use violence to achieve his ends: Mafia style,
he presents Joab with an offer he can't refuse.

32 field that belongs to me?" And Absalom said to Joab, "Look, I sent to you, saying, 'Come here that I may send you to the king, saying, Why did I come from Geshur? It would be better for me were I still there. And now, let me see the face of the king, and if there be guilt in me, let

33 him put me to death.'" And Joab came to the king and told him. And he called to Absalom and he came to the king and bowed down to him, his face to the ground before the king, and the king kissed Absalom.

---

32. *if there be guilt in me, let him put me to death.* Absalom of course knows he is responsible for the killing of Amnon, but he construes that act as something other than "guilt" because it was done to avenge the violation of Tamar—a crime David left unpunished.

33. *he . . . bowed down to him, his face to the ground.* Fokkelman notes that there is a series of three acts of prostration before the king—first the Tekoite woman, then Joab, and now Absalom, the third bowing-down ostensibly consummating the reconciliation of father and son toward which all three acts are directed.

and the king kissed Absalom. The noun used (rather than "David") may suggest that this is more a royal, or official, kiss than a paternal one. It clearly gives Absalom no satisfaction, as his initiative of usurpation in the next episode strongly argues.

CHAPTER 15

A nd it happened thereafter that Absalom made himself a chariot with   1
horses and fifty men running before him. And Absalom would rise early   2
and stand by the gate road, and so, to every man who had a suit to appear
in judgment before the king, Absalom would call and say, "From what
town are you?" And he would say, "From one of the tribes of Israel is your
servant." And Absalom would say to him, "See, your words are good and   3
right, but you have no one to listen to you from the king." And Absalom   4

---

1. *a chariot with horses and fifty men running before him.* All this vehicular pomp
and circumstance, as other biblical references to chariots, horses, and runners
in conjunction with kings suggest, is a claim to royal status. The gestures of
usurpation are undertaken in Jerusalem, under David's nose, yet the king, who
has been described by the Tekoite woman as "knowing everything in the land,"
does nothing.

2.–5. This whole tableau of Absalom standing at the gate to the city, accost-
ing each newcomer, professing sympathy for his cause, and announcing that
were he the supreme judicial authority, he would rule in the man's favor, is a
stylized representation of the operation of a demagogue. It is hard to imagine
realistically that Absalom would tell each person so flatly that, whatever the
legal case, he would declare in his favor, but the point of the stylization is clear:
the demagogue enlists support by flattering people's special interests, leading
them to believe that he will champion their cause, cut their taxes, increase their
social security benefits, and so forth.

3. *you have no one to listen to you from the king.* The heart of Absalom's demagogic pitch is his exploiting what must have been widespread dissatisfaction
over the new centralized monarchic bureaucracy with its imposition of taxes
and corvées and military conscription: there is no one in this impersonal palace
to listen to you with a sympathetic ear, as I do.

would say, "Would that I were made judge in the land, and to me every
man would come who had a suit in justice, and I would declare in his
5 favor." And so, when a man would draw near to bow down to him, he
6 would reach out his hand and take hold of him and kiss him. And Absalom would act in this fashion to all the Israelites who appeared in judgment before the king, and Absalom stole the hearts of the men of Israel.

7 And it happened at the end of four years that Absalom said to the king,
"Let me go, pray, and pay my vow that I pledged to the LORD in Hebron.
8 For your servant made a vow when I was staying in Geshur in Aram,
saying, "If the LORD indeed brings me back to Jerusalem, I shall wor-
9 ship the LORD." And the king said to him, "Go in peace to Hebron."
10 And he arose and went to Hebron. And Absalom sent agents through
all the tribes of Israel, saying, "When you hear the sound of the ram's

---

5. *he would reach out his hand and take hold of him and kiss him.* The odd "rhym-
ing" of Absalom's kiss to each man he seduces and David's kiss to Absalom at
the end of the immediately preceding chapter is obvious. Could it suggest,
retrospectively, that David's kiss has an element of falseness that recurs, grossly
magnified, in Absalom's kiss? It should also be noted that Absalom's gesture of
"taking hold" of each of his political victims is verbally identical with Amnon's
"taking hold" of Tamar before the rape.

7. *at the end of four years.* The Masoretic text has "forty years," an untenable
number in this narrative context, but four different ancient versions show "four
years."
  pay my vow that I pledged to the LORD in Hebron. Haim Gevaryahu proposes
that the vow is to offer an exculpatory sacrifice for the crime of manslaughter.
With three years in Geshur and another four in Jerusalem, Absalom would have
come to the end of the period of seven years of penance that, according to some
ancient parallels, might have applied to such crimes. Absalom of course wants
to go off to Hebron—David's first capital city—in order to proclaim himself
king at a certain distance from his father's palace. It also appears that he feels
he can call on a base of support from Judah, his father's tribe. But why is not
David suspicious when his son proposes to pay his cultic vow in Hebron rather
than in Jerusalem? Gevaryahu, citing Greek analogues, makes the interesting
suggestion that a fratricide who had not yet atoned for his crime was not per-
mitted to worship in the same sanctuary as his father and brothers.

horn, you shall say, 'Absalom has become king in Hebron.'" And with 11
Absalom two hundred men went from Jerusalem, invited guests going
in all innocence, and they knew nothing. And Absalom sent Ahitophel 12
the Gilonite, David's counselor, from his town, from Giloh, while he
was offering the sacrifices, and the plot was strong, and the people
with Absalom were growing in number. And the informant came to 13
David, saying, "The hearts of the men of Israel are following Absalom."
And David said to all his servants who were with him in Jerusalem, 14
"Rise and let us flee or none of us will escape from Absalom. Hurry
and go, lest he hurry and overtake us and bring down harm upon us
and strike the town with the edge of the sword." And the king's ser- 15
vants said to the king, "Whatever my lord the king chooses, look, we are
your servants." And the king went out, and all his household with him, 16
on foot, and the king left his ten concubines to watch over the house.

---

11. *invited guests going in all innocence.* In a shrewd maneuver, Absalom takes
with him a large contingent of people not known to be his partisans, and not
willing participants in the conspiracy, and in this way he wards off suspicion
about the aim of his expedition. Once in Hebron, the two hundred men would
presumably be caught up in the tide of insurrection.

14. *Rise and let us flee.* Suddenly, under the pressure of crisis, with intelligence
that Absalom has overwhelming support, David shakes himself from his slumber of passivity, realizing he must move at once if he is to have any chance
of surviving. Against superior forces, the walled city of Jerusalem would be a
death trap. As Fokkelman aptly puts it, "Once again he is in contact with his
old self. . . . Once again men seek his death and he enters the wilderness both
figuratively and literally."

15. *Whatever my lord the king chooses, look, we are your servants.* As the episode unfolds, there is a constant counterpoint between those who reveal their
unswerving loyalty to David no matter how grim the outlook and the betrayal
of David by his son and all those who have rallied to the usurper.

16. *the king left his ten concubines to watch over the house.* This gesture sounds
as though it might be an expression of hope that David will return to Jerusalem.
In the event, it produces a disastrous consequence that fulfills one of the dire
terms of Nathan's curse in Chapter 12.

17 And the king, and all the people with him, went out on foot, and they
18 stopped by the outlying house. And all his servants were crossing over
alongside him, and all the Cherethites and the Pelethites and all the
Gittites, six hundred men who had come at his heels from Gath, were
19 crossing over before the king. And the king said to Ittai the Gittite,
"Why should you too go with us? Go back, stay with the king. For you

---

17. *the king, and all the people with him, went out on foot.* This restatement of
the first clause of the previous verse reflects the device that biblical scholars
call "resumptive repetition": after an interruption of the narrative line—here,
the introduction of the information about the concubines—the words just
before the interruption are repeated as the main line of the narrative resumes.
Moreover, the emphasis through repetition on going by foot suggests how David
and his entourage have been reduced from royal dignity in this abrupt flight.

the outlying house. The literal meaning of the Hebrew is "the house of distance." It clearly means the last house in the settled area beyond the walls of
the city.

18. *all his servants were crossing over.* The verb "to cross over" (*'avar*), abundantly
repeated, is a thematic focus of the episode. David and his followers are crossing over eastward from Jerusalem, headed first up the Mount of Olives and
then down the long declivity to the Jordan, which they will cross (the verb *'avar*
is often used for Jordan crossing) in their flight. The entire episode is unusual
in the leisurely panoramic view it provides of the eastward march from the
city. Instead of the preterite verb form ordinarily used for narration, participial
forms ("were crossing over") predominate, imparting a sense of something like
a present tense to the report of the action.

Cherethites . . . Pelethites . . . Gittites. This elite palace guard, which we
have encountered before, are Philistine warriors who became David's followers,
probably when he was residing in Gath. Ittai's expression of loyalty suggests
that they were more than mere mercenaries.

19. *Ittai.* His name is close to the preposition *'iti,* "with me." Both Moshe Garsiel and Robert Polzin have proposed that the name has a symbolic function:
Ittai is the loyalist who insists on remaining with David. Polzin notes that this
preposition is constantly reiterated in the episode, rather than its synonym *'im:*
David, for example, says to Ittai, "Why should you, too, go with us [*'itanu*]?"

stay with the king. This designation of the usurping son would be especially
painful for David to pronounce. He does it in order to try to persuade Ittai that
he should cast his fate with the person exercising the power of king.

are a foreigner, and you are also in exile from your own place. Just   20
yesterday you came, and today should I make you wander with us,
when I myself am going to wherever I may go? Turn back, and bring
back your brothers. Steadfast kindness to you!" And Ittai answered   21
the king and said, "As the LORD lives, and as my lord the king lives,
whatever place that my lord the king may be, whether for death or for
life, there your servant will be." And David said, "Go and cross over."
And Ittai crossed over, and all his men and all the children who were   22
with him. And all the land was weeping loudly and all the people were   23
crossing over, and the king was crossing over the Wadi Kidron, and all
the people were crossing over along the road to the wilderness. And,   24
look, Zadok and all the Levites were also with him, bearing the Ark of
the Covenant of God, and they set down the Ark of God, and Abiathar
came up, until all the people had finished crossing over from the town.
And the king said to Zadok, "Bring back the Ark of God to the town.   25
Should I find favor in the eyes of the LORD, He will bring me back
and let me see it and its abode. And should He say thus, 'I want no   26

---

20. *Steadfast kindness to you!* The translation reproduces the elliptical character
of the Masoretic text at this point. The Septuagint has an easier reading: "May
the LORD show steadfast kindness to you."

21. *whether for death or for life.* Given the grim circumstances, this loyal soldier
unflinchingly puts death before life in the two alternatives he contemplates.

23. *and the king was crossing over the Wadi Kidron.* In the slow-motion report of
the flight, reinforced by the participial verbs, David is now crossing the Kidron
brook at the foot of the slope descending eastward from the walled city. He will
then make his way up the Mount of Olives.

25. *Bring back the Ark of God to the town.* Given the difficulties David encountered in bringing the Ark to Jerusalem in the first place, and given the disastrous
consequences at the time of Eli in carrying it out to the battlefield, it is understandable that he should want the Ark left in Jerusalem. He makes this act a
token of his reiterated fatalism about his predicament.

27   part of you,' let Him do to me what is good in His eyes." And the king
said to Zadok the priest, "Do you see? Go back to the town in peace,
and Ahimaaz your son and Jonathan son of Abiathar—your two sons
28   with you. See, I shall be tarrying in the steppes of the wilderness until
29   word from you reaches me to inform me." And Zadok, and Abiathar
with him, brought back the Ark of God to Jerusalem, and they stayed
30   there. And David was going up the Slope of Olives, going up weeping, his head uncovered, and he walking barefoot, and all the people
who were with him, everyone with his head uncovered, went on up
31   weeping the while. And to David it was told, saying, "Ahitophel is
among the plotters with Absalom." And David said, "Thwart, pray, the
32   counsel of Ahitophel, O LORD." And David had come to the summit,
where one would bow down to God, and, look, coming toward him
33   was Hushai the Archite, his tunic torn and earth on his head. And

---

27. *and the king said to Zadok the priest.* Again we see the distinctive biblical
convention in the deployment of dialogue: when the first party speaks and
the second party does not respond, and a second speech of the first party is
introduced, there is an intimation of some sort of failure of response. Zadok is
nonplussed by David's instructions to return the Ark and also by David's fatalism. Now, in his second speech, David provides a practical, strategic rationale
for Zadok's going back to the city with the Ark—he and his two acolytes will
then be able to act as spies for David (see the end of his speech in verse 28).

30. *his head uncovered.* There is a difference of philological opinion as to
whether the verb here means covered or uncovered. The usual meaning of the
root is "to cover," but an uncovered head is more likely as a gesture of mourning—which is clearly intended—and this could be an instance of the same
term denoting antonyms, like the English verb "cleave."

31. *And to David it was told.* The Masoretic text reads, "And David told," but
both the Qumran Samuel and the Septuagint reflect the more likely idea—a
difference of one Hebrew letter—that someone told David.

32. *the summit, where one would bow down to God, and, look, coming toward him
was Hushai.* This crucial moment in the story is an especially deft manifestation
of the system of double causation that Gerhard von Rad and others after him
have attributed to the David narrative: everything in the story is determined by
its human actors, according to the stringent dictates of political realism; yet,

David said, "If you cross over with me, you will be a burden to me. But if you go back to the town and say to Absalom, 'Your servant, O 34 king, I will be. Your father's servant I always was, and now I am your servant,' you shall overturn Ahitophel's counsel for me. And are not 35 Zadok and Abiathar the priests there with you? And so, whatever you hear from the king's house you shall tell to Zadok and to Abiathar the priests. Look, there with them are their two sons, Ahimaaz, who is 36 Zadok's, and Jonathan, who is Abiathar's, and you shall send to me by their hand whatever you hear." And Hushai, David's friend, came to 37 the city, as Absalom was coming into Jerusalem.

---

simultaneously, everything is determined by God, according to a divine plan in history. David, informed that his own shrewd political advisor Ahitophel is part of Absalom's conspiracy, urgently and breathlessly invokes God, "Thwart, pray, the counsel of Ahitophel, O LORD." Then he reaches a holy site, an altar on the crest of the Mount of Olives ("where one would bow down to God"), and here he sees Hushai, his loyalty betokened by the trappings of mourning he has assumed, coming toward him. Theologically, Hushai is the immediate answer to David's prayer. Politically, David seizes upon Hushai as the perfect instrument to thwart Ahitophel's counsel, so from a certain point of view David is really answering his own prayer through his human initiative. Yet the encounter with Hushai at a place of worship leaves the lingering intimation that Hushai has been sent by God to David.

34. *say to Absalom, 'Your servant, O king, I will be.'* David, passive to a fault in the preceding episodes, now improvises in the moment of crisis a detailed plan for subverting Absalom, even dictating to Hushai the exact script he is to use when he comes before the usurper.

35. *are not Zadok and Abiathar the priests there with you?* David is both offering encouragement to Hushai, assuring him that he will not be the sole, isolated undercover agent in Jerusalem, and indicating to him what every spy needs to know, that there will be a reliable network for transmitting intelligence to the command center for which the spy is working.

CHAPTER 16

$\mathcal{A}$nd when David had crossed over a little beyond the summit, look, Ziba, Mephibosheth's lad, was there to meet him, with a yoke of saddled donkeys and on them two hundred loaves of bread and a hundred raisin cakes and a hundred of summer fruit and a jug of wine. And the king said to Ziba, "What would you with these things?" And Ziba said, "The donkeys are for the king's household to ride upon, and the

---

1. *David had crossed over.* The verbal motif of "crossing over," which virtually defines David's flight eastward from Jerusalem to trans-Jordan, is continued here. It will be given another odd turn in verse 17 when the bloody-minded Abishai volunteers to "cross over" and lop off Shimei's head.

a little beyond the summit. The summit in question is of course the top of the Mount of Olives, where David has just encountered Hushai and sent him off to Jerusalem as an undercover agent. Polzin acutely observes that the two low points of David's abasement—his humiliation by Shimei and the sexual possession of his concubines by his son—both take place on an elevation: near the summit and on the palace roof. The Hebrew term for summit used here is *ro'sh*, which is the ordinary word for "head," and as Polzin goes on to note, "head" is an organizing image of the entire episode: David goes up the mountainside with his head uncovered in a sign of mourning, as do the people with him. Hushai puts dirt on his head as a related expression of mourning. Both Hushai and Ziba are encountered on or near the head of the mountain. Abishai is prepared to cut off Shimei's head. And, as in other languages, head also designates political leader—an ironic verbal background to his moment when the head of all Israel has been displaced. Finally, Absalom's usurpation will come to a violent end when his head—the narrator does not say hair—is caught in the branches of a tree.

2. *for the king's household.* That is, for a couple of members of the king's immediate family. David, it should be recalled, has set off on foot.

bread and the summer fruit for the lads to eat, and the wine for the
exhausted to drink in the wilderness." And the king said, "And where   3
is your master's son?" And Ziba said to the king, "Why, he is staying in
Jerusalem, for he has said, 'Today the house of Israel will give back to
me my father's kingdom.'" And the king said to Ziba, "Look, everything   4
of Mephibosheth's is yours!" And Ziba said, "I am prostrate! May I find
favor in your eyes, my lord the king."

And King David came as far as Bahurim, and, look, from there out came   5
a man from the clan of the house of Saul, Shimei son of Gera was his

---

   the exhausted. The Hebrew term *ya 'ef*—also, by metathesis, *'ayef*, as in verse
14—straddles the two meanings of exhausted and famished.

3. *And where is your master's son?* Mephibosheth, who is crippled in both
legs, would scarcely have been up to joining the flight from Jerusalem. But
David, overwhelmed by betrayals from within his own court, is suspicious of
Mephibosheth's absence, and it is clear that Ziba has been counting on this
suspicion in his scheme to discredit Mephibosheth and take over his property.
It is noteworthy that, at this late date, David still refers to Mephibosheth as
"your master's son," still thinks of the long-dead Jonathan as Ziba's real master.
   Today the house of Israel will give back to me my father's kingdom. There is
no corroborating evidence in the story that Mephibosheth actually said these
words. What in fact seems to be happening is that Ziba is flatly lying about
his master in order to make himself appear to be the only loyal subject worthy
of David's benefactions, and of title to Saul's property. The notion Ziba puts
forth that Absalom would have turned over the throne to the surviving Saulide
is highly improbable, but what he proposes to David is that the purportedly
treacherous Mephibosheth sees in the general political upheaval of the rebellion an opportunity to reinstate the house of Saul.

5. *as far as Bahurim*. This is a village in the vicinity of Jerusalem on the eastern
slope of the Mount of Olives.

6 name, and he came cursing. And he hurled stones at David and at all
   King David's servants, and all the troops and all the warriors were at his
7 right and at his left. And thus said Shimei as he cursed, "Get out, get
8 out, you man of blood, you worthless fellow! The LORD has brought back
   upon you all the blood of the house of Saul, in whose place you became
   king, and the LORD has given the kingship into the hand of Absalom
   your son, and here you are, because of your evil, for you are a man of
9 blood." And Abishai son of Zeruiah said to the king, "Why should this
   dead dog curse my lord the king? Let me, pray, cross over and take off

---

6. *and all the troops and all the warriors were at his right and at his left.* Perhaps
Shimei is counting on the abject mood of David and his men to guarantee
his safety in this act of extreme provocation. Yet he is clearly playing a very
dangerous game—the history of David's warriors and of the sons of Zeruiah in
particular as ruthless and implacable enemies is well known to him, as the very
language of his words of revilement attest. Only a great, pent-up rage against
David, joined now with gloating over David's being thrust from power, could
explain Shimei's act.

7. *Get out, get out, you man of blood, you worthless fellow!* The blood that,
according to the narrative itself, David has on his hands is that of Uriah the
Hittite, and of the fighting men of Israel who perished at Rabbath Ammon with
Uriah. But the Benjaminite Shimei clearly believes what David himself, and
the narrative with him, has taken pains to refute—that the blood of the house
of Saul is on David's hands: Abner, Ish-Bosheth, and perhaps even Saul and
Jonathan (for David was collaborating with the Philistine Achish when they fell
at Gilboa). Hence the phrase Shimei hurls at David in his next sentence, "all
the blood of the house of Saul, in whose place you became king," suggesting a
conjunction of murder and usurpation.

8. *and here you are, because of your evil.* Most translations understand the last
phrase (a single word in the Hebrew) to mean "You are in evil circumstances,"
but the prefix *bet*, which can mean "in," also has a *causal* meaning, and that
makes more sense here: David has come into dire straits, losing the throne,
displaced by his own son, because of his own evil actions.

9. *Why should this dead dog curse my lord the king?* We have seen previously
the idiomatic use of "dead dog" to mean the lowest of the low, David applying
this designation to himself in his speech to Saul at Ein-Gedi. Here the polar
contrast between "dead dog" and "my lord the king" is striking. But Abishai is
also reviving the literal force of the idiom, since he proposes to deal swift death

his head." And the king said, "What do I have to do with you, O sons   10
of Zeruiah? If he curses, it is because the LORD has said to him, 'Curse
David,' and who can say, 'Why have you done this?'" And David said to   11
Abishai and to all his servants, "Look—my son, the issue of my loins,
seeks my life. How much more so, then, this Benjaminite. Leave him
be and let him curse, for the LORD has told him. Perhaps the LORD will   12
see my affliction and the LORD may requite me good for his cursing this
day." And David, and his men with him, went off on the way, and Shimei   13
was walking round the side of the mountain alongside him, cursing and
hurling stones at him and flinging dirt. And the king came, and all the   14
troops who were with him, exhausted, and took a breathing stop there.

---

to the snarling Shimei. This is not the first time that Abishai has been prepared
to kill someone on the spot: when he accompanied David into Saul's camp (1
Samuel 26:8), he had to be restrained from his impulse to dispatch Saul with
a single thrust of the spear.

10. *If he curses, it is because the LORD has said to him, 'Curse David.'* This is one
of the most astonishing turning points in this story that abounds in human
surprises. The proud, canny, often implacable David here resigns himself to
accepting the most stinging humiliation from a person he could easily have his
men kill. David's abasement is not a disguise, like Odysseus's when he takes on
the appearance of a beggar, but a real change in condition—from which, however, he will emerge in more than one surprising way. The acceptance of humiliation is a kind of fatalism: if someone commits such a sacrilegious act against
the man who is God's anointed king, it must be because God has decreed it.
Behind that fatalism may be a sense of guilt: I am suffering all this because of
what I have done, for taking Bathsheba and murdering her husband, for my
inaction in Amnon's rape of Tamar and Absalom's murder of Amnon. The guilt
is coupled with despair: as David goes on to say, When my own son is trying to
kill me, what difference could it make if this man of a rival tribe, who at least
has political grounds for hostility toward me, should revile me?

13. *cursing and hurling stones at him and flinging dirt.* It is with this image that
the episode concludes—Shimei walking along, angrily persisting in his insults,
the dirt flung a material equivalent of the words uttered.

14. *came.* Some indication of where he came seems to be required. One version of the Septuagint supplies "to the Jordan" as the answer. That would be a
plausible stopping place.

15 And Absalom and all the troops, the men of Israel, had come to Jerusalem, and Ahitophel was with him.

16 And it happened when Hushai the Archite, David's friend, came to
Absalom, that Hushai said, "Long live the king, long live the king!"
17 And Absalom said to Hushai, "Is this your loyalty to your friend? Why
18 did you not go with your friend?" And Hushai said to Absalom, "On the
contrary! Whom the LORD has chosen, and this people and every man of
19 Israel—his I will be and with him I will stay. And, besides, whom should
I serve? Should it not be his son? As I served your father, so will I be in
20 your service." And Absalom said to Ahitophel, "Give you counsel: what

---

15. *And Absalom . . . had come to Jerusalem, and Ahitophel was with him.* This
brief switch of narrative tracks, in a pluperfect verbal form, lays the ground for
the fateful clash of counsels between Ahitophel and Hushai and also provides
the necessary indication that David and his people have succeeded in fleeing a
good many miles to the east by the time Absalom's forces enter the city.

16. *David's friend.* As we have noted, *rea'* "friend" or "companion," is a court
title, but when Absalom uses it, he leans on the ordinary sense of friendship.
   Long live the king. Fokkelman nicely observes that "what he particularly does
not say is 'long live King Absalom.'" Thus, in a dramatic irony evident to the
audience of the story and of course concealed from Absalom, Hushai is really
wishing long life to *his* king—David. And again in his response to Absalom's
question about his disloyalty to David, he avoids the use of Absalom's name in
a sentence that he secretly applies to David: "Whom the LORD has chosen . . .
his I will be and with him I will stay."

19. *And, besides, whom should I serve? Should it not be his son?* Only now does
Hushai invoke the line of explanation that David instructed him to use when
he came before Absalom.

20. *Give you counsel.* Both the verb and the ethical dative "you" are in the
plural, though Absalom is said to be speaking to Ahitophel. Shimon Bar-Efrat
proposes that the language implies Absalom is addressing both Ahitophel and
Hushai, though it is from Ahitophel as his official advisor that he expects to
receive counsel. The plural forms, then, suggest that Absalom has been persuaded by Hushai and has accepted him into his circle of court counselors.
That inference helps make sense of the immediately following encounter in
which both men appear as members of Absalom's national security council.

shall we do?" And Ahitophel said to Absalom, "Come to bed with your ²¹
father's concubines whom he left to watch over the house, and let all
Israel hear that you have become repugnant to your father, and the hand
of all who are with you will be strengthened." And they pitched a tent for ²²
Absalom on the roof, and he came to bed with his father's concubines
before the eyes of all Israel. And the counsel of Ahitophel that he would ²³
give in those days was as one would inquire of an oracle of God, even
so was every counsel of Ahitophel, for David and for Absalom as well.

---

21. *Come to bed with your father's concubines.* Cohabiting with the sexual
consorts of a ruler is an assertion of having taken over all his prerogatives of
dominion. Ahitophel's shrewd counsel especially addresses the effect on public
opinion of the action proposed: after it, no one will be able to imagine a reconciliation between Absalom and his father ("let all Israel hear that you have
become repugnant to your father"), and so the hand of Absalom's supporters
will be strengthened, for no one will hedge his support, thinking that David and
Absalom will somehow come to terms.

22. *he came to bed with his father's concubines before the eyes of all Israel.* The
tent on the roof ensures sexual privacy, but Absalom's entering into it with
each of the women is a public display of the act of cohabitation. Either this
is to be accepted as an unrealistic event, given that there are ten concubines,
or Absalom is supposed to be not only beautiful and hirsute but also a sexual
athlete. His act, of course, is a fulfillment of Nathan's dire curse in Chapter
12. As several commentators have noted, the usurper's sexual transgression of
David's women takes place on the very palace roof from which his father first
looked lustfully at Bathsheba.

23. *the counsel of Ahitophel . . . was as one would inquire of an oracle of God.*
This quasi-religious trust in Ahitophel's counsel is obviously from the point of
view of those who seek it, there being a sour irony in likening the sordid, if pragmatic, counsel to have sex with the king's concubines to a divine oracle. In any
event, this observation throws a retrospective light on David's disturbance over
the news that Ahitophel was among the conspirators and his prayer to God to
confound Ahitophel's counsel (15:31). Ahitophel, it seems, is a kind of Israelite
Metternich or Bismarck, and David fears that in losing him he has lost a vital
strategic resource. The canniness of Ahitophel's military advice will be evident
in his clash with Hushai.

CHAPTER 17

And Ahitophel said to Absalom, "Let me pick, pray, twelve thousand men, and let me rise and pursue David tonight. And let me come upon him when he is tired and slack-handed, and I shall panic him, and all the troops who are with him will flee, and I shall strike down the king alone. And let me turn back all the troops to you, for it is one man you seek,

---

1. *Let me pick . . . twelve thousand men . . . and pursue David tonight.* Ahitophel not only offers counsel but proposes to undertake the command of the expedition himself, in striking contrast to Hushai, who begins with a lengthy descriptive statement and then uses a third-person verbal form (verse 11, "let all Israel gather round you") to express his recommended course of action. It seems as though the urgent Ahitophel has taken on the attribute of his rival's name, which carries the verb *ḥush*, "hurry."

2. *let me come upon him when he is tired and slack-handed.* This is, of course, very sound advice: David and his men are in fact fatigued from their flight to the banks of the Jordan (16:14), and are likely to be vulnerable to a surprise attack.
   I shall strike down the king alone. Ahitophel seeks to avoid a protracted civil war: if he can panic David's forces into a general retreat, the death of David will then put an end to the opposition, and his troops are likely to transfer their loyalty to Absalom. The image of one man struck down as the troops flee may ironically echo David's plan for doing away with Uriah.

3. *for it is one man you seek.* The Masoretic text has three simple Hebrew words here that make no sense as a syntactic sequence: *keshuv hakol ha'ish* ("as-return all the-man"). Many modern interpreters follow the Septuagint, which rearranges the Hebrew letters to read *keshuv kalah le'ishah*, "as a bride returns to her husband." But, as Bar-Efrat contends, this would be a strange image for the movement of troops to the opposite side and it would violate the pointedly unmetaphoric, businesslike character of Ahitophel's language, which stands in sharp contrast to Hushai's elaborately figurative rhetoric of persua-

and all the troops will be at peace." And the thing seemed right in the 4
eyes of Absalom and in the eyes of all the elders of Israel. And Absalom 5
said, "Call, pray, to Hushai the Archite, too, and let us hear what he,
too, has to say." And Hushai came to Absalom, and Absalom said to him, 6
saying, "In the following manner Ahitophel has spoken. Shall we act on
his word? If not, you must speak." And Hushai said to Absalom, "The 7
counsel that Ahitophel has given is not good this time." And Hushai said, 8
"You yourself know of your father and his men that they are warriors and
that they are bitter men, like a bear in the field bereaved of its young.

---

sion. This translation therefore adopts Bar-Efrat's proposal that *keshuv hakol* is
an inadvertent scribal repetition of *we'ashiva kol* ("let me turn back all") at the
beginning of the verse; that phrase is omitted here, and *'ish 'ehad*, "one man,"
is presumed instead of *ha'ish 'asher*, "the man who."

4. *the elders of Israel*. This term clearly designates an official group, a kind of
royal council. Ahitophel, addressing this group, acts as national security advisor.

5. *Hushai the Archite, too*. Although Hushai does not have Ahitophel's official
standing, he has sufficiently won Absalom's trust that the usurper is at least
curious to see whether Hushai will concur with Ahitophel. This will prove to
be a fatal error.

7. *not good this time*. Shrewdly, Hushai begins by implicity conceding that as a
rule Ahitophel's counsel is good—but in this specific instance, the trusty advisor has exhibited a lapse in judgment.

8. *And Hushai said*. Absalom is silent, astounded that anyone should deny the
self-evident rightness of Ahitophel's counsel. So the formula for introducing
direct discourse, according to the biblical convention, must be repeated, and
now Hushai launches upon his cunningly devised argument.
  You yourself know. Hushai's opening rhetorical move is to flatter his interlocutor: I hardly have to tell you what you yourself well know, that your father is
a very dangerous adversary who cannot be attacked impulsively, without proper
preparation.
  warriors . . . bitter men . . . like a bear in the field . . . a seasoned fighter. Hushai
uses language that, as Bar-Efrat and others have noted, recapitulates a series
of moments from the earlier story of David. What he is doing in effect is invoking the legend of the heroic David, who as a boy slew bear and lion (compare
the lion simile in verse 10), and who gathered round him bitter men, warriors,
seasoned fighters.

And your father is a seasoned fighter and he will not spend the night with
9 the troops. Look, he will now be hiding in some hollow or some other
place, and it will happen when they fall from the very first that he who
hears of it will say, 'There's a rout among the troops who follow Absalom.'
10 And though he be a valiant fellow whose heart is like the heart of a lion,
he will surely quail, for all Israel knows that your father is a warrior,
11 and valiant men are those who are with him. And so I counsel you—
let all Israel gather round you, from Dan to Beersheba, multitudinous
as the sand that is on the seashore, and you in person will go forward
12 into battle. And we shall come upon him in whatever place that he may
be, and we shall light upon him as the dew falls upon the ground, and

---

he will not spend the night with the troops. This image of David as the constantly wakeful, elusive guerilla leader scarcely accords with the figure David
has cut in the last several years of reported narrative—sleeping through the
long afternoon while his army fights in Ammon, sedentary in his palace while
internecine struggle goes on between his own children.

9. *he will now be hiding in some hollow or some other place.* Hushai's rather
vague language once again evokes the time when David was a fugitive from
Saul, hiding in caves and wildernesses.
   when they fall from the very first. The unspecified subject of the verb—actually emended by some as "the troops"—clearly refers to Absalom's forces:
ambushed by the wily David, they will quickly panic.

10. *he will surely quail.* The literal meaning of the Hebrew is "he will surely
melt."

11. *multitudinous as the sand . . . on the seashore.* This traditional simile is
used to convey the idea that only overwhelmingly superior numbers, achieved
through a general (and time-consuming!) conscription, can prevail against so
formidable a foe as David.

12. *we shall light upon him as the dew falls upon the ground.* Hushai, as Fok-
kleman has observed, pairs the traditional simile of the sands of the seashore
with a more innovative, yet related simile of dew on the field. The dew falls
silently, effortlessly, and this is how this huge army will "light upon" David's
forces. Dew, elsewhere an image of peacetime blessing, is here associated with
destruction.

not a single one will be left of all the men who are with him. And should 13
he withdraw into a town, all Israel will bear ropes to the town and haul
it away to the wadi until not a stone remains there." And Absalom said, 14
and every man of Israel with him, "The counsel of Hushai the Archite
is better than the counsel of Ahitophel." And the LORD had ordained
to overturn Ahitophel's good counsel in order for the LORD to bring evil
upon Absalom.

And Hushai said to Zadok and to Abiathar the priests, "Such and such 15
did Ahitophel counsel Absalom and the elders of Israel, and such and
such I on my part counseled. And now, send quickly and inform David, 16

---

not a single one will be left of all the men who are with him. Ahitophel proposed a strategy through which it might be possible to kill David alone and then
to enlist the support of his followers. Hushai's counsel is to annihilate David's
forces, a much more violent means of preventing civil war. The bloodthirsty
alternative evidently appeals to something in Absalom, who is unwilling to trust
the future loyalty of the troops who have remained with David.

13. *should he withdraw into a town.* This little addendum to Hushai's scenario
is intended to anticipate an obvious objection to it: the recommended course of
action would give David time to pull back his forces to a strong defensive position in a fortified town. Hushai's counterargument is that with so huge an army,
Absalom's people could easily take down the walls of the town stone by stone.

14. *The counsel of Hushai . . . is better than the counsel of Ahitophel.* This entire
episode turns on an ingenious reversal of values. The straight-talking, clear-
seeing advisor is defeated by the lying secret agent who musters the resources
of a figurative, psychologically manipulative rhetoric to achieve his ends. Yet it
is the master of deception who serves the forces of legitimacy while the plain
dealer looks out for the interests of a usurper and would-be parricide.
  the LORD had ordained to overturn Ahitophel's good counsel. This theological
explanation can be viewed as adding an overarching perspective, or as merely secondary, to the thoroughly human machinations of Hushai, instigated by David.

16. *And now, send quickly and inform David.* Although Zadok and Abiathar
presumably know that Absalom has chosen to follow Hushai's counsel, they
appear to be nervous that he may change his mind and implement Ahitophel's
strategy, for they urge David not to waste a moment but to flee eastward across
the Jordan.

saying, 'Spend not the night in the steppes of the wilderness, but rather cross over onward, lest disaster engulf the king and all the troops who

17 are with him.'" And Jonathan and Ahimaaz were stationed at Ein-Rogel, and the slavegirl would go and inform them and they would go and inform King David, for they could not be seen coming into the town.

18 And a lad saw them and informed Absalom, and the two of them went quickly and came to the house of a man in Bahurim who had a well in

19 his courtyard, and they went down into it. And the woman took a cloth and stretched it over the mouth of the well and spread groats on top of

20 it, so that nothing could be noticed. And Absalom's servants came to the woman in the house and said, "Where are Ahimaaz and Jonathan?" And she said to them, "They've crossed over past the water reservoir." And they searched and they found nothing and they went back to Jerusalem.

---

17. *Ein-Rogel.* The site of this village has not been confidently identified, but it would have to be near Jerusalem to the east.

18. *the house of a man in Bahurim.* This village on the eastern slope of the Mount of Olives is the hometown of Shimei, who cursed David. What appears to be reflected is a political reality in which the populace is divided between loyalists and supporters of the usurper.

19. *And the woman took a cloth.* The woman is evidently the wife of the man from Bahurim (the same Hebrew word means both "woman" and "wife," like *femme* in French and *Frau* in German). This is still another instance in the David story in which the enterprising intervention of a shrewd woman saves the day. As has often been noted, this moment alludes to the story told in Joshua 2 of Rahab the harlot, who hides the two spies sent out to Jericho by Joshua. In Joshua, the spies are hidden up above, in the roof thatch; here they hide below in the well. There may be a certain agricultural affinity between the covering of thatch and the cloth covered with groats (if that is what the anomalous Hebrew *rifot* means) under which the pairs of spies hide. In any case, the destruction of all the men of Jericho who sought Joshua's spies foreshadows the destruction of Absalom's army.

20. *They've crossed over past the water reservoir.* Rahab, too, gives the pursuers false directions about where the spies have gone. Here, the thematically crucial "cross over" is again invoked. The meaning of *mikhal*, the word rendered here as "reservoir," is a little doubtful, though it could be derived from a verbal root that means "to contain."

And it happened after they had gone that Ahimaaz and Jonathan came 21
up from the well and went and informed King David, and they said to
David, "Rise and cross over the water quickly, for thus has Ahitophel
counseled against you." And David rose, and all the troops with him, 22
and they crossed over the Jordan. By the light of morning not a single
one was missing who had not crossed over the Jordan.

And Ahitophel saw that his counsel was not acted on, and he saddled 23
his donkey and arose and went to his home to his town, and he left a
charge for his household, and he hanged himself and died. And he was
buried in the tomb of his father. And David had come to Mahanaim 24
when Absalom crossed over the Jordan, he and every man of Israel
with him. And Absalom had placed Amasa instead of Joab over the 25
army, and Amasa was the son of a man named Ithra the Ishmaelite,

---

21. *cross over the water quickly, for thus has Ahitophel counseled against you*. The
two couriers now assume the worst-case scenario, that Ahitophel's counsel will
after all be followed. The reference to crossing over the water is a clear indication that David is encamped on the west bank of the Jordan.

23. *he saddled his donkey and arose and went to his home to his town, and he
left a charge for his household, and he hanged himself*. This haunting notice of
Ahitophel's suicide shows him a deliberate, practical man to the very end,
making all the necessary arrangements for his family and being sure to do away
with himself in his hometown, where he knows he will be readily buried in the
ancestral tomb. Ahitophel kills himself not only because, in quasi-Japanese
fashion, he has lost face, but also out of sober calculation: he realizes that
Hushai's counsel will enable David to defeat Absalom, and with the old king
returned to the throne, an archtraitor like Ahitophel will surely face death.
Thus, in tying the noose around his own neck, he anticipates the executioner's
sword.

24. *Mahanaim*. This is an Israelite walled city in trans-Jordan.

25. *Ithra the Ishmaelite*. There are two different problems with the identification of Amasa's progenitors in the Masoretic text. The Masoretic version has
"Israelite," but this national label (rather than identification by tribe) would be
strange here, and the same Ithra in 1 Chronicles 2:17 is said, more plausibly,
to be the son of an Ishmaelite. The fact that the father is a member of another
national-ethnic group accords with the report that he "had come to bed with

who had come to bed with Abigail daughter of Jesse, sister of Zeruiah,
26 Joab's mother. And Israel and Absalom camped in the land of Gilead.
27 And it happened when David came to Mahanaim that Shobi son of
Nahash from Rabbath Ammon and Machir son of Amiel from Lo-
28 Debar and Barzillai the Gileadite from Rogelim brought couches and
basins and earthenware, and wheat and barley and flour and parched
29 grain and beans and lentils and honey and curds from the flock and
cheese from the herd. These they offered to David and the troops with
him to eat, for they thought, "The troops are hungry and exhausted and
thirsty in the wilderness."

Abigail," for that sexual term by no means necessarily implies marriage. The
Masoretic text makes Nahash, an Ammonite, Abigail's father, but it looks as
though that name may have drifted into this verse in scribal transcription from
verse 27. 1 Chronicles 2 more plausibly reports that Jesse was Abigail's father.
She would then be the sister of David and of Zeruiah, Joab's mother; and so
Amasa and Joab, the two army commanders, are first cousins, and both of them
David's nephews.

28. *beans and lentils.* The received text adds "and parched grain" at the end
of the list, an apparent scribal duplication of the word that occurs just before
"beans and lentils." This detailed catalogue of vitally needed victuals, preceded
by the utensils required to serve them and something like bedrolls, is a vivid
expression of loyalty to David's beleaguered forces on the part of the trans-
Jordanian Israelites and their Ammonite vassals. Barzillai's faithfulness will be
singled out when David returns.

29. *curds from the flock.* This reflects a very minor emendation of the Masoretic
text, which says "curds and flock." In the next phrase, the Hebrew word for
"cheese" (*shefot*) has no precedent but is usually understood as cheese because
of the alimentary context and the likely root of the word.

CHAPTER 18

And David marshaled the troops that were with him and set over 1
them commanders of thousands and commanders of hundreds. And 2
David sent out the troops—a third under Joab and a third under Abishai son of Zeruiah, Joab's brother, and a third under Ittai the Gittite.
And the king said to the troops, "I, too, will surely sally forth with you."
And the troops said, "You shall not sally forth. For if we must flee, 3
they will pay us no mind, and should half of us die, they will pay us no
mind, for you are like ten thousand of us, and so it is better that you
be a help for us from the town." And the king said to them, "What- 4
ever is good in your eyes I shall do." And the king stood by the gate

---

2. *I, too, will surely sally forth with you.* The aging David, as we have had occasion to note (see comment on 11:1), has long been a sedentary monarch rather
than a field commander. In the present crisis, he imagines he can rise again
to his old role, but the troops, who diplomatically make no reference to age or
infirmity, clearly recognize he is not up to it.

3. *should half of us die, they will pay us no mind.* Like Ahitophel, the troops
assume that the real object of Absalom's attack is David. But they essentially
propose an opposite scenario to Absalom's: David will remain safe inside the
fortified town, well behind the lines, while the troops—not panicked, as Ahitophel would have had it, but strategically deployed—will do battle against
Absalom's army.

for you are like ten thousand of us. This is the reading of numerous Hebrew
manuscripts and the Septuagint and Vulgate. The Masoretic text reads "for now
we are like ten thousand."

4. *the king stood by the gate.* Fokkelman has noted a wry correspondence here
with the beginning of Absalom's usurpation, when he took a stance by the gate of
the city and accosted each man who came by in order to enlist him to his cause.

and all the troops sallied forth by their hundreds and their thousands.
5 And the king charged Joab and Abishai and Ittai, saying, "Deal gently
for me with the lad Absalom." And all the troops heard when the
6 king charged the commanders concerning Absalom. And the troops
sallied forth to the field to meet Israel, and the battle took place in
7 the forest of Ephraim. And the troops of Israel were routed there by
David's servants, and great was the slaughter there, twenty thousand.
8 And the battle spread out over all the countryside, and the forest
devoured more of the troops than the sword devoured on that day.
9 And Absalom chanced to be in front of David's servants, Absalom
riding on his mule, and the mule came under the tangled branches
of a great terebinth, and his head caught in the terebinth, and he

---

5. *Deal gently.* This is the time-honored and eloquent rendering of the King
James Version. But some philologists derive the rare verb here from a root that
means "to cover" and hence construe it in context as "protect." This construction would make it a closer synonym of the verb used in the soldier's repetition
of David's injunction in verse 12, "watch over."

7. *the troops of Israel were routed there.* The elision of the precise details of the
battle is entirely consistent with the narrative treatment of battles elsewhere
in the Bible. One may assume that the three divisions of seasoned fighters,
led by their experienced commanders, attacked the Israelite army from three
different sides, panicking it into disorderly flight—an outcome indicated in
the "devouring" forest, where presumably the fleeing soldiers lost their way,
stumbled, became entangled in the undergrowth, perhaps even slashed at each
other in the dark of the wood. Throughout this episode, Absalom's forces are
"Israel" and David's are his "servants." The former are numerically superior, but
they behave like a poorly organized conscript army facing professional soldiers.

9. *his head caught in the terebinth, and he dangled between heaven and earth,
while the mule which was beneath him passed on.* This striking and bizarre image
of Absalom's penultimate moment provides a brilliant symbolic summation of
his story. Most obviously, the head of hair that was his narcissistic glory is now
the instrument of his fatal entrapment, Absalom the commander microcosmi-
cally enacting the fate of his army "devoured" by the forest. There is nothing
supernatural here—David's forces have shrewdly taken advantage of the irregu-
lar terrain—yet there is a sense that nature is conspiring against Absalom and
his men. The mule is in this period the usual mount for princes and kings (one
should recall that all the king's sons ride away on their mules after Absalom

dangled between heaven and earth, while the mule which was beneath him passed on. And a certain man saw and informed Joab and said, 10 "Look, I saw Absalom dangling from the terebinth." And Joab said to 11 the man informing him, "And look, you saw, and why did you not strike him to the ground there, and I would have had to give you ten pieces of silver and a belt?" And the man said to Joab, "Even were I to heft in 12 my palms a thousand pieces of silver, I would not reach out my hand against the king's son, for within our hearing the king charged you and

---

has Amnon killed), so Absalom's losing his mule from under him is an image of his losing his royal seat. Having climbed from exile and rejection to the throne, he now dangles helplessly between sky and earth. The mule's "passing on" (*'avar*), as Polzin notes, picks up the key verb ("cross over") that has characterized David's flight from the royal city. Fokkelman brilliantly shows that there is also a whole series of contrastive parallels between Absalom's fate and that of his counselor Ahitophel: "The counselor rides calmly on his ass to his home while the prince is abandoned by his mule, a fatal loss. He is thrown into an unknown, nameless and ignominious grave while Ahitophel is 'buried in his father's grave'. . . . With all these contrasts, they have one detail in common: both finally hang."

he dangled. The Masoretic text has "he was given," but ancient translations into Aramaic, Syriac, Greek, and Latin, now confirmed by the Qumran Samuel scroll, read "dangled," a difference of a single consonant in the Hebrew.

11. *And look, you saw.* The contemptuous Joab throws the soldier's own words back into his face: if that's what you really saw, why didn't you have the brains to finish him off on the spot and get the reward I would have given you? Joab, in his unflinching resolution to kill Absalom in defiance of David's explicit orders to the contrary, remains the consummately calculating political man—something David once was but no longer is. When Joab thought it was politically prudent to reconcile David with Absalom, he took elaborate steps to achieve that end. Now he realizes that an Absalom allowed to survive is likely to be a source of future political dissension and that the only sure way to eliminate this threat is Absalom's death.

12. *were I to heft in my palms a thousand pieces of silver.* The soldier responds to Joab's contempt with righteous indignation, multiplying the hypothetical reward a hundredfold and turning the general act of giving silver into a concrete hefting of its weight in order to express how sacred he holds the king's injunction, which, we now see, has in fact been heard by "all the troops" (verse 5).

13 Abishai and Ittai, saying, 'Watch for me over the lad Absalom.' Otherwise, I would have wrought falsely with my own life, and nothing can
14 be concealed from the king, while you would have stood aloof." And
   Joab said, "Not so will I wait for you!" And he took three sticks in his
   palm and he thrust them into Absalom's heart, still alive in the heart
15 of the terebinth. And ten lads, Joab's armor bearers, pulled round and
16 struck down Absalom and put him to death. And Joab sounded the
   ram's horn, and the troops came back from pursuing Israel, for Joab
17 held back the troops. And they took Absalom and flung him into the
   big hollow in the forest, and they heaped up over it a very big mound
   of stones. And all Israel had fled, each to his tent.

---

14. *he took three sticks in his palm.* Over against the soldier's palms hyperbolically hefting a thousand pieces of silver, Joab's palm grasps a blunt instrument
of violence. The Hebrew *shevatim* means "sticks," not "darts," as it is often
translated, and had they been darts, the blow would surely have been fatal. On
the contrary, it seems probable that Joab's intention is not to kill the prince—
after all, this military man is an experienced killer—but rather to stun him and
hurt him badly, and then to spread the responsibility for the death by ordering
the warriors to finish him off. Fokkelman proposes that the three sticks jibe
with the three divisions of the army, so that Joab performs a deliberately symbolic act, "executing the rebellious prince on behalf of the whole army."
   into Absalom's heart, still alive in the heart of the terebinth. The two hearts,
one a vulnerable human organ, the other the dense of center of the tangle of
branches, produce an unsettling effect.

15. *lads.* The Hebrew *ne'arim*, "lads," in its sense of elite fighting men, rings
dissonantly against David's repeated paternal designation of Absalom as *na'ar*,
"lad."

16. *sounded.* The Hebrew reflects an untranslatable pun because the verb *taqa'*,
"to make a piercing sound with a horn," also means to thrust or stab, and is the
word just used to report Joab's blow to the heart.

17. *the big hollow.* An alternative rendering is "pit," but "hollow" is used here to
preserve the verbal identity in the Hebrew between this moment and Hushai's
imaginary description in Chapter 17 of David's hiding in "one of the hollows."
To be flung into a hole in the field and covered with a heap of stones is a shameful burial.

And Absalom had taken and heaped up a cairn for himself in his life- 18
time, which is in the Valley of the King, for he said, "I have no son to
make my name remembered." And he called the cairn after his name,
and it is called Absalom's Monument to this day.

And Ahimaaz son of Zadok had said, "Let me run, pray, and bear tidings 19
to the king that the LORD has done him justice against his enemies."
And Joab said to him, "You are no man of tidings this day. You may bear 20
tidings on another day, but this day you shall bear no tidings, for the
king's son is dead." And Joab said to the Cushite "Go, inform the king of 21
what you have seen," and the Cushite bowed down before Joab and ran

---

18. *Absalom had . . . heaped up a cairn.* This brief notice, in the pluperfect
tense, draws a pointed contrast with Absalom's ignominious grave. The same
verb, "to heap up," is used for both, and the cairn, or commemorative pile of
stones (*not* a "pillar") is the grandiose image that is transformed into the pile
of stones over Absalom's body.

   I have no son to make my name remembered. Faulkner's *Absalom, Absalom!*,
with reference to both its David figure and its Absalom figure, beautifully
catches the pathos of these words. Those who have sought to harmonize this
verse with 14:27, where Absalom is said to have fathered three sons, propose
that the sons died, their early death explaining why they are left unnamed.

21. *the Cushite.* This Nubian is the third foreign messenger introduced into the
story (the other two are the Egyptian slave who informs David of the whereabouts of the Amalekite raiding party and the Amalekite who reports Saul's
death to David). Joab appears to exhibit a certain paternal concern for Ahimaaz,
a priest and a faithful agent of David's during the insurrection—in the next
verse he addresses him as "my son." Joab is keenly aware that David has in the
past shown himself capable of killing the bearer of ill tidings in a fit of rage, and
so the commander prefers to let a foreigner take the risk.

22 off. And Ahimaaz son of Zadok once again said to Joab, "Whatever may
    be, let me, too, pray, run after the Cushite." And Joab said, "Why should
23 you run, my son, when yours are not welcome tidings?" "Whatever may
    be, I will run!" And he said to him, "Run." And Ahimaaz ran by the way
    of the Plain, and he overtook the Cushite.

24 And David was sitting between the gates, and the lookout went up on
    the roof of the gate on the wall, and he raised his eyes and saw and,
25 look, a man was running alone. And the lookout called and told the
    king, and the king said, "If he's alone, there are tidings in his mouth."

---

22. *yours are not welcome tidings*. The Hebrew—literally, "finding tidings"—is
anomalous, and has inspired both emendation and excessively ingenious interpretation. The immediate context suggests "welcome" as the most plausible
meaning, and this could easily be an idiom for which there are no other occurrences in the biblical corpus, which, after all, provides only a small sampling of
ancient Hebrew usage. In fact, these two words, *besorah motsei't*, could well be
an idiomatic ellipsis for *besorah motsei't ḥen*, "tidings finding favor (in his eyes)."

23. *by the way of the Plain*. The Plain in question is the Jordan Valley on the
east side of the river. Some have suggested that Ahimaaz overtakes the Cushite
not by speed but by running along a flatter, if less direct, route in the Jordan
Valley riverbed, but verses 25–27 indicate that Ahimaaz outruns the Cushite.

24. *David was sitting between the gates*. Walled cities in ancient Israel and
environs often had double walls, with an inner and outer gate and a small plaza
between them. Moshe Garsiel neatly observes that David's ambivalence about
the armed struggle is spatially figured by his physical location: he wanted to
sally forth with the army; the troops wanted him within the town; he stations
himself in between. Before the battle he stood by the gate; now he is seated
by the gate, awaiting the news from the front—as Polzin notes, exactly like Eli,
who is told of the death of his two sons.
      the lookout went up on the roof of the gate . . . and he raised his eyes and saw.
This moment is quite exceptional, and striking, in representing the arrival of
the two messengers visually, from the perspective of the lookout on the wall
reporting to David down below in the gate plaza. David's troubles with all his
sons, it should be remembered, began when he himself looked down from a
roof and saw a woman bathing.

25. *If he's alone, there are tidings in his mouth*. A solitary runner is likely to be
a courier. Soldiers, whether in retreat or maneuvering, would travel in groups.

And he came on, drawing nearer. And the lookout saw another man   26
running, and the lookout called to the gatekeeper and said, "Look, a
man is running alone." And the king said, "This one, too, bears tidings."
And the lookout said, "I see the running of the first one as the running   27
of Ahimaaz son of Zadok," and the king said, "He is a good man and
with good tidings he must come." And Ahimaaz called out and said to   28
the king, "All is well." And he bowed down to the king, his face to the
ground, and he said, "Blessed is the LORD your God Who has delivered
over the men who raised their hand against my lord the king." And the   29
king said, "Is it well with the lad Absalom?" And Ahimaaz said, "I saw
a great crowd to send the king's servant Joab, and your servant, and I
know not what . . ." And the king said, "Turn aside, stand by!" And he   30

---

27. *He is a good man and with good tidings he must come.* This obvious non
sequitur suggests that the desperately anxious David is grasping at straws. In
fact, as revelatory dialogue, it shows us just how desperate he feels.

28. *All is well.* This is one word in the Hebrew, *shalom*. That word is the last two
syllables of Absalom's name in Hebrew, *'Avshalom*, a link David will reinforce
when he nervously asks, "Is it well [*shalom*] with the lad Absalom ['*Avshalom*]?"

    *Who has delivered over the men who raised their hands against my lord the
king.* Ahimaaz hastens to report, in terms that express both his Israelite piety
and his loyalty to the king, the general defeat of the usurper's army. He of course
says nothing of Absalom's fate.

29. *Is it well with the lad Absalom?* This seems to be David's overriding concern,
not the military victory. Again and again, he insists on the term of affection,
"lad," for the rebel son who would have killed him. The tension between his
political role, which, as Joab understood, requires Absalom's destruction, and
his paternal role, is painfully palpable. In this connection, it is noteworthy that
David, so much the emotionally vulnerable father here, is consistently referred
to as "the king," not as "David."

    I saw a great crowd to send the king's servant. This is nearly gibberish but not
because of any corruption of the text. Ahimaaz has been posed a question he
does not dare answer, and so he begins to talk nervously and incoherently ("and
I know not what . . .").

30. *Turn aside, stand by!* David, realizing he is unlikely to extract anything from
the babbling Ahimaaz, decides to wait and interrogate the second messenger,
whose arrival is imminent.

31 turned aside and took his place. And, look, the Cushite had come and
the Cushite said, "Let my lord the king receive the tidings that the LORD

32 has done you justice against all who rose against you." And the king said
to the Cushite, "Is it well with the lad Absalom?" And the Cushite said,
"May the enemies of my lord the king be like the lad, and all who have
risen against you for evil!"

---

31. *Let my lord the king receive the tidings.* The Cushite is considerably more
brusque than his predecessor. He does not begin with a reassuring "All is well."
There is no indication of his bowing down before the king. He proceeds quickly
to the report of the victory, and though the language of that report approximately parallels Ahimaaz's language, it is briefer, and ends with "against you"
instead of the more deferential "against my lord the king."

32. *May the enemies of my lord the king be like the lad.* The Cushite promptly
and clearly responds by reporting Absalom's death, though even he has enough
sense to phrase it indirectly, neither mentioning Absalom by name nor using the
word "died." In referring to the usurper as "the lad," he is quoting David, but
without having picked up the crucial cue of David's paternal feelings reflected
in the word. He blithely assumes that because Absalom was at the head of
"all who have risen against" the king, the news of his death will be welcome.
It strikes exactly the right note that the Cushite's very last word is "evil" (or,
"harm").

CHAPTER 19

And the king was shaken. And he went up to the upper room over the   1
gate and he wept, and thus he said as he went, "My son, Absalom! My
son, my son, Absalom! Would that I had died in your stead! Absalom,
my son, my son!" And it was told to Joab, "Look, the king is weeping and   2
he is grieving over Absalom." And the victory on that day turned into   3
mourning for all the troops, for the troops had heard on that day, saying,

---

1. *My son, my son, Absalom!* Much of the way experience transforms David in
the course of his story can be seen through his changing responses to the deaths
of those close to him. When Jonathan and Saul died, he intoned an eloquent
elegy. When Abner was murdered, he declaimed a much briefer elegy, coupled
with a speech dissociating himself from the killing. When his infant son by
Bathsheba died, he spoke somber words about his own mortality and the irreversibility of death. Now, the eloquent David is reduced to a sheer stammer of
grief, repeating over and over the two Hebrew words, *beni 'Avshalom*, "my son,
Absalom." Although the narrator continues to refer to David only as "the king,"
in the shifting conflict between his public and private roles the latter here takes
over entirely: Absalom is not the usurper who drove him from the throne but
only "my son," and David is the anguished father who would rather have died,
that his son might have lived.

3. *for the troops had heard on that day.* Before the battle they had all heard
David's admonition to his commanders to do no harm to Absalom. Now they
hear of his grief and are smitten with shame and apprehension—whether out
of empathy for their beloved leader, or guilt over the complicity some of their
number share in Absalom's death, or fear of potential violence between David
and Joab.

4 "The king is pained over his son." And the troops stole away on that day to come to the town as troops disgraced in their flight from the battle

5 would steal away. And the king covered his face, and the king cried out with a loud voice, "My son, Absalom! Absalom, my son, my son!"

6 And Joab came to the king within the house and said, "You have today shamed all your servants who have saved your life today and the lives of your sons and daughters and the lives of your wives and the lives of

7 your concubines, to love those who hate you and to hate those who love you. For you have said today that you have no commanders or servants.

---

4. *the troops stole away . . . as troops disgraced in their flight from the battle*. This striking image of victory transformed into the bitterness of defeat picks up verbal threads, as Moshe Garsiel has perceptively noted, from the beginning of Absalom's insurrection (Chapter 15). There, the usurper stood at the gate, as David is here made to go out and sit in the gate. Absalom was said to "steal the heart" of the men of Israel as here the men steal away, and in order to recover dominion David is enjoined to speak to their heart (verse 8). The disheartened slipping away of the troops suggests that Joab is addressing an imminent danger of the disintegration of the army.

5. *the king covered his face*. The gesture makes perfect psychological sense, while the verb used, *la'at,* is the same one David chose when he said "Deal gently [*le'at*] with the lad Absalom."

6. *within the house*. The implication is that Joab speaks with David in private. The thematic opposition to this term is "in the gate," where Joab will send David.
    You have today shamed all your servants who have saved your life today. Again and again here Joab insists on the word "today." It is this very moment, he suggests, this crucial turning point, that you must seize in order to reestablish your reign. You cannot allow yourself to think of the past, of your history as Absalom's father: as king, you must confront *today*, with its challenge and its political responsibilities.

7. *to love those who hate you and to hate those who love you*. Joab uses rhetorical exaggeration in order to elevate David's paternal attachment to Absalom into a generalized, perverse political principle: if you show such extravagant fondness for the usurper who sought your life, then you are behaving as though all your enemies were your friends and your friends your enemies.
    For you have said today that you have no commanders or servants. That is, by exhibiting such love for your archenemy, you are showing flagrant disregard for the loyal officers and followers to whose devotion you owe your life.

For I know today that were Absalom alive and all of us today dead, then
would it have been right in your eyes! And now, rise, go out, and speak   8
to the heart of your servants. For by the Lᴏʀᴅ I have sworn, if you go
not out, that not a man shall spend the night with you, and this will be
a greater evil for you than any evil that has befallen you from your youth
until now." And the king arose and sat in the gate, and to all the troops   9
they told, saying, "Look, the king is sitting in the gate." And all the troops
came before the king, while Israel had fled each man to his tent.

And all the people were deliberating throughout the tribes of Israel,   10
saying, "The king rescued us from the clutches of our enemies and he
saved us from the clutches of the Philistines, but now he has fled the
land before Absalom, and Absalom, whom we anointed over us, has died   11

---

8. *speak to the heart of your servants.* This personal act of rallying the men is
deemed urgently necessary by Joab because the army has already begun to
disperse ("steal away").

   if you go not out . . . not a man shall spend the night with you. These words
are a naked threat: if David does not follow Joab's order, the commander will
encourage the army to abandon the king, and he will be alone, without power or
troops, engulfed in "a greater evil" than any that has befallen him in his long and
arduous career. In all this, Joab's verbal assault on David, however motivated by
pressing considerations of practical politics, is also a defense of his own flouting
of David's injunction to protect Absalom. David at this point knows only the
bare fact of his son's death, not who was responsible for it. This is something
that he will inevitably soon learn, and that bitter knowledge is surely registered
in his decision to replace Joab with Amasa (verse 14).

9. *the king arose and sat in the gate.* Fokkelman brilliantly observes the disparity
between Joab's exhortation and the report of David's action. Joab had said, "go
out, and speak to the heart of your servants." Instead of these active gestures,
we see David passively sitting in the gate while the troops come to him, and we
are given no reported speech for him. In Fokkelman's reading, this gap between
command and act "call[s] up the image of a man beaten to a pulp, who can
barely stand, and does only the minimum requested or expected of him."

10. *deliberating.* The verb *nadon* in this verse is conventionally related to the
noun *madon,* "quarrel" or "contention." But in fact what the people say is not
contentious, and it is preferable to derive the passive (perhaps implicitly reflexive) verbal form here from *dun,* to judge, consider, or deliberate.

12 in battle. And now why do you not speak up to bring back the king?" And
King David had sent to Zadok and to Abiathar the priests, saying, "Speak
to the elders of Judah, saying, 'Why should you be the last to bring back
the king to his house when the word of all Israel has come to the king
13 regarding his house? You are my brothers. You are my bone and my flesh,
14 and why should you be the last to bring back the king?' And to Amasa
you shall say, 'Are you not my bone and my flesh? So may the LORD do
to me, and even more, if you will not be commander of the army before
15 me for all time instead of Joab,'" And he inclined the heart of all the
men of Judah as a single man, and they sent to the king: "Come back,
you and all your servants."

---

12. *Why should you be the last to bring back the king.* Throughout this episode,
there is a central focus on who will be first and who will be last to show support
for the Davidic restoration. The northern tribes, Israel, have already evinced
support (verse 10), and David is concerned to enlist the backing of his own
tribe, Judah, which had largely swung to Absalom during the insurrection.

regarding his house. Or simply, "to his house." Many textual critics regard this
phrase as a mistaken scribal duplication of the same phrase earlier in this verse.

13. *You are my bone and my flesh.* That is, you are Judahites, just as I am, and
so there is actual kinship between us.

14. *to Amasa . . . 'Are you not my bone and my flesh?'* Now the phrase is no longer
hyperbolic, for Amasa is David's nephew. The extraordinary offer of the post of
commander of the army to Absalom's general in the rebellion reflects David's
knack for combining personal and political motives. It is a slap in the face to
Joab, the killer of David's son, against whom David evidently does not dare to
take any more direct steps of vengeance. At the same time, the hesitation of the
Judahites in rallying behind the restored king suggests that an act such as the
appointment of Amasa as commander may be required to enlist their support.
Joab, not surprisingly, will not quietly acquiesce in his abrupt dismissal from
the office he has held since the beginning of David's career.

15. *he inclined the heart.* It is not clear whether the Hebrew, characteristically
overgenerous in its use of pronouns, intends the "he" to refer to David or to
Amasa. In either case, David's overture succeeds in bringing the tribe of Judah
into his camp.

And the king turned back, and he came to the Jordan, and Judah had   16
come to Gilgal to go to meet the king to bring the king across the Jordan.
And Shimei son of Gera the Benjaminite from Bahurim hastened and   17
went down with the men of Judah to meet King David. And a thousand   18
men were with him from Benjamin, and Ziba, the lad of the house
of Saul and his fifteen sons and his twenty slaves with him, and they
rushed down to the Jordan before the king. And as the crossing over was   19
going on, to bring across the king's household and to do what was good
in his eyes, Shimei son of Gera flung himself before the king as he was
crossing the Jordan and he said to the king, "Let not my lord reckon it a   20
crime, and do not remember the perverse thing your servant did on the
day my lord the king went out from Jerusalem, that the king should pay
it mind. For your servant knows that it was I who offended, and, look, I   21
have come today first of all the house of Joseph to go down to meet my
lord the king." And Abishai son of Zeruiah spoke out and said, "For this   22
should not Shimei be put to death? For he cursed the Lord's anointed."

---

16. *to bring the king across the Jordan.* The verb *'avar,* "cross over," and its caus-
ative form, *ha'avir,* "to bring across," which thematically defined David's exodus
from Jerusalem in Chapter 15, dominates this episode, too, as the crossing over
in flight to the east is reversed by the crossing over westward back to Jerusalem.

17. *Shimei son of Gera.* There is an approximate symmetry between David's
encounters in his exodus from Jerusalem and those that now occur in his return.
Then he met a hostile Shimei, now he meets a contrite Shimei. Then he met
Ziba, who denounced his master Mephibosheth; now he meets Mephibosheth
himself, who defends his own loyalty. Then he spoke with Ittai, the loyalist who
insisted on accompanying him; now he speaks with Barzillai, the proven loyalist
who refuses to accompany him back to the capital. The encounter with Hushai,
who becomes David's secret agent, has no counterpart here.

21. *first of all the house of Joseph to go down to meet my lord the king.* Shimei, who
has rushed down to the Jordan in order to demonstrate his newfound loyalty
to David, uses "the house of Joseph" loosely to refer to the northern tribes. He
is, of course, actually from the tribe of Benjamin. He "goes down" because his
hometown of Bahurim is in the high country near Jerusalem.

22. *For this should not Shimei be put to death?* Abishai remains true to character,
for the third time prepared to kill someone on the impulse of the moment.

23 And David said, "What do I have to do with you, sons of Zeruiah, that
you should become my adversary today? Should today a man of Israel
24 be put to death? For I surely know that today I am king over Israel." And
the king said to Shimei, "You shall not die." And the king swore to him.

25 And Mephibosheth son of Saul had come down to meet the king, and he
had not dressed his feet or trimmed his moustache, and his garments he
had not laundered from the day the king had gone until the day he came
26 back safe and sound. And it happened when he came from Jerusalem to
meet the king, that the king said to him, "Why did you not go with me,
27 Mephibosheth?" And he said, "My lord the king! My servant deceived
me. For your servant thought, 'I'll saddle me the donkey and ride on it
28 and go with the king,' for your servant is lame. And he slandered your

---

23. *What do I have to do with you, sons of Zeruiah.* These words by now are a
kind of refrain, as David seeks to dissociate himself from the murderous sons
of Zeruiah. It is noteworthy that though Abishai alone has just spoken, David,
mindful of the killing of Absalom, includes Joab as well in his protest by using
the plural "sons of Zeruiah."

Should today a man of Israel be put to death? David's "today" is an implicit
rejoinder to Joab's "today" in the confrontation over his mourning Absalom.
This day of victorious return is a moment for national reconciliation and hence
for a general amnesty for both the Saulides and the supporters of Absalom. In
the course of time, it will appear that David in effect restricts his pledge not to
harm Shimei to an extended "today."

25. *he had not dressed his feet or trimmed his moustache, and his garments he
had not laundered.* These acts of mourning, reported to us by the authoritative
narrator, are an indication that in fact Mephibosheth remained loyal to David
throughout the insurrection, and that Ziba's denunciation was a self-interested
calumny. (Some interpret "dressing"—literally "doing"—the feet as cutting the
toenails, though the parallel usage often cited from Deuteronomy has "toenails," not "feet," as the object of the verb "to do.")

26. *when he came from Jerusalem.* The Masoretic text simply says "Jerusalem" but
this encounter presumably takes place down by the Jordan. One version of the
Septuagint removes the word from this verse and places it at the end of verse 25.

27. *I'll saddle me the donkey . . . for your servant is lame.* The evident implication
is that it would have taken the crippled Mephibosheth some time to get ready

servant to my lord the king, and my lord the king is like a messenger of God, and do what is good in your eyes. For all my father's house are 29
but men marked for death to my lord the king, yet you set your servant among those who eat at your table. And what right still do I have to cry out still in appeal to the king?" And the king said to him, "Why should 30
you still speak your words? I say—you and Ziba shall divide the field. And Mephibosheth said to the king, "Let him even take all, seeing that 31
my lord the king has come safe and sound to his house."

---

to go after the fleeing king. Meanwhile, his servant headed out before him in order to denounce him, perhaps actually leaving his master awaiting his help to saddle the donkey.

29. *For all my father's house are but men marked for death to my lord the king.* Mephibosheth's choice of words—the literal phrasing of the Hebrew is "men of death"—is an oblique, perhaps inadvertent, concession that he shares what must have been the general suspicion among the Saulides that David was responsible for the chain of violent deaths in the house of Saul.

30. *Why should you still speak your words?* David cuts off Mephibosheth impatiently, picking up the "still" that the anxious supplicant has just twice used.
   you and Ziba shall divide the field. This "Solomonic" judgment may actually be another sign that David has lost his ruler's grip. For if Ziba has told the truth about his master, Mephibosheth as a traitor would deserve nothing, except perhaps capital punishment. And if Ziba was lying, then the servant would deserve nothing except a harsh legal penalty for defamation. Perhaps Mephibosheth is paying a price for having betrayed that he thought David was responsible for the Saulide deaths: in this reading, David knows Mephibosheth is telling the truth, but he punishes him for assuming David was involved in the killings by decreeing Mephibosheth will lose half his property.

31. *Let him even take all.* By this verbal gesture, Mephibosheth shows himself loyal to David to the end, regardless of personal benefit. These words could well be an implicit judgment on the unwisdom of David's decree.

32 And Barzillai the Gileadite had come down from Rogelim, and he crossed over the Jordan with the king to send him off from the Jordan.

33 And Barzillai was very aged, eighty years old, and he had provided for the

34 king during his stay in Mahanaim, for he was a very wealthy man. And the king said to Barzillai, "You, cross over with me, and I shall provide

35 for you by me in Jerusalem." And Barzillai said to the king, "How many are the days of the years of my life that I should go up with the king to

36 Jerusalem? Eighty years old I am today. Do I know between good and evil? Does your servant taste what I eat and what I drink? Do I still hear the voice of men and women singing? And why should your servant still

37 be a burden on my lord the king? Your servant can barely cross over the

38 Jordan, and why should the king give me this recompense? Let your servant, pray, turn back, that I may die in my own town by the tomb of my father and my mother, and, look, let your servant Chimham cross over with my lord the king, and do for him what is good in your eyes."

39 And the king said, "With me shall Chimham cross over, and I will do for him what is good in your eyes, and whatever you choose for me, I will

40 do for you." And all the troops crossed over the Jordan, and the king crossed over, and the king kissed Barzillai and blessed him, and he went

---

32. *Barzillai the Gileadite.* David's three encounters at the ford of the Jordan from a progressive series on the scale of loyalty: first Shimei, who has heaped insults on him and now pleads for forgiveness; then Mephibosheth, whose loyalty, though probably genuine, has been called into question by Ziba; and then the unswervingly devoted old man, Barzillai.

35. *How many are the days of the years of my life.* Though this rhetorical question literally echoes the question that Pharaoh asks the aged Jacob, the meaning is the opposite—not "How long have I lived?" but "How long could I possibly have left to live?"

38. *your servant Chimham.* This is presumably Barzillai's son.

40. *the king kissed Barzillai.* This entire catastrophic sequence in the David story began with David's cold kiss to the son from whom he had been estranged, followed by Absalom's calculated kiss for every man he enlisted to his cause at the gate of the city. Now the king bestows a kiss of true affection upon the loyal old man who provided for him and his troops in their moment of need.

back to his place. And the king crossed over to Gilgal, and Chimham 41
crossed over with him, and all the people of Judah, they brought the
king across, and half of the people of Israel as well. And, look, all the 42
men of Israel were coming toward the king, and they said to the king,
"Why have our brothers, the men of Judah, stolen you away, bringing
the king across the Jordan with his household, and all David's men
with him?" And all the men of Judah answered the men of Israel, "For 43
the king is kin to us. And why should you be incensed over this thing?
Have we eaten anything of the king's? Have we been given any gift?"
And the men of Israel answered the men of Judah and they said, "We 44
have ten parts in the king, even in David, more than you, and why have

---

41. *the king crossed over . . . and Chimham crossed over with him, and . . . they
brought the king across.* The crossing over eastward of the banished king, which
never should have occurred, is now decisively reversed, as David and all his
people come across the Jordan and head for Jerusalem. But, as the immediately
following dialogue intimates, David's political troubles are far from over.

   to Gilgal. This is the gathering place where Saul was consecrated as king and
later severed by Samuel from his role as God's anointed.

   half of the people of Israel as well. In all likelihood, "half" is used loosely to
indicate simply that some members of the northern tribes took part in bringing
David to Gilgal.

42. *and they said to the king.* Although their complaint is addressed to the king,
he never answers them. Instead, as Fokkelman notes, the scene breaks down
into a squabble between Israelite and Judahite. Once again, David appears to
be losing his regal grip.

43. *the king is kin to us.* That is, David is actually a member of the tribe of
Judah.

44. *We have ten parts in the king, even in David, more than you.* Though ten
to one might merely be idiomatic for great preponderance, it seems likely that
they allude to the fact that they are ten tribes to Judah's one—if David is king
of the entire nation, this gives them ten times the claim to the king that Judah
has. The phrase "even in David" (or, "also in David") is a little odd, and the Septuagint reads instead, "also I am firstborn more than you." It should be noted
that all the pronouns in this dialogue in the Hebrew are cast in the first person
singular, referring to a singular, collective "man of Israel" and "man of Judah,"
but that usage doesn't quite work in English.

you treated us with contempt? Was not our word first to bring back the king?" And the word of the men of Judah was harsher than the word of the men of Israel.

---

the word of the men of Judah was harsher than the word of the men of Israel. The episode concludes in a clash of words, to be followed by a clash of swords. The implication of the greater "harshness" (or, "hardness") of the Judahite words is aptly caught by the medieval Hebrew commentator David Kimchi: "Their word was harsher and stronger than the word of the men of Israel, and the men of Judah spoke harshly to the men of Israel, with the king saying nothing to them. Therefore the men of Israel were incensed and they followed after [the rebel] Sheba son of Bichri."

CHAPTER 20

And there chanced to be there a worthless fellow named Sheba son of   1
Bichri, a Benjaminite. And he blew the ram's horn and said,

> "We have no share in David,
>> no portion have we in Jesse's son—
>>> every man to his tent, O Israel!"

And all the men of Israel turned away from David to follow Sheba son   2
of Bichri, but the men of Judah clung to their king from the Jordan to
Jerusalem.

---

1. *there chanced to be there.* The narrative is a direct continuation of the end of
the previous chapter, and so "there" is the national assembly grounds at Gilgal
where the northern tribes, Israel, and the tribe of Judah have just quarreled.
The northerners, resentful of the harshness of the Judahites' words, in which
the members of David's own tribe claimed a special proprietary relationship
with the king, are ripe for the appeal of a demagogue such as Sheba, who is at
once identified as "a worthless fellow."

    We have no share in David. This is a defiant reversal of the claim just made
by the Israelites that they had "ten parts" in the king. Later, in 1 Kings, when
the monarchy actually splits in two, the same rallying cry will be used by the
secessionists.

2. *the men of Judah clung to their king.* David is, of course, "their" king because
he is from the tribe of Judah. The reach of the tribe stretches west to east, from
the Jordan to Jerusalem, and also to the south of Jerusalem, while the rebel
forces are to the north.

3 And David came to his house in Jerusalem, and the king took his ten
concubine women whom he had left to watch over the house, and he
placed them in a house under watch, but he did not come to bed with
them, and they were shut up till their dying day in living widowhood.

4 And the king said to Amasa, "Muster me the men of Judah, in three days,
5 and you take your stand here." And Amasa went to muster Judah, and he
6 missed the appointed time that was set for him. And David said to Abishai, "Now Sheba son of Bichri will do us more harm than Absalom. You,
take your master's servants and pursue him, lest he find him fortified

---

3. *David came to his house in Jerusalem, and . . . took his ten concubine women.*
The concubines have become taboo to David because they cohabited with
Absalom his son. But this whole sad notice suggests that David now cannot
fully "come back to his house." The women he left, perhaps foolishly and surely
futilely, "to watch over the house" are now sequestered "in a house under
watch." There is a wry echo in all this of that early moment of David's investment of Jerusalem when he was confronted by another wife he had left behind
who had slept with another man—Michal. She had no child "till her dying
day"—an image of interrupted conjugality that is multiplied tenfold here with
the concubines.

4. *the king said to Amasa.* Amasa, Absalom's commander in the rebellion, has
been designated by David to replace Joab. At the margins of the narrative report
lurks the question, Where is Joab? The answer forthcoming will be savage.
     take your stand. That is, report to me.

6. *Now Sheba son of Bichri will do us more harm than Absalom.* Although it is
not clear why Amasa is late for his appointed meeting with David (perhaps
his appearance at Gibeon in verse 8 suggests that he decided, out of military
considerations, to pursue Sheba at once without reporting back to the king),
David's unjustified panic is another indication that he has lost his political
composure. By sending out Abishai, Joab's brother, to give chase after Sheba,
he sets up the circumstances for Joab's murder of Amasa and his subsequent
return to power.
     You, take your master's servants. The obtrusively imperative "you" is very
brusque, at the same time expressing David's intention to designate Abishai,
and not his brother, to command the pursuit.

towns, and elude our gaze." And Joab's men sallied forth after him, and   7
the Cherethites and the Pelethites and all the warriors. And they sallied forth from Jerusalem to pursue Sheba son of Bichri. They were just   8
by the great stone which is in Gibeon when Amasa came before them,
and Joab was girt in his battle garb, and he had on a belt for a sword
strapped to his waist in its sheath, and as he came forward, it slipped out.

---

and elude our gaze. The two Hebrew words here, *wehitsil 'eynenu*, are problematic. They might mean "and save [himself] [from] our eyes (the bracketed
words would be implied via ellipsis by the Hebrew); or, if the verb here is
vocalized differently, the words might mean "and cast a shadow over our eyes."
Needless to say, many emendations have been proposed. In any case, the idea
strongly suggested by the context is that Sheba would place himself beyond the
reach of pursuit by withdrawing into fortified towns. In the event, he is trapped
inside just such a town.

7. *Joab's men sallied forth.* J. P. Fokkelman must be credited with seeing what
an extraordinary designation this is. David has dismissed Joab. The elite warriors are in any case David's men (note how David has just referred to them
in addressing Abishai as "your master's servants"). The fact that they are here
called "Joab's men" suggests where the real power is, and where Joab's brother
Abishai assumes it must be. The clear implication is that the supposedly dismissed Joab is actually leading his men in the pursuit.

8. *They were just by the great stone which is in Gibeon.* Gibeon, it should be
recalled, is the very place where the civil war between the house of Saul (Israel)
and the house of David (Judah) began. That first battle (2 Samuel 2) began with
a choreographed duel between twelve champions from each side, each warrior
clasping the head of his adversary and stabbing him in the side. Joab's posture
in the killing of Amasa strikingly recalls those lethal gestures.
*he had on a belt for a sword strapped to his waist . . . and as he came forward, it
slipped out.* The sword—often, as here, a weapon closer to a long dagger—was
customarily strapped against the left thigh, for easy unsheathing across the lower
belly by a right-handed fighter. Joab may have deliberately fastened the sword to
his waist so that it would slip out of the scabbard as he leaned forward to embrace
Amasa. The last two verbs here are rather cryptic in the Hebrew: literally "he/
it went out and she/it fell/slipped." Since "sword" is feminine in Hebrew, that is
the only likely subject for "slipped," and "he" (Joab) is the plausible masculine
subject for "went out" (or, "came forward"), though it could also be the scabbard.
Josephus's reading of this verse remains the most persuasive one: the wily Joab,
deliberately allowing his dagger to slip to the ground as he bends forward, then
snatches it up with his left hand while his right hand grasps Amasa's beard.

9 And Joab said to Amasa, "Is it well with you, my brother?" And Joab's
10 right hand grasped Amasa's beard so as to kiss him. And Amasa did not
watch out for the sword which was in Joab's hand, and he struck him
with it in the belly and spilled his innards to the ground—no second
blow did he need—and he died. And Joab with Abishai his brother pur-
11 sued Sheba son of Bichri. And a man stood over him, one of Joab's lads,
and said, "Whoever favors Joab and whoever is for David—after Joab!"
12 And Amasa was wallowing in blood in the midst of the road, and the
man saw that all the troops had come to a halt, and he moved Amasa
aside from the road to the field and flung a cloak over him when he saw

---

9. *so as to kiss him*. We remember David's cool kiss to Absalom, then Absalom's
demagogic kiss, as we witness this kiss, which is a prelude to murder.

10. *Amasa did not watch out for the sword which was in Joab's hand*. His attention
caught by Joab's gesture of affection, Amasa does not think to look at Joab's
left hand, which one would not normally expect to hold a weapon. (Has Joab
learned the lesson of Ehud, Judges 3, who takes the Moabite king Eglon by surprise with a dagger thrust to the belly delivered by the left hand?) Joab's manual
proficiency as a killer reinforces the perception that he struck at Absalom in
the heart with sticks, not "darts," in order to hurt him badly but deliberately
not to finish him off. The phrase "did not watch out" rhymes ironically with the
plight of the ten concubines left to watch over the house and condemned to a
house under watch.
  he struck him with it in the belly and spilled his innards to the ground. It is
by a blow to the belly (*ḥomesh*) that Abner's brother Asahel died at this same
place, Gibeon, and by a thrust to the belly that Joab killed Abner in revenge.
The spilling of the innards implies a horrendous welter of blood, and that gruesome image of violent death will then pursue Joab through the story to his own
bloody end.

11. *Whoever favors Joab and whoever is for David*. In dismissing Joab, David
had severed himself from his longtime commander. This henchman of Joab's
smoothly sutures the rift by bracketing Joab and David in these parallel clauses,
publicly assuming that Joab is once more David's commander.

12. *Amasa was wallowing in blood . . . and . . . all the troops had come to a halt*.
The soldiers come to a halt because they are confounded by seeing their commander reduced to a bloody corpse, and they also recoil from the idea of treading on the blood of the murdered man, who lies in the midst of the roadway.

that all who came upon him had come to a halt. When he had been 13
removed from the road, every man passed on after Joab to pursue Sheba
son of Bichri. And he passed through all the tribes of Israel to Abel of 14
Beth-Maacah, and all the Bichrites assembled and they, too, came in
after him. And all the troops who were with Joab came and besieged 15
him in Abel of Beth-Maacah, and they heaped up a siege mound against
the town and it stood up against the rampart, and they were savaging
the wall to bring it down. And a wise woman called out from the town, 16

"Listen, listen—speak, pray, to Joab,
approach here, that I may speak to you."

---

14. *And he passed through.* The switch in scene is effected, in accordance with
an established technique of biblical narrative, by a repetition of the verb in a
slightly different meaning: the Judahite soldiers "pass on" beyond the corpse
at Gibeon; the object of their pursuit "passes through" the territories of the
northern tribes.

Abel of Beth-Maacah. "Abel" means "brook." Thus "Beth-Maacah" is required
in order to distinguish it from other place-names that have a brook component.
This fortified town is located near the northern border of ancient Israel.

they, too, came in after him. That is, they withdraw with him into the shelter
of the fortified town.

15. *savaging the wall.* This is the first of several verbal clues intended to establish a link between this episode involving a "wise woman" and the episode of
the wise woman of Tekoa that prepared the way for Absalom's return to Jerusalem, which then eventuated in the rebellion. Both women seek to deflect an
impulse of vengeful violence. The Tekoite implores the king to take steps "that
the blood avenger not savage this much" (2 Samuel 14:11). She fears those
bent on "destroying me and my son together from God's heritage" (14:16), just
as the wise woman of Abel Beth-Maacah asks Joab, "Why should you engulf
the LORD's heritage?" He responds by saying "Far be it from me . . . that I
should engulf and that I should destroy [the same root as the verb rendered as
"savage"].

16. *Listen, listen—speak, pray, to Joab.* As befits a professional wise woman in
a place evidently famous for its oracle (see verse 18), she speaks in poetry, in
a style that is elevated, ceremonially repetitive, hieratic, and at least a little
obscure.

17 And he approached her, and the woman said, "Are you Joab?" And he
said, "I am." And she said to him, "Listen to the words of your servant."

18 And he said, "I am listening," And she said, saying,

"Surely would they speak in days of old, saying:
'Surely will they ask counsel of Abel, and thus conclude.'

19 I am of the peaceable steadfast of Israel.
You seek to put to death a mother city in Israel.
Why should you engulf the LORD's heritage?"

---

18. *Surely would they speak . . . Surely will they ask counsel.* The Hebrew
expresses this emphasis by repeating the verbal root, first as infinitive, then
in conjugated form: *daber yedaberu, sha'ol yesha'alu.* Since the woman extravagantly uses this sort of initial reiteration three times in four clauses, the effect
is incantatory. The burden of what she says here is that Abel has long been a
revered city, so why would Joab think of destroying it?

and thus conclude. This might mean, come to a conclusion regarding the
question posed to the oracle at Abel, but the Hebrew is rather enigmatic, perhaps because the wise woman herself is quoting an ancient proverb, in archaic
language, about the town.

19. *I am of the peaceable steadfast of Israel.* She at once affirms her loyalty
to the national cause ("I am no rebel," she implies) and her commitment to
peace rather than violence. Some interpreters understand the first term of this
construct chain, *shelumey 'emuney yisra'el,* as "whole" (from *shalem*), but the
context argues for a reference to peace.

to put to death a mother city in Israel. The literal Hebrew is "town and
mother," a hendyadis that clearly means something like "principal town." (The
phrase would remain idiomatic in later Hebrew.) Since in biblical Hebrew the
suburbs or outlying villages around a town are called "daughters," the logic of
the idiom is evident. It is, however, an idiom that appears only here in the entire
biblical corpus, and there is thematic point in its use. In this narrative reflecting a male warrior culture and acts of terrible violence, from decapitation to
evisceration, a series of female figures—Abigail, the Tekoite, the wise woman
of Abel—intervene to avert violence. The city itself is figured as a mother; its
destruction would be a kind of matricide, and the wise woman speaks on behalf
of the childbearers and nurturers of life in Israelite society to turn aside Joab's
terrible swift sword.

And Joab answered and said, "Far be it from me, far be it, that I should 20
engulf and that I should destroy. It isn't so. But a man from the high 21
country of Ephraim named Sheba son of Bichri has raised his hand
against the king, against David. Give over him alone, that I may turn
away from the town." And the woman said to Joab, "Look, his head is
about to be flung to you from the wall." And the woman came in her 22
wisdom to all the people, and they cut off the head of Sheba son of
Bichri and flung it to Joab. And he blew the ram's horn and they dispersed from the town, every man to his tent, but Joab came back to
Jerusalem.

---

20. *But a man from the high country of Ephraim.* This region is part of the
territory of Benjamin, Saul's tribe. By providing this identification, Joab distinguishes the rebel who is the object of his pursuit from the non-Benjaminite
inhabitants of Abel Beth-Maacah.

against the king, against David. By using this apposition (instead of the usual
"King David") Joab implicitly responds to some doubt as to whether in fact it is
David who is the king. Recent political events might well have triggered general
questioning about David's grip on the monarchy.

21. *Look, his head is about to be flung to you.* This decisive woman, instead of
using a simple future form, employs a participial form introduced by the presentative *hineh,* as if to say: it's already on the way to being done.

22. *in her wisdom.* The wisdom is her shrewdness in finding a way to avert a
general massacre (as the wise Abigail had done in mollifying David, bent on
vengeance) and perhaps also in the aptness of rhetoric she no doubt employs
to persuade the people.

he blew the ram's horn and they dispersed . . . every man to his tent. These
phrases echo the ones used in verse 1 to report the beginning of Sheba's rebellion, and thus conclude the episode in a symmetric envelope structure.

but Joab came back to Jerusalem. He comes back to Jerusalem, not to his
house ("tent") in nearby Bethlehem. The implication, as Bar-Efrat notes, is
that he now resumes his post as David's commander. David evidently has little
say in the matter, being confronted with a fait accompli of military power. This
clause then provides a motivation for the introduction of the notice of David's
governing council in the next three verses.

23 And Joab was over all the army of Israel and Benaiah son of Johoiada
24 was over the Cherethites and the Pelethites. And Adoram was over the
25 corvée, and Jehoshaphat son of Ahilud was recorder. And Sheva was
26 scribe, and Zadok and Abiathar, priests. And Ira the Jairite was also a
priest to David.

---

23. *Joab was over all the army of Israel.* This list of David's royal bureaucracy
parallels the one in 8:16–18, with a couple of instructive differences. The two
serve as bookends to David's reign in Jerusalem. The first is introduced after
he has consolidated his mini-empire, and this one after the suppression of two
successive rebellions and just before the account of David's last days in 1 Kings
1–2. (As we shall see, the remaining four chapters of 2 Samuel are actually a
series of appendices to the story proper and not a direct continuation of it.) In
Chapter 8, Joab was simply "over the army." Here, after the defeat of the seces-
sionist northern tribes, he is said to be "over all the army of Israel." Adoram as
supervisor of the corvée does not appear in the earlier list but is inserted here
to anticipate the role he will play in Solomon's grand building projects, and he
may in fact have been a much later appointment by David. The name of the
royal scribe, Sheva, is anomalous in the Hebrew, and may be the same person
identified in Chapter 8 as Seraiah.

26. *And Ira the Jairite was also a priest to David.* In addition to the hereditary
priests of the public cult just mentioned, David has a kind of special royal
chaplain. In Chapter 8, it is David's sons who are said to perform this service.
Either later editors were uneasy with this intimation of priestly dynasty in the
royal family, or David, after all the tribulations he has suffered because of two
of his sons, decided to designate someone else as his chaplain.

CHAPTER 21

And there was a famine in the days of David three years, year after   1
year. And David sought out the presence of the LORD. And the LORD

Chapters 21–24. these chapters appear to be a series of appendices to the David story proper, manifestly written by different writers in styles that exhibit notable differences from that of the main narrative, and also certain differences in ideological assumptions and even in what are presumed to be the narrative data of David's history. It should, however, be kept in mind that creating a collage of disparate sources was an established literary technique used by the ancient Hebrew editors and sometimes by the original writers themselves. Recent critics have abundantly demonstrated the compositional coherence of Chapters 21–24 and have argued for some significant links with the preceding narrative. For that reason, it may be preferable to think of this whole unit as a coda to the story rather than as a series of appendices. The structure of the chapters is neatly chiastic, as follows: a story of a national calamity in which David intercedes; a list (Chapter 21); a poem (Chapter 22); a poem; a list (Chapter 23); a story of a national calamity in which David intercedes (Chapter 24). The temporal setting of these materials is unclear but they seem to belong somewhere in the middle of David's career, and do not follow from the late point in his reign reported in the immediately preceding account of the rebellion of Sheba son of Bichri. The editors placed these chapters here, rather than after David's death, and then set the account of his last days, which they interrupt, at the beginning of 1 Kings in order to underline the dynastic continuity between David's story and Solomon's, which then immediately follows as the first large unit of the Book of Kings.

1. *David sought out the presence of the LORD.* The idiom means to seek an audience (with a ruler), though what is referred to in practical terms is inquiry of an oracle. The rest of the verse gives God's response to the question put to the oracle. At the very outset, a difference in idiom from the main narrative, where people consistently "inquire of the LORD," is detectable. The idiom preferred by this new author emphasizes hierarchical relationship rather than the practical business of putting a question to the oracle.

said, "On account of Saul and on account of the house of blood guilt,
2 because he put the Gibeonites to death." And the king called to the
Gibeonites and said to them—and the Gibeonites were not of Israelite stock but from the remnant of the Amorites, and the Israelites had
vowed to them, but Saul sought to strike them down in his zeal for
3 the Israelites and for Judah. And David said to the Gibeonites, "What
shall I do for you and how shall I atone, that you may bless the LORD's
4 heritage?" And the Gibeonites said to him, "We have no claim of silver
and gold against Saul and his house, and we have no man in Israel to
5 put to death." And he said, "Whatever you say, I shall do for you." And

---

2. *and the Gibeonites were not of Israelite stock.* The syntactic looseness of this
long parenthetical sentence (compare the similar syntax in verse 5) is uncharacteristic of the David story proper.

the Israelites had vowed to them. The story of the vow to do no harm to this
group of resident aliens is reported in Joshua 9:15.

but Saul sought to strike them down. There is no way of knowing whether
this massacre of Gibeonites by Saul reflects historical fact, but there is not the
slightest hint of it in the story of Saul recounted in 1 Samuel. As with the differences of style, one sees here the presence of a distinctly different literary source.

3. *What shall I do for you and how shall I atone.* The speech and acts of David
in this story show nothing of the psychological complexity of the experience-
torn David whose story we have been following. He speaks in flat terms, almost
ritualistically, fulfilling his public and cultic functions as king. And after this
brief initial exchange with the Gibeonites, the writer entirely abandons dialogue, which had been the chief instrument for expressing emotional nuance
and complication of motive and theme in the David story.

4. *We have no claim of silver and gold . . . we have no man in Israel to put to death.*
The second clause is really an opening ploy in negotiation: they say they have
no claim to execute any Israelite ("claim" in the first clause is merely implied
by ellipsis in the Hebrew), suggesting that they are waiting for David to agree
to hand Israelites over to them in expiation of Saul's crime.

Whatever you say, I shall do for you. David's submissiveness to the Gibeonites
reflects a notion of causation and the role of human action scarcely evident in
the main narrative. A famine grips the land because its former ruler violated a
national vow. Collective disaster can be averted only by the expiatory—indeed,
sacrificial—offering of human lives. This archaic world of divine retribution
and ritual response is very far from the historical realm of *Realpolitik* in which
the story of David has been played out.

they said to the king, "The man who massacred us and who devastated us—we were destroyed from having a stand in all the territory of
Israel—let seven men of his sons be given to us, that we may impale   6
them before the Lord at Gibeah of Saul, the Lord's chosen." And the
king said, "I will give them." And the king spared Mephibosheth son of   7
Jonathan son of Saul because of the Lord's vow that was between them,
between David and Jonathan son of Saul. And the king took the two   8
sons of Rizpah daughter of Aiah, whom she had borne to Saul, Armoni
and Mephibosheth, and the five sons of Merab daughter of Saul, whom
she had borne to Adriel son of Barzillai the Meholathite. And he gave   9
them into the hands of the Gibeonites, and they impaled them on the
hill before the Lord, and the seven of them fell together. And they were
put to death in the first days of the harvest, the beginning of the barley
harvest. And Rizpah daughter of Aiah took sackcloth and stretched it   10

---

6. *impale*. There is no scholarly consensus on the exact form of execution,
except that it obviously involves exhibiting the corpses. Some understand it as
a kind of crucifixion.

before the Lord at Gibeah of Saul, the Lord's chosen. "Before the Lord" is an
explicit indication of the sacrificial nature of the killings. Many scholars have
doubted that the Saulides would be executed in Saul's own town and emend
this to read "at Gibeon, on the mount of the Lord." If the phrase "the Lord's
chosen" is authentic, it would be spoken sarcastically by the Gibeonites.

8. *Merab*. This is the reading of one version of the Septuagint and of many
Hebrew manuscripts. The Masoretic text has "Michal," who had no children
and who, unlike her sister Merab, was not married to Adriel son of Barzillai.

9. *the seven of them fell together*. Polzin neatly observes that this phrase precisely
echoes "they fell together" of 2:16—the account of the beginning of the civil
war at this very same place, Gibeon. He also notes how this whole episode is
organized around recurring units of three and seven, the latter number *shiv'ah*
punning on the reiterated *shevu'ah*, vow.

the beginning of the barley harvest. This would be in April. The bereaved
Rizpah then watches over the corpses throughout the hot months of the summer,
until the rains return—heralding the end of the long famine—in the fall.

10. *Rizpah . . . took sackcloth and stretched it out over herself*. The verb here is
the one generally used for pitching tents, so the translations that have Rizpah
spreading the cloth over the rock are misleading. What she does is to make a
little lean-to with the sackcloth to shield herself from the summer sun.

out over herself on the rock from the beginning of the harvest till the
waters poured down on them from the heavens, and she did not allow
the birds of the heavens to settle on them by day nor the beasts of the
11 field by night. And David was told what Rizpah daughter of Aiah, Saul's
12 concubine, had done. And David went and took the bones of Saul and
the bones of Jonathan his son from the notables of Jabesh-Gilead who
had stolen them from the square of Beth-Shan, where the Philistines
had hanged them on the day the Philistines struck down Saul at Gilboa.
13 And he brought up from there the bones of Saul and the bones of Jona-
14 than his son, and they collected the bones of the impaled men. And
they buried the bones of Saul and of Jonathan his son in the territory of

---

she did not allow the birds of the heavens to settle on them. The antecedent
of "them" is of course the corpses. As in the ancient Greek world, leaving a
corpse unburied is a primal sacrilege, a final desecration of the sacredness of
the human person. Rizpah, watching over the unburied corpses, is a kind of
Hebrew Antigone. David had delivered the seven descendants of Saul to the
Gibeonites with the single-minded intention of expiating the crime that had
caused the famine. Evidently, he gave no thought to the possibility that the
Gibeonites would desecrate the bodies of the Saulides after killing them by
denying them burial.

11. *And David was told what Rizpah . . . had done.* Rizpah's sustained act of
maternal heroism finally achieves its end: the king is shaken out of his acquiescence in the Gibeonite inhumanity.

12. *David went and took the bones of Saul and the bones of Jonathan.* According
to the account in 1 Samuel 31, they were cremated. Either this report reflects
a conflicting tradition or "bones" here has to be understood as "ashes."

14. *they buried the bones of Saul and of Jonathan his son. . . . And God then
granted the plea for the land.* It should be noted that the end of the famine does
not come with the sacrificial killing of the seven Saulides but only after all of
them, together with Saul himself and Jonathan, are given fitting burial in their
own place (a biblical desideratum). In this strange story, David is seen handing
over the surviving offspring of Saul to be killed, but only for the urgent good
of the nation, after which he pays posthumous respect to the line of Saul. It
is conceivable that this story reflects an alternative narrative tradition to the
more politically complex one of the David story proper through which David
is exonerated from what may well have been a widespread accusation that he
deliberately liquidated all of Saul's heirs, with the exception of Mephibosheth.

Benjamin in Zela, in the tomb of Kish his father, and they did all that the king had charged. And God then granted the plea for the land.

And once again there was fighting between the Philistines and Israel, 15 and David went down, and his servants with him, and they did battle with the Philistines, and David grew weary. And Ishbi-Benob, who was 16 of the offspring of the titan, the weight of his weapon three hundred weights of bronze, and he was girded with new gear—he meant to strike down David. And Abishai son of Zeruiah came to his aid and struck 17 down the Philistine and put him to death. Then David's men swore to him, saying, "You shall not sally forth with us again to battle, lest you snuff out the lamp of Israel."

And it happened thereafter that once again there was fighting with 18 the Philistines, at Gob. Then did Sibbecai the Hushathite strike down

---

15. *David grew weary.* This phrase probably indicates an aging David, though not yet the vulnerable sedentary monarch of the conflict with Absalom.

16. *Ishbi-Benob.* This name looks as bizarre in the Hebrew as in transliteration and probably betrays a corrupt text. (The textual obscurities that abound in this section in all likelihood reflect the fact that this is an old literary document imperfectly transmitted.) There have been attempts to revocalize the name as a verb, but those in turn necessitate extensive tinkering with other parts of the verse.

of the offspring of the titan. The Hebrew *rafah* (with a definite article here) elsewhere means "giant." The ending is feminine and it is not clear whether the reference is to a progenitrix or a progenitor.

the weight of his weapon. The Hebrew for "weapon," *qayin,* appears only here, and so the translation is merely inference from context. It might be related to a word that means "metalsmith." The invocation of the titanic weight of the weapon (spear?) is of course reminiscent of the earlier description of Goliath.

girded with new gear. The Hebrew says simply "girded with new [feminine ending]." Some assume the reference is to sword, which is feminine in Hebrew.

17. *You shall not sally forth with us again.* This fragmentary episode is obviously remembered because it marks a turning point in David's career. It is at least consonant with the image of David at Mahanaim asked by his men to stay behind as they go out to the battlefield.

19 Saph, who was of the offspring of the titan. And once again there was fighting with the Philistines at Nob, and Elhanan son of Jair the Bethlehemite struck down Goliath the Gittite, and the shaft of his spear was like a weaver's beam.

20 And once again there was fighting, at Gath. And there was a man of huge measure, who had six fingers on each hand and six toes on each
21 foot, twenty-four in all, and he, too, was sprung from the titan. And he insulted Israel, and Jonathan son of Shimei, David's kinsman, struck
22 him down. These four were sprung from the titan, and they fell at the hand of David and at the hand of his servants.

---

19. *Elhanan son of Jair*. So he is identified in the parallel report in Chronicles. The Masoretic text here reads "Elhanan son of Ja'arey 'Orgim," but the last word, *'orgim*, means "weavers," and seems clearly a scribal duplication of *'orgim* at the very end of the verse.

Elhanan. . . struck down Goliath the Gittite. This is one of the most famous contradictions in the Book of Samuel. Various attempts, both ancient and modern, have been made to harmonize the contradiction—such as the contention that "Goliath" is not a name but a Philistine title—but none of these efforts is convincing. Of the two reports, this one may well be the more plausible. In the literary shaping of the story of David, a triumph originally attributed, perhaps with good reason, to Elhanan was transferred to David and grafted onto the folktale pattern of the killing of a giant or an ogre by a resourceful young man. The writer used this material, as we have seen, to shape a vivid and arresting portrait of David's debut.

22. *These four were sprung from the titan, and they fell at the hand of David*. Stylistically, the entire unit from verse 15 to the end of the chapter has the feel of a deliberately formulaic epic catalogue (rather than an actual epic narrative, which the earlier Goliath story in 1 Samuel 17 more closely approximates). Formally, the predominant number three of the famine story is succeeded by four here—just as in biblical poetic parallelism three is conventionally followed by four (for example, Amos 1:3, "For three crimes of Damascus, / and for four, I will not revoke it").

CHAPTER 22

And David spoke to the LORD the words of this song on the day the   1
LORD rescued him from the clutches of his enemies and from the
clutches of Saul, and he said:

---

1. *And David spoke to the LORD the words of this song.* It was a common literary practice in ancient Israel to place a long poem or "song" (*shirah*) at or near
the end of a narrative book—compare Jacob's Testament, Genesis 49, and the
Song of Moses, Deuteronomy 32. In the case of the Book of Samuel, David's
victory psalm and Hannah's psalm, respectively a song of the male warrior's triumph and a song contextualized as an expression of maternal triumph, enclose
the large narrative like bookends, and there is even some interechoing of language between the two poems. These long concluding poems were presumably
selected by the editor or composer of the book from a variety of texts available
in the literary tradition and then ascribed to a principal character of the story.
There is, of course, a persistent biblical notion of David the poet as well as
of David the warrior-king, and the idea that he actually composed this poem,
though unlikely, cannot be categorically dismissed. In any case, most scholars
(Albright, Cross and Friedman, Robertson) detect relatively archaic language in
the poem and date it to the tenth century, David's time. The archaic character
of the language makes the meaning of many terms conjectural. Even in the
ancient period, some of the older locutions may already have been obscure to
the scribes, who seem to have scrambled many phrases in transmission; but in
contrast to the confident practice of many biblical scholars, caution in presum-
ing to reconstruct the "primitive" text is prudent. It should be noted that this
same poem occurs in the Book of Psalms as Psalm 18, with a good many minor
textual variants. In several instances, the reading in Psalm 18 seems preferable,
but here, too, methodological caution is necessary: Psalm 18 appears to be a
secondary version of the poem, and its editor at least in some cases may have
clarified obscurities through revision.

2   "The Lord is my crag and my fortress
        and my own deliverer.

3   God, my rock where I shelter,
        my shield and the horn of my rescue,
    My bulwark and refuge,
        my rescuer, saves me from havoc.

4   Praised! did I call the Lord,
        and from my enemies I was rescued.

5   For the breakers of death beset me,
        the underworld's torrents dismayed me.

6   The snares of Sheol coiled round me,
        the traps of death sprang against me.

7   In my strait I called to the Lord,
        to my God I called,
    And from His palace He heard my voice,
        My cry in His ears.

8   The earth heaved and quaked,
        the heavens' foundations shuddered,
        they heaved, for He was incensed.

---

2. *my crag and my fortress*. Albright notes that many of the Northwest Semitic gods were deified mountains. Thus the imagery of the god as a lofty rock or crag abounds in the poetic tradition upon which the biblical poet drew. It also makes particular sense for a poem of military triumph, since a warrior battling in the mountainous terrain of the land of Israel would keenly appreciate the image of protection of a towering cliff or a fortress situated on a height.

3. *horn*. The idiom is drawn from the goring horn of a charging ram or bull. In keeping with the precedent of the King James Version, it is worth preserving in English in order to suggest the concreteness and the archaic coloration of the poem.

5. *For the breakers of death beset me*. The condition of being mortally threatened is regularly figured in the poetry of Psalms as a descent, or virtual descent, into the terrifying shadows of the underworld.

8. *The earth heaved and quaked*. God's descent from His celestial palace to do battle on behalf of his faithful servant is imagined as a seismic upheaval of the whole earth.

Smoke went up from His nostrils,   9
      consuming fire from His mouth,
         coals before Him blazed.
He tilted the heavens, came down,   10
      dense mist beneath His feet.
He mounted a cherub and flew,   11
      He soared on the wings of the wind.
He set darkness as shelters around Him,   12
      a massing of waters, the clouds of the skies.
From the radiance before Him,   13
      fiery coals blazed.
The LORD from the heavens thundered,   14
      the Most High sent forth His voice.
He let loose arrows and routed them,   15
      lightning, and struck them with panic.
The channels of the sea were exposed,   16
      the world's foundations laid bare,
by the LORD's roaring,
      the blast of His nostrils' breath.

---

9. *Smoke went up from His nostrils.* The poetic representation of God, drawing on pre-monotheistic literary traditions such as the Ugaritic Baal epic, is
unabashedly anthropomorphic. One must be cautious, however, in drawing
theological inferences from this fact. Modes of literary expression exert a powerful momentum beyond their original cultural contexts, as Milton's embrace
of the apparatus of pagan epic in *Paradise Lost* vividly demonstrates. The LORD
figures as a fierce warrior, like Baal, because that works evocatively as poetry.
This God of earthquakes and battles breathes fire: in an intensifying narrative
progression from one verset to the next and then from line to line, smoke comes
out of His nostrils, His mouth spews fire, in His awesome incandescence coals
ignite before Him, and then He begins his actual descent from on high.

11. *He mounted a cherub and flew.* The cherub is a fierce winged beast, the
traditional mount of the deity.
    He soared on the wings of the wind. The translation reads with Psalm 18
wayeda', instead of the weaker *wayera'*, "He was seen" (the Hebrew graphemes
for *d* and *r* being very close).

17   He reached from on high and He took me,
        He drew me out of vast waters,

18   saved me from enemies fierce,
        from my foes who had overwhelmed me.

19   They sprang against me on my most dire day,
        but the LORD was a stay then for me.

20   He led me out to an open place.
        He freed me for He took up my cause.

21   The LORD dealt with me by my merit,
        by the cleanness of my hands, requited me.

22   For I kept the ways of the LORD,
        I did no evil before my God.

23   For all His statutes are before me,
        from His laws I have not swerved.

24   I have been blameless before Him,
        I kept myself from sin.

25   The LORD requited me by my merit,
        by the cleanness of my hands before His eyes.

---

19. *They sprang against me.* The verb here—its basic meaning is to meet or greet, sometimes before the person is ready—repeats "the traps of death sprang against me" in verse 6: first that act of being taken by surprise occurs metaphorically, and now again in the literal experience of the speaker on the battlefield.

21. *The LORD dealt with me by my merit.* It is often claimed that verses 21–25 are a Deuteronomistic interpolation in the poem—that is, seventh century or later. The evidence is not entirely persuasive because the theological notion of God's rewarding the innocence of the individual by rescuing him from grave danger is by no means a Deuteronomistic innovation, and adherence to "statutes" and "laws" (verse 23), though encouraged in the Deuteronomistic literary environment, is neither its unprecedented invention nor its unique linguistic marker.

25. *by the cleanness of my hands.* The Masoretic text has merely "by my cleanness" (*kevori*), but the parallel version in Psalm 18 shows *kevor yadai* "by the cleanness of my hands," as do the Septuagint and other ancient translations of this line. The concrete juxtaposition of idioms anchored in body parts— "cleanness of hands" for "innocence" and "before Your eyes" for "in Your sight"— is characteristic of biblical usage.

With the loyal You act in loyalty,   26
      with the blameless warrior You are without blame.
With the pure You show Your pureness,   27
      with the perverse You twist and turn.
A lowly people You rescue,   28
      You cast Your eyes down on the haughty.
For You are my lamp, O Lord!   29
      The Lord has lit up my darkness.
For through You I rush a barrier,   30
      through my God I vault a wall.
The God Whose way is blameless,   31
      the Lord's speech is without taint,
            a shield He is to those who shelter in him.
For who is god but the Lord,   32

---

26. *with the blameless warrior You are without blame.* Many textual critics consider "warrior" to be an interpolation and either delete it or substitute for *gibor*, "warrior," *gever*, "man." The parallelism of these four versets, in each of which God, in a verb, answers in kind to the adjectivally defined human agent, is better preserved without "warrior." The profession of blamelessness scarcely accords with David's behavior in the body of the story.

27. *twist and turn.* This English phrase represents a single reflexive verb in the Hebrew. It is the sole instance in this series of four versets in which the verb describing God's action has a root different from the adjective characterizing the kind of person to whom God responds, though there is still a manifest semantic connection between the two terms here, and this works quite nicely as a small variation on the pattern to conclude the series.

28. *A lowly people You rescue, / You cast Your eyes down on the haughty.* The opposition between low and high is conventional in the poetry of Psalms— it also figures in Hannah's Song—but is nonetheless effective. The speaker's people is "lowly" in the sense that it is miserable, afflicted, endangered by superior forces. God on high looks down on the lofty who seem to have the upper hand and, as the triumphant images from verse 39 onward make clear, brings them low.

30. *I rush a barrier . . . vault a wall.* The speaker who has just been seen among "a lowly people" and then vouchsafed a beam from God's lantern as he gropes in the dark now suddenly takes the offensive, charging the enemies' ramparts.

　　　　who is a rock but our God?
33　The God, my mighty stronghold,
　　　　　　He frees my way to be blameless,
34　makes my legs like a gazelle's,
　　　　　　and stands me on the heights,
35　trains my hands for combat,
　　　　　　makes my arms bend a bow of bronze.
36　You gave me Your shield of rescue,
　　　　　　Your battle cry made me many.

---

33. *The God, my mighty stronghold.* Although this phrase, *ma'uzi ḥayil*, is intel-ligible as it stands, the variant in Psalm 18, supported by the Qumran Samuel scroll, is more fluent and sustains a parallelism of verbs between the two halves of the line. That reading is *hame'azreni ḥayil*, "Who girds me with might."

He frees my way to be blameless. The verb here, *wayater*, is problematic. The most obvious construction would be as a term that generally means "to loosen," though the syntactic link with "blameless" (there is no explicit "to be" in the Hebrew) is obscure. The version in Psalm 18 substitutes *wayiten*, "He made" (or "set"), but the use of that all-purpose verb may simply reflect the scribe's bafflement with the original verb.

34. *makes my legs like a gazelle's, / and stands me on the heights.* The swiftness of the gazelle accords nicely with the image in verse 30 of the warrior sprinting in assault against the ramparts of the foe. Standing secure on the heights, then, would mark the successful conclusion of his trajectory of attack: the victorious warrior now stands on the walls, or within the conquered bastion, of the enemy. The *ai* suffix of *bamotai*, "heights," normally a sign of the first-person possessive, is an archaic, or poetic, plural ending. The sense proposed by some scholars of "my back [or, thighs?]" is very strained, and destroys the narrative momentum between versets that is a hallmark of biblical poetry.

35. *makes my arms bend a bow of bronze.* The verb *niḥat* has not been satisfac-torily explained, nor is its syntactic role in the clause clear. This translation, like everyone else's, is no more than a guess, based on the possibility that the verb reflects a root meaning "to come down," and so perhaps refers to the bending down of a bow.

36. *Your battle cry.* This noun, *'anotkha*, is still another crux. The least far-fetched derivation is from the verbal steam '-*n*-*h*, which means either "to answer," thus yielding a sense here of "answering power," or "to call out," "speak

You lengthened my stride beneath me,   37
    and my ankles did not trip.
I pursued my foes and destroyed them,   38
    never turned back till I cut them down.
I cut them down, smashed them, they did not rise,   39
    they fell beneath my feet.
You girt me with might for combat,   40
    those against me You brought down beneath me,
You showed me my enemies' nape,   41
    my foes, I demolished them.
They cried out—there was none to rescue,   42
    to the LORD, He answered them not.

---

up." Given the sequence of concrete warfare images in these lines, from bronze bow to saving shield, this translation proposes, conjecturally, "battle cry," with the established verbal noun *'anot*, "noise" or "calling out" in mind. Compare Exodus 32:18: "The sound of crying out in triumph" (*qol 'anot gevurah*). The battle cry would use God's name (perhaps something like "sword of the LORD and of David") with the idea that it had a potency that would infuse the warrior with strength and resolution and strike fear in the enemy. Thus the battle cry makes the solitary fighter, or the handful he leads, "many" against seemingly superior forces.

37. *You lengthened my stride beneath me, / and my ankles did not trip.* This focus on the long, firm stride jibes with the previous images of rapid running against the enemy and anticipates the evocation in the lines that follow of the victorious warrior's feet trampling the foe.

38. *till I cut them down.* The English phrase, chosen to reflect the rhythmic compactness of the original, represents a Hebrew verb that means "to destroy them utterly," or, "to finish them off," but the former phrase is too much of a mouthful and the latter is the wrong level of diction. In any event, the narrative sequence of being provided with armor and weapons and charging against a fleeing enemy is now completed as the victor overtakes his adversaries and tramples them to death.

42. *there was none to rescue, / to the LORD, He answered them not.* The frustration of the enemies desperate prayers is meant to be a pointed contrast to the situation of the speaker of the poem, who calls out to the LORD and is saved (verse 4).

43   I crushed them like dust of the earth,
                    like street mud, I pounded them, stomped them.
44   You delivered me from the strife of peoples,
                    kept me at the head of nations
                             a people I knew not did serve me.
45   Foreigners cowered before me,
                    by what the ear heard they obeyed me.
46   Foreigners did wither,
                    filed out from their forts.
47   The LORD lives and blessed is my Rock,
                    exalted the God, Rock of my rescue!
48   The God Who grants vengeance to me
                    and brings down peoples beneath me,
49   frees me from my enemies,
                    from those against me You raise me up,
                             from a man of violence You save me.

---

44. *the strife of peoples.* The translation follows the minor variation of the parallel reading in Psalm 18, *merivey 'am*, literally, "the strife of people." The Masoretic text here reads *merivey 'ami*, "the strife of my people," which may simply
mean the battles in which my people is embroiled, but it also inadvertently
suggests internal strife. Despite the presence of Saul in the poem's superscrip-
tion, the immediately following lines here indicate external enemies.

kept me at the head of nations. This phrase and the language of the next
verset are perfectly consonant with David's creation of an imperial presence
among the peoples of the trans-Jordan region.

45. *Foreigners cowered before me.* All that can be said in confidence about the
Hebrew verb is that it indicates something negative. The common meaning of
the root is "to deny" or "to lie." Perhaps that sense is linked in this instance with
the foreigners' fawning on their conqueror.

46. *filed out from their forts.* The meanings of both the verb and the noun are in
dispute. The verb *hagar* usually means "to gird," but the text in Psalm 18, more
plausibly, inverts the second and third consonants, yielding *harag*, which is generally taken to mean "emerge from," or "pop out from," a restrictive framework.
The noun *misgerotam* is clearly derived from the root s-g-r, "to close," and "fort"
(an enclosure) seems fairly plausible. (The proposal of "collar" has little biblical
warrant and makes rather bad sense in context.)

Therefore I acclaim You among nations, O Lord,   50
        and to Your name I would hymn.
Tower of rescue to His king,   51
              keeping faith with His anointed,
                       for David and his seed, forever."

---

50. *Therefore I acclaim You . . . O Lord.* In keeping with a formal convention of the thanksgiving psalm, or *todah*, the poem concludes by explicitly stating that the speaker has acclaimed or given thanks (the verb cognate with the noun *todah*) to God.

and to your name I would hymn. The pairing in poetic parallelism of the two verbs, *hodah*, "acclaim," and *zimer*, "hymn," is common in the conclusion of thanksgiving psalms.

51. *Tower of rescue.* The variant reading in Psalm 18, supported by the consonantal text here but not by its Masoretic vocalization, is "He magnifies the rescues [or victories]" of—(instead of the noun, *migdol*, "tower," the verb *magdil*, "to make big"). The one attraction of the Masoretic reading here of this word is that it closes the poem with an image that picks up the multiple metaphors of a lofty stronghold at the beginning.

keeping faith with His anointed, / for David and his seed, forever. Many critics have seen the entire concluding verse as an editorial addition, both because of the switch to a third-person reference to the king and because of the invocation of dynasty, beyond the temporal frame of the warrior-king's own victories. The inference, however, is not inevitable. Switches in grammatical person, even in a single clause, occur much more easily in biblical Hebrew than in modern Western languages, and if the triumphant speaker of the poem is actually David or in any event is imagined to be David, it is quite possible that he would conclude his account of attaining imperial greatness by a prayer that the dynasty he has founded will continue to enjoy God's steadfast support for all time.

CHAPTER 23

₁ A nd these are the last words of David:

"Thus spoke David son of Jesse,
                    thus spoke the man raised on high,
anointed of the God of Jacob,
                    and sweet singer of Israel.

---

1. *these are the last words of David.* David's victory psalm in the preceding chapter is now followed by a second archaic poetic text, quite different in style, unrelated to the psalm tradition, and a good deal obscurer in many of its formulations. Although there is scholarly debate about the dating of this poem, the consensus puts it in or close to David's own time in the tenth century. The mystifying features of the language certainly suggest great antiquity, and it is just possible that the poet was really by David. The exact application of "the last words of David" is unclear. In terms of the narrative, they are not literally his last words because he will convey a deathbed testament to Solomon (1 Kings 2). The phrase might be intended to designate the last pronouncement in poetry of David the royal poet.

Thus spoke David. This introductory formula is a mark of prophetic or oracular language—compare the beginning of Balaam's third oracle in Numbers 24:3.

raised on high. The two Hebrew words reflected in this translation, *huqam 'al*, have a gorgeous strangeness as compacted idiom—so strange that both the Septuagint and the Qumran Samuel prefer a more common Hebrew locution, *heqim 'el*, "God has raised up." In either case, the phrase refers to David's elevation to the throne.

sweet singer of Israel. The eloquent and famous wording of the King James Version (KJV) seems worth retaining because the divergent proposals for understanding the phrase are scarcely more certain than that of the KJV. The literal meaning of *ne'im zemirot yisra'el* is "sweet one [or, favorite] of the chants of

574

The LORD's spirit has spoken in me,   2
       his utterance on my tongue.
The God of Israel has said,   3
       to me the Rock of Israel has spoken:
He who rules men, just,
       who rules in the fear of God.
Like morning's light when the sun comes up,   4
       morning without clouds,
           from radiance, from showers—grass from
           earth.
For is not thus my house with God?   5

Israel." The root z-m-r has a homonymous meaning—strength—which has encouraged some interpreters to construe this as "preferred of the Strong One [or, Stronghold] of Israel" in parallel to "anointed of the God of Israel." It must be said, however, that there are no instances in which the root z-m-r in the sense of strength serves as an epithet for the deity.

2. *The LORD's spirit has spoken in me.* This does not mean, as some have understood, that David is claiming actual status as a prophet but rather that he is attesting to an access of oracular elevation as he proclaims his lofty (and enigmatic!) verse.

3. *He who rules men, just.* The translation reproduces the cryptic (elliptic?) syntax of the Hebrew, adding a clarifying comma (the Hebrew of course has no punctuation).

   who rules in the fear of God. The compacted syntax of the Hebrew has no "in," but most interpreters assume it is implied.

4. *from radiance, from showers—grass from earth.* The meaning of these images is much disputed, and some critics move "from radiance" altogether back to the preceding clause. The tentative reading presumed by the translation is as follows: The anointed king has been compared to the brilliant rising sun on a cloudless morning (solar imagery for kings being fairly common in ancient Near Eastern literature). The poet now adds that from the sun's radiance, coupled with rainfall, grass springs forth from the earth. Thus the rule of the just king is a source of blessed fruitfulness to his subjects.

5. *For is not thus my house with God?* The Hebrew grammar here is a little confusing. It is most plausible to construe both this clause and the one at the end

An eternal covenant He gave me,
   drawn up in full and guaranteed.
For all my triumph and all my desire
  will He not bring to bloom?
6 And the worthless man is like a thorn—
  uprooted every one,
    they cannot be picked up by hand.
7 Should a man touch them,
   he must get himself iron
    or the shaft of a spear.
And in fire they'll be utterly burned where they are."

---

of the verse not as negative statements but as affirmative questions. The image of bringing to bloom in the concluding clause suggests that David's dynasty in relation to God is to be imagined like the earth in relation to sun and showers and like the people in relation to the king: because of the everlasting covenant with David, God will make his house blossom.

6. *the worthless man is like a thorn— / uprooted every one.* The antithesis between flourishing soft grass and the prickly thorn torn from its roots is manifest (though it must be said that "uprooted" for the obscure *munad* is conjectural, if widely accepted).

7. *he must get himself iron.* The translation adopts the common proposal that the verb *yimale'* (literally, "he will fill") is an ellipsis for *yimale' yado*, "he will fill his hand," "equip himself with"). Others emend it to read '*im lo'*, "except [with]."
 or the shaft of a spear. The Hebrew is usually construed as "and the shaft," but the particle *waw* does occasionally have the force of "or," which is more plausible here.
 in fire they'll be utterly burned. The only suitable disposition of these nasty thorns is to rake them up with an iron tool or a spear shaft and make a bonfire of them, in order to get entirely rid of the threat they pose. The fact that weapons are used for the raking suggests the political referent of the metaphor. Such will be the fate of mischief makers ("the worthless")—evidently all who would presume to oppose the legitimate monarchy.
 where they are. This phrase reflects a single, highly dubious word in the Masoretic text, *bashavet.* That word may well be an inadvertent repetition by a baffled scribe of the seventh Hebrew word in the following verse. The whole phrase in which that term occurs is itself textually problematic.

These are the names of the warriors of David: Josheb-Basshebeth, a 8
Tahchemonite, head of the Three, he is Adino the Eznite. He brandished his spear over eight hundred slain at a single time. And after him 9
Eleazar son of Dodo son of Ahohi, of the three warriors with David when
they insulted the Philistines gathered there for battle and the Israelites
decamped. He arose and struck down Philistines until his hand tired 10
and his hand stuck to the sword. And the LORD wrought a great victory
on that day, and the troops came back after him only to strip the slain.

---

8. *These are the names of the warriors of David.* This list of military heroes and
their exploits is perhaps the strongest candidate of any passage in the Book
of Samuel to be considered a text actually written in David's lifetime. The
language is crabbed, and the very abundance of textual difficulties, uncharacteristic for prose, reflects the great antiquity of the list. These fragmentary
recollections of particular heroic exploits do not sound like the invention of
any later writer but, on the contrary, like memories of remarkable martial acts
familiar to the audience (for example, "he . . . killed the lion in the pit on the
day of the snow") and requiring only the act of epic listing, not of narrative
elaboration. It should also be noted that the list invokes the early phase of
David's career—when the Philistines were the dominant military force in the
land, when David was at Adullam and in "the stronghold," and when Asahel,
destined to perish at the hands of Abner at the beginning of the civil war, was
an active member of David's corp of elite fighters.

Josheb-Basshebeth a Tahchemonite. So reads the Masoretic text. But this
looks quite dubious as a Hebrew name. One version of the Septuagint has
Ish-Baal (alternately, Jeshbaal), which by scribal euphemism also appears as
Ish-Bosheth and hence may have produced the confusion in the Masoretic
text. Many authorities prefer the gentilic "Hachmoni," in accordance with the
parallel verse in Chronicles.

the Three. Throughout the list, there are confusions between three, third,
and thirty. The received text at this point seems to read *shalishim*, "commanders
of units of thirty," but "three" makes far better sense.

He brandished his spear. This whole phrase, which seems strictly necessary
to make the sentence intelligible, is lacking in the Masoretic text but appears
in the parallel verse in Chronicles.

10. *to strip the slain.* No object of the verb "to strip" appears in the Hebrew,
but this may be a simple ellipses for a common military idiom rather than a
scribal omission.

11 And after him Shammah son of Agei the Ararite. And the Philistines
gathered at Lehi, and there was a plot of land there full of lentils, and
12 the troops had fled before the Philistines. And he took a stand in the plot
and saved it and struck down the Philistines. And the LORD wrought a
13 great victory. And three of the Thirty, at the head, went down in the harvest to David at the cave of Adullam, with the Philistine force camped
14 in the Valley of Rephaim. And David was then in the stronghold and the
15 Philistine garrison then at Bethlehem. And David had a craving and said,
"Who will give me water to drink from the well of Bethlehem, which is
16 by the gate?" And the three warriors broke through the Philistine camp
and drew water from the well of Bethlehem, which is by the gate, and
they bore it off and brought it to David. But he would not drink it, and he
17 poured it out in libation to the LORD. And he said, "Far be it from me that
I should do such a thing. Shall I drink the blood of men who have gone

---

11. *at Lehi.* The translation presupposes a minor emendation of the Masoretic *laḥayah* (meaning obscure, though some understand it as "in a force") to *leḥi*, a place-name, which the rest of the clause seems to require.

there was a plot of land there full of lentils. The homey specificity of the detail is another manifestation of the feeling of remembered anecdote in this catalogue of exploits.

13. *at the head.* The Hebrew says only "head," but the word seems to have an adverbial function, and so "at the head" is not unlikely.

15. *Who will give me water to drink from the well of Bethlehem.* Or, "Would that I might drink water . . ." Bethlehem, of course, is David's hometown, at this juncture a headquarters of the occupying Philistine forces. David expresses a sudden yen to taste the sweet water he remembers from that well by the gate of his native town, though he scarcely intends this as a serious invitation to his men to undertake anything so foolhardy as to attempt breaking through the Philistine lines in order to get it. Presumably, the three warriors—it is unclear as to whether they are identical with the Three just named, for they are said to be part of the Thirty—do not misunderstand David's intentions. Rather, as daring fighters, they decide to take him at his word and risk their necks in raiding the Philistine garrison at Bethlehem in order to prove they can execute a seemingly impossible mission. It is easy to understand how such an exploit would be vividly recalled and registered in the epic list.

17. *Shall I drink the blood of men.* The verb (one word in the Hebrew) "shall I drink" is missing from the Masoretic text, though present in both the paral-

at the risk of their lives?" And he would not drink it. These things did
the three warriors do. And Abishai brother of Joab son of Zeruiah—he 18
was chief of the Thirty. And he brandished his spear over three hundred
slain, and he had a name with the Three. Of the Thirty he was most 19
honored and so he became their captain, but he did not attain to the
Three. And Benaiah son of Jehoida from Kabzeel, son of a valiant man, 20
great in deeds—he struck down the two sons of Ariel of Moab and he
went down and killed the lion in the pit on the day of the snow. And he 21
struck down an Egyptian man, a man of daunting appearance, a spear
was in the hand of the Egyptian. And he went down to him with a staff
and stole the spear from the hand of the Egyptian and he killed him
with his own spear. These things did Benaiah son of Jehoida do, and he 22
had a name with the Three Warriors. Of the Thirty he was honored but 23
he did not attain to the Three. And David put him over his royal guard.
Asahel brother of Joab was in the Thirty, and Elhanan son of Dodo 24

lel verse in Chronicles and in the Septuagint. It is possible that some ancient
scribe recoiled from an expression that had David drinking human blood, even
in a hyperbolic verbal gesture.

18. *he was chief of the Thirty*. The received text here and in verse 19 reads
"Three," but this makes no sense, as we are told that Abishai "did not attain to
the Three."
　with the Three. Or, "in the three." Since Abishai is not a member of the
Three, this would have to mean that his prowess won him a reputation even
among the legendary Three. Another solution is to emend the initial *ba* ("in,"
"among") to *ka* ("like"), yielding "he had a name like the Three."

20. *son of a valiant man*. Many textual critics conclude that "son of" (*ben*) is an
erroneous scribal addition.
　he struck down the two sons of Ariel of Moab. These words are among the
most enigmatic in the report of the exploits of David's heroes. The words "two
sons of" (*sheney beney*) are supplied from the Septuagint in an effort to make
this clause at least a little intelligible. "Ariel" is probably a cultic site or object
in Moab.

22. *he had a name with the Three Warriors*. See the comment on verse 18. The
same problem is reflected here.

25,26 of Bethlehem. Shammah the Harodite, Elika the Harodite, Helez the
27 Paltite, Ira son of Ikkesh the Tekoite, Abiezer the Anathothite, Mebun-
28 nai the Hushathite. Zalmon the Ahohite, Maharai the Netophathite,
29 Heleb son of Baanah the Netophathite, Ittai son of Ribai from Gibeah
30 of the Benjaminites, Benaiah the Pirathonite, Hiddai from Nahalei-
31,32 Gaash, Abi-Albon the Anbathite, Azmaveth the Barhumite, Eliahba the
33 Shaalbonite, sons of Jashen Jonathan, Shammah the Hararite, Ahiam
34 son of Sharar the Ararite, Eliphelet son of Ahasbai son of the Maaca-
35 thite, Eliam son of Ahitophel the Gilonite, Hezrai the Carmelite, Paarai
36,37 the Arbite, Igal son of Nathan from Zobah, Bani the Gadite, Zelek
the Ammonite, Naharai the Beerothite, armor bearer to Joab son of
38,39 Zeruiah, Ira the Ithrite, Gareb the Ithrite, Uriah the Hittite—thirty-
seven in all.

---

25. *the Harodite.* All these identifying terms in the list designate the villages
from which the warriors come. A likely location of the biblical Harod would be
not far from Bethlehem. The earlier names in the list cluster geographically in
the territory of Judah, David's tribe. Some of the later names indicate places
in the territories of tribes to the north—perhaps reflecting new recruits to the
elite unit after the conclusion of the civil war. Toward the end of the list there
are also non-Israelites: these could have been mercenaries, or perhaps rather
naturalized subjects of the new monarchy.

32. *sons of Jashen Jonathan.* This identification definitely looks scrambled. "Sons
of" appears not to belong, and many textual critics omit it. "Jonathan," as a
second proper name immediately after "Jashen," is also problematic, and one
wonders whether Jashen (Hebrew *yashen* means "sleeping") was ever a name.

34. *Eliam son of Ahitophel.* One notes that the son of the state counselor who
betrayed David for Absalom was a member of David's elite corps. He might also
be the same Eliam who is Bathsheba's father.

39. *Uriah the Hittite.* Is it an intended irony that the list of David's picked warriors concludes with the man he murdered? The irony may be an artifact of
the editor, if this list was composed after the events recorded in the Bathsheba
story.
    thirty-seven in all. As elsewhere in biblical tabulations, it is hard to make
this figure compute. One system of counting yields a total of thirty-six, and the
addition of Joab—rather surprisingly, omitted from the list—would produce
thirty-seven.

CHAPTER 24

And once more the wrath of the LORD was kindled against Israel, and 1
He incited David against them, saying, "Go, count Israel and Judah."
And the king said to Joab, commander of the force that was with him, 2
"Go round, pray, among all the tribes of Israel, from Dan to Beersheba,
and take a census of the people, that I may know the number of the
people." And Joab said to the king, "May the LORD your God add to the 3
people a hundred times over with the eyes of my lord the king behold-

---

1. *And once more the wrath of the LORD was kindled against Israel.* The reason
for God's wrath is entirely unspecified, and attempts to link it to events in the
preceding narrative are quite unconvincing. In fact, this entire narrative unit
(which some scholars claim is itself composite) is strikingly different in theological assumptions, in its imagination of narrative situation and character, and
even in its style from the David story proper as well as from the tale of David
and the Gibeonites in Chapter 21 with which it is symmetrically paired. Perhaps, indeed, there is no discernible reason for God's fury against Israel. The
God of this story has the look of acting arbitrarily, exacting terrible human costs
in order to be placated. Unlike the deity of 1 Samuel 1–2 Samuel 20, He is
decidedly an interventionist God, pulling the human actors by strings, and He
may well be a capricious God, here "inciting" David to carry out a census that
will only bring grief to the people.

2. *Joab, commander of the force.* A different vocabulary is another indication
that a different writer is at work here. Throughout the David narrative, Joab
is designated *sar hatsava'*, "commander of the army," but here the terminology
changes to the unusual *sar haḥayil*, "commander of the force." Similarly, the
verb for "go round," *sh-w-t*—it is attached to the Adversary in the frame story
of Job—is distinctive of this narrative.

4 ing. But why should my lord the king desire this thing?" And the king's
word prevailed over Joab and over the commanders of the force, and
Joab, and the commanders of the force with him, went out from the
5 king's presence to take a census of the people, of Israel. And they
crossed the Jordan and camped in Aroer south of the town, which is in
6 the middle of the wadi of Gad and by Jazer. And they came to Gilead
and to the region of Tahtim-Hodshi, and they came to Dan-Jaan and
7 round toward Sidon. And they came to the fortress of Tyre and to
all the towns of the Hivite and the Canaanite, and they went out to
8 the Negeb of Judah, to Beersheba. And they went round through all

---

3. *But why should my lord the king desire this thing?* Underlying the story is both
a cultic and a superstitious fear of the census, reflected in Joab's objection to it.
Several commentators have noted that according to Exodus 30:12 every Israelite counted in a census was required to pay a half shekel as "ransom" (*kofer*)
for his life. Since such payment could not be realistically expected in a total
census of the nation, masses of people would be put in a condition of violation
of ritual. But there is also a folkloric horror of being counted as a condition of
vulnerability to malignant forces. In Rashi's words: "For the evil eye holds sway
over counting." Beyond these considerations, Joab the commander may have
a political concern in mind: the census served as the basis for conscription
(compare the notation in verse 9 of those counted as "sword-wielding men"),
and thus imposing the census might conceivably have provoked opposition to
the threatened conscription and to the king who was behind it. It is noteworthy
that the census is carried out by army officers.

5. *they crossed the Jordan and camped in Aroer.* Aroer is roughly fifteen miles east
of the Dead Sea. The trajectory of the census takers describes a large ellipsis:
first to the southeast from Jerusalem, then north through trans-Jordan to Gilead
and beyond, then west through the northernmost Israelite territory to the sea,
then all the way south to Beersheba, and back to Jerusalem. All this, which will
lead to wholesale death, is accomplished in nine months and twenty days—the
human gestation period.

6. *Tahtim-Hodshi.* The name is suspect, but efforts to recover an original name
behind it remain uncertain.

7. *the fortress of Tyre.* Evidently a mainland outpost to the south of Tyre proper,
which was on an island.

the land and returned at the end of nine months and twenty days to Jerusalem. And Joab gave the number of the census of the people to 9 the king, and Israel made up eight hundred thousand sword-wielding men, and Judah five hundred thousand men. And David was smitten 10 with remorse afterward for having counted the people. And David said to the LORD, "I have offended greatly in what I have done. And now, LORD, remit the guilt of your servant, for I have been very foolish." And David arose in the morning, and the word of the LORD had come 11 to Gad the prophet, David's seer, saying, "Go and speak to David— 12 'Thus says the LORD: Three things I have taken against you. Choose you one of them, and I shall do it to you. Seven years of famine in your 13 land, or three months when you flee before your foes as they pursue you, or let there be three days of plague in your land.' Now, mark and see, what reply shall I bring back to Him Who sent me?" And David 14 said to Gad, "I am in great straits. Let us, pray, fall into the LORD's hand, for great is His mercy, and into the hand of man let me not fall."

---

9. *sword-wielding.* The Hebrew says literally "sword-drawing."

10. *I have offended greatly in what I have done.* In contrast to the cogent sense of moral agency and moral responsibility in the David story proper, there is a peculiar contradiction here: David confesses deep contrition, yet he has, after all, been manipulated by God ("incited") to do what he has done.

11. *Gad the prophet, David's seer.* Gad was mentioned earlier (1 Samuel 22:5). His appearance here by no means warrants the claim of Kyle McCarter, Jr., and others that this story is the work of a "prophetic" writer. Visionary inter-mediaries between king and God were a common assumption in the ancient world. Gad is called "seer" (*ḥozeh*), not the way prophetic writers would ordi-narily think of prophets (and also not the term used for Samuel in 1 Samuel 9). Above all, the prophetic current in biblical literature does not presuppose either this kind of arbitrarily punitive God or the accompanying hocus-pocus with choices of punishment and divine messengers of destruction visible to the human characters.

14. *Let us . . . fall into the LORD's hand . . . and into the hand of man let me not fall.* There is a puzzle in David's choice because only one of the three pun-ishments—the flight from enemies—clearly involves human agency. Perhaps David has in mind that an extended famine would lead to absolute dependence

15   And the LORD sent a plague against Israel from morning until the fixed
time, and from Dan to Beersheba seventy-seven thousand men of the
people died.

16   And the messenger reached out his hand against Jerusalem to destroy
it, and the LORD regretted the evil and said to the messenger who was
sowing destruction among the people, "Enough! Now stay your hand."
And the LORD's messenger was at the threshing floor of Araunah the

---

on those foreign nations unaffected by the famine, as in the story of Joseph's
brothers going down to Egypt. In all this, it should be noted that David is
scarcely the same character we have seen in the body of his story. Instead of
that figure of conflicting feelings and emotions so remarkable in psychological depth, we have a flat character instigated to act by God, then expressing
remorse, then speaking in rather official tones in his role as political ruler and
cultic chief responsible for all the people.

15. *the fixed time*. There is some question about what this refers to, though the
grounds for emending the text to solve the problem are shaky. The phrase ought
logically to refer to the end of the ordained three days of the plague. Yet David's
intercession to stop the plague short before it engulfs Jerusalem suggests that
the plague does not go on for the full three days. The difficulty might be resolved
simply by assuming that the initial verb—"and the LORD sent a plague against
Israel"—refers to the initiating of the process according to the promised time
limitations: God sends a plague against Israel intended to rage for the stipulated
time of three days, but after it has devastated the people on a terrible scale for
a certain time (perhaps two days?), David, aghast that these horrors should visit
his own city as well, takes steps to induce God to cut the plague short.

16. *And the messenger reached out his hand against Jerusalem to destroy it*. Once
again, the apparatus and the theology of this story reflect a different imaginative
world from that of the main narrative about David, in which there are no divine
emissaries of destruction brandishing celestial swords. The text of the Qumran
Samuel scroll, paralleled in 1 Chronicles 21, makes the mythological character
of this story even clearer: "and David raised his eyes and saw a messenger of the
LORD standing between earth and heaven, his sword unsheathed in his hand
reaching out against Jerusalem, and David and the elders fell on their faces,
covered with sackcloth."
    stay your hand. Literally, "let your hand go slack, unclench it."
    the LORD's messenger was at the threshing floor of Araunah the Jebusite. In this
fashion, the last-minute averting of the destruction of Jerusalem is linked with
the etiological tale explaining how the site of the future temple was acquired.

Jebusite. And David said to the LORD when he saw the messenger who   17
was striking down the people, thus he said, "It is I who offended, I who
did wrong. And these sheep, what have they done? Let your hand be
against me and my father's house." And Gad came to David on that day   18
and said to him, "Go up, raise to the LORD an altar on the threshing floor
of Araunah the Jebusite." And David went up according to the word of   19
Gad, as the LORD had charged. And Araunah looked out and saw the   20
king and his servants crossing over toward him, and Araunah went out
and bowed down to the king, his face to the ground. And Araunah said,   21
"Why has my lord the king come to his servant?" And David said, "To
buy the threshing floor from you to build an altar to the LORD, that the

---

(Although the temple is not explicitly mentioned, this acquisition of an altar
site in Jerusalem is clearly placed here to prepare the way for the story of Solomon the temple builder that is to follow.) Thus, the first sacrifice offered on this
spot is associated with a legendary turning away of wrath from Jerusalem—a
token of the future function of the temple. The name Araunah it is not Semitic
and is generally thought to be Hittite or Hurrian. Some scholars claim it is
a title, not a name. In any event, Araunah's presence indicates that the conquered Jebusites were not massacred or entirely banished but continued to live
in Jerusalem under David as his subjects.

17. *It is I who offended.* The Qumran text reads here, "It is I, the shepherd, who
did evil." That, of course, neatly complements "these sheep" in the next clause,
but it is hard to know whether "shepherd" was original or added by a later scribe
to clarify the sheep metaphor.

21. *Why has my lord the king come to his servant?* Isaac Abravanel aptly notes
that it would not have been customary for the king to come to his subject: "You
should have sent for me, for the lesser man goes to the greater and the greater
does not go to the lesser." Abravanel, a councillor to Ferdinand and Isabella
who was in the end exiled by them, would have been keenly familiar with such
protocol.

    to build an altar to the LORD, *that the scourge may be held back.* According to
the ritualistic assumptions of this narrative, it requires not merely contrition
but a special sacrifice to placate the deity. This leads one to suspect that the
story, far from being prophetic literature, may have originated in some sort of
priestly circle.

22 scourge may be held back from the people. And Araunah said to David, "Let my lord the king take and offer up what is good in his eyes. See the oxen for the burnt offering and the threshing boards and the oxen's gear
23 for wood. All of it has Araunah, O king, given to the king." And Araunah
24 said to the king, "May the LORD your God show you favor." And the king said to Araunah, "Not so! I will surely buy it from you for a price, and I will not offer up burnt offerings to the LORD my God at no cost." And David bought the threshing floor and the oxen for fifty shekels of
25 silver. And David built there an altar to the LORD and offered up burnt offerings and well-being sacrifices, and the LORD granted the plea for the land and the scourge was pulled back from Israel.

---

22. *Let my lord . . . take . . . what is good in his eyes.* In this whole exchange, there is a distinct parallel to Abraham's bargaining with Ephron the Hittite for the purchase of a grave site at Hebron in Genesis 23. Ephron, too, first offers to make a gift to Abraham of what he requires, but the patriarch, like David here, insists on paying full price in order to have undisputed possession of the property.

the oxen for the burnt offering and the threshing boards and the oxen's gear. What Araunah does not offer David is the land itself, which he clearly wants. Both the threshing board and the "gear" (presumably, the yoke) would have been wooden. Since the sacrifice needs to be performed at once in order to avert the plague, Araunah is quick to offer not only the sacrificial beasts but firewood on the spot.

23. *All of it has Araunah, O king, given to the king.* The Hebrew, with the repeated "king," looks peculiar, though it is intelligible if the first "king" is construed as a vocative. Some emend the verse to read "all of it has Araunah your servant given to my lord the king."

25. *the LORD granted the plea for the land.* This is, of course, a near-verbatim repetition of the words that conclude the story of David and the Gibeonites' execution of the descendants of Saul (21:14). The repetition may well be an editorial intervention intended to underscore the symmetry between the tale of a scourge averted by David's intercession at the beginning and at the end of this large composite coda to 1 and 2 Samuel. Although neither of these stories is especially continuous with the David story proper, both reflect a connection with it in the emphasis on guilt that the king incurs, which brings disaster on the nation and which requires expiation. But the writer of genius responsible for the larger David narrative imagines guilt in far more probing moral terms and does not assume that the consequences of moral offenses and grave political misjudgments can be reversed by some ritual act.

KINGS

TO THE READER

THE BOOK OF KINGS, like the Book of Samuel, as Josephus and early rabbinic sources indicate, was originally one book, not two. Its first two chapters, moreover, are clearly a completion of the story of David, showing the masterful hand of the great writer who fashioned the long narrative of Israel's founding king. The ancient editors set this material at the beginning of the Book of Kings because it reports Solomon's accession to the throne, though that story is intertwined with the wrenching portrait of the aging and failing David and his troubled relationship with his henchman Joab and his actual and potential enemies within and without the court. Once this story is completed, the Book of Kings proper exhibits an approach to politics, character, and historical causation that is quite different from the one that informs the David story.

Kings proves to be the most miscellaneous of the books assembled as the Former Prophets, though all of them are composite at least to some degree. The encompassing redactional framework is patently Deuteronomistic. The measure of every king is whether he did evil in the eyes of the LORD, and doing evil, with only a few limited exceptions, is conceived in cultic terms. The Deuteronomistic compiler repeatedly invokes the stipulation that there can be only one legitimate place of worship, which is the temple in Jerusalem—an idea that became firmly entrenched only with King Josiah's reforms around 621 BCE, scant decades before the Babylonian exile. Through most of these stories, the editor holds clearly in view the destruction of the Northern Kingdom of Israel in 721 BCE and evidently also the destruction of the Southern Kingdom of Judah in 586 BCE. Since there is no hint, even at the end of the narrative, of any return to Zion after the exile, scholars have plausibly inferred that the book as a whole was put together in the early decades after the destruction of Judah.

It was put together, however, from a variety of widely disparate sources, which is why it is best to think of the person or persons responsible for its final form as a compiler or compilers. The large unit at the very beginning (1 Kings 1–11) in itself illustrates the composite character of the book as a whole. The first two chapters, as I have noted, belong to the end of the David story, exhibiting its brilliant deployment of dialogue and of techniques of narrative repetition and its shrewd sense of *Realpolitik*. Chapter 3 begins with an emphatically theological story of God's appearance to Solomon in a dream and the king's request for the gift of wisdom. This encounter with the divine is followed in the second half of the chapter by the often recalled Judgment of Solomon, a fable obviously meant to illustrate his wisdom and clearly reflecting a different narrative genre, the folktale. Chapter 4 is a roster of Solomon's royal bureaucracy, quite different from anything that precedes it.

The first half of Chapter 5 is taken up with a report of the material grandeur of Solomon's court and of his unsurpassed wisdom, manifested in his composition of proverbs and poems. The next two and half chapters focus on Solomon's great building projects, the temple and the palace, undertaken with the collaboration of Hiram king of Tyre. Chapter 8 recounts the dedication of the temple, most of it being the grand speech delivered by Solomon on that occasion (and deemed by many scholars to be a later composition). Chapter 9 begins with God's theologically freighted response to Solomon, then moves on to more of his royal projects. In Chapter 10 we get the enchanting folktale of the visit to Solomon's court of the queen of Sheba. The following chapter, the last in Solomon's story, switches gears to show us the hitherto exemplary king led into the encouraging of pagan practices by his sundry foreign wives.

At the very end of the Solomon narrative, the editor informs us that "The rest of the acts of Solomon and all that he did, and his wisdom, are they not written in the Book of the Acts of Solomon?" (1 Kings 11:42). We may infer that at least some of the material in Chapters 3–11 was drawn from this source, which seems to have been some sort of court annal. The reports of the royal bureaucracy and of Solomon's building projects, including a great abundance of architectural details and catalogues of furnishings, and of his marriage to Pharaoh's daughter, are likely candidates for this annalistic source. Other sources appear to have been tapped for the two folktales and probably also for the account at the end of Solomon's backsliding into pagan ways.

The sundry stories of the kings that come after the Solomon narrative approximately follow this pattern of drawing together disparate documents. More than any other narrative book of the Bible, the stories in Kings are repeatedly and insistently framed by formulaic declarations. Wayward monarchs being preponderant, one king after another is said to swerve from the ways of the LORD, and in the case of the northern kingdom, to follow the dire path of its founder, Jeroboam son of Nebat, who offended and led Israel to offend. Again and again, the compiler, with his overriding concern for the exclusivity of the cult in the Jerusalem temple, inveighs against both northern and southern kings in formulaic language for allowing the people to burn incense and offer sacrifice on "the high places," that is, local rural altars. And the story of each king is concluded, like Solomon's, by a notation that the rest of the acts of this monarch are recorded in the Book of the Acts of the Kings of Judah or the Book of the Acts of the Kings of Israel, depending on whether the king is southern or northern.

The reasonable inference from this editorial procedure is that much of the factual material of the Book of Kings was drawn from these two annalistic sources, one for the Kingdom of Judah and the other for the Kingdom of Israel. There is no way of knowing how much of the two lost annals was left out of the canonical text, though it seems likely that a good deal of circumstantial detail about the various kings was deemed irrelevant to this narrative, encompassing four centuries of Israelite history, that is meant to expound the cumulative chain of actions that led to two nationally traumatic events, the destruction of the northern kingdom in 721 BCE and, 135 years later, the destruction of its southern counterpart.

But we should not think of the Book of Kings merely as a series of extracts from two sets of royal annals. The Deuteronomistic editor provides a good deal of interpretation of the events, especially in his repeated insistence that cultic disloyalty to YHWH brought about the national catastrophes, and in all likelihood he also introduces some of his own narrative invention in order to support his interpretation of the history he conveys. Beyond these interventions, he incorporates materials from sources that are clearly not annalistic. In the later chapters of 2 Kings, there are a few extended passages taken directly from a narrative section of Isaiah, and, at the very end, a short section is drawn from Jeremiah (though it may be the other way around—that the two prophetic books drew from Kings). Elsewhere, there are numerous stories about prophets—not "writing prophets" but men of God who roam the countryside and are active players in the political realm—that have a strong folkloric stamp. Scholars have conjectured that there were collections of tales about prophets, probably produced in prophetic circles, which the later compiler decided to include in the large narrative. However, the fact that these stories are about prophets does not necessarily mean that they were the product of a prophetic milieu, and I would propose that what is most salient about them is their generic character as folktales—stories spun out by the people awestruck by the remembered or imagined powers of these men of God.

There is, in fact, a palpable tension between the narrative of the kings and the tales of the prophets, however they intersect. The royal narrative appears to be historical, at least in its broad outlines. The kingdom did split in two after the death of Solomon around 930 BCE. There is no reason to doubt the reports of chronic political instability, especially in the northern kingdom where there was no authorized dynasty, involving a long and bloody sequence of court conspiracies, assassinations of kings, and usurpations. Israel's and Judah's struggles with the Arameans, the Assyrians, and finally the Babylonians were actual historical events, many of them attested in the Assyrian and Babylonian annals that have been uncovered by modern archeology. The compiler of Kings, then, registers the course of historical events in the two kingdoms, making efforts to synchronize their chronology with reference to regnal spans, though his commitment to theological historical causation leads him occasionally to introduce a supernatural event into the historical account. Thus, the Assyrian emperor Sennacherib did in fact conduct a campaign against Judah and neighboring regions toward the end of the seventh century BCE and laid siege against Jerusalem in 601 BCE, then withdrew for reasons that remain uncertain. The author of Kings, however, chooses to represent the lifting of the siege as the result of an act of divine intervention in which the Assyrian army is suddenly stricken with a mysterious plague. This retreat of the Assyrian forces confirms his view that Jerusalem is a divinely protected city, the exclusive place that God has chosen to set his name upon. In this view, it is only the pagan outrages and the murderous practices of King Manasseh that later tip the balance and determine the destruction of Jerusalem.

If the accounts of the kings are by and large historical, the tales of the prophets—preeminently, the cycle of stories about Elijah and Elisha—abound in displays of supernatural powers that set them off not only from the royal history but also from virtually everything that precedes them in the Book of Samuel. Fire is brought down from the heavens to consume a sacrifice in a confrontation with the prophets of Baal; a dead child is revived; a cruse of oil becomes bottomless to provide for a destitute widow; a precious borrowed axehead, sunk in the Jordan, floats to the surface; Elijah does not die but ascends in a chariot of fire to the heavens. In the actual miracle-count, Elisha somewhat surpasses his master Elijah, but it is Elijah who is embraced by later tradition, singled out at the end of Malachi as the man who will announce the coming of the redeemer; serving as a model for the Gospel writers in their stories of the miraculous acts performed by Jesus; and becoming a cherished folk-hero in later Jewish tradition. It is Elijah rather than Elisha who enjoys this vivid afterlife because he is the master, not the disciple, and perhaps also because he is finally the more sympathetic figure of the two—it is hard to forget Elisha's initial act of sending bears to devour the boys who mock him, an event that already caused discomfort among the early rabbis.

The Elijah stories, it should be said, are not only a chronicle of signs and wonders but the representation of a rather arresting character. First we see him in flight, hiding out from Ahab's wrath. Then he shows himself as the iron-willed spokesman of God, denouncing Ahab to his face as "the troubler of Israel." After his triumph over the Baal prophets on Mount Carmel, finding himself nevertheless again mortally threatened by Ahab and Jezebel, he flees to the wilderness where he despairs, asking God, "Enough, now, LORD. Take my life, for I am no better than my fathers" (1 Kings 19:4). But the despair is countered by the epiphany vouchsafed him in the wilderness, and he climbs back from his nadir again to confront Ahab after the judicial murder of Naboth contrived by Jezebel—"Have you murdered and also taken hold?" (1 Kings 21:19).

In all this, as in the Samson stories and elsewhere in the Bible, the folktale fondness for wondrous acts is interfused with a subtle narrative art in which dialogue, cunning patterns of repetition, and intimations of the character's inwardness are impressively deployed. Among all the narratives of monarchs, southern and northern, in the Book of Kings, pride of place is accorded to two characters—King Solomon and Elijah the prophet. Solomon is the embodiment of the regal grandeur of Israel's divinely elected monarchy, and as such great attention is lavished on his wealth, his grand royal enterprises, and his wisdom. He, like Elijah, will survive in later tradition as a figure both unmatched and revered. At the end of his story, he is seen falling away from his high calling, thus providing a rationale for the dividing of the kingdom and, ultimately, for its destruction. Elijah's story ends in a fiery ascent, assuring his future standing as the harbinger of the messiah and the folk-hero who will come to the wretched of his people in their hour of distress.

The compiler who put Kings together for posterity above all sought to provide an account of the nation's history and an explanation of why that history took the course it finally did. The artful crafting of narrative was not one of his conscious aims. The deep-seated storytelling impulse, however, that drives so much biblical narrative manifests itself in this book as well, in some degree in the luminous tales about King Solomon and even more in the cycle of stories marked by confrontation, triumph, and dejection about Elijah the Tishbite.

1 Kings

CHAPTER 1

And King David had grown old, advanced in years, and they covered ₁ him with bedclothes, but he was not warm. And his servants said to him, ₂ "Let them seek out for my lord the king a young virgin, that she may wait upon the king and become his familiar, and lie in your lap, and my lord

---

1. *And King David had grown old.* Although an editor, several centuries after the composition of the story, placed this episode and the next one at the beginning of the Book of Kings, and after the coda of 2 Samuel 21–24, because of the centrality in them of Solomon's succession, they are clearly the conclusion to the David story and bear all the hallmarks of its author's distinctive literary genius. There are strong stylistic links with the previous David narrative; the artful deployment of dialogue and of spatial shifts is very similar; and there are significant connections of phrasing, motif, and theme.

they covered him with bedclothes, but he was not warm. This extraordinary portrait of a human life working itself out in the gradual passage of time, which began with an agile, daring, and charismatic young David, now shows him in the extreme infirmity of old age, shivering in bed beneath his covers.

2. *Let them seek out for my lord the king a young virgin.* The language used by the courtiers recalls that of the mentally troubled Saul's courtiers, "Let them seek out a man skilled in playing the lyre" (2 Samuel 16:16)—the very words that were the prelude to the young David's entrance into the court.

become his familiar. The exact meaning of the Hebrew noun *sokhenet* is uncertain. Some translate it as "attendant" on the basis of the context. The verbal stem from which the word is derived generally has the meaning of "to become accustomed," hence the choice here of "familiar"—of course, in the social sense and not in the secondary sense linked with witchcraft. The only other occurrence of this term in the biblical corpus, Isaiah 22:15, seems to designate a (male) court official.

and lie in your lap. Nathan in his denunciatory parable addressed to David represented the ewe, symbolic of Bathsheba, lying in the poor man's lap (2 Samuel 12:3).

3   the king will be warm." And they sought out a beautiful young woman
through all the territory of Israel, and they found Abishag the Shunamite
4   and brought her to the king. And the young woman was very beautiful,
and she became a familiar to the king and ministered to him, but the
king knew her not.

5   And Adonijah son of Haggith was giving himself airs, saying, "I shall be
king!" And he made himself a chariot and horsemen with fifty men run-
6   ning before him. And his father never caused him pain, saying, "Why
have you done thus?" And he, too, was very goodly of appearance, and
7   him she had borne after Absalom. And he parlayed with Joab son of
Zeruiah and with Abiathar the priest, and they lent their support to

---

4. *the young woman was very beautiful . . . but the king knew her not.* David,
lying in bed with this desirable virgin, but now beyond any thought or capacity
of sexual consummation, is of course a sad image of infirm old age. At the same
time, this vignette of geriatric impotence is a pointed reversal of the Bathsheba
story that brought down God's curse on the house of David, triggering all the
subsequent troubles of dynastic succession. There, too, David was lying in
his bed or couch (*mishkav*, as in verse 47 here), and there, too, he sent out
emissaries to bring back a beautiful young woman to lie with him, though to
antithetical purposes.

5. *was giving himself airs.* The reflexive verb has a root that means to raise up
(hence the King James Version, "exalting himself"). Since a common noun
derived from that verb, *nasi'* means "prince," the reflexive verb might even have
the sense of "acting the part of a prince."
   he made himself a chariot and horsemen with fifty men running before him.
These acts of regal presumption are the same ones carried out by the usurper
Absalom, Adonijah's older brother.

6. *his father never caused him pain.* The obvious sense of the verb in context is
"reprimand." The Septuagint reads "restrained him" (*'atsaro* instead of *'atsavo*),
either because the Greek translators had a better Hebrew version here or were
smoothing out the Hebrew.
   And he, too, was very goodly of appearance. As the second clause of this
sentence makes clear, the "too" refers to Absalom, the son Haggith bore David
before Adonijah.

Adonijah. But Zadok the priest and Benaiah son of Jehoiada and Nathan   8
the prophet and Shimei and Rei and David's warriors were not with
Adonijah. And Adonijah made a sacrificial feast of sheep and oxen and   9
fatlings by the Zoheleth stone which is near Ein-Rogel, and he invited
all his brothers, the king's sons, and all the men of Judah, the king's
servants. But Nathan the prophet and Benaiah and the warriors and   10
Solomon his brother he did not invite.

---

8. *Shimei and Rei.* The Septuagint reads "Shimei and his companions" (*re'aw*
instead of *re'i*).

9. *made a sacrificial feast.* The Hebrew verb *z-b-ḥ* refers both to the sacrifice of the
animals, the greater part of which was kept to be eaten, and to the feast. This is
clearly a ceremonial feast at which the monarchy is to be conferred on Adonijah.

the Zoheleth stone which is near Ein-Rogel. The spring (Hebrew *'ayin*) of
Rogel is within a couple of miles of Jerusalem. The spatial proximity becomes
important later in the story because Adonijah's supporters, after they finish
their feast, are able to hear the shouting from the city. Zoheleth means "creeping thing," which has led some scholars to conjecture that this location was a
sacred site dedicated to the worship of a snake deity.

and all the men of Judah, the king's servants. Like his brother Absalom, Adonijah draws on a base of support from his own tribe, Judah. In political and royal
contexts, the phrase "the king's servants" usually refers to courtiers, members
of the king's inner circle.

10. *But Nathan the prophet and Benaiah.* In keeping with the established convention of biblical narrative, this list of the uninvited and the report of Adonijah's self-coronation feast will be repeated more or less verbatim, with subtle
and significant changes reflecting who the speaker is.

and the warriors. One should remember that Joab, commander of the army,
was not listed in 2 Samuel 23 as a member of "the warriors," David's elite fighting corps. Though few in number, they would have been a formidable counter-
force in a struggle for the throne.

11 And Nathan said to Bathsheba, Solomon's mother, saying, "Have you not heard that Adonijah son of Haggith has become king, and our lord
12 David knows it not? And now, come let me give you counsel that you
13 may save your own life and the life of your son Solomon. Go and get you to King David and say to him, 'Has not my lord the king sworn to your servant, saying: Solomon your son shall be king after me, and he shall
14 sit on my throne. And why has Adonijah become king?' Look, while you are still speaking there, I shall come after you and fill in your words."

---

11. *Bathsheba, Solomon's mother.* After her fatal affair with David, she disappears from the narrative. Now, after some two decades or perhaps more of elapsed time, she resurfaces. Whereas the beautiful young wife was accorded no dialogue except for her report to David of her pregnancy, the mature Bathsheba will show herself a mistress of language—shrewd, energetic, politically astute.

Adonijah . . . has become king, and our lord David knows it not. Fokkelman notes the play on words in the Hebrew between 'Adoniyah ("my lord is Yah") and 'adoneinu ("our lord"). Playing also on the double sense of the Hebrew verb "to know," the writer represents David in a state of both sexual and cognitive impotence: he knows not Abishag and he knows not Adonijah's initiative to assume the throne.

13. *Has not my lord the king sworn to your servant.* The script that Nathan dictates to Bathsheba invokes a central ambiguity, which the writer surely intends to exploit. Perhaps David actually made a private vow to Bathsheba promising that Solomon would succeed him. There is, however, no mention of such a vow anywhere in the preceding narrative, including the report of Solomon's God-favored birth, where one might expect it. This opens up a large, though by no means certain, possibility that Nathan the man of God has invented the vow and enlists Bathsheba's help in persuading the doddering David that he actually made this commitment.

Solomon your son shall be king after me, and he shall sit on my throne. The verse-like parallelism of David's purported vow has the effect of impressing it on memory. It is repeated three times: here by Nathan, then by Bathsheba as she carries out Nathan's orders, then by David, who will make one small but crucial change in the wording of the formula.

14. *fill in your words.* Many translate the Hebrew verb that means "to fill" as "confirm." But in fact what Nathan will do is to complement Bathsheba's speech, adding certain elements and not repeating certain others.

And Bathsheba came to the king in the inner chamber, and the king 15
was very old, with Abishag the Shunamite ministering to the king. And 16
Bathsheba did obeisance and bowed down to the king, and the king
said, "What troubles you?" And she said to him, "My lord, you yourself 17
swore by the LORD your God to your servant, 'Solomon your son shall
be king after me, and he shall sit on my throne.' And now, look, Adoni- 18
jah has become king and my lord the king knows it not. And he has 19
made a sacrificial feast of oxen and fatlings and sheep in abundance
and has invited all the king's sons and Abiathar the priest and Joab
commander of the army, but Solomon your servant he did not invite.

---

15. *the inner chamber.* At an earlier moment, a figure from David's house, Amnon, was seen lying ill (or pretending) while a beautiful woman came to him in the inner chamber.

16. *Bathsheba did obeisance and bowed down to the king.* Whatever the actual relationship between Bathsheba and David at this very late point in his life, it seems reduced to a punctilious observance of palace protocol. In the background, silent, stands the beautiful young Abishag, now the king's bedmate but not really his consort.

17. *My lord, you yourself swore by the* LORD *your God.* Bathsheba edits the script Nathan has given her in two ways: the third-person address to the king is switched to the second person, allowing her to introduce an emphatic, "you yourself" (in the Hebrew the addition of the pronoun *'atah* before the conjugated verb); and the vow is said to have been made solemnly "by the LORD your God." If in fact the vow is a fabrication, perhaps Nathan the prophet was leery of invoking God's name in connection with it.

19. *oxen and fatlings and sheep in abundance.* The last term, "in abundance," is added to the verbal chain from the narrator's initial report of the feast, a small magnification of the scale of the event that Adonijah has staged.

but Solomon your servant he did not invite. Nathan had not incorporated a list of the excluded in his instructions to her. Bathsheba singles out only her own son among the uninvited, but she is careful to identify him to David not as "my son" but as "your servant," emphasizing Solomon's status as loyal subject.

20 And you, my lord the king, the eyes of all Israel are upon you to tell them
21 who will sit on the throne of my lord the king after him. And it will come
about when my lord king lies with his fathers, that I and my son Solo-
22 mon will be held offenders." And, look, she was still speaking with the
23 king when Nathan the prophet came in. And they told the king, saying,
"Here is Nathan the prophet." And he came before the king and bowed
24 to the king, his face to the ground. And Nathan said, "My lord the king,
have you yourself said, 'Adonijah shall be king after me and he shall sit
25 on my throne?' For he has gone down today and made a sacrificial feast
of oxen and fatlings and sheep in abundance, and he has invited all the
king's sons and the commanders of the army and Abiathar the priest, and

---

20. *the eyes of all Israel are upon you to tell them who will sit on the throne.*
Now improvising, Bathsheba uses words that strongly evoke David's authority,
though in fact he has been out of the picture, failing and bedridden.

21. *when my lord the king lies with his fathers . . . I and my son Solomon will be
held offenders.* With admirable tact, she uses a decorous euphemism for dying,
and then expresses her perfectly plausible fear that as king, Adonijah would
take prompt steps to eliminate both her and Solomon. (Compare Nathan's
"save your own life and the life of your son.")

23. *Here is Nathan the prophet.* Nathan in his role as prophet is formally
announced to David by the courtiers. According to biblical convention, there
are no three-sided dialogues. Bathsheba presumably withdraws as soon as she
sees Nathan enter. In verse 28, after the conversation with Nathan, David has
to summon her back. All this takes place not in the throne room but in the
"inner chamber," where David lies in bed.

24. *have you yourself said, 'Adonijah shall be king . . . ?'* Unlike Bathsheba,
Nathan makes no reference to a vow regarding Solomon, presumably because
it would have been a private vow to her. Instead, he refers to observable public
events: have you authorized the succession of Adonijah? He uses the identical
formula for succession that has already twice been attached to Solomon ("shall
be king after me . . . shall sit on my throne").

25. *he has invited all the king's sons and the commanders of the army.* Nathan's
more political version of the unfolding usurpation adds to the list of Adonijah's
supporters the whole officer corps of the army, not just Joab.

there they are eating and drinking before him, and they have said, 'Long live King Adonijah!' But me—your servant—and Zadok the priest and Benaiah son of Jehoiada and Solomon your servant he did not invite. Has this thing been done by my lord the king without informing your servant who will sit on the throne of my lord the king after him?" And King David answered and said, "Call me Bathsheba." And she came before the king and stood before the king. And the king swore and said, "As the LORD lives Who rescued me from every strait, as I swore to you by the LORD God of Israel, saying, 'Solomon your son shall be king after me, and he shall sit on my throne in my stead,' even so will I do this day." And Bath-

26

27

28

29

30

31

Long live King Adonijah! This vivid acclamation of Adonijah's kingship, not reported by the narrator, is calculated to rouse David's ire. The evocation of the coronation feast ("they are eating and drinking before him") is similarly more vivid than Bathsheba's account.

26. *But me—your servant.* Nathan takes pains, in righteous indignation as prophet to the throne, to highlight his own exclusion, at the very beginning of the list.

30. *as I swore to you by the LORD God of Israel.* Whether or not David actually made this vow to Bathsheba, by now he is thoroughly persuaded that he did. Note that he raises Bathsheba's language to still another level of politically efficacious resonance: Nathan had made no mention of God in invoking the vow; Bathsheba had said "you . . . swore by the LORD your God"; David now encompasses the whole national realm in declaring, "as I swore to you by the LORD God of Israel."

he shall sit on my throne in my stead. David introduces a crucial change into the formula for the promise of succession, as Fokkelman shrewdly observes: to the understandable "after me" of the first clause he adds "in my stead," implying not merely that Solomon will succeed him but that Solomon will replace him on the throne while he is still alive. Accordingly, David then proceeds to give instructions for an immediate ceremony of anointment. In the face of Adonijah's virtual coup d'état, David appears to realize that he is no longer physically capable of acting as monarch and protecting himself against usurpation, and that the wisest course is to put his chosen successor on the throne without a moment's delay.

sheba did obeisance, her face to the ground, and bowed to the king and
32 said, "May my lord King David live forever." And David said, "Call to me
Zadok the priest and Nathan the prophet and Benaiah son of Jehoiada."
33 And they came before the king. And the king said to them, "Take with
you your lord's servants and mount Solomon my son on my special mule
34 and bring him down to the Gihon. And Zadok the priest shall anoint
him there, with Nathan the prophet, as king over Israel, and sound the
35 ram's horn and say, 'Long live King Solomon.' And you shall come up
after him, and he shall come and sit on my throne, and he shall be king
after me, him have I charged to be prince over Israel and over Judah."
36 And Benaiah son of Jehoiada answered the king and said, "Amen! May
37 thus, too, say the LORD, my lord the king's God. As the LORD has been
with my lord the king, thus may He be with Solomon and make his
throne even greater than the throne of my lord King David."

---

31. *May my lord King David live forever.* Bathsheba's tact remains flawless.
Now that she has extracted from David exactly the commitment she wanted,
she wishes him, hyperbolically, eternal life, even as he teeters on the edge of
the grave.

33. *your lord's servants.* That is, David's courtiers.
   my special mule. Literally, "the mule that is mine." Seating Solomon on the
royal mule is the first public expression of the conferral of the kingship on him.
   the Gihon. This is a brook just outside the city walls. David enjoins his officials to act rapidly in anointing Solomon while Adonijah's coronation feast is
still under way a couple of miles off.

35. *he shall come and sit on my throne.* This reiterated symbolic statement is
now literalized: after the anointment at the Gihon brook, Solomon is to be
brought to the palace and publicly seated on the throne.
   him have I charged to be prince. The term *nagid*, prince, previously attached
to Saul and now to David, appears for the last time to designate the monarch.
He is to be prince over Judah, where Adonijah has gathered support, as well
as over Israel.

And Zadok the priest, with Nathan the prophet and Benaiah son of 38
Jehoiada and the Cherethites and the Pelethites, went down and
mounted Solomon on King David's mule and led him to the Gihon. And 39
Zadok the priest took the horn of oil from the Tent and anointed Solomon, and they blew the ram's horn and all the people said, "Long live
King Solomon!" And all the people went up after him, and the people 40
were playing flutes and making such revelry that the very earth split
apart with their noise. And Adonijah heard, and all the invited guests 41
who were with him, and they had finished eating, and Joab heard the
sound of the ram's horn and said, "Why this sound of the town in an
uproar?" He was still speaking when, look, Jonathan son of Abiathar the 42
priest came. And Adonijah said, "Come! For you are a valiant fellow and

---

38. *the Cherethites and the Pelethites.* These members of the palace guard of
Philistine origin provide a show of arms for the act of anointing Solomon.

39. *took the horn of oil from the Tent.* The Tent in question is obviously the
cultic site where the Ark of the Covenant is kept—the emphasis is that the oil
of anointment is sanctified oil.

40. *the people were playing flutes and making such revelry that the very earth split
apart with their noise.* This hyperbolic report of the public rejoicing over Solomon's succession to the throne serves two purposes: the tremendous clamor is
so loud that the sound reaches Adonijah and his supporters at Ein-Rogel (verse
41), and it is a vocal demonstration that the choice of Solomon immediately
enjoys extravagant popular support. This latter consideration is crucial for the
politics of the story because it makes clear that Adonijah has no hope of mustering opposition to Solomon.

41. *Adonijah heard, and all the invited guests . . . and Joab heard the sound of the
ram's horn.* As a couple of commentators have noted, Adonijah and his followers
hear only the hubbub from the town, whereas Joab, the military man, picks up
the sound of the *shofar*, the ram's horn. This would be either a call to arms or
the proclamation of a king.

42. *For you are a valiant fellow and you must bear good tidings.* This obvious non
sequitur ominously echoes David's anxious words about Ahimaaz (2 Samuel
18), "he is a good man and with good tidings he must come." Jonathan's very
first word, "alas," shows how mistaken Adonijah is.

43 you must bear good tidings." And Jonathan answered and said to Adoni-
44 jah, "Alas, our lord King David has made Solomon king. And the king
has sent with him Zadok the priest and Nathan the prophet and Benaiah
son of Jehoiada and the Cherethites and the Pelethites, and they have
45 mounted him on the king's mule. And Zadok the priest and Nathan
the prophet have anointed him king at the Gihon, and they have gone
up from there reveling, and the town is in an uproar. This is the sound
46 you heard. And what's more, Solomon is seated on the royal throne.
47 And what's more, the king's servants have come to bless our lord King
David, saying, 'May your God make Solomon's name even better than
your name and make his throne even greater than your throne.' And the
48 king bowed down on his couch. And what's more, thus has the king said,
'Blessed is the LORD God of Israel Who has granted today someone sit-
49 ting on my throne with my own eyes beholding it.'" And all of Adonijah's
50 invited guests trembled and rose up and each man went on his way. And

---

43. *our lord King David has made Solomon king.* Jonathan flatly begins with the
brunt of the bad news, then fleshes out the circumstances to make it all the
worse. He at once identifies David as "our lord," conceding that, after all, David
retains a monarch's authority to determine his successor.

46, 47, 48. *And what's more, Solomon is seated. . . . And what's more, the king's
servants have come. . . . And what's more, thus has the king said.* Jonathan's long,
breathless account of the installation of Solomon as king, with its reiterated
"what's more" (*wegam*), conveys an excited cumulative sense of the chain of
disasters that have destroyed all of Adonijah's hopes. He goes beyond what the
narrator has reported to depict Solomon actually seated on the throne, receiving his father's blessing.

48. *someone sitting on my throne.* Some textual critics propose instead the Masoretic reading "a son sitting on my throne."

49. *each man went on his way.* Terrified, the supporters of Adonijah's claim to
the throne disperse. This moment is reminiscent of the dispersal and flight of
"all the king's sons" from Amnon's feast after Absalom's men murder Amnon.

Adonijah was afraid of Solomon, and he rose up and went off and caught
hold of the horns of the altar. And it was told to Solomon, saying, "Look, 51
Adonijah is afraid of King Solomon and, look, he has caught hold of the
horns of the altar, saying, 'Let King Solomon swear to me today that he
will not put his servant to death by the sword.'" And Solomon said, "If 52
he prove a valiant fellow, not a hair of his will fall to the ground, but if
evil be found in him, he shall die." And King Solomon sent, and they 53
took him down from the altar, and he came and bowed to King Solomon,
and Solomon said to him, "Go to your house."

---

50. *caught hold of the horns of the altar*. The typical construction of ancient
Israelite altars, as archeology has confirmed, featured a curving protuberance at
each of the four corners, roughly like the curve of a ram's horn. The association
of horn with strength may explain this design. Gripping the horns—actually,
probably one horn—of the altar was a plea for sanctuary: at least in principle,
though not always in practice, a person in this posture and in this place should
be held inviolable by his pursuers.

51. *Let King Solomon swear . . . that he will not put his servant to death*. Adonijah, compelled by force majeure, fully acknowledges Solomon's kingship and
his own status as subject in his plea for mercy.

52. *And Solomon said*. Until this point, Solomon has been acted upon by others,
and no dialogue has been assigned to him. Now that he is king, he speaks with
firm authority.
    If he prove a valiant fellow. In immediate context, the force of the idiom
ben ḥayil is obviously something like "a decent fellow." But its usual meaning
is worth preserving because it precisely echoes the term Adonijah addressed
to Jonathan (verse 42), and it also points up ironically that Adonijah now is
trembling with fear.
    if evil be found in him, he shall die. The evil Solomon has in mind would be
further political machinations. He thus does not agree to swear unconditionally,
as Adonijah had pleaded, not to harm his half brother, and he will make due use
of the loophole he leaves himself.

53. *Go to your house*. This injunction concludes the episode on a note of ambiguity. Solomon is distancing Adonijah from the palace. He sends him to the
presumed safety of his own home, or is it to a condition of virtual house arrest?
In any case, Adonijah is surely meant to be kept under surveillance, and Solomon has already put him on warning.

CHAPTER 2

1   And David's time to die grew near, and he charged Solomon his son,
2   saying: "I am going on the way of all the earth. And you must be strong,
3   and be a man. And keep what the LORD your God enjoins, to walk in
    His ways, to keep His statutes, His commands, and His dictates and

---

3.–4. These two relatively long verses are an unusual instance of the intervention of a Deuteronomistic editor in the dialogue of the original David story
that was composed perhaps nearly four centuries before him. The language
here is an uninterrupted chain of verbal formulas distinctive of the Book of
Deuteronomy and its satellite literature: *keep what the* LORD *your God enjoins,
walk in His ways, keep His statutes, His commands, and His dictates and admonitions, so that you may prosper in everything you do and in everything to which you
turn, walk before Me in truth with their whole heart and with their whole being.*
The very mention of the Teaching [*torah*] of Moses is a hallmark of the Deuteronomist, and as phrase and concept did not yet have currency in the tenth
century. The long sentences loaded with synonyms are also uncharacteristic
of the author of the David story, and there is no one in that story—least of all,
David himself—who speaks in this high-minded, long-winded, didactic vein.
Why did the Deuteronomistic editor choose to intervene at this penultimate
point of the David story? It seems very likely that he was uneasy with David's
pronouncing to Solomon a last will and testament worthy of a dying Mafia capo:
be strong and be a man, and use your savvy to pay off all my old scores with my
enemies. In fact, David's deathbed implacability, which the later editor tries to
mitigate by first placing noble sentiments in his mouth, is powerfully consistent
with both the characterization and the imagination of politics in the preceding
narrative. The all too human David on the brink of the grave is still smarting
from the grief and humiliation that Joab's violent acts caused him and from the
public shame Shimei heaped on him, and he wants Solomon to do what he
himself was prevented from doing by fear in the one case and by an inhibiting
vow in the other. In practical political terms, moreover, either Joab, just recently
a supporter of the usurper Adonijah, or Shimei, the disaffected Benjaminite,
might threaten Solomon's hold on power, and so both should be eliminated.

His admonitions, as it is written in the Teaching of Moses, so that you may prosper in everything you do and in everything to which you turn. So that the Lord may fulfill His word that He spoke unto me, saying, 4 'If your sons keep their way to walk before Me in truth with their whole heart and with their whole being, no man of yours will be cut off from the throne of Israel.' And, what's more, you yourself know what Joab 5 son of Zeruiah did to me, what he did to the two commanders of the armies of Israel, Abner son of Ner and Amasa son of Jether—he killed them, and shed the blood of war in peace, and put the blood of war on his belt that was round his waist and on his sandals that were on his feet. And you must act in your wisdom, and do not let his gray head go 6

---

5. *what he did to the two commanders of the armies of Israel.* David is silent about the third murder perpetrated by Joab, and the one that caused him the greatest grief—the killing of Absalom. Perhaps he does not mention it because it was a murder, unlike the other two, that served a reason of state. But it was surely the one act he could not forgive.

shed the blood of war in peace, and put the blood of war on his belt . . . and on his sandals. Both killings were done on the roadway, Joab approaching his victim with gestures of peace. In the case of Abner, his rival had come to make peace with David, and the phrase "went in peace [*shalom*]" was attached to Abner in a triple repetition (2 Samuel 3). In the case of Amasa, Joab's last words to him before stabbing him in the belly were "Is it well [*shalom*] with you, my brother?" (2 Samuel 20). The virtually visual emphasis of blood on belt and sandals recalls in particular the murder of Amasa, who lay in the middle of the road wallowing in blood, while the mention of Joab's belt looks back to his strategem of belting his sword to his waist so that it would fall out when he bent over, to be picked up by his left hand. The reference to Joab's waist and feet conveys an image of a man splashed all over with blood. Beyond this integration of details from the preceding narrative in the words David chooses, the concentration on blood reflects a general belief that blood shed in murder lingers over not only the murderer but also over those associated with the victim like a contaminating miasma until it is "redeemed" or "taken away" by vengeance.

6. *you must act in your wisdom.* The wisdom of Solomon in the subsequent narrative is proverbial, but what David already has in mind here is political shrewdness: Joab is, after all, a formidable adversary, and Solomon will have to choose the right time and place, when Joab is without allies or protection, to dispatch him.

do not let his gray head go down in peace to Sheol. This proverbial phrase is actualized here because we realize that Joab, after half a century as David's

7 down in peace to Sheol. And with the sons of Barzillai the Gileadite
keep faith, and let them be among those who eat at your table, for did
8 they not draw near me when I fled from Absalom your brother? And,
look, with you is Shimei son of Gera the Benjaminite from Bahurim, and
he cursed me with a scathing curse on the day I went to Mahanaim.
And he came down to meet me at the Jordan, and I swore to him by the
9 LORD, saying, 'I will not put you to death by the sword.' And now, do not
hold him guiltless, for you are a wise man, and you will know what you
10 should do to him, and bring his gray head down in blood to Sheol!" And
11 David lay with his fathers and he was buried in the city of David. And
the time that David was king over Israel was forty years—in Hebron he
was king seven years and in Jerusalem he was king thirty-three years.
12 And Solomon sat on the throne of David like his father, and his kingdom
was wholly unshaken.

---

commander—forty regnal years plus several years before that in David's guerilla
band—is now an old man. He who shed the blood of war in peace will not be
allowed to go down in peace to the underworld.

9. *for you are a wise man, and you will know what you should do to him.* In regard
to Shimei, the "wisdom" Solomon must exercise is to find some legal loophole
to obviate his father's vow not to harm the Benjaminite. In the event, Solomon
does this with considerable cleverness. David's vow to Shimei was made at a
moment when it seemed politically prudent to include the man who had cursed
him in what was probably a general amnesty after the suppression of the rebellion. It is understandable that later on David would regret this binding act of
forgiveness to a vile-spirited enemy.
   bring his gray head down in blood to Sheol. Shimei had screamed at the fleeing David, "man of blood." Now David enjoins Solomon to send him to the
netherworld in blood. In his long career, David has had noble moments as well
as affectingly human ones, but it is a remarkable token of the writer's gritty
realism about men in the vindictive currents of violent politics that the very last
words he assigns to David are *bedam She'ol*, "in blood to Sheol."

11. *forty years.* One may assume this is no more than an approximation of
David's regnal span since forty years, as the Book of Judges repeatedly shows,
is a formulaic number for a full reign.

And Adonijah son of Haggith came to Bathsheba, Solomon's mother, 13
and she said, "Do you come in peace?" And he said, "In peace." And he 14
said, "There is something I have to say to you." And she said, "Speak."
And he said, "You yourself know that mine was the kingship, and to me 15
did all Israel turn their faces to be king, yet the kingship was brought
round and became my brother's, for from the LORD was it his. And 16
now, there is one petition I ask of you, do not refuse me." And she said,
"Speak." And he said, "Pray, say to Solomon the king, for he would not 17
refuse you, that he give me Abishag the Shunamite as wife."

---

13. *Adonijah son of Haggith*. The reappearance of Solomon's rival follows hard
upon the report that his kingdom was unshaken, introducing a potential dissonance. Adonijah was not included in David's list of enemies to be eliminated
because he is Solomon's problem, not David's.

Do you come in peace? After Adonijah's attempt to seize the throne that was
then given to her son, Bathsheba is understandably uncertain about Adonijah's
intentions in coming to see her.

15. *You yourself know that mine was the kingship . . . yet the kingship was brought
round and became my brother's, for from the LORD was it his.* Adonijah tries to
have it both ways in his overture to Bathsheba: on the one hand, the kingship really was his, and he enjoyed popular support; on the other hand, he is
prepared to be reconciled with the idea that it was God's determination that
the crown should pass on from him to his brother. There may be a note of
petulance here: Adonijah speaks of his situation as though he deserved some
sort of consolation prize. It will prove a fatal imprudence that he should have
addressed this complaint to the mother of the man he sought to anticipate in
seizing the throne.

17. *that he give me Abishag the Shunamite as wife.* The promotion of fruit-
ful ambiguity through narrative reticence so characteristic of the author of
the David story is never more brilliantly deployed. What is Adonijah really up
to? He approaches Solomon's mother because he thinks she will have special
influence over the king and because he is afraid to go to Solomon himself.
Perhaps, Adonijah imagines, as a mother she will have pity for him and do him
this favor. But in taking this course, Adonijah betrays the most extraordinary
political naivete. Why does he want Abishag? The political motive would be
that by uniting with a woman who had shared the king's bed, though merely
as a bedwarmer, he was preparing the ground for a future claim to the throne.
(The act of his brother Absalom in cohabiting with David's concubines stands

18,19 And Bathsheba said, "Good, I myself shall speak for you to the king." And Bathsheba came to King Solomon to speak to him about Adonijah. And the king arose to greet her and bowed to her and sat down on his throne and set out a throne for the queen mother, and she sat down to his

20 right. And she said, "There is one small petition that I ask of you, do not refuse me." And the king said to her, "Ask, Mother, for I shall not refuse

21 you." And she said, "Let Abishag the Shunamite be given to Adonijah

22 your brother as wife." And King Solomon answered and said to his mother, "And why do you ask Abishag the Shunamite for Adonijah? Ask the kingship for him, as he is my older brother, and Abiathar the priest

---

in the background.) If this motive were transparent, as it turns out to be in Solomon's reading of the request, it would be idiotic for Adonijah to ask for Abishag. Perhaps he feels safe because Abishag was not technically David's consort. Perhaps the political consideration is only at the back of his mind, and he really is seeking consolation in the idea of marrying a beautiful young woman who has, so to speak, a kind of association by contiguity with the throne. In any case, he will pay the ultimate price for his miscalculation.

18. *I myself shall speak for you to the king.* As with Adonijah, there is no explanation of her motive. But given the shrewdness with which Bathsheba has acted in the previous episode, it is entirely plausible that she immediately agrees to do this favor for Adonijah because she quickly realizes what escapes him—that it will prove to be his death sentence, and thus a threat to her son's throne will be permanently eliminated.

19. *and bowed to her.* The Septuagint has "and kissed her" because of the anomaly of a king's bowing to his subject.

20. *There is one small petition that I ask of you.* In accordance with the established convention of biblical narrative, she uses the very same words Adonijah has spoken to her, adding only the adjective "small." This is just a tiny request, she appears to say, full knowing that Solomon is likely to see it, on the contrary, as a huge thing—a device that could be turned into a ladder to the throne on which Solomon sits. One should note that this whole large narrative begins when a woman who is to become a mother (Hannah) puts forth a petition (*she'eilah*, the same word used here).

22. *as he is my older brother, and Abiathar . . . and Joab . . . are for him.* If he makes the dead king's consort his wife, that, together with the fact that he is my elder and has powerful supporters in the court, will give him a dangerously

and Joab son of Zeruiah are for him." And King Solomon swore by the 23
LORD, saying, "Thus may God do to me and even more, for at the cost
of his life has Adonijah spoken this thing! And now, as the LORD lives, 24
Who seated me unshaken on the throne of David my father, and Who
made me a house just as He had spoken, today shall Adonijah be put to
death." And King Solomon sent by the hand of Benaiah son of Jehoiada, 25
and he stabbed him and he died. And to Abiathar the priest did the 26
king say, "Go to Anathoth to your own fields, for you are a doomed
man, but on this day I shall not put you to death, for you bore the Ark
of the LORD God before David my father and you suffered through all
that my father suffered." And Solomon banished Abiathar from being 27
priest to the LORD, so as to fulfill the word of the LORD that He spoke
concerning the house of Eli at Shiloh.

---

strong claim to the throne. In the Hebrew, the second clause appears to say
"and for him and for Abiathar . . . and for Joab," which makes little sense, and
so the small emendation, deleting the second and third occurrence of "for" (a
single-letter prefix in the Hebrew), is presumed in the translation.

26. *to Abiathar the priest*. Throughout this episode centering on Adonijah, Solomon shows himself to be decisive, emphatic, and ruthless—a worthy son of his
father. The moment he hears of Adonijah's pretentions to the late king's nurse/
bedmate, he orders him to be killed immediately. He then proceeds to remove
from office and banish the key priestly supporter of Adonijah, and he will go on
to deal with Joab as well.

on this day I shall not put you to death. There is a veiled threat in this formulation: right now I shall not kill you, and in any case you had better stay away
from Jerusalem on the farm at Anathoth.

*for you bore the Ark of the LORD . . . and you suffered through all that my father
suffered*. Solomon is circumspect in not ordering the execution of a priest—in
sharp contrast to Saul, who thought he might protect his kingship from a perceived threat by massacring a whole town of priests who he imagined were
allied with his rival. Solomon also honors the fact that Abiathar has shared
many years of danger and hardship with David, and during that time never
betrayed David, as Joab did.

27. *so as to fulfill the word of the LORD . . . concerning the house of Eli*. One sees
how this chapter concludes a grand narrative that begins in 1 Samuel 1, and is
not merely the end of a supposedly independent Succession Narrative.

28 And the news reached Joab, for Joab had sided with Adonijah, though with Absalom he had not sided, and Joab fled to the Tent of the LORD,
29 and he grasped the horns of the altar. And it was told to the king that Joab had fled to the Tent of the LORD, and there he was by the altar,
30 and Solomon sent Benaiah son of Jehoiada, saying, "Go, stab him." And Benaiah came to the Tent of the LORD and said to him, "Thus says the king, 'Come out.'" And he said, "No, for here I shall die." And Benaiah brought back word to the king, saying, "Thus did Joab speak and thus did he answer me." And the king said, "Do as he has spoken, and stab
31 him and bury him, and you shall take away the blood that Joab shed for no cause, from me and from my father's house. And the LORD will bring
32 back his blood guilt on his own head, for he stabbed two men more righteous and better than himself and he killed them by the sword,

---

28. *And the news reached Joab . . . and Joab fled to the Tent of the* LORD. With Adonijah dead and Abiathar banished, Joab realizes that all who remain from the recent anti-Solomon alliance have been isolated and cut off. This relentlessly political general recognizes that he has no power base left to protect him against the resolute young king. He has only the desperate last remedy of seeking sanctuary at the altar.

30. *Thus says the king, 'Come out.'* Solomon's blunt order was simply to stab Joab, but Benaiah, steely executioner though he has shown himself, is loath to kill a man clinging to the altar, and so he directs Joab to come down out of the Tent of the LORD.

31. *stab him and bury him.* Solomon's command is to take Joab's life in the very place of sanctuary ("for here shall I die"), a decision that is in accordance with biblical law: "And should a man scheme against his fellow man to kill him in cunning, from My altar you shall take him to die" (Exodus 21:14). But Solomon also enjoins Benaiah to see to it that Joab, who was after all a stalwart soldier and once David's boon companion, should have a proper burial and not be thrown to the scavengers of sky and earth—the ultimate indignity in ancient Mediterranean cultures.

32. *for he stabbed two men more righteous and better than himself . . . unbeknownst to my father David.* Solomon in his "wisdom" has thus used the purported renewal of the Adonijah conspiracy to carry out the will of vengeance his father conveyed to him, and for the precise reasons David stipulated.

unbeknownst to my father David—Abner son of Ner, commander of
the army of Israel, and Amasa son of Jether, commander of the army of
Judah. And their blood will come back on the head of Joab and on the 33
head of his seed forever, but for David and his seed and his house and
his throne there will be peace evermore from the LORD." And Benaiah 34
son of Jehoiada went up and stabbed him and put him to death, and he
was buried at his home in the wilderness. And the king put Benaiah son 35
of Jehoiada in his stead over the army, and Zadok the priest did the king
put instead of Abiathar.

And the king sent and called to Shimei and said to him, "Build yourself 36
a house in Jerusalem and dwell in it, and do not go out from there hither

---

33. *their blood will come back on the head of Joab and on the head of his seed.* The
miasma of blood guilt settles on the house of Joab for all time: a curse on the
house of Joab was not part of David's injunction, but perhaps Solomon means
to ward off any prospect that resentful descendants of Joab will seek to marshal
forces against the Davidic line.

   but for David and his seed and his house there will be peace evermore. There
is an emphatic contrast between permanent blessing on the line of David and
an everlasting curse on the line of Joab, with "peace" counterpointed to "blood,"
as in verse 5.

34. *he was buried at his home in the wilderness.* This notation has puzzled commentators because one would assume that Joab's home (like David's original
home) was in the town of Bethlehem. The Hebrew for "wilderness," *midbar*,
has the basic meaning of uninhabited terrain, and it is not improbable that Joab
would have had a kind of hacienda removed from the town. Nevertheless, the
report of Joab's burial in the wilderness concludes his story on a haunting note.
That resonance has been nicely caught by the medieval Hebrew commentator Gersonides: "he was buried in the wilderness, which was the home fitting
for him, for it would not be meet for a man like him to be part of civil society
[*lihyot medini*] because he had killed men by devious means and by deception."

37 and yon. For should you cross the Wadi Kidron, on the very day you go
    out, you must surely know that you are doomed to die, your blood will
38 be on your own head." And Shimei said to the king, "The thing is good.
    Even as my lord the king has spoken, so will his servant do." And Shimei
39 dwelled in Jerusalem a long while. And it happened at the end of three
    years that two of Shimei's slaves ran away to Achish son of Maacah, king
    of Gath, and they told Shimei, saying, "Look, your slaves are in Gath."
40 And Shimei arose and saddled his donkey and went to Gath, to Achish,
    to seek his slaves, and Shimei went and brought his slaves from Gath.
41 And it was told to Solomon that Shimei had gone from Jerusalem and
42 had come back. And the king sent and called Shimei and said to him,
    "Did I not make you swear by the LORD and warn you, saying, 'The day

---

37. *should you cross the Wadi Kidron*. This brook runs at the foot of Jerusalem
to the east, and Shimei would have to cross it to go back to his native village
of Bahurim.

    Your blood will be on your own head. Again, behind these words lies the
spectacle of Shimei reviling David with the epithet "man of blood" and asking
that the blood of the house of Saul come down on his head.

38. *The thing is good*. Shimei has no alternative but to agree—better virtual
confinement in the capital city than death.

40. *Shimei arose and saddled his donkey and went to Gath . . . to seek his slaves*.
According to several ancient Near Eastern codes (though not Israelite law),
authorities were obliged to return a runaway slave. Evidently, by this point
peaceful relations obtained between Israel and the Philistine cities. Lulled into
a false sense of security by the passage of three years ("a long while"), Shimei
may be allowing his cupidity for recovering lost property to override the concern
he should have preserved about Solomon's injunction not to leave Jerusalem.
Or he may be a bad reader of Solomon's oral text, construing the ban on crossing the Wadi Kidron as implicit permission to leave the city temporarily in the
opposite direction, so long as he does not try to return to his hometown.

42. *Did I not make you swear by the LORD*. In the actual report, only Solomon
swore (the Septuagint supplies an oath for Shimei), though perhaps Shimei's
taking a solemn oath is implied in verse 38.

    The thing is good. I do hear it. Solomon adds "I do hear it" (*shamaʻti*) to the
actual report in verse 38 of Shimei's words, in order to emphasize that Shimei
gave full and knowing assent to Solomon's terms. Fokkelman notes that there
is a pun on Shimei's own name—*Shimʻi/shamaʻti*.

you go out and move about hither and yon, you must surely know that you are doomed to die,' and you said to me, 'The thing is good. I do hear it.' And why have you not kept the Lord's oath and the command 43 with which I charged you?" And the king said to Shimei, "You yourself 44 know all the evil, which your own heart knows, that you did to David my father, and the Lord has brought back your evil on your own head. But King Solomon shall be blessed and the throne of David shall be 45 unshaken before the Lord forevermore." And the king charged Benaiah 46 son of Jeohaiada, and he went out and stabbed him, and he died.

And the kingdom was unshaken in Solomon's hand.

---

43. *And why have you not kept the Lord's oath.* Here, then, is Solomon's wisdom in carrying out his father's will: he has set Shimei up, waiting patiently until he violates the oath, which then frees Solomon of any obligation lingering from David's earlier oath to do no harm to Shimei.

45. *But King Solomon shall be blessed.* As in the killing of Joab, the imprecation pronounced over the doomed man is balanced by the invocation of the Lord's perpetual blessing on the house of David.

46. *And the kingdom was unshaken in Solomon's hand.* This seemingly formulaic notice at the very end of the story is a last touch of genius by that unblinking observer of the savage realm of politics who is the author of the David story: Solomon's power is now firmly established, blessed by the God Who has promised an everlasting covenant with David and his descendants; but the immediately preceding actions undertaken so decisively and so shrewdly by the young king involve the ruthless elimination of all potential enemies. The solid foundations of the throne have been hewn by the sharp daggers of the king's henchmen.

CHAPTER 3

1 And Solomon became son-in-law to Pharaoh king of Egypt, and he took Pharaoh's daughter and brought her to the city of David till he could finish building his house and the house of the LORD and the wall of Jeru-
2 salem all around. But the people were sacrificing on the high places, for a
3 house had not been built for the LORD as yet in those days. And Solomon loved the LORD, going by the statutes of David his father, but on the
4 high places he was sacrificing and burning incense. And the king went to Gibeon to sacrifice there, for it was a great high place—a thousand

---

1. *And Solomon became son-in-law to Pharaoh.* The Hebrew verb, though it involves marriage, indicates an establishment of relationship between the groom and the father of the bride. The marriage is thus politically motivated and will be the first of many such unions for Solomon in his effort to consolidate the mini-empire created by his father.

took. This ordinary verb often has the force of "marry," as here.

2. *But the people were sacrificing on the high places.* Since the temple was not yet built, there was no alternative to these local altars on hilltops. But the notation reveals the unease of the Deuteronomist with a moment when both the people and Solomon himself offered sacrifices at sites other than the center of the cult in Jerusalem. The strong presence of the Deuteronomist and the shift that reveals itself in the subsequent passages to a different kind of narrative suggest that the book has now moved on from the David story to the work of very different writers.

3. *Solomon loved the LORD.* This is not said of David. There may be a play on Solomon's other name, Jedidiah, which means friend, or lover (though different from the verb used here) of the LORD.

4. *for it was a great high place.* Evidently, the altar at Gibeon was much larger than the one Solomon had available in Jerusalem, hence his move to Gibeon to offer a huge sacrifice.

burnt offerings would Solomon offer up on that altar. In Gibeon did the 5
LORD appear to Solomon in a night dream, and God said, "Ask. What
shall I give you?" And Solomon said, "You Yourself did great kindness 6
with Your servant David my father, as he walked in Your presence in
truth and in justice and in the heart's rightness with You. And You kept
for him this great kindness and gave him a son sitting on his throne to
this day. And now, O LORD my God, You Yourself made Your servant 7
king in place of my father when I was a young lad, not knowing how to
lead into the fray. And Your servant was in the midst of Your people that 8
You chose, a multitudinous people that could not be numbered and
could not be counted for all its multitude. May You give Your servant 9
an understanding heart to discern between good and evil, for who can
judge this vast people of Yours?" And the thing was good in the eyes 10
of the LORD that Solomon had asked for this thing. And God said to 11
him, "In as much as you have asked for this thing and you did not ask
long life for yourself and did not ask wealth for yourself and did not ask
for the life of your enemies, but you asked to discern and understand
justice, look, I am doing according to your words. Look, I give you a 12

---

5. *a night dream.* This is a lesser form of divine revelation, one even vouchsafed
the pagan king Abimelech (Genesis 20). In the David story, God calls upon
Nathan the prophet in a night vision, but it is Nathan as intermediary who then
goes to deliver the message to David (2 Samuel 7).

6. *David my father . . . walked in Your presence in truth and in justice.* The
words assigned here to Solomon adopt the Deuteronomist's revisionist portrait
of David (see the comment on 2:3–4) as an exemplary servant of God. The
actual representation of David gives us a much more mixed picture of the man
with all his calculations of power and his weaknesses and moral failings.

7. *not knowing how to lead into the fray.* The account of Solomon's reign does
not represent him as a military leader combating surrounding nations, but in
assuming the throne he does have dangerous enemies in the court who could
have contested the succession.

9. *May You give Your servant an understanding heart.* Solomon's legendary
wisdom is here given a divine etiology: it is the one gift he asks of God, and it
is granted.

　　vast. Elsewhere this term usually means "heavy."

wise and discerning heart, so that your like there will not have been
13 before you, and after you none like you shall arise. And even what you
did not ask I give to you—both wealth and honor, so that there will not
14 have been any man like you among kings all your days. And if you go in
My ways, to keep My statutes and My commands, as David your father
15 went, I shall grant you length of days." And Solomon awoke and, look,
it was a dream. And he came to Jerusalem and stood before the ark of
the Lord's covenant and offered up burnt offerings and prepared well-
16 being sacrifices and made a feast for all his servants. Then two whore-
17 women did come to the king and stood in his presence. And the one
woman said, "I beseech you, my lord. I and this woman live in a single
18 house, and I gave birth alongside her in the house. And it happened on
the third day after I gave birth that this woman, too, gave birth, and we
were together, no stranger was with us in the house, just the two of us

---

13. *wealth and honor, so that there will not have been any man like you among
kings.* This statement, of course, is a fantastic exaggeration because the head
of a small kingdom like Israel could scarcely compare with the monarchs who
commanded the great empires to the east and the south. Solomon, quite unlike
David, is manifestly woven out of the stuff of legend in this literary account.

16. *Then two whore-woman.* The introduction of the story with "then," 'az, is
unusual in Hebrew narrative. It clearly serves to mark a direct link with the
preceding episode: the gift of wisdom that God has granted Solomon will now
be exemplified in this tale.

    stood in his presence. A primary function of the monarch, in the Bible and
in the Ugaritic texts before it, is to administer justice, and so the two whores
come before him to make their case against each other.

17. *a single house . . . gave birth alongside her in the house.* The repetition of
"house" (which recurs still again twice in the next verse) both underlines the
idea of their sharing quarters and reflects the style of this story, which abounds
in symmetrical repetitions. It may not be coincidental that the larger narrative
of Solomon begins (verse 1) by twice using the same word, "house."

18. *no stranger was with us.* There are therefore no witnesses.

in the house. And this woman's son died during the night, as she had 19
lain upon him. And she rose in the middle of the night and took my son 20
from by me, your servant being asleep, and she laid him in her lap, and
her dead son she laid in my lap. And I rose in the morning to nurse my 21
son, and, look, he was dead, and when I examined him in the morning,
look, he was not my son whom I had borne." And the other woman 22
said, "No, for my son is the living one and your son is dead." And the
other said, "No, for your son is dead and my son is the living one." And
they spoke before the king. And the king said, "This one says, 'This is 23
my live son and your son is dead,' and this one says, 'No, for your son
is dead and my son is the living one.'" And the king said, "Fetch me a 24
sword." And they brought a sword before the king. And the king said, 25
"Cut the living child in two, and give half to one and half to the other."

---

19. *as she had lain upon him.* There is thus a suggestion that the mother of
the dead child may have been negligent, and at any rate she was inadvertently
responsible for her infant's death.

22. *"No, for my son . . . And the other said, "No, for your son."* This inter-echoing
dialogue, heightened by the fact that neither woman is given a name, underscores the seeming undecidability of the case: each is saying exactly the same
thing, so how can anyone know which one is lying? Solomon's repetition of their
words in the next verse amplifies this effect.

25. *Cut the living child in two.* This momentarily shocking decree, which then
will be seen to be a manifestation of Solomon's wisdom, is a clear expression of
the fabulous or folktale character of the whole story. There is an approximate
equivalent of the Judgment of Solomon in Indian literature that some scholars
think may even have been its ultimate source, reaching ancient Israel through
oral transmission. In any case, it sounds very much like a tale of surprising
wisdom told among the people, or perhaps among many peoples, that was
eventually attributed to Solomon.

26 And the woman whose son was alive said to the king, for her compassion welled up for her son, and she said, "I beseech you, my lord, give her the living newborn but absolutely do not put him to death." And the other
27 was saying, "Neither mine nor yours shall he be. Cut him apart!" And the king spoke up and said, "Give her the living newborn, and absolutely
28 do not put him to death. She is his mother." And all Israel heard of the judgment that the king had judged, and they held the king in awe, for they saw that God's wisdom was within him to do justice.

---

26. *Neither mine nor yours will he be.* Finally, the bewildering symmetry between the two women is shattered, and the false mother reveals herself.

Cut him apart. This plural imperative is a single word in the Hebrew, *gezoru* ("cut"), exposing the brutal lack of maternal feeling of the lying woman.

28. *for they saw that God's wisdom was within him.* This concluding flourish confirms that God's promise to Solomon of a discerning heart has been amply realized.

CHAPTER 4

And Solomon was king over all Israel.   1
And these are the names of the officials he had: 2
Azariah son of Zadok the priest.
Elihoreph and Ahijah sons of Shisha, scribes.   3
Jehoshaphat son of Ehilud, recorder.
And Benaiah son of Jehoiada, over the army.   4
And Zadok and Abiathar, priests.
And Azariah son of Nathan, over the prefects.   5

---

1. *And Solomon was king over all Israel.* This declaration of his sovereignty over the entire nation prefaces the catalogue of his royal bureaucracy.

2. *And these are the names of the officials he had.* Everything that follows in this chapter is another indication of the composite character of the Solomon narrative. First we have the story of his ascent to the throne, which is actually the last episode of the David story and manifestly written by its brilliant author. Then we are given the report of Solomon's dream-vision in which he asks for the gift of wisdom, which is followed by the folktale of Solomon's Judgment, illustrating the exercise of that wisdom. Now we are presented with two documents listing the royal bureaucracy. The first lists the members of his cabinet in the Jerusalem court, and the second the prefects overseeing the sundry regions of the country and making sure each supplies its due provision—a form of taxation—to the royal court. Both these sections may be old documents, though there are at least a few seemingly scrambled entries and probably some later additions.
    son of Zadok. Zadok is the priest who sided with Solomon in his struggle for the throne. Not surprisingly, several of the members of the king's inner circle listed here are either his supporters, or the sons of his supporters, in that struggle.

4. *Benaiah.* He is the man Solomon sent to kill Joab.

And Zabud son of Nathan the priest, the king's companion.

6   And Ahishar, over the house,
and Adoniram son of Abda, over the forced labor.

7 And Solomon had twelve prefects over all Israel, and they provisioned
the king and his household—one month in a year each one had to pro-
8 vision. And these were their names: Ben-Hur, in the high country of
9 Ephraim. Ben-Deker, in Makaz and in Shaalbim and Beth-Shemesh and
10 Elon-Beth-Hanan. Ben-Hesed, in Arubboth, his was Socho and all the
11 land of Hepher. Ben-Abinadab, all Naphath-Dor. Taphath daughter of
12 Solomon became his wife. Baana son of Ahilud, Taanach and Megiddo
and all Beth-She'an, which is by Zarethon below Jezreel, from Beth-
She'an as far as Abel-Meholah, as far as the other side of Jokneam.
13 Ben-Geber, in Ramoth-Gilead. His were the hamlets of Jair son of
Manasseh that were in Bashan. His was the region of Argob which is
14 in Bashan, sixty great towns with walls and bronze bolts. Ahinadab son
15 of Iddo, at Mahanaim. Ahimaaz in Naphtali. He, too, took a daughter
16 of Solomon, Bosmath, as wife. Baanah son of Hushi, in Asher and
17,18 Bealoth. Jehoshaphat son of Paruah, in Issachar. Shimei son of Ela in
19 Benjamin. Geber son of Uri, in the land of Gilead, the land of Shihor
king of the Amorites and Og king of Bashan. And one prefect who was

---

6. *forced labor.* Conscripted labor on behalf of the king was another instrument
of taxation.

8. *Ben-Hur.* An oddity of the list of prefects is that many names are given with
patronymic only and no first name.

19. *And one prefect who was in the land of Judah.* The Masoretic text reads
"And one prefect who was in the land." The next verse then begins "Judah and
Israel were multitudinous." That division of the text is problematic for two
reasons: it is unclear what a prefect "in the land," with no specified territory to
supervise, would be doing; beginning a new sentence without an introductory
"and" (simply, "Judah") diverges from the norm of biblical narrative style. The
assumption of this translation is that in addition to the twelve prefects named,
there was to be a thirteenth prefect, perhaps designated ad hoc by the king,
over the king's own tribal territory, which would also be obliged to make an
annual contribution to the court.

in the land of Judah. And Israel was multitudinous as the sand of the   20
sea in multitude, eating and drinking and rejoicing.

---

20. *eating and drinking and rejoicing*. The last term of this series could also
mean "making merry." Although all the regions of the country have to make
annual contributions to the court, the implication of this verse is that the pros-
perity—contrary to Samuel's dire warnings about the monarchy in 1 Samuel
8—was shared by the entire country as its population swelled.

CHAPTER 5

1 And Solomon ruled over all the kingdoms from the River to the land of the Philistines and as far as the border of Egypt. They offered 2 tribute and served Solomon all the days of his life. And Solomon's fare for a single day was thirty *kors* of fine flour and sixty *kors* of plain flour, 3 ten fatted oxen and twenty pasture-fed oxen and a hundred sheep, 4 besides deer and gazelle and roebuck and fatted geese. For he held sway over all that was west of the River from Tiphsah as far as Gaza, over all the kings west of the River. And he had peace on all sides 5 round about. And Judah and Israel dwelled secure, each man under his vine and under his fig tree, from Dan to Beersheba, all the days of 6 Solomon. And Solomon had forty thousand horse stalls for his chari-7 ots and twelve thousand horsemen. And those prefects provisioned King Solomon and all who were adjoined to King Solomon's table,

---

1. *ruled . . . offered.* The Hebrew uses a participial form of the verb, suggesting sustained activity over an extended time-span.

2. *fare.* The literal sense is "bread," a synecdoche for all kinds of food, and the list that follows includes meat and fowl.

   kors. The *kor* is a large measure, so thirty *kors* would have been hundreds of pounds.

3. *geese.* In modern Hebrew, *barbur* means "swan," but swans were rare in ancient Israel, and the likely fowl is the goose.

4. *the River.* As throughout the Bible, this means the Euphrates. It is highly unlikely that all the kingdoms to the east as far as the Euphrates could have been subject to Solomon.

each one for his month, they let nothing lack. And they would bring 8
the barley and the straw for the horses and for the chargers to the place
where each was, each man according to his regimen. And God gave very 9
great wisdom and discernment to Solomon and breadth of understanding like the sand that is on the shore of the sea. And Solomon's wisdom 10
was greater than the wisdom of all the easterners and all the wisdom
of Egypt. And he was wiser than all men, than Ethan the Ezrahite and 11
Heman and Calcol and Darda, the sons of Mahol, and his fame was
in all the nations round about. And he spoke three thousand proverbs, 12
and his poems came to five thousand. And he spoke of the trees, from 13
the cedar that is in Lebanon to the moss that springs from the wall, and
he spoke of beasts and birds and creeping things and fish. And from all 14
peoples they came to listen to Solomon's wisdom, from all the kings of
the earth who had heard of his wisdom.

---

10. *greater than the wisdom of all the easterners and all the wisdom of Egypt.*
Wisdom was a known international activity, and both Mesopotamia and Egypt
were renowned for their wisdom schools, their achievements in astronomy,
mathematics, and much else. Here the celebration of Solomon's unmatched
wisdom is properly referred to the broad Near Eastern context.

11. *Ethan . . . and Heman and Calcol and Darda.* The first two are temple poets
to whom, respectively, Psalm 88 and Psalm 89 are attributed, and the last two
are mentioned in 1 Chronicles 2:6 as temple choristers. The link between
wisdom and the fashioning of poetry or song is a commonly shared assumption
in the ancient Near East.

12. *proverbs.* The proverb was thought of as a quintessential expression of
wisdom, a notion evident in the Book of Proverbs, attributed by tradition to Solomon, in part because of this passage. The proverb was formulated in verse, and
other kinds of poetry as well are supposed to have been composed by Solomon.

13. *trees . . . beasts . . . birds . . . creeping things . . . fish.* Solomon's wisdom
includes a mastery of the whole realm of nature. The words here gave rise to
later legends that Solomon was able to speak the language of animals.

15 And Hiram king of Tyre sent his servants to Solomon, for he had heard
that they had anointed him king in his father's stead, for Hiram was
16 friendly toward David always. And Solomon sent to Hiram, saying.
17 "You yourself knew of David my father that he could not build a house
for the LORD his God because of the fighting that was all round him,
18 until the LORD should set them under his footsoles. And now, the
LORD my God has granted me rest all around. There is no adversary
19 nor evil chancing. And I am about to build a house for the name of the
LORD my God as the LORD spoke to David my father, saying, 'Your son
whom I put in your stead on your throne, he shall build the house for
20 My name. And now, charge that they cut down cedars from Lebanon,
and my servants will be with your servants, and the wages of your
servants I shall give you, whatever you say, for you yourself know that
there is no man among us who knows how to cut down trees like the

---

15. *Hiram king of Tyre.* Tyre is the principal city on the Phoenician coast.

Hiram was friendly toward David always. These words may reflect an actual
historical alliance. It was David who subdued the Philistines, the great enemies
of the Phoenicians on the Mediterranean coast, and that victory might conceivably have enabled the commercial and colonial impetus enjoyed by Phoenicia
in the tenth century BCE.

17. *should set them under his footsoles.* This posture of subjugation appears in
quite a few ancient Near Eastern bas-reliefs celebrating the victory of a king.

20. *my servants will be with your servants.* This proposal of joint labor may have
been motivated by a desire to expedite the costly work. Hiram doesn't mention
it in his response, perhaps because he is not enthusiastic about the idea, but
verse 27 reports that ten thousand Israelite workers were sent each month to
Lebanon.

no man among us . . . knows how to cut down trees like the Sidonians. Sidon
is another Phoenician city, and "Sidonians" is often used as a general term for
Phoenicians. It is in their territory that there are large stands of timber, which
they used to build ships and as a valuable export, and so they were experienced
lumberjacks.

Sidonians." And it happened when Hiram heard Solomon's words that 21
he greatly rejoiced, and he said, "Blessed is the LORD today, that He
has given David a wise son over this large people." And Hiram sent 22
to Solomon, saying, "I have heard what you sent to me. I will meet all
you desire in cedar wood and in cypress wood. My servants will come 23
down from Lebanon to the sea, and I will turn the wood into rafts in
the sea, to the place that you will tell me, and I will break it up there
and you will bear it off. And you on your part will meet my desire to
provide the bread of my house." And so Hiram gave to Solomon cedar 24
trees and cypress trees, all he desired. And Solomon gave to Hiram 25
twenty thousand *kors* of wheat as provision for his house and twenty
thousand *kors* of fine-pressed oil. Thus would Solomon give to Hiram
year after year. And the LORD had given wisdom to Solomon as He had 26

---

21. *when Hiram heard Solomon's words.* A possible though not necessary inference from this formulation is that Solomon's message was oral, but the emissary
or a courtier might have read out a written message to the king.

he greatly rejoiced. He has good reason to rejoice because he sees here the
opportunity for a lucrative agreement. The words that immediately follow are
his exclamation and not part of his message in response to Solomon.

23. *My servants will come down from Lebanon to the sea.* They will take charge
of transporting the timber from the mountainsides to the seashore.

the wood. This word is added in the translation for clarity. The Hebrew says
"them," a plural accusative suffix referring to "the trees."

turn the wood into rafts. Binding the cut logs together into improvised rafts
is a widespread device for transporting timber by water.

meet my desire to provide the bread of my house. Solomon had offered to pay
the wages of Hiram's workers. Hiram now counters this proposal by stipulat-
ing a much higher price—the cost of provisions for the Phoenician court with
all its entourage for the entire period in which the labor is done. In this whole
exchange, there is an element of canny bargaining reminiscent of the negotiations over a gravesite between Abraham and Ephron the Hittite in Genesis 25.

25. *twenty thousand* kors *of wheat . . . twenty thousand* kors *of fine-pressed oil.*
The price exacted, one notes, is very high. Solomon provides wheat and olive
oil, which the Land of Israel had in abundance. The mountainous terrain of
Lebanon did not favor the cultivation of these crops but was ideally suited for
timber, which Israel lacked.

spoken to him. And there was peace between Hiram and Solomon,
27 and the two sealed a pact. And King Solomon exacted forced labor
28 from all Israel, and the forced labor came to thirty thousand men. And
he sent them to Lebanon—ten thousand a month, by turns they were
a month in Lebanon and two months at his house. And Adoniram was
29 over the forced labor. And Solomon had seventy thousand porters and
30 eighty thousand quarriers in the mountains, besides Solomon's prefect
officers who were over the labor, three thousand three hundred, who
31 held sway over the people doing the labor. And the king gave the order,
and they moved great stones, costly stones, for the foundation of the
32 house, hewn stones. And Solomon's builders and Hiram's builders and
the Gebalites carved and readied the timber and the stones to build
the house.

---

31. *they moved great stones.* The stones, of course, would have been a much
bigger challenge to transport than the wood, which was floated most of the
way, but there were quarries in the Judean mountains not far from Jerusalem.

32. *And Solomon's builders and Hiram's builders and the Gebalites.* It emerges
that there was a blended labor force of Phoenicians and Israelites both in Lebanon and in Jerusalem. The Gebalites are residents of the Phoenician town
of Gebal. One may infer from the separate reference to them here that they
constituted a kind of guild with special building skills, perhaps as stonemasons.

CHAPTER 6

And it happened in the four hundred and eightieth year after the 1
Israelites came out of Egypt, in King Solomon's fourth year in the
month of Ziv, which is the second month, that he set out to build a
house to the LORD. And the house that King Solomon built was sixty 2
cubits in length and twenty in width and thirty cubits in height. And 3
the outer court that was in front of the great hall of the house was
twenty cubits in length along the width of the house, ten cubits in
width along the house. And he made inset and latticed windows for 4

---

1. *the four hundred and eightieth year.* This is a manifestly schematic figure, produced by multiplying two formulaic numbers, forty and twelve. In fact, the number of years from the exodus to the building of the temple would be not much more than half 480.

in the month of Ziv. This name for the second month, which would roughly correspond to May, is borrowed from the Phoenician, and that may be why an explanatory gloss is added, "which is the second month." The term for month is also not the standard term, *ḥodesh*, but rather *yareaḥ* (literally, "moon"). *Ziv* means "brilliance," "bright light."

2. *sixty cubits.* This would be less than 120 feet, perhaps as little as 100 feet, which makes Solomon's temple a relatively intimate structure—the Chartres cathedral is three times as long, and the great mosque at Cordova, before its conversion into a church, still larger. These dimensions may be historically accurate.

4. *he made inset and latticed windows for the house.* The reader should be warned that the precise meaning of these and other architectural terms here is uncertain. Because of the perennial fascination with Solomon's temple, many elaborate attempts to reconstruct its exact configuration have been made, in analytic descriptions, drawings, and scale models, but all of these remain highly

5 the house. And he built on the wall of the house a balcony all around
    the walls of the house in the great hall and in the sanctuary, and he
6 made supports all around. And the lowest balcony was five cubits
    in width and the middle one six cubits in width and the third one
    seven cubits in width, for he set recesses in the house all around on
7 the outside so as to fasten nothing to the walls of the house. And the
    house when it was built, of whole stones brought from the quarry it
    was built, and no hammers nor axes nor any iron tools were heard in
8 the house when it was built. The entrance at the middle support was
    on the right side of the house, and on spiral stairs they would go up
9 to the middle chamber and from the middle to the third. And he built
    the house and finished it, and he paneled the house with cedar beams
10 and boards. And he built the balcony over all the house, five cubits
11 in height, and it held the house fast in cedar wood. And the word of
12 the LORD came to Solomon, saying: "This house that you build—if
    you walk by My statutes and do My laws and keep all My commands
    to walk by them, I shall fulfill My word with you that I spoke to
13 David your father, and I shall dwell in the midst of the Israelites, and

---

conjectural. What is clear is that, like the sanctuary in Exodus, it had a tripartite
structure: an outer court (*'ulam*), a great hall (*heikhal*), and an inner sanctuary
(*devir*) in which the Ark of the Covenant was placed.

5. *balcony . . . supports.* The meaning of both these Hebrew terms, *yatsia'* and
tsela'ot, is much disputed.

7. *of whole stones . . . it was built, and no hammers nor axes nor any iron tools were
heard in the house.* The stones were dressed at the site of the quarry and then
set in place in Jerusalem. This procedure in part picks up the instructions for
building the altar in Exodus 20:25: "You shall not build them of hewn stones,
for your sword you would brandish over it and profane it."

9. *And he built the house and finished it.* This report of completion marks the
finishing of the stone structure. What follows is an account of the paneling,
carving, and finishing of the structure.

12. *if you walk by My statutes and do My laws.* The language in God's speech is
preeminently Deuteronomistic.

I shall not forsake My people Israel." And Solomon built the house 14
and finished it. And he built the walls of the house from within with 15
cedar supports from the floor of the house to the ceiling, overlaid it
with wood within, and he overlaid the floor of the house with cypress
supports. And he built the twenty cubits from the corners of the house 16
with cedar supports from the floor to the walls, and he built it from
within the sanctuary, the Holy of Holies. And the house was forty 17
cubits, which was the great hall. And cedar was the house inside, a 18
weave of birds and blossoms. Everything was cedar, no stone was seen.
And the sanctuary in the innermost part of the house he readied to 19
place there the Ark of the Covenant of the LORD. And before the sanc- 20
tuary twenty cubits in length and twenty cubits in width and twenty
cubits in height he overlaid with pure gold, and he overlaid the altar
with cedar. And Solomon overlaid the house from within with pure 21
gold, and he fastened gold chains in front of the sanctuary and overlaid
it with gold. And the house he overlaid with gold till the whole house 22
was finished, and the whole altar which was in the inner sanctum he
overlaid with gold. And in the sanctuary he made two cherubim of 23

---

14. *And Solomon built the house and finished it.* These words are what scholars
call a "resumptive repetition" of verse 9. That is, when the continuity of a narrative is interrupted—here, by God's address to Solomon—phrases or sentences
from just before the break are repeated as the narrative resumes its forward
momentum.

16. *and he built it from within the sanctuary, the Holy of Holies.* This is the first of
several places in this chapter where the Hebrew syntax seems a little doubtful.

18. *a weave.* The "weave" of course is a carving of interlaced ornamental figures.
    Everything was cedar, no stone was seen. The cedarwood paneling entirely
covered the stone surfaces. The pervasive use of wooden elements made the
stone structure thoroughly flammable, as the Babylonian army would demonstrate when it destroyed the temple in 586 BCE.

23. *two cherubim.* In a borrowing from Canaanite mythology, the cherubim
were imagined, at least in poetry, as God's mounts. (The word *keruv* means
either "mount" or "hybrid".) They were fierce-looking winged beasts, probably
with leonine bodies and heads, perhaps resembling the Egyptian sphinx and
other bas-relief figures that have been found across the Near East.

24 olivewood, one cherub with a five-cubit wing and the other wing five
25 cubits, ten cubits from one edge of its wings to the other. And the
second cherub was ten cubits, a single measure and shape for both
26 cherubim. The height of the one cherub was ten cubits, and the same
27 for the second cherub. And he placed the cherubim within the inner
chamber. And the wings of the cherubim were spread, and the wing of
the one touched the wall and that of the second cherub touched the
28 other wall, and their inner wings touched wing to wing. And he over-
29 laid the cherubim with gold. And all the walls of the house all round
he wove in carvings of intertwined cherubim and palms and birds,
30 within and without. And the floor of the house he overlaid with gold,
31 within and without. And the entrance of the sanctuary he made of
32 olive wood doors, five-sided capitals and doorposts, and two olive wood
doors. And he wove on them a weave of cherubim and buds and overlaid them with gold, and he worked the gold down over the cherubim
33 and the palms. And the same he did for the entrance of the great hall,
34 four-sided olive wood doorposts. And the two doors were cypress wood,
the two supports of the one door cylindrical and the two supports of
35 the other door cylindrical. And he wove cherubim and palms and buds
36 and overlaid them with gold directly over the incising. And he built the
37 inner court in three rows of hewn stone and a row of cut cedars. In
the fourth year did he lay the foundations of the LORD's house, in the

---

30. *the floor of the house he overlaid with gold*. From what can be made out
from the preceding description, the gold would have been overlaid on the cedar
paneling.

31. *five-sided capitals and doorposts*. The translation of the three Hebrew words
here is conjectural, and the text looks suspect. It may well be that the ancient
scribes were as confused as we moderns by the architectural details and thus
scrambled words at some points.

33. *four-sided*. The Hebrew term is problematic in the same way that "five-
sided" is in verse 31.

35. *directly over the incising*. This is still another architectural indication of
uncertain meaning.

month of Ziv. And in the eleventh year, in the month of Bul, which is 38
the eighth month, he finished the house in all its details and in all its
designs, and he was seven years building it.

---

38. *in the eleventh year*. Thus the years of the building of the temple are reported
to conform to the sacred number seven, as the end of this verse confirms with
a flourish.

in the month of Bul. This is still another Phoenician month name, accompanied by an explanatory gloss, as is *Ziv* in verse 1, and again the unusual term
yeraḥ is used for "month." As the eighth month, it would come in the late fall,
and the name *Bul* may derive from a word that means "harvest."

CHAPTER 7

And his own house Solomon was building for thirteen years, and he
finished his house. And he built the Lebanon Forest House, a hundred
cubits in length and fifty cubits in width and thirty cubits in height with
four rows of cedar columns and cedar beams on the columns. And it
was paneled in cedarwood from above on the supports, which were on
the columns, forty-five, fifteen in each row. And there were windows in
three rows, three tiers face to face. And all the entrances and the doorposts were square-windowed, three tiers face to face. And the Court of
Columns he made fifty cubits in length and thirty cubits in width, and
the court was in front of the columns, and the columns with a beam

---

1. *his own house.* Solomon's two main building projects were the temple and
the palace. No date is given for the inception of the palace, but the notation
in 9:7 that the building of the two structures together took twenty years would
indicate that the palace was begun after the temple was completed. The palace,
the bigger of the two structures, took almost twice as long to build.

2. *the Lebanon Forest House.* This structure is evidently so called because of
the rows of Lebanon cedar it contained. Some think it may have served as an
armory.

4. *three tiers face to face.* This is the first of many places in this chapter where
the architectural indications are quite obscure in the Hebrew, whether because
of scribal scrambling or because we have lost the precise applications of this
technical vocabulary. In much of what follows, then, any translation, including
this one, is no more than educated guesswork.

6. *beam.* The Hebrew *'av* usually means "cloud," leading some to speculate that
here it might refer to some sort of canopy or cover.

over them. And the Court of the Throne, where he meted out justice, 7
the Court of Justice, did he make, and it was paneled in cedarwood from
floor to roof-beams. And in his house in which he would dwell, there 8
was another court besides the outer court made in the same fashion,
and he made a house for Pharaoh's daughter whom Solomon had married, like this court. All these were of costly stones, hewn in measure, 9
smoothed with an adz inside and out, and from the foundation up to the
coping and on the outside up to the great court, and founded with costly 10
stones, great stones, stones of ten cubits and stones of eight cubits. And 11
above were costly stones hewn in measure, and cedar wood. And the 12
great court all around had three rows of hewn stone and a row of cedar
planks, as for the inner court of the House of the LORD and for the outer
court of the house.

And King Solomon sent and fetched Hiram from Tyre. He was the 13,14
son of a widow-woman from the tribe of Naphtali, and his father was
a Tyrean man who was a coppersmith, and he was filled with wisdom

---

7. *from floor to roof-beams.* The Masoretic text reads "from floor to floor," but
the Septuagint, more plausibly, has "from floor to roof-beams."

8. *he made a house for Pharaoh's daughter.* Although the ground-plan of the
palace is hard to reconstruct, the fact that a separate residence was built for one
of Solomon's wives reflects the grandeur of the overall construction.

13. *and King Solomon sent and fetched Hiram from Tyre.* The legendary and
schematic character of the narrative at this point is manifest: it is highly unlikely
that the Phoenician king himself would come to Jerusalem to perform or even
supervise the building work. What this refers to is that Hiram may have sent
master artisans from Tyre to participate in the project.

14. *He was the son of a widow-woman from the tribe of Naphtali.* It is even
more unlikely that a Phoenician king would have had an Israelite mother, and
a woman previously married, besides. The narrative here may be reaching to
establish a genetic connection between Israel and the foreign king who helped
to build both the temple and the palace.
   his father was a Tyrean man who was a coppersmith. The notion of an artisan
king (both Hiram's father and Hiram are represented as that) sounds odd, but
the idea is that the king is imagined to embody the distinctive skills and expertise of his people.

and discerning and knowledge to do every task in bronze. And he came
15 to King Solomon and did all his task. And he fashioned the two pillars
of bronze, eighteen cubits the height of each column, and a twelve-
16 cubit line went round the second pillar. And he made two capitals to
put on the tops of the pillars, cast in bronze, five cubits the height of the
17 one capital and five cubits the height of the other capital. Nets of meshwork, chainwork wreathes for the capitals that were on the top of the
18 pillars, seven for the one capital and seven for the other. And he made
the pillars, with two rows around over the one net to cover the capitals that were on top of the pomegranates, and so he did for the other
19 capital. And the capitals that were on top of the pillars in the outer
20 court were a lily design, four cubits high. And the capitals on the two
pillars above as well, opposite the curve that was over against the net,
and the pomegranates were in two hundred rows around on the second
21 capital. And he set up the pillars for the great hall and set up the right
pillar and called its name Jachin and set up the left pillar and called
22 its name Boaz. And on the top of the pillars was a lily design. And the
23 task of the pillars was finished. And he made the cast-metal sea ten
cubits from edge to edge, circular all around, and five cubits in height,
24 and a line of thirty cubits going all around. And birds beneath its edge
going all around it, ten cubits, encompassing the sea all around, two
25 rows cast in its casting. It stood on twelve oxen, three facing north and
three facing west and three facing south and three facing east. And

---

20. *the curve.* The Hebrew is literally "belly," and its architectural meaning is
uncertain.

21. *Jachin . . . Boaz.* The naming of pillars and altars was not uncommon in the
ancient Near East. These two names mean "he will firmly found" (*yakhin*) and
"strength in him" (the latter is an attested personal name). Both names appear
to refer to the stability of the royal dynasty.

23. *the cast-metal sea.* This is essentially a metal pool, to be used by the priests
to bathe hands and feet before they perform their ritual duties. The Hebrew
uses the rather grand term "sea" (*yam*) perhaps to suggest a cosmic correspondence between the structure of the temple and of creation at large.
a line. The translation reads, with many Hebrew manuscripts, *qaw* for the
incomprehensible Masoretic *qawoh*.

the sea was on top of them, and their hind parts were inward. And its 26
thickness was a handspan, and its rim like the design of a cup's rim,
blossom and lily, two thousand *bats* did it hold. And he made ten stands 27
of bronze, four cubits in length each stand and four cubits in width and
three cubits in height. And this was the design of the stands: they had 28
frames, and there were frames between the rungs. And on the frames 29
between the rungs were lions, oxen, and cherubim on the bevels, so it
was above and below the lions and the oxen, hammered metal spirals.
And each stand had four bronze wheels and bronze axeltrees. And 30
its four legs had brackets beneath the laver. The brackets were cast
in spirals opposite each. And its spout was within the capital a cubit 31
above it, and its spout was round in the design of a stand, a cubit and
a half. And on its spout, too, there was woven-work. And their frames
were square, not round. And the four wheels were beneath the frames, 32
and the axeltrees of the wheels inserted in the stand. And the height
of each wheel was a cubit and a half. And the design of the wheels was 33
like the design of a chariot's wheels. Their axeltrees and rims and their
spokes and their hubs were all of cast metal. And the four brackets 34
at the four corners of each stand, of a piece with the stand were its
brackets. And on top of the stand was a circular form all around, and 35
on top of the stand its brackets and its frames were of a piece with it.
And he carved on the panels of its brackets and on its frames cheru- 36
bim, lions, and palms, each laid bare, and a spiral all around. Thus did 37

---

26. *bats*. The *bat* is a relatively large unit of liquid measure, but the precise
quantity is uncertain.

28. *rungs*. The meaning of the Hebrew *shelabim* is conjectural, but a laddered
structure may be involved.

30. *four bronze wheels*. Wheeled ritual vessels have been uncovered across the
Near East.
   in spirals opposite each. The Hebrew here is particularly obscure.

31. *woven-work*. As elsewhere, the term refers to carved interlaced figures.

36. *each laid bare*. The Hebrew *kema'ar 'ish* is not intelligible. The translation is
based on a tentative guess that the first of these words is a verbal noun derived
from the root '-r-h, "lay bare."

he make the ten stands, each cast the same, a single measure and a
38 single shape they all had. And he made ten lavers of bronze, each laver
would hold forty *bats*, four cubits each laver on each stand, for the ten
39 stands. And he placed the stands, five on the right side of the house
and five on the left side of the house. And the sea he placed on the
40 right side of the house to the east, facing south. And Hiram made the
lavers and the shovels and the basins. And Hiram completed doing the
41 task that he had done for King Solomon in the house of the LORD: two
pillars and two globes of the capitals that were on top of the pillars
and two nets to cover the two globes of the capitals that were on top of
42 the pillars, and four hundred pomegranates for the nets, two rows of
pomegranates for every net to cover the globes of the capitals that were
43,44 on the pillars, and the ten stands and the ten lavers on the stands, and
45 the one sea and the twelve oxen beneath the sea. And the bowls and
the shovels and the basins and those vessels that Hiram made for King
46 Solomon in the house of the LORD, burnished bronze. In the plain of
the Jordan did the king cast them, in the thick of the ground, between
47 Succoth and Zarethan. And Solomon left all the vessels unweighed on
account of their very great abundance; the measure of the bronze was
48 not taken. And Solomon made all the vessels that were in the House
of the LORD, the gold altar and the gold table on which was the bread
49 of display, and the pure gold lampstands, five on the right and five on
the left in front of the sanctuary, and the gold blossoms and lamps

---

40. *And Hiram completed doing the task that he had done.* This is an explicit
echoing of Genesis 2:2, suggesting that the work of building the temple is
analogous to the work of building the world.

41. *two pillars and two globes.* What begins here is a summarizing catalogue of
all the sacred furniture fashioned for the temple.

45. *those.* The translation reads, with many Hebrew manuscripts, *ha'eleh* for the
incomprehensible Masoretic *ha'ehel* (a simple reversal of consonants, which is
a common scribal error).

46. *in the thick of the ground.* The casting was done in earthen molds.

47. *unweighed.* This term is merely implied in the Hebrew.

and tongs, and the pure gold bowls and the snuffers and the basins 50
and the ladles and firepans, and the gold sockets for the doors of the
inner house, for the Holy of Holies, for the doors of the great hall of
the house. And the task that King Solomon had done was finished in 51
the House of the LORD, and Solomon brought the dedicated things of
David his father, the silver and the gold, and he placed the vessels in
the treasury of the House of the LORD.

---

50. *snuffers*. Others, including many Jewish commentators from late antiquity
on, construe this to mean "musical instruments."

51. *And the task that King Solomon had done was finished*. Through both this
long chapter and the preceding one, it should be observed that Solomon virtually disappears as an individualized character: the king here functions as an
impersonal royal "he" who directs these elaborate building projects.

CHAPTER 8

Then did Solomon assemble the elders of Israel, all the heads of the tribes, the patriarchal chieftains of the Israelites, round King Solomon in Jerusalem, to bring up the Ark of the Covenant of the LORD from the City of David, which is Zion. And every man of Israel assembled round Solomon in the month of Ethanim, which is the seventh month, at the festival. And all the elders of Israel came, and the priests carried the Ark. And they brought up the Ark of the LORD and the Tent of Meeting and all the sacred vessels that were in the Tent, and the priests and the Levites brought them up. And King Solomon and all the community of Israel who had gathered round him were with him before the Ark, sacrificing sheep and oxen that could not be numbered for their abundance. And the priests brought the Ark of the Covenant of the LORD to its place, to the sanctuary of the house, to the Holy of Holies, beneath the

---

1. *the City of David, which is Zion.* Though part of Jerusalem, this area is distinct from the temple mount, to its west. The Ark was kept here in a temporary structure (probably the Tent of Meeting) after David brought it up to Jerusalem (see 2 Samuel:6),

2. *the month of Ethanim, which is the seventh month.* Again, a non-standard nomenclature for the months is used, necessitating the explanatory gloss. The seventh month would correspond approximately to October, and the festival celebrated on this occasion (see verse 65) is Sukkot, which, because it was a seven-day festival at the end of the fall harvest, was of the three pilgrim festivals the one for which the greatest number of celebrants came to Jerusalem from all over the country. Solomon thus chooses wisely the time for dedicating the temple.

wings of the cherubim. For the cherubim spread wings over the place of 7
the Ark, and the cherubim sheltered the Ark and its poles from above.
And the poles extended, and the ends of the poles could be seen from 8
the Holy Place in the front of the sanctuary, but they could not be seen
from without, and they have been there to this day. There was nothing in 9
the Ark except the two stone tablets that Moses had put there on Horeb,
which the LORD had sealed as a covenant with the Israelites when they
came out of the land of Egypt. And it happened when the priests came 10
out of the Holy Place, that a cloud filled the house of the LORD. And 11
the priests could not stand up to minister because of the cloud, for the
LORD's glory filled the house of the LORD. Then did Solomon say: 12

"The LORD meant to abide in thick fog.
    I indeed have built You a lofty house, 13
        a firm place for Your dwelling forever."

---

7. *its poles*. The Ark was a portable structure, carried on poles.

9. *as a covenant*. These words are merely implied by the verb "sealed."

11. *the LORD's glory filled the house*. The manifestation of God's glory, as is clear
from a number of biblical texts, is a dense cloud. The ultimate source of this
idea may be the poetic image of God, drawn from the Canaanite representation
of Baal, as a dweller or rider of the clouds.

12. *Then did Solomon say*. This solemn declaration about where God abides is
cast in a triadic line of poetry.
    The LORD meant to abide in thick fog. What tradition—especially, poetic
tradition—tells us of Him is that He abides in the clouds above.

13. *I indeed have built You a lofty house*. But with the erection of the temple, a
new era is inaugurated in which the God of Israel has an earthly abode.
    a firm place for Your dwelling. This phrase, which will be repeated in Solo-
mon's lengthy address, occurs at the end of the Song of the Sea, Exodus 15:17.

14 And the king turned his face and blessed all the assembly of Israel with
15 all the assembly of Israel standing. And he said: "Blessed is the LORD
God of Israel Who spoke with His own mouth to David my father, and
16 with His own hand has fulfilled it, saying, 'From the day that I brought
out My people Israel from Egypt, I have not chosen a town from all the
tribes of Israel to build a house for My name to be there, but I chose
17 David to be over My people Israel.' And it was in the heart of David my
18 father to build a house for the name of the LORD God of Israel. And the
LORD said to David my father, 'In as much as it was in your heart to
build a house for My name, you have done well, for it was in your heart.
19 Only you will not build the house, but your son, who issues from your
20 loins, he will build the house for My name.' And the LORD has fulfilled
His word that He spoke, and I arose in place of David my father and
sat on the throne of Israel as the LORD spoke and I have built the house
21 for the name of the LORD God of Israel. And I have set there a place
for the Ark in which is the covenant of the LORD that He sealed with
22 our fathers when He brought them out of the land of Egypt." And Solomon stood before the LORD's altar over against all the assembly of Israel

---

15. *to David my father.* This weighted designation is reiterated throughout the speech: Solomon, consolidating his own rule through the construction of the temple, repeatedly emphasizes that he is David's son and sole heir and that God's promises to his father are now fulfilled in him.

20. *I arose in place of David my father.* It should be recalled, as Solomon's phrasing here invites us to recall, that he was designated by his father to assume the throne while his father was still alive.

for the name of the LORD. The temple is understood to enhance the glory or reputation ("the name") of the LORD.

21. *in which is the covenant.* The two stone tablets are conceived as the material equivalent of the covenant between God and Israel (see verse 9).

and spread his palms toward the heavens. And he said, "Lord God of 23
Israel! There is no god like You in the heavens above and on the earth
below, keeping the covenant and the kindness for Your servants who
walk before You with all their heart, which You kept for David my father, 24
what You spoke to him, and You spoke with Your own mouth, and with
Your own hand You fulfilled it, as on this day. And now, Lord God of 25
Israel, keep for Your servant David my father what You spoke to him,
saying, 'No man of yours will be cut off from before Me, sitting on the
throne of Israel, if only your sons will keep their way to walk before Me
as you have walked before Me.' And now, God of Israel, may Your 26
words, pray, be shown true that You spoke to David my father. But can 27
God really dwell on earth? Look, the heavens and the heavens beyond
the heavens cannot contain You. How much less this house that I have
built. Yet turn to the prayer of Your servant and to his plea, Lord God 28
of Israel, to hearken to the glad song and to the prayer that Your servant
prays before You today, so that Your eyes be open to this house night 29
and day, to this place of which You have said, 'My name is there,' to

---

22. *spread his palms toward the heavens.* This conventional gesture of prayer is
visible in many ancient Near Eastern statues and bas-reliefs.

23. *Lord God of Israel!* The first part of Solomon's speech is an address to Israel
in which he reminds the people that God's promise to David is now fulfilled
through his acts. At this point, he proceeds to voice a prayer to God.
   There is no god like You in the heavens above and on the earth below. This wording may, like the Song of the Sea, reflects an older concept in which there are
gods besides YHWH, but they are insubstantial and cannot compete with Him.
   walk before You with all their heart. The language here is Deuteronomistic. The idiom "walk before" suggests entering into a relationship of devoted
servitude.

27. *can God really dwell on earth?* Solomon now touches on a theological problem raised by the building of the temple: it is figuratively and symbolically
God's dwelling-place, but Solomon wants to deflect any literal notion that God
actually abides in a human structure.

30 hearken to the prayer that Your servant prays in this place. And may You
hearken to the plea of Your servant and of Your people Israel, which
they will pray in this place, and may You hearken in Your dwelling-place
31 in the heavens, and hearken and forgive what a man offends against his
fellow and bears an oath against him to bring a curse on him, and the
32 oath comes before Your altar in this house. But You will hearken in the
heavens and judge Your servant to condemn the guilty, to bring down
his way on his head, and to vindicate him who is right, to mete out to
33 him according to his righteousness. When Your people Israel are routed
by an enemy, for they will offend You, and they come back to You and
34 acclaim Your name and pray and plead to You in this house, You will
hearken in the heavens and forgive the offense of Your people Israel,
35 and bring them back to the land that You gave to their fathers. When
the heavens are shut up and there is no rain, for the Israelites will have
offended against You, and they pray in this place and acclaim Your
name, You shall forgive the offense of Your servants and turn back from
36 their offense, for You will answer them. You will hearken in the heavens
and forgive the offense of Your servants, Your people Israel, for You will
teach them the good way in which they should walk, and You will give

---

30. *hearken to the plea of Your servant and of Your people.* Throughout Solomon's
prayer, the emphasis is on the temple as a place of prayer and supplication,
a kind of terrestrial communications center for speaking with God. Sacrifice
is not mentioned. It is possible, though not demonstrable, that the stress on
prayer rather than sacrifice reflects some influence of the Prophets, beginning
with Isaiah in the late seventh century. There are other features of Solomon's
speech that look late.

34. *bring them back to the land.* It is unlikely that the historical Solomon in the
mid-tenth century BCE, at the very moment of his royal grandeur, with peace
all around, should have introduced into his prayer, in the hearing of all Israel,
this stark intimation of a future exile. The plausible inference is that the speech,
or at the very least this part of it, was composed after the exile of the northern
kingdom in 721 BCE and perhaps even after the destruction of the southern
kingdom in 586 BCE.

35. *the Israelites.* The Hebrew says simply "they," but this implied antecedent
is introduced in the translation to avoid the impression that it is the heavens
that have offended.

rain upon Your land that You have given to Your people in estate. Should 37
there be famine in the land, should there be plague, blight, mildew,
locusts, caterpillars, should his enemy besiege him in the gates of his
land, any affliction, any disease, any prayer, any plea that any man have 38
in all Your people Israel, that every man know his heart's affliction, he
shall spread out his palms in this house. And You shall hearken in the 39
heavens, the firm place of Your dwelling, and You shall forgive and act
and give to a man according to his ways, as You know his heart, for You
alone know the heart of all men. So that they may fear You all the days 40
that they live on the land that You gave to their fathers. And the for- 41
eigner, too, who is not from Your people Israel and has come from a
distant land for the sake of Your name, if he hearkens to Your great 42
name and Your strong hand and Your outstretched arm and comes and
prays in this house, You will hearken in the heavens, the firm place of 43
Your dwelling and do as all that the foreigner will call out to You, so that
all the peoples of the earth may know Your name to fear You as does
Your people Israel, to know that Your name has been called on this
house that I have built. Should your people go out to battle against its 44
enemy on the way that You send them, they shall pray to the LORD
through the city that You have chosen and the house that I have built

---

37. *Should there be famine in the land.* This long run-on sentence—and there
are more like it as the speech continues—is not typical of biblical prose style,
though the Book of Deuteronomy exhibits a fondness for lengthy, periodic sentences, most of them more syntactically controlled that this one.

39. *And You shall hearken in the heavens, the firm place of Your dwelling.* This
refrain-like clause picks up the previous notion that God does not actually
dwell in the temple but in the heavens above, from which He is disposed
to listen to the prayers enunciated in the temple because He regards it as a
favored focal point for prayer.

41. *and the foreigner, too.* This sympathetic attitude toward the devoutness
of foreigners who join the community of Israel sounds rather like a theme in
Deutero-Isaiah, though one might argue that Solomon's cordial relations, political, commercial, and marital, with surrounding nations might be reflected here.

44. *through the city.* Others understand the preposition as "in the direction of."

45 for Your name. And You shall hearken in the heavens to their prayer and
46 to their plea, and You shall do justice for them. Should they offend
against You, for there is no man who does not offend, and You are furious with them and give them to the enemy, and their captors take them
47 off to a distant or nearby land, and they turn their heart back to You in
the land in which they are captive, and turn back to You and plead with
You in the land of their captors, saying, 'We have offended and have
48 done wrong, we have been evil,' and they turn back to You with all their
heart and all their being in the land of their enemies who took them in
captivity, and they pray to you through their land that You gave to their
fathers, the city that You chose and the house that I have built for Your
49 name, You shall hearken from the heavens, the firm place of Your dwell-
50 ing, to their prayer and to their plea, and do justice for them. And You
shall forgive Your people who have offended against you for all their
crimes that they committed, and You shall grant them mercy before
51 their captors, who will have mercy upon them. For they are Your people
and Your estate that You brought out of the land of Egypt from the forge
52 of iron. So that Your eyes be open to the plea of Your servant and the
pleas of Your people Israel, to listen to them whenever they call to You.
53 For You set them apart for You as an estate from all the peoples of the
earth as You spoke through Moses Your servant when You brought out

---

46. *their captors take them off.* At this point, the prospect of exile becomes more explicit and emphatic.

47. *We have offended and have done wrong, we have been evil.* These words were incorporated in the short confession of sins in the Yom Kippur liturgy.

48. *through their land.* Again, the translation understands this to mean that they will invoke their land, though it could mean that they will turn in the direction of the land as they pray.

50. *their captors, who will have mercy upon them.* It is noteworthy that the defeat or humiliation of Israel's enemies is not envisaged but rather the prospect that the captors will have compassion and treat them kindly. It is tempting to see in these words a reflection of Cyrus's beneficence toward the exiled Israelites, though it is hard to know whether any of the speech could have been written that late.

our fathers from Egypt, O Master Lord." And it happened when Solo- 54
mon finished praying to the Lord all this prayer and plea, that he rose
from before the Lord's altar from kneeling on his knees with his palms
stretched out to the heavens. And he stood and blessed all the assembly 55
of Israel in a loud voice, saying: "Blessed is the Lord Who has granted 56
to his people Israel as all that He spoke. Not a single thing has failed of
all His good word that He spoke through Moses His servant. May the 57
Lord our God be with us as He was with our Fathers. May He not
forsake us and not abandon us, to incline our heart to Him to walk in 58
all His ways and to keep His commands and His statutes and His laws
with which He charged our fathers. And may these words that I pleaded 59
before the Lord be near the Lord our God day and night to do justice
for His servant and justice for His people Israel day after day, so that all 60
the peoples of the earth may know that the Lord is our God, there is
none else. And may your heart be whole with the Lord our God to walk 61
in His statutes and to keep His commands as on this day." And the king 62
and all Israel with him were offering sacrifice before the Lord. And 63
Solomon offered up the well-being sacrifices that he sacrificed to the
Lord, twenty-two thousand oxen and a hundred twenty thousand sheep.
And the king and all the Israelites dedicated the house of the Lord. On 64
that day the king sanctified the midst of the court that was before the
house of the Lord, for he did there the burnt offering and the grain
offering and the fat of the well-being sacrifices. For the bronze altar that
was before the Lord was too small to hold the burnt offering and the

---

56. *Blessed is the* Lord. This last part of Solomon's quoted words, to the end of
verse 61, is a kind of peroration that concludes his long address, appropriately
invoking the divine promises to Moses and the importance of continuing loyalty
to the covenant, framed once again in Deuteronomistic language.

63. *twenty-two thousand oxen and a hundred twenty thousand sheep.* These
imposing numbers are surely a fantastic embellishment of the actual ceremony.

65 grain offering and the fat of the well-being sacrifices. And at that time Solomon performed the festival and all Israel his people was with him, a great assembly from Lebo-Hamath to the wadi of Egypt, seven days

66 and seven days—fourteen days. On the seventh day he sent off the people, and they blessed the king and went to their tents, rejoicing and of good cheer over all the good that the LORD had done for David his servant and for Israel His people.

---

65. *from Lebo-Hamath.* This town was at the border of Lebanon in the north.

seven days and seven days—fourteen days. The wording is a little confusing. The designated span of the pilgrim festival of Sukkot was seven days. Solomon evidently doubled the time, adding a second week of celebration. But the report in the next verse that he sent the people home on the seventh day might suggest that he continued a more private celebration, perhaps involving only the royal house and priests, for the second week. Alternately, "he sent off the people on the seventh day" might mean the seventh day of the second week

CHAPTER 9

Ａnd it happened when Solomon finished building the house of the   1
LORD and the house of the king and all Solomon's desire that he was
pleased to do, that the LORD appeared to Solomon a second time as He   2
had appeared to him in Gibeon. And the LORD said to him: "I have hear-   3
kened to your prayer and to your plea that you pleaded before Me. I have
sanctified this house that you built to set My name there forever, and
My eyes and My heart shall be there for all time. As for you, if you walk   4
before Me, as David your father walked, wholeheartedly and uprightly,
to do as all that I have charged you, My statutes and My laws to keep, I   5
shall raise up the throne of your kingdom over Israel forever as I spoke
to David your father, saying, 'No man of yours shall be cut off from the
throne of Israel.' If you and your sons actually turn back from Me and   6
you do not keep My commands, My statutes that I gave you, and you

---

2. *the LORD appeared to Solomon a second time.* Solomon's royal enterprise is
framed by two revelations. Early in his reign, God appears to him at Gibeon and
grants him the gift of wisdom (3:5–14). The wisdom is first manifested in the
episode of the Judgment of Solomon and in his composing proverbs. His great
building projects, now completed, may reflect another kind of wisdom because
they consolidate his rule. Now God comes to him to tell him that the sanctity
of the temple is divinely ratified.

4. *if you walk before Me, as David your father walked.* The legitimacy of the
dynasty necessitates this idealized representation of David. In fact, the older—
and probing—narrative of David shows him to be deeply flawed—an adulterer,
a murderer, and a man beset with weaknesses.

to do as . . . I have charged you, My statutes and My laws to keep. As in Solomon's speech at the dedication of the temple, the language is emphatically
Deuteronomistic.

7 go and serve other gods and bow down to them, I shall cut Israel off
from the land that I gave them, and the house that I have sanctified for
My name will I send away from My presence, and Israel shall become a
8 byword and a mockery among all the peoples. And this house will turn
into ruins—all who pass by it will be dismayed and whistle in derision
9 and say, 'Why did the LORD do thus to this land and to this house?' And
they will say, 'Because they forsook the LORD their God Who brought
their fathers out of the land of Egypt and held fast to other gods and
bowed down to them and served them. Therefore has the LORD brought
upon them all this harm.'"

10 And it happened at the end of the twenty years that Solomon was building the two houses, the house of the LORD and the house of the king,
11 that Hiram king of Tyre had furnished Solomon with cedar wood and
cypress wood and gold as all that he desired, then did Solomon give

---

7. *I shall cut Israel off from the land.* The invocation of the specter of exile, as
earlier, looks like the reflection of a later historical moment.

I will send away from My presence. This is a slightly odd idiom to attach to
the temple. Its usual connotation is divorce, a trope often used by the Prophets
for God's disaffection with Israel.

a byword and a mockery. This phrase is also fairly common in the Prophets
to indicate Israel's national humiliation.

8. *this house will turn into ruins.* The received text reads, "this house will be
exalted." This translation reads instead of *'elyon*, "exalted" or "high," *'iyyim*,
"ruins," along with the Syriac and two versions of the Vulgate.

9. *Because they forsook the LORD.* In keeping with the Deuteronomistic theology,
it is cultic infidelity that will cause the catastrophe of exile.

10. *the twenty years.* That is, seven for the building of the temple and another
thirteen for the palace.

11. *gold.* This precious substance, which was needed for the furnishings of the
temple and the palace, was not mentioned in the initial negotiations between
Solomon and Hiram. Though Tyre did not have its own gold mines, it would
have accumulated stockpiles of gold through its flourishing international trade.

Solomon give Hiram twenty towns in the land of the Galilee. In the original
agreement, Solomon was to pay for the cedar wood and cypress wood with

Hiram twenty towns in the land of the Galilee. And Hiram went out   12
from Tyre to see the towns that Solomon had given him, and they were
not right in his eyes. And he said, "What are these towns that you have   13
given me, my brother?" And they have been called the Land of Cabul
to this day. And Hiram had sent to the king a hundred twenty talents   14
of gold. And this is the aim of the forced labor that Solomon exacted: 15
to build the house of the LORD and his house and the citadel, and the
wall of Jerusalem and Hazor and Megiddo and Gezer. Pharaoh king   16
of Egypt had gone up and taken Gezer and burnt it in fire and killed
the Canaanites who dwelled in the town, and he gave it as a dowry to
his daughter, Solomon's wife. And Solomon rebuilt Gezer and Lower   17

---

wheat and olive oil. Perhaps Hiram's providing gold came afterward and thus
required additional payment.

13. *What are these towns that you have given me, my brother?* Hiram obviously
regards these paltry towns on his southern border as poor recompense, but he
maintains his diplomatic relationship with Solomon by adding "my brother" to
his objection.

    the Land of Cabul. No satisfactory explanation for the enigmatic *kabul* has
been offered, though it clearly indicates something quite negative, mirroring
Hiram's disappointment. It could mean "land of the chained one" (the one
chained to a bad agreement?). It could also mean "land like the produce" (land
offered in payment, like the wheat and oil?). Perhaps an explanatory clause in
Hiram's speech has dropped out of the text.

14. *And Hiram had sent to the king a hundred twenty talents of gold.* It would
make no sense for Hiram to send Solomon gold after his dismissing the twenty
towns as poor payment. Thus, though the form of the Hebrew verb does not
indicate a pluperfect, one is compelled to understand this as a reference to his
earlier shipments of gold to Solomon.

15. *And this is the aim of the forced labor.* The connection with what precedes
is associative: in the great building enterprise in which Hiram was Solomon's
partner, Israelite forced labor was used.

    the citadel. The Hebrew *milo'* derives from a root that means "to fill," perhaps
suggesting a raised citadel erected on landfill.

    Hazor and Megiddo and Gezer. Solomon's building projects thus extended far
beyond Jerusalem, involving fortified towns around the country.

18 Beth-Horon, and Baalath and Tamor in the wilderness, in the land,
19 and all the storehouse towns that were Solomon's, and the towns for the
chariots and the towns for the horsemen, and every desire of Solomon
that he desired to build in Jerusalem and in Lebanon and in all the land
20 of his dominion. All the people remaining in the land, the Amorite, the
Hittite, the Perizzite and the Jebusite, who were not of the Israelites,
21 their sons who remained after them whom the Israelites could not wholly
22 destroy, Solomon put to forced labor to this day. And of the Israelites
Solomon made no slave, for they were men of war, and his servants and
his commanders and his captains and the officers of his chariots and
23 his horsemen. These were the commander-prefects who were over the
tasks of Solomon, five hundred fifty holding sway over the people who
24 performed the tasks. But Pharaoh's daughter had gone up from the city
of David to her house that he built for her. Then did he build the citadel.

---

18. *Tamor.* The Masoretic marginal note (*qeri*) reads this as "Tadmor," which is
Palmyra in Syria. That would be an improbable place for Solomon to build, so
the translation adheres to the consonantal text, indicating a town in the Negev.

19. *in Lebanon.* This might mean on the border of Lebanon.

21. *Solomon put to forced labor.* This notion that the indigenous inhabitants of
the land became forced laborers, subject to Israel, is put forth in the Book of
Joshua.

22. *And of the Israelites Solomon made no slave.* The Israelite forced laborers
paid what amounted to a tax through their labor for a limited period of time.
    for they were men of war. Here, however, a different reason is offered for not
enslaving Israelites—their value as warriors.

And three times in the year Solomon offered up burnt offerings and well- 25
being sacrifices on the altar that he had built for the LORD, and turned
it to smoke before the LORD and made the house whole. And a fleet 26
did Solomon make in Etzion-Geber, which is by Eloth on the shore of
the Red Sea in the land of Edom. And Hiram sent his servants to the 27
fleet—shipmen, adept in the sea—with Solomon's servants. And they 28
came to Ophir and took four hundred twenty talents of gold from there
and brought it to King Solomon.

---

25. *and turned it to smoke*. The Masoretic text adds "with him that," which is
syntactically incoherent and looks like a scribal error.

   made the house whole. The verb *shilem*, which elsewhere means "requite,"
derives from a root meaning "whole" and here may refer to an affirmation or
restoration of the integrity of the temple through the act of sacrifice.

26. *Eloth*. This place-name is evidently identical with Eilath.

27. *shipmen, adept in the sea*. The Phoenicians, of course, were a great seafaring
nation, and Solomon could well have used the expertise of his northern ally.

28. *Ophir*. This location, somewhere to the south by the shore of the Red Sea,
is repeatedly identified in the Bible as a source of gold—so much so that in
poetry the name "Ophir" alone can mean "fine gold."

CHAPTER 10

¹ And the Queen of Sheba heard the rumor of Solomon for the name of
² the LORD, and she came to try him with riddles. And she came to Jerusalem with a very great retinue—camels bearing a very great abundance of
spices and gold and precious stones, and she came to Solomon and spoke
³ to him all that was in her heart. And Solomon told her all her questions.

---

1. *the Queen of Sheba*. The consensus is that Sheba is far to the south of ancient
Israel, somewhere on the Arabian Peninsula along the shore of the Red Sea.
This episode is linked associatively with the immediately preceding passage
in which Solomon builds fleets on the Red Sea and carries on trade in rich
materials with the South.

for the name of the LORD. This phrase, repeatedly used for the building of the
temple, is a little cryptic in the present context. It might mean that Solomon's
fabulous wisdom, granted to him as a special gift by God, was because of its
divine source "for the name of the LORD."

2. *And she came to Jerusalem with a very great retinue*. This encounter between
the queen of a southern kingdom and the great King Solomon has gripped
the imagination of readers, writers, and artists over the ages. Among countless
elaborations of the story in poetry and painting, an especially memorable one
is "The Visit of the Queen of Sheba," a cycle of poems by the great Israeli poet,
Yehuda Amichai, which highlights the grand voyage over the Red Sea and teases
out an erotic subtext from the biblical tale.

spoke to him all that was in her heart. The heart here is the locus of intel-
lection, not emotion, so what she speaks are all the riddles she had carefully
prepared to pose to him.

3. *And Solomon told her all her questions*. The verb "told," is regularly used for
pronouncing the solution to a riddle, as in the Samson story. "Questions" here
is the term that usually means "words" but has to be rendered as "questions" to
make the sentence intelligible. It is something of a tease that the story does not
divulge any of her riddles—of course, leaving much room for later interpreters.

There was no question hidden from the king that he did not tell her. And 4
the Queen of Sheba saw all Solomon's wisdom and the house that he had
built, and the food on his table and the seat of his servants and the stand- 5
ing of his attendants and their garments and his cupbearers and the burnt
offering he would offer up in the house of the LORD—and she was breathless. And she said to the king: "The word that I heard in my land about 6
your doings and about your wisdom is true. And I did not believe these 7
words until I came and my own eyes saw, and, look, the half of it was not
told me. You exceed in wisdom and bounty beyond the rumor that I heard.
Happy are your men, happy your servants, those who stand in your pres- 8
ence perpetually, listening to your wisdom. May the LORD your God be 9
blessed, Who has desired you to set you on the throne of Israel through the
LORD's love of Israel forever, and has made you king to do judgment and
justice." And she gave the king a hundred and twenty talents of gold and 10

---

4. *And the Queen of Sheba saw all Solomon's wisdom.* Scholars conventionally
classify this story as a Wisdom text, a judgment that might be questioned.
Wisdom is celebrated as a value, but in fact there is no Wisdom content in this
story (in contrast to Proverbs or Qohelet).

and the house that he had built. She is impressed not only by Solomon's
wisdom but—perhaps just as much—by the material splendor and affluence
of his palace and his court. One extravagantly wealthy monarch duly recognizes
the tremendous wealth of the other.

5. *the burnt offering.* Two ancient versions vocalize this word differently to yield
"the ascent on which he would go up to the house of the LORD," though a grand
abundance of daily sacrifices would certainly be evidence of his regal wealth.

9. *May the LORD your God be blessed.* The dazzling impression that Solomon
makes on the Queen of Sheba is thus seen as a confirmation of the greatness of
YHWH, the God of Israel. At the same time, the whole story of the triumphal
encounter of Israel's king with a great queen from the distant South is a vivid
illustration of Solomon's supreme regal grandeur, which has been a repeated
theme in the preceding chapters.

10. *And she gave the king a hundred and twenty talents of gold.* There is no
indication that a wager was involved in solving the riddles, as in the Samson
story, though that is possible. The more likely explanation of her act is that
she is moved to offer a generous gift from her own great wealth as a gesture
of appreciation to the wise and great king. In verse 13, we learn that she on
her part asks for an exchange of gifts, to which Solomon readily agrees. Some

a very great abundance of spices and precious stones—never again did
such an abundance of spice come as the Queen of Sheba gave to King
11   Solomon. And Hiram's fleet as well that bore gold from Ophir brought
12   from Ophir a great abundance of sandalwood and precious stones. And
the king made from the sandalwood beams for the house of the LORD
and the house of the king and lutes and lyres for the singers—the like
13   of the sandalwood has not come nor been seen to this day. And King
Solomon gave to the Queen of Sheba all she desired, for which she had
asked, besides what Solomon had given her in royal bounty. And she
turned and went off to her land, she and her servants.

14   And the weight of gold that came to Solomon in a single year was six hun-
15   dred and sixty-six talents of gold, besides what he had from the merchants
and the traffic of the traders and all the kings of Arabia and the governors
16   of the land. And King Solomon made two hundred shields of hammered
17   gold, six hundred measures of gold he put on each shield, and three hundred bucklers of hammered gold, three hundred measures of gold on each
18   buckler. And the king put them in the House of the Lebanon Forest. And

---

interpreters see this part of the story as an oblique reflection of trade relations
between Israel and Sheba, though it may be more plausible to read it simply as
a diplomatic exchange of regal generosity.
   a very great abundance of spices. The Arabian Peninsula was in fact known in
the ancient world for its spices and perfumes, something of which Shakespeare
was still aware when he had Lady Macbeth say, "All the perfumes of Araby will
not sweeten this little hand."

11. *And Hiram's fleet . . . that bore gold from Ophir.* The obvious associative
connection is the bringing of precious materials from southern regions. Ophir
probably was also in the Arabian Peninsula.

16. *two hundred shields of . . . gold.* These shields and bucklers (the precise distinction between the two Hebrew terms cannot be determined) made of gold are
obviously not fashioned to be used in combat but as ornamental objects, evoking
by their form the king's military power and by their substance his great wealth.

17. *three hundred.* The received text reads "three," too little if six hundred are
used for the shields, but two ancient versions show "three hundred."
   the House of the Lebanon Forest. If this evidently impressive hall in the palace
was, as some claim, an armory, it might have been a symbolic armory because

the king made a great ivory throne and overlaid it with choicest gold. Six steps the throne had, and a round top behind it the throne had, and arms on each side at the seat and two lions standing by the arms. And twelve lions stood there on the six steps on each side. Its like was not made in all the kingdoms. And all King Solomon's drinking vessels were gold, and all the vessels of the House of the Lebanon Forest pure gold. There was no silver—in Solomon's days it was counted as naught. For the king had a Tarshish fleet in the sea together with Hiram's fleet bearing gold and silver, ivory, apes, and parrots. And King Solomon was greater than all the kings of the earth in wealth and in wisdom. And the whole earth sought Solomon's presence to hear his wisdom that God had put in his heart. And they would bring each his tribute, vessels of silver and vessels of gold and cloaks and arms and spices, horses and mules, the set amount year by year. And Solomon gathered chariots and horsemen, and he had a thousand four hundred chariots and

19
20
21

22
23
24

25

26

---

the shields displayed in it were not actually for military use. Verse 20 notes that *everything* in the House of Lebanon was made of pure gold, so it could even have been a kind of treasury.

22. *a Tarshish fleet.* Tarshish is generally thought to be a Mediterranean port far to the west, though scholars differ about its precise location. The allied fleets of Solomon and Hiram, however, were plying the Red Sea, so it is more likely that the term refers to a kind of ship—the sort built in Tarshish or outfitted to reach far-off Tarshish. It has also been proposed that the term derives from the Greek *tarsos*, "oar," and so designates a sailing ship that is also equipped with oars.

parrots. Others understand the term to mean "peacocks," though parrots are a better pairing with apes.

23. *And King Solomon was greater than all the kings of the earth in wealth and in wisdom.* This stature has just been demonstrated in the story of the Queen of Sheba.

26. *And Solomon gathered chariots and horsemen.* The reiterated emphasis on Solomon's chariots and horses might reflect historical reality, but it also echoes, perhaps a little ominously, the warning in Deuteronomy 17:16 for the future king, "Only let him not get himself many horses." The text in Deuteronomy, of course, might be a response to Solomon's royal extravagances.

twelve thousand horsemen, and he led them to the chariot towns, and
27 with the king in Jerusalem. And the king made silver in Jerusalem as
28 abundant as stones, and cedar as the sycamores in the lowlands. And
the source of Solomon's horses was from Muzri and from Kue. The
29 king's merchants would take them from Kue for a set price. And a chariot coming up out of Muzri cost six hundred silver shekels and a horse
a hundred fifty. And thus by the sea to all the kings of the Hittites and
to the kings of Aram they would bring them out.

---

twelve thousand horsemen. The fact that the number of horsemen is so much
greater than the number of chariots suggests that the term *parashim* refers both
to charioteers and to cavalrymen.

28. *And the source of Solomon's horses was from Muzri and from Kue.* Both the
geography and the terminology for Solomon's international horse trading in
these last two verses of the chapter are rather obscure. The received text reads
Mitsrayim, Egypt, which was not known for the export of horses, but many
scholars emend this to *Mutsri,* a town in northern Syria (Kue is in Asia Minor).
The substitution of a familiar term for an unfamiliar word is one of the most
common causes of scribal error.

29. *coming up.* Literally, "would come up and go out." Some interpreters take
this as an idiom for "export," but that is not entirely clear.
 by the sea. The Masoretic text reads *beyadam,* "in their hand," which is
obscure because there is no clear antecedent for "their." This translation follows
the Septuagint, which appears to have used a Hebrew text that read *bayam,* a
difference of a single consonant. The transportation of horses from the north
by ship along the Mediterranean coast seems plausible.
 to all the kings of the Hittites and to the kings of Aram. This would mean that
Solomon not only purchased horses for his own use but engaged in an international trade of horses. It is also possible that the preposition "to" (a single-
consonant particle) is a scribal error for "from."

CHAPTER 11

And King Solomon loved many foreign women—Pharaoh's daughter 1
and Moabites, Ammonites, Edomites, Sidonians, Hittites, from the 2
nations of which the LORD had said to the Israelites, "You shall not
come among them and they shall not come among you, for they will
surely lead your heart astray after their gods." To these did Solomon
cling in love. And he had seven hundred princess wives and three hun- 3
dred concubines, and his wives led his heart astray. And it happened 4

---

1. *And King Solomon loved many foreign women.* These words mark a strong
shift in the perception of Solomon. Up to this point, he had been portrayed as
an ideally wise and fabulously wealthy king to whom God gave rousing promises and who built God's house in Jerusalem. The previous mentions of his
marriage to Pharaoh's daughter do not put that alliance in any negative light.
(Later prohibitions on intermarriage were not operative in the early centuries
of Israelite national existence.) Here, however, the legendary profusion of Solomon's foreign wives—a full thousand—leads to the sin of idolatry. The Deuteronomistic editor, for all the inherited stories of Solomon's grandeur, needed an
explanation for the splitting of the kingdom after Solomon's death, and he now
provides it in a manner in keeping with Deuteronomy's conception of historical
causation, in which idolatry leads to national disaster.

2. *from the nations of which the LORD had said . . . , "You shall not come among
them."* The Moabites and the Ammonites in particular were singled out for
this ban.

To these did Solomon cling in love. This expression suggests that the wise
Solomon was besotted with his foreign wives and hence ready to follow their
lead in cultic practice.

3. *his wives led his heart astray.* One may infer that he initially allowed them
freedom of worship and then was drawn into their pagan ways.

in Solomon's old age that his wives led his heart astray after other gods,
and his heart was not whole with the Lord his God like the heart of
5 David his father. And Solomon went after Ashtoreth goddess of the
6 Sidonians and after Milcom abomination of the Ammonites. And Solomon did evil in the eyes of the Lord, and he did not obey the Lord like
7 David his father. Then did Solomon build a high place for Chemosh
the abomination of Moab on the mountain facing Jerusalem and for
8 Molech the abomination of the Ammonites. And, thus did he do for all
his foreign wives who would burn incense and would sacrifice to their
9 gods. And the Lord was furious with Solomon, for his heart had gone
astray from the Lord God of Israel, Who had appeared to him twice,
10 and had charged him about this thing not to go after other gods, and
11 he had not kept what the Lord had charged. And the Lord said to
Solomon: "In as much as this was with you and you did not keep My
covenant and my statutes that I charged to you, I will surely tear away
12 the kingdom from you and give it to your servant. But in your days I will
not do it, for the sake of David your father. From the hand of your son
13 I will tear it away. Only the entire kingdom I will not tear away. One
tribe I will give to your son, for the sake of David my servant and for the

---

7. *Then did Solomon build a high place for Chemosh.* The building of "high
places"—typically rural hilltop altars—is a bête noir of the Deuteronomist both
because he insists on the exclusivity of the Jerusalem temple and because such
altars were vulnerable to pagan influences. Here Solomon is seen taking an
active role in the pagan cult, actually promulgating it.

11. *give it to your servant.* In royal contexts, "servant," *'eved*, usually means
"courtier." Jeroboam, who will appear later in the story, is a member of the royal
bureaucracy and hence Solomon's "servant."

13. *One tribe I will give to your son.* It should be two tribes because the break-
away kingdom in the north will have ten. Either "one" is used hyperbolically, to
emphasize how little will be left to Solomon's line, or it reflects the assimilation
of Simeon into Judah, which became to all intents and purposes the only tribe
of the southern kingdom.

sake of Jerusalem, which I have chosen." And the LORD raised up an 14
adversary against Solomon, Hadad the Edomite, who was of the royal
seed in Edom. And it had happened when David was in Edom, when 15
Joab commander of the army went up to bury the fallen, that he struck
down every male in Edom. For six months Joab had stayed there, and all 16
Israel with him, until he cut off every male in Edom. And Hadad fled, 17
and Edomite men of his father's servants with him, and went to Egypt,
and Hadad was a young lad. And they arose from Midian and came to 18
Paran, and they took men with them from Paran and came to Egypt to
Pharaoh king of Egypt, and he gave him a house, and he decreed food
for him, and he gave him land. And Hadad found great favor in the eyes 19
of Pharaoh, and he gave him a wife, the sister of his own wife Tahpanes
the royal consort. And Tahpanes's sister bore him his son Genubath, 20

---

14. *adversary*. The Hebrew *satan* does not strictly mean "enemy" but something like "troublemaker," someone who is a stumbling-block.

18. *from Midian*. This kingdom to the southeast of Israel would have been a way-station between Edom, farther north, and Egypt.

   came to Paran. Paran is in the Sinai desert, south of Midian and on the way to Egypt.

   Pharaoh . . . gave him a house . . . food . . . and land. The Pharaoh in David's time, unlike the successor who gave his daughter to Solomon, was hostile to Israel. His providing refuge and sustenance to this Edomite refugee from David's onslaught is politically motivated, with the calculation that at some future point Hadad might prove useful in the conflict with David.

19. *the royal consort*. Translations invariably render this as "the queen." But the Hebrew does not call her queen, *malkah*, but rather *gevirah*, a term that elsewhere (including 15:13 in this book) designates the queen-mother. Tahpenes could not be the king's mother because she is his wife, but *gevirah* seems to be extended to a woman intimately related to the king though lacking the full authority and status of queen.

20. *Tahpanes weaned him*. This looks odd because as his aunt, she certainly would not have suckled the child. The attachment of this verb to her might suggest that she had a kind of adoptive relationship with the infant, a child fathered by a foreigner, and so in some symbolic or even legal fashion could be said to preside over his weaning.

and Tahpanes weaned him in Pharaoh's house, and Genubath was in
21 Pharaoh's house in the midst of Pharaoh's sons. And Hadad had heard
in Egypt that David lay with his fathers and that Joab the commander
of the army was dead, and Hadad said to Pharaoh, "Send me off, that I
22 may go to my land." And Pharaoh said to him, "Why, what are you lacking with me that you should seek to go to your land?" And he said, "No.
23 Send me off." And God raised up against him as adversary Rezon son of
24 Eliadu, who had fled from Hadadezer his master, king of Zoba. And he
gathered men about him and became the commander of a troop after
David killed them, and they went to Damascus and dwelled there, and
25 they reigned in Damascus. And he was an adversary against Israel all
the days of Solomon, together with all the harm that Hadad had done,
and he loathed Israel and reigned over Aram.

26 And Jeroboam son of Nebat, an Ephraimite from Zeredah, whose
mother's name was Zeruah, a widow woman, was a servant to Solomon.
27 And he raised his hand against the king. And this is how he raised his
hand against the king: Solomon had built the Citadel, had closed the

---

22. *No. Send me off.* No continuation of the story is given, so there is no way of
knowing whether Hadad was repatriated. If he was, then he would presumably
have taken up his role as "adversary" to Solomon, son of the man who had massacred the male population of Edom. Verse 25 suggests that in fact he played
this role.

23. *who had fled from Hadadezer his master.* Rezon is not referred to as being "of
the royal seed." The implication may be that he was a plebian who may have
been part of a conspiracy against the king.

24. *they reigned in Damascus.* The use of the plural may make sense in this
context: Rezon is not of royal stock; he has gathered around him a private militia; and it is this group of fighting men who have seized control of Damascus.

25. *together with.* The Hebrew preposition looks a little strange but could
simply mean that the harm perpetrated by Rezon was in addition to the harm
done by Hadad.

26. *a servant to Solomon.* The precise nature of the service he performs in Solomon's court is spelled out in verse 28.

breaches of the City of David his father. And the man Jeroboam was an   28
able fellow and Solomon saw that the lad could carry out tasks, and he
appointed him over all the heavy labor of the house of Joseph. And it   29
happened at that time that Jeroboam went out from Jerusalem, and the
prophet Ahijah the Shilonite found him on the way, he covering himself
in a new cloak and the two of them alone in the field. And Ahijah caught   30
hold of the new cloak and tore it into twelve pieces. And he said to   31
Jeroboam, "Take you ten pieces, for thus said the Lord God of Israel: 'I
am about to tear away the kingdom from Solomon's hand and give it to
the ten tribes. And the one tribe shall be his for the sake of My servant   32
David and for the sake of Jerusalem, the city that I have chosen from
all the tribes of Israel, in as much as they have forsaken Me and have   33
bowed down to Ashtoreth goddess of the Sidonians and to Chemosh
god of Moab and to Milcom god of the Ammonites, and they have not
walked in My ways to do what is right in My eyes and My statutes and

---

28. *an able fellow*. The Hebrew *gibor ḥayil* in military contexts means "valiant warrior," but it can also indicate in pacific contexts either competence or
wealth.

   the lad. The Hebrew *na'ar* here might refer not to youth but to subordinate
position.

   could carry out tasks. More literally, "was a carrier-out of tasks."

   the heavy labor. This activity is linked with the building and the repair of
breaches in the wall mentioned in the previous verse. The Hebrew *sevel* derives
from a root that means bearing burdens.

29. *the prophet Ahijah*. The only prophet who has appeared in this story till now
is Nathan, but from this point there will be many. Unlike the so-called literary
prophets, they do not deliver extensive poetic messages of rebuke or consolation, but they do pronounce what the future will be.

   the two of them alone in the field. By its subversive nature, Ahijah's communication to Jeroboam has to be in a clandestine setting.

30. *tore it into twelve pieces*. Turning the torn cloak into a sign picks up Saul's
tearing of Samuel's cloak, which Samuel immediately turns into a sign that
God will tear the kingship away from Saul. The earlier tearing of the garment
was inadvertent whereas this act is deliberately carried out as a symbol of what
will happen.

34 My laws, like David his father. But I will not take the entire kingdom from his hand, for I will keep him as a prince all the days of his life for the sake of David whom I chose, who kept My commands and My stat-
35 utes. And I will take the kingship from the hand of his son and give it
36 to you—the ten tribes. And to his son I will give one tribe, so that there be a lamp for David my servant for all time before Me in Jerusalem, the
37 city that I have chosen to set My name there. And you will I take, and you shall reign over all that you desire, and you shall be king over Israel.
38 And it shall be, if you hearken to all that I charge you and walk in My ways and do what is right in My eyes to keep My statues and My commands as did David My servant, I shall be with you and build for you a
39 lasting house, as I built for David, and I shall give Israel to you. And I
40 shall afflict the seed of David because of this, but not for all time.'" And Solomon sought to put Jeroboam to death, and Jeroboam arose and fled to Egypt, to Shishak king of Egypt, and he stayed in Egypt until Solo-

---

34. *prince*. God's words, as quoted by Ahijah, avoid the authoritative title "king" and instead use an ambiguous word that often designates a tribal chieftain. Solomon's kingship, one sees, is already slipping away.

36. *so that there be a lamp for David my servant*. The language of the prophecy labors to preserve the notion of a divinely elected Davidic dynasty even as most of the kingdom is about to be shorn from the line of David.

38. *if you hearken to all that I charge you*. Once again, the language is explicitly Deuteronomistic.

39. *because of this*. Presumably the reference is to the idolatrous backsliding under the rule of Solomon.

40. *And Solomon sought to put Jeroboam to death*. No report is given of the actions by Jeroboam that might have provoked the king's attempt to kill him (the Septuagint supplies details, but these are of doubtful authority), but one must assume that after the encounter with Ahijah, Jeroboam took steps—like Macbeth after the prophecy of the witches—to secure the throne for himself.
    Shishak king of Egypt. This is clearly a Pharaoh who has come after the one who gave his daughter to Solomon, and who regards Solomon's kingdom with suspicion, if not hostility.

mon's death. And the rest of the acts of Solomon and all that he did, and 41
his wisdom, are they not written in the Book of the Acts of Solomon?
And the time that Solomon reigned in Jerusalem over all Israel was forty 42
years. And Solomon lay with his fathers and was buried in the City of 43
David his father. And Rehoboam his son reigned in his stead.

---

41. *the Book of the Acts of Solomon*. This text would seem to be some sort of
court annals. It is quite possible that the writer or writers responsible for Solomon's story beginning with 1 Kings 3 drew materials from this book, though
that remains in the realm of conjecture.

42. *forty years*. This is, of course, a formulaic number—one frequently used to
designate the length of time a leader in the Book of Judges remained in power.
In all likelihood, it reflects knowledge that Solomon reigned for a relatively long
time, a full generation in biblical terms.

CHAPTER 12

1 And Rehoboam came to Shechem, for all Israel had come to Shechem
2 to make him king. And it happened when Jeroboam son of Nebat heard,
and he was still in Egypt where he had fled from King Solomon, and
3 Jeroboam had stayed in Egypt, that they sent and called to him, and
Jeroboam and all the assembly of Israel came and spoke to Rehoboam,
4 saying, "Your father made our yoke heavy, and you, now lighten the hard
labor of your father and his heavy yoke that he put on us, that we may
5 serve you." And he said to them, "Go off another three days and come
6 back to me," and the people went off. And King Rehoboam took counsel
with the elders who stood in the service of his father while he was alive,

---

1. *for all Israel had come to Shechem to make him king.* Shechem was a frequent
assembly-point in the tribal period. One might have expected, however, that the
coronation would take place in Jerusalem. In this national meeting at Shechem
there appears to be an intimation that Rehoboam's succession to the throne
was not an automatic matter, or to put this differently, that the Davidic rule
over what had been, barely half a century earlier, a federation of tribes was not
entirely assured. Thus Rehoboam comes out from Jerusalem to an assembly
that he hopes will acclaim or ratify his succession. His knowledge of Jeroboam's
ambitions for the throne may be a motivator.

4. *made our yoke heavy.* The literal sense of the Hebrew verb is "made hard,"
but in all the subsequent occurrences of "yoke" in this story, the more expected
"heavy" is used.

   now lighten the hard labor. The people refer, of course, to the punishing
taxation through forced labor necessitated by Solomon's vast building projects.
Requests for remission of taxes and obligations to the crown when a new king
assumed the throne were common in the ancient Near East.

6. *the elders.* These would be a group of state councilors, experienced men who
are not necessarily aged but knowledgeable.

saying, "How do you counsel to respond to this people?" And, they spoke 7
to him, saying, "If today you will be a servant to this people and serve
them and answer them and speak good words to them, they will be servants to you always." And he forsook the counsel of the elders that they 8
had given him and took counsel with the young men with whom he had
grown up, who stood in his service. And he said to them, "What do you 9
counsel that we should respond to this people that has spoken to me,
saying, 'Lighten the yoke that your father put on us?'" And the young 10
men with whom he had grown up spoke to him, saying, "Thus shall you
say to these people who have spoken to you, saying, 'Your father made
our yoke heavy, and you, lighten it for us.' Thus shall you say to them,
'My little finger is thicker than my father's loins. And now, my father 11
burdened you with a heavy yoke, and I will add to your yoke. My father
scourged you with whips, and I will scourge you with scorpions.'" And 12
Jeroboam, and all the people with him, came to Rehoboam on the third
day, as the king had said, "Return to me on the third day." And the king 13
answered the people harshly and forsook the counsel of the elders that
they had given him. And he spoke to them according to the counsel of 14

---

7. *this people*. They are referred to by all parties in this story with the demonstrative pronoun, distancing them and indicating them as a refractory group
with which one must know how to deal properly.

8. *the young men with whom he had grown up*. The word for "young men,"
yeladim, usually means "child" or even "infant." Since we later learn that
Rehoboam was forty when he became king, these are actually middle-aged
men. The term may have been chosen to underscore their puerile behavior. In
any case, the episode surely reflects the ancient predisposition to seek wisdom
from elders, as Job's three friends repeatedly stress.

10. *My little finger is thicker than my father's loins*. This extravagant metaphor
is the advice of arrogance. In the event, Rehoboam deletes these words in his
response to the people. A few interpreters have seen a sexual allusion here,
perhaps because of the proximity to loins, with "little finger" a euphemism for
the male member (in rabbinic Hebrew, "little member" means "penis"). That
would be in keeping with the macho brashness of these words.

11. *I will scourge you with scorpions*. These would either be actual scorpions,
perhaps poisonous, or an iron implement with a ragged head, perhaps one
carved to resemble a scorpion.

the young men, saying, "My father made your yoke heavy and I will add to your yoke. My father scourged you with whips and I will scourge you

15 with scorpions." And the king did not hearken to the people, for it was brought about by the LORD in order to fulfill His word that the LORD

16 had spoken through Ahijah the Shilonite to Jeroboam son of Nebat. And all Israel saw that the king had not hearkened to them, and the people responded to the king, saying,

> "We have no share in David
> > nor an estate in the son of Jesse.
> To your tents, O Israel!
> > See to your house, O David!"

17 And Israel went to their tents. As to the Israelites dwelling in the towns

18 of Judah, Rehoboam was king over them. And King Rehoboam sent out Adoram, who was over the forced labor, and all Israel stoned him and he died. Then King Rehoboam hastened to mount a chariot to flee to

19 Jerusalem. And Israel has rebelled against the house of David to this

20 day. And it happened when all Israel heard that Jeroboam had come back, that they sent and called him to the community and made him king over all Israel. There was no one following the house of David save

---

15. *for it was brought about by the* LORD. Rehoboam's alienating the people has been reported in realistic—possibly historical—terms as a very unwise policy decision. Now, however, it is given a theological explanation: this is the means through which God causes Ahijah's prophecy to be fulfilled.

16. *See to your house, O David!* The people's response, in two lines of poetry, vividly expresses the distance they now feel from the Davidic monarchy: Rehoboam's brutal language makes them realize that this recently founded dynasty has been a bad idea, and that they owe no fealty to it.

18. *Adoram.* Earlier, his name was given a longer form, Adoniram.
who was over the forced labor. It is precisely the forced labor that had been the people's chief complaint. Rehoboam, not yet realizing that his writ no longer extends over the whole people, sends out the chief overseer over the forced labor, unwittingly consigning him to his death.
Then King Rehoboam hastened to mount a chariot. Adoram's murder by the mob makes Rehoboam realize that his own life is in danger.

Judah alone. And Rehoboam came to Jerusalem and assembled all the   21
house of Judah and the tribe of Benjamin, a hundred eighty thousand
picked warriors to do battle with the house of Israel to bring back the
kingship to Rehoboam son of Solomon. And the word of the LORD came   22
to Shemaiah man of God, saying, "Say to Rehoboam son of Solomon   23
king of Judah and to all the house of Judah and Benjamin and the rest
of the people, saying, Thus said the LORD, 'You shall not go up and you   24
shall not do battle with your Israelite brothers. Go back each man to his
house, for from Me has this thing come about.'" And they heeded the
LORD's word and turned back from going, according to the LORD's word.

And Jeroboam rebuilt Shechem in the high country of Ephraim and-   25
dwelled in it. And he went out from there and rebuilt Penuel. And   26
Jeroboam said in his heart, "Now the kingdom will turn back to the

---

21. *the tribe of Benjamin.* Part of Benjamin remained loyal to the house of
David.

   the house of Israel. Henceforth, this phrase will refer to the northern tribes,
in contradistinction to Judah.

22. *Shemaiah man of God.* He is clearly a prophet, precisely like Ahijah, but
here an alternate designation is used.

24. *And they heeded the LORD's word.* It is not clear that they would automatically concede the divine authority of words pronounced by a particular prophet
or man of God. In this instance, however, the prospect of a bloody civil war
and of a military confrontation between two tribes and ten may have disposed
them to accept the prophecy. It is noteworthy that "they"—the people—heed
the prophecy, while no explicit mention is made of the king. It may be that the
force of the prophetic injunction swayed the people, leaving Rehoboam no
choice but to acquiesce.

25. *rebuilt Shechem . . . rebuilt Penuel.* Penuel was destroyed by Gideon to
revenge the failure of its elders to give provisions to his troops (see Judges 8).
In the case of Shechem, fortification may be what is indicated.

26. *Now the kingdom will turn back to the house of David.* Jeroboam clearly
understands what Josiah in the seventh century will understand, that possession of a cultic center is also a claim to centralized political authority. Thus he
takes steps to create cultic places in the north.

27 house of David, if this people go up to do sacrifices in the house of
the LORD in Jerusalem, the heart of this people will turn back to their
master, to Rehoboam king of Judah, and they will kill me and turn back
28 to Rehoboam king of Judah." And the king took counsel and made two
golden calves and said to the people, "Enough for you to go up to Jerusalem! Here are your gods, Israel, who brought you up from the land of
29,30 Egypt." And he placed one in Bethel and the other he set in Dan. And
this thing became an offense; and the people marched before the one
31 in Bethel and the other in Dan. And he made buildings for the high

---

28. *two golden calves . . . Here are your gods, Israel, who brought you up from the
land of Egypt*. The representation of Jeroboam's act as idolatrous—underscored
by the use of "gods" in the plural—is tendentious. Calves or bulls were often
conceived as a mount or a throne of God, precisely like those winged leonine
figures, the cherubim. In all historical likelihood, Jeroboam's intention was not
to displace the worship of YHWH but merely to create alternate cultic centers
to Jerusalem with an alternate temple iconography. But the narrator pointedly
represents all this in precisely the terms, with an explicit quotation, of Aaron's
golden calf (Exodus 32).

29. *one in Bethel and the other . . . in Dan*. Bethel was a well-known cultic site,
and archeologists have uncovered the remnants of a substantial cultic site at
Dan in the far north. Jeroboam's decision to create two cultic centers may be a
concession on his part to the loose and disparate nature of the constellation of
tribes that constituted his new kingdom.

30. *And this thing became an offense*. It is important for the Deuteronomistic
writer to establish that the first king of Israel, despite the admonition of Ahijah,
initiated idolatry in his realm, thus setting the stage for the eventual destruction
of the northern kingdom.
    and the people marched before the one in Bethel and the other in Dan. The
Masoretic text lacks "the one in Bethel," surely an inadvertent omission. One
might have expected the phrase "to go after," the preposition used for idolatry
in 11:2 and 4. Here "to go" is rendered as "to march," presupposing that the
reference is to a procession before the cultic calves.

31. *he made buildings for the high places*. The literal sense of the Hebrew is "he
made a house of high places." The reference may be to the erection of sanctuaries around the hilltop altars.

places and made priests from the pick of the people who were not from
the sons of Levi. And Jeroboam made a festival in the eighth month on ₃₂
the fifteenth day of the month like the festival that was in Judah, and he
went up on the altar. Thus did he do in Bethel to sacrifice to the calves
that he had made, and he set up in Bethel the priests of the high places
he had made. And he went up on the altar that he had made in Bethel ₃₃
on the fifteenth day of the eighth month, in the month he had devised
from his own heart. And he made a festival for the Israelites and went
up on the altar to burn incense.

---

the pick of the people. This is what this Hebrew phrase indicates elsewhere,
though others understand it in an opposite sense, "the common people."
Jeroboam, however, would have had no motivation to enlist priests from the
peasantry. His waywardness is rather reflected in bypassing the priestly caste.
See Genesis 47:2, where this same expression appears to mean "the pick" or
"the best."

32. *a festival in the eighth month*. Calendric differences have often been the
lever of sectarian or political divisions among Jews. The festival referred to is
Sukkot, the most densely attended of the three pilgrim festivals. Its designated
date is on the fifteenth of the seventh month, so Jeroboam, by pushing it a
month later, is marking a pointed difference between his realm and the southern kingdom.

to sacrifice to the calves that he had made. The wording again represents the
cult Jeroboam had set up as sheer idolatry.

CHAPTER 13

1   **A**nd, look, a man of God came from Judah through the word of the
    LORD to Bethel, with Jeroboam standing on the altar to burn incense.
2   And he called out against the altar by the word of the LORD and said,
    "Altar, altar! Thus says the LORD: 'Look, a son is to be born to the house
    of David, Josiah his name, and he shall sacrifice upon you the priests of
    the high places who burn incense upon you, and they shall burn upon
3   you human bones.'" And he gave a portent on that day, saying, "This
    is the portent, that the LORD has spoken: look, the altar is about to be
4   torn asunder, and the ashes that are upon it will be spilled." And it hap-
    pened when the king heard the word of the man of God that he had
    called out against the altar in Bethel, Jeroboam reached out his hand,

---

1. *a man of God.* As before, this is an alternate designation for prophet. In this
story, however, the man who comes from Judah to Bethel is consistently called
a man of God, whereas the old man who will go after him and bring him home
to dine is called a prophet. Verse 26 is the one seeming exception, but that may
reflect a textual problem.

2. *Altar, altar!* This sort of apostrophe to an inanimate object is not a usual
form of prophetic address. The man of God adopts it for shock effect, to direct
attention to what he understands to be an entirely illegitimate altar and cult.
    a son is to be born to the house of David, Josiah his name. Josiah was king
of Judah three centuries after the time of this story, which thus was surely
composed no earlier than the late seventh century BCE. The continuation of
this story appears in 2 Kings 23, where Josiah is reported to have undertaken a
sweeping campaign to destroy idols and the apparatus of pagan worship. In the
course of that campaign, he slaughters the idolatrous priests and also exhumes
bones from graves and burns them on the altar of Bethel in order to make it
forever ritually impure.

saying, "Seize him." And the hand he reached out against him withered, and he could not pull it back. And the altar was torn asunder and the ashes were spilled from the altar according to the portent that the man of God had given by the word of the LORD. And the king spoke out and said to the man of God, "Entreat, please, the LORD your God and pray for me, that my hand come back to me." And the man of God entreated the LORD, and the king's hand came back to him and was as it had been before. And the king spoke to the man of God, "Come into the house with me and dine, that I may give you a gift." And the man of God said to the king, "Should you give me half your house, I would not come with you and I would not eat bread and I would not drink water in this place. For thus it was charged me by the word of the LORD, saying, 'No bread shall you eat nor water shall you drink nor shall you go back on the way that you went.'" And he went off on another way, and he did not return on the way that he had come to Bethel. And a certain old prophet was dwelling in Bethel, and his sons came and recounted to him the whole deed that the man of God had done that day in Bethel, the words that he

---

7. *Come into the house with me and dine.* Jeroboam, having seen the man of God's fearsome power both in the destruction of the altar and the paralyzing and restoring of his arm, seeks to make him an ally.

9. *No bread shall you eat nor water shall you drink.* This prohibition is understandable as an expression of God's absolute rejection of Jeroboam's wayward kingdom: the man of God must shun the king, not breaking bread with him or even drinking water in his house.

nor shall you go back on the way you went. This third prohibition is less transparent. Perhaps the fact that he must take a different route back to Judah is meant to indicate that the dire prophecy he has pronounced is irreversible, though it looks rather like the kind of arbitrary injunction one often encounters in folktales: if you fail to follow these precise stipulations for your mission, disaster will ensue.

11. *a certain old prophet.* The fact that the old prophet lies to the man of God (verse 18) may raise questions about his legitimacy as prophet, but in verse 21 he is represented as the authentic vehicle for the word of the LORD.

his sons. The Masoretic text has a singular here, but two Hebrew manuscripts and three ancient versions show a plural, the form that appears in the rest of the verse and in the next one.

12 had spoken to the king, they recounted them to their father. And their father spoke to them, "By what way did he go?" And his sons showed him the way on which the man of God who had come from Judah had gone.
13 And he said to his sons, "Saddle the donkey for me." And they saddled
14 the donkey for him and he mounted it. And he went after the man of God and found him sitting under a terebinth. And he said to him, "Are
15 you the man of God who came from Judah?" And he said, "I am." And
16 he said, "Come home with me and eat bread." And he said, "I cannot go back with you, nor will I eat bread nor will I drink water in this place.
17 For a word came to me, by the word of the LORD, 'You shall eat no bread nor shall you drink water nor shall you go back to go on the way that you
18 went.'" And he said to him, "I, too, am a prophet like you, and a divine messenger spoke to me with the word of the LORD, saying, 'Bring him back with you to your house, that he may eat bread and drink water.'"
19 He lied to him. And he went back with him and ate bread in his house
20 and drank water. And it happened as they were sitting at the table, that the word of the LORD came to the prophet who had brought him back,
21 and he called out to the man of God who had come from Judah, saying, "Thus said the LORD: 'In as much as you have flouted the word of the LORD and not kept the command that the LORD your God commanded

---

14. *And he went after the man of God.* The man of God, as the sons have reported to the old man, has just demonstrated his credentials by performing two spectacular portents. It would appear that, as a result, the old prophet wants to associate himself with the man of God from Judah, perhaps enhancing his own prophetic status in this fashion.

18. *He lied to him.* Although the lie has fatal consequences, it may have been impelled by a good intention. The old man might well have imagined that the stern prohibition was directed against the king's house but not against the house of a prophet like himself—a professional colleague of the man of God. Seeing how determined the man from Judah is to observe the prohibition, he permits himself to fabricate the story about the divine messenger.

20. *the word of the LORD came to the prophet.* The old man, now made the conduit of the prophecy of doom pronounced upon the man of God, is forced to see how drastically mistaken he was in bringing the man home with him under false pretenses.

you, and you came back and ate bread and drank water in the place of 22
which He spoke to you, Do not eat bread nor drink water, your carcass
shall not come to the grave of your fathers.'" And it happened after he 23
had eaten bread and after he had drunk water that the prophet who had
brought him back saddled the donkey for him. And he went off, and a 24
lion found him on the way and killed him, and his carcass was flung
down on the way with the donkey standing by him and the lion standing by the carcass. And, look, people were passing by, and they saw the 25
carcass flung down on the way and the lion standing by the carcass, and
they came and spoke of it in the town in which the old prophet lived.
And the prophet who had brought him back from the way heard and he 26
said, "It is the man of God who flouted the word of the LORD, and the

---

22. *your carcass.* The Hebrew *neveilah* usually refers to an animal carcass, not
to a human corpse. Its repeated use here may emphasize the abject condition
of the slaughtered man of God, his body flung down on the way.

23. *the prophet who had brought him back saddled the donkey for him.* The
Masoretic text reads: "and he saddled the donkey for the prophet which he
had brought back." This reading is problematic because throughout the story
only the old man is called a prophet, and the other is invariably referred to as
the man of God. The emendation on which the translation rests involves the
change of a single consonant, *hanavi'* instead of *lanavi'* with no alteration of
the Hebrew word-order.

24. *a lion found him on the way.* This part of the story is not miraculous because
in ancient Israel there was an abundance of lions in the countryside, a fact
reflected in the currency of five different terms for "lion" in biblical Hebrew.
  *his carcass was flung down on the way with the donkey standing by him and
the lion standing by the carcass.* It is in this bizarre tableau that the miraculous
character of the event is manifested. As we learn in verse 28, the lion kills the
man but does not eat him and does not harm the donkey. Moreover, he remains
standing by the body and the donkey instead of going off, as one would expect.

26. *who flouted the word of the LORD.* It must be said that the old prophet plays a
rather ambiguous role in this story. After all, it was his lie about having received
instructions from a divine messenger that led the man of God to go back with
him to his house and thus flout the word of the LORD. His pronouncement here
does not appear to express any remorse or any sense of guilt about the death
that he has caused. Perhaps he still feels that he acted out of good intentions

LORD has given him over to the lion, and it has torn him apart and killed

27 him, according to the word of the LORD that He spoke to him." And he
spoke to his sons, saying, "Saddle the donkey for me," and they saddled

28 it. And he went and found his carcass flung down on the way. The lion

29 had not eaten the carcass and had not torn apart the donkey. And the
prophet lifted the man of God's carcass and laid it on the donkey, and he
brought him back to the town of the old prophet to keen for him and to

30 bury him. And he lay his carcass in his grave and keened for him, "Woe,

31 my brother." And it happened after he had buried him that he said to
his sons, saying, "When I die, bury me in the grave in which the man of

32 God is buried; by his bones lay my bones. For the word will surely come
about that he called by the word of the LORD concerning the altar which
is in Bethel and concerning all the buildings of the high places that are

33 in the towns of Samaria." Yet after this thing Jeroboam did not turn back
from his evil way, and again he made priests from the pick of the people.
Whoever desired was ordained and became one of the priests of the high

---

and that the man of God should have strictly observed the divine prohibitions, whatever the persuasive force of an argument to the contrary.

31. *bury me in the grave in which the man of God is buried.* He had wanted to have communion with this prophetic colleague through an act of hospitality. Now he wants to have solidarity with him after his death through a common grave. In the completion of this story in 2 Kings 23, this joint burial will have a positive posthumous consequence for the old prophet because Josiah will spare the bones buried in the man of God's grave from being exhumed and burnt on the Bethel altar.

32. *For the word will surely come about.* The old prophet appears to have foreseen the means by which human bones will be burnt on this altar in order to render it impure—the exhumation of bones from local graves—and so he may be buying himself a kind of burial insurance by having his body buried together with the man who pronounced the dire prophecy about the altar. This entire story remains bizarre to the end.

places. And this thing became an offense for the house of Jeroboam, to 34
wipe it out and destroy it from the face of the earth.

---

34. *to wipe it out and destroy it from the face of the earth.* The late writer,
formulating his story more than a century after the total destruction of the
northern kingdom, has that historical catastrophe in mind (though the immediate reference is to the house of Jeroboam) and here offers a theological
explanation, in keeping with his Deuteronomistic outlook—the offense of
cultic disloyalty.

CHAPTER 14

$_{1,2}$ At that time Abijah son of Jeroboam fell ill. And Jeroboam said to his
wife, "Rise, pray, and disguise yourself, that they will not know you are
Jeroboam's wife, and go to Shiloh, for Ahijah the prophet is there, who
$_3$ spoke to me to become king over this people. And take in your hand ten
loaves of bread and cakes and a jar of honey and come to him. He will
$_4$ tell you what will happen to the lad." And so did Jeroboam's wife do: she
rose and went to Shiloh and came to Ahijah's house, but Ahijah could
$_5$ not see, for his eyes had gone blind from old age. And the LORD had
said to Ahijah, "Look, Jeroboam's wife is about to come to you to ask an
oracle concerning her son, for he is ill, and thus and so shall you speak

---

1. *At that time*. This particular temporal reference is a generalized formulaic
phrase that does not indicate that what follows happened precisely at the same
time as the preceding events in the narrative.

3. *ten loaves of bread and cakes and a jar of honey*. It was customary to bring gifts
to a prophet or seer when seeking oracular counsel from him. These in effect
constituted his professional income.

4. *but Ahijah could not see*. This is the first indication that Jeroboam's plan has
gone awry. He has instructed his wife to go in disguise, but the disguise proves
to be pointless because the prophet is blind. In any case, God will expose the
disguise in speaking to the blind prophet. The blindness, a consequence of
old age, is also an indication that a good deal of time has passed since Ahijah's
fateful encounter on the road with Jeroboam.

5. *thus and so shall you speak to her*. This convention of using a phrase like this
of summary without stipulation of the actual words is not infrequent in biblical
dialogue and reflects its formal bias of stylization. In this case, it is a means of
postponing the revelation of the prophecy of doom that Ahijah will pronounce
against the house of Jeroboam.

to her. And when she comes she will feign to be another." And it hap- 6
pened when Ahijah heard the sound of her footsteps coming through
the entrance, he said, "Come in, wife of Jeroboam. Why should you
feign to be another when I have been sent to you with harsh tidings?
Go, say to Jeroboam, 'Thus said the Lord God of Israel: In as much 7
as I have raised you up from the people and made you prince over My
people Israel, and I have torn the kingdom from the house of David 8
and given it to you, but you have not been like My servant David, who
kept My commands and who walked after Me with all his heart to do
only what was right in My eyes, and you have done evil more than all 9
who were before you and have gone and made yourself other gods and
molten images to vex Me, and Me have you flung behind your back,
therefore am I about to bring evil on the house of Jeroboam, and I 10
shall cut off from Jeroboam every pisser against the wall, bondsman
and freeborn in Israel, and I will burn out from the house of Jeroboam

---

6. *when Ahijah heard the sound of her footsteps.* This detail nicely captures the
perspective of the blind man, who has to depend on his acute sense of hearing.
Though sightless, he of course knows who has come, why she has come, and
the fact that she is disguised, because God has told him all this.

7. *prince.* In God's words, the term *melekh*, king, is avoided, and the vaguer
term *nagid*, prince (etymologically, he who takes the place in front of others),
is used instead for Jeroboam.

8. *My servant David, who kept My commands.* As before, this is an idealized
image of David that does not square with the narrative in 1 and 2 Samuel.

9. *and you have done evil more than all who were before you.* In light of the fact
that there is only one king between Jeroboam and David, the reference here is
probably to all the bad behavior of the people of Israel from the backslidings in
the Wilderness stories onward.

10. *I shall cut off from Jeroboam every pisser against the wall.* This coarse epithet
for males, which David uses in vowing to destroy Nabal and all the males of
his household (1 Samuel 25:22), may well have been formulaic in pronouncing
resolutions of total destruction, so that even God uses it.
    bondsman and freeborn. The meaning of these two Hebrew terms is much
in dispute.

11 as one burns dung till it is gone. Jeroboam's dead in the town the dogs
    will eat, and the dead in the field, the fowl of the heavens, for the Lord
12 has spoken.' And you, rise, go to your house. As your feet come into the
13 town, the child will die. And all Israel shall keen for him and bury him,
    for he alone of Jeroboam shall come to a grave in as much as in him
    alone in the house of Jeroboam a good thing is found before the Lord
14 God of Israel. And the Lord will raise up for Himself a king over Israel
    who will cut off the house of Jeroboam this day and, indeed, even now.
15 And the Lord will strike Israel as a reed sways in the water, and He
    will uproot Israel from the good land that He gave to their fathers and
    will scatter them beyond the River in as much as they have made their
16 sacred poles that vex the Lord. And He shall give Israel up because of
    the offenses of Jeroboam that he committed and that he led Israel to
17 commit." And Jeroboam's wife rose and went off and came to Tirzah.
18 She was coming over the threshold of the house when the lad died. And
    all Israel buried him and keened for him, according to the word of the

---

as one burns dung. The Hebrew verb can mean "root out," "eradicate," but
since pieces of dried dung were used as fuel, it is fairly likely that the sense of
burning is activated here, or that there is a punning relationship between root-
ing out the house of Jeroboam and burning dung. The simile of dung obviously
conveys a withering sense of the value of the house of Jeroboam.

11. *Jeroboam's dead in the town the dogs will eat*. As in the Greek world, leaving a corpse to the degradation of scavengers was conceived as a fundamental
violation of the sanctity of the human body.

12. *As your feet come into the town*. This slightly odd phrase for arrival picks up
the sound of the woman's feet that the blind prophet heard as she came into
his house.

13. *a good thing is found before the Lord*. The virtue in the sick child that earns
him a proper burial is left unspecified.

14. *this day and, indeed, even now*. The Hebrew words—each of them perfectly
ordinary—sound a little peculiar, but the gist seems to be that the end of the
house of Jeroboam is very imminent.

15. *beyond the River*. The Euphrates.

LORD that He had spoken through His servant Ahijah the prophet. And 19
the rest of the acts of Jeroboam, wherein he did battle and whereby he
reigned, why they are written in the Book of the Acts of the Kings of
Israel. And the time that Jeroboam reigned was twenty-two years. And 20
he lay with his fathers, and Nadab his son was king in his stead.

And Rehoboam son of Solomon king of Judah was forty-one years old 21
when he became king, and seventeen years he was king in Jerusalem,
the city that the LORD chose to set His name there from all the tribes of
Israel. And his mother's name was Naamah the Ammonite. And Judah 22
did what was evil in the eyes of the LORD, and they provoked Him more
than all that their fathers had done in their offenses that they committed. And they, too, built high places and steles and sacred poles on every 23
high hill and under every lush tree. And male cult-harlots, too, there 24
were in the land. They did like all the abominations of the nations that

---

19. *the Book of the Acts of the Kings of Israel.* As with the Book of the Acts of
Solomon, this appears to be some sort of royal annals that was probably drawn
on as a source by the author of our narrative.

20. *And he lay with his fathers.* Since, according to the terms of the curse on the
house of Jeroboam, he was not supposed to come to a proper burial, this must
be taken as a general idiom for dying.

21. *And Rehoboam son of Solomon king of Judah.* From this point onward, the
narrative will switch back and forth between the kings of Israel and the kings
of Judah.

22. *And Judah did.* In contrast to Jeroboam, Rehoboam is not said to be directly
responsible, so he may have been seen as merely permissive about pagan
practice.

23. *on every high hill and under every lush tree.* This is a formulaic phrase, obviously reflecting the writer's view that the only legitimate place for the cult was
in the Jerusalem temple. But the phrase also marks what is seen as a dangerous
intertwining between worship and nature: "high places" or shrines on hilltops,
rituals under sacred trees, in some instances may have been associated with a
fertility cult. There is an easy segue from the lush trees of this verse to the male
cult-harlots in the next verse.

25 the LORD had dispossessed before Israel. And it happened in the fifth
year of Rehoboam's reign that Shishak king of Egypt came up against
26 Jerusalem. And he took the treasures of the house of the LORD and the
treasures of the house of the king, and everything did he take, and he
27 took all the gold bucklers that Solomon made. And Rehoboam made
bronze bucklers in their stead and entrusted them to the officers of
28 the royal sentries who guarded the entrance of the king's house. And
it happened, when the king would come to the house of the LORD, the
royal sentries would carry them and bring them back to the chamber
29 of the royal sentries. And the rest of the acts of Rehoboam, and all
that he did, are they not written in the Book of the Acts of the Kings of
30 Judah? And there was constant war between Rehoboam and Jeroboam.

---

25. *Shishak king of Egypt came up against Jerusalem*. Finally, the biblical text
gives us a Pharaoh with a name. An inscription at one entrance of a sanctuary
at Karnak in fact offers a list of towns in Judah and Israel that Shishak attacked
in the course of a sweeping military campaign in 926 BCE. Jerusalem, however, does not appear in the list. The language of the biblical text here is a little
vague: Shishak "came up against Jerusalem" and "took the treasures." This
leaves open the possibility that he besieged the city without conquering it and
that he extorted the treasures from Rehoboam in return for lifting the siege.

27. *the royal sentries*. The Hebrew *ratsim* means "runners," but men put in
charge of palace treasures would scarcely be couriers, and it is immediately
stated that they served as guards. Perhaps the Hebrew term was used because
they also had some function of running before the king's chariots in royal
processions.

29. *the Book of the Acts of the Kings of Judah*. See the comment on verse 19.

30. *And there was constant war between Rehoboam and Jeroboam*. This brief
notice suggests how selective the narratives of the kings are. Nothing is reported
of the course of war between the two kingdoms. For Jeroboam, we get only his
backsliding into idolatry and the consequent prophecies of doom for his house.
For the shorter narrative about Rehoboam, again we are told of the spread
of pagan worship, and of the surrender of the treasures to Shishak—nothing
more. The story of the kings, in keeping with the Deuteronomistic perspective,
is more focused on cultic dereliction, always seen as the cause of historical
disaster, than on political history.

And Rehoboam lay with his fathers and was buried with his fathers in 31
the City of David. And his mother's name was Naamah the Ammonite.
And Abijam his son reigned in his stead.

---

31. *and was buried with his fathers.* Pointedly, this phrase is absent from the
report of Jeroboam's death in verse 20.

And his mother's name was Naamah the Ammonite. This verbatim repetition
of the identification of Rehoboam's mother from verse 21 may seem a bit odd,
and could be the result of an editorial glitch, though perhaps the writer meant
to underscore both at the beginning and the end of Rehoboam's story the link
of this king with the world of idolatry.

CHAPTER 15

And in the eighteenth year of King Jeroboam son of Nebat, Abijam
was king over Judah. Three years he was king in Jerusalem, and his
mother's name was Maacah daughter of Absalom. And he went in all the
offenses of his father that he had done before him, and his heart was not
whole with the LORD his God like the heart of David his forefather. For
the LORD his God for David's sake had given him a lamp in Jerusalem
to raise up his son after him and to make Jerusalem stand, as David had
done what was right in the eyes of the LORD and had not swerved from
all that He charged him all the days of his life, except for the matter of
Uriah the Hittite. And there was war between Rehoboam and Jeroboam
all the days of his life. And the rest of the acts of Abijam and all that he
did, are they not written in the Book of the Acts of the Kings of Judah?
And there was war between Abijam and Jeroboam. And Abijam lay with

---

2. *his mother's name was Maacah daughter of Absalom.* There is a problem in
this notice because Maacah is also said (verse 10) to be the mother of the next
king, Asa, who is Abijam's son, and there is no warrant for the use of "mother" to
mean "grandmother." (In 2 Chronicles 13:2 it is reported that Abijam's mother
was Michaiahu, daughter of Uriel from Gibeah. It is unlikely that the Absalom
mentioned here is the same person as David's son who usurped the throne.)

5. *except for the matter of Uriah the Hittite.* The murder of Uriah is David's
great crime, but even this notation reflects a rather selective reading of his
checkered history.

6. *And there was war between Rehoboam and Jeroboam.* This would have to
mean the house of Rehoboam because it is the reign of Abijam that is being
discussed. The repetition of this whole sentence at the end of the next verse
looks redundant and may reflect a scribal error.

his fathers, and they buried him in the City of David, and Asa his son
was king in his stead.

And in the twentieth year of Jeroboam king of Israel, Asa king of Judah 9
became king. And forty-one years he was king in Jerusalem, and his 10
mother's name was Maacah daughter of Absalom. And Asa did what 11
was right in the eyes of the LORD like David his forefather. And he rid 12
the land of male cult-harlots and removed the vile idols that his fathers
had made. And Maacah his mother, too, he removed from being queen- 13
mother, as she had made a horror for Asherah. And Asa cut down her
horror, and burnt it in the Kidron wadi. But the high places did not 14
disappear, only the heart of Asa was whole with the LORD all his days.
And he brought his father's consecrated things and his own consecrated 15
things into the house of the LORD—silver and gold and vessels. And 16
there was war between Asa and Baasha king of Israel all their days.
And Baasha king of Israel came up against Judah and built Ramah so as 17
not to allow anyone to come or go who belonged to Asa king of Judah.
And Asa took all the silver and the gold remaining in the treasuries of 18
the house of the LORD and the king's treasuries and put them in the
hand of his servants, and King Asa sent them to King Ben-Hadad son of

---

12. *vile idols.* The vocabulary of the Deuteronomistic writers, for understandable ideological reasons, is rich in invective terms for idols, some of them perhaps original coinages. The Hebrew *gilulim* is formed on a root that suggests
"dung."

13. *he removed from being queen-mother.* From this we may infer that the role of
queen-mother, *gevirah*, had certain ceremonial or perhaps even legal functions
attached to it. See the comment on 11:19.
   horror. The Hebrew *mifletset* is clearly derived from a verbal root that means
to suffer spasms of horror. Its use as an epithet for "idol" is similar to *gilulim*
in verse 12.
   And Asa cut down her horror. Some sort of sacred pole was employed in the
cult of Asherah—hence the verb "cut down."

14. *But the high places did not disappear.* The reason would be either that Asa
regarded them as acceptable sites for the worship of YHWH or because they
were spread across the countryside and hence resistant to royal control.

Tabrimmon son of Hezion of Aram, who dwelled in Damascus, saying,
19 "There is a pact between you and me, between your father and my father.
Look, I have sent you a payment of silver and gold. Go, revoke your pact
20 with Baasha king of Israel, that he withdraw from me." And Ben-Hadad
heeded King Asa and sent the commanders of the troops that he had
against the towns of Israel, and he struck down Ijon and Dan and all
21 Abel-Beth-Maacah and all Kinroth, with all the land of Naphtali. And
it happened, when Baasha heard, that he left off building Ramah, and
22 he stayed in Tirzah. And King Asa had mustered all Judah, none was
exempt. And they bore off the stones of Ramah and its timbers with
which Baasha had built, and King Asa built with them Geba-Benjamin
23 and Mizpah. And the rest of all the acts of Asa and all his valor and all
that he did and the towns that he built, are they not written in the Book
of the Acts of the Kings of Judah? Only in his old age he was ailing in
24 his feet. And Asa lay with his fathers and was buried with his fathers
in the City of David his forefather. And Jehoshaphat his son was king
in his stead.

---

19. *I have sent you a payment.* The noun *shohad* in most other contexts means
"bribe." Either the writer put this word in Asa's mouth to convey his own judgment that the payment to turn Ben-Hadad against Baasha was a nasty business,
or—perhaps more likely—the semantic range of *shohad* extended to mean any
payment offered in order to persuade someone to serve one's purposes.

20. *he struck down Ijon and Dan . . . with all the land of Naphtali.* Ben-Hadad's
attack is to the north, whereas Baasha's troops are concentrated in the south.
This would have the effect of making them withdraw from their positions
around Ramah. (See the next verse.)

23. *Only in his old age he was ailing in his feet.* This notice of foot disease
(or perhaps paralysis in the feet) is by no means essential to the story and so
appears to reflect an actual historical memory about the later years of King
Asa, perhaps made poignant by the fact that he had previously been a valiant
military commander.

And Nadab son of Jeroboam had become king over Israel in the second 25
year of Asa king of Judah, and he was king over Israel two years. And 26
he did evil in the eyes of the LORD and went in the way of his father
and his offense that he had led Israel to offend. And Baasha son of 27
Ahijah of the house of Issachar plotted against him, and Baasha struck
him down in Gibethon, which was the Philistines', when Nadab and
all Israel were besieging Gibethon. And Baasha put him to death in the 28
third year of Asa king of Judah, and he became king in his stead. And it 29
happened when he became king that he struck down the whole house
of Jeroboam, he did not leave Jeroboam any breathing creature, until
he destroyed him, according to the words of the LORD which He had
spoken through His servant Ahijah the Shilonite, for the offenses of 30
Jeroboam that he committed and that he led Israel to commit, through
the vexation through which he vexed the LORD God of Israel. And the 31
rest of the acts of Nadab and all that he did, are they not written in the
Book of the Acts of the Kings of Israel? And there was constant war 32
between Asa and Baasha king of Israel. In the third year of Asa king 33
of Judah, Baasha son of Ahijah became king over all Israel in Tirzah,
for twenty-four years. And he did evil in the eyes of the LORD, and he 34
went in the way of Jeroboam and in his offense that he had led Israel
to commit.

---

25. *And Nadab son of Jeroboam had become king over Israel.* Both the form of the
verb and the content of the statement mark this as a pluperfect: the narrative
now backtracks in order to explain how it came about that Baasha supplanted
Jeroboam's son Nadab as king of Israel.

29. *he struck down the whole house of Jeroboam.* This liquidation of all the males
in the house of Jeroboam is both the fulfillment of the prophet Ahijah's curse
and common ancient Near Eastern practice when someone usurps a royal
house. One recalls Macbeth's impulse to kill Banquo and any of his offspring
in order to eliminate anyone who might lay claim to the throne.

CHAPTER 16

₁   And the word of the Lᴏʀᴅ came to Jehu son of Hanani about Baasha,
₂ saying: "In as much as I have raised you from the dust and have made
you prince over My people Israel, yet you went in the way of Jeroboam
₃ and led My people Israel to offend, to vex Me with their offenses. I am
about to root out Baasha and his house, and I will make your house like
₄ the house of Jeroboam son of Nebat. The dogs will eat Baasha's dead
in the town, and his dead in the field the fowl of the heavens will eat."
₅ And the rest of the acts of Baasha and that which he did and his valor,
₆ are they not written in the Book of the Acts of the Kings of Israel? And
Baasha lay with his fathers, and he was buried in Tirzah, and Elah his
₇ son was king in his stead. And indeed through the prophet Jehu son of
Hanani the word of the Lᴏʀᴅ had come against Baasha and against his
house, because of the evil he had done in the eyes of the Lᴏʀᴅ to vex
Him by the work of his hands, to become like the house of Jeroboam,
and because he had struck him down.

---

1. *about Baasha.* The Hebrew preposition could also mean "against" and even
"to." In any case, God's address in the words of the prophecy is directed to
Baasha, not to the prophet.

4. *The dogs will eat Baasha's dead in the town.* For the force of this curse, which
will recur in connection with Ahab and Jezebel, it should be kept in mind that
in ancient Israel dogs were semi-feral scavengers, not pets, and thus an apt
match for "the fowl of the heavens," which would be vultures and related aerial
scavengers.

7. *and because he had struck him down.* This clause is a little cryptic. The initial
"he" has to be Baasha, and so the person he struck down is Jeroboam. Since the
destruction of the house of Jeroboam for the offense of idolatry was announced

In the twenty-sixth year of Asa king of Judah, Elah son of Baasha became 8
king over Israel for two years. And his servant Zimri commander of half 9
the chariotry plotted against him when he was in Tirzah in a drunken
stupor at the house of Arzah, who was appointed over the palace, in
Tirzah. And Zimri came and struck him down and put him to death in 10
the twenty-seventh year of Asa king of Judah, and he became king in his
stead. And it happened when he became king, when he took his seat 11
on the throne, that he struck down the whole house of Baasha, he did
not leave him a pisser against the wall, nor a blood-redeemer or companion. And Zimri destroyed the whole house of Baasha according to 12
the word of the LORD that He had spoken against Baasha through Jehu

---

in a divinely authorized prophecy, one might have thought that there was no sin
in Baasha's killing Jeroboam and all the males of his house. Perhaps the writer
means to suggest that ruthless murder, even if it is the enactment of deserved
retribution, remains ruthless murder, especially if the motives of the killer are
far from noble, as appears to be the case with Baasha. In all these reports,
the writer manifestly struggles with putting forth a theological explanation for
political upheavals. The history of the kingdom of Judah, whatever its vulner-
abilities and cultic derelictions, reflects relative stability: Asa's reign lasts forty
years, while a series of kings in the rival kingdom of Israel are assassinated,
with one regnal span as little as two years and another only seven days. One
might infer that this instability goes back to the fact that the northern kingdom
was established by a usurper, Jeroboam, in contrast to the Davidic dynasty in
the south with its claim of divine election and the heroic figure of David as
its iconic founder. The writer, however, feels constrained to explain that each
murdered monarch perished because of his idolatrous ways.

9. *commander of half the chariotry*. The inevitable inference is that the royal
chariotry was divided into two units, but the "half" here anticipates the hostile
division between factions that will occur.

when he was in . . . a drunken stupor. Zimri shrewdly waits for this moment
when Elah will be an easy target for attack.

who was appointed over the palace. More literally, "over the house." Elah is
attending a feast at the house of his court official.

11. *blood-redeemer*. "Blood" is merely implied. The "redeemer" is a relative who
in the code of vendetta justice has the obligation to avenge a murdered kinsman. No avenger is left alive by Zimri.

13 the prophet, for all the offenses of Baasha and the offenses of Elah his
son, which they committed and which they led Israel to commit, to vex

14 the LORD God of Israel with their empty idols. And the rest of the acts
of Elah and all that he did, are they not written in the Book of the Acts
of the Kings of Israel?

15 In the twenty-seventh year of Asa king of Judah, Zimri became king in
Tirzah for seven days, while the troops encamped at Gibbethon, which

16 was the Philistines'. And the encamped troops heard, saying, "Zimri
has hatched a plot and actually struck down the king." And all Israel
made Omri, commander of the army, king over Israel on that day in the

17 camp. And Omri, and all Israel with him, came up from Gibbethon and

18 besieged Tirzah. And it happened when Zimri saw that that town was
taken, he came into the palace, the king's house, and he burnt down the

19 king's house upon himself and died for the offenses that he had committed to do evil in the eyes of the LORD, to go in the way of Jeroboam and

20 in his offense that he had done to lead Israel to commit. And the rest of
the acts of Zimri and the plot that he had hatched, are they not written

---

13. *for all the offenses of Baasha and the offenses of Elah his son.* As noted above,
a theological explanation is offered for what appears to be a self-interested act
of assassination on the part of a person who wants to seize power.

16. *And all Israel.* Since Israel is now clearly split into two warring factions, this
formulaic phrase must mean all the Israelites present in the military encampment at Gibethon.
  made Omri, commander of the army, king. One sees the rapidity with which
people rise to, or claim, the throne. What this amounts to in this case is a military coup: the troops, seeing that Zimri has assassinated Elah son of Baasha,
who himself assassinated the second monarch of the northern kingdom, decide
to proclaim their own commander king. Omri prevails over Zimri because he
has a large part of the army behind him.

18. *the palace, the king's house.* This is the first time in a narrative book that the
term 'armon, "palace," appears. The only other occurrence in a narrative text is
in Chronicles, though it is frequently used in poetry. The usual narrative designation for "palace" is "the king's house," which here appears as an apposition
or perhaps even as a gloss on 'armon.

in the Book of the Acts of the Kings of Israel? Then was the people of 21
Israel divided in two—half the people followed Tibni son of Ginath to
make him king and the other half followed Omri. And the people who 22
followed Omri were stronger than the people who followed Tibni son of
Ginath, and Tibni died, and Omri became king.

In the thirty-first year of Asa king of Judah, Omri became king over 23
Israel for twelve years. In Tirzah he was king six years. And he bought 24
the Mount of Samaria from Shemer for two talents of silver and built
up the mount and called the name of the town that he had built up
after the name of Shemer master of Mount Samaria. And Omri did 25
evil in the eyes of the LORD, and he was more evil than all who were
before him. And he went in all the way of Jeroboam son of Nebat and 26
in his offenses that he had led Israel to commit, to vex the LORD God
of Israel with their empty idols. And the rest of the acts of Omri and 27
his valor which he did, are they not written in the Book of the Acts of
the Kings of Israel? And Omri lay with his fathers and was buried in 28
Samaria, and Ahab his son was king in his stead.

And Ahab son of Omri became king over Israel in the thirty-eighth year 29
of Asa king of Judah, and Ahab son of Omri was king over Israel in
Samaria twenty-two years. And Ahab son of Omri did evil in the eyes 30

---

21. *half the people followed Tibni son of Ginath.* No information is provided
about Tibni, so it is unclear whether he is a follower of the dead Zimri or simply
an opportunist who seeks to seize the kingship in a moment of political chaos.

22. *And the people who followed Omri were stronger.* Again, it appears that Omri
prevails because he can muster more troops.

24. *Shemer . . . Samaria.* In Hebrew, the connection between the two names is
more transparent because the Hebrew for Samaria is *Shomron.*

29. *Ahab . . . was king over Israel in Samaria twenty-two years.* Despite being the
most flagrantly idolatrous of all the kings of Israel, he enjoys a relatively long
reign, though he will come to an ignominious end.

31 of the L ORD more than all who were before him. And it happened, as
though it were a light thing for him to follow in the offenses of Jeroboam
son of Nebat, that he took as wife Jezebel, daughter of Ithbaal king of
the Sidonians, and he went and served Baal and bowed down to him.
32 And he set up an altar to Baal in the house of Baal that he had built in
33 Samaria. And Ahab made a sacred pole, and Ahab continued to act so as
to vex the L ORD God of Israel more than all the kings of Israel who were
34 before him. In his days Hiel the Bethelite built up Jericho. At the cost
of Abiram his firstborn he laid its foundation and at the cost of Segib his
youngest he put up its gates, according to the word of the L ORD that He
spoke through Joshua son of Nun.

---

31. *Jezebel, daughter of Ithbaal king of the Sidonians.* Her name and lineage
proclaim her roots in the world of idolatry. She is a Phoenician (Sidon being
a principal Phoenician city); her father's name contains the pagan theophoric
element "Baal"; her name means "Where is the prince." The Masoretic texts
polemically revocalize the name of the Phoenician god Zebul as *zebel,* "dung."

he went and served Baal and bowed down to him. Ahab, outdoing his royal
predecessors in Judah and Israel, does not merely tolerate the idolatry of a foreign wife but becomes an active worshipper of Baal, even establishing a temple
and altar dedicated to Baal (the next verse) in his capital city.

34. *Hiel the Bethelite.* He appears to be a royal official.

built up Jericho. Joshua, after the destruction of Jericho, had pronounced a
curse (Joshua 6:26) on whoever might presume to rebuild Jericho. The violation of that solemn prohibition by one of Ahab's people is of a piece with Ahab's
building a site of worship to a pagan god.

At the cost of Abiram his firstborn he laid its foundation. The probable meaning is that according to the terms of Joshua's curse, his firstborn died when he
laid the town's foundations and his youngest when the gates were put up, marking the completion of the building. But the ghost of the ancient Near Eastern
practice of a foundation sacrifice, in which a ruler sacrificed his firstborn to
ensure the well-being of the city, flickers through this grim verse.

CHAPTER 17

And Elijah the Tishbite, of the inhabitants of Gilead, said to Ahab,   1
"As the LORD God of Israel lives, Whom I have served, there shall be
no rain or dew except by my word." And the word of the LORD came to   2
him saying, "Go from here and turn you eastward and hide in the wadi   3
of Cherith, which goes into the Jordan. And it shall be, that from the   4
wadi you shall drink, and the ravens have I charged to sustain you there."
And he went and did according to the word of the LORD, and he went   5
and stayed in the wadi of Cherith, which goes into the Jordan. And the   6
ravens would bring him bread and meat in the morning and bread and

---

1. *Elijah the Tishbite.* Elijah springs into the narrative, like several previous
prophets, with no introduction or explanation. Part of the role he will play is like
that of his predecessors; another part is quite new, as we shall see.

Whom I have served. Literally, before Whom I have stood.

there shall be no rain or dew except by my word. A persistent drought is the
background of the stories that follow. It will be broken only at the climax of
Elijah's confrontation with the priests of Baal on Mount Carmel. He tells Ahab
that he has the power to bring a drought through his own word—a posture that
previous prophets have not assumed. The implication appears to be that the
drought is a punishment for Ahab's idolatry, but Elijah does not spell that out
in his brief and peremptory speech.

3. *Go from here and turn you eastward.* God's instruction to Elijah presupposes
that the prophet is in mortal danger after his harsh words to the king and so
must take refuge in a wilderness region along the Jordan.

which goes into the Jordan. The literal sense is "which is by" or "which faces."
This wadi, unidentified by scholars, is obviously a tributary of the Jordan.

4. *the ravens have I charged to sustain you.* This is the first in a series of miraculous notes that mark the Elijah story.

7   meat in the evening, and from the wadi he would drink. And it happened
    after a time that the wadi dried up, for there was no rain in the land.
8,9 And the word of the LORD came to him, saying, "Rise, go to Zarephath,
    which belongs to Sidon, and stay there. Look, I have charged a widow-
10 woman there to sustain you." And he rose and went to Zarephath and
    came to the entrance of the town, and, look, a widow-woman was there
    gathering sticks. And he called to her and said, "Fetch me, pray, a bit of
11 water in a vessel that I may drink." And she went to fetch and he called
12 to her and said, "Fetch me, pray, a crust of bread in your hand." And she
    said, "As the LORD your God lives, I have no loaf but only a handful of
    flour in the jar and a bit of oil in the cruse and I am about to gather a
    couple of sticks, and I shall make it for me and for my son and we shall
13 eat it and die." And Elijah said to her, "Fear not. Come, do as you have
    spoken, only first make me from there a little loaf and bring it out to me,

---

7. *after a time.* This elastic indication of time might also mean "at the end of
a year."

9. *Zarephath, which belongs to Sidon.* The second place of flight for Elijah is in
Phoenician territory, a little north of the Israelite border. Thus the widow for
whom Elijah miraculously intervenes is not Israelite. Her coming to recognize
the God of Israel is an ironic contrast to Ahab, Israel's king. The closeness of
Phoenician to Hebrew (if the writer thought of such things) would have made
conversation between them possible.
    I have charged a widow-woman. God has not actually spoken to the widow,
as will become evident, but rather has designated her to play this role.

10. *gathering sticks.* Her intention is to make a fire over which she can bake,
bedouin-style, the bit of flour she carries with her.
    Fetch me, pray, a bit of water in a vessel that I may drink. This request is remi-
niscent of the request of Abraham's servant to Rebekah in Genesis 24. In this
case, however, water would have to be scarce because of the extended drought.

12. *we shall eat it and die.* This telescoped clause is a vivid expression of the
woman's desperation. The little flour that she possesses is scarcely enough to
sustain two starving people; it will provide no more than a teasing taste, a mere
scrap of flatbread baked over embers.

13. *only first make me from there a little loaf.* The order of feeding he stipulates
is deliberately perverse: first the prophet then the woman and last her son,

and for you and for your son make afterward. For thus the LORD God 14
of Israel has said, 'The jar of flour will not go empty nor will the cruse
of oil be drained until the day the LORD sends rain over the land.'" And 15
she went and did according to Elijah's word, and she ate, she and he and
her household, many days. The jar of flour did not go empty nor was the 16
cruse of oil drained, according to the word of the LORD that He spoke
through Elijah. And it happened after these things that the son of the 17
woman, mistress of the house, fell ill, and his illness was very grave, till
no breath was left in him. And she said to Elijah, "What is between you 18
and me, O man of God? You have come to me to recall my crime and to

---

instead of the other way around when there is not enough flour even for two. It
challenges the woman to place implicit faith in the prophet.

14. *the* LORD *God of Israel.* This set phrase has special force in being addressed
to a Phoenician woman: it is Israel's uniquely powerful God, YHWH, who has
the power to perform these wonders.

The jar of flour will not go empty nor will the cruse of oil be drained. This is
the point at which Elijah's role as a miracle worker becomes explicit. Unlike the
figure cut by Nathan or Ahijah, Elijah looks very much like the protagonist of a
cycle of folktales, providing sustenance in time of famine through supernatural
means and reviving the dead. It is obviously Elijah, not Moses or Isaiah, who
establishes the template for many of the stories about Jesus in the Gospels. It
was also this aspect of Elijah as a miraculous and compassionate intervener on
behalf of the wretched of the earth that was picked up by later Jewish folklore.
His other role, as implacable reprover, was not embraced by folk tradition.

until the day the LORD *sends rain over the land.* The inexhaustible jar of flour
and cruse of oil thus provide continuing drought insurance for the widow and
her son.

17. *till no breath was left in him.* The somewhat ambiguous phrasing in which
the breath, *neshamah*, has gone out of the boy leaves it unclear whether he has
actually died or whether he is in a comatose state in which breathing is barely
detectable. In verses 21 and 22, it is the "life-breath," *nefesh*, that is said to
return to the child. *Neshamah* and *nefesh* are close synonyms, though the former
may be more closely associated with breathing and the latter with life itself.

18. *What is between you and me.* This idiom, rendered literally, could mean either,
What quarrel is there between you and me? or What should I have to do with you?

You have come to me to recall my crime. One need not assume that she
has actually committed any heinous crime. Ancient Near Eastern people, both

19 put my son to death." And he said to her, "Give me your son." And he
took him from her lap and brought him up to the upper chamber where
20 he was staying and laid him in his bed. And he called out to the LORD
and said, "LORD my God, have You actually done harm to the widow with
21 whom I sojourn to put her son to death?" And he stretched out over the
child three times and called out to the LORD and said, "LORD my God,
22 let the life-breath, pray, of the child go back into him." And the LORD
heeded Elijah's voice, and the child's life-breath went back into him, and
23 he revived. And Elijah took the child and brought him down from the
upper chamber and gave him to his mother, and Elijah said, "See, your
24 son is alive." And the woman said to Elijah, "Now I know that you are a
man of God, and the word of the LORD in your mouth is truth."

Israelites and their neighbors, usually assumed that affliction came as retribution for wrongdoing. The woman thus feels that the very presence of a man of
God has exposed to God's attention some transgression, however inadvertent
or unconscious, for which she is now punished by the death of her only son.

19. *the upper chamber where he was staying.* In a piece of delayed exposition,
we are now informed that Elijah has not only miraculously provided flour and
oil for the widow but has taken refuge—still hiding from Ahab's wrath—in the
upper chamber of her house.

21. *he stretched out over the child.* Some interpreters see here, as in the parallel
story about Elisha, an act of resuscitation through artificial respiration, though
the writer probably conceived it as a miraculous intervention, the prophet
imparting the supernatural vitality of his own body to the boy. Elijah's prayer to
God obviously supports the notion of a divine miracle.

24. *Now I know that you are a man of God, and the word of the LORD in your
mouth is truth.* She had previously addressed him as "man of God," but in anger.
Now the positive force of this identity has been confirmed by his act. The
two aspects of Elijah's mission—wonder-worker and prophesier/reprover—
are interdependent, the former demonstrating to skeptics the authority of the
latter. This pattern, which will be picked up in the stories about Jesus, does not
appear in the reports about the prophets before Elijah. Sometimes one detects
a belief that the prophet has the power to project a kind of spiritual force-field
as when Samuel zaps the messengers Saul sends to him (1 Samuel 19), but
Samuel does not go around the countryside performing acts of resurrection and
miraculous provision of food.

CHAPTER 18

And it happened after a long time, that the word of the LORD came to 1
Elijah in the third year, saying, "Go and appear before Ahab, that I may
send rain over the land." And Elijah went to appear before Ahab, and 2
the famine was severe in Samaria. And Elijah called to Obadiah, who 3
was appointed over the palace, and Obadiah feared the LORD greatly.
And it had happened, when Jezebel cut off the prophets of the LORD, 4
that Obadiah had taken a hundred prophets, fifty men to a cave, and
sustained them with bread and water. And Ahab said to Obadiah, "Go 5
through the land to all the water-springs and to all the wadis. Perhaps we
shall find grass and we can keep horse and mule alive and will not lose

---

1. *in the third year.* This is clearly the third year of the drought. Some interpreters think the story is evenly divided in thirds—a year at the wadi of Cherith, a
year in the house of the widow at Zarephath, and a year in which Elijah moves
across the country, finally confronting Ahab—but there is no explicit indication
of such a division.

3. *Obadiah, who was appointed over the palace, and Obadiah feared the* LORD
greatly. Obadiah's name means "servant of God," a role he affirms in the risky
business of hiding and sustaining the hundred prophets of the LORD. At the
same time, he is a high official in Ahab's court.

4. *a hundred prophets.* This large number suggests they are not prophets directly
assigned a specific mission by God, like Elijah, but rather members of a kind of
guild of prophets, probably figuring as ecstatics, like the prophets in the Saul
story, though with the assumption that the ecstasy is inspired by YHWH. Ahab's
swerving from God, then, is seen to have taken a new deadly turn—not only
does he foster the worship of Baal but also he takes violent steps to extirpate
devotion to YHWH.

6 all our beasts." And they divided up the land for them to pass through—
Ahab went one way by himself and Obadiah went another way by him-
7 self. And it happened, when Obadiah was on the way, that, look, Elijah
was coming toward him, and he recognized him and fell on his face and
8 said, "Are you my lord Elijah?" And he said to him, "I am. Go and say
9 to your lord, 'Elijah is here.'" And he said, "How have I offended, that
10 you should place your servant in Ahab's hands to put me to death? As
the LORD lives, there is no nation or kingdom to which my lord has not
sent to seek you out, and they said, 'He is not here,' and he made the
11 kingdom or nation swear that you were not found. And now you say to
12 me, 'Go, say to your lord, Elijah is here?' And so, I shall go away from you

---

6. *And they divided up the land for them to pass through*. The cause of their
separation is the pressing severity of the drought, but it is also important that
they be separated—Obadiah would normally have remained in the palace—so
that Elijah can speak to him in Ahab's absence.

7.–8. *my lord Elijah . . . say to your lord*. There is an ironic interplay between this
designation of two different men—Elijah, recognized by Obadiah as his lord
through the force of his spiritual authority, and Ahab, who is Obadiah's lord in
the political hierarchy as his king.

9. *How have I offended*. The exchange between Obadiah and Elijah is one of the
most spectacular deployments of the biblical technique of contrastive dialogue,
in which the two speakers are sharply differentiated by antithesis in tone and
attitude and, often, by an opposition between brevity and prolixity (see, for
example, Joseph and Potiphar's wife in Genesis 39). Elijah expresses a concise
imperative, "Go and say to your lord Elijah is here," and then the steely resolution at the end of the dialogue, "As the LORD of Armies lives, Whom I have
served, today I will appear before him." Obadiah, on the other hand, terrified by
the prospect of conveying this message to Ahab, spouts a stream of highly nervous volubility, anxiously repeating twice what he regards as Elijah's impossible
order to him and at the same time defending his own record as a God-fearing
man. The effect is almost comical: he is a good man and has incurred danger
in his loyalty to the LORD, but he is also an ordinary man, susceptible to fear.
The contrast to the iron-willed Elijah is striking. At the same time, Obadiah's
terror vividly reflects Ahab's ruthlessness as a paganizing monarch.

and the LORD's spirit will bear you off to I know not where, and I shall
come to tell Ahab and he won't find you, and he will kill me. And your
servant has feared the LORD from his youth. Why, it has been told to my   13
lord what I did when Jezebel killed the prophets of the LORD, fifty men
to a cave, and I sustained them with bread and water. And now you say   14
to me, 'Say to your lord, Elijah is here,' and he will kill me!" And Elijah   15
said, "As the LORD of Armies lives, Whom I have served, today I will
appear before him." And Obadiah went to meet Ahab and told him, and   16
Ahab went to meet Elijah. And it happened, when Ahab saw Elijah, that   17
he said to him, "Is it you, troubler of Israel?" And he said, "I have not   18
troubled Israel but rather you and your father's house in your forsaking
the LORD's commands and going after the Baalim. And now, send out,   19
gather for me all Israel at Mount Carmel, and the four hundred fifty
prophets of Baal and the four hundred prophets of Asherah, who eat at
Jezebel's table. And Ahab sent out among all the Israelites and gathered   20
the prophets at Mount Carmel. And Elijah approached all the people   21
and said, "How long will you keep hopping between the two crevices?

---

12. *the LORD's spirit will bear you off to I know not where.* For nearly three years,
Elijah has proven to be a successfully elusive fugitive from Ahab's wrath, and so
Obadiah feels it is safe to assume that the prophet will continue on this path.

19. *And now, send out, gather . . . all Israel at Mount Carmel.* Ahab may be willing to accept this challenge instead of having Elijah killed on the spot because
it presents itself as the opportunity for a grand public triumph. Nine hundred
pagan prophets will surely overwhelm one prophet of the LORD in any contest,
and even the place of confrontation is favorable to the pagan cause, Mount
Carmel near the northern coast and close to the border of Lebanon being in
proximity to the Phoenician sphere and a place where an altar of YHWH lies
in ruins, presumably replaced by Baal worship. The king's calculation is probably first to humiliate Elijah before the assembled people and then to kill him.

21. *How long will you keep hopping between the two crevices?* This is obviously
an idiom that means trying to have it both ways. The Hebrew noun has three
different meanings: *se'if* can be a "thought" (hence "opinions" in the King James
Version), a "branch," or a "crevice." This translation assumes that the idiom
invokes a concrete image, and opts for "crevices" because of the physical evocation of a person awkwardly jumping between two cracks in a rock.

If it's the Lord God, go follow Him, and if it's Baal, go follow him." And
22 the people answered him not a word. And Elijah said to the people, "I
alone remain a prophet of the Lord, and the prophets of Baal are four
23 hundred fifty men. Let them give us two bulls, and let them choose for
themselves one bull and cut it up and put it on the wood, but let them
set no fire, and I on my part will prepare the other bull and put it on the
24 wood, but I will set no fire. And you shall call in the name of your god,
and I on my part will call in the name of the Lord, and it shall be that
the god who answers with fire, he is God." And all the people answered
25 and said, "The thing is good." And Elijah said to the prophets of Baal,
"Choose one of the bulls for yourselves and go first, for you are the many,
26 and call in the name of your god, but set no fire." And they took the bull
that he had given them, and they prepared it and called in the name of
Baal from morning to noon, saying, "O Baal, answer us!" But, there was
no voice and none answering, and they hopped about on the altar that
27 he had made. And it happened at noon that Elijah mocked them and
said, "Call out in a loud voice, for he is a god. Perhaps he is chatting
or occupied or off on a journey. Perhaps he is sleeping and will awake."

---

22. *I alone remain a prophet of the* Lord. The hundred prophets hidden in caves,
who have no mission and are not standing on Mount Carmel confronting the
450 prophets of Baal, would not count.

four hundred fifty men. The 450 prophets of the goddess Asherah appear to
be out of the picture.

25. *Choose one of the bulls for yourselves.* He creates the impression of giving
them the advantage of, one might say, serving first.

26. *the bull that he had given them.* That is, he offered two bulls and allowed
them to choose.

they hopped about on the altar. The verb here satirically picks up the "hopping between two crevices" in verse 21.

27. *Perhaps he is chatting.* Though both the Prophets and Psalms denounce
idols as having ears and mouth but without the capacity for hearing or speech,
Elijah turns this notion into biting sarcasm in dialogue.

And they called out in a loud voice and gouged themselves with swords   28
and spears as was their wont till blood spilled upon them. And it hap-   29
pened, as the morning passed, that they prophesied until the hour of
the afternoon offering, but there was no voice and none answering and
none hearing. And Elijah said to all the people, "Draw near me." And   30
all the people drew near him, and he mended the wrecked altar of the
LORD. And Elijah took twelve stones, like the number of the tribes of   31
Jacob's sons, to whom the word of the LORD came saying, "Israel shall
be your name." And he built with the stones an altar in the name of the   32
LORD and made a trench wide enough for two *seahs* of seed around
the altar. And he laid out the wood and cut up the bull and put it on   33
the wood. And he said, "Fill four jugs with water and pour it on the   34
offering and on the wood," and he said, "Do it a second time," and they
did it a second time, and he said, "Do it a third time," and they did it a
third time. And the water went round the altar, and the trench, too, was   35
filled with water. And it happened at the hour of the afternoon offering   36
that Elijah the prophet approached and said, "LORD, God of Abraham,
Isaac, and Israel, this day let it be known that You are God in Israel

---

28. *gouged themselves.* This is an attested pagan cultic practice, prohibited in
the Torah, and is either a gesture of self-immolation or an act of sympathetic
magic (blood spurting to stimulate fire springing out from the wood).

29. *prophesied.* The reflexive conjugation of the verb associated with prophecy
that is used here means to fling oneself into a state of ecstasy or frenzy.
    none hearing. Literally, "no hearing."

34. *Fill four jugs with water.* Pouring water over the wood and the sacrificial
animal magnifies the miraculous nature of the appearance of fire that is about
to occur. Elijah, together with his gift of rhetoric and satire, is a grand stage
manager at this event.

36. *at the hour of the afternoon offering.* This would be late afternoon.
    approached. This is the same verb as "draw near" in verse 30 but here has
the technical sense of approaching a sacred zone.

and I am Your servant, and by Your word have I done all these things.
37 Answer me, LORD, answer me, that this people may know that You are
38 the LORD God, and that it is You Who turned their heart backward." And
the LORD's fire came down and consumed the offering and the wood and
39 the dirt, and the water that was in the trench it licked up. And all the
people saw and fell on their faces and said, "The LORD, He is God; the
40 LORD, He is God." And Elijah said to them, "Seize the prophets of Baal.
Let no man of them escape." And they seized them and Elijah took them
41 down to the wadi of Kishon and slaughtered them there. And Elijah said
to Ahab, "Go up, eat and drink, for it is the rumbling sound of rain."
42 And Ahab went up to eat and to drink, while Elijah had gone up to the
top of Carmel and stooped to the ground and put his head between his
43 knees. And he said to his lad, "Go up, pray, look out to the sea." And he
went up and looked out and said, "There is nothing." And he said "Go

---

37. *it is You Who turned their heart backward.* The clause is ambiguous. It could
mean, given the narrative context: it is You Who made them again realize that
YHWH alone is God. But "backward," *aḥoranit*, often has a negative connotation, so the clause could mean: it was You Who allowed them to fall back into
idolatry, for God causes all things.

39. *The LORD, He is God.* This awestruck proclamation of faith has, appropriately, been introduced into the Yom Kippur liturgy at the very end of the
concluding service.

40. *Elijah . . . slaughtered them there.* The verb used is singular, so the slaugh-
terer is Elijah. There are other verbs for killing—this particular verb is generally
used for animals. Elijah is as ruthless in his zealotry for YHWH as Ahab in his
pagan despotism.

41. *Go up, eat and drink.* Feasting is in order because the drought is about to
come to an end.

42. *stooped.* Usually the verb *gahar* means to stretch out, but he could scarcely
be stretched out if his head is between his knees.

back" seven times. And it happened on the seventh time that he said, 44
"Look, a little cloud like a man's palm is coming up from the sea." And
he said, "Go up, say to Ahab, 'Harness and come down, and let not the
rain hold you back.'" And it happened, meanwhile, that the heavens 45
grew dark with clouds, and there was wind, and there was heavy rain.
And Ahab rode off and went to Jezreel. And the hand of the LORD had 46
come upon Elijah, and he girded his loins and ran before Ahab till you
come to Jezreel.

---

44. *Harness and come down.* Ahab has "gone up" to eat and drink, perhaps
somewhere on the slopes of Mount Carmel. Now he will descend by chariot
into the Valley of Jezreel.

46. *he girded his loins and ran before Ahab till you come to Jezreel.* Some interpret
Elijah's running ahead of Ahab's chariot as a gesture of alliance with the king.
More probably, he is again demonstrating a power superior to the king's: filled
with the divine afflatus, he sprints ahead of the king's chariot all the way to
Jezreel, outstripping the galloping horses.

CHAPTER 19

A nd Ahab told Jezebel all that Elijah had done and all about how he
2 killed all the prophets by the sword. And Jezebel sent a messenger to
Elijah saying, "So may the gods do to me, and even more, if by this time
3 tomorrow I do not make your life like the life of one of them." And he
was afraid, and he arose and went off to save himself, and he came to
4 Beersheba, which is Judah's, and he left his lad there. And he had gone
a day's journey into the wilderness, and he came and sat under a certain
broom-tree, and he wanted to die, and he said, "Enough now LORD. Take

---

1. *all*. This word is repeated three times in the report of Ahab's speech to
Jezebel, probably to suggest his emphasis in speaking to her of the enormity
perpetrated by Elijah—all the things he did.

all the prophets. In this instance, the repeated phrase "the prophets of Baal"
is not used. Moshe Garsiel has aptly observed that this usage reflects the viewpoint of Ahab and Jezebel, who see the prophets of Baal as prophets *tout court*,
with no need of a qualifier.

3. *And he was afraid*. The received text reads "And he saw" (a difference of a
single vowel in the Hebrew), but several Hebrew manuscripts and most of the
ancient translations have "And he was afraid." One suspects that the Masoretic
editors balked at the notion that the iron-willed Elijah could have shown fear.
In fact, this turn in the narrative is by no means implausible: Elijah has spent
two years or more hiding out from Ahab's wrath. He then decides to confront
him in the conviction that a show of divine force on Mount Carmel will dis-
abuse the king of his idolatrous illusions and make him bend to Elijah's spiritual
authority. But Elijah has not reckoned with Jezebel's implacability, and now,
finding that she seeks his life despite the spectacular public triumph on Mount
Carmel, he is afraid and flees.

4. *Enough now LORD. Take my life*. The fear for his life inspired by Jezebel is,
here, followed by despair. If, after his tremendous performance publicly dem-

my life, for I am no better than my fathers." And he lay down and slept 5
under a certain broom-tree, and look, a divine messenger was touching
him, and he said to him, "Arise, eat." And he looked, and there at his 6
head was a loaf baked on hot coals and a cruse of water. And he ate
and he drank and he lay down once more. And the LORD's messenger 7
came back again and touched him and said, "Arise, eat, for your way is
long. And he rose and ate and drank and walked in the strength of that 8
eating forty days and forty nights as far as the mountain of God, Horeb.
And he came into a cave and spent the night there, and, look, the word 9
of the LORD came to him and said to him, "What are you doing here,
Elijah?" And he said, "I have been very zealous for the LORD God of 10
Armies, for the Israelites have forsaken Your covenant—Your altars they
have destroyed, Your prophets they have killed by the sword, and I alone
remain, and they have sought to take my life." And He said, "Go and 11
stand on the mountain before the LORD, and, look, the LORD is about

---

onstrating that YHWH is God, the royal couple still seek to kill him and remain
unrepentant in the idolatrous ways they have fostered in Israel, his prophetic
mission has been a failure, and there is no point in his going on.

6. *a loaf baked on hot coals.* This is the immemorial bedouin method of making
flatbread (modern-day *pitah*).

7. *your way is long.* As the next verse explains, his journey on foot will take forty
days, recalling Moses's forty days on the mountain.

9. *What are you doing here, Elijah?* This might be a challenge to Elijah for
abandoning his people to flee to the wilderness, or it might mean, in view of
the attention to the details of epiphany that will follow: what are you doing following in Moses's footsteps to Mount Horeb?

10. *and I alone remain.* As before, the hundred prophets hidden by Obadiah are
not taken into account because they are not on a prophetic mission.

11. *Go and stand on the mountain before the LORD.* Elijah is commanded to
assume the stature of Moses, but the epiphany he is vouchsafed vigorously
revises the details of Moses's epiphany: God will reveal himself not in storm
or fire or the shaking of the mountain but in a small, barely audible sound. On
Mount Carmel, God spoke through fire; here at Horeb, he speaks in a more
subtle language, for the deity is by no means limited to seismic manifestations.

to pass over, with a great and strong wind tearing apart mountains and smashing rocks before the LORD. Not in the wind is the LORD. And after

12 the wind an earthquake. Not in the earthquake is the LORD. And after the earthquake—fire. Not in the fire is the LORD. And after the fire, a

13 sound of minute stillness." And it happened, when Elijah heard, that he covered his face with his mantle and he went out and stood at the entrance to the cave, and, look, a voice came to him and said, "What are

14 you doing here, Elijah?" And he said, "I have been very zealous for the LORD God of Armies, for the Israelites have forsaken Your covenant— Your altars they have destroyed, and your prophets they have killed by the sword, and I alone remain, and they have sought to take my life."

15 And the LORD said to him, "Go, return on your way to the wilderness of

16 Damascus, and you shall come and anoint Hazael king over Aram. And Jehu son of Nimshi you shall anoint king over Israel, and Elisha son of Shephat from Abel Meholah you shall anoint prophet in your stead.

17 And it shall be, that who escapes the sword of Hazael, Jehu shall put

---

13. *What are you doing here, Elijah?* These words, and Elijah's response, replicate the exchange between "the word of the LORD" and the prophet in verse 9. Either the repetition is intended to frame Elijah's encounter with God symmetrically, before and after the epiphany in a virtually still voice, or it reflects a duplication in scribal transmission.

15. *you shall come and anoint Hazael king over Aram.* Perhaps this act is meant to manifest God's sovereignty over all nations, but it seems strange, and historically altogether unlikely, that a Hebrew prophet could have taken upon himself to anoint an Aramean king.

16. *you shall anoint prophet in your stead.* The term "in your stead" is the same one used for royal succession. Elisha, then, is designated not merely as ministrant to Elijah but as his successor, so there is an intimation that Elijah's days are now numbered.

17. *who escapes the sword of Hazael, Jehu shall put to death.* The prophetic campaign against Ahab and Jezebel is now to take a new path. Since they have demonstrated that no proof of God's power will deflect them from the promotion of idolatry, they must be destroyed—first by a foreign enemy, then by an Israelite who will depose Ahab, and in the last instance by Elisha, who will follow Elijah's prophetic precedent in slaughtering Baal worshipers.

to death, and who escapes the word of Jehu, Elisha shall put to death.
And I shall leave in Israel seven thousand, every knee that did not bow   18
to Baal and every mouth that did not kiss him." And he went from there   19
and found Elisha son of Shaphat while he was plowing with twelve yoke
of oxen before him, and he was with the twelfth. And Elijah crossed over
to him and flung his mantle upon him. And he abandoned the cattle   20
and ran after Elijah. And he said, "Let me, pray, kiss my father and my
mother and I will come after you." And he said to him, "Go, return, for
what have I done to you?" And he turned back from him and took the   21
yoke of oxen and slaughtered them, and with the wood from the gear
of the oxen he cooked the meat and gave it to the people, and they ate.
And he arose and went after Elijah and ministered to him.

---

19. *twelve yoke of oxen.* This would make him a rather prosperous farmer,
though the number twelve is obviously symbolic of the twelve tribes of Israel.

flung his mantle upon him. This act, which would produce an English idiom,
is a clear indication that Elijah is passing on the authority of the prophet's role
to Elisha. In the Samuel story, the prophet's vocation is similarly associated
with a distinctive garment.

20. *Let me, pray, kiss my father and my mother.* This gesture of filial affection is
a contrast to the idolatrous kissing of Baal icons mentioned in verse 18.

Go, return, for what have I done to you? It seems more plausible not to
construe these words as a rebuke for hesitancy on the part of Elisha but as an
assent: Why shouldn't you go back to take fond leave of your parents? I have
made no unreasonable demands of you.

21. *the gear of the oxen.* That is, the plow. Elisha's turning the wooden plow into
firewood is a sign that he is definitively putting behind him his life as a farmer
to assume the role of prophet.

he cooked the meat and gave it to the people. The slaughtering of the two
oxen, then, is not a sacrificial act, or at any rate not primarily a sacrificial act,
but rather Elisha's means of providing a kind of farewell feast for his parents
and kinsmen.

CHAPTER 20

₁ **A**nd Ben-Hadad king of Aram gathered all his forces, and thirty-two kings were with him, and horses and chariots, and he came up ₂ and besieged Samaria and battled against it. And he sent messengers ₃ to Ahab king of Israel in the town and said to him, "Thus says Ben-Hadad: 'Your silver and your gold are mine and your wives and your ₄ goodly sons are mine.'" And the king of Israel answered and said, "As ₅ you have spoken, my lord the king. Yours am I and all I have." And the messengers came back and said, "Thus says Ben-Hadad, saying: "As I sent to you, saying, 'Your silver and your gold and your wives and your ₆ sons are mine,' give them over. For at this time tomorrow I will send my servants to you and they will search your house and your servants'

---

1. *thirty-two kings were with him.* This large number suggests that these "kings" may have been no more than local warlords.

4. *the king of Israel.* From this point on in the story, he will be referred to only by this title and not as "Ahab." It may be that the writer made this choice because in this entire episode of the conflict with Aram, Ahab plays a very different role from the one in which he has been seen up to now as Elijah's adversary. It is also possible that this entire episode, editorially set in the Ahab story, was originally about a different king.

As you have spoken, my lord the king. Ahab's absolute submission to Ben-Hadad's imperious demands is surprising. After all, the Aramaen king has asked him not only to hand over his treasure but his sons (presumably to be slaves) and his wives, including Jezebel (presumably to become Ben-Hadad's consorts). Perhaps he feels that the overwhelming numerical superiority of the Aramean forces leaves him no alternative.

houses, and it shall be that whatever is precious in their eyes they will put in their hand and take." And the king of Israel called in all the elders 7 of Israel and said, "Mark, pray, and see that he intends this harm, for he has sent to me for my wives and for my sons and for my silver and for my gold, and I did not withhold them from him." And the elders 8 and all the people said to him, "Do not listen, nor should you agree." And he said to the messengers of Ben-Hadad, "Everything concerning 9 which you sent at first to your servant I will do, but this thing I cannot do." And the messengers went off, and brought him the response. And 10 Ben-Hadad sent to him and said, "So may the gods do to me and even more, if the ground of Samaria will be enough for the footsteps of all the troops that are at my heels." And the king of Israel answered 11 and said, "Let not the buckler of armor boast like the unfastener."

---

6. *whatever is precious in their eyes*. The received text reads "your eyes." The translation here reflects the reading of the Septuagint. The added demand of Ben-Hadad that becomes a deal-breaker is that the prized possessions of the king's servants—that is, his courtiers—are also to be expropriated. Ahab had been willing to sacrifice what was his own, but now everyone around him is asked to submit to the same exorbitant demands of the Aramean king.

9. *but this thing I cannot do*. Ahab will not agree to the confiscation of his courtiers' possessions. Surrendering what is his own would reduce him to a vassal king; surrendering the treasures of those around him might make him the object of a palace coup.

10. *if the ground of Samaria will be enough for the footsteps of all the troops that are at my heels*. English translations since the seventeenth century have rendered this as "if the dust of Samaria will suffice for handfuls." But the Hebrew word that means "handfuls" is *sho'alim*, whereas the word here is *she'alim*, "footsteps." This actually yields a more coherent image: the troops commanded by Ben-Hadad are so numerous that there will scarcely be enough space on the soil of Samaria for all of them to stand. The use of "at my heels" (literally, "at my feet") reinforces this focus on feet.

11. *Let not the buckler of armor boast like the unfastener*. The Hebrew has a ter-rific compactness that, alas, is impossible in English: just four weighted words, *'al-yithalel hoger kemefateah*. A very different side of Ahab is manifested here. In the face of Ben-Hadad's intimidating threat, he responds coolly with a pithy proverb: do not arrogantly presume before the battle is joined to know who will be the victor when the fighting is done.

12 And it happened when he heard this thing he was drinking, he and the kings, at Succoth—that he said to his servants, "Set forth," and they set
13 forth against the town. And, look, a certain prophet approached Ahab king of Israel and said, "Thus says the LORD: 'Have you seen all this great throng? I am about to give it into your hand today, and you shall know
14 that I am the LORD.'" And Ahab said, "Through whom?" And he said, "Thus says the LORD, 'Through the aides of the provincial commanders.'
15 And he said, "Who will join battle?" And he said, "You." And he mustered the aides of the provincial commanders, and they came to two hundred and thirty. And after them he mustered all the troops, all the Israelites,
16 seven thousand. And they sallied forth at noon while Ben-Hadad was in a drunken stupor at Succoth, he and the thirty-two kings aiding him.
17 And the aides of the provincial commanders sallied forth first. And they sent to Ben-Hadad and told him, saying, "Men have sallied forth from
18 Samaria." And he said, "If in peace they have come forth, seize them
19 alive, and if for war they have come forth, alive seize them." And these had sallied forth from the town, the aides of the provincial command-
20 ers and the forces that were behind them. And each man struck down his man, and the Arameans fled and Israel pursued them, and Ben-
21 Hadad escaped on a horse with horsemen. And the king of Israel sallied forth and struck down the horses and the chariots, and struck a great
22 blow against Aram. And the prophet approached the king of Israel and said, "Go, summon strength, and mark and see what you should do,

---

12. *he was drinking, he and the kings*. The fact that Ben-Hadad is drinking with his allies just before the battle is a vivid expression of his overconfidence. In verse 16, we learn that he is in fact dead drunk when the Israelite forces attack.

17. *And they sent to Ben-Hadad*. The implied referent of "they" is presumably Aramean scouts.

18. *If in peace they have come forth*. This is the same verb, "to go out," which is rendered above as "sally forth," its technical sense in military contexts. But since Ben-Hadad is unsure whether they are coming out to surrender or to fight, the unambiguous "sally forth" would not make sense here. In either case, he unquestionably assumes he can take them as prisoners.

for at the turn of the year the king of Aram will be coming up against
you." And the servants of the king of Aram said to him, "Their god is a   23
mountain god. Therefore they prevailed over us. But when we do battle
with them on the plain, we will surely prevail over them." And this thing   24
do: remove the kings each from his place and set governors in their stead.
And as for you, assemble a force like your force that fell, and horses like   25
the horses and chariots like the chariots, that we may do battle against
them on the plain. We will surely prevail over them." And he heeded
their voice and thus he did. And it happened at the turn of the year, that   26
Ben-Hadad mustered Aram and went up to Aphek for battle with Israel.
And the Israelites had been mustered and had been provisioned. And   27
they went to meet them, and the Israelites encamped opposite them like
two little flocks of goats, but the Arameans filled the land. And the man   28
of God approached and said to the king of Israel, "Thus says the LORD:
'In as much as the Arameans have said, The LORD is a mountain god
and not a valley god, I will give all this great throng into your hand and

---

22. *for at the turn of the year the king of Aram will be coming up against you.* The
same phrase is used in 2 Samuel 12:1 for the time of year when kings go forth
to do battle. This would be the spring—the spring month Nissan is the first
month in the biblical calendar—when the winter rains are over.

23. *Their god is a mountain god.* Their remark reflects the pagan view that different gods have jurisdiction over different realms of nature. But they are also
making a strategic calculation: the Aramean chariots and cavalry will give them
an advantage in fighting on the plain that they would lose on mountainous
terrain.

24. *remove the kings . . . and set governors in their stead.* The governors might be
military officials more directly answerable to Ben-Hadad as their commander
than the kings.

26. *Aphek.* Located near the Jordan, this would be on more level land than
Mount Samaria and in keeping with the courtiers' counsel.

27. *like two little flocks of goats.* The unusual Hebrew locution is a little uncertain in meaning (at least the "little flocks" component), though it clearly
expresses the small size of the Israelite forces in relation to Aram, a theme
throughout this story.

29 you shall know that I am the LORD.'" And they encamped each opposite
the other seven days. And it happened on the seventh day that the battle
was joined, and the Israelites struck down a hundred thousand Aramean
30 foot soldiers in a single day. And the remaining ones fled to Aphek to the
town, and the wall fell on twenty-seven thousand men of those remaining, and Ben-Hadad fled and came into the town, to an inner chamber.
31 And his servants said to him, "Look, pray, we have heard that the kings
of Israel are merciful kings. Let us, pray, put sackcloth on our loins and
ropes on our heads and go out to the king of Israel. Perhaps he will let us
32 live." And they bound sackcloth on their loins and ropes on their heads
and came to the king of Israel and said, "Your servant Ben-Hadad has
said, 'Let me, pray, live.'" And he said, "Is he still alive? He is my brother."
33 And the men divined and quickly and firmly said, "Ben-Hadad is your
brother!" And he said, "Come, fetch him." And Ben-Hadad came out to
34 him, and he put him up on a chariot. And he said, "The towns that my
father took from your father I will give back, and you may place markets
for yourself in Damascus as my father placed in Samaria, and as for me,
I will send you off with a pact," and he sealed a pact with him and sent

---

30. *Ben-Hadad fled and came into the town, to an inner chamber.* The boastful
Ben-Hadad tries to hide in an inner chamber within a town that has already
fallen to the Israelites.

32. *Is he still alive? He is my brother.* This expression of concern and solidarity
is surely odd after Ben-Hadad has demanded Ahab to hand over all his treasure
and his wives and children, and then promised to destroy him. Ahab appears
to act out of political calculation—which will prove misguided. He may think
that the Arameans are too numerous for him to hold them under long-term
subjugation by occupying Aram, and that therefore he is better off showing
generosity to Ben-Hadad while obliging him to relinquish the towns his father
had taken from Israel.

34. *you may place markets for yourself in Damascus.* These would be something
like trade missions. The implication is that in such a peace agreement the
superior power is allowed to conduct trade on favorable terms in the territory
of the other kingdom.

him off. And a certain man among the followers of the prophets had said 35
to his companion by the word of the Lord, "Strike me, pray," but the
man had refused to strike him. And he said to him, "In as much as you 36
did not heed the voice of the Lord, you are now about to go away from
me, and a lion will strike you." And he went away from him and a lion
encountered him and struck him down. And he encountered another 37
man and said, "Strike me, pray," and he struck him, hitting and wounding him. And the prophet went and stood before the king on the road 38
and disguised himself with a scarf over his eyes. And as the king was 39
passing by, he cried out to the king and said, "Your servant sallied forth
in the midst of the battle, and, look, a man turned aside and brought
me a man and said, 'Guard this man. If he should indeed be missing,
it is your life instead of his, or you will weigh out a talent of silver.'

---

35. *Strike me, pray*. This bizarre exchange between two members of a guild of
prophets, *beney hanevi'im*, proposes a rather loose analogy for Ahab vis-à-vis
Ben-Hadad. If the word of the Lord prompts you to strike someone, even if
you are disinclined, you must do it or face dire consequences.

36. *a lion will strike you*. Though "strike" is not a verb one would expect to be
attached to a lion, it is used here to convey the idea of a quid pro quo: he who
failed to strike will be struck down. Though the Hebrew verb does have the
primary sense of delivering a blow, it has an extended meaning of "to kill."

37. *he struck him, hitting and wounding him*. The second person obeys the word
of the Lord, though it may go against his better instincts.

38. *a scarf*. The Hebrew noun occurs only here, but it is clearly some sort of
head-cloth or scarf (perhaps the sort that Bedouins use in a sandstorm) that
can be pulled down over the eyes.

39. *brought me a man*. The context would indicate that this is an enemy captive, which brings the parable close to the situation of Ahab and Ben-Hadad.
    or you will weigh out a talent of silver. This is an enormous amount, far more
than the value of a captive slave. The silver is "weighed out" because this is an
era before coinage, when payment is made in weights of silver and gold.

40 And it happened, as your servant was doing one thing and another that, look, he was not there." And the king of Israel said to him, "So be your
41 judgment. You yourself have decreed it." And he hastened to remove the scarf from over his eyes, and the king recognized him, that he was
42 of the prophets. And he said to him, "Thus says the Lord. 'In as much as you set free from My hand the man I condemned, it will be your life
43 instead of his and your people instead of his people.'" And the king of Israel went off to his house sullen and morose and came to Samaria.

---

40. *So be your judgment. You yourself have decreed it.* The story of the captured enemy whom the man allows to escape functions quite like Nathan's parable of the poor man's ewe in 2 Samuel 12: the king, having condemned the reported act, does not realize until the prophet tells him that the tale is about his own malfeasance.

41. *the king recognized him.* Ahab evidently has had some personal acquaintance with the members of this group of prophets. It is even possible that they are the hundred prophets whom Obadiah hid in the caves.

42. *you set free from My hand the man I condemned.* The Masoretic text reads "from a hand," but two ancient versions and a Hebrew manuscript have "My hand," which is more plausible. It is God Who has granted the victory to Ahab, and so the defeated king is in God's hand. It must be said that there has been no direct indication in the story until now that God has condemned Ben-Hadad to death or told Ahab he must kill him, though the prophet assumes that Ahab should have known this. Behind the theological reasoning lies a political calculation: allowing Ben-Hadad to go free will lead to a new attack on Israel.

CHAPTER 21

A̲nd it happened after these things, that Naboth the Jezreelite had a   1
vineyard that was in Jezreel near the palace of Ahab king of Samaria.
And Ahab spoke to Naboth, saying, "Give me your vineyard that I may   2
have it as a garden of greens, for it is close to my house, and let me give
you in its stead a better vineyard, or should it be good in your eyes, let
me give you silver as its price." And Naboth said to Ahab, "The Lord   3
forbid that I should give away the estate of my fathers." And Ahab came   4
to his house sullen and morose over this thing that Naboth the Jezreelite had spoken to him and said, "I will not give away the estate of my

---

1. *And it happened after these things.* As elsewhere, this vague temporal formula
introduces a new narrative unit.

2. *Give me your vineyard.* The verb "give" sometimes means "to sell," as Ahab's
subsequent words here make clear.
    a better vineyard . . . silver as its price. Ahab initially offers fair value for the
vineyard. The alternative of a better vineyard, stated first, is the more attractive
because Naboth will still possess real estate (and a favorable possession), which
was a prime consideration in Israelite society.

3. *The Lord forbid that I should give away the estate of my fathers.* Naboth is
thinking in traditional tribal terms rather than in those of a fluid economy in
which property is fungible for value. Hanging on to inherited land is conceived
as a sacred obligation.

4. *sullen and morose.* This phrase is pointedly picked up from the last sentence
of the previous episode.

fathers." And he lay down on his couch and turned away his face and
5 ate no food. And Jezebel his wife came to him and said, "What is this?
6 You are sullen in spirit and eat no food." And he spoke to her, "When I
spoke to Naboth the Jezreelite and said to him, 'Give me your vineyard
for silver, or if you wish, I shall give you a vineyard in its stead,' he said,
7 'I will not give you my vineyard.'" And Jezebel his wife said to him, "You,
now, must act like a king over Israel! Rise, eat food, and be of good cheer.
8 I myself will give you the vineyard of Naboth the Jezreelite." And she
wrote letters in Ahab's name and sealed them with his seal and sent the
letters to the elders and the notables who were in his town, who dwelled
9 with Naboth. And she wrote in the letters, saying, "Proclaim a fast and

---

And he lay down on his couch and turned away his face and ate no food.
Ahab, who in the preceding episode had shown martial resolution against Ben-
Hadad's threats, now acts like a petulant adolescent. He has a child's fixation
on the desired object he can't have, but it does not occur to him to wield royal
power in order to seize it.

6. *Give me your vineyard for silver.* In his repetition of his own words to Jezebel,
he pointedly switches the order, representing himself as having made the lesser
offer first.
   I will not give you my vineyard. This seeming repetition is a drastic recasting
of Naboth's actual words: there is no pious "The Lord forbid" and no mention
of the sacred obligation to retain the estate of his fathers. In this version, for
Jezebel's benefit, Naboth sounds merely obstinate.

7. *act like a king.* The literal sense of the Hebrew is "act [or do] kingship."
   I myself will give you the vineyard of Naboth. She is careful not to explain the
means by which she will effect this transaction.

8. *she wrote letters in Ahab's name and sealed them with his seal.* She in effect
usurps his royal power, "acting like a king" instead of him.
   who were in his town, who dwelled with Naboth. The seeming redundancy
underlines the idea that his own neighbors, alongside of whom he had always
lived, will be complicit in betraying him.

9. *Proclaim a fast.* A common function of an ad hoc communal fast was to sup-
plicate God when some ill had befallen the community because of an offense
committed within the community. In all likelihood, the occasion of the fast,
which would have been a reason for assembling the community, sets the stage
for exposing the purported crime committed by Naboth.

seat Naboth at the head of the people. And seat two worthless fellows   10
opposite him, that they may bear witness against him, saying, 'You have
cursed God and king.' And take him out and stone him to death." And   11
the men of his town, the elders and the notables, who dwelled in his
town, did as Jezebel had sent to them as was written in the letters that
she had sent them, "Proclaim a fast and seat Naboth at the head of the   12
people." And the two worthless fellows came and sat opposite him, and   13
the worthless fellows bore witness against Naboth before the people,
saying, "Naboth has cursed God and king." And they took him outside
the town and stoned him to death. And they sent to Jezebel, saying,   14
"Naboth has been stoned and he is dead." And it happened when Jeze-   15
bel heard that Naboth had been stoned to death, Jezebel said to Ahab,
"Rise, take hold of the vineyard of Naboth the Jezreelite, who refused
to give it to you for silver, for Naboth is not alive, for he is dead." And   16
when Ahab heard that Naboth was dead, Ahab rose to go down to the
vineyard of Naboth the Jezreelite to take hold of it. And the word of the   17

---

10. *seat two worthless fellows opposite him.* Her written instructions, fully accepted by the elders, are candid about using scoundrels willing to perjure themselves in a false accusation against Naboth.

13. *the worthless fellows bore witness against Naboth.* Unlike the altered repetitions in Ahab's report of his interchange with Naboth, every item of Jezebel's murderous instructions is precisely carried out.

15. *for Naboth is not alive, for he is dead.* Her repetition at this point of what was first her written instructions, then the narrative report of their implementation, entirely omits reference to the stoning to death or to the false accusation that led to the stoning. The redundancy of her statement to Ahab is dramatically apt: she tells her fearful husband he is no longer alive, he's actually dead, so you have nothing to worry about and can seize the vineyard.

18 LORD came to Elijah the Tishbite saying, "Rise, go down to meet Ahab
king of Israel, who is in Samaria. Look, he is in the vineyard of Naboth
19 where he has gone down to take hold of it. And you shall speak to him,
saying, 'Thus says the LORD: Have you murdered and also taken hold?'
And you shall speak to him saying, 'Thus says the LORD: Where the dogs
20 licked Naboth's blood they will lick your blood, too.'" And Ahab said to
Elijah, "Have you found me, O my enemy?" And he said, "I have found
you. In as much as you have given yourself over to doing evil in the eyes
21 of the LORD, I am about to bring evil upon you, and I will root you out,
and I will cut off every pisser against the wall of Ahab's, and ruler and
22 helper in Israel. And I will make your house like the house of Jeroboam
son of Nebat and like the house of Baasha son of Ahijah for the vexa-
23 tion with which you have vexed Me, leading Israel to offend." And for
Jezebel, too, the word of the LORD came, saying, "The dogs shall devour
24 Jezebel in the flatland of Jezreel. Ahab's dead in the town the dogs shall

---

19. *Have you murdered and also taken hold?* The Hebrew evinces the power of
compressed statement—*haratsahta wegam yarashta*—just three words. Though
Ahab was unaware of Jezebel's scheme, these words of denunciation name him
directly as the murderer.
    Where the dogs licked Naboth's blood. We learn that not only was Naboth
stoned to death on a false accusation but also that his body was left in the open
to be desecrated by scavengers.

20. *In as much as you have given yourself over to doing evil.* Ahab's previously
condemned transgressions were all cultic. Now an act of moral turpitude is
excoriated, and it will be this that dooms his royal line.

21. *I will cut off every pisser against the wall.* This coarse epithet for males is
reserved for curses.
    ruler and helper. The Hebrew term is somewhat obscure, but it appears to
refer to political leadership. Compare Deuteronomy 32:36.

23. *flatland.* The received text reads *ḥel*, "rampart," not a likely place for the
devouring of Jezebel's body, but many Hebrew manuscripts show *ḥeleq* (one
additional consonant), which means something like "cultivated field."

devour, and the dead in the field the fowl of the heavens shall devour."
Surely there was none like Ahab, who gave himself over to doing evil in   25
the eyes of the LORD, as Jezebel his wife had enticed him to do. And   26
he acted most loathsomely to go after foul idols, as all that the Amorites
had done, whom the LORD had dispossessed before the Israelites. And   27
it happened when Ahab heard these words that he rent his garments and
put sackcloth on his flesh and fasted and lay down in the sackcloth and
walked meekly. And the word of the LORD came to Elijah the Tishbite,   28
saying, "Have you seen that Ahab has humbled himself before Me?   29
Because he has humbled himself before Me, I will not bring the evil in
his days. In his son's days will I bring the evil upon his house."

---

26. *he acted most loathsomely to go after foul idols.* Here the chief reason for the
condemnation of Ahab shifts back from ethical to cultic infraction.

29. *I will not bring the evil in his days.* This postponement of retribution proves
to be rather qualified. In the event, Ahab does not die peacefully in his bed,
as one might infer from these words, but, after the passage of some time, he is
killed in battle, after which the dogs lick his blood, in keeping with the terms
of the initial prophetic curse.

CHAPTER 22

And they stayed three years with no war between Aram and Israel.
2 And it happened in the third year that Jehoshaphat king of Judah came
3 down to the king of Israel. And the king of Israel said to his servants,
"Did you know that Ramoth-Gilead is ours? Yet we refrain from taking
4 it from the hand of the king of Aram. And he said to Jehoshaphat, "Will
you go with me to battle at Ramoth-Gilead?" And Jehoshaphat said to
the king of Israel, "I am like you, my people like your people, my horses
5 like your horses." And Jehoshaphat said to the king of Israel, "Inquire,
6 pray, now the word of the LORD." And the king of Israel gathered the

---

2. *Jehoshaphat king of Judah came down to the king of Israel.* The verb here is
slightly odd for a movement from south to north. It could reflect the high elevation of the Judean capital in Jerusalem.

3. *the king of Israel.* Throughout this long episode, with just one exception,
the northern monarch is referred to as "king of Israel," not "Ahab," in a striking divergence from most of the preceding stories about Ahab. Some scholars,
citing the contradiction of this need to retake Ramoth-Gilead when the king of
Aram had agreed to return all Israelite towns in his terms of surrender, propose
that the king of Israel here is Ahab's son Ahaziah, with that story then being
attached to the Ahab narrative. The fact that it is not Elijah but a different
prophet, Micaiah, who confronts the king, may support this view.

4. *Will you go with me to battle.* The northern and southern kingdoms had long
been at war with each other, but now they become allies, perhaps because of
the threat to both of Aram.

5. *Inquire, pray, now the word of the LORD.* As we have seen before, it was standard practice in the biblical world and throughout the ancient Near East to
inquire of an oracle before a battle.

prophets, about four hundred men, and he said to them, "Shall I go against Ramoth-Gilead for battle or should I desist?" and they said, "Go up, that the Master may give it into the king's hand." And Jehoshaphat 7 said, "Is there no prophet of the LORD left here, that we might inquire of him?" And the king of Israel said to Jehoshaphat, "There is still one 8 man through whom to inquire of the LORD, but I hate him, for he will not prophesy good about me but evil—Micaiah son of Imlah." And Jehoshaphat said, "Let not the king say thus." And the king of Israel 9 called to a certain eunuch and said, "Hurry here Micaiah son of Imlah." And the king of Israel and Jehoshaphat king of Judah were sitting each 10 on his throne dressed in royal garb on the threshing-floor at the entrance gate of Samaria, and all the prophets were prophesying before them. And Zedekiah son of Chenaanah made himself iron horns and said, 11 "Thus says the LORD: 'With these shall you gore the Arameans until you destroy them.'" And all the prophets were prophesying thus, saying, 12 "Go up to Ramoth-Gilead and prosper, and the LORD shall give it into

---

7. *Is there no prophet of the* LORD *left here.* The precise cultic identify of the four hundred prophets is ambiguous. Jehoshaphat's words here suggest that he does not regard them as prophets of the LORD. In their own words, they invoke "the Master," which could be YHWH or another deity. Three possibilities emerge: they are actually pagan prophets; they are syncretistic prophets, alternately turning to YHWH and to other gods; they are purported prophets of the LORD, claiming to speak in the name of YHWH with no actual access to Him. It is plausible that this king of Israel, whether Ahab or his son, would keep a throng of dubious court prophets around him.

8. *Micaiah son of Imlah.* The king withholds this name till the very end of his speech, as though he could barely bring himself to utter it.

10. *each on his throne dressed in royal garb.* This display of royal regalia, rather odd in this threshing floor location, sets the stage for the battle scene, when one of the two will dress as a commoner in a futile effort to protect himself from harm.

11. *made himself iron horns.* This use of symbolic props to illustrate the prophecy is occasionally taken up by the literary prophets. Here, however, it is made to stand in contrast to Micaiah's mode of operation: he resorts to no symbols but simply reports his prophetic vision.

13 the hand of the king." And the messenger who had gone to call Micaiah
spoke to him, saying, "Look, pray, the words of the prophets as with one
mouth are good for the king. Let your word, pray, be like the word of
14 one of them, and you should speak good things." And Micaiah said, "As
15 the LORD lives, that which the LORD says to me will I speak." And he
came to the king and the king said to him, "Micaiah, shall we go up to
Ramoth-Gilead to battle or shall we refrain?" and he said to him, "Go
up and prosper, and the LORD shall give it into the hand of the king."
16 And the king said to him, "How many times must I make you swear
17 that you shall speak to me only truth in the name of the LORD?" And he
said, "I saw all Israel scattered over the mountains like sheep that have
no shepherd. And the LORD said, 'These have no master. Let each go
18 back home in peace.'" And the king of Israel said to Jehoshaphat, "Did
19 I not say to you, he will not prophesy good about me but evil?" And he
said, "Therefore hear the word of the LORD: I saw the LORD sitting on
His throne with all the army of the heavens standing in attendance by

---

13. *Let your word, pray, be like the word of one of them.* The messenger is perfectly aware that the king anticipates only bad news from Micaiah, and he tries
to ward off trouble by encouraging him to deliver a positive prophecy.

14. *that which the LORD says to me will I speak.* His words are reminiscent of
the ones spoken by the pagan seer Balaam in Numbers 22:39. Balaam was
summoned to pronounce doom on Israel but blessed them instead; Micaiah,
when the king of Israel would like him to prophesy good, will deliver a message
of doom.

17. *like sheep that have no shepherd . . . 'These have no master.'* In the first
instance, evidently following the messenger's instructions, Micaiah prophe-
sies victory, in a vague formulation. Now, pressed by the suspicious king, he
couches his true prophecy in oblique terms, but the response of the king of
Israel in the next verse indicates his clear understanding that the sheep without
a shepherd is a prediction of his own death.

19. *And he said.* Jehoshaphat does not answer the rhetorical question of the
king of Israel. Instead, Micaiah picks up the moment of silence by pronouncing
a second prophecy of doom, far more explicit than the first.
    *I saw the LORD sitting on His throne with all the army of the heavens standing
in attendance.* There is a convergence between the visionary scene and the
actual one. As armies assemble below, the celestial army stands in attendance

Him at His right and at His left. And the LORD said, 'Who will entice 20
Ahab, that he go up and fall at Ramoth-Gilead?' And one said this way
and one said another way. And a spirit came out and stood before the 21
LORD and said, 'I will entice him.' And the LORD said, 'How?' And it said, 22
'I will go out and become a lying spirit in the mouth of all his prophets.'
And He said, 'You shall entice and you shall also prevail. Go forth and
thus do.' And now, look, the LORD has placed a lying spirit in the mouth 23
of all these prophets of yours, but the LORD has spoken evil against you."
And Zedekiah son of Chenaanah approached and struck Micaiah on the 24
cheek and said, "How has the spirit of the LORD passed from me to speak
to you?" And Micaiah said, "You are about to see on that day when you 25
will enter the innermost chamber to hide." And the king of Israel said, 26
"Take Micaiah and bring him back to Amon commander of the town and
to Joash the king's son, and say, 'Thus said the king: Put this fellow in the 27
prison-house and feed him meager bread and meager water until I return
safe and sound.'" And Micaiah said, "If you really return safe and sound, 28
the LORD has not spoken through me." And he said, "Hear, all peoples!"

---

on God (He is LORD of Armies, or LORD of Hosts). The two kings have been sitting on their thrones, which, as Moshe Garsiel has aptly observed, is precisely how Micaiah sees the LORD in his vision.

20. *Who will entice Ahab*. This story puts forth a theological explanation of false prophecy. A celestial spirit answers God's call and volunteers to lure Ahab to his destruction by putting a false message in the mouths of the four hundred prophets claiming to speak the word of the LORD. By means of this contrivance, everything in this story is seen to be determined by God, and the false prophecy is not merely the human initiative of prophets seeking to curry the king's favor. It is only here that the monarch is named as Ahab, not "king of Israel."

28. *And he said, "Hear, all peoples!"* The "he" is Micaiah speaking again. The repetition of the formula for introducing direct speech, with no intervening response from the king, suggests that the king is flabbergasted by the prophet's obduracy, even in the face of imprisonment. But the hortatory "Hear, all peoples!" is an odd thing for the prophet to say in this narrative context. In fact, these three words are borrowed from the beginning of Micah's prophecies (Micah 1:2) and are almost certainly an editorial interpolation intended to establish a link between Micaiah son of Imlah and the literary prophet Micah (the same name without the theophoric suffix, who lived a century later). Some versions of the Septuagint lack these three words.

29 And the king of Israel went up, and Jehoshaphat king of Judah with
30 him, to Ramoth-Gilead. And the king of Israel said, "I will disguise
myself and go into battle, but you, don your royal garb." And the king
31 of Israel disguised himself and went into the battle. And the king of
Aram had charged the commanders of his thirty-two chariots, saying,
"You shall battle against neither small nor great but against the king of
32 Israel alone." And it happened, when the commanders of the chariots
saw Jehoshaphat, that they said, "He must be the king of Israel," and
33 they swerved against him to do battle, and Jehoshaphat cried out. And
it happened, when the commanders of the chariots saw that he was not
34 the king of Israel, they turned back from him. But a man drew the bow
unwitting and struck the king of Israel between the joints of the armor.
And he said to his charioteer, "Turn your hand back and take me out of
35 the fray, for I am wounded." And the battle surged on that day, and the
king was propped up in the chariot facing Aram. And he died in the evening, and the blood of the wound spilled out onto the floor of the chariot.
36 And the rumor passed through the camp as the sun was setting, saying,

---

30. *I will disguise myself.* The Masoretic text reads "disguise yourself," which
is flatly contradicted by the next clause, in which the king of Israel tells
Jehoshaphat to wear royal garb. Three ancient versions have the king of Israel
and not Jehoshaphat disguising himself, and this is surely the original reading.

34. *drew the bow unwitting.* He is simply targeting an Israelite in a chariot,
unaware that the man in commoner's clothes is the king of Israel.

35. *the king was propped up in the chariot facing Aram.* His initial command
to the charioteer to carry him away from the front is not carried out, either
because the fighting is so thick that the chariot cannot get away or because the
charioteer decides on his own that the removal of the king would demoralize
the troops. The dying king, propped up in the chariot, appears to be continuing
to battle.
    the floor of the chariot. The Hebrew uses an anatomical term, literally
"bosom." The passage of several hours indicates that the king dies of loss of
blood from the wound, so there would have been a considerable quantity of
blood on the floor of the chariot.

"Each man to his town and each man to his land." And the king died, and   37
they came to Samaria and buried the king in Samaria. And they flushed   38
out the chariot by the pool of Samaria, and the dogs licked his blood, and
the whores had bathed, according to the word of the LORD that He had
spoken. And the rest of the acts of Ahab and all that he did, and the ivory   39
house that he built and all the towns that he built, are they not written in
the Book of the Acts of the Kings of Israel? And Ahab lay with his fathers,   40
and Ahaziah his son was king in his stead.

And Jehoshaphat son of Asa had become king over Judah in the fourth   41
year of Ahab king of Israel. Jehoshaphat was thirty-five years old when   42
he became king, and he was king in Jerusalem twenty-five years. And his
mother's name was Azubah daughter of Shilhi. And he went in all the   43
ways of Asa his father, he did not turn away from them, to do what was
right in the eyes of the LORD. Only the high places were not removed.   44

---

36. *Each man to his town and each man to his land.* This flight of the troops on
the news of the king's death is an explicit fulfillment of Micaiah's prophecy. "I
saw all Israel scattered over the mountains like sheep that had no shepherd"
and "Let each go back to his home in peace."

38. *And they flushed out the chariot by the pool of Samaria, and the dogs licked his
blood.* This is only an approximate fulfillment of Elijah's prophecy to Naboth.
Elijah had said the dogs would lick Ahab's blood in the place they had licked
Naboth's blood, which would be in Jezreel, not Samaria. Also, the dogs evidently do not lick the blood from the corpse or from the chariot but from the
bloodied water of the pool used to clean the chariot. This indirection was no
doubt necessary because the royal attendants would not have allowed the king's
body to be desecrated or the chariot to be invaded by dogs.
    and the whores had bathed. Presumably, they used the pool to bathe and
thus the king's blood, however diluted, passed over their bodies. This added
indignity was not part of Elijah's prophecy of doom, at least not in the versions
we have in the received text.

39. *ivory house.* This is a house with ivory panels or ornamentation, as ivory would
have not been a suitable material for the structural elements of the building.

44. *Only the high places were not removed.* This refrain reflects the view of the
Deuteronomist that the local altars were a kind of paganism, though they could
well have been legitimate places for the worship of YHWH.

The people were still sacrificing and burning incense on the high places.
45,46 And Jehoshaphat made peace with the king of Israel. And the rest of
the acts of Jehoshaphat and his valor that he performed and with which
he fought, are they not written in the Book of the Acts of the Kings of
47 Judah? And the rest of the male cult-harlots who were left in the days
48 of Asa his father he rooted out from the land. And there was no king in
49 Edom but a royal governor. Jehoshaphat had fashioned Tarshish ships
to go to Ophir for gold, but they did not go, for the ships had broken
50 up in Ezion-Geber. Then did Ahaziah son of Ahab say to Jehoshaphat,
"Let my servants go with your servants in ships," but Jehoshaphat did
51 not agree. And Jehoshaphat lay with his fathers and was buried with
his fathers in the city of David his father, and Jehoram his son became
52 king in his stead. Ahaziah son of Ahab had become king over Israel in
Samaria in the seventeenth year of Jehoshaphat king of Judah, and he
53 was king over Israel two years. And he did what was evil in the eyes of
the Lord and went in the way of his father and in the way of his mother
and in the way of Jeroboam son of Nebat, who had led Israel to offend.
54 And he worshipped Baal and bowed down to him and vexed the Lord
God of Israel as all that his father had done.

---

48. *but a royal governor*. The Hebrew lacks "but" and sounds a little crabbed.

49. *Tarshish ships*. Since the destination of the ships is on the Red Sea, it is clear at least in this instance that "Tarshish ships" refers to a particular design of ship, not to a geographical location.

50. *Let my servants go with your servants in ships*. Perhaps the northern kingdom had greater proficiency in seafaring because of its proximity to Phoenicia. In any case, Jehoshaphat rejects the proposal, probably because he doesn't want to share the gold of Ophir.

54. *And he worshipped Baal*. If this scarcely seems a proper ending for the book, that is because Kings, like Samuel, was originally one book, the division into two reflecting merely the limits of the length of a scroll.

2 Kings

CHAPTER I

A nd Moab rebelled against Israel after Ahab's death. And Ahaziah fell 1,2
through the lattice in his upper chamber and became ill, and he sent
messengers and said, "Go, inquire of Baal-Zebub god of Ekron whether
I shall survive this illness." But the LORD had spoken to Elijah the Tish- 3
bite: "Rise, go up to meet the messengers of the king of Samaria and
speak to them: 'Is it for lack of a god in Israel that you go to inquire of
Baal-Zebub god of Ekron?' And therefore, thus said the LORD: 'From the 4
bed you mounted you shall not come down, for you are doomed to die.'"
And Elijah went off. And the messengers came back to him, and he said 5

---

1. *And Moab rebelled against Israel after Ahab's death.* This notation locates
the story temporally but is not otherwise linked to it, except to indicate that
Israel's dominance over vassal states was shaken in the political uncertainty
after Ahab's death.

2. *inquire.* The Hebrew verb *darash* is the technical term used for inquiring of
an oracle. From the monotheistic point of view, it is of course outrageous that
a king of Israel should go out of his way to inquire of a pagan oracle.
   Baal-Zebub. This appears to mean "Lord of the flies," and in the New Testament Baal-Zebub, or Beelzebub, is demoted from pagan deity to demon. A
plausible scholarly proposal is that the original name was Baal-Zebul, "Baal the
Prince," and that the final consonant was changed by the Hebrew writers in
order to make it a term of opprobrium.

3. *But the LORD had spoken to Elijah.* The entire episode is constructed through
dialogue, with further cited speech nesting within the dialogue, and the verb
"to speak" is repeated again and again.
   the king of Samaria. This epithet diminishes the sphere of the king of Israel.
   for lack of a god. The wording also could mean "for lack of gods."

6 to them, "Why have you come back?" And they said to him, "A man
  came up to meet us and said to us, 'Go back to the king who sent you
  and speak to him: Thus said the LORD—Is it for lack of a god in Israel
  that he sent to inquire of Baal-Zebub god of Ekron? Therefore, from
  the bed you mounted you shall not come down, for you are doomed to
7 die.'" And he said to them, "What is the manner of the man who came
8 up to meet you and spoke to you these words?" And they said to him,
  "He is a hairy man, and a leather belt is bound round his waist." And
9 he said, "It is Elijah the Tishbite." And he sent to him a captain of fifty
  with his men, and he went up to him, and, look, he was sitting on the
  hilltop. And he spoke to him: "Man of God! The king has spoken—
10 come down." And Elijah answered and spoke to the captain of the fifty:
  "And if I am a man of God, let fire come down from the heavens and
  consume you and your men!" And fire came down from the heavens and
11 consumed him and his men. And he persisted and sent him another
  captain of fifty with his men, and he spoke out and said to him, "Man

---

6. *Go back to the king who sent you.* In the reiterated pattern of verbatim repetition in this story, this clause stands out as an added element that was not part of Elijah's speech to the messengers. The clause has the effect of underscoring the king's responsibility for sending the messengers to a pagan oracle.

8. *He is a hairy man, and a leather belt is bound round his waist.* This is the first indication in the whole cycle of stories of Elijah's appearance. There is something roughhewn and perhaps forbidding in his distinctive look.

9. *with his men.* Literally, "with his fifty." The usage is repeated.

10. *let fire come down from the heavens.* Celestial fire is Elijah's prophetic medium. It came down to consume the sacrifice in the contest with the prophets of Baal at Mount Carmel. At the end of his story, he will ascend to the heavens in a fiery chariot.

11. *And he persisted.* The literal sense is "and he went back."

of God! Thus said the king: 'Quick, come down.'" And Elijah answered 12
and spoke to him: "If I am a man of God, let fire come down from the
heavens and consume you and your men." And fire came down from
the heavens and consumed him and his men. And he persisted and sent 13
a third captain of fifty with his men, and the third captain of the fifty
went up and came and kneeled before Elijah and pleaded with him:
"Man of God! May my life, pray, and the lives of these fifty servants
of yours be precious in your eyes. Look, fire has come down from the 14
heavens and consumed the two captains of the fifty and their men,
and now, may my life be precious in your eyes." And the LORD's mes- 15
senger spoke to Elijah: "Go down with him. Do not fear him." And he
rose and went down with him to the king. And he spoke to him: "Thus 16
said the LORD—'In as much as you have sent messengers to inquire of
Baal-Zebub god of Ekron—is it for lack of a god in Israel?—to inquire

---

Quick, come down. In the verbatim repetition, "quick" is added, suggesting
a mounting urgency after the failure of the first contingent of fifty.

12. *spoke to him.* The Masoretic text has "to them," but Elijah's answer ("you
and your men") makes clear he is speaking to the captain, and two Hebrew
manuscripts as well as the Septuagint and the Syriac show the singular.

13. *these fifty servants of yours.* The pleading captain is careful to address Elijah
in deferential terms, as would a subject to his monarch, referring to his own
troops as Elijah's servants.

15. *Do not fear him.* The captain's expressed terror of Elijah confirms that the
prophet has nothing to fear from him.

16. *is it for lack of a god in Israel?* In the two preceding repetitions of this clause,
it appeared at the beginning of the sentence, "Is it for lack of a god in Israel that
you go . . . ?" Here, instead, it appears as an outraged interjection in the middle
of the sentence after the mention of Baal-Zebub.

of his word, therefore from the bed you mounted you shall not come
17 down, for you are doomed to die." And he died according to the word
of the LORD that Elijah had spoken, and Jehoram became king in his
stead in the second year of Jehoram son of Jehoshaphat king of Judah,
18 for he had no son. And the rest of the acts of Ahaziah that he did, are
they not written in the Book of the Acts of the Kings of Israel?

---

therefore from the bed you mounted you shall not come down. The sentence
of doom is an invariable element in the three repetitions, and always occurs at
the end of the prophetic statement. The three repetitions of the prophecy are
joined by the three repeated reports of a captain and his fifty men going up to
Elijah. The folktale pattern, often deployed in the Bible, is used in which there
are two identical repetitions and then a third that diverges from the first two
(as in Goldilocks and the Three Bears),

17. *And he died according to the word of the LORD.* In the narrative report, nothing is allowed to intervene between Elijah's pronouncement of the prophecy of
doom directly to the ailing king and the king's death.

*and Jehoram became king . . . in the second year of Jehoram . . . king of Judah,
for he had no son.* The seeming confusion is the result of a historical coinci-
dence: Jehoram, brother of the heirless Ahaziah, happened to have the same
name as the king reigning in Judah at that time. In a culture that favored
theophoric names, this one, which means "God is exalted," might have been
fairly common.

CHAPTER 2

And it happened, when the LORD was going to take Elijah up to the 1
heavens in a whirlwind, that Elijah, and Elisha with him, went from
Gilgal. And Elijah said to Elisha, "Stay here, pray, for the LORD has sent 2
me to Bethel." And Elisha said, "As the LORD lives and as you live, I will
not forsake you." And they went down to Bethel. And the acolyte proph- 3
ets who were in Bethel came out to Elisha and said to him, "Did you
know that today the LORD is about to take your master from over you?"
And he said, "I, too, know. Be still!" And Elijah said to him, "Elisha, stay 4
here, pray, for the LORD has sent me to Jericho." And he said, "As the

---

2. *Stay here, pray, for the LORD has sent me to Bethel.* Elijah seems to have fore-
knowledge of his own departure from the earthly realm, and his initial sense
is that this should be a private encounter between him and God, not to be
witnessed by anyone else, not even by his disciple.
   I will not forsake you. By this pronouncement, to be repeated twice, Elisha
affirms that he is Elijah's loyal follower and heir. In the event, his being able
actually to see his master's fiery ascension will justify his request of a double
portion of the spirit investing Elijah.

3. *the acolyte prophets.* Literally, "the sons of the prophets." The prefix "sons"
suggests they are not full-fledged prophets, which means they are either acolytes or members of a professional guild of prophets rather than independent
prophetic agents.
   Did you know that . . . the LORD is about to take your master. Evidently, Elijah's
imminent departure has become general news, at least in prophetic circles.
   from over you. The literal sense is "from your head."

4. *stay here, pray, for the LORD has sent me.* This episode follows the folktale
patterns manifested in the previous episode of three repetitions with verbatim
restatements. Here, too, there is a swerve in the third repetition: in the third

Lord lives and as you live, I will not forsake you." And they came to Jeri-
5 cho. And the acolyte prophets who were in Jericho approached Elisha
and said to him, "Do you know that today the Lord is about to take your
6 master from over you?" And he said, "I, too, know. Be still!" And Elijah
said to him, "Stay here, pray, for the Lord has sent me to the Jordan."
And he said, "As the Lord lives and as you live, I will not forsake you."
7 And the two of them went. And fifty men of the acolyte prophets had
gone and stood opposite at a distance, and the two of them stood by the
8 Jordan. And Elijah took his mantle and rolled it up and struck the water,
and it parted on both sides, and the two of them crossed over on dry
9 ground. And it happened as they crossed over that Elijah said to Elisha,
"Ask, what may I do for you before I am taken from you?" And Elisha
10 said, "Let there be, pray, a double portion of your spirit upon me." And
he said, "You have asked a hard thing. If you see me taken from you, let

---

instance, Elijah and Elisha do not go to a town but to the Jordan, so there is
no group of acolyte prophets for them to encounter, and this third iteration
concludes with Elijah's ascent to the heavens in a chariot of fire.

6. *the Lord has sent me to the Jordan.* The town of Jericho is close to the Jordan,
as is clear in the next verse, when the fifty acolyte prophets can see Elijah and
Elisha from a distance.

8. *and it parted on both sides.* This is, of course, a small-scale reenactment of the
miracle performed by Moses in parting the waters of the Sea of Reeds. Here it
is executed not with an upraised staff but with the rolled-up prophet's mantle,
which Elisha will then inherit from Elijah. The point of crossing the Jordan is
to have Elijah pass through this liminal zone and thus to be on the other side,
beyond the land of Israel proper, when he is taken up into the heavens.

9. *a double portion of your spirit.* Though this may seem to be a presumptuous
wish by Elisha to surpass his master, it could just as easily reflect a sense of
inadequacy: feeling himself to be no more than an ordinary man, Elisha wants
a supercharge of the spirit in order to be Elijah's successor.

10. *If you see me taken from you, let it be thus for you.* Elijah himself is not
entirely sure that Elisha is worthy to bear a double portion of the spirit. If God
unveils his eyes to witness Elijah's miraculous ascension, that will be proof of
his worthiness.

it be thus for you, and if not, it will not be." And it happened as they 11
were going along speaking, that, look, there was a chariot of fire, and
horses of fire, and they separated the two of them, and Elijah went up to
the heavens in a whirlwind. And Elisha was watching and he was crying 12
out, "My father, my father, Israel's chariot and its horsemen!" And he
saw him not again. And he had clung to his garments and torn them in
two. And he lifted up Elijah's mantle, which had fallen from him, and 13
he went back and stood on the bank of the Jordan. And he took Elijah's 14
mantle that had fallen from him and struck the water and said, "Where
is the LORD, God of Elijah?" And he, too, struck the water, and it parted

---

11. *a chariot of fire, and horses of fire.* As noted above, fire has been an important
instrument for Elijah's prophetic activities.

Elijah went up to the heavens in a whirlwind. This story takes us into new
territory. Everywhere in the Hebrew Bible, death is the definitive end, Sheol,
the underworld, a hole in the ground into which the once living person goes
down. The single previous intimation of Elijah's ascension is the cryptic notation about Enoch's being "taken" by God in Genesis 5:24. Elijah does not die
but rides up to the celestial sphere in a fiery chariot. His ascension prepares
the way for the idea of Christ's resurrection in Christian Scripture, and it is
significant that Elijah and Moses are represented in the New Testament as the
two chief precursors of Jesus.

12. *My father, my father, Israel's chariot and its horsemen.* Elisha obviously refers
to Elijah as his father because he is his master and mentor. The metaphor of
the chariot and horsemen, suggested to him by the vision of the chariot of fire
before his eyes, registers the idea that Elijah has been Israel's true power, as
chariotry is the driving power of an army.

And he had clung to his garments and torn them in two. Since Elijah had
removed his mantle, this would be the tunic worn beneath the mantle. Elisha's clinging to it reflects his impassioned desire not to part from his master.
It seems that as Elijah left him for his ascent, part of the tunic tore away in
Elisha's hands. This is an ironic reversal of the request for a double portion of
the spirit because he now holds half a garment.

14. *Where is the LORD, God of Elijah?* If the LORD is now to be with him as
He was with Elijah, He will enable Elisha to replicate the miracles that Elijah
performed.

he, too. There is an evident glitch in the Hebrew syntax. These two words
in the Hebrew should appear after "and he struck." The word-order in the
received text produces an odd bumpiness: "He too and he struck."

15 on both sides, and Elisha crossed over. And the acolyte prophets who were in Jericho saw him from the other side and said, "Elijah's spirit has rested upon Elisha." And they came to meet him and bowed down

16 before him to the ground. And they said to him, "Look, pray, your servants have fifty stalwart men. Let them go, pray, and seek your master, lest the spirit of the LORD has borne him off and flung him down on

17 some hill or into some valley." And he said, "You shall not send." And they urged him incessantly, and he said, "Send." And they sent fifty men

18 and sought him three days but did not find him. And they came back to him while he was still staying in Jericho, and he said to them, "Did I not say to you, do not go?"

19 And the men of the town said to Elisha, "Look, pray, it is good to live in the town as my master sees, but the water is bad and the land bereaves."

20 And he said, "Fetch me a new bowl and put salt in it." And they fetched

21 it for him. And he went out to the water source and flung the salt there and said, "Thus said the LORD: 'I have healed these waters. There will

22 no longer be death and bereaving.'" And the waters have been healed

---

15. *And the acolyte prophets . . . saw him from the other side.* Elisha's parting of the waters, in full sight of the assembled Jericho prophets, becomes a public demonstration that he is Elijah's prophetic heir.

19. *Look, pray, it is good to live in the town.* Having recognized Elisha as Elijah's successor, endowed with his powers, the townsmen promptly turn to him with a request for help.
   the water is bad and the land bereaves. This is cause and effect: the bad water contaminates the land, which then brings death to man and beast.

21. *he . . . flung the salt there.* The agency of the miracle is deliberately paradoxical. Salt water is not drinkable, but Elisha's salt purifies the spring of its blight.
   Thus said the LORD: 'I have healed these waters.' Elisha pointedly attributes the purification of the spring to God's intervention, not to a magical act on his part.

to this day, according to the word of Elisha that he spoke. And he went 23
up from there to Bethel, and as he was coming up on the road, young
lads came out from the town and jeered at him and said to him, "Away
with you, baldy, away with you, baldy!" And he turned behind him and 24
saw them and cursed them in the name of the LORD, and two she-bears
came out of the forest and ripped apart forty-two boys. And he went 25
from there to Mount Carmel and from there he came back to Samaria.

---

23. *Away with you, baldy.* Literally, "Go up, baldy." We learn incidentally that
Elisha is bald, in contrast to Elijah, who was a hairy man.

24. *two she-bears came out of the forest and ripped apart forty-two boys.* This
murderous response to the boys' mockery is morally scandalous. Is it meant to
suggest that Elisha does not make responsible use of his prophetic powers, that
after turning death to life at the spring he now spreads death? The early rabbis
were so outraged by this story that they felt constrained to assert it never really
happened. Their formulation, "neither bears nor forest," became idiomatic in
Hebrew for a cock-and-bull story.

CHAPTER 3

1 And Jehoram son of Ahab had become king over Israel in Samaria in the eighteenth year of Jehoshaphat king of Judah. And he was king 2 twelve years. And he did what was evil in the eyes of the LORD, though not like his father nor like his mother, and he removed the pillar of Baal 3 that his father had made. But he clung to the offenses of Jeroboam son of Nebat, who had led Israel to offend, he did not swerve from them. 4 And Mesha king of Moab was a sheep-breeder and he would bring back to the king of Israel the wool of a hundred thousand lambs and of a 5 hundred thousand rams. And it happened when Ahab died that the king 6 of Moab rebelled against the king of Israel. And King Jehoram sallied 7 forth from Samaria on that day, and he mustered all Israel. And he went and sent to Jehoshaphat king of Judah, saying, "The king of Moab has rebelled against me. Will you go with me against Moab to battle?" And he said, "I will go. I am like you, my people like your people, my horses

---

4. *he would bring back to the king of Israel.* The context suggests that the verb here has an iterative sense: this is the tribute that Mesha, as vassal to Israel, would give annually to the king of Israel. David had initially reduced Moab to vassal status. At some point, perhaps during the reign of Baasha, Moab drove out the Israelite overlords, but King Omri again subjugated it.

a hundred thousand lambs. As with the numbers given for troops and casualties in these narratives, the figures here are hyperbolic.

5. *when Ahab died.* Mesha exploits the political disorder following upon Ahab's death to rebel against Israel.

7. *I am like you, my people like your people.* This speech repeats verbatim Jehoshaphat's words to the king of Israel in 1 Kings 22:4. Verse 11 then repeats exactly Jehoshaphat's words in 1 Kings 22:7. All this has the look of a story

like your horses." And he said, "By what way shall we go up?" And he 8
said, "The way of the Wilderness of Edom." And the king of Israel went, 9
and the king of Judah and the king of Edom with him, and they swung
round on the way seven days, and there was no water for the camp or
for the beasts that were at their heels. And the king of Israel said, "Woe, 10
for the LORD has called forth these three kings to give them into the
hand of Moab." And Jehoshaphat said, "Is there no prophet of the LORD 11
here, that we might inquire of the LORD through him?" And one of the
servants of the king of Israel answered, "Elisha son of Shaphat is here,
who attended Elijah." And Jehoshaphat said, "The word of the LORD is 12
with him." And the king of Israel and Jehoshaphat and the king of Edom
went down to him. And Elisha said to the king of Israel, "What do you 13
and I have to do with one another? Go to your father's prophets and to
your mother's prophets." And the king of Israel said to him, "Don't! For
the LORD has called forth these three kings to give them into the hand

---

floating around in the scribal archives that was first ascribed to Ahab (though,
perhaps symptomatically, without using his name) and then, in different circumstances with a different enemy and a different prophet, to Jehoram (though
here, again, in the body of the story, he is not referred to by name). It is possible
that the original story was actually about a third king whose identity, however,
remains conjectural.

8. *The way of the Wilderness of Edom.* The allied forces, instead of taking a
direct route by crossing the Jordan and then driving south to Moab, swing
round (that verb is used in the next verse) in a long arc through the Negev and
then the wilderness of Edom to the east of the Dead Sea, thus approaching
Moab from the south. Their likely intention would have been to avoid Moabite
troops stationed along the northern and western perimeters of Moabite territory. But this move takes them on a seven-day march through the desert, during
which they run out of water.

11. *attended.* The literal sense of the Hebrew idiom is "poured water on the
hands of."

13. *Go to your father's prophets and to your mother's prophets.* He is referring to
the sycophantic court-prophets or actually pagan prophets who surrounded
Ahab and Jezebel.

14 of Moab." And Elisha said, "As the LORD of Armies lives, in Whose
    attendance I have stood, were I not showing favor to Jehoshaphat king
15 of Judah, I would not so much as look at you nor see you, but now, fetch
    me a lyre-player." And it happened, as the lyre-player played, the hand
16 of the LORD was upon him, and he said, "Thus said the LORD: 'Dig out
17 this wadi into hollows.' For thus said the LORD: 'You will not see wind
    and you will not see rain, but that wadi will fill with water, and you and
18 your cattle and your beasts will drink.' And this is easy in the eyes of
19 the LORD, and he shall give Moab into your hand. And you shall strike
    every fortified town and every fine town, and every goodly tree you shall
    fell, and all the springs of water you shall stop up, and every goodly field
20 you shall spoil with stones." And it happened in the morning, as the
    meal offering was being offered up, that, look, water was coming from
21 the way to Edom, and the land was filled with water. And all Moab had

---

14. *were I not showing favor to Jehoshaphat.* Elisha grudgingly agrees to seek a
propitious oracle only for the sake of Jehoram's Judean ally Jehoshaphat.

15. *as the lyre-player played, the hand of the LORD was upon him.* The use of
stringed instruments and percussion instruments to induce a vatic trance
through their hypnotic rhythm is known in many different traditions of ecstatic
religion. In the Bible, it is typically linked with bands of professional prophets
(see, for example, 1 Samuel 10:5–6). What is unusual here is that an individual
prophet feels he has to have recourse to these musical stimuli in order to gain
access to God's word.

16. *Dig out this wadi into hollows.* In the rocky gulches in this region, rain water
would gather in the little hollows and crevices in the rock. In this miraculous
instance, however, there will be no rain.

18. *this is easy in the eyes of the LORD.* Just as the LORD can easily provide water
where there is no rain, He will be able to effect the defeat of the Moabites
with no difficulty.

19. *every fine town.* The word for "fine" (or "choice"), *mivhor*, is an odd formation (it should be *mivhar*), and some scholars think it is an erroneous scribal
duplication of the previous phrase, "every fortified town," *kol 'ir mivtsar.*
   every goodly tree you shall fell. This is in direct contradiction to Deuteronomy
20:9, which prohibits cutting down an enemy's fruit trees.

heard that the kings had come up to do battle with them, and every
man of sword-wielding age was mustered, and they stood at the border.
And they rose early in the morning, and the sun had dawned over the   22
water, and from a distance Moab saw the water red as blood. And they   23
said, "This blood is because the kings have surely been destroyed, each
striking down his fellow, and they are now Moab's booty." And they came   24
into the camp of Israel, and Israel rose up and struck Moab, and they
fled before them, and they struck Moab again and again. And they laid   25
waste the towns, and in every goodly field each of them flung stones and
filled it, and every spring of water they stopped up, and every goodly tree
they felled, till they left only the stones of Kir-Hareseth, and the slingers
swung round and struck it. And the king of Moab saw that the battle   26
was hard against him, and he took seven hundred sword-wielding men
with him to break through to the king of Edom, but they were not able.

---

22. *from a distance Moab saw the water red as blood.* The red look of the water is
a result of the early light of dawn, perhaps reinforced, as many have proposed,
by the reddish sandstone surrounding the wadi and its bed. God's miraculous
providing of water, then, serves a double purpose: first it revives the troops and
their animals after the long march in the desert, and then it sets a trap for the
Moabites.

23. *each striking down his fellow.* The Moabites assume that the potentially
fragile alliance put together by the king of Israel has fallen apart violently.
    and they are now Moab's booty. They conclude that most, if not all, of the
enemy are dead, and that they have no one to fight, only corpses to despoil.

24. *and they struck Moab again and again.* The Hebrew text looks defective at
this point (with a confusing divergence between the consonantal text and the
marginal correction), but this is the likely sense.

25. *Kir-Hareseth.* This is an alternate name for Kir-Moab, the Moabite capital.

26. *he took seven hundred sword-wielding men with him to break through to the
king of Edom.* He musters an elite fighting unit in an attempt to break through
the besieging forces, probably driving against the vassal king of Edom as the
weakest element in the alliance of three kings. The attempt is foiled, and the
Moabites are driven back into the town.

27 And he took his firstborn son, who would have been king after him, and offered him up as a burnt-offering on the wall, and a great fury came against Israel, and they journeyed away from him and went back to the land.

---

27. *he took his firstborn.* A king's sacrifice of his own child, in an effort to placate the gods at a moment of military emergency, was a familiar practice in the ancient Near East.

and a great fury came against Israel. This denouement is surely perplexing from a monotheistic point of view. "Fury" (*qetsef*) is usually the term for God's devastating rage against Israel when the people has transgressed. Here, however, Israel has done no wrong. And the descent of the fury explicitly reverses Elisha's favorable prophecy. This turn of events might reflect an early tradition that accords Chemosh, the Moabite god, power that must be propitiated by human sacrifice, so that he will then blight the enemies of Moab. In any case, the story means to explain why Israel and its allies, after an initial victory, were obliged to retreat. A Moabite inscription on a stele, discovered in 1868, in which Mesha speaks in the first person, triumphantly proclaims a sweeping victory over Israel, though it is not altogether clear whether this victory is over Jehoram or his predecessor.

CHAPTER 4

And a certain woman from the wives of the acolyte prophets had cried 1
out to Elisha, saying, "Your servant, my husband, died. And you know
that your servant was a LORD fearer. And the creditor has come to take
my two children to be his slaves." And Elisha said to her, "What shall 2
I do for you? Tell me, what do you have in the house?" And she said,
"Your servant has nothing at all in the house except a cruse of oil." And 3
he said, "Go, borrow vessels for yourself from outside, from all your
neighbors—empty vessels, and not just a few. And you shall come and 4
close the door behind you and behind your sons, and you shall pour into
these vessels, and the full ones you shall set aside." And she went from 5
him and closed the door behind her and behind her sons. They were
bringing the vessels to her and she was pouring. And it happened when 6
the vessels were full that she said to her son, "Bring me another vessel,"
and he said to her, "There are no more vessels." And the oil stopped. And 7
she came and told the man of God, and he said, "Go, sell the oil and pay
your debt, and you and your sons will live off what is left."

---

1. *Your sevant, my husband.* Almost everyone in these stories addresses Elisha
deferentially. In this case, Elisha may have actually been the master of this
group of acolyte prophets. In the story of the almost poisoned stew in verses
38–41, he appears to take upon himself the responsibility of providing food
for them.

3. *Go, borrow vessels.* All these stories about Elisha's performing miracles to aid
people in distress have a strong folkloric character. They would provide direct
inspiration for the stories about Jesus's miracles in the Gospels—the cruse of
oil that is constantly full, the raising of Lazarus from the dead, the multiplica-
tion of the fish and loaves.

8   And one day Elisha was passing through Shunem, and there was a
    wealthy woman there. And she urged him to break bread, and so, when-
9   ever he passed through, he would turn aside there to break bread. And
    she said to her husband, "Look, pray, I know that he is a holy man of
10 God who always passes by us. Let us make, pray, a little upper chamber
    and put a bed there for him and a table and chair and lamp, and so when
11 he comes to us, he will turn aside there." And one day he came there
12 and turned aside to the upper chamber and slept there. And he said
    to Gehazi his lad, "Call this Shunammite," and he called her, and she
13 stood before him. And he said to him, "Say to her, pray: 'Look, you have
    gone to all this bother for us. What can be done for you? Shall a word
    be said for you to the king or to the commander of the army?'" And she
14 said, "In the midst of my people I dwell." And he said, "What can be

---

8. *a wealthy woman.* The usual sense of the Hebrew adjective is "great," but
it also has the meaning of "wealthy." The fact that she has the means to add a
room to her house and furnish it argues for the sense of "wealthy."

9. *a holy man of God.* Throughout these stories, Elisha is referred to as a man of
God, not prophet. That designation does not mean "clergyman," as in modern
English, but rather someone with divine powers, and those are manifested in
the sundry miracles he performs.

12. *Gehazi his lad.* This is the first mention of him. Elisha's elevated status is
reflected in his having an attendant or factotum who performs sundry tasks for
him and acts as his intermediary.
    Call this Shunammite. This form of reference seems a bit condescending,
and if he has taken the trouble to learn her name, he is not disposed to use it.

13. *Say to her, pray.* Even though the woman is now standing before Elisha, he
does not address her directly but instead has Gehazi put the question to her
on his behalf.
    In the midst of my people I dwell. Though some understand this to mean that
she has no need for royal favors because she has the support of people around
her, the more likely meaning is that she views herself as an ordinary person,
dwelling among the people, and thus wants no part of special treatment from
the court.

done for her?" And Gehazi said, "Why, she has no son, and her husband
is an old man." And he said, "Call her," and he called her, and she stood 15
in the doorway. And he said, "At this fixed time, at this very season, you 16
will embrace a son." And she said, "Don't, my lord, man of God, don't
mislead your servant." And the woman conceived and bore a son at that 17
fixed time, at that very season, as Elisha had spoken to her. And the 18
child grew, and one day he went out to his father, to the reapers. And 19
he said to his father, "My head, my head!" And he said concerning the
lad, "Carry him to his mother." And he was carried and brought to his 20
mother, and he stayed on her knees till noon, and he died. And she went 21
up and laid him on the bed of the man of God, and closed the door on
him and went out. And she called to her husband and said, "Send me, 22
pray, one of the lads and one of the donkeys, that I may hurry to the man

---

14. *Why, she has no son.* It seems a little suspect that Elisha needs Gehazi to
point out the fact of her childlessness. One wonders how much attention he
has been paying to her.

   and her husband is an old man. This might well be the source of her fertility
problems. The phrase is a reminiscence of Sarah's words in Genesis 18:12.

16. *At this fixed time, at this very season, you will embrace a son.* These formulaic
words signal the unfolding of the annunciation type-scene. This one differs
from all the others in that the word from the man of God is not dictated from
above but is his own initiative as recompense for the woman's kindness to him.
This is also the only annunciation that does not lead to the birth of someone
destined to play a significant role in the national story: the boy is never named,
and he remains no more than the son of a prosperous farmer.

17. *And the woman conceived and bore a son.* In another divergence from the
set pattern of the annunciation, there is no mention of the necessary fact that
the husband "knew" his wife. Could there be further play here with the fact of
his advanced age?

19. *My head, my head!* Like Isaac, another son born after an annunciation, this
child is threatened with death out in the open.

20. *and he stayed on her knees till noon, and he died.* Her anguish is magnified by
his still being alive when he is brought to her, then expiring as she desperately
tries to succor him.

23 of God and come back. And he said, "Why are you going to him? Today
24 is neither new moon nor Sabbath." And she said, "Farewell." And she
saddled the donkey and said to her lad, "Drive it and go. Do not hold me
25 back in riding unless I say to you." And she went and came to the man of
God at Mount Carmel, and it happened, when the man of God saw her
from a distance, that he said to Gehazi, "Here is that Shunammite. Now
26 hurry to meet her, pray, and say to her, 'Is it well with you? Is it well with
27 your husband? Is it well with the child?'" And she said, "It is well." And
she came to the man of God on the mountain and clung to his legs. And
Gehazi approached to push her back, and the man of God said, "Let her
be, for she is deeply embittered, and the Lord has hidden it from me
28 and not told me." And she said, "Did I ask of my lord for a son? Did I
29 not say, 'You should not deceive me'?" And he said to Gehazi, "Gird your
loins and take my staff in your hand and go. Should you meet a man,
do not greet him, and should a man greet you, do not answer him. And
30 you shall put my staff on the lad's face." And the lad's mother said, "As

---

23. *Why are you going to him? Today is neither new moon nor Sabbath.* The
husband is surely being obtuse, for it is obvious enough why she wants to hurry
off to the man of God. Sabbaths and new moons were times when special sacrifices were offered, which one could bring to a man of God so that he might
partake of the part of the animal not burnt on the altar.

Farewell. The Hebrew is *shalom,* the same word Gehazi used when he asked
whether it is "well" with her and her family. In saying farewell, she simply
ignores her husband's obtuse question.

24. *Drive it and go.* The servant's job is to run behind the donkey on which she
is riding and prod it to move quickly with a switch or goad.

26. *And she said, "It is well."* She says these words to Gehazi because she does
not want to be detained in explaining the disaster but instead means to head
directly to Elisha.

27. *and the Lord has hidden it from me.* Elisha is, after all, a prophet, but he
seems in many respects out of touch with the woman's life.

29. *And you shall put my staff on the lad's face.* Elisha assumes that his staff is
imbued with supernatural powers, but this effort to revive the child through an
act of pure magic does not work.

the LORD lives and as you live, I will not forsake you." And he rose and
went after her. And Gehazi had gone before them and put the staff on 31
the lad's face, but there was no voice and no sound, and he turned back
to meet him, and he told him, saying, "The lad has not awakened." And 32
Elisha came into the house, and, look, the lad was dead, laid out on his
bed. And he came in and closed the door behind the two of them and 33
prayed to the LORD. And he climbed up and lay over the child and put 34
his mouth over his mouth and his eyes over his eyes and his palms over
his palms and stretched out over him, and the child's body grew warm.
And he went back and walked in the house this way and that, and he 35
climbed up and stretched out over him, and the lad sneezed a full seven
times, and the lad opened his eyes. And he called to Gehazi and said, 36
"Call this Shunammite," and he called her, and she came to him, and he
said, "Carry away your son." And she came and fell at his feet and bowed 37
to the ground, and she carried away her son and went out.

And Elisha had gone back to Gilgal. And there was famine in the land, 38
and the acolyte prophets were sitting before him. And he said to his lad,
"Put the big pot on the fire and cook a stew for the acolyte prophets."
And one of them went out to the field to gather sprouts and found a 39
field vine and gathered from it field gourds, as much as his garment
could hold, and he came and sliced them into the stew pot, for they did

---

30. *I will not forsake you.* She puts her trust not in magic staffs but in the person
of Elisha and so wants him to stick with her and come back to Shunem with
her, to which he agrees.

32. *laid out on his bed.* That is, laid out on Elisha's bed.

34. *and lay over the child and put his mouth over his mouth.* Though this detail
may look to a modern reader like mouth-to-mouth resuscitation, the intention
of the ancient writer was more likely that the prophet imparted his own vital
warmth, fueled by prophetic aura, to the child, reviving him in this fashion.

39. *sprouts . . . field gourds.* As with many other flora mentioned in the Bible,
the exact identification of these plants remains uncertain. What is clear is that
instead of a plant that would have been a proper ingredient for the stew, the
ignorant gatherer brings back a poisonous plant.

40 not know. And they poured for the men to eat, and it happened, as they were about to eat, they cried out, "Death is in the pot, man of God!"

41 And they could not eat. And he said, "Fetch flour." And he flung it into the pot, and he said, "Pour for the people, that they may eat." And there was nothing harmful in the pot.

42 And a man had come from Baal-Shalishah, and he brought the man of God first fruits, twenty loaves of barley bread and fresh grain in his sack.

43 And he said, "Give it to the people, that they may eat." And his attendant said, "What? Shall I set this before a hundred men?" And he said, "Give it to the people that they may eat. For thus said the LORD, 'Eat and leave

44 over.'" And he set it before them, and they ate and left over, according to the word of the LORD.

---

41. *Fetch flour.* It is highly unlikely that flour would have the property of neutralizing the poison, so one must take this as a purely miraculous act.

42. *sack.* This is the traditional rendering of the unique Hebrew term *tsiqalon*, from whence it has passed into general usage in the language. But some scholars, proposing a Ugaritic cognate, argue that it refers to a kind of grain.

CHAPTER 5

And Naaman, commander of the army of the king of Aram, was a great 1
man in the presence of his master and highly esteemed, for through
him the LORD had granted victory to Aram, and the man was a valiant
warrior stricken with skin-blanch. And Aram had sallied forth in raiding 2
parties and captured a young girl from the land of Israel. And she said 3
to her mistress, "Would that my master might come before the prophet
who is in Samaria. Then he could cure him of his skin-blanch." And 4

---

1. *for through him the LORD had granted victory to Aram.* This clause establishes
the universalist perspective of the story, in which a prophet of Israel will perform a wonder for a non-Israelite. From the viewpoint of the Hebrew writer, it
is the LORD, the God worshipped by Israel, Who determines all events, though
of course the Aramean general could not be aware that he owes his victories
to YHWH.

2. *the land of Israel.* This designation is actually unusual and in all likelihood
reflects the perception of the Arameans.

3. *Would that my master might come before the prophet.* The Hebrew has only
the implied verb "be." To be or stand before someone implies a relationship of
deference or even subservience, and the idiom recurs in the story. One notes
that the captive Israelite girl appears to be on good terms with her Aramean
mistress, evincing solicitude for her mistress's husband.
   skin-blanch. The Hebrew *tsara 'at* is traditionally translated as "leprosy," but
the leading symptom mentioned in this narrative and elsewhere is a complete
loss of pigmentation, whereas leprosy involves lesions and lumps in the skin
and sometimes a slightly paler color but not the ghastly whiteness of which
the biblical texts speak. This is, then, a disfiguring skin disease that remains
unidentified, and hence the present translation, here and elsewhere, coins a
name not to be found in dermatological manuals that refers to the whiteness.

he sent and told his master, "Thus and so did the girl who is from the
5 land of Israel speak." And the king of Aram said, "Go forth, and I shall
send a letter to the king of Israel." And he went, and he took in his hand
ten talents of silver and six thousand pieces of gold and ten changes of
6 garments. And he brought the letter to the king of Israel, saying, "And
now, when this letter comes to you, look, I have sent to you my servant
7 Naaman, and you shall cure him of his skin-blanch." And it happened
when the king of Israel read the letter, he rent his garments and said,
"Am I God, to deal death and life, that this person has sent to me to
cure a man from his skin-blanch? For you must surely know and mark,
8 pray, that he is seeking a pretext against me." And it happened when
Elisha, the man of God, heard that the king of Israel had rent his garments, he sent to the king, saying, "Why did you rend your garments?
Let him come, pray, to me, that he may know there is a prophet in
9 Israel." And Naaman came with his horses and his chariot and stood
10 at the entrance to Elisha's house. And Elisha sent a messenger to him,

---

5. *I shall send a letter to the king of Israel.* The king of Aram decides to intervene on behalf of his general on the highest diplomatic level, king to king. He
barely registers the advice that came from the captive girl to turn to the prophet
because his letter to the king of Israel makes no mention of it, in consequence
of which the Israelite king is panicked.

ten talents of silver and six thousand pieces of gold. This vast treasure is meant
to be a gift or payment to the Israelite prophet.

7. *he is seeking a pretext against me.* Confronted with the bare request from
the Aramean king in his very brief missive to cure Naaman, the Israelite king
construes the entire maneuver as a trap: when he fails to cure Naaman, the
king of Aram will attack him.

8. *when Elisha . . . heard that the king of Israel had rent his garments.* Word of
this public gesture of mourning or grief would have quickly spread.

9. *And Naaman came with his horses and his chariot.* Now we learn that the
general has come to Samaria with a full military retinue.

and stood at the entrance of Elisha's house. Nevertheless, the distinguished
general does not presume to march into the house of the man of God, but
stands at the entrance, awaiting word. The word comes to him only through an
intermediary, a messenger (evidently not Elisha's personal attendant Gehazi).

saying, "Go and bathe seven times in the Jordan, and your flesh will
be restored, and you will be clean." And Naaman was furious, and he   11
went off and said, "Look, I thought to myself, he will surely come out
and stand and call in the name of the LORD his God and wave his hand
toward the place and cure the skin-blanched person. Are not Amanah   12
and Parpar the rivers of Damascus better than all the waters of Israel?
Could I not bathe in them and be clean?" And he turned and went off
incensed. And his servants approached and said, "Father! The prophet   13
has spoken a great thing to you. Shall you not do it? How much more so
as he said to you, bathe and be clean?" And he went down and dipped   14
in the Jordan seven times, according to the word of the man of God,
and his flesh was restored, like the flesh of a young lad, and he was
clean. And he went back to the man of God, he and all his camp, and he   15
came and stood before him and said "Now, pray, I know that there is no
god in all the earth except in Israel, and so, take, pray, a gift from your

---

11. *he will surely come out and stand and call in the name of the* LORD *his God
and wave his hand*. Naaman had expected personal intervention by the prophet
that involved invocation of the deity's powerful name and magical hand gestures, probably over the "place" of the disease.

12. *Are not Amanah and Parpar the rivers of Damascus better than all the waters
of Israel?* Damascus, after all, is situated at a fertile confluence of rivers, and
to the Damascene eye, the Jordan is no more than a muddy rivulet. If simple
bathing could cure the disease, he would have been better off doing it in Aram.

13. *The prophet has spoken a great thing to you*. They intuit that the ostensibly
simple command to dip seven times in the Jordan is actually the direction for
a miraculous cure.
    How much more so. It is a great thing that can be effected through an easy
act.

14. *like the flesh of a young lad*. There is an interesting echo of the phrase here,
na'ar qaton, with the designation of the captive girl who gave the advice, *na'arah
qetanah*, "a young girl."

15. *stood before him*. The posture, as noted above, is deferential.
    there is no god in all the earth except in Israel. The miraculous cure converts
the Aramean general into a monotheist.

16 servant." And he said, "As the LORD lives, in Whose attendance I have stood, I will not take it." And he pressed him to take it but he refused.
17 And Naaman said, "If not, let your servant be given two mules' load of soil, for your servant will no longer perform burnt offering or sacrifice
18 to other gods but to the LORD. For this thing may the LORD forgive me: when my master comes to the house of Rimmon to worship there and he leans on my arm and I worship in the house of Rimmon, may the LORD forgive me in this thing for my worshipping in the house of
19 Rimmon." And he said to him, "Go in peace." And he went away from
20 him some distance. And Gehazi, lad of Elisha man of God, thought: "Look, my master has held back Naaman the Aramean, not taking from his hand what he brought. As the LORD lives, I will run after him and
21 take something from his hand." And Gehazi chased after Naaman, and Naaman saw him running after him and alighted from the chariot to

---

16. *I will not take it.* Elisha does not seek payment for services. His payment is in the triumph of Naaman's conversion.

17. *let your servant be given two mules' load of soil.* Naaman assumes that proper sacrifice to YHWH can be offered only on the soil of Israel, and so he requests permission to take some of it back with him to Aram. Some scholars see in this a reflection of the quandary of the Israelites exiled after 721 BCE, though that is not a necessary inference.

18. *the house of Rimmon.* This is the temple of the national god of Aram, evidently a storm-god.
    to worship. Literally, "to bow down," this gesture being a synecdoche for worship.
    and he leans on my arm. Given Naaman's position as accompanier of the king in the temple, which would be an official duty, he can scarcely avoid going through the outward motions of Rimmon worship.

meet him and said, "Is all well?" And he said, "It is well. My master sent   22
me, saying, 'Look, just now two lads from the high country of Ephraim
of the acolyte prophets have come to me. Give them, pray, a talent of
silver and two changes of garments.'" And Naaman said, "Be so kind   23
as to take two talents." And he pressed him, and he wrapped the two
talents of silver in two bags, and the two changes of garments, and he
gave them to his two lads, and they bore them off before him. And he   24
came to the citadel and took them from their hand and lay them aside
in the house and sent away the men, and they went off. And he had   25
come and was standing by his master, and Elisha said to him, "From
where have you come, Gehazi?" And he said, "Your servant has not gone
anywhere." And he said to him, "Did not my heart come along when a   26
man turned back from his chariot to meet you? Is this the time to take
silver and to take garments and olive trees and vineyards and sheep and
cattle and slaves and slave-girls? May Naaman's skin-blanch cling to   27
you and to your seed forever!" And he went out from before him skin-
blanched as snow.

---

21. *Is all well?* Seeing Elisha's attendant running after him, Naaman is alarmed
that something may be amiss as far as the prophet is concerned.

22. *My master sent me.* Gehazi is obliged to implement his greedy act by an
outright lie: that his master needs some of the proffered gift for two newly
arrived acolyte prophets. He does not dare ask for the whole splendid gift,
though Naaman generously gives him twice the amount of silver he requested.

26. *Did not my heart come along.* At this juncture, for purposes necessary to
the plot in which Gehazi's base act is exposed, Elisha exercises clairvoyance.
    olive trees and vineyards and sheep and cattle and slaves and slave-girls. These
items, of course, are not part of the gift Gehazi extracted from Naaman, but
Elisha implies that the talents of silver could serve to purchase these standard
markers of wealth in the agricultural-pastoral society.

27. *May Naaman's skin-blanch cling to you.* In the final turn of the universalist
screw in this story, the rapacious and dishonest Israelite is stricken with the
disease of which the Aramean general, now a devout follower of the God of
Israel, has been cured.

CHAPTER 6

₁ And the acolyte prophets said to Elisha, "Look, the place where we
₂ dwell is too cramped for us. Let us, pray, go to the Jordan and each of
us take from there one beam and make us a place to dwell there." And
₃ he said, "Go." And one of them said, "Be so kind, pray, as to go with
₄ your servants." And he said, "I will go." And he went with them, and
₅ they came to the Jordan and cut down trees. And it happened, as one of
them was felling the beam, that the iron blade dropped into the water,
₆ and he cried out, "Woe, my master, it is borrowed!" And the man of God
said, "Where did it fall?" and he showed him. And he cut off a stick and
₇ flung it there, and the iron blade floated up. And he said, "Lift it up for
yourself," and he stretched out his hand and took it.

---

1. *Look, the place where we dwell is too cramped for us.* From this petition, one
may infer that Elisha as master prophet was responsible for decisions regarding
the living arrangements of the acolyte prophets as well as for providing them
with food. It also is evident that they constituted a sizable group.

3. *Be so kind, pray, as to go with your servants.* They feel dependent on his guidance and his sustaining presence.

5. *Woe, my master, it is borrowed!* An axe-head was a valuable item, and we have
already seen that the acolyte prophets were relatively poor.

6. *the iron blade floated up.* This particular intercession on behalf of a follower
is, even more transparently than the previous one, an act of pure magic.

And the king of Aram had been battling against Israel, and he took coun- 8
sel with his servants, saying, "At such and such a place is my encampment." And the man of God said to the king of Israel, saying, "Keep 9
yourself from passing through this place, for the Arameans are deployed
there." And the king of Israel sent to the place of which the man of God 10
had spoken to him and warned about it, and he kept himself from there
more than once. And the king of Aram's heart stormed over this thing, 11
and he called to his servants and said to them, "'Will you not tell me?
Who of ours is for the king of Israel?" And one of his servants said, "No, 12
my lord the king! Rather, it is Elisha, the prophet who is in Israel, who
can tell the king of Israel the very words you speak in your bedchamber."
And he said, "Go, see where he is, that I might send and fetch him." And 13
it was told to him, saying, "Look, he is in Dothan," and he sent horses 14
there and chariots and a heavy force, and they came by night and surrounded the town. And the man of God's attendant woke early to rise 15
up, and he went out, and, look, a force was drawn round the town, and
horses and chariots. And his lad said to him, "Woe, my master, what can
we do?" And he said, "Do not fear, for there are more with us than with 16

---

8. *And the king of Aram had been battling against Israel.* It is not possible to
determine with any confidence which kings they are from these generalized
terms. It also looks as if these episodes in sequence were originally independent
stories collected and strung together editorially. There is no hint here that in
the previous episode an Israelite prophet cured an Aramean general, who then
went off happily, converted to monotheism.

his servants. The Hebrew term that has the general meaning of "servants" or
"slaves" refers in royal contexts to the king's courtiers, who may well be high
officials.

9. *Keep yourself from passing through this place.* Elisha again exercises prophetic
clairvoyance, a power duly recognized by the Aramean king's courtiers in verse 12.

16. *Do not fear, for there are more with us than with them.* At this point, it is
not yet clear that he is referring to supernatural forces. Elisha, more than any
other of the early prophets, repeatedly resorts to miraculous powers. His master
Elijah was obliged to flee for his life when Ahab sought to kill him, but Elisha
when mortally threatened can immediately count on chariots of fire and mysterious cavalry.

17 them." And Elisha prayed and said, "LORD, open his eyes, pray, that he may see." And the LORD opened the lad's eyes, and he saw, and look, the mountain was filled with horses and chariots of fire around Elisha.
18 And they came down to him, and Elisha prayed to the LORD and said, "Strike this nation with blinding light." And he struck them with blind-
19 ing light according to the word of Elisha. And Elisha said to them, "This is not the way, and this is not the town. Come after me, that I may lead you to the man whom you seek." And they went after him to Samaria.
20 And it happened, when they came to Samaria, that Elisha said, "LORD, open the eyes of these people, that they may see." And the LORD opened their eyes and they saw, and, look, they were in the midst of Samaria.
21 And the king of Israel said to Elisha when he saw them, "Shall I indeed
22 strike them down, my father?" And he said, "You shall not strike. Whom you have captured with your sword and your bow you may strike. Set out bread and water before them, that they may eat and drink and go
23 to their master." And he made a great feast for them, and they ate and

---

17. *LORD, open his eyes, pray, that he may see.* Elisha, with his prophet's vision, has already seen the supernatural army on the mountains. The narrative will go on to play with a counterpoint of opening the eyes and blinding them with dazzling light.

18. *Strike this nation with blinding light.* Blinding light, *sanweirim*, is also what the divine messengers at Sodom (Genesis 19) use to disable the mob of would-be rapists, and a connection between these two groups impelled by nefarious intention may be suggested.

19. *the man whom you seek.* Your targeting of a man of God is misconceived. If you are Israel's enemy, let me show you Israel's king.

20. *And the LORD opened their eyes and they saw.* Unlike the opening of the servant's eyes, which enables him to see supernatural allies, what they see is that they are in the heart of the enemy capital, a potentially fatal place for them, as the king's words in the next verse make clear.

23. *And he made a great feast for them.* The king, taking Elisha's cue that these miraculously captured warriors are not legitimate prisoners of war, goes one better than the prophet's instructions and lays out a generous feast for the Arameans, not merely bread and water.

they drank, and he sent them off, and they went to their master. And the raiding parties of Aram no longer came into the land of Israel.

And it happened afterward that Ben-Hadad king of Aram gathered 24 all his camp and came up and laid siege against Samaria. And there 25 was a great famine in Samaria, and, look, they laid siege against it till a donkey's head cost eighty pieces of silver and a quarter of a *qab* of pigeon-droppings five pieces of silver. And as the king of Israel was 26 passing on top of the wall, a woman cried out to him, saying, "Rescue me, my lord the king!" And he said, "Don't! Let the LORD rescue you. 27 From where can I rescue you, from the threshing floor or from the winepress?" And he said to her, "What's the matter with you?" And she 28 said, "This woman said to me, 'Give over your son, that we may eat him today, and my son we shall eat tomorrow.' And we cooked my son and 29

---

25. *And there was a great famine in Samaria.* Starvation in besieged towns cut off from all food supplies was one of the great terrors on ancient warfare, a fact reflected in many biblical texts. The famine here is a counterpoint to the royal feast at the end of the preceding episode.

till a donkey's head cost eighty pieces of silver and a quarter of a qab *of pigeon-droppings five pieces of silver.* The besieged population is so desperate for food that even the most inedible part of an unclean animal commands a prince's ransom. Some scholars understand the term for pigeon-droppings as a reference to carob pods, but that dilutes the hyperbolic power of the statement— that even animal filth was consumed by the starving people, and at a stiff price. *Qab* is a unit of dry measure, probably a little over a liter.

26. *Rescue me.* This cry, *hoshia'*, was the set term in pleading for justice from the king.

27. *From where can I rescue you, from the threshing floor or from the winepress?* These are, of course, places where food and drink are produced, and they are inaccessible to anyone in the besieged town. Thus the king assumes she is pleading for food. The phrase has the ring of a set idiom.

28. *Give over your son, that we may eat him today.* Cannibalism in time of siege is invoked a number of times in prophetic poetry, and it appears to have been a reality in the ancient world, but only here do we get a direct representation of the grisly act in dialogue, as part of a narrative.

ate him and I said to her the next day, 'Give over your son, that we may
30 eat him,' but she has hidden her son." And it happened when the king of
Israel heard the woman's words, he rent his garments as he was passing
on top of the wall, and the people saw, and, look, sackcloth was on his
31 flesh underneath. And he said "So may God do to me and even more, if
32 the head of Elisha son of Shaphat stays on him today." And Elisha was
sitting in his house and the elders were sitting with him. And he sent
a man ahead of him before the messenger could come to him. And he
had said to the elders, "Do you see that this murderer's son has sent to
take off my head? See, when the messenger comes, close the door and
squeeze him against the door. Is that not the sound of his master's foot-

---

30. *when the king of Israel heard . . . the woman's words, he rent his garments.*
The situation of the two women, one asking for justice from the king after her
child has been cannibalized, is reminiscent of the two whores with the dead
child and the living child in 1 Kings 3. This king, however, has no option to exercise Solomonic wisdom after the woman's child has been eaten, and instead,
despairing, he rends his garments in an act of mourning.

sackcloth was on his flesh underneath. The king is wearing some sort of royal
robe, but it has now been torn open, and the sackcloth beneath is visible.

31. *So may God do to me and even more, if the head of Elisha son of Shaphat stays
on him today.* The king's fury against Elisha may be triggered by his recognition
of the prophet's supernatural powers. If the man of God is able to blind and
capture a heavy force of Aramean warriors, his failure to intervene on behalf of
the besieged town must be a deliberately hostile act.

32. *the elders were sitting with him.* The elders would constitute a political group
outside the monarchy, and harking back to the pre-monarchic period. They may
even be a center of opposition to the king.

And he sent a man ahead of him. Again, he sees what is about to happen
through clairvoyance.

the messenger. The term, which designates any agent, human or divine, here
refers to an assassin, not to someone bringing a message.

this murderer's son. This could well refer to Jehoram, the son of Ahab, whom
Elijah excoriated as a murderer, though some scholars prefer to understand it
as "murderous person."

close the door and squeeze him against the door. Elisha reduces the would-be
hitman to an object of farce, pinned between the door and the wall.

steps after him?" He was still speaking with them when, look, the king 33
came down to him and said, "This evil is from the LORD. What more can
I hope for from the LORD?"

---

33. *the king came down to him.* The received text says "messenger," *mal'akh,*
but the king has been following close after his messenger, his footsteps audible,
and in the next moment in this scene (7:2), we see the king, who has just been
addressed by Elisha, leaving on the arm of his official. *Mal'akh,* then, is in all
likelihood a scribal error for *melekh,* "king." See the note on the beginning of 2
Samuel 11:1, where the orthographic closeness of these two words is pointedly
put into play.

CHAPTER 7

₁ And Elisha said, "Hear the word of the LORD. Thus said the LORD:
'At this time tomorrow, a *seah* of fine flour will sell for a shekel, and two
₂ *seahs* of barley for a shekel in the gate of Samaria.'" And the official on
whose arm the king was leaning answered the man of God and said,
"Look, the LORD is about to make casements in the heavens! Can this
thing be?" And he said, "You are about to see with your own eyes, but
₃ you shall not eat from there." And four men stricken with skin-blanch

---

1. *a* seah *of fine flour will sell for a shekel*. The prices stipulated here are the
antithesis of the astronomic prices for virtually inedible stuff mentioned in
6:25. This is, then, a concrete way of saying that the deadly famine will suddenly come to an end. It should be kept in mind that in this early period, the
shekel is not a coin but a weight of silver (about 11.5 grams). A *seah* is roughly
7.3 liters.

2. *the official on whose arm the king was leaning*. Since Naaman performs the
same function for the king of Aram, one may infer that this was a set court
duty for a high-ranking figure. But Naaman in mentioning this role of his has
become a convinced believer in the power of YHWH, whereas this official is
a doubter.
   Look, the LORD is about to make casements in the heavens! This remark, which
invokes a memorable phrase from the Flood story, is obviously sarcastic, the
idea being that Elisha imagines the LORD will somehow rain down food from
the sky for the starving Israelites.
   but you shall not eat from there. Elisha's words are veiled, ominously hinting
at the dire fate that will befall the official.

3. *And four men stricken with skin-blanch were at the entrance to the gate.* This
disfiguring skin-disease was thought to be contagious, requiring quarantine,
according to the laws of Leviticus. (But the requirement of quarantine is

were at the entrance to the gate, and they said to one another, "Why are
we sitting here till we die? Should we say, 'Let us come into the town,' 4
with famine in the town, we would die there, and if we stay here, we
shall die. And now, come, let us slip off to the camp of Aram. If they let
us live, we shall live, and if they put us to death, we shall die." And they 5
rose at twilight to go into the camp of Aram, and they came to the edge
of the camp of Aram, and, look, there was no one there. And the LORD 6
had made the sound of chariots, the sound of horses heard in the camp
of Aram, the sound of a great force, and every man said to his comrade,
"Look, the king of Israel has hired against us the Hittite kings and the
kings of Egypt to come against us." And they rose and fled at twilight, 7
and they abandoned their tents and their horses and their donkeys in the
camp just as it was, and they ran for their lives. And these men stricken 8
with skin-blanch came to the edge of the camp and came into one tent
and ate and drank and carried away silver and gold and garments, and
they went off and hid them, and they returned and came into another

---

ignored in the case of a high-ranking figure such as Naaman.) The diseased
men are thus outside the town, in a liminal space between the besieged city
and the Aramean camp. The Schadenfreude in this account of the flight of
the Arameans is heightened by the fact that the discovery of their precipitous
retreat is made by outcasts.

4. *If they let us live, we shall live.* Given that they are bound to die of starvation
either inside the town or outside the walls, they decide that they may as well
throw themselves on the mercy of the Arameans, who might just feed them and
let them live rather than kill them.

6. *the king of Israel has hired against us the Hittite kings and the kings of Egypt.*
If this story of an Aramean army renouncing a siege has a historical kernel, it
would be here—that an alliance of kings induced the Arameans to retreat. In
their fearful dialogue, they make the monarchs of both Egypt and the Hittites
plurals.

7. *they . . . fled at twilight.* As in many languages, the Hebrew word for twilight,
neshef, can refer either to sunset or dawn. Here the likely scenario is that the
Arameans depart as the sun sets, their flight thus unseen from the town; the
diseased men enter the camp just after the besiegers have fled; they then bring
the report of what they have seen to the king in the middle of the night.

tent and carried things away from there and went off and hid them.
9 And they said to each other, "We are not doing right. This day is a day
of good tidings and we remain silent. If we wait till morning's light, guilt
will befall us. And now, come, let us go and tell it at the king's house."
10 And they came and called out to the gatekeepers of the town and told
them, saying, "We came into the camp of Aram, and, look, there was
no one there and no human sound, only horses tethered and donkeys
11 tethered, and tents just as they had been." And the gatekeepers called
12 and told it at the king's house within. And the king arose in the night
and said to his servants, "Let me tell you, pray, what the Arameans have
done to us: they knew we were starving, and they have gone out of the
camp to hide in the field, saying, 'When they come out of the town we
13 shall catch them alive and enter the town.'" And one of his servants
answered and said, "Let them take, pray, five of the remaining horses
that are left in the town—look, they are like all the multitude of Israel

---

9. *guilt will befall us.* The Israelites will berate them, or worse, for not having
brought the news at once of the flight of the Arameans.

10. *the gatekeepers.* The Hebrew shows a singular noun, but "to them" is unambiguously plural. In the next verse, "gatekeepers" has the plural ending. The
gates of the town were of course bolted, and so the diseased men had to make
a special plea to the gatekeepers to be admitted within in order to bring their
great news to the king. The gatekeepers do not let them in, but carry the news
to the king.

12. *Let me tell you, pray, what the Arameans have done to us.* True to the fearful
character that the king of Israel exhibited when he received the letter from the
king of Aram about curing Naaman, he now concludes that this is a trap the
Arameans have set to lure the Israelites outside the town.

13. *five of the remaining horses that are left in the town.* The implication is that
most of the horses have been eaten. Some scholars think that "five" does not
indicate a precise number but means "a few."
   look, they are like all the multitude of Israel. The repetition of this clause in
immediate sequence might be an inadvertent scribal duplication (dittography),
though it could equally be an expression of the speaker's emotional turmoil in
contemplating the terrible fact that there are so few survivors in the town.

who are left in it; look, they are like all the multitude of Israel who have
come to an end, and let us send and see." And they took two teams of   14
horses, and the king sent after the camp of Aram, saying, "Go and see."
And they went after them to the Jordan, and, look, the whole road was   15
filled with garments and gear that the Arameans had flung down in their
haste, and the messengers came back and told the king. And the people   16
went out and plundered the camp of Aram, and so, a *seah* of fine flour
sold for a shekel and two *seahs* of barley for a shekel, according to the
word of the LORD. And the king had appointed over the gate the official   17
on whose arm he had leaned, and the people trampled him in the gate
and he died, as the man of God had spoken, as he had spoken when the

---

they are like all the multitude of Israel who have come to an end. In the first
iteration of this clause, the verb is "who are left." Now it is "who have come
to an end." There is a grim overlap between surviving and dying: if the horses
are like the people, barely surviving and on the way to joining those who have
already died, there is nothing lost in sending them out on this mission.

14. *two teams of horses.* This seems the likely sense of the Hebrew, which is
literally "two chariots of horses."

15. *And they went after them to the Jordan.* What may be happening is that the
horses are sent down the road, with the king's men driving them from behind
with cries and perhaps long whips, ready to fall back if the horses are spotted
by Aramean troops. They evidently bypass the empty camp, where they fear
an ambush, and discover—a significant use of the presentative "look" to mark
their visual point of view—evidence that the flight is real in the garments and
gear strewn over the road.

17. *the people trampled him in the gate.* This is a credible detail: the people,
on the point of death by starvation, stampede through the gate to get at the
food and riches they have heard are available in the Aramean camp (or to get
to those who have already expropriated the flour and are selling it at the prices
announced in the previous verse), and so they inadvertently trample the official. Elisha's obscure prophecy is now violently fulfilled.

18 king came down to him. And it happened when the man of God spoke
    to the king, saying, "Two *seahs* of barley will sell for a shekel and a *seah*
    of fine flour for a shekel at this time tomorrow in the gate of Samaria,"
19 the official answered the man of God and said, "And look, the LORD is
    about to make casements in the heavens! Can such a thing be?" And
    he said, "You are about to see with your own eyes, but you shall not eat
20 from there." And so it happened to him, and the people trampled him
    and he died.

---

18. *two* seahs *of barley will sell for a shekel and a* seah *of fine flour for a shekel.*
The story concludes with an elaborate verbatim repetition of Elisha's prophecy
and the words of the official. The only variation is that here the barley is first,
the fine flour second, and the particle that means "and" is added to the official's first word. In this instance, the point of the verbatim repetition with no
substantive changes is to underscore how the general prophecy, and then the
prophecy specifically addressed to the official in rebuke of his skepticism, are
literally and completely fulfilled.

CHAPTER 8

And Elisha had spoken to the woman whose son he revived, saying, 1
"Arise and go, you and your household, and sojourn wherever you
would sojourn, for the LORD has called forth famine and it actually
has come to the land for seven years." And the woman arose and did 2
according to the man of God's word, and she went, she and her household, and sojourned in the land of the Philistines seven years. And it 3
happened at the end of seven years that the woman came back from
the land of the Philistines, and she went out and cried to the king for
her house and for her field. And the king was speaking to Gehazi, the 4
man of God's lad, saying, "Recount to me, pray, all the great things

---

1. *And Elisha had spoken to the woman.* The syntax and the form of the Hebrew
verb indicate a pluperfect, as reflected in the translation—a careful indication
of tense because the action about to be reported unfolds seven years after
Elisha's words to the woman. Oddly, in this episode she is never referred to as
"the Shunammite."

4. *And the king was speaking to Gehazi.* There is no hint here that Gehazi has
been stricken with a ghastly skin disease. This is one of several indications
that the stories about Elisha brought together in this cycle probably originated
independently. The fact that Gehazi is a presence in the court recounting the
great acts of his master has led some interpreters to infer that in this particular
story Elisha is assumed to have died.

5 that Elisha did." And it happened as he was recounting to the king
that Elisha revived the dead, that, look, the woman whose son he
had revived came crying out to the king for her house and for her field.
And Gehazi said, "This is the woman, and this is her son whom Elisha
6 revived." And the king asked the woman, and she recounted to him, and
he gave her a certain eunuch, saying, "Return all that is hers and all the
yield of the field from the day she left the land till now."

7 And Elisha came to Damascus, with Ben-Hadad king of Aram ill, and
8 it was told to him, saying, "The man of God has come here." And the
king said to Hazael, "Take tribute in your hand and go to meet the man
of God and inquire of the LORD through him, saying, 'Will I survive
9 this illness?'" And Hazael went to meet him and took tribute in his
hand, from all the bounty of Damascus, a load of forty camels, and
he came and stood before him and said, "Your son Ben-Hadad king

---

5. *crying out to the king*. The Hebrew verb used here has a technical sense of
making a plea for justice from the king.
   for her house and for her field. These substantial possessions have obviously
been seized by others during her seven years' absence.

6. *a certain eunuch*. Though this is the plain meaning of the Hebrew noun *saris*,
it is possible that the term came to designate a particular kind of court official,
without reference to genital mutilation.
   all the yield of the field from the day she left the land till now. She is legally
entitled not only to resume possession of the land but to receive all the profit
made from it during her absence.

8. *Take tribute in your hand and go to meet the man of God*. If there is any continuity between this story and the story of Naaman, Elisha's powers would be
well-known and respected in the Aramean court.
   inquire of the LORD through him. Ben-Hadad does not assume that YHWH is
the one and only God, but he has reason to think that this Hebrew deity served
by Elisha has great potency.

9. *a load of forty camels*. This makes the tribute a very grand gift.

of Aram has sent me to you, saying, 'Will I survive this illness?'" And 10
Elisha said to him, "Go, say to him, 'You will surely survive,' but the
LORD has shown me that he is doomed to die." And his face froze and 11
he was dumbfounded a long time, and the man of God wept. And 12
Hazael said, "Why is my lord weeping?" And he said, "Because I know
the harm that you will do to the Israelites. Their fortresses you will
send up in flames, and their young men you will slay by the sword, and
their infants you will smash, and their pregnant women you will split
open." And Hazael said, "How could your servant, a dog, do this great 13
thing?" And Elisha said, "The LORD has showed you to me as king over
Aram." And he went from Elisha and came to his master, and he said 14

---

10. *Go, say to him, 'You will surely survive,' but the LORD has shown me that he
is doomed to die.* Elisha's response is devious: you can tell him he will survive
his grave illness, which will be technically true because he is to die from quite
a different cause. Some interpreters imagine that Elisha is encouraging Hazael
to assassinate Ben-Hadad, but this is implausible because Elisha foresees that
when he becomes king, Hazael will ravage the people of Israel. What has happened is simply that God has revealed to him both Ben-Hadad's fate and the
future course of war between Aram and Israel.

11. *And his face froze.* This is the likely sense of the somewhat obscure Hebrew,
which is literally, "and he made his face stand [still]."
    and he was dumbfounded. The received text shows *wayasem*, "and he put."
But two Hebrew manuscripts and the Vulgate have *wayishom*, to be desolate
or dumbfounded, which is much more likely. The subject of both these verbs
must be Hazael, who is astounded, and at a loss, to hear Elisha's stark prophecy.

13. *How could your servant, a dog, do this great thing?* The humble self-desig-
nation reflects the fact that Hazael, though he is some sort of court official, is
not of the royal line. In an inscription by the Assyrian king Shalmaneser III,
Hazael is in fact referred to as "son of no one." One notes that he has no moral
compunctions about the prospect of perpetrating the most barbaric cruelties
on the men, women and infants of Israel; on the contrary, these were common
acts in military conquest and thus part of what constituted a "great thing" that
he is not sure he is worthy to do.
    The LORD has showed you to me as king over Aram. These words may not be
intended to instigate the assassination, but they certainly have the effect of
giving Hazael the idea.

to him, "What did Elisha say to you?" And he said, "He said, 'You will
15 surely survive.'" And it happened the next day that he took a cloth and
soaked it in water and spread it over his face, and he died. And Hazael
became king in his stead.

16 And in the fifth year of Jehoram son of Ahab king of Israel—Jehoshaphat
had been king of Judah—Jehoram son of Jehoshaphat became king, king
17 of Judah. He was thirty-two years old when he became king, and he was
18 king in Jerusalem eight years. And he went in the way of the kings of
Israel, as the house of Ahab had done, for Ahab's daughter had become
19 his wife, and he did what was evil in the eyes of the LORD. But the LORD
did not want to destroy Judah, for the sake of David His servant, as He
20 had said to him to grant a lamp for his sons perpetually. In his days did
Edom rebel from under the hand of Judah, and they set a king over
21 themselves. And Jehoram crossed over to Zair, all the chariots with him,
and it happened that as he arose in the night, the Edomites surrounding
him struck him, and the captains of the chariots, and the troops fled to
22 their tents. And Edom has rebelled from under the hand of Judah until
23 this day. Then did Libneh rebel at that time. And the rest of the acts
of Jehoram and all that he did, are they not written in the Book of the
24 Acts of the Kings of Judah? And Jehoram lay with his fathers and was
buried in the City of David, and Ahaziah his son became king in his

---

15. *he took a cloth and soaked it in water and spread it over his face.* The subject
of the verb is Hazael. He kills the king by suffocating him (there will be no
blood visible and perhaps the courtiers will conclude that Ben-Hadad died of
his illness). The king, of course, in his greatly weakened state is in no shape to
resist the murderous act.

21. *as he arose in the night, the Edomites surrounding him struck him.* The
Masoretic text reads: as he arose in the night, he struck the Edomites surrounding him. This reading may reflect scribal wishful thinking. To begin with,
it is syntactically peculiar, and the clear indication is that the Israelites were
defeated in a successful rebellion by the Edomites. Furthermore, the "troops,"
'am, who flee to their tents, that is, to their homes, is a term generally referring
to Israelite troops, not, as it appears here in the received text, to Edomites.

stead. In the twelfth year of Jehoram son of Ahab king of Israel, Ahaziah 25
became king, king of Judah. Ahaziah was twenty-two years old when he 26
became king, and he was king one year in Jerusalem. And his mother's
name was Athaliah daughter of Omri king of Israel. And he went in 27
the way of the house of Ahab and did what was evil in the eyes of the
LORD like the house of Ahab, for he was kin by marriage to the house of
Ahab. And Jehoram son of Ahab went to battle with Hazael king of Aram 28
at Ramoth-Gilead, and the Arameans struck down Jehoram. And King 29
Jehoram came back to heal in Jezreel from the blows that the Arameans had struck him at Ramah when he did battle with Hazael king of
Aram, and Ahaziah son of Jehoram king of Judah had gone down to see
Jehoram son of Ahab in Jezreel, for he was ill.

---

26. *his mother's name was Athaliah daughter of Omri.* In verse 18 she is identified as Ahab's daughter, though perhaps the Hebrew *bat* could encompass
granddaughter. In any case, the familial connection through marriage with the
house of Ahab leads to trouble.

CHAPTER 9

1 And Elisha the prophet had called to one of the acolyte prophets and said to him, "Gird your loins and take this cruse of oil in your hand and 2 go to Ramoth-Gilead. And you shall come there and see there Jehu son of Jehoshaphat son of Nimshi. And you shall come and raise him up from the midst of his brothers and bring him into the inner chamber. 3 And you shall take the cruse of oil and pour it on his head and say, Thus said the LORD: 'I have anointed you king over Israel.' And you shall 4 open the door and flee and you shall not wait.'" And the lad went, the 5 prophet lad, to Ramoth-Gilead. And he came and, look, the commanders of the force were sitting there, and he said, "I have a word for you, commander." And Jehu said, "For whom among all of us?" And he said, 6 "For you, commander." And he rose and entered the house and poured oil on his head and said to him, "Thus said the LORD God of Israel: 'I 7 have anointed you king over the LORD's people, over Israel. And you shall strike down the house of Ahab your master, and I will be avenged for the blood of My servants the prophets and for the blood of all the

---

2. *you shall come there and see there Jehu son of Jehoshaphat.* All along, prophets have been involved in power struggles around the throne, but Elisha's initiative in this instance is the most blatant of these involvements: he sends one of his people to anoint Jehu as king and to prompt Jehu to assassinate the reigning king, Jehoram.

bring him into the inner chamber. The actual anointment is clandestine, and the acolyte prophet is accordingly enjoined to flee once he has performed the act, lest there be an adverse reaction on the part of the military people around Jehu when they learn what has occurred.

LORD's servants from the hand of Jezebel. And all the house of Ahab 8 shall perish, and I will cut off from Ahab every pisser against the wall and ruler and helper in Israel. And I will make the house of Ahab like 9 the house of Jeroboam son of Nebat and like the house of Baasha son of Ahijah. And Jezebel the dogs shall devour in the field of Jezreel, with 10 none to bury her.'" And he opened the door and fled. And Jehu had gone 11 out to his master's servants, and someone said to him, "Is all well? Why did this madman come to you?" And he said to them, "You know this man and how he talks." And they said, "It's a lie! Tell us, pray." And he 12 said, "Thus and so he said to me, saying, 'Thus said the LORD: "I have anointed you king over Israel."'" And they hastened and each of them 13 took his garment and they put them beneath him on the top of the stairs,

---

8. *I will cut off from Ahab ever pisser against the wall.* This pungent epithet for males, reserved for curses, is usually pronounced by human speakers but here is used by God in the momentum of the curse-formula.

11. *his master's servants.* There is an ironic point in the use of this designation for Jehu's fellow officers. "His master" would have to be the king, against whom Jehu is about to rebel, abetted by the other commanders of the army.
   Why did this madman come to you? The groups of prophets, bonded together in a kind of guild, were known for working themselves into ecstatic states, often with the help of musical instruments, as the two stories of Saul among the prophets in 1 Samuel illustrate. Calling a prophet a madman, then, makes perfect sense, and that equation occurs elsewhere in biblical literature.

12. *It's a lie!* The other officers immediately see that Jehu's response to their question about the acolyte prophet ("You know the man and how he talks") is an evasion. Jehu then feels constrained to divulge the truth about his clandestine anointment, counting on their support.

13. *each of them took his garment.* What they appear to be doing is constructing a kind of improvised throne, seating him on the top of the stairs. This is a literal realization of Elisha's injunction regarding Jehu to "raise him up from the midst of his brothers."
   the top of the stairs. The Hebrew *gerem hama'alot* is unique to this verse and its meaning has been inferred from the context. In modern Hebrew, *gerem* has been adopted for "stairwell."

14 and they blew the ram's horn and said, "Jehu is king." And Jehu son of
Jehoshaphat son of Nimshi plotted against Jehoram, and Jehoram had
been on watch at Ramoth-Gilead—he and all Israel—against Hazael
15 king of Aram. And King Jehoram had gone back to Jezreel to heal from
the blows that the Arameans struck him when he did battle with Hazael
king of Aram. And Jehu said, "If you agree, let no fugitive come out of
16 the town to tell in Jezreel." And Jehu mounted and went to Jezreel, for
Jehoram was in bed there, and Ahaziah king of Judah had gone down
17 to see Jehoram. And the lookout was stationed on the tower in Jezreel,
and he saw Jehu's throng as it came, and he said, "I see a throng." And
Jehoram said, "Take a horseman and send out to meet them and say,
18 "Do you come in peace?" And the horseman went to meet him and said,
"Thus said the king: 'Do you come in peace?'" And Jehu said, "What do
you have to do with peace? Turn round behind me!" And the lookout told,
19 saying, "The messenger came to them and has not come back." And he
sent a second horseman, and he came to them and said, "Thus said the
king: 'Do you come in peace?'" And Jehu said, "What do you have to do

---

14. *Jehu . . . plotted against Jehoram.* As the details of the narrative make clear,
the conspiracy is a military coup whereby Jehu, as one of the army officers,
seizes the throne after killing its occupant.

Jehoram. The Hebrew here and at several other points uses a shortened
form, Joram, but the translation, to avoid confusion, shows the full form of the
name throughout.

15. *If you agree.* This is probably no more than a polite way of delivering an
order, though it is possible that Jehu does not fully trust his fellow officers to
follow his commands in implementing the coup, despite their gesture of support in elevating him on the improvised throne.

17. *Jehu's throng.* The word-choice is realistic: from the distance, the lookout
is able to identify a crowd of advancing soldiers, which he correctly assumes
to be led by Jehu.

18. *What do you have to do with peace?* Jehu's implacably hostile intentions are
manifest in his dialogue.

Turn round behind me! He also makes clear that he is the stronger party, and
that the messenger had better abandon Jehoram and join the usurper.

with peace? Turn round behind me." And the lookout told, saying, "He ₂₀
came to them and has not come back, and the driving is like Jehu son
of Nimshi's driving, for he drives madly." And Jehoram said, "Hitch up!" ₂₁
And his chariot was hitched up, and Jehoram king of Israel, and Ahaziah
king of Judah went out, each in his chariot, and they went out to meet
Jehu and found him in the field of Naboth the Jezreelite. And it happened ₂₂
when Jehoram saw Jehu that he said, "Do you come in peace, Jehu?"
And he said to him, "What do the whoring of Jezebel your mother and
her abundant witchcraft have to do with peace?" And Jehoram whipped ₂₃
round the reins and fled, and he said to Ahaziah, "Treachery, Ahaziah!"
And Jehu bent the bow in his hand and struck Jehoram between his ₂₄
shoulders, and the arrow came out through his heart, and he collapsed

---

20. *the driving is like Jehu son of Nimshi's driving, for he drives madly.* The lookout is too far off to see Jehu's face but can recognize his wild style of driving a
chariot. In this we get a new element of characterization of Jehu: he is known,
at least in royal circles, for riding in his chariot at breakneck speed. This wild
energy is of a piece with his quickness as an assassin, about to be manifested.

21. *And Jehoram said, "Hitch up!"* In still another instance of the pattern of
two repetitions with a divergence in the third repetition, Jehoram, after the
defection of the two messengers, goes out himself to parlay with Jehu, naively
imagining they can come to terms.
    and Ahaziah king of Judah went out. Exhibiting what will prove to be fatal
imprudence, Ahaziah chooses to express his solidarity with Jehoram by joining
him in going to meet Jehu.

22. *What do the whoring of Jezebel your mother and her abundant witchcraft
have to do with peace?* In this switch from the twice-repeated formula, Jehu
makes himself the mouthpiece of Elisha's prophetic wrath against the whole
house of Ahab. "Whoring" may mean, as it often does elsewhere in the Bible,
going after strange gods, though an innuendo of sexual promiscuity is distinctly
possible—calling a man's mother a whore to his face is, after all, an especially
blatant insult.

23. *whipped round the reins.* The literal sense is "turned over his hands."

24. *struck Jehoram between his shoulders.* There is no chivalry in this efficient
killing: Jehu shoots the fleeing Jehoram in the back.

₂₅ in his chariot. And he said to Bidkar his officer, "Bear him off, fling him into the field of Naboth the Jezreelite. For remember! You and I rode side by side after Ahab his father, and the LORD delivered this message about ₂₆ him: 'I surely saw the blood of Naboth and his sons last night,' says the LORD, 'and I will pay you back in this field,' says the LORD. And, now, bear him off, fling him into the field according to the word of the LORD." ₂₇ And Ahaziah king of Judah had seen, and he fled on the road to Beth-Gan, and Jehu pursued him and said, "Him, too, strike down." And they struck him in the chariot on the Ascent of Gur which is by Jibleam, and ₂₈ he fled to Megiddo and died there. And his servants took him by chariot to Jerusalem and buried him there in his grave with his fathers in the ₂₉ City of David. And in the eleventh year of Jehoram son of Ahab, Ahaziah ₃₀ had become king over Judah. And Jehu came to Jezreel, and Jezebel had heard, and she put kohl round her eyes and did up her hair and looked

---

25. *You and I rode side by side after Ahab his father*. This is a piece of delayed exposition that sharpens our sense of Jehu's animus toward Jehoram: he and Bidkar were actually present when Ahab expropriated the field of Naboth after his judicial murder.

26. *the blood of Naboth and his sons*. No sons were mentioned in the story of the killing of Naboth. Either this detail reflects a variant version of the story, or the sons, fatherless and landless, are considered as good as dead.

27. *Him, too, strike down*. Jehu shows Machiavellian ruthlessness here. Ahaziah king of Judah was in no way involved in the egregious crimes, cultic and moral, of the house of Ahab, but he became Jehoram's ally, and, as such, he might be a potential threat to Jehu, who therefore makes sure to have him killed.

And they struck him. This phrase (a single Hebrew word) is absent from the received text but appears in three ancient versions as well as in two Hebrew manuscripts. Without it, the sentence is semantically and syntactically incoherent.

28. *buried him there in his grave with his fathers*. Unlike Jehoram, who is flung into the field his father stole, there to be devoured by scavengers, Ahaziah is granted a proper burial.

30. *she put kohl round her eyes and did up her hair*. Though some interpreters take this as an expression of her desire to show a noble appearance, it looks more like an effort at the very end to exhibit her female attractiveness, thus picking up the sexual sense of "the whoring of Jezebel."

out through the window. And Jehu had entered the gate, and she said,   31
"Is all well, you Zimri, killer of his master?" And he lifted his face toward   32
the window and said, "Who is with me, who?" And two or three eunuchs
looked down at him. And he said, "Push her out." And they pushed her   33
out, and her blood splattered against the wall and on the horses, and they
trampled her. And he came and ate and drank, and he said, "Look to this   34
cursed creature and bury her, for she is the daughter of a king." And they   35
went to bury her, but they found of her only the skull and the legs and
the palms of the hands. And they came back and told him, and he said,   36
"It is the word of the LORD that He spoke through His servant Elijah the
Tishbite, saying, 'In the field of Jezreel the dogs shall devour the flesh of
Jezebel. And Jezebel's carcass shall be like dung upon the ground in the   37
field of Jezreel, so that they cannot say, This is Jezebel.'"

---

31. *you Zimri, killer of his master*. Confronted by the man who has killed her son
and who she must know is now determined to kill her, Jezebel remains fierce
and contemptuous. Zimri (1 Kings 16:8–18) slaughtered the whole house of
Baasha and usurped the throne but was himself killed seven days later.

32. *Who is with me, who?* As with Jehoram's two messengers, Jehu counts on
the fact that the attendants of the house of Ahab, seeing his superior force, will
turn against their masters. Pointedly, Jehu does not deign to answer Jezebel's
biting words to him.
    two or three eunuchs. As before, these may simply be court officials.

34. *Look to this cursed creature*. The Hebrew uses merely the feminine indica-
tive *ha'arurah hazo't* ("this cursed one") to express contempt.
    bury her, for she is the daughter of a king. Though Jehu despises Jezebel, he is
conscious of the respect due to royal personages—perhaps out of self-interest
since he has just become king himself. For the moment, he puts out of his mind
the explicit prophecy that has been delivered to him (verse 10), "And Jezebel
the dogs shall devour in the field of Jezreel, with none to bury her."

36. *It is the word of the LORD*. After the fact, Jehu, though he has just appeared
to be concerned that Jezebel receive a proper burial, affirms her being consumed by canine scavengers as a fitting fulfillment of God's curse on her.

37. *so that they cannot say, This is Jezebel*. There may be a political angle to this
fulfillment of the curse: nothing recognizable of Jezebel's body is left, nothing
for any potential loyalists to venerate (as the Bolsheviks reduced the murdered
family of the Czar to ashes for just this reason).

CHAPTER 10

And Ahab had seventy sons in Samaria. And Jehu wrote letters and sent them to the rulers of Samaria, to the elders of the town and to Ahab's tutors, saying, "And now, when this letter comes to you, and the sons of your master are with you, and the chariots and the horses are with you, and the fortified towns and the weapons, you shall see to the best and the most fitting of your master's sons and put him on his father's throne, and battle for your master's house." And they were very, very afraid, and they thought, "Look, two kings could not stand up against him, and how can we stand?" And he who was appointed over the palace and he who was appointed over the town and the elders and the tutors sent to Jehu, saying, "We are your servants, and all that you say to us we shall do. We

---

1. *And Ahab had seventy sons.* The number is formulaic, as in the case of the seventy sons of Gideon in the story of Abimelech (Judges 9). "Sons" in this instance probably refers to all the descendants of Ahab, encompassing at least two generations.

Ahab's tutors. These are the tutors engaged by Ahab to look after the education and well-being of his sons and grandsons.

3. *you shall see to the best and the most fitting of your master's sons.* With characteristic deviousness, Jehu does not initially present the elders and tutors with a command but with an ostensible exhortation to elect a new king who can lead the loyalists of the house of Ahab against the forces of Jehu. He of course counts on their knowledge of his just manifested lethal efficiency that will make this proposal strike terror in their hearts.

shall make no one king. Do what is good in your eyes." And he wrote 6
them a letter again, saying, "If you are mine and heed my voice, take off
the heads of the men who are your master's sons and bring them to me
at this time tomorrow in Jezreel." And the king's sons, seventy men, were
with the town's notables who had reared them. And it happened, when 7
the letter came to them, that they took the king's sons and slaughtered
the seventy men and put their heads in baskets and sent them to him
in Jezreel. And the messenger came and told him, saying, "They have 8
brought the heads of the king's sons." And he said, "Put them in two
piles at the entrance of the gate until morning." And it happened in the 9
morning that he came out and stood and said to all the people, "Well,
you are innocent! Look, I plotted against my master and killed him, but
who struck down all these? Know, then, that nothing will fail of the word 10
of the LORD that He spoke against the house of Ahab, but the LORD has
done what He spoke through his servant Elijah." And Jehu struck down 11

---

6. *take off the heads of the men who are your master's sons.* After his oblique
opening move, Jehu confronts them with the brutal command to commit mass
murder on his behalf.

   bring. The received text reads "come" (a different conjugation of the same
verbal stem), but three ancient versions and a few Hebrew manuscripts show
"bring," which is more plausible because the killers send the heads in baskets
rather than coming themselves.

8. *Put them in two piles at the entrance of the gate.* This grisly detail is another
stroke of Jehu's ruthless calculation: the bloody evidence of the elimination of
the whole house of Ahab is set out for public exhibition. Presumably, no one
will now dare to oppose Jehu.

9. *Well, you are innocent!* This declaration is of course sarcastic (and "well"
has been added in the translation to intimate the tone). Jehu has managed to
make the leaders of the Samaritan establishment his accomplices in murder:
they can scarcely condemn him for killing the two kings when they are directly
responsible for many more deaths.

10. *the LORD has done what He spoke through His servant Elijah.* Throughout the
bloody trajectory Jehu traces, he justifies his acts as the fulfillment of the dire
prophecy against the house of Ahab. At the same time, the ruthless elimination of any conceivable claimant to the throne from the line he has overthrown
surely serves his political interests.

all who were left of the house of Ahab in Jezreel, and all his notables and
12 his intimates and his priests, till he left him no remnant. And he rose
and went and came to Samaria. When he was at Beth-Eked-ha-Roim
13 on the way, Jehu encountered the kinsmen of Ahaziah king of Judah,
and he said, "Who are you?" And they said, "We are the kinsmen of
Ahaziah, and we are going down to see if all is well with the king's sons
14 and the sons of the queen mother." And he said, "Seize them alive," and
they seized them alive, and they slaughtered them at the pit of Beth-
15 Eked, forty-two men, he did not leave a man of them. And he went
from there and encountered Jehonadab son of Rechab coming toward
him, and he greeted him and he said to him, "Is your heart steadfast
with me as my heart is with yours?" And he said to him, "It certainly is."
"Give me your hand." And he gave him his hand, and he took him up
16 to him in the chariot. And he said, "Come with me and see my zeal for
17 the LORD." And he drove him in his chariot. And he came to Samaria
and struck down all who were left of Ahab in Samaria till he destroyed
18 them, according to the word of the LORD that He spoke to Elijah. And

---

13. *kinsmen.* Though the Hebrew noun has the primary meaning of "brothers,"
the narrative context here suggests that the more extended sense of the word
is being used.

*we are going down to see if all is well with the king's sons and the sons of the
queen mother.* All of these sons have just been beheaded. The kinsmen of Ahaziah, perhaps because they have been on their way to visit the royal family of
their allies in Samaria, appear not to have heard about the murder of Jehoram
and Ahaziah, or they scarcely would be going to visit Jehoram's kinfolk.

14. *he did not leave a man of them.* Jehu is absolutely consistent in this.

15. *Jehonadab son of Rechab.* The Rechabites were known for their ascetic
practice (see Jeremiah 35:6–7), so perhaps Jehu embraces Jehonadab as an ally
because he feels he can count on Jehonadab's fanatic devotion to YHWH and
his concomitant animosity toward the followers of Baal.

Give me your hand. These words are evidently spoken by Jehu, though there
is no formula here for the introduction of speech.

17. *he . . . struck down all who were left of Ahab.* After the murder of the seventy
sons, there evidently were still relatives of Ahab's left to eliminate, unless "of
Ahab" refers more broadly to people loyal to Ahab.

Jehu gathered all the people and said to them, "Ahab served Baal a little. Jehu will serve him abundantly. And now, call to me all the prophets 19 of Baal, all his servants and all his priests, let no one be missing, for I am about to have a great sacrifice to Baal—whoever is missing shall not live." But Jehu dealt deviously in order to destroy the servants of Baal. And Jehu said, "Call a solemn assembly to Baal," and they called. And 20,21 Jehu sent out through all Israel, and all the servants of Baal came, and not a man remained who did not come. And they came to the house of Baal, and the house of Baal was filled from corner to corner. And he said 22 to the one appointed over the wardrobe, "Bring out garments for all the servants of Baal," and he brought out garments for them. And he came 23 into the house of Baal, and Jehonadab son of Rechab with him, and he said to the worshippers of Baal, "Search and see if there are here with you any servants of the LORD besides the servants of Baal alone." And 24 they came to perform sacrifices and burnt offerings, and Jehu had set for himself eighty men outside. And he said, "Any man who escapes of the men whom I have brought into your hands—his life for that man's life!" And it happened when he finished performing the burnt offering, 25 that Jehu said to the sentries and to the captains, "Come, strike them down. Let no man get away." And they struck them down by the sword, and the sentries and the captains flung them out, and they went to the town of the house of Baal. And they brought out the sacred pillars of 26

---

19. *But Jehu dealt deviously.* The narrator wants to make sure the audience immediately understands that Jehu's proposal of a great sacrifice to Baal is mere subterfuge.

22. *Bring out garments for all the servants of Baal.* Extending the deception, Jehu presents festive garments to the followers of Baal, as if to enhance the pomp and ceremony of the occasion. "Servants" throughout this passage of course means "worshippers."

24. *his life for that man's life!* "That man" has been added for the sake of clarity.

25. *they went to the town of the house of Baal.* "Town" here is a little confusing because presumably the temple of Baal is in Samaria, where they all are (unless one assumes it was located in a nearby suburb). One proposed emendation is instead of *'ir*, town, to read *devir*, inner sanctum.

27 the house of Baal and burned them. And they smashed the sacred pillar
    of Baal, and they smashed the house of Baal and turned it into latrines,
28,29 to this very day. And Jehu destroyed Baal from Israel. But Jehu did not
    swerve from the offenses of Jeroboam son of Nebat, who had led Israel
30 to offend—the golden calves that were in Bethel and in Dan. And the
    LORD said to Jehu, "In as much as you have done well what is right in
    My eyes, according to all that was in My heart you have done to the
    house of Ahab, four generations of your sons shall sit on the throne of
31 Israel." But Jehu did not watch out to go by the teaching of the LORD
    God of Israel with all his heart. He did not swerve from the offenses of
32 Jeroboam, who had led Israel to offend. In those days the LORD began
    to trim away Israel, and Hazael struck them down through all the bor-
33 derland of Israel, from the Jordan, where the sun rises, all the land of
    Gilead, the Gadites and the Reubenites and the Manassites, from Aroer,
34 which is by the wadi of Arnon, and Gilead and Bashan. And the rest of
    the acts of Jehu, and all that he did, and all his valor, are they not writ-
35 ten in the Book of the Acts of the Kings of Israel? And Jehu lay with his
    fathers, and they buried him in Samaria, and Jehoahaz his son became
36 king in his stead. And the time Jehu had been king over Israel in Samaria
    was twenty-eight years.

---

27. *they smashed the sacred pillar.* There may be a textual confusion here, not
only because of the switch from plural to singular pillar but also because a
burnt pillar does not need to be smashed.

29. *the golden calves that were in Bethel and in Dan.* From the viewpoint of the
Judahite writer, these cultic objects were pagan images, though in historical
fact they were probably only an alternative iconography (in Judahite worship
cherubim were used) to represent the sanctuary where YHWH dwelled. The
failure to "swerve from the offenses of Jereboam" mentioned in the next verse
probably refers to the golden calves.

32. *trim away Israel.* The verb refers, quite accurately, to chopping off fringe
areas.
    through all the borderland of Israel. The noun *gevul* can mean either "border"
or "territory." Since the incursions of the Aramean king were limited to the area
east of the Jordan occupied by the two and a half tribes, the word as it is used
here probably is intended to make us think of a border region.

CHAPTER 11

 nd Athaliah, Ahaziah's mother, saw that her son was dead, and she 1
arose and destroyed all the royal seed. And Jehosheba, Ahaziah's sister, 2
the daughter of King Jehoram, took Joash, Ahaziah's son, and stole him
away from the king's sons who had been put to death—him and his
nurse—in the bedchamber, and they hid him from Athaliah, and he
was not put to death. And he was with her hiding in the house of the 3
LORD six years, while Athaliah was reigning over the land. And in the 4
seventh year Jehoiada sent and took the commanders of the hundreds

---

1. *saw.* The Masoretic text shows, in defiance of Hebrew grammar, "and saw,"
but many Hebrew manuscripts omit the "and."

    and destroyed all the royal seed. This shocking act, which makes Athaliah far
more horrendous than Medea, is not explained. One should keep in mind that
Athaliah appears to be the daughter of Ahab and Jezebel, and she takes after
her mother in viciousness. Seeing that her son Ahaziah has been killed, she
ruthlessly grasps an opportunity for herself by murdering her sons and grandsons so that she can seize the throne without rivals.

2. *Jehosheba.* She is both the aunt of the infant Joash whom she saves and wife
of Jehoiada the priest, who plots the overthrow of Athaliah.

3. *hiding in the house of the LORD.* Jehosheba's husband, as priest (evidently, high
priest), would have had jurisdiction over the temple precincts and would have
been able to devise a safe hiding-place within the temple.

    while Athaliah was reigning over the land. Given that she has violently
usurped the throne, her reign is indicated only through a participial aside, and
the formulaic statement ("and X was king/queen in his stead") is avoided.

4. *And in the seventh year Jehoiada sent.* Perhaps the initiative occurs in the seventh year merely because it is the formulaic number for several years, though

of the Cherithites and the sentries and brought them to him at the
house of the Lᴏʀᴅ and made a pact with them and imposed a vow on
them in the house of the Lᴏʀᴅ. And he showed them the king's son.
5 And he charged them, saying, "This is the thing that you must do: a
third of you, who begin your weekly duty, are to keep guard at the king's
6 house, and a third in the Horse Gate and a third in the gate behind
7 the sentries, and you shall keep watch over the house. And the two
contingents among you, all who have finished their weekly duty, shall
8 keep guard over the house of the Lᴏʀᴅ for the king. And you shall draw
round the king, every man with his weapons in his hand. And whosoever enters the colonnades shall be put to death. And be you with the
9 king when he goes out and when he comes in." And the commanders of
the hundreds did as all that Jehoiada the priest had charged, and each
took his men, those beginning their weekly duty with those finishing
10 their weekly duty, and they came to Jehoiada the priest. And the priest
gave to the commanders of the hundreds the spears and the shields
11 that were King David's, which were in the house of the Lᴏʀᴅ. And
the sentries stood, each with his weapons in his hand, from the south
corner of the house to the north corner of the house, by the altar and

---

seven years would have given Joash time to grow from infant to young boy,
at which point he could be placed on the throne with a regent as political
executive.

the Cherithites. The received text says "Charite," but this is in all likelihood
a shortened form or error for Cherithites, Cretan warriors who served as a
palace guard.

the sentries. This may be a designation for a particular group of palace guards.
The literal sense of the Hebrew is "runners."

6. the Horse Gate. The Hebrew says the Sur Gate, but the meaning of *Sur* is
obscure, and verse 16 speaks of "the Horse Entrance," *mevo' hasusim*. Thus, *sur*
may well be an error for *sus*, "horse."

8. be you with the king when he goes out and when he comes in. Jehoida pointedly
refers to Joash as "the king," even before his coronation, in order to publicly
confirm his royal status. Joash, after having been kept in hiding almost seven
years, must be zealously protected in this moment of transfer of power.

10. the shields. Others interpret the Hebrew term as "quivers" or "lances."

by the house, all round the king. And he brought out the prince and put   12
the crown on him and the regalia, and he made him king and anointed
him, and they clapped their hands and said, "Long live the king!" And   13
Athaliah heard the sound of the sentries and the people, and she came
to the people at the house of the LORD. And she saw, and, look, the   14
king was standing by the pillar as was the custom, and the commanders
and the trumpets were by the king, and all the people of the land were
rejoicing and blowing the trumpets. And Athaliah rent her garments
and called out, "A plot, a plot!" And Jehoiada the priest charged the   15
commanders of the hundreds, the mustered men of the force, and said
to them, "Take her out from the colonnades, and put to death by the
sword whoever comes after her," for the priest said, "Let her not be put
to death in the house of the LORD." And they locked hands on all sides   16
of her, and she came into the king's house by way of the Horse Entrance
and was put to death there. And Jehoiada made a pact between the   17
LORD and the king and the people to be a people of the LORD, between
the king and the people. And all the people of the land came to the   18
house of Baal and smashed it, its altars and its images they utterly shat-

---

12. *the regalia*. The Hebrew *'edut* usually means "covenant," but it is hard
to imagine that any form of the covenant could be placed on the new king,
so it seems more likely that the word here is a homonym, derived from *'adi*,
"ornament."

14. *all the people of the land*. Some scholars contend that the Hebrew *'am
ha'arets* refers to a particular group of Davidic loyalists in Jerusalem.

15. *Let her not be put to death in the house of the* LORD. Jehoiada, conscious of
a cultic taboo, wants no blood shed within the temple.

17. *between the king and the people*. Though this phrase sounds redundant, it
may be that the repetition is deliberate, in order to emphasize the new solidarity
between king and people that stands in contrast to Athaliah's autocratic seizure
of power.

18. *the house of Baal*. This is new information: that during Athaliah's reign a
functioning temple of Baal stood in Jerusalem. We are probably meant to infer
that Athaliah, in addition to her murderous lust for power, followed the pagan
ways of her mother Jezebel and encouraged a cult of Baal in Jerusalem.

tered, and Mattan priest of Baal they killed in front of the altars. And
19 the priest appointed guards over the house of the LORD. And he took
the commanders of the hundreds and the Cherethites and the sentries
and all the people of the land, and they brought the king down from the
house of the LORD, and they entered the king's house through the Gate
20 of the Sentries, and he sat on the royal throne. And all the people of the
land rejoiced, while the town was quiet. And Athaliah they had put to
death in the king's house.

Mattan priest of Baal. He has a good Hebrew name, so the functionaries of
the cult of Baal in Jerusalem are Judahites, not foreign priests.

19. *they brought the king down from the house of the LORD, and they entered
the king's house through the Gate of the Sentries*. With the vicious queen dead,
they can now bring Joash from the temple, where he was hidden, in a grand
triumphal march to the palace.

20. *And Athaliah they had put to death in the king's house*. This concluding
notice is not redundant. Cast in the pluperfect, it is a recapitulative statement
of Athaliah's death that also reminds us that as Joash is brought into the palace,
the usurper who occupied it for seven years has been eliminated.

CHAPTER 12

Seven years old was Joash when he became king. In the seventh year [1,2] of Jehu, Joash became king, and he was king in Jerusalem forty years. And his mother's name was Zibiah from Beersheba. And Joash did what [3] was right in the eyes of the LORD all his days, as Jehoiada the priest had taught him. But the high places were not removed—the people [4] were still sacrificing and burning incense on the high places. And Joash [5] said to the priests, "All the silver of sacred gifts that is brought to the house of the LORD, silver currency for each person the value in silver,

---

3. *as Jehoiada the priest had taught him*. This clause is an addition to the recurrent formula about the behavior of the virtuous kings. It surely reflects a political reality in which Jehoiada the high priest served as regent while the child-king was growing up.

4. *But the high places were not removed*. This repeated formula registers the view of the editor of the Book of Kings that worship on the high places constituted actual or at least potential paganism and violated the principles of the exclusive legitimacy of the cult in the Jerusalem temple. In point of historical fact, Jehoiada as regent could certainly have taken steps to eliminate the local altars on the high places if he regarded them as sinful, so we may infer that he, his priestly colleagues, and the king did not think worship on the high places was forbidden.

5. *All the silver*. Though many translations represent *kesef* as "money" (its later sense), in the ninth century BCE there were no coins in Israelite society, and probably still not in the period when this narrative was composed. What the writer has in mind are small weights of silver.
   silver currency for each person the value in silver. The exact meaning of the entire formulation about silver, persons, and sacred gifts is somewhat obscure, and widely different interpretations have been proposed.

and any silver that a man's heart prompts him to bring to the house of
6 the L ORD — let the priests take, every man from his acquaintance, and
they shall repair the breaches of the house wherever a breach is found
7 there." And it happened in the twenty-third year of King Joash, that
8 the priests did not repair the breaches of the house. And King Joash
called to Jehoiada the priest and to the priests and said to them, "Why
are you not repairing the breaches of the house? And now, do not take
silver from your acquaintances but give it for repairing the breaches of
9 the house." And the priests agreed not to take silver from the people,
10 and not to repair the breaches of the house. And Jehoiada took a certain
chest and bored a hole in its door and set it by the altar on the right.
When a man came into the house of the L ORD , the priests, guardians of
the threshold, put into it all the silver brought to the house of the L ORD .
11 And so, when they saw there was abundant silver in the chest, the king's
scribe came up, and the high priest, and they wrapped it in bundles and
12 counted the silver that was found in the house of the L ORD . And they

---

6. *let the priests take, every man from his acquaintance.* The gist of this royal
order is that the gifts in silver brought to the temple are no longer to be passed
on to the priests for their personal use but are to be dedicated to repairs of the
temple building. These new instructions may reflect a power struggle between
the king and the priests, with the adult Joash seeking to break loose from the
domination of his guardian and uncle, Jehoiada, as his direct challenge to the
high priest in verse 8 seems to suggest.

9. *and not to repair the . . . house.* This is only an ostensible contradiction.
The idea is that Joash doesn't trust the priests to use the funds for the repair
of the temple. Instead, he will have all the collected silver placed in a chest,
to be duly counted and paid out to the workers by a committee of two, one
being the king's scribe and personal representative and the other the high
priest. They in turn pass the silver on to an appointed group (verse 12) that
pays it out to the work crews.

11. *they wrapped it in bundles and counted the silver.* There would probably
be bundles of like weights of silver. One sees that all precautions are taken
that none of the donated silver be diverted for any use except the repair of the
temple.

gave the silver that had been measured out to those performing the
tasks, who were appointed for the house of the LORD, and they brought
it out to the carpenters and to the builders working in the house of the
LORD, and to the masons and to the quarriers of stone to buy timber   13
and quarried stone to repair the breaches of the house of the LORD,
whatever was laid out for repair of the house. But no silver bowls, snuff-   14
ers, basins, trumpets, nor golden vessels nor silver vessels were made
in the house of the LORD from the silver brought to the house of the
LORD. But they would give it to those performing the tasks, that with it   15
they should restore the house of the LORD. And they made no reckon-   16
ing for the men to whom they gave the silver, to those performing the
tasks, as they worked in good faith. Silver for guilt-offerings and silver   17
for offense-offerings would not be brought to the house of the LORD. It
would be for the priests.

Then did Hazael king of Aram come up and do battle against Gath   18
and take it. And Hazael set his face to go up against Jerusalem. And   19
Joash king of Judah took all the consecrated things that Jehoshaphat and
Jehoram and Ahaziah his fathers, kings of Judah, had consecrated, all
his consecrated things, and all the gold that was found in the treasuries
of the house of the LORD and in the house of the king, and he sent them
to Hazael king of Aram, and he went away from Jerusalem. And the rest   20
of the acts of Joash, and all that he did, are they not written in the Book

---

17. *It would be for the priests*. This verse indicates a compromise with the
priests. They no longer have access to general donations, but silver given for
guilt-offerings and offense-offerings still goes to them.

19. *And Joash king of Judah took all the consecrated things*. This amounts to the
payment of a high ransom to Hazael in order that he abandon his siege of Jerusalem. The title "king of Judah" is perhaps added here to make an ironic point,
for Joash is scarcely behaving in a kingly fashion in emptying out the royal and
temple treasuries in order to persuade a hostile king to relinquish his attack.

21 of the Acts of the Kings of Judah? And his servants rose up and hatched
22 a plot and struck down Joash in Beth-Millo going down to Silla. And
Jozabad son of Shimat and Jehozabad son of Shomer his servants struck
him down, and he died. And they buried him with his fathers in the City
of David, and his son Amaziah became king in his stead.

---

21. *his servants*. As elsewhere in royal contexts, these are court officials.

hatched a plot and struck down Joash. No explanation is given here for the
conspiracy and regicide. In the parallel passage in 2 Chronicles 24:25, the
killing of Joash is said to be an act of revenge for his killing the son of the now
deceased Jehoiada. It is hard to know whether the report in Chronicles has
a historical basis, but it does suggest a tradition in which the conspiracy was
motivated by a conflict between king and priests, and it is possible that the two
assassins were priests. Joash's surrendering of the temple treasures and not
just the royal treasures to the king of Aram could easily have alienated priestly
circles.

CHAPTER 13

I n the twenty-third year of Joash son of Ahaziah king of Judah, Jehoahaz 1
son of Jehu became king over Israel in Samaria, for seventeen years.
And he did what was evil in the eyes of the LORD and went after the 2
offenses of Jeroboam son of Nebat, who had led Israel to offend. He
did not swerve from it. And the LORD's wrath flared up against Israel, 3
and He gave them continuously into the hand of Hazael king of Aram
and into the hand of Ben-Hadad son of Hazael. And Jehoahaz implored 4
the LORD, and the LORD heeded him, for He saw Israel's oppression, for
the king of Aram oppressed them. And the LORD gave Israel a rescuer, 5
and they came out from under the hand of Aram, and the Israelites
dwelled in their tents as in former days. But they did not swerve from 6
the offenses of the house of Jeroboam, who had led Israel to offend, the
way in which he had gone, and the Asherah, too, stood in Samaria. For 7
Jehoahaz was left no troops except fifty horsemen and ten chariots and
ten thousand foot-soldiers, for the king of Aram had destroyed them and

---

5. *the LORD gave Israel a rescuer*. The appearance of this familiar formula recurring in the Book of Judges is a little surprising here in the Book of Kings. It is
unlikely that the formula would refer to an Israelite king. Though the "rescuer"
might conceivably be an ad-hoc military leader, it is doubtful that the political
arrangements of the monarchy would have allowed the operation of such a
judge-like figure. One scholarly proposal is that the reference is to the Assyrian
king, Adad-Nirari III, who assumed the throne in 810 BCE and four years later
launched a campaign against Aram. His incursions would have had the effect
of loosening Aram's grip on Israel.

7. *ten thousand foot-soldiers*. Because the cavalry and the chariots of Israel,
which has become a vassal to Aram, are reduced to a symbolic number (fifty

8 made them like dust to be trampled. And the rest of the acts of Jehoahaz
   and all that he did and his valor, are they not written in the Book of the
9 Acts of the Kings of Israel? And Jehoahaz lay with his fathers, and they
   buried him in Samaria. And Joash his son was king in his stead.

10 In the thirty-seventh year of Joash king of Judah, Joash son of Jehoahaz
11 became king over Israel in Samaria for sixteen years. And he did what
   was evil in the eyes of the LORD, he did not swerve from all the offenses
   of Jeroboam son of Nebat, who had led Israel to offend, the way in
12 which he had gone. And the rest of the acts of Joash and all that he
   did, and his valor with which he battled against Amaziah king of Judah,
13 are they not written in the Book of the Acts of the Kings of Israel? And
   Joash lay with his fathers, and Jeroboam sat on his throne, and Joash
   was buried in Samaria with the kings of Israel.

14 And Elisha had fallen ill with the illness of which he would die, and Joash
   king of Israel went down to him and wept in his presence and said, "My
15 father, my father, the chariot of Israel and its horsemen!" And Elisha said
   to him, "Fetch a bow and arrows." And he fetched him a bow and arrows.

---

and ten, respectively), it is unlikely that so large a number of infantry as ten
thousand would have been allowed by their conquerors. Perhaps the text originally read not 'aseret 'alafim, "ten thousand," but 'alpayim, "two thousand."

10.–13. These four verses are a striking testimony to the use of formulas in the
Book of Kings. Except for the names, there is not a word in the four verses that
is not part of the recurrent formula. But there may be an editorial glitch here
because after Joash receives his formulaic burial, he becomes an active figure
in the narrative (13:14–25, 14:8–14), and then a second notice of his death is
introduced (14:15–16),

14. *My father, my father, the chariots of Israel and its horsemen!* This evidently
proverbial epithet for a leader, which Elisha himself had applied to Elijah when
he was about to die (2 Kings 2:12), expresses Joash's perception that Elisha has
been a source of power and guidance for his kingdom.

15. *Fetch a bow and arrows.* As the king despairs because he is about to lose
Elisha, the prophet gives him a portent that Joash will continue to triumph after
the death of the man of God.

And he said to the king of Israel, "Set your hand on the bow." And he 16
set his hand, and Elisha placed his hands over the king's hands. And he 17
said, "Open the window to the east," and he opened it. And Elisha said,
"Shoot!" And he shot. And he said, "An arrow of rescue for the LORD,
and an arrow of rescue against Aram! And you shall strike Aram in Aphek
till its destruction." And he said, "Take the arrows." And he took them. 18
And he said to the king of Israel, "Strike to the ground!" And he struck
three times and he stopped. And the man of God was furious with him, 19
and he said, "To strike five or six times—then you would have struck
Aram till its destruction! And now, three times you shall strike Aram."
And Elisha died and they buried him, and the raiding parties of Moab 20
came into the land, they came for a year. And as they were burying a 21
man, they saw a raiding party and they flung the man into Elisha's grave,
and the man went and touched Elisha's bones, and he revived and rose
up on his feet. And Hazael king of Aram oppressed Israel all the days 22

---

16. *and Elisha placed his hands over the king's hands.* This looks like an act
through which the prophet—repeatedly seen as a wonder-worker—imparts
something of his supernatural power to the king.

17. *An arrow of rescue for the LORD.* The shooting of the arrow thus becomes a
prophetic symbol, a metonymy for the exercise of military might. The Hebrew
teshu'ah, usually "rescue," can mean "victory" in military contexts, but because
Israel has been subjugated by Aram, "rescue" may be the more salient meaning
here.

19. *And now, three times you shall strike Aram.* Joash will drive back Aram three
times but fail to destroy it utterly. This detail of the beating of the arrows on
the ground is meant to explain a historical difficulty: Elisha, given his unique
power, could have prophesied, and intended to prophecy, total victory over
Aram. In point of historical fact, Israel's military success against Aram was
partial and temporary. This failure is explained in folktale fashion as the failure
of the principal agent to carry out the entire magical act expected of him by
the man of God.

21. *and the man went and touched Elisha's bones, and he revived and rose up.*
The first clause is formulated as a kind of prolepsis: instead of "the body," we
have "the man"; and "he went and touched" makes the corpse sound as though
it were already a living person. It should be noted that Elisha's miracle-working
power is imagined to be invested in his body, so that even after death he is able

23 of Jehoahaz, and the LORD showed grace to them and pitied them and
turned to them for the sake of His covenant with Abraham, Isaac, and
Jacob, and He did not desire to destroy them, He did not fling them
24 away from His presence till now. And Hazael king of Aram died, and
25 Ben-Hadad his son became king in his stead. And Joash came back and
took the towns from the hand of Ben-Hadad son of Hazael which he
had taken from the hand of Jehoahaz his father in battle. Three times
did Joash strike him, and he brought back Israel's towns.

---

to work wonders. The Elisha cycle began with a (scandalous) episode in which
he summoned bears to kill forty-two boys. Now, at the end of the cycle, his
bones perform the opposite act of reviving the dead.

25. *Three times did Joash strike him.* The Elisha cycle concludes with two different manifestations of the posthumous power of the prophet. First, his bones
impart life to the man who has died; then, the explicit terms of his prophecy to
Joash, marked by the triple pounding of the arrows on the ground, are fulfilled
on the battlefield.

CHAPTER 14

In the second year of Joash son of Joahaz king of Israel, Amaziah the son 1
of Joash had become king, king of Judah. He was twenty-five years old 2
when he became king, and twenty-nine years he was king in Jerusalem,
and his mother's name was Jehoaddan from Jerusalem. And he did what 3
was right in the eyes of the LORD, but not like David his forefather; as all
that Joash his father had done he did do. But the high places were not 4
removed—the people were sacrificing and burning incense on the high
places. And it happened, when the kingdom was firmly in his hand, that 5
he struck down his servants who had struck down the king his father.
But the sons of the killers he did not put to death, as it is written in the 6
Book of the Teaching of Moses, as the LORD charged, saying, "Fathers
shall not be put to death over sons, and sons shall not be put to death
over fathers, but each man shall be put to death for his own offense." He 7
struck down Edom in Salt Valley, ten thousand of them, and he seized

---

5. *when the kingdom was firmly in his hand.* After Amaziah's father Joash was
murdered, the son was installed on the throne because evidently the quarrel of
the conspirators was with Amaziah personally and not with the Davidic dynasty.
(In the northern kingdom, where there was no authorized dynasty, one royal
line was repeatedly replaced by another after a coup.) But, understandably, the
new king did not feel safe to move against his father's killers until he had fully
consolidated his power.

6. *the Book of the Teaching of Moses.* This designation almost certainly refers to
Deuteronomy, which is here quoted verbatim (Deuteronomy 24:16). Deuteronomy, or its initial core, was not composed until around 621 BCE, so the comment here is an intervention in the older story of the Deuteronomistic editor. In
point of political fact, Amaziah may have refrained from killing the offspring of
the conspirators in order not to alienate the court circles from which they came.

8 the Rock in the battle and called its name Jokthel to this day. Then did
   Amaziah send messengers to Joash son of Jehoahaz son of Jehu king
9 of Israel, saying, "Come let us face each other down." And Joash king
   of Israel sent to Amaziah king of Judah, saying, "The thistle which is
   in Lebanon sent to the cedar which is in Lebanon, saying, 'Give your
   daughter to my son as wife,' and the beast of the field which is in Leba-
10 non came by and trampled the thistle. You indeed have struck down
   Edom, and you are carried away by your own heart. Enjoy your glory,
   and stay in your house. Why should you provoke evil, and you will fall,
11 you and Judah with you?" But Amaziah did not heed. And Joash king of
   Israel came up, and they faced each other down, he and Amaziah king
12 of Judah, in Beth-Shemesh, which is Judah's. And Judah was routed by
13 Israel, and every man fled to his tent. But Joash king of Israel caught
   Amaziah son of Joash son of Ahaziah king of Judah in Beth-Shemesh,
   and he came to Jerusalem and breached the wall of Jerusalem from the
14 Gate of Ephraim as far as the Corner Gate, four hundred cubits. And
   he took all the gold and the silver and all the vessels that were found in
   the house of the LORD and in the treasuries of the house of the king,

---

8. *Come let us face each other down.* No reason is given for this provocative
and imprudent military challenge. It has been suggested that Amaziah's success against Edom (verse 7) may have encouraged him to think he could right
old wrongs—perhaps a territorial dispute—with the northern kingdom. Joash's
words in verse 10 lend evidence to this interpretation.

9. *The thistle . . . the cedar.* This homey parable is vaguely reminiscent of the
one declaimed by Jotham in Judges 9. As is often the case in biblical parables,
the parabolic details match the situation to which they refer somewhat loosely.
The request for the hand of the daughter does not entirely fit Amaziah's eagerness for military confrontation, and both the cedar and the wild beast have to
refer, rather awkwardly, to Joash.

13. *Joash king of Israel caught Amaziah.* From the subsequent narrative, one
must infer that he then returned Amaziah to his Judahite subjects, but it is
not explained why. Perhaps Joash thought it sufficient to humiliate the king
of Judah and strip him of his treasures but did not want to give cause for still
further embitterment between the two kingdoms.
   breached the wall of Jerusalem. This huge breach in the walls of the town
would of course have left it entirely exposed to attack.

and all the hostages, and he went back to Samaria. And the rest of the 15
acts of Joash that he did, and his valor with which he battled against
Amaziah king of Judah, are they not written in the Book of the Acts of
the Kings of Israel? And Joash lay with his fathers and was buried in 16
Samaria with the kings of Israel. And Jeroboam his son became king in
his stead. And Amaziah son of Joash king of Judah lived fifteen years 17
after the death of Joash son of Joahaz king of Israel. And the rest of the 18
acts of Amaziah, are they not written in the Book of the Acts of the Kings
of Judah? And they hatched a plot against him in Jerusalem, and he fled 19
to Lachish, and they sent after him to Lachish, and they sent after him
to Lachish and put him to death there. And they bore him off on horses, 20
and he was buried in Jerusalem with his fathers in the City of David.
And all the people of Judah took Azariah, when he was sixteen years old, 21
and they made him king in Amaziah his father's stead. He it was who 22
built Eilath and settled it for Judah after the king lay with his fathers.

In the fifteenth year of Amaziah son of Joash king of Judah, Jeroboam son 23
of Joash became king, king over Israel, in Samaria, for forty-one years.
And he did what was evil in the eyes of the LORD, he did not swerve from 24
all the offenses of Jeroboam son of Nebat, who had led Israel to offend.
He it was who brought back the territory of Israel from Lebo-Hamath to 25
the Arabah Sea, according to the word of the LORD God of Israel which
He spoke through His servant Jonah son of Amittai the prophet, who

---

19. *And they hatched a plot against him.* Once again, no reason is given for the
determination of the conspirators—presumably people in the royal court—to
kill the king. One possibility would be simmering resentment over his rash
military provocation of the northern kingdom and its disastrous results—the
breaching of the wall, the emptying of royal and temple treasuries. As with the
assassination of Amaziah's father, the hostility is directed against the king, not
the dynasty, for his son is allowed to ascend the throne.

25. *Jonah son of Amittai.* The name of this prophet, about whom nothing is
known beyond the mention of his prophecy here, is then picked up by a writer
of the Second Commonwealth period for the central figure of the narrative
Book of Jonah.

26 was from Gath Hepher. For the LORD had seen the very bitter affliction
27 of Israel, and there was no ruler or helper, and none aiding Israel. And
the LORD had not spoken to wipe out the name of Israel from under the
heavens, but He rescued them by the hand of Jeroboam son of Joash.
28 And the rest of the acts of Jeroboam and all that he did, and his valor
with which he battled and brought back Damascus and Hammath to
Judah in Israel, are they not written in the Book of the Acts of the Kings
29 of Israel? And Jeroboam lay with his fathers, with the kings of Israel,
and Zachariah his son became king in his stead.

---

26. *For the* LORD *had seen the very bitter affliction of Israel.* The writer faces a
quandary here: this Jeroboam is said to follow all the evil ways of Jeroboam I,
yet the historical record evidently shows military triumphs in his reign. These
are explained as God's compassion for suffering Israel and His promise not to
allow them to be destroyed, even under an evil king.

27. *the* LORD *had not spoken to wipe out the name of Israel from under the heavens.* One cannot be sure exactly when these words were written. In effect, with
the Assyrian conquest of the northern kingdom in 721 BCE (just two decades
after the end of Jeroboam's reign), Israel was wiped out, though perhaps one
could say that its name remained.

28. *brought back Damascus.* The verb here is an extravagant flourish, for Damascus had not once been a possession of Israel. What is realistically indicated is
some military success against the kingdom of Aram.
    to Judah in Israel. This formulation of the Masoretic text is enigmatic because
only the most forced explanation could place Judah within Israel. The Peshitta
lacks "to Judah" and reads "to Israel," and this could be what the original text
had.

CHAPTER 15

In the twenty-seventh year of Jeroboam king of Israel, Azariah son of 1
Amaziah became king, king of Judah. Sixteen years old he was when 2
he became king, and fifty-two years he was king in Jerusalem. And his
mother's name was Jecoliah from Jerusalem. And he did what was right 3
in the eyes of the LORD as all that Amaziah his father had done. But 4
the high places were not removed—the people were still sacrificing and
burning incense on the high places. And the LORD infected the king 5
and he was stricken with skin-blanch till his dying day, and he dwelled
in the quarantine house, and Jotham the king's son was appointed over
the palace, judging the people of the land. And the rest of the acts of 6
Azariah and all that he did, are they not written in the Book of the Acts
of the Kings of Judah? And Azariah lay with his fathers, and they buried 7

---

5. *he was stricken with skin-blanch till his dying day*. No reason is given for this
terrible affliction: Azariah is said to have done what was right in the eyes of
the LORD, apart from allowing worship on the high places to continue, as all
his predecessors had done. One may conclude that we have here the report
of a historical datum—that Azariah suffered from a disfiguring skin-disease,
presumed to be contagious, all his life. The fact that God is said to have done
the afflicting simply reflects the general assumption of this and other biblical
writers that all things are caused by God.

the quarantine house. The Hebrew name of this place appears to reflect
a term that means "free." It is a "free house" either because the condition of
freedom is associated, as in one Ugaritic text, with death (here, a living death),
or because someone in such a place is free of all civic obligations.

Jotham the king's son was appointed over the palace. The Hebrew for "palace"
is simply "house," but it is clearly the king's house, and here it is rendered as
"palace" in order to avoid its seeming to refer to the quarantine house. In any
case, Jotham becomes a kind of regent because of his father's illness. Upon his
father's death (verse 7), he officially becomes king.

him with his fathers in the City of David, and Jotham his son became king in his stead.

8 In the thirty-eighth year of Azariah king of Judah, Zachariah son of
9 Jeroboam became king of Israel for six months. And he did what was evil in the eyes of the LORD as his forefathers had done. He did not swerve from the offenses of Jeroboam son of Nebat, who had led Israel to offend.
10 And Shallum son of Jabesh hatched a plot against him and struck him down in the presence of the people and put him to death, and he became
11 king in his stead. And the rest of the acts of Zachariah, are they not writ-
12 ten in the Book of the Acts of the Kings of Israel? This was the word of the LORD that He spoke to Jehu, saying, "A fourth generation of yours
13 shall sit on the throne of Israel." And so it was. Shallum son of Jabesh had become king in the thirty-ninth year of Uziah king of Judah, and he
14 was king in Samaria for a month. And Menahem son of Gadi came up from Tirzah and came to Samaria and struck down Shallum son of Jabesh
15 and put him to death, and he became king in his stead. And the rest of the acts of Shallum and his plot that he hatched, why they are written
16 in the Book of the Acts of the Kings of Israel. Then did Menahem strike Tapuah and everything in it and its territories from Tirzah, for it had not
17 yielded, and he struck it, and its pregnant women he ripped apart. In

---

13. *he was king . . . for a month*. The northern kingdom by this point in history, in the eighth century BCE, exhibits extreme political instability—monarch after monarch is assassinated as coup follows coup. The Deuteronomistic editor makes some attempt to provide a theological explanation for these upheavals—"This was the word of the LORD that he spoke to Jehu"—but he cannot encompass all the rapid changes in this way. Thus no reason is given for the fact that Shallum reigns only a month before he is murdered by Menahem.

16. *Tapuah*. The received text reads "Tipsah," a city on the eastern bank of the Euphrates that Menahem surely could not have reached. One version of the Septuagint shows, more plausibly, Tapuah, a town in the tribal region of Ephraim and Manasseh.

for it had not yielded. The Hebrew wording, literally, "it had not opened," is a little odd.

and its pregnant women he ripped apart. This barbaric practice seems to have been embraced by several nations in the ancient Near East. See 2 Kings 8:13 and Amos 1:13, where it is vehemently denounced.

the thirty-ninth year of Azariah king of Judah, Menahem son of Gadi became king over Israel in Samaria for ten years. And he did what was 18 evil in the eyes of the LORD. He did not swerve all his days from the offenses of Jeroboam son of Nebat who had led Israel to offend. Pul king 19 of Assyria came against the land, and Menahem gave Pul a thousand talents of silver so that his hand would be with him to make the kingdom firm in his hand. And Menahem exacted the silver from Israel, from all 20 the prosperous men, to give to the king of Assyria, fifty shekels of silver from each man. And the king of Assyria turned back and did not stay there in the land. And the rest of the Acts of Menahem and all that he 21 did are they not written in the Book of the Acts of the Kings of Israel? And Menahem lay with his fathers, and Pekahiah his son became king 22 in his stead. In the fiftieth year of Azariah, king of Judah, Pekahiah son 23 of Menahem became king over Israel in Samaria for two years. And he 24 did what was evil in the eyes of the LORD. He did not swerve from the offenses of Jeroboam son of Nebat who led Israel to offend. And Pekah 25 son of Remaliah his officer hatched a plot against him and struck him down in the king's house, with Argob and Arieh, and with him were fifty men of the Gildeadites. And he put him to death and became king in his stead. And the rest of the Acts of Pekahaiah and all that he did, why 26 they are written in the Book of the Acts of the Kings of Israel.

In the fifty-seventh year of Azariah king of Judah, Pekah son of Remaliah 27 became king over Israel in Samaria, for twenty years. And he did what 28 was evil in the eyes of the LORD. He did not swerve from the offenses

---

19. *Menahem gave Pul a thousand talents of silver so that his hand would be with him to make the kingdom firm in his hand.* Menahem pays a huge tribute to Pul, thus accepting vassal status. Having seized the throne by assassinating his predecessor, he could well need foreign support against opposing groups in the court.

25. *Pekah.* This actually is the same first name as Pekahiah, simply without the theophoric suffix.

with Argob and Arieh. These mystifying names have variously been interpreted as names of architectural structures within the palace, towns from which the killers came, and personal names.

29   of Jeroboam son of Nebat, who had led Israel to offend. In the days of
Pekah king of Israel, Tiglath-Pileser king of Assyria came and took Ijon
and Abel-Beth-Maacah and Janoah and Kedesh and Hazor and Gilead
and the Galilee, the whole land of the Naphtalite, and he exiled them
30   to Assyria. And Hosea son of Elah hatched a plot against Pekah son of
Remaliah and struck him down and put him to death, and he became
31   king in his stead in the twentieth year of Jotham son of Uziah. And the
rest of the acts of Pekah and all that he did, why they are written in the
Book of the Acts of the Kings of Israel.

32   In the second year of Pekah son of Remaliah king of Israel, Jotham
33   son of Uziah became king, king of Judah. Twenty-five-years-old he was
when he became king, and sixteen years he was king in Jerusalem. And
34   his mother's name was Jerusha daughter of Zadok. And he did what was
35   right in the eyes of the LORD as all that Uziah his father had done. But
the high places were not removed. The people were still sacrificing and
burning incense on the high places. He did build the Upper Gate of the
36   house of the LORD. And the rest of the acts of Jotham that he did, are
37   they not written in the Book of the Acts of the Kings of Judah? In those
days the LORD began to let loose against Judah Rezin king of Aram and
38   Pekah son of Remaliah. And Jotham lay with his fathers and was buried
with his fathers in the City of David his father. And Ahaz his son became
king in his stead.

---

29. *and he exiled them to Assyria.* Although the Assyrians sometimes merely
reduced conquered kingdoms to vassal status, they followed a general imperial
policy of exiling the conquered population in order to integrate the new territory as a province of the Assyrian empire. Assyrian inscriptions indicate that
the westward thrust recorded here took place in 732 BCE, just a decade before
the final destruction of the kingdom of Israel by Assyria and the exile of a large
part of its population.

CHAPTER 16

In the seventeenth year of Pekah son of Remaliah, Ahaz son of Jotham 1
became king, king of Judah. Twenty years old was Ahaz when he became 2
king, and sixteen years he was king in Jerusalem, and he did not do what
was right in the eyes of the LORD his God like David his forefather. And 3
he went in the way of the kings of Israel, and even his son he passed
through the fire like the abominations of the nations that the LORD had
dispossessed before the Israelites. And he sacrificed and burnt incense 4
on the high places and on the hills and under every lush tree. Then did 5
Rezin king of Aram and Pekah son of Remaliah king of Israel come up
to Jerusalem for battle, but they were not able to battle against it. At 6
that time Rezin king of Aram restored Eilath to Aram and drove out the

---

3. *and even his son he passed through the fire.* This expression, featuring the verb
"to pass through" (or "pass over"), is used elsewhere in reference to the pagan
cult of the Molech. It is unclear whether the expression refers to actually burning the son as an offering to the god or to a symbolic act of passing him through
or over the fire. The translation preserves the ambiguity of the Hebrew, avoiding
a rendering such as "consigned to the fire" that some modern translators favor.

4. *under every lush tree.* This phrase, which recurs in a number of different
biblical texts, evidently refers to the worship of nature deities.

6. *Rezin king of Aram restored Eilath to Aram.* It is puzzling that Rezin, in the
midst of laying siege against Jerusalem, should have gone on an expedition
to Eilath in the far south. This difficulty is compounded by the fact that the
consonantal text has Arameans settling in Eilath, but the Masoretic marginal
gloss corrects this to Edomites. (The graphic difference in Hebrew between
"Aram" and "Edom" is minimal because the letters *reish* and *dalet* are similar
in appearance.) The original verse may have read: the king of Edom restored
Eilath to Edom. The Edomites could easily have taken advantage of the fact
that the Judahite forces were distracted by the siege of Jerusalem.

Judeans from Eilath, while the Edomites came to Eilath and dwelled
7 there till this day. And Ahaz sent messengers to Tiglath Pileser king of
Assyria saying, "I am your servant and your son. Come up and rescue
me from the hand of the king of Aram and from the hand of the king
8 of Israel, who are risen against me." And Ahaz took the silver and the
gold that were in the house of the LORD and the treasuries of the king's
9 house, and he sent them to the king of Assyria as a bribe. And the king of
Assyria heeded him, and the king of Assyria went up against Damascus
10 and seized it and exiled its people to Kir, but Rezin he put to death. And
King Ahaz went to meet Tiglath Pileser in Damascus, and he saw the
altar that was in Damascus, and Ahaz sent to Uriah the priest the image
11 of the altar and its design in all its fashioning. And Uriah the priest built
an altar according to all that King Ahaz had sent from Damascus, so did
12 Uriah the priest do, until the return of King Ahaz from Damascus. And

7. *I am your servant and your son.* This is obviously an expression of subservience or vassaldom.

8. *Ahaz took the silver and the gold that were in the house of the LORD.* The
mechanics of this act are spelled out in verses 17–18.
   as a bribe. This amounts to protection-money. The Hebrew *shoḥad* always
has a negative connotation and it is a mistake to translate it as "gifts." Tiglath
Pileser was in any case engaged in a series of campaigns against Aram, Israel,
Phoenicia, and the Philistines and thus scarcely needed encouragement, but
the payment of silver and gold would have been an expression of Ahaz's fealty
to Assyria.

9. *exiled its people.* The Hebrew merely says "exiled it," but since "it," though
grammatically referring to the city, actually refers to its inhabitants, an expan-
sion in translation is called for here.

10. *Ahaz sent to Uriah the priest the image of the altar and its design in all its
fashioning.* In the present instance, this is not an attempt to adapt pagan practice, for the narrator makes no critical comment, and the new altar erected in
Jerusalem is adapted for the cult of YHWH and is not subsequently destroyed.
Instead, Ahaz, a provincial monarch, comes to the metropolis of Damascus,
where, as a kind of cultic tourist, he sees and marvels at the large and impressive altar constructed according to the most modern design, and he decides to
adopt it for his own temple.

the king came from Damascus, and the king saw the altar, and the king approached the altar and went up on it. And he turned his burnt offer-   13 ing and his grain offering to smoke and poured out his libation and cast the blood of his well-being sacrifices on the altar. And the bronze altar   14 that was before the Lord he moved forward from the front of the house, from between the altar and the house of the Lord and set it along with the altar to the north. And King Ahaz charged Uriah the priest, saying,   15 "On the large altar, turn to smoke the morning's burnt offering and the evening's grain offering and the king's burnt offering and his grain offer-ing and the burnt offering of all the people and their grain offering and their libations, and all the blood of the burnt offering and all the blood of the sacrifice you shall cast upon it, and the bronze altar shall be to gaze upon." And Uriah the priest did as all that King Ahaz had charged   16 him. And King Ahaz cut off the frames of the laver stands and removed   17 the lavers from them and took down the basin from the bronze oxen that were beneath it and set it on the stone pavement. And the covered   18 passage for Sabbath that they had built in the house and the king's outer entrance he took away from the house of the Lord—because of the king of Assyria. And the rest of the acts of Ahaz that he did, are they   19 not written in the Book of the Acts of the Kings of Judah? And Ahaz lay   20 with his fathers and was buried with his fathers in the City of David, and Hezekiah his son became king in his stead.

---

13. *he turned his burnt offering and his grain offering to smoke.* There are indi-cations elsewhere that the king, on special ceremonial occasions such as the dedication of a new altar, officiated at the sacrifices, which otherwise were the province of the priests.

15. *the large altar.* This is the new altar, built according to the model of the altar in Damascus.

17. *cut off the frames of the laver stands.* As in the account of the sacred furnish-ings of Solomon's temple, it is difficult to reconstruct the details of the cultic vessels, but the general idea is that Ahaz stripped the precious metals from them to send as his tribute to Tiglath Pileser.

CHAPTER 17

In the twelfth year of Ahaz king of Judea, Hosea son of Elah became king in Samaria over Israel, for nine years. And he did what was evil in the eyes of the LORD though not like the kings of Israel who were before him. Against him did Shalmaneser king of Assyria come up, and Hosea became vassal to him and rendered tribute to him. And the king of Assyria discovered a plot of Hosea's, that he had sent messengers to So king of Egypt and had not brought up tribute to the king of Assyria as every year, and the king of Assyria seized him and locked him in the prison-house. And the king of Assyria went up through all the land and

---

2. *not like the kings of Israel who were before him*. The destruction of the northern kingdom, then, is not attributed to egregious behavior on the part of its last king but rather to the cumulative transgressions of its inhabitants, which are duly set forth in verses 7–23.

3. *Shalmaneser king of Assyria*. Though Shalmaneser in fact attacked Israel and other territories in Canaan-Phoenicia in 725 BCE, he died in 721 and, according to Assyrian royal inscriptions, the actual conquest was consummated by Sargon II. Either this information was not available to the Hebrew historian, writing perhaps a century and a half after the events, or he chose to simplify his narrative by speaking of a single "king of Assyria" invading Samaria.

4. *So*. No such royal name appears in Egyptian records, and this may be a distortion of an Egyptian title or of a different Egyptian name.
  the king of Assyria seized him. If Hosea was the Assyrian emperor's prisoner, one must assume that the court officials in Samaria remained loyal to him (no replacement is mentioned) and thus continued the battle against the Assyrians during the three years of siege.

went up to Samaria and besieged it for three years. In the ninth year of 6
Hosea, the king of Assyria took Samaria and exiled Israel to Assyria and
settled them in Halah and in Habor by the river of Gozan and in the
towns of Media. And so, because the Israelites had offended the Lord 7
their God who brought them up from the land of Egypt from under the
hand of Pharaoh king of Egypt, and they had feared other gods and had 8
gone by the statutes of the nations whom the Lord had dispossessed
before Israel, and that the kings of Israel had made for them, and the 9
Israelites had done acts that were not right against the Lord their God
and had built themselves high places in all their towns from watchtowers to fortress-towns. And they had set up for themselves pillars and 10
sacred poles on every high hill and under every lush tree. And they had 11
burnt incense there on all the high places like all the nations that the
Lord had exiled before them, and they did evil things to vex the Lord.

---

6. *the king of Assyria . . . exiled Israel to Assyria and settled them.* This was a general imperial policy of the Assyrians. They removed the native population of a
conquered territory—though it is not clear whether in fact the entire Israelite
population was exiled, as is implied here—and replaced it with people from the
existing empire in order to make the territory an Assyrian province. The sundry
groups enumerated in verse 24 who are brought to Samaria are all inhabitants
of territories conquered by the Assyrians, and so the verb "exiled" is properly
applied to their displacement from their native lands to Samaria.

7. *because the Israelites had offended the Lord their God.* The catastrophic event
of the utter destruction of the kingdom of Israel calls for a grand theological
explanation, cast in Deuteronomistic terms, and so a ringing sermonic catalogue of the transgressions of the Israelites is introduced that runs all the way to
verse 23. It is notable that all the transgressions are cultic—there is no mention
of ethical failings or injustice.
  feared. This is the core meaning of this reiterated Hebrew verb, though in
cultic contexts it obviously refers to modes of worship rather than to the emotion of fear.

8. *and that the kings of Israel had made for them.* The syntactic connection of
this clause to the rest of the sentence is ambiguous in the Hebrew. "For them"
has been added in the translation as an interpretive guess, assuming that the
clause refers to the two molten images of calves.

12 And they had worshipped the foul idols about which the LORD said, "You
13 shall not do this thing." And the LORD had made every prophet, every
seer, warn Israel, saying, "Turn back from your evil ways and keep My
commands and My statutes, according to all the teaching that I charged
your fathers, and that I sent to you through My servants the prophets."
14 But they did not heed, and they stiffened their necks like the necks of
15 their fathers, who did not trust the LORD their God. And they spurned
His statutes and His covenant that He had sealed with their fathers,
and His precepts that He imparted to them, and they went after empty
breath and did empty things, and after the nations that were all round
16 them, of whom the LORD had charged not to do like them. And they
forsook the LORD their God and made themselves a molten image of two
calves, and they made a sacred pole and bowed down to all the array of
17 the heavens, and they worshipped Baal. And they passed their sons and
their daughters through the fire and worked sorcery and divined, and
they gave themselves over to do what was evil in the eyes of the LORD
18 to vex him. And the LORD was greatly incensed against Israel, and He
removed them from His presence. None remained but the tribe of Judah
19 alone. Judah, too, had not kept the commands of the LORD their God,
and they went in the way of the statutes of Israel which they had done.
20 And the LORD spurned all the seed of Israel, and He abused them and
gave them into the hand of plunderers, until He flung them from His
21 presence. For He had torn Israel from Judah, and they made Jeroboam
son of Nebat king, and he drove Israel away from following the LORD

---

14. *like the necks of their fathers*. The reference is in all likelihood to the stubborn and rebellious Wilderness generation.

16. *a molten image of two calves*. As before, the writer construes this as idol worship, though these were very probably icons of the throne of YHWH, like the cherubim in the southern kingdom.
　the array of the heavens. Worship of celestial deities was a prominent feature of the last phase of First Commonwealth history.

19. *Judah, too, had not kept the commands of the LORD*. Evidently, it was not destroyed—rather, not yet—because of God's promises to David. "Commands," here and below, is singular in the Hebrew but is in effect a collective noun.

and led them to commit a great offense. And the Israelites went in all 22
the offenses of Jeroboam that he had done, they did not swerve from
it, until the LORD had removed Israel from His presence, as He had 23
spoken through His servants the prophets, and He exiled Israel from its
land to Assyria, till this day. And the king of Assyria brought people from 24
Babel and from Kirthah and from Ivvah and from Hammath and from
Sepharvaim and settled them in the towns of Samaria instead of the
Israelites, and they took hold of Samaria and settled in its towns. And 25
it happened at the beginning of their settling there, that they did not
fear the LORD, and the LORD sent lions against them, and they set about
killing them. And they said to the king of Assyria, saying, "The nations 26
that you exiled and resettled in the towns of Samaria do not know the
rules of the god of the land, and he sent lions against them, and here
they are killing them, for they do not know the rules of the god of the
land." And the king of Assyria charged, saying, "Bring there one of the 27
priests whom you have exiled from there, and let him settle there and
teach the rules of the god of the land." And one of the priests whom they 28
had exiled from Samaria came and settled in Bethel, and he set about
teaching them how they should fear the LORD. And each nation would 29
make its own god and put it in one of the houses on the high places
that the Samaritans had made, each nation in the town in which it had
settled. And the people of Babel made Succoth-Benoth, and the people 30
of Kith made Nergal, and the people of Hammath made Ashima. And 31
the Avvites made Nibhaz and Tirhak, and the Sepharvites were burning
their children in fire to Adrammelech and Anammelech, the gods of
Sepharvaim. And they were fearing the LORD, and they made priests for 32
the high places for themselves from their pick, and they would officiate

---

25. *the LORD sent lions against them.* Lions were abundant in ancient Israel, a
fact reflected in the five different terms for "lion" in biblical Hebrew; and so it
is possible that the displacement of population, with hunting perhaps in abeyance, created the circumstances for an incursion of lions. In any case, the lion
attacks seem to be represented as a miraculous intervention against the new
inhabitants of Samaria.

32. *they were fearing the LORD, and they made priests for the high places.* That
is, they added YHWH to their cult while continuing to worship pagan gods.

33 in the houses of the high places. The Lord they would fear but their
gods they would serve according to the practice of the nations from
34 which they had been exiled. Till this day they do according to their first
practices. They do not truly fear the Lord and they do not act according
to their statutes and their practice and the teaching and the commands
that the Lord charged the sons of Jacob, whose name He set as Israel.
35 And the Lord sealed a covenant with them and charged them, saying,
"You shall not fear other gods nor shall you bow down to them, nor shall
36 you serve them nor shall you sacrifice to them. But the Lord Who
brought you up from the land of Egypt with great power and with an
outstretched hand, Him shall you fear and to Him shall you bow down
37 and to Him shall you sacrifice. And the statutes and the laws and the
teaching and the commands that He wrote for you, you shall keep to

---

34. *Till this day they do according to their first practices.* The whole account of
the cultic practices of the Samaritans, as many scholars have inferred, looks
suspiciously like the work of a post-exilic Judean writer promoting a separatist
view of the Samaritans. In this representation, the population of Samaria after
721 BCE was entirely a foreign implant, and the cult performed in Samaria
was not a legitimate worship of YHWH but a promiscuous mingling of pagan
and Yahwistic practices. Historically, this perception may have been wrong both
in regard to the composition of the Samaritan population and in regard to the
nature of its cult.

They do not truly fear the Lord. The adverb "truly" has been added in the
translation to spell out what the Hebrew implies because otherwise there might
be a confusion—earlier the Samaritans are said to fear the Lord, that is, to
perform the outward offices of the Lord's service.

they do not act according to their statutes and their practice. It would make
better sense if this read "His statutes and His practice," though there is no
textual warrant for this reading.

Jacob, whose name He set as Israel. This reminder of Jacob's portentous name
change underscores the notion that the people of Israel have a grand divinely
ordained destiny in which the paganizing Samaritans have no part.

35. *You shall not fear other gods nor shall you bow down to them.* This entire
sentence is an approximate quotation of the first of the Ten Commandments.

do always, and you shall not fear other gods. And the covenant that I   38
sealed with you, you shall not forget, and you shall not fear other gods.
But the LORD your God shall you fear, and He will save you from the   39
hand of all your enemies." But they did not heed; rather, they went on   40
doing according to their first practice. And these nations would fear the   41
LORD and serve their idols. Their children too, and the children of their
children, as their fathers had done, they do till this day.

---

38. *and you shall not fear other gods.* This prohibition against worshipping other
gods is repeated here three times, strongly stamping the Samaritans as a show-
case instance of dereliction from the God Who gave the Decalogue to Israel.

41. *fear the* LORD *and serve their idols.* The verbs "fear" and "serve" are clearly
equivalent terms for performing acts of worship. In this instance, instead of the
pejorative designation, *gilulim* ("foul idols") associated with *gelalim*, "turds," as
in verse 12, the more neutral general noun, *pesilim*, "idols," is used. This may be
because when Israelites worship idols (verse 12), the act is especially disgust-
ing, whereas one would expect benighted pagans to serve idols.

CHAPTER 18

1 And it happened in the third year of Hosea son of Elah king of Israel
2 that Hezekiah son of Ahaz became king, king of Judah. Twenty-five
years old he was when he became king, and twenty-nine years he was
king in Jerusalem. And his mother's name was Avi daughter of Zacha-
3 riah. And he did what was right in the eyes of the LORD as all that David
4 his forefather had done. He it was who took away the high places and
smashed the pillars and cut down the sacred pole and pulverized the
bronze serpent that Moses had made, for at that time the Israelites had
5 been burning incense to it, and it was called Nehushtan. In the LORD
God of Israel he put his trust, and after him there was none like him
among all the kings of Judah and among those that were before him.
6 And he clung to the LORD, he did not swerve from Him, and he kept

---

4. *He it was who took away the high places.* Hezekiah is the first king to do this.
As with Josiah a century later, the motive may have been political as well as
religious, for an exclusive cult in Jerusalem would clearly consolidate the power
of the Judean king. One can assume that there was some resentment against
this new policy, for the high places were popularly viewed as legitimate—and
convenient—locations for the worship of YHWH. In Rabshakeh's provocative
speech, he appears to play to this resentment by describing the removal of the
high places as an offense against YHWH.

the bronze serpent that Moses had made. The fashioning of the bronze serpent
to counter the plague of serpents is reported in Numbers 21. Archeologists
have found numerous serpents, evidently cultic objects, and it looks as if these
were objects of worship in popular religion, which were then retrojected on
Moses in the story told in Numbers 21.

Nehushtan. The name is transparently derived from *nehoshet*, bronze, with
a probable pun on *nahash*, serpent.

His commands that the LORD had charged Moses. And the LORD was   7
with him. Wherever he sallied forth, he prospered. And he rebelled
against the king of Assyria and did not serve him. He it was who struck   8
down the Philistines as far as Gaza and its territories, from watchtowers
to fortress-towns. And it happened in the fourth year of King Hezekiah,   9
which was the seventh year of Hosea son of Elah king of Israel, that
Shalmaneser king of Assyria went up against Samaria and laid siege
against it. And he took it at the end of three years, in the sixth year of   10
Hezekiah, which was the ninth year of Hosea king of Israel—Samaria
was taken. And the king of Assyria exiled Israel to Assyria and led them   11
to Halah and Habor at the River of Gozan and to the towns of Media.
Because they had not heeded the voice of the LORD their God and had   12
broken His covenant, all that Moses servant of the LORD had charged,
yet they did not heed and they did not do it. And in the fourteenth year   13
of King Hezekiah, Sennacherib king of Assyria went up against all the
fortified towns of Judah and took them. And Hezekiah king of Judah   14
sent to the king of Assyria at Lachish, saying. "I have offended. Turn
back from me. Whatever you fix for me I will bear." And the king of

---

7. *he rebelled against the king of Assyria.* After the death of Sargon II, there was
widespread rebellion against the Assyrian overlords in the northern regions of
the empire, and Hezekiah evidently exploited the upheaval to reject his own
vassal condition.

9. *Shalmaneser king of Assyria went up against Samaria.* The report beginning
here and concluding in verse 12 is a recapitulation of 17:6ff. Evidently, the
historical context of the Assyrian conquest of the northern kingdom needs to
be recalled here as Judah is threatened with a similar fate.

13. *in the fourteenth year of King Hezekiah.* Sennacherib's campaign in Phoenicia, Philistia, and Judea in 701 BCE is elaborately documented in Assyrian
annals and bas-reliefs.
      all the fortified towns of Judah. According to the Assyrian annals, the imperial
forces captured forty-six Judean towns—which may be an imperial exaggeration. The principal one was Lachish, where Sennacherib is headquartered in
the next verse. The Assyrians left a vivid bas-relief of their archers, in characteristic high-pointed caps, assaulting this town.

14. *Whatever you fix for me I will bear.* Hezekiah's act of submission, expressed
in his readiness to pay whatever tribute Sennacherib imposes, is contradicted

Assyria imposed upon Hezekiah king of Judah three hundred talents
15 of silver and thirty talents of gold. And Hezekiah gave all the silver that
was in the house of the LORD and in the treasuries of the house of the
16 king. At that time Hezekiah cut away the doors of the LORD's temple
and the columns that Hezekiah king of Judah had overlaid, and he gave
17 them to the king of Assyria. And the king of Assyria sent Tartan and
Rabsaris and Rabshakeh from Lachish to King Hezekiah in Jerusalem
with a heavy force. And they went up and came to Jerusalem, and they
went up and came and took a stance at the conduit of the Upper Pool,
18 which is by the road to the Fuller's Field. And they called out to the
king, and Eliakim son of Hilkiah who was appointed over the house
came out to them, with Shebnah the scribe and Joah son of Asaph the
19 recorder. And Rabshakeh said to them, "Say, pray, to Hezekiah, Thus
says the great king, the king of Assyria: 'What is this great trust that you
20 show? You thought, mere words are counsel and valor for battle. Now,
21 in whom did you trust that you should have rebelled against me? Now,
look, you have trusted in this shattered reed, in Egypt, which when a
man leans on it, enters his palm and pierces it. So is Pharaoh king of
22 Egypt to all who trust in him. And should you say to me, In the LORD

---

by the narrative episode that begins in verse 17, where Hezekiah is represented
as part of an alliance with Egypt opposing the Assyrians. It would appear that
two different sources, for reasons that are unclear, have been spliced together
rather than blended.

17. *And the king of Assyria sent.* This entire episode appears, with only minor
variations, in Isaiah 36. The compiler of Kings evidently drew on the Book of
Isaiah as a source.
   Tartan and Rabsaris and Rabshakeh. Although these three terms are presented
in the Hebrew text without definite articles, as though they were proper names,
each is actually a title: vizier, high chamberlain (literally, "head eunuch"), and
head steward. In any case, all are clearly high officials in the Assyrian court.

18. *who was appointed over the house.* That is, the palace.

21. *this shattered reed.* Reeds, of course, grow in abundance along the Nile.
   which when a man leans on it, enters his palm and pierces it. The metaphor is
quite realistic. The reed looks as if it could provide support, but it easily breaks
when you lean on it, and the jagged edges of the break can pierce the skin.

our God we trust, is it not He Whose high places and altars Hezekiah took away, and he said to Judah and to Jerusalem: Before this altar you shall bow down in Jerusalem?' And now, wager, pray, with my master, 23 with the king of Assyria, and I shall give you two thousand horses if you can give yourself riders for them. And how could you turn away 24 the agent of one of the least of my master's servants and trust Egypt for chariots and horses? Now, was it without the LORD that I have come 25 up against this place to destroy it? The LORD said to me, Go up against this land and destroy it." And Eliakim son of Helkiah, and Shebnah and 26 Joah with him, said to Rabshakeh, "Speak, pray, to your servants Aramaic, for we understand it, and do not speak Judean in the hearing of the people who are on the wall." And Rabshakeh said to them, "Did my 27 master send me to you and to your master to speak these words? Did he not send to these men sitting on the wall—to eat their own turds and to drink their own urine—together with you?" And Rabshakeh stood and 28 called out in a loud voice in Judean and spoke and said, "Listen to the words of the great king, the king of Assyria. Thus said the king. 'Let not 29

---

23. *I shall give you two thousand horses if you can give yourself riders for them.* Hezekiah's attempted rebellion is so hopelessly pathetic, Rabshakeh says, that he could not even muster sufficient cavalrymen were he given the horses.

24. *agent.* The Hebrew aptly uses an Assyrian imperial administrative title, *paḥat* (compare the English "pasha," which has a shared linguistic background).

26. *Speak, pray, to your servants Aramaic.* Aramaic was the most widely shared language in the lands of the Assyrian empire east of the Jordan, and so by the late eighth century it had been adopted as the diplomatic lingua franca. Thus, an educated Judean court official would have been fluent in Aramaic.

do not speak Judean. "Judean," of course, is Hebrew, but that term for the language never appears in the Bible. It is not explained how an Assyrian court official had a command of Hebrew.

27. *Did he not send to these men sitting on the wall.* The verb "send" is merely implied in the Hebrew. Rabshkeh makes clear that his entire speech—itself a brilliant deployment of political rhetoric—is precisely intended for the ears of the people. His purpose is to drive a wedge between the rebellious Hezekiah and the people, convincing them that the uprising is hopeless, and that, in fact, the fate of deportation to Assyria will be a happy one.

Hezekiah deceive you, for he will not be able to save you from my hand.
30 And let not Hezekiah have you trust in the LORD, saying, the LORD will
surely save us, and this city will not be given into the hand of the king
31 of Assyria.' Do not listen to Hezekiah, for thus said the king of Assyria:
'Make terms with me and come out to me, and eat each man of his
vine and each man of his fig tree, and drink each man the water of his
32 well, until I come and take you to a land like your land—a land of grain
and new wine, a land of bread and vineyards, a land of olive trees and
oil and honey. And live, and do not die, and do not listen to Hezekiah
33 when he misleads you, saying, the LORD will save us. Did the gods of
the nations ever save each its land from the hand of the king of Assyria?

---

30. *let not Hezekiah have you trust in the* LORD. Rabshakeh appears to be
shifting grounds. First he claimed that it was YHWH Who sent the Assyrians
against Judah (verse 25), which was a way of conveying to the people the idea
that their destruction was divinely ordained and irreversible. Now he takes a
different tack: no national god has ever availed against the great king of Assyria.

31. *Make terms with me.* The literal sense is "make a gift [or blessing] with me,"
but in context, as Rashi and the King James Version after him understood, the
expression means to offer terms of surrender.
  *eat each man of his vine and . . . his fig tree and drink each man the water of his
well.* The vine and the fig tree appear in a repeated proverbial expression about
peaceful and prosperous life. Eating from the vine and the fig tree and drinking
well-water are a vivid antithesis to the representation of the starving besieged
population eating its own excrement and drinking its own urine.

32. *a land like your land.* The catalogue of agricultural bounty that follows
closely resembles the recurrent list of all the good things of the Land of Israel.
Rabshakeh in this fashion depicts life in exile in Assyria as a new Promised
Land.

Where were the gods of Hammath and Arpad? Where were the gods 34
of Sepharvaim, Hena and Ivvah? And where were the gods of Samaria?
Did they save Samaria from my hand? Who is there of all the gods of 35
the lands that saved their land from my hand, that the Lord should
save Jerusalem from my hand?'" And the people were silent and did not 36
answer a word to him, for it was the king's command, saying, "You shall
not answer him." And Eliakim son of Hilkiah, who was appointed over 37
the house, and Shebna the scribe and Joah son of Asaph the recorder
with him, came to Hezekiah, their garments rent, and they told him
Rabshakeh's words.

---

34. *where were the gods of Samaria.* The Masoretic text merely has "that they
saved Samaria from my hand" immediately after the question about the sundry
gods of the lands in the northern region of the empires. One version of the
Septuagint and a fragment of Kings from the Cairo Genizah show the clause
here translated, which makes the verse coherent.

CHAPTER 19

1 And it happened when King Hezekiah heard, that he rent his garments and covered himself in sackcloth and went into the house of the 2 LORD. And he sent Eliakim, who was appointed over the house, and Shebna the scribe and the elders of the priest, covered in sackcloth, to 3 Isaiah the prophet son of Amoz. And they said to him, "Thus said Hezekiah: 'A day of distress and chastisement and insult is this day.

> For children have come to the birthstool,
> > and there is no strength to give birth.

4 Perhaps the LORD will have heard all the words of Rabshakeh, whom his master the king of Assyria sent, to defame the living God, and He will chastise for the words that the LORD your God heard, and you will

---

3. *For children have come to the birthstool.* The poetic style makes these words seem initially cryptic, but the obvious meaning is that the children about to be born cannot emerge because when the mothers come to the birthstool, they do not have the strength to push the babies out. The delegation from the king may want to speak to the prophet in his own characteristic language by first addressing him in a line of verse. In any case, the line forcefully frames their message to Isaiah with an image of desperate impotence that represents the plight of the people. As in the previous chapter, this entire episode is taken, with only minor textual variants, from the Book of Isaiah (Chapter 37). Isaiah in this narrative resembles Elijah and Elisha in being seen by others as a holy man who has the power to intercede on their behalf with God. Unlike them, however, he is a "literary prophet" who delivers his prophecies in the form of poetry, as he does here in the poem that runs from verse 21 to verse 28.

offer prayers for the remnant that still exists.'" And the servants of King 5
Hezekiah came to Isaiah. And Isaiah said to them, "Thus shall you say to 6
your master: 'Thus said the LORD: Do not fear the words that you have
heard, with which the flunkeys of the king of Assyria reviled Me. I am 7
about to send an ill spirit into him, and he shall hear a rumor and go back
to his land, and I shall make him fall by the sword in his land." And Rab- 8
shakeh went back and found the king of Assyria battling against Libneh,
for he had heard that he had journeyed on from Lachish. And he heard 9
about Tirhakah king of Cush, saying, "Look, he has sallied forth to do
battle with you." And he turned back and sent messengers to Hezekiah,
saying, "Thus shall you say to Hezekiah king of Judah, saying, 'Let not 10
your god in whom you trust deceive you, saying, Jerusalem will not be
given into the hand of the king of Assyria.' Look, you yourself have heard 11
what the king of Assyria did to all the lands, annihilating them—and will
you be saved? Did the gods of the nations save them, when my fathers 12
destroyed Gozan and Haran and Rezeph and the Edomites who are in
Telassar? Where is the king of Hammath, and the king of Arpad and the 13

---

5. *And the servants of King Hezekiah came to Isaiah.* Their arrival was clearly
implied by the end of verse 2. Perhaps one should construe the verb as a pluperfect, though its form does not indicate that. The same seemingly redundant
clause appears in Isaiah 37.

6. *flunkeys.* The Hebrew *ne'arim*, youths or people in a subservient status, is
usually represented in this translation as "lads," but its use here by Isaiah,
instead of the expected *'avadim*, "servants," has a pejorative connotation.

7. *an ill spirit.* The Hebrew says only "a spirit," but since it induces fear followed
by flight, it appears to be a troubling spirit.
   he shall hear a rumor. What this might be is never spelled out. If the prophecy is to be consistent with what is reported at the end of the chapter, it would
be the news that his army has been stricken with a plague.

9. *king of Cush.* Cush is Nubia, just south of Egypt and politically linked with
it. Egypt was a key player in the uprising against the Assyrian imperial forces,
and so it is not surprising that the Nubian king would oppose Sennacherib. The
connection of this report with the story of the siege against Jerusalem is not
entirely clear. Perhaps Sennacherib is impelled to finish off Jerusalem quickly
so that he can turn his forces to the south.

14 king of Lahir, Sepharvaim, Hena, and Ivvah?" And Hezekiah took the letters from the hand of the messengers and read them, and Hezekiah went up to the house of the LORD and spread them out before the LORD.

15 And Hezekiah prayed before the LORD God of Israel enthroned on the cherubim: "You alone are God of all the kingdoms of the earth. You it

16 was made heaven and earth. Incline Your ear and listen; open, LORD, Your eyes and see; and listen to the words of Sennacherib that he sent

17 to insult the living God. Indeed, LORD, the kings of Assyria destroyed

18 nations and their lands and consigned their gods to the fire—because they are not gods but the work of human hands, wood and stone, and

19 they destroyed them. And now, O LORD our God, rescue us, pray, from his hand, that all the kingdoms of the earth may know that You alone are

20 the LORD our God." And Isaiah son of Amoz sent to Hezekiah, saying, "Thus said the LORD God of Israel: 'Of which you prayed to Me about

21 Sennacherib king of Assyria I have listened.' This is the word that the LORD spoke about him:

> She scorns you, mocks you,
> > the maiden, Zion's daughter.
> She wags her head at you,
> > Jerusalem's daughter.

---

14. *spread them out*. The Hebrew reads "spread it out," but the first part of the verse speaks of multiple letters.

15. *You alone are God of all the kingdoms of the earth*. These words are a direct rebuttal of the arrogant words spoken by Rabshakeh in verse 12. Hezekiah will make his rejoinder to the Assyrian boast still more explicit in verse 17.

21. *She scorns you, mocks you*. The "you" is of course Sennacherib. Zion, scorned by Sennacherib's spokesman, has nothing but contempt for the presumptuous Assyrian king.
   She wags her head at you. In biblical poetry, this is a conventional gesture of scorn.

Whom did you insult and revile,   22
     and against whom have you lifted your voice,
and raised your eyes up high
     against Israel's Holy One.
By your messengers you insulted the Master   23
     and thought, 'When I ride in my chariots,
I will go up to the heights of the mountains,
     the far reaches of Lebanon.
I will cut down its lofty cedars,
     its choicest cypresses
and will come to its uttermost heights,
     and the woods of its undergrowth.
It is I who have dug and drunk   24
     the waters of foreigners,

---

22. *raised your eyes up high / against Israel's Holy One.* Isaiah ups the ante of denunciation: Sennacherib's presumption in declaring that he will destroy the Judean kingdom is cast as an assault on the God of heaven and earth.

23. *I will go up the heights of the mountains, / the far reaches of Lebanon.* Although Sennacherib's imperial campaign did include Phoenicia, here he is besieging Jerusalem. The mountains of Lebanon, however, are the proverbial loftiest heights in biblical poetry, and *yarketey levanon*, "the far reaches of Lebanon," contains an echo of *yarketey tsafon*, "the far reaches of Tsafon," the dwelling-place of the gods. Sennacherib's declaration at this point sounds rather like that of the overweening king who is brought down to Sheol in Isaiah 15. The cutting down of lofty cedars also figures in Isaiah 15.

    its uttermost heights. The received text here reads *melon*, "night encampment," but the parallel phrase in Isaiah 37 as well as one Hebrew manuscript shows *merom*, "heights" (a singular rendered here as a plural for the sake of the English idiom).

    the woods of its undergrowth. The Hebrew *karmel* usually means "farmland," which would be anomalous on the Lebanon heights, but as Yehuda Felix has noted, it can also mean "low shrubs" (compare Isaiah 29:17). This would be the sparse vegetation on the mountaintops above the treeline.

24. *the waters of foreigners.* The phrase, slightly opaque, is part of Sennacherib's boast of conquest: he has seized the territories of nations and even sunk wells to exploit their water resources.

and dried up with the soles of my feet
    all Egypt's rivers.
25   Have you not heard from afar
        that which I did from time of old?
I fashioned it, brought it to pass—
    and fortified towns
        have turned into heaps of ruins.
26   Their inhabitants, impotent,
        are cast down and put to shame,
become the grass of the field
    and green growth,
thatch on the roofs
    by the east wind blasted.
27   And your stayings and comings and goings I know
    and your raging against Me.
28   Because of your raging against Me,
        and your din that came up in My ears
I will put My hook in your nose
    and My bit between your lips,
and will turn you back on the way
    on which you came.

---

and dried up with the soles of my feet / all Egypt's rivers. This is an antithetical act to the digging of wells—Egypt, blessed by the Nile, abounds in water. Here the Assyrian king makes himself, at least through the hyperbole, a divine figure with the power to dry up rivers as he trods upon them.

26. *thatch on the roofs / by the east wind blasted.* The speech Isaiah attributes to Sennacherib concludes with a metaphor common in biblical poetry of the nations as mere grass, blasted by the hot wind blowing from the eastern desert.

28. *I will put My hook in your nose / and My bit between your lips.* Sennacherib had imagined himself a god. Now the God of Israel describes him as a dumb helpless beast to be driven where God wants.
    turn you back. This is Isaiah's prophecy of Sennacherib's flight back to Assyria.

And this is the sign for you: eat aftergrowth this year, and in the second 29
year stubble, and in the third year sow and harvest and plant vineyards
and eat their fruit. And the remnant of the house of Judah shall add root 30
beneath and put forth fruit above. For from Jerusalem shall come forth 31
the surviving remnant from Mount Zion. The LORD's zeal shall do this.
Therefore, thus said the LORD about the King of Assyria: 'He shall not 32
enter this city and he shall not shoot an arrow there, and no shield shall
go before him, nor shall he raise a siege-work against it. In the way he 33
comes he shall go back, and he shall not enter this city, said the LORD.
And I will defend this city to rescue it, for My sake and for the sake of 34
David My servant.'"

And it happened on that night that the LORD's messenger went out 35
and struck down the Assyrian camp, a hundred eighty-five thousand.
And when they rose early in the morning—look, they were all dead
corpses. And Sennacherib king of Assyria pulled up stakes and went 36

---

29. *eat aftergrowth this year.* The "you" now is Hezekiah, and the verbs will then
switch to the plural, referring to the people. Because the invading army has laid
waste to the countryside, there will be no crops for two years—and yet, as a
"sign," the Judeans will survive.

35. *the LORD's messenger went out and struck down in the Assyrian camp, a hundred eighty-five thousand.* The lifting of the siege is a historical event, though the
reason for it is uncertain. If the report here is authentic, it would be because
of a plague that swept through the Assyrian camp. But one must say that the
writer has a vested interest in representing this event as a miraculous intervention, demonstrating God's commitment to protect Jerusalem (in contrast to
Samaria, destroyed by an Assyrian king twenty years earlier).

37 off and returned to Nineveh. And it happened as he was bowing down in the house of his god Nisroch, that Adrammelech and Sarezer struck him down with the sword, and they escaped to the land of Ararat. And Esharaddon his son became king in his stead.

---

37. *Adrammelech and Sarezer struck him down with the sword.* The two figures named were Sennacherib's sons. One gets the impression from the narrative report that the assassination took place directly after the emperor's return to Nineveh. In fact, Sennacherib was murdered twenty years after the military campaign of 701 BCE. The writer, however, wants to present this killing in the temple of a pagan god as an immediate fulfillment of Isaiah's prophecy (verse 7) and a prompt retribution against the boasting conqueror depicted in Isaiah's poem.

And Esharaddon his son became king in his stead. Esharaddon had been Sennacherib's chosen successor. It was evidently this choice that led Adrammelech, abetted by one of his brothers, to kill his father, hoping to seize the throne. One infers that he then discovered no support in the court for his claim to the crown and thus was obliged to flee with his brother to Ararat in the far north.

CHAPTER 20

I n those days Hezekiah fell mortally ill, and Isaiah son of Amoz the   1
prophet came to him and said to him, "Thus said the LORD: 'Charge
your household, for you are about to die and you will not live.'" And   2
he turned his face to the wall and prayed to the LORD, saying, "Please,   3
O LORD, recall, pray, that I walked before You truthfully and with a
whole heart and did what was good in Your eyes." And Hezekiah wept.
And it happened that Isaiah had not gone out of the central court,   4
when the word of the LORD came to him, saying, "Go back, and you   5
shall say to Hezekiah prince of My people, 'Thus said the LORD God
of David your forefather: I have heard your prayer, I have seen your
tears. I am about to heal you. On the third day you shall go up to the

---

1. *In those days Hezekiah fell mortally ill.* The historian of Kings continues to
splice into his narrative material from the Book of Isaiah—in the case of this
chapter from Isaiah 38 and 39. Again, we have integral citation with only minor
textual variants. The formulaic phrase at the beginning, "In those days," is a
noncommittal temporal indicator, and it is unclear whether Hezekiah's grave
illness occurred before or after the siege of Jerusalem reported in the previous
chapter.

5. *the LORD God of David your forefather.* This epithet serves as a reminder
of God's commitment to preserve the Davidic dynasty, and Hezekiah is presented as a king who does what is right in the eyes of the LORD, like David his
forefather.

6 house of the LORD. And I shall add to your days fifteen years, and from the hand of the king of Assyria I shall save you and this city, and I shall defend this city for My sake and for the sake of David My 7 servant.'" And Isaiah said, "Fetch a clump of figs." And they fetched it 8 and put it on the burning rash, and he revived. And Hezekiah said to Isaiah, "What is the sign that the LORD will heal me and I will go up 9 on the third day to the house of the LORD?" And Isaiah said, "This is the sign for you from the LORD that the LORD will do the thing which He spoke: should the shadow go down ten steps or should it go back 10 ten steps?" And Hezekiah said, "It is easy for the shadow to incline down ten steps and not for the shadow to go backward ten steps."

---

6. *and from the hand of the king of Assyria I shall save you.* This clause could be an indication that Hezekiah's illness preceded the siege of Jerusalem, but the inference is not entirely certain because even after the lifting of the siege, Assyria would have remained a potential threat.

7. *Fetch a clump of figs.* Isaiah here appears not to be performing a miracle but practicing folk medicine. Hezekiah, however, in the next verse requests a portent that he will be cured.

burning rash. Only here do we learn that *shehin*, burning rash, which is Job's affliction, is a potentially fatal disease.

and he revived. Given that Hezekiah in the next verse remains uncertain that he will recover, the sense of "revived" (literally, "lived") here is that after the application of the fig poltice he experienced some relief from the torment of the burning rash.

9. *should the shadow go down ten steps.* What is evidently in question is a kind of sundial, but one that is not a horizontal disk but rather a series of steps set into a wall, ten on the left side to show the shadow of the ascending sun and ten on the right side for the descending sun. A device of this sort has been found in Egypt. The King James Version and modern Hebrew understand *ma'alot* as "degrees," but these were probably actual steps, which is what the word usually means.

10. *It is easy for the shadow to incline down ten steps.* This would be the natural course of the shadow, so Hezekiah chooses instead the miraculous reversal of the progress of the shadow. That also becomes a figure for the reversal of his seemingly imminent death.

And Isaiah the prophet called out to the LORD, and He turned back   11
the shadow that had gone down on the Steps of Ahaz, backward ten
steps. At that time Berodach-Baladan son of Baladan king of Babylonia   12
sent letters and a gift to Hezekiah, for he heard that Hezekiah had fallen
ill. And Hezekiah heard of the envoys and showed them all his house of   13
precious things, the silver and the gold and the spices and the goodly oil,
and his armory and all his treasuries. There was nothing that Hezekiah
did not show them in his house and in his kingdom. And Isaiah the   14
prophet came to King Hezekiah and said to him, "What did these men
say to you and from where did they come to you?" And Hezekiah said,
"From a distant land, from Babylonia." And he said, "What did they see   15
in your house?" And Hezekiah said, "All that is in my house they saw.
There was nothing that I did not show them of my treasuries." And   16
Isaiah said, "Listen to the word of the LORD: 'Look, a time is coming   17
when everything that is in your house and that your fathers stored up
till this day will be borne off to Babylonia. Nothing will remain,' said

---

11. *the Steps of Ahaz.* The sundial in question proves to be a well-known marker
in Jerusalem commissioned by King Ahaz.

12. *king of Babylonia.* The Babylonians were threatened by the Assyrian empire to
the north and so were eager to make common cause with the kingdom of Judah.

13. *the envoys.* The received text has only "about them," and this identification
is added in the translation for clarity.

17. *a time is coming when everything that is in your house . . . will be borne off
to Babylonia.* This dire prophecy is presented as punishment for Hezekiah's
imprudence in exposing all his treasures to the eyes of the Babylonians visi-
tors. Many scholars think that the episode was added over a century later in an
effort to explain the despoiling of Jerusalem during the reign of Jehoiakim in
597 BCE or in the final destruction of the city in 586 BCE.

18 the LORD. 'And from your sons who will issue from you, whom you will
beget, he will take and they will become eunuchs in the palace of the
19 king of Babylonia.' And Hezekiah said to Isaiah, "The word of the LORD
that you have spoken is good." And he thought, "Why, there will be
20 peace and trust in my days." And the rest of the acts of Hezekiah and
all his valor, and his making the pool and the conduit so that he could
bring water into the town, are they not written in the Book of the Acts
21 of the Kings of Judah? And Hezekiah lay with his fathers, and Manasseh
his son was king in his stead.

---

18. *they will become eunuchs in the palace of the king of Babylonia.* Although
sarisim sometimes may refer to court officials who are not necessarily castrated,
one suspects that the core meaning that involves castration is invoked here:
there could be no greater curse for a king than to have his sons turned into
eunuchs, incapable of begetting offspring.

19. *The word of the LORD that you have spoken is good.* This response by Hezekiah to the grim prophecy is astonishing. On the surface, he seems to be saying
to Isaiah that he accepts the word of the LORD, that it must be good because
it is God's will. In the next sentence, however, he thinks to himself that what
is good about it is that the disaster will not happen in his lifetime—something
that in fact Isaiah has not clearly told him. This self-centered view of national
catastrophe puts the virtuous Hezekiah in a somewhat questionable light.

20. *his making the pool and the conduit so that he could bring water into the town.*
The conduit is a remarkable engineering feat that one can walk through to this
day. It is a tunnel sloping gradually down from outside to inside, devised to
introduce water into the town in time of siege. It is roughly 550 yards in length,
not at all in a straight line, and showing evidence that two teams of workers
hewed the tunnel out of the underground rock from opposite directions, somehow managing to meet each other in the middle.

CHAPTER 21

Twelve years old was Manasseh when he became king, and fifty-five years he was king in Jerusalem, and his mother's name was Hephzibah. And he did what was evil in the eyes of the LORD, like the abominations of the nations that the LORD had dispossessed before the Israelites. And he rebuilt the high places that Hezekiah his father had destroyed, and he made a sacred pole as Ahab king of Israel had made, and he bowed down to all the array of the heavens and worshipped them.

---

2. *like the abominations of the nations.* The formulaic language for reporting the cultic divagations of an Israelite king is stepped up here, and it will continue to be intensified in the verses to follow. Manasseh, the son of one of the two most virtuous kings of Judah, is cast as the most egregious of evil kings. It is historically plausible that he would have encouraged pagan cults—he was a vassal to Assyria, a fact not mentioned in our text but registered in Assyrian inscriptions—but it appears that his religious and moral turpitude is stressed in order to explain how the kingdom of Judah was destroyed four generations later, despite Hezekiah and his virtuous grandson Josiah. This impending destruction is the burden of the dire prophecy in verses 11–15.

3. *he made a sacred pole.* The Hebrew *'asherah* can refer either to a special pole used in the pagan cult or to the goddess Asherah, depending on the context. In verse 7, the reference is clearly to Asherah because there could not be a statue of a sacred pole.
   and he bowed down to all the array of the heavens. The worship of astral deities, not especially prominent in Canaanite religion, was widespread in Assyria, and the biblical literature produced in the last century of the First Temple period abounds in objections to it.

4 And he built altars in the house of the Lord, of which the Lord had
5 said, "In Jerusalem I will set My name. And he built altars to all the
6 array of the heavens in both courts of the house of the Lord. And he
passed his son through the fire and performed sorcery and divined and
conjured ghosts and familiar spirits. He did abundantly what was evil in
7 the eyes of the Lord, to vex Him. And he placed the statue of Asherah
that he had made in the house of which the Lord had said to David
and to Solomon his son, "In this house and in Jerusalem, which I have
8 chosen from all the tribes of Israel, will I set My name forever. And I
will no longer make Israel's foot go wandering from this land that I gave
to their fathers—but only if they keep to do all that I have charged them
9 and as all the teaching that My servant Moses charged them." But they
did not heed, and Manasseh led them astray to do what was evil more
10 than the nations that the Lord had destroyed before the Israelites. And
11 the Lord spoke through His servants the prophets, saying, "In as much
as Manasseh king of Judah has done these abominations, he has done
more evil than all that the Amorites did before him, and he has led Judah,

---

4. *And he built altars in the house of the* Lord. Introducing pagan worship into
the Jerusalem temple was an especially heinous act, far worse than reestablish-
ing the cult of the high places.

5. *both courts of the house of the* Lord. These are the inner and outer courts of
the temple.

6. *And he passed his son through the fire.* The ambiguity of the Hebrew wording, as noted earlier, allows one to construe this either as child sacrifice or as a
non-lethal magical/cultic rite.
   to vex Him. The object of the verb is merely implied in the Hebrew.

7. *Jerusalem, which I have chosen from all the tribes of Israel.* The language of
the election of Jerusalem is emphatically Deuteronomistic.

9. *to do what was evil more than the nations that the* Lord *had destroyed.*
Manasseh's offenses are so great that they even outdo those of the surrounding
nations. A grim *a fortiori* notion is intimated here: if the Canaanite nations were
dispossessed because of their evil acts, how much more so will this be the fate
of Judah, which under their king surpassed the Canaanites in culpable behavior.

too, to offend with his foul idols. Therefore, thus said the LORD God   12
of Israel, I am about to bring an evil upon Jerusalem and Judah, about
which any who hears of it, both his ears will ring. And I will stretch over   13
Jerusalem the line of Samaria and the weight of the house of Ahab, and I
will wipe out Jerusalem as one wipes a bowl clean, wiping and turning it
on its face. And I will abandon the remnant of My estate and give them   14
into the hand of their enemies, and they will become plunder and spoils
for all their enemies. In as much as they have done what is evil in My   15
eyes and have been vexing Me from the day their fathers came out of
Egypt to this day." And Manasseh also had shed innocent blood in great   16
abundance until he filled Jerusalem with it from one end to the other,
besides his offense with which he led Judah to offend, to do what was
evil in the eyes of the LORD. And the rest of the acts of Manasseh and   17

---

11. *foul idols*. As before, the writer uses an invented invective term, *gilulim*,
coined from *gelalim*, "turds."

13. *the line . . . and the weight*. In the construction of buildings, in order to
ensure that the walls would be vertical, walls were measured against a plumb
line—a line with a weight attached to its bottom end. The line and the weight
are thus a metaphor for the rigorous measuring of the integrity of Jerusalem.
Ironically, it is not a correction in building that will ensue but destruction, as
Samaria was measured and destroyed.

   as one wipes a bowl clean, wiping and turning it on its face. This is a homey
and vivid image of total destruction: when the last remnant of food is wiped
from the bowl, leaving no drop or crumb, the bowl can be turned upside down.

15. *and have been vexing Me from the day their fathers came out of Egypt to this
day*. In the explanation put forth here for the imminent national catastrophe,
the evil Manasseh is not unique but rather the culmination of all the backsliding and rebellion of the Israelites from the generation of the wilderness
wanderings onward.

16. *Manasseh also had shed innocent blood in great abundance*. Moral offense
compounds the cultic offenses. The victims of these many murders are in all
likelihood loyalists to YHWH, perhaps the prophets of the LORD just mentioned, who were slaughtered as Jezebel slaughtered the prophets of the LORD.
It may have been this that led the Israeli biblical scholar Yehezkel Kaufmann
to describe Manasseh as "The Jezebel of the South."

all that he did and his offense that he committed, are they not written
18 in the Book of the Acts of the Kings of Judah? And Manasseh lay with
his fathers, and he was buried in the garden of his house, in the Garden
of Uzzah, and his son Amon became king in his stead.

19 Twenty-two years old was Amon when he became king, and two years
he was king in Jerusalem, and his mother's name was Meshullemeth
20 daughter of Haraz from Jotbah. And he did what was evil in the eyes of
21 the LORD as Manasseh his father had done. And he went in all the way
in which his father had gone, and he worshipped the foul idols that his
22 father had worshipped, and he bowed down to them. And he forsook
23 the LORD God of his fathers and did not go in the way of the LORD. And
Amon's servants hatched a plot against him and put the king to death in
24 his house. And the people of the land struck down the plotters against
King Amon, and the people of the land made Josiah his son king in his
25 stead. And the rest of the acts of Amon that he did, are they not written
26 in the Book of the Acts of the Kings of Judah? And they buried him in
his grave in the Garden of Uzzah, and Josiah his son became king in
his stead.

---

23. *And Amon's servants hatched a plot against him.* Whenever the connection is
with a king, "servants" means "courtiers." The reason for the court conspiracy is
not stated. Some have interpreted the regicide as a response to Amon's paganizing ways, and the fact that "the people of the land" (whether the phrase
indicates the general populace or a particular political group within it) kill the
conspirators and promote Josiah to the throne argues for this understanding.
Josiah was only eight years old at the time, and given his later record of unflag-
ging loyalty to YHWH and his devotion to the centrality of the Jerusalem cult,
those who instated him and looked after his education must surely have themselves been loyalists to YHWH.

CHAPTER 22

Eight years old was Josiah when he became king, and thirty-one years 1
he was king in Jerusalem, and his mother's name was Jedidah daughter
of Adaiah from Bozkath. And he did what was right in the eyes of the 2
LORD, and he went in all the way of David his forefather and did not
swerve to the right or to the left. And it happened in the eighteenth year 3
of King Josiah that the king sent Shaphan son of Azaliah son of Meshul-
lam the scribe to the house of the LORD, saying, "Go up to Hilkiah the 4
high priest, that he melt down the silver brought to the house of the
LORD, which the guards of the threshold had gathered from the people.

---

2. *And he did what was right in the eyes of the* LORD. Since Josiah was a child
when he became king, one must assume that his virtuous behavior at first must
have been through the dictates of the regents who would have had to manage
the affairs of state for the first eight to ten years of his reign.

3. *the scribe.* As elsewhere, this title, in court circles, designates not someone who copies manuscripts but a high royal official with administrative
responsibilities.

4. *that he melt down the silver.* The verb as it appears here in the received text,
yatem, is of uncertain meaning. When this same activity is reported in verse 9, a
different verb is used, meaning "to melt down," suggesting that the original text
here read *yatekh*. (The differing last consonants resemble each other in appearance in paleo-Hebrew script.) Several ancient versions show "melt down" at
this point. People would have brought contributions to the temple in the form
of silver ornaments, and these then had to be melted down and broken into
small weights of silver that could be used for payment of labor and materials.

5 And let them give it to those doing the tasks appointed over the house
of the LORD, that they give it to those doing the tasks in the house of
6 the LORD, to repair the breaches of the house, to the carpenters and
to the builders and to the masons, to buy wood and quarried stone to
7 repair the house. But the silver given them need not be accounted for,
8 for they deal honestly." And Hilkiah the high priest said to Shaphan
the scribe, "I have found a book of teaching in the house of the LORD."
9 And Hilkiah gave the book to Shaphan and he read it. And Shaphan
came to the king and brought back word to the king and said, "Your
servants melted down the silver that was in the house and gave it to
10 those doing the tasks appointed over the house of the LORD." And
Shaphan told the king, saying, "Hilkiah the priest gave me a book,"
11 and Shaphan read it to the king. And it happened when the king heard
12 the words of the book of teaching, that he rent his garments. And
the king charged Hilkiah the priest and Ahikam son of Shaphan and

---

5. *those doing the tasks appointed over the house of the* LORD *. . . those doing the
tasks.* The first group, distinguished by the term "appointed," are administra-
tors and foremen, probably part of the permanent staff of the temple, and the
second group are the sundry skilled workmen, in all likelihood brought into the
temple to perform these specific jobs.

8. *I have found a book of teaching.* The identical designation *sefer hatorah* occurs
in Deuteronomy 30:10. The term *sefer* can mean "scroll" or "book" or indeed
any written document, even a letter, but its force as "book" seems especially
relevant here. For two centuries, the scholarly consensus, despite some dissent,
has been that the found book is Deuteronomy. Though attributed to Moses, it
would have been written in the reign of Josiah, perhaps drawing on some earlier materials. The book "found" in 621 BCE was also not altogether identical
with Deuteronomy as we have it, which almost certainly included some later
elements, and was not edited in the form that has come down to us until the
Babylonian exile. The major new emphases of the book brought to Josiah were
the repeated stress on the exclusivity of the cult in Jerusalem ("the place that
I shall choose") and the dire warnings of imminent disaster and exile if the
people fail to fulfill its covenant with God.

11. *he rent his garments.* The most likely reason would be his hearing the grim
warnings of impending catastrophe if Judah did not mend its ways. This reaction would then provide the impetus for Josiah's rigorous reforms.

Achbor son of Michaiah and Shaphan the scribe and Asaiah the king's
servant, saying, "Go, inquire of the LORD on my behalf and on behalf of   13
the people and on behalf of all Judah concerning the words of this book
that has been found, for great is the LORD's wrath that is kindled against
us because our fathers have not heeded the words of this book to do as
all that is written in it." And Hilkiah the priest went, and Ahikam and   14
Achbor and Shaphan, and Asaiah with him, to Hulda the prophetess,
wife of Shallum son of Tikvah son of Harhas, keeper of the wardrobe,
and she was living in the Mishneh, and they spoke to her. And she   15
said to them, "Thus said the LORD God of Israel: 'Say to the man who
sent you to me, Thus said the LORD: I am about to bring evil on this   16
place and on its inhabitants, by all the words of the book that the king
of Judah read, in return for their forsaking Me and burning incense to   17
other gods so as to vex Me with all their handiwork, and My wrath will

---

13. *Go, inquire of the* LORD. This is the usual idiom for inquiring of an oracle.

for great is the LORD's *wrath*. This sounds very much like a direct response to
the great catalogue of hair-raising curses (see Deuteronomy 28:15–68) in the
book read out to Josiah.

14. *Hulda the prophetess*. She is the only female prophet mentioned in the Book
of Kings. She performs in every respect like the male prophets, quoting God's
words directly with the introductory messenger-formula, "Thus said the LORD,"
and the large royal delegation that comes to her clearly accepts her authority as
fully as they would that of a male prophet.

Mishneh. The term means "repetition" or "addition" and was a western addition in Jerusalem.

15. *Say to the man who sent you to me*. Pointedly avoiding in her initial speech
reference to Josiah by name or title, she reduces him to a mere sender of messages. In verse 18, she refers to him as "the king of Judah" but continues to
suppress his name.

16. *by all the words of the book that the king of Judah read*. Since the contents of
the book at this point would be known only to Josiah and Shaphan and perhaps
some courtiers who heard the reading of the text, Hulda must be presumed to
know the book through her prophetic gifts.

17. *all their handiwork*. The reference is to idols, fashioned by human hands.

18 kindle against this place and will not be extinguished.' And to the king of
Judah who sends you to inquire of the LORD, thus shall you say to him:

19 'Thus said the LORD God of Israel: the words that you heard, in as much
as your heart quailed and you humbled yourself before the LORD when
you heard what I said about this place and about its inhabitants, that
they will become a desolation and a curse, and you rent your garments

20 and wept before Me, I, too, have heard, said the LORD. Therefore I am
about to gather you to your fathers, and you shall be gathered to your
grave in peace, and your eyes shall not see all the evil that I am about to
bring on this place.'" And they brought back word to the king.

---

20. *you shall be gathered to your grave in peace.* In fact, Josiah will be killed in
battle at Megiddo at the age of thirty-nine. Some scholars cite the discrepancy
between Hulda's prophecy and what is reported in 23:29 as evidence that the
terms of the prophecy are authentic, with Hulda's actual reassurance at the
time to Josiah then contradicted by historical events.

CHAPTER 23

And the king sent out, and all the elders of Judah and Jerusalem gathered round him. And the king went up to the house of the LORD, and every man of Judah and all the inhabitants of Jerusalem were with him, and the priests and the prophets and all the people from the smallest to the greatest. And he read in their hearing all the words of the book of the covenant that was found in the house of the LORD. And the king stood on a platform and sealed a covenant before the LORD to walk after the LORD and to keep His commands and His precepts and His statutes with a whole heart and with all their being, to fulfill the words of this covenant written in this book. And all the people entered into the covenant. And the king charged Hilkiah the high priest and the assistant priests and the guards of the threshold to bring out from the LORD's temple the vessels made for Baal and Asherah and for all the array of the heavens, and he burnt them outside Jerusalem in the Kidron

---

3. *with a whole heart and with all their being.* These are signature formulas of the Book of Deuteronomy. They occur again, expanded, in verse 25.

And all the people entered into the covenant. The received text here has the verb *waya'amed,* literally "stood," but this may be a scribal error for *waya'avor,* literally, "pass through."

4. *he burnt them outside Jerusalem.* Because these objects of pagan worship are impure, they are taken outside Jerusalem to be destroyed in an open space where purity does not obtain.

5 fields and bore off their ashes to Bethel. And he put down the pagan priests that the kings of Judah had set up to burn incense on the high places in the towns of Judah and in the environs of Jerusalem, and those burning incense to Baal and to the sun and to the moon and 6 to the constellations and to all the array of the heavens. And he took out the sacred pole from the house of the LORD outside of Jerusalem to the Kidron wadi and burnt it in the Kidron wadi and ground it to 7 dust and flung its ashes on the graves of the common people. And he smashed the houses of the male cult-harlots that were within the house of the LORD where women would weave fabrics for Asherah.

---

and bore off their ashes to Bethel. Bethel was one of the two main sanctuaries of the northern kingdom. Scattering the ashes of the statues of Baal and Asherah on that site would be a way of confirming its illegitimacy or impurity. Josiah's access to Bethel and, later in this chapter, to other northern sites probably reflects the decline of Assyrian power in the latter part of the seventh century BCE. It would appear that the Assyrians at this point had vacated much of the northern kingdom that it conquered in 721 BCE and that Josiah attached these regimes to his own kingdom. Many scholars suspect that his campaign to establish the absolute exclusivity of the Jerusalem cult was at least in part an effort to consolidate his rule over the entire country, in effect reviving the united kingdom that existed in the era of Solomon.

5. *put down.* The Hebrew verb *hishbit*, literally, "put an end to," is a little ambiguous (hence the translation choice), but the slaughter of pagan priests reported in verse 20 suggests that the verb in this context may mean "to kill."
   to Baal and to the sun and to the moon and to the constellations. The worship of the old Canaanite god Baal is joined with the later fashionable worship of the astral deities, probably under Assyrian influence.

6. *dust . . . ashes.* Two processes of destruction are involved here, grinding down and burning. The Hebrew terms *'afar* and *'efer* exhibit a degree of interchangeability.
   the graves of the common people. The context suggests a kind of potters' field, so that the casting of the ashes of the *'asherah* here would do further dishonor to it.

7. *fabrics for Asherah.* The Hebrew reads *batim*, "houses," probably a scribal error for *badim*, "fabrics," influenced by the appearance of "houses" at the beginning of this verse.

And he brought all the priests from the towns of Judah and defiled 8
the high places where the priests from Geba to Beersheba had been
burning incense. And he smashed the high places of the gates that
were at the entrance of the gate of Joshua commander of the town,
which were to a man's left at the town gate. Only, the priests of the 9
high places would not go up to the LORD's altar in Jerusalem, but they
ate flatbread in the midst of their kinsmen. And he defiled the Topheth 10
that was in the Valley of Hinnom, so that no man would pass his son or
his daughter through the fire to Molech. And he put down the horses 11
that the kings of Judah would dedicate to the sun, from the entrance of
the house of the LORD to the chamber of Nathan-Melech the eunuch,
which is in the precincts. And the chariots of the sun he burnt in fire.
And the altars that were on the roof of the Upper Chamber of Ahaz, 12
which the kings of Judah had made, and the altars that Manasseh had
made in the two courts of the house of the LORD, the king smashed,
and he hurried off their dust from there and flung it into the Kidron

---

8. *the high places of the gates that were at the entrance of the gate of Joshua.* The
Hebrew wording here is a little confusing and may reflect scribal scrambling
of the text.

9. *Only, the priests of the high places would not go up to the LORD's altar . . . but
they ate flatbread in the midst of their kinsmen.* These priests had officiated in
the worship of YHWH on the high places. Their involvement in a cult located in
an unauthorized place disqualifies them from serving in the Jerusalem temple,
but they are nevertheless entitled to receive sustenance—the flatbread—with
other members of the priestly caste in Jerusalem.

11. *And he put down the horses that the kings of Judah would dedicate to the sun.*
Horses were associated with worship of the solar deity, probably because the
Hebrews, like the Greeks, imagined the sun riding across the sky in a chariot.
The verb translated as "dedicate" is literally "gave," and probably indicates sacri-
ficing the horses to the sun—an especial abomination in Israelite eyes because
the horse is an impure beast, prohibited as food.

13 wadi. And the high places facing Jerusalem that were to the right of
the Mount of the Destroyer, which Solomon king of Israel had built for
Ashtoreth foulness of the Sidonians and Chemosh foulness of Moab
14 and Milcom abomination of the Ammorites—the king defiled. And
he shattered the steles and cut down the sacred poles and filled their
15 place with human bones. And also the altar that was in Bethel, the
high place that Jeroboam son of Nebat had made, who had led Israel
to offend, that altar, too, and the high places he smashed and burnt
16 the high place, grinding it to dust, and he burnt the sacred pole. And
Josiah turned and saw the graves that were there on the mountain, and
he sent and fetched the bones from the graves and burnt them on the
altar and defiled it, according to the word of the LORD that the man of
17 God called out, who had called out these words. And he said, "What
is that marker which I see?" And the townspeople said to him, "It is
the grave of the man of God who came from Judah, and who called out
18 these things that you did on the Bethel altar." And he said, "Let him
be. Let no man touch his bones." And they rescued his bones, with the
19 bones of the prophet who had come from Samaria. And the structures,
too, of the high places that were in the mountains of Samaria which
the kings of Israel had made to vex, did Josiah remove, like all the acts
20 that he had done in Bethel. And he slaughtered all the priests of the
high places who were there on the altars, and he burnt human bones

---

13. *the Mount of the Destroyer.* Many scholars infer that this designation, *har hamashhit*, is a polemic distortion of *har hamishhah*, the Mount of Anointment.

16. *fetched the bones from the graves.* Burning human bones on an altar would permanently defile it.
    according to the word of the LORD. What follows is the fulfillment of the prophecy of the man of God from Judah reported in 1 Kings 11.

18. *with the bones of the prophet who had come from Samaria.* In the story in 1 Kings 11, he is a prophet who lives in Bethel, and the reference to coming from Samaria, evidently triggered by the phrase "who came from Judah," is not in keeping with the original story (which in fact occurred before the building of Samaria).

on them. And he went back to Jerusalem. And the king charged all 21
the people, saying, "Make a Passover to the LORD your God, as it is
written in this book of the covenant. For it has not been done like this 22
Passover from the days of the judges who judged Israel and all the days
of the kings of Israel and the kings of Judah." But in the eighteenth 23
year of King Josiah this Passover to the LORD was done in Jerusalem.
And the ghosts, too, and the familiar spirits and the household gods 24
and the foul idols and all the vile things that were seen in the land of
Judah and in Jerusalem, Josiah rooted out, in order to fulfill the words
of the teaching written in the book that Hilkiah the priest had found
in the house of the LORD. And like him there was no king before him 25
who turned back to the LORD with all his heart and with all his being
and with all his might according to all the teaching of Moses, and
after him none arose like him. Yet the LORD did not turn back from 26
His great smoldering wrath, His wrath that had kindled against Judah,
for all the vexations with which Manasseh had vexed Him. And the 27
LORD said, "Judah, too, will I remove from My presence, as I removed
Israel, and I will spurn this city Jerusalem that I chose, and the house
of which I said, Let My name be there." And the rest of the acts of 28
Josiah and all that he did, are they not written in the Book of the Acts
of the Kings of Judah? In his days Pharaoh Neco king of Egypt had 29

---

21. *Make a Passover to the* LORD *your God, as it is written in this book of the covenant.* Passover was the great rite that affirmed national purpose and belonging to the nation (compare Joshua 1). Josiah suggests that the exacting stipulations for observing Passover are made fully clear only in the book found in the temple.

26. *Yet the* LORD *did not turn back from His great smoldering wrath.* The writer struggles with a dilemma: Josiah is in his view the supremely virtuous king, and yet three generations after him Judah is destroyed. The explanation offered is that because of the cumulative offenses of the kings of Judah, with Manasseh the most egregious, Josiah's virtue cannot save the nation.

29. *In his days Pharaoh Neco King of Egypt had come up.* This two-verse notice of Josiah's death on the battlefield seems out of place, coming after the formulaic concluding statement about "the rest of the acts of Josiah." Perhaps it was tacked on at the end here because it was a historical fact that had to be reported but with which the historian was uncomfortable, contradicting as it does both Hulda's prophecy and Josiah's exemplary virtue.

come up against the king of Assyria by the Euphrates River, and King Josiah sallied forth to meet him, and he put him to death at Megiddo

30 when he saw him. And his servants took him off dead on a chariot from Megiddo and brought him to Jerusalem and buried him in his grave. And the people of the land took Jehoahaz son of Josiah and anointed

31 him and made him king in his father's stead. Twenty-three years old was Jehoahaz when he became king, and three months he was king in Jerusalem, and his mother's name was Hamutal daughter of Jeremiah

32 from Libnah. And he did what was evil in the eyes of the LORD as all

33 that his fathers had done. And Pharaoh Neco put him in bonds at Riblah in the land of Hammath, removing him as king in Jerusalem, and he imposed a levy on the land of a hundred talents of silver and

---

against the king of Assyria. Something is awry here in regard to historical facts. We know from Babylonian annals that it was against Babylonia that Pharaoh Neco led his expeditionary force in 600 BCE, and Babylonia was aligned against Assyria, then in serious decline. Some scholars suggest reading "to," *'el,* instead of "against," *'al.*

and King Josiah sallied forth to meet him. Though the geopolitics of the confrontation at Megiddo may be a little obscure, it appears that Josiah sought to associate himself with Babylonia and block Neco's passage to the east. In the event, he proved no match for the Egyptians and was immediately killed.

30. *And the people of the land took Jehoahaz . . . and anointed him.* The action of *'am ha'arets,* the people of the land, in this instance does make it look like a particular political force in the Judean populace, capable of choosing kings.

33. *And Pharaoh Neco put him in bonds.* There were political divisions in Judah between a pro-Babylonian party (with which Josiah would have been linked) and a pro-Egyptian group. Neco, with commanding military force, saw to it that a pro-Egyptian king would be set on the throne.

in the land of Hammath. The location is northern Mesopotamia, conquered by the Egyptian forces.

he imposed a levy on the land. Neco has clearly reduced Judah to a vassal state.

talents of gold. And Pharaoh Neco made Eliakim, son of Josiah, king 34
in Josiah his father's stead, and changed his name to Jehoiakim. And
he took Jehoahaz and brought him to Egypt, and he died there. And 35
Jehoiakim gave the silver and the gold to Pharaoh, but he assessed the
land so as to give the silver according to Pharaoh's decree—every man
according to his assessment, he wrested the silver and the gold from
the people of the land to give to Pharaoh Neco. Twenty-five years old 36
was Jehoiakim when he became king, and eleven years he was king in
Jerusalem. And his mother's name was Zebudah daughter of Pedaiah
from Rumah. And he did what was evil in the eyes of the Lord as all 37
that his fathers had done.

---

34. *changed his name to Jehoiakim.* Name-changing when someone assumed
the throne was fairly common in the ancient Near East. The two names in this
case are essentially the same name with different theophoric designations—*'el*
and *yeho* (which is the same as *yah / Yahweh*).

35. *he wrested the silver and the gold.* The Hebrew verb has the connotation of
extracting by main force.

CHAPTER 24

1 In his days Nebuchadnezzar king of Babylonia came up, and Jehoiakim was his vassal for three years, and he turned back and rebelled against 2 him. And the Lord sent against him the Chaldean brigades and the Aramean brigades and the Moabite brigades and the Ammonite brigades, and He sent them against Judah to destroy it, according to the word of the Lord which He had spoken through his servants the proph- 3 ets. Only by the Lord's decree was this in Judah, to remove it from His presence for the offense of Manasseh, according to all that he had done. 4 And also for the innocent blood that he had shed and filled Jerusalem 5 with innocent blood. And the Lord did not want to forgive. And the rest of the acts of Jehoiakim and all that he did, are they not written in 6 the Book of the Acts of the Kings of Judah? And Jehoiakim lay with his 7 fathers, and Jehoiachin his son was king in his stead. And the king of Egypt no longer went out from his land, for the King of Babylonia had taken all that was the king of Egypt's, from the Wadi of Egypt to the

---

2. *And the* Lord *sent against him.* According to the notion of historical causa- tion promoted by the writer, all historical events are directly dictated by God. In point of fact, the sundry peoples of the trans-Jordan region mentioned here, all vassals to Babylonia, would have dispatched their troops against Judah at the behest of Nebuchadnezzar.

3. *was this in Judah.* The Hebrew preposition could also mean "against."

7. *And the king of Egypt no longer went out from his land.* Pharaoh Neco had sent a large expeditionary force against Babylonia in 609 BCE that took up a position along the Euphrates. Now, a decade later, after the defeat at the battle of Carchemish, the Egyptians were compelled to retreat and remain within their own borders.

Euphrates River. Eighteen years old was Jehoiachin when he became 8
king, and three months he was king in Jerusalem, and his mother's name
was Nehushta daughter of Elnathan from Jerusalem. And he did what 9
was evil in the eyes of the LORD, as all that his father had done. At that 10
time the servants of Nebuchadnezzar king of Babylonia went up against
Jerusalem, and the city came under siege. And Nebuchadnezzar king of 11
Babylonia came against the city, and his servants were besieging it. And 12
Jehoiachin king of Judah went out to the king of Babylonia—he and his
mother and his servants and his commanders and his eunuchs—and
the king of Babylonia took him in the eighth year of his reign. And he 13
took out from there all the treasures of the house of the LORD and the
treasures of the house of the king, and he cut up all the golden vessels
that Solomon king of Israel had made in the temple of the LORD, as the
LORD had spoken. And he exiled all Jerusalem and all the command- 14
ers and all the valiant warriors, ten thousand exiles, and no artisan nor
metalsmith remained, only the poor people of the land. And he exiled 15
Jehoiachin to Babylonia, and the king's mother and the king's wives and
his eunuchs and the nobles of the land he led into exile to Babylonia.
And all the fighting men, seven thousand, and the artisans and the met- 16
alsmiths a thousand, all of them battle-tested warriors. And the king of
Babylonia brought them in exile to Babylonia. And the king of Babylonia 17
made Mattaniah his uncle king in his stead, and he changed his name
to Zedekiah. Twenty-one years old was Zedekiah when he became king, 18
and eleven years he was king in Jerusalem, and his mother's name was
Hamutal daughter of Jeremiah from Libnah. And he did what was evil 19

---

12. *he and his mother and his servants and his commanders and his eunuchs.* This
retinue of notables, including not only military men but court officials and the
queen mother, suggests that the king has come out in order to submit himself
and those around him to Nebuchadnezzar.

14. *And he exiled all Jerusalem.* What this means is not the entire population
but a substantial part of its elite and its skilled workers.

16. *all of them battle-tested warriors.* The syntactical position of this phrase is
slightly confusing because it has to refer to the fighting men at the beginning of
the sentence but not to the artisans and eunuchs who come afterward.

20   in the eyes of the Lord as all that Jehoiakim had done. For because of
the Lord's wrath, it was against Jerusalem and against Judah, till He
flung them from His presence. And Zedekiah rebelled against the king
of Babylonia.

---

20. *And Zedekiah rebelled against the king of Babylonia.* As usual, the writer
provides no political explanation—in this case, for the fact that Zedekiah,
having been installed by Nebuchadnezzar as vassal king, now decides to rebel.
From the Book of Jeremiah, from Ezekiel, and from extra-biblical sources, we
know that there were sharp divisions within the kingdom of Judah between a
pro-Egyptian faction and a pro-Babylonian faction. Zedekiah at this moment,
counting on Egyptian support, joined an alliance of trans-Jordanian kingdoms
plotting to overthrow Babylonian rule. In the event, Egypt did not provide support, and the rebellion failed to materialize. The consequence was Nebuchadnezzar's assault on Jerusalem and the destruction of the kingdom of Judah.

CHAPTER 25

And it happened in the ninth year of his reign, in the tenth month, 1
on the tenth of the month, that Nebuchadnezzar king of Babylonia
came—he and all his forces—against Jerusalem and camped against
it and built siege-towers all around it. And the city came under siege 2
till the twelfth year of King Zedekiah. On the ninth of the month the 3
famine was severe in the city and there was no bread for the people
of the land. *In the eleventh year of Zedekiah in the fourth month on the* 4
ninth day the city was breached. *And all the commanders of the king of*
Babylonia came and sat in the central gate, Nergal-Sarezer, Samgur-Nebo,
Sarsechim, the chief eunuch, *Nergal-Sarezer the chief magus,* and all
the rest of the king of Babylonia's commanders. *And it happened when*
Zedekiah saw them and all the men of war, *that they fled* by night through

---

1. *Nebuchadnezzar king of Babylonia came.* It appears that Nebuchadnezzar
was so incensed by the betrayal on the part of his vassal king Zedekiah that
he personally led the siege against Jerusalem. At some point, however, before
the actual conquest of the city, he withdrew to a Mesopotamian outpost in
Riblah (verse 5), leaving the completion of the siege to his military deputy,
Nebuzaradan (verse 9ff.).

3. *bread.* As elsewhere, this word is probably a synecdoche for food in general.

4. *In the eleventh year of Zedekiah.* The text at this point is clearly defective,
exhibiting a subject ("all the men of war") with no predicate and lacking some
narrative information. The entire passage is transcribed from Jeremiah 39—at
this point, a faulty transcription—and so the translation incorporates, italicized, elements from the text in Jeremiah.
    Nergal-Sarezer. This name occurs twice in the list in Jeremiah, which must
be a scribal duplication.

the gate between the double walls which is by the king's garden, and the Chaldeans were upon the city all around. And they went through the

5 Arabah. And the Chaldean force pursued the king and overtook him on the plain of Jericho, and all his force scattered from around him.

6 And they seized the king and brought him up to the king of Babylonia

7 at Riblah and pronounced judgment against him. And Zedekiah's sons they slaughtered before his eyes, and Zedekiah's eyes they blinded, and

8 they bound him in fetters and brought him to Babylonia. And in the fifth month on the seventh of the month, which was the nineteenth year of King Nebuchadnezzar, king of Babylonia, Nebuzaradan the high chamberlain, servant of the king of Babylonia, came to Jerusalem.

9 And he burnt the house of the LORD and the house of the king and all

10 the houses of Jerusalem, and every great house he burnt in fire. And the wall of Jerusalem all around did the Chaldean force that was the

---

6. *pronounced judgment against him.* This would scarcely have been a proper trial but summary judgment of a vassal king who had proved himself a traitor.

7. *And Zedekiah's sons they slaughtered before his eyes.* In a pointed device of ancient Near Eastern barbarity, the last thing he is made to see before they blind him is the slaughter of his sons. The act is political as well as sadistic: no one is left in the line of Zedekiah to claim the throne after him.

8. *the high chamberlain.* This is the same title attached to Potiphar in Genesis 39:1. The Hebrew *sar hatabaḥim* literally means "commander of the slaughter" ("slaughter" in the culinary sense). The title might have originally designated a head steward of chef, but it clearly came to mean someone exercising high authority in the political and military realm.

9. *every great house.* These are the houses of the nobility, as the Aramaic translation, *batey revavaia*, properly registers.

10. *And the wall of Jerusalem . . . did the Chaldean force . . . shatter.* Destroying the wall rendered the city totally indefensible, eradicating any possibility that it could continue to be the capital of an independent state.

high chamberlain's shatter. And the rest of the people remaining in the 11
city and the turncoats who had gone over to the king of Babylonia and
the rest of the masses, Nebuzaradan the high chamberlain exiled. And 12
of the poorest of the land the high chamberlain left to be vinedressers
and field workers. And the bronze pillars that were in the house of the 13
Lord and the stands and the bronze sea that was in the house of the
Lord the Chaldeans smashed and bore off their bronze to Babylonia.
And the pails and the scrapers and the snuffers and the ladles and 14
all the bronze vessels with which one ministered they took. And the 15
firepans and the sprinkling bowls, whatever was of gold and whatever

---

11. *the turncoats.* Literally, "those who fell." One should recall that there was
a strong group among the Judeans (including Jeremiah) who thought that the
rebellion against Babylonia was greatly ill-advised, and so it is not surprising
that some of these should defect to the Babylonians.

the masses. The Hebrew *hamon*, which in biblical usage generally refers to a
loud hubbub, may be doubtful. The parallel passage in Jeremiah 52:15 shows
ha'amon, a collective noun for artisans, and that looks like the more likely
reading.

12. *And of the poorest of the land.* The impression given here that only the
poor agricultural workers were spared the fate of exile is probably misleading.
Although the Babylonians appear to have exiled a large part of the nation's elite,
both Gedaliah, who is appointed regent by the Babylonians, and the conspirators who kill him are from the nobility. The burial center at Katef-Hinnom, in
western Jerusalem, which contains epigraphic and other evidence of having
been in continuous use through the sixth century BCE, was clearly a burial
place for Judean aristocracy.

13. *And the bronze pillars.* It was common procedure in conquests to cart off the
temple treasures of the conquered. At the same time, this catalogue of precious
sacred vessels seized by the Babylonians reverses everything reported in 1 Kings
6–7 about the splendid furnishings for the temple and the palace that Solomon
caused to be fashioned. Everything that the grand first king after David built or
made is either reduced to rubble or taken off by the enemy,

the bronze sea. This is a large cast-metal pool, mentioned in 1 Kings 7:23
and elsewhere.

16 was of silver, the high chamberlain took. The two pillars, the one sea, the stands that Solomon had for the house of the LORD—all these ves-
17 sels were beyond measure. Eighteen cubits was the height of one pillar with a bronze capital on its top, and the height of the capital was three cubits, and there were pomegranates on the capital all around of bronze,
18 and like these was the second pillar with the meshwork. And the high chamberlain took Seraiah the head priest and Zephaniah the assistant
19 priest and the three guards of the threshold. And from the city he took one eunuch who was the official over the men of war and five men of those who attended in the king's presence and the scribe of the army commander who mustered the people of the land, and sixty men from
20 the people of the land who were in the town. And Nebuzaradan the high chamberlain took them and led them to the king of Babylonia at Riblah.
21 And the king of Babylonia struck them down and put them to death in
22 Riblah in the land of Hammath. And he exiled Judah from its land. And as to the people remaining in the land of Judah whom Nebuchadnezzar king of Babylonia had left, he appointed over them Gedaliah son of
23 Ahikam son of Shaphan. And all the commanders of the forces, they and the men, heard that the king of Babylonia had appointed Gedaliah, and they came to Gedaliah at Mizpah—Ishmael son of Nethaniah and Johanan son of Kareah and Seraiah son of Tanhumeth the Netophah
24 thite, and Jaazaniah son of the Maachite, they and their men. And Gedaliah swore to them and to their men and said to them, "Do not be afraid to serve the Chaldeans. Stay in the land and serve the king of Babylonia,

16. *beyond measure.* More literally, "beyond weighing."

18. *And the high chamberlain took Seraiah the head priest and Zephaniah the assistant priest.* The obvious intention is to prevent a renewal of the cult in Jerusalem. The usual term for high priest (in the Hebrew, "great priest") is not used but rather "head priest," *kohen haro'sh.*

21. *And the king of Babylonia struck them down and put them to death.* No Geneva convention obtains for these ancient prisoners of war, and since they constitute the nation's military and sacerdotal elite, Nebuchadnezzar wants to eliminate them entirely,

24. *Do not be afraid to serve the Chaldeans.* Gedaliah is obviously a member of the pro-Babylonian faction among the Judeans who assumed that military

that it may go well with you." And it happened in the seventh month   25
that Ishmael son of Nethaniah son of Elishama of the royal seed, and ten
men with him, came and struck down Gedaliah, and he died, as well as
the Judeans and the Chaldeans who were with him in Mizpah. And all   26
the people arose, from the smallest to the greatest, and the commanders
of the forces, and they went to Egypt, for they feared the Chaldeans.

And it happened in the twenty-seventh year of the exile of Jehoiachin   27
king of Judah in the twelfth month, on the twenty-seventh of the month,
that Evil-Merodach king of Babylonia, in the year he became king,
lifted up the head of Jehoiachin king of Judah from the prison-house.

---

resistance was not feasible and that cooperation would lead to kind treatment
by the Babylonians. The men who come to see him clearly belong to the opposing faction, and they regard Gedaliah as a quisling and thus proceed to kill him.

25. *of the royal seed*. He may well have hoped to claim the throne after the
death of Gedaliah.
    as well as the Judeans and the Chaldeans who were with him in Mizpah. These
killings are a mark of their ruthlessness and of their thoroughness as insurgents.
They murder all of Gedaliah's attendants and staff as vile collaborators, and
they also kill the Chaldeans stationed with him, perhaps to eliminate them as
witnesses and certainly as an act of defiance against the conquerors.

26. *And all the people arose, from the smallest to the greatest*. This is again a
patent exaggeration: the historical evidence argues strongly against the notion
that the entire country was emptied of its Judean population. The logic of the
flight to Egypt is that the Egyptians were the adversaries of Babylonia and the
allies of the anti-Babylonian faction.

27. *Evil-Merodach*. He assumed the throne of Babylonia in 562 BCE. Granting
pardons when one becomes king was a common ancient Near Eastern practice.
Jehoiachin was taken into captivity in 597. His quarter-century as prisoner may
actually have been a form of house arrest because a Babylonian document from
592 records the provision of food for Jehoiachin king of Judah and his five sons,
suggesting that some recognition of his royal status was accorded all along.
    lifted up the head. This is the same idiom, intimating pardon, that is used for
the imprisoned chief steward in the Joseph story (Genesis 40:13).

28 And he spoke kindly to him and gave him a throne above the thrones of
29 the kings who were with him in Babylonia. And he changed his prison
garments, and Jehoiachin ate bread perpetually in his presence all the
30 days of his life. And his provision was a perpetual provision given him
by the king day after day, all the days of his life.

---

28. *gave him a throne above the thrones of the kings who were with him.* This is probably a nationalistic flourish of the writer's because it is unlikely that Jehoiachin would have been granted a higher status than other kings held in Babylonian captivity.

29. *And he changed his prison garments.* This detail is probably a deliberate reminiscence of the Joseph story: when Joseph is freed from prison, he is clothed by Pharaoh in fine garments.
   Jehoiachin. The Hebrew says merely "he," and the proper name has been added in order to avoid confusion of pronominal reference.

30. *And his provision was a perpetual provision . . . day after day.* The historical event with which the Book of Kings ends is of course a complete catastrophe—the utter destruction of Jerusalem, including temple and palace; the massacre of the royal line and the military and priestly elite; and the exile of a large part of the population. This concluding image, however, seeks to intimate a hopeful possibility of future restoration: a Davidic king is recognized as king, even in captivity, and is given a daily provision appropriate to his royal status. As he sits on his throne elevated above the thrones of the other captive kings, the audience of the story is invited to imagine a scion of David again sitting on his throne in Jerusalem.